The Art of Fashion Draping

The Art of Fashion Draping

SECOND EDITION

Connie Amaden-Crawford
Fashion Design Department
The Fashion Institute of Design and Merchandising
Los Angeles, California

Fairchild Publications / New York

Third Printing © 2000
Second Printing © 1998
Fairchild Publications is a division of
ABC Media, Inc.

Library of Congress Catalog
Card Number: 95-61082
ISBN: 1-56365-017-8
GST R 133004424

Printed in the United States of America

Cover & Interior Design:
Dutton & Sherman Design

Chapter Opening Illustration:
Kichisaburo Ogawa

Contents

Extended Contents

Preface

The second edition of *The Art of Fashion Draping* has been significantly reorganized and expanded for fashion design professionals and students. It has been revised with the following objectives in mind:

- To appreciate the importance of the grain of fabric in relationship to the desired design.
- To manipulate fabric on a three-dimensional form and obtain harmony between the fabric and design.
- To stimulate creativity by feeling and sculpting with fabric.
- To develop a keen sense of proportion and placement of style lines.
- To evaluate the fit, hang and balance of garments on live models.
- To create foundation patterns for the basic bodice, skirt, shift, and sleeve from which other more complicated designs with details such as collars, yokes and cowls may be designed.

I have maintained my original concept of step-by-step written instructions accompanied by illustrations to outline the principles involved in draping fabric on the dress form. However, in response to the comments from users of the first edition, the chapters and projects from the first edition are now organized into parts. The techniques and styles in each part for the second edition are aimed at learning draping skills from beginning to intermediate to advanced to stimulate an endless variety of ideas. For the sake of time, some technical work is accomplished using flat pattern drafting methods. However, the designs developed from flat patternmaking would not be complete unless they were checked for balance, fit, and hang in muslin and draped directly on the dress form. Instructions and illustrations on how to transfer the finished drape into a complete pattern are included for all projects.

Organization of the Text

Chapter 1 in Part One begins with a discussion of the tools and equipment necessary for all designers. A full-size illustration of the dress form and its components is provided in chapter 2. The elements of fabric, particularly acquiring an understanding of the relationship of grain to draping fabrics, are discussed in Chapter 3. A short glossary of important draping terminology completes this section.

Chapters in Part Two are the foundation for a sound understanding of manipulating, molding, and shaping fabric into basic garments on the dress form. Each chapter in Part Two completes the draping skills for basic garments - the bodice, skirt, shift (torso) and sleeve. The sense of seeing and feeling a simple design, which cannot be achieved by creating patterns flat on the table, is accomplished. The steps discuss how to drape the fabric from neck to hem, maintaining a smooth and easy-flowing design, while at the same time not overworking a piece of fabric. Instructions for the basic sleeve are also included in this section. Here to save time and maintain accuracy, the basic sleeve is drafted. Sleeves are pinned and checked for balance, fit, and hang when the garment is placed on the dress form. Step-by-step principles discussed in Part Two enable students to understand: accurate placement of the grain and darts, tucks, and pleats on the figure; necessary ease amounts, and the correct shape of the flat pattern.

After mastering the basic principles of draping explained in Part Two the designer can continue with the intermediate projects in Part Three, such as: dartless and princess shapes and variations of bodices, skirts and sleeves. Draping principles for collars - basic and fashion-oriented - and pants are covered. Part Two ends with draping asymmetric designs - introducing the student to more advanced designs. Projects in Part two encourage the students to identify which draping steps are most flattering to the various figures while at the same time allows them to continue to refine their ability to handle pliable fabrics. Projects explore how to define styles and silhouettes over the bust, hip, and waist and how to utilize folds, darts, pleats, and fullness to emphasize the design.

Designers derive a great deal of pleasure and satisfaction when creating original styles. The chapters in Part Four apply the information discussed in previous parts to more unusual and complicated cuts. Students approaching the draping projects in this section must understand thoroughly the basic and intermediate principles covered earlier. All the draping projects in this section discuss how to retain the figure's most pleasing attributes and how to emphasize them through subtle illusion. Designs are more challenging and work towards the entire effect while paying attention to the most minute detail. Draping bias and sculptured dresses, the bustier, and design details such as yokes, midriffs, cowls, ruffles and flounces are discussed and illustrated. As a result of the fibers and construction in knit fabrics, the designer must use a great deal of finesse and be expert in technique to accurately drape these styles. A chapter is devoted to the step-by-step guidelines for draping such knit designs as the bodice, sleeve, halter, bodysuit and leotard.

As in the previous edition an arm pattern which when sewn and stuffed with polyfill can be attached to the dress form to drape sleeves is included. Instructions of the preparation of this fabric arm are now listed in the appendix.

Acknowledgments

I wish to express appreciation for the assistance, information, and love given to me by colleagues, students and friends. Their many ideas and suggestions have been useful in presenting this text. My grateful appreciation to the following: Mary Stephens, Chairperson of the Fashion Design Department at Fashion Institute of Design and Merchandising, Moira Doyle, Wayne Fuller, Alice Kaku, Betty Morales, Anahid Sultanian, Vivian Tellefson, and Terry Werdan. A very warm and loving thank you to my husband, Wayne, for so much patience and help while writing this book.

I wish to thank reviewers selected by the publisher: Janet Hethorn, University of California-Davis; Paula Sampson, Ball State University; Carolyn Schactler, Central Washington University; Elaine Zarse, Mount Mary College-Milwaukee.

My deepest appreciation to Tiffin Dove and Kelle Schaeffel for their untiring efforts in drawing the technical illustrations.

Connie Amaden-Crawford
Los Angeles, California
1996

The Art of Fashion Draping

Part One

Practical Draping Skills

Many designers prefer to use draping methods to create their original designs. In the early twentieth-century, Madeleine Vionnet created a half-scale wooden doll that could be used to design and drape bias garments. Throughout Alix Gres career, she used creative draping techniques to design asymmetrical jersey drapes, molded silhouette dresses, and many other creative fashions. Working with actual materials gives a designer greater inspiration and indication of the flow and performance of a fabric. A designer can easily see the proportion, fit, balance, and style lines of a design, exactly as it will look on the bodice.

Chapters in this section identify appropriate tools and equipment, define grain and its relationship to design, list terms and basic principles applicable to the development of draped garments. The importance of the dress form to draping is illustrated and discussed in this section. The dress form is used to manipulate flat fabric to fit the curves of the body accurately. It is used to visualize what a pattern should look like in relationship to the figure. The material covered in this section if carefully applied to any of the projects in the text will result in the accurate and professional production of draped garments.

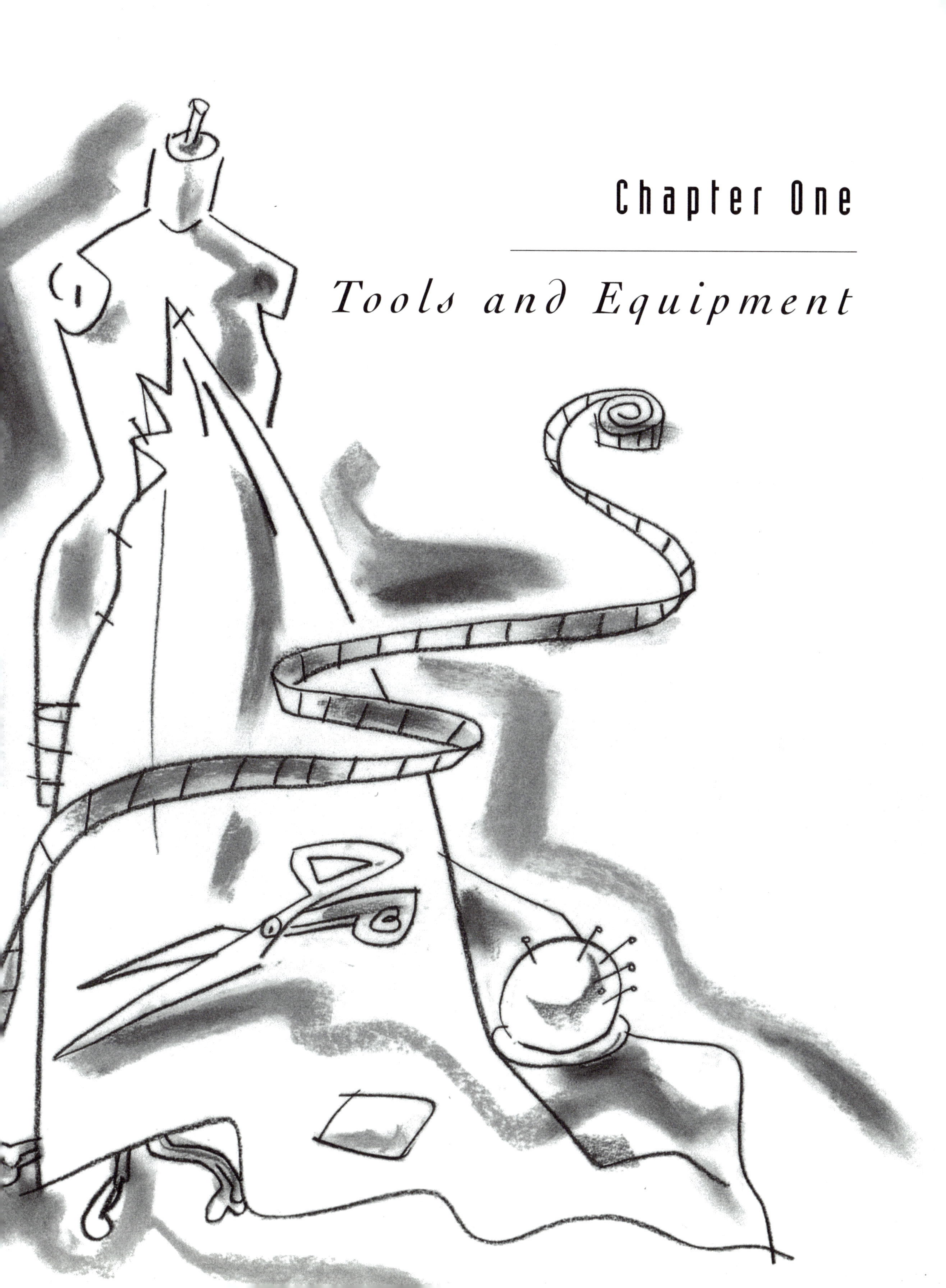

Chapter One

Tools and Equipment

A few basic supplies are needed for any draping project. Draping tools are necessary to drape, measure, mark, and draft designs. Keep all necessary supplies on hand and keep them neatly together to use at any time.

Awl A pointed metal instrument used for punching holes for belt eyelets and other clean, sharp holes in fabric or leather.

18-Inch Clear Plastic Ruler A two-inch wide ruler divided into 1/8 inch grids. It is clear and perfect for truing and adding seam allowances. Available through C-thru Ruler Co.

French Curve Ruler An irregular curve with an edge describing a spiral curve used to shape and curve edges of curved collars, necklines, crotch seams, and armholes.

Hip Curve Ruler A 24-inch ruler with a long, slightly shaped curve that finishes with a strong circular shape. This hip curve ruler is marked in both inches and centimeters, along with fractional measurements. It is used to shape lapels, seams, flares, godets, princess lines, and pant crotch seams.

Iron A steam-and-dry iron used to smooth and aid in blocking muslin.

Ironing Board A flat, adjustable board about 54-inches long by 15-inches wide that tapers to 6 inches at one end to provide a stable, soft surface on which to iron or press.

L-Square A metal or plastic ruler with two arms of different lengths meeting at right angles. These rulers are marked in both inches and centimeters, along with fractional measurements.

Muslin An inexpensive fabric, on which the grain and crossgrain are quite visible, used to drape garments made of woven goods. The quality and hand of the muslin should represent the texture and characteristics of the actual fabric chosen for the garment design. *Soft muslin* will simulate the draping quality of natural or synthetic silk, lingerie fabric, and fine cottons. *Medium-weight muslin* will simulate the draping quality of wool and medium-weight cottons. *Coarse muslin* will simulate the draping quality of heavyweight wools and cottons. Also, canvas muslin will simulate the draping qualities of such heavyweight fabrics as denim, fur, or imitation fur.

Garments made of *knitted fabrics* should be draped in less expensive knit fabric. However, the sample knit should have the same stretch value as the fabric selected for the finished garment.

Notcher A punching tool used to mark the edge of a sloper or paper pattern.

Pattern Drafting Paper Strong, white drafting paper, with 1-inch grids of pattern dots, of a good quality and thickness available in rolls of various widths.

Pencils Soft 2B or 5H pencils used in developing muslin patterns.

Pin Cushion or Pin Dispenser A sewing tool that keeps pins organized in a convenient place. The most common pin cushion is in the shape of a tomato. However, other types and sizes are available. Choose the pin cushion that will be easiest to use.

Scissors and Shears Shears are usually four-to-eight inches long and made of steel. Bent-handled shears are excellent for easy and correct cutting. A three-to-six inch scissor is smaller than shears. The difference between shears and scissors is that one handle on a pair of shears is larger than the other. The handles on a pair of scissors are the same size.

Style Tape A narrow, woven tape that is used to delineate style lines on the dress form.

Straight Pins Satin dressmaker pins #17 with sharp tapering points that will not rust are used to anchor muslin or fabric to the dress form while draping.

Tailor's Chalk A small piece of chalk, approximately 1 1/2" square, with two tapered edges. It is used to mark lines temporarily on garment hems and other alteration points.

Tape Measure A flexible, narrow, firmly woven, 60-inch reversible tape marked with measurements indicating both inches and metric terms used to take dress form, muslin, and body measurements.

Tracing Wheel A sharp, spike-edged circular wheel with a handle that is used to transfer markings from the drape to the pattern paper.

Yardstick A wooden or metal ruler one yard in length (36 inches) that is marked in inches or metric terms. An aid for laying pattern pieces on the straight of grain of the fabric or for measuring hem lines.

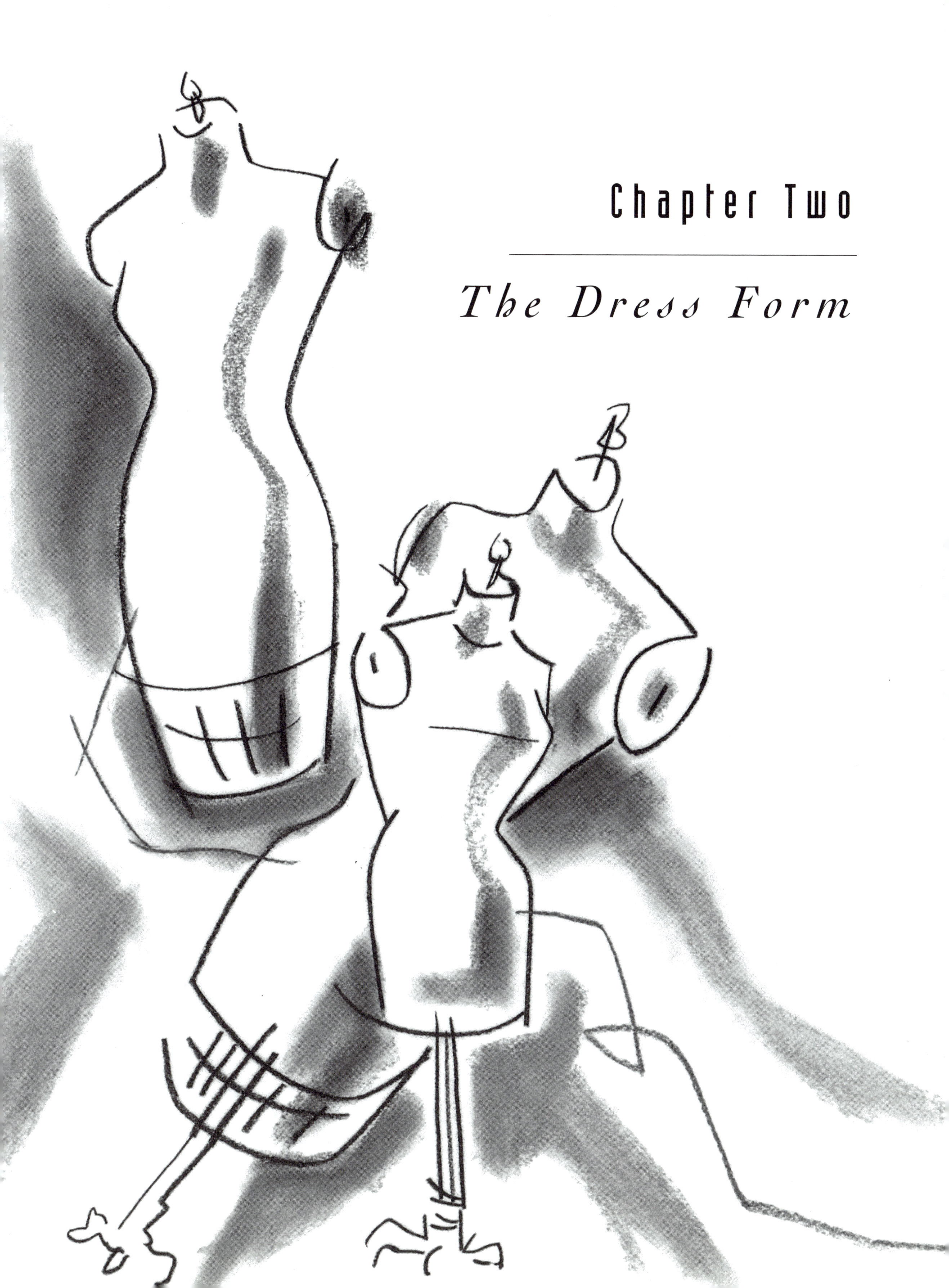

Chapter Two

The Dress Form

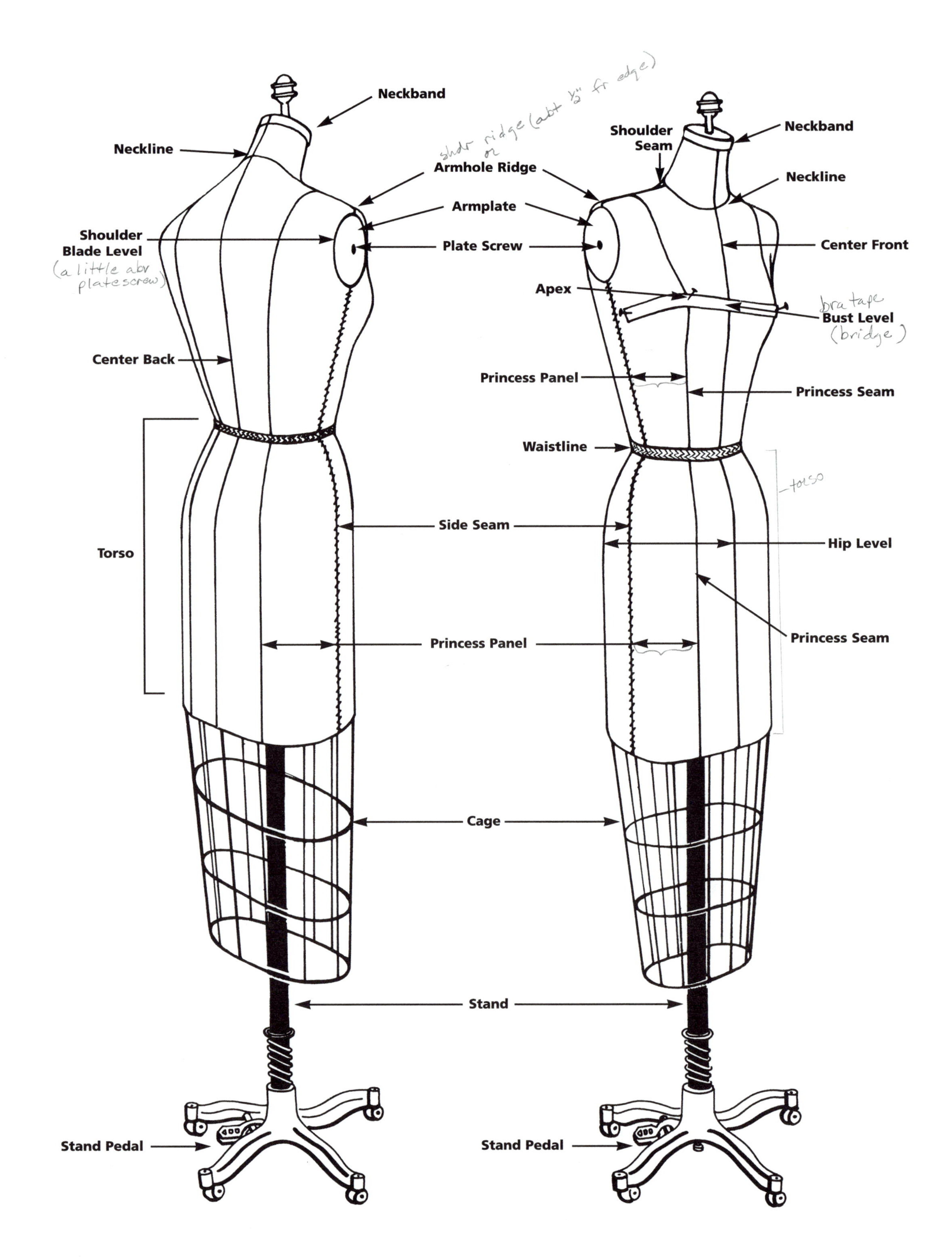
Neckband
Neckline
Armhole Ridge
Armplate
Shoulder Blade Level
Plate Screw
Center Back
Torso
Side Seam
Princess Panel
Cage
Stand
Stand Pedal
Shoulder Seam
Neckband
Neckline
Center Front
Apex
Bust Level
Princess Panel
Princess Seam
Waistline
Hip Level
Princess Seam
Princess Panel
Cage
Stand
Stand Pedal

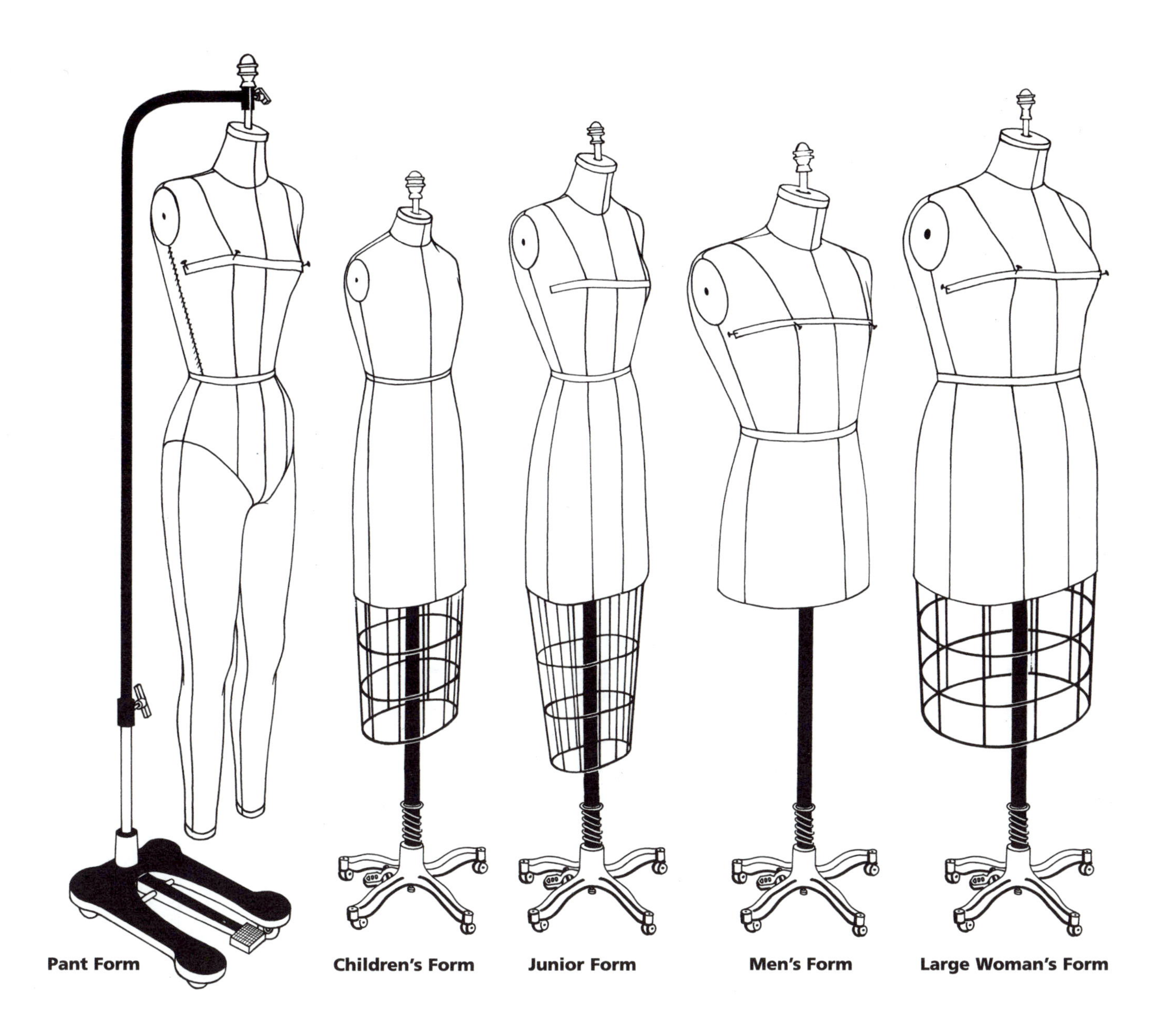

There are several types and manufacturers of dress forms on the market. The most commonly used form for both the novice and the designer/manufacturer is the muslin-padded dress form (see illustration). This form, set on a movable, height-adjustable stand, duplicates the shape of the human body. It is firm, yet resilient, and does not resist pins. The right and left sides are exactly alike.

Garment manufacturers use this type of dress form to drape and perfect most basic blocks and original designs. Because sample garments are fitted, checked, and corrected on this same form, much care and thought should be given to the purchase of the appropriate model, size, and proportion of dress form. Manufacturers must be selective because their basic patterns and subsequent designs are proportioned to fit many customers without too many alterations.

A dress form conforms to the measurements of a particular size and type of figure for an individual or specific manufacturer. Although dress forms are updated every year according to government standards and silhouette changes, any newly purchased dress form should be tested and checked for alignment, relationship, and proper balance of the shoulder and side seams.

A variety of dress forms are available in standard sizes for junior, missy, children's, and men's figures. Some manufacturers use "special dress forms" for their customers, depending on the type of clothes designed, the fit required, and the figure shape necessary. Illustrated here are examples of forms other than the standard size 8 or 10 that are used to design various garments headed for the retail marketplace.

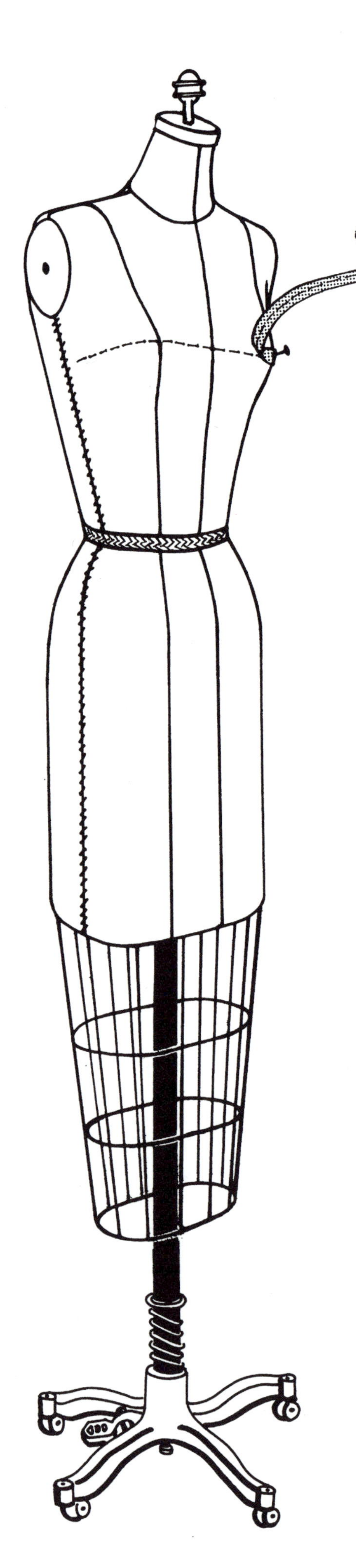

Attaching the Bustline Tape

In many cases the dress form needs a bustline tape in order to achieve a correctly fitted drape. This bustline tape represents the same fit on the dress form as a bra does on the human body. This tape is sometimes referred to as the *bra tape.*

1. Pin the bustline tape to the dress form in the middle of the princess panel on the left side of the dress form.
2. Drape the bustline tape tightly across the bustline. Do not secure tape at center front.
3. Finish pinning the bustline tape, across the front only, in the middle of the princess panel on the right side of the dress form.

NOTE: The tape should be tight and pinned securely.

4. Pin and crossmark the apex on the bustline tape. (The apex is the highest point of the bustline at the princess seam.)

Balancing the Armhole

The armhole side seam and the armplate screw level should be in perfect alignment.

Shift the shoulder and side seam positions if they need adjusting. Draw the new lines with a dark pen.

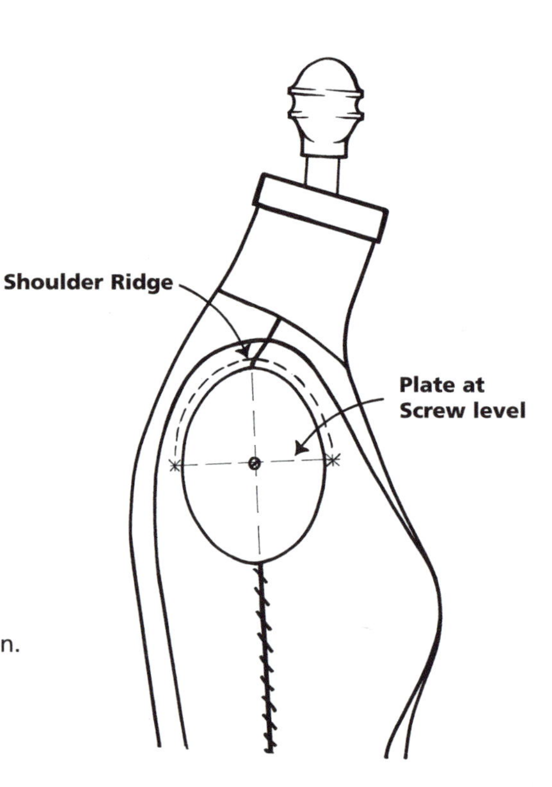

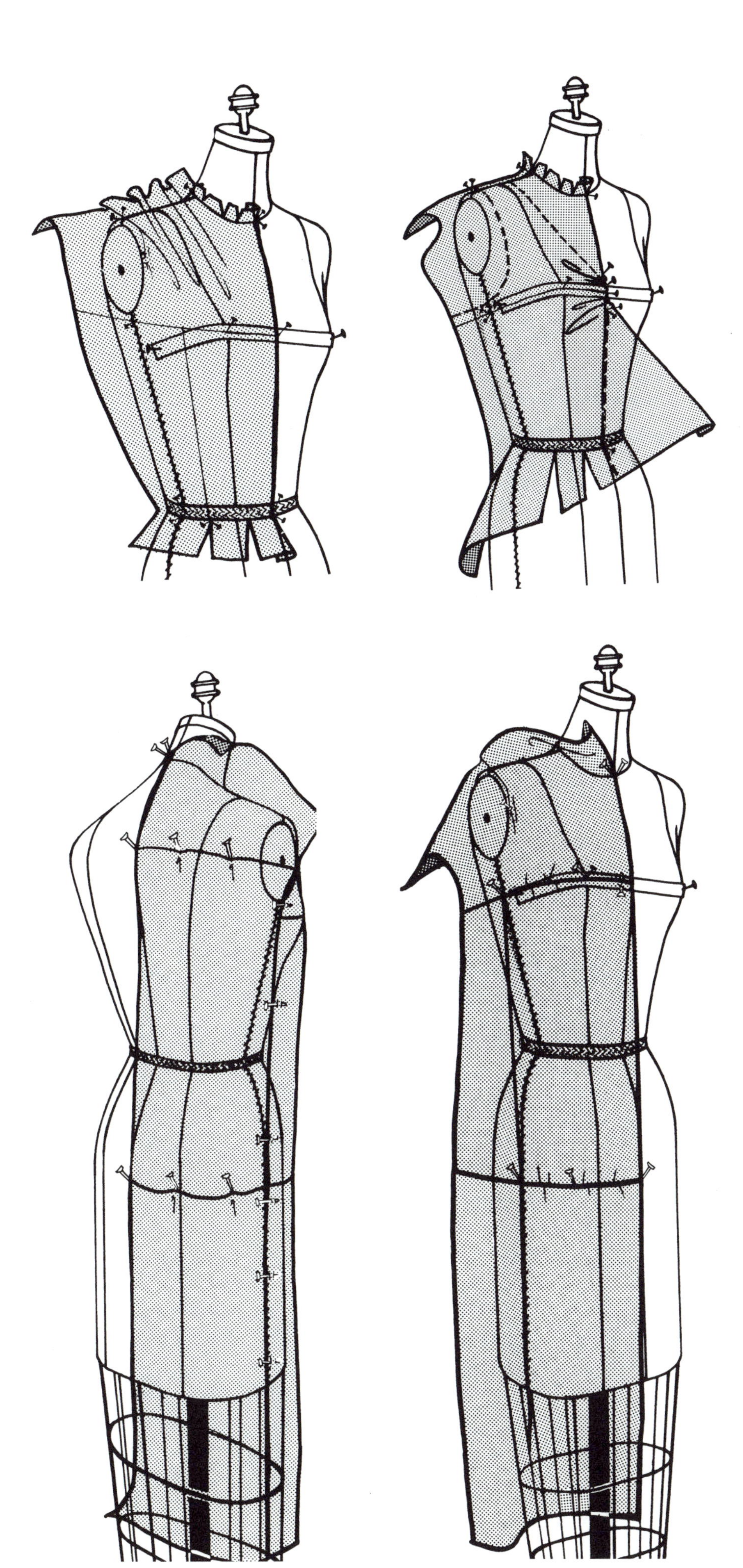

Draping Fabric on the Dress Form

The right side of the front dress form is used to drape the front basic pattern or garment and the left side of the back dress form for the back basic pattern or garment. Although the procedure may vary, this is the "standard" rule when fitting and draping.

Chapter Three

Elements of Fabrics

Elements of Fabrics

New approaches to dressing have combined with the new technological age to produce fabrics that are flatter, crisper, smoother, firmer, and stretchier than ever before. These versatile fabrics fit the lifestyles and the moods of the new fashion age.

Fabrics and clothes should relate to our lifestyles and our need for greater variety and diversity in dressing. Thus, clothes for our active lifestyles are made of many different stretch knits. All around us sportswear garments are made of denim, single knits, and a variety of woven cottons and synthetics. Sheer, see-through fabrics capture the body's sleek line, while tulle, organza, and sheer cottons and knits are used for discreetly revealing effects. Special evening fabrics, such as chiffon, crepe de chine, silk, voile, and brocade, capture the elegant lifestyles of modern women. In contrast, linen, seersucker, homespun plaids, natural cottons, corduroy, woolens, and a variety of woven synthetics are appealing fabrics for realistic, durable, and longer-lasting quality clothes.

Before beginning any draping steps, consider the large selection of available fabrics. The fabric selected for a garment greatly influences the finished look. A good designer is not only aware of the fiber content, weave, and finish of a fabric, but analyzes and understands its structure and characteristics to create the proper ease and balance of the garment or pattern drape.

Selecting a fabric of correct quality and suitability is important because it will determine the appearance, durability, maintenance, and comfort of the finished garment. A designer selects the fabric with the following criteria in mind: color, texture, hand, weight, comfort, and price.

Approach each design with a positive attitude and a clear fashion sense.

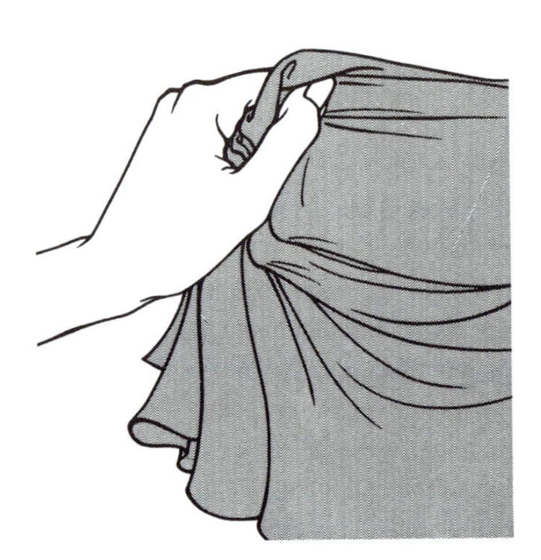

Hand, Appearance, and Texture

The feel of a fabric is referred to as the hand. The appearance is the flexibility of the fabric. Texture refers to the weight, body, or drape of fabrics. It is created by different types and combinations of fibers and yarns and methods of construction as well as colorings and finishes.

Regardless of hand, appearance, and texture, fibers are usually twisted together to form yarns, which are then woven or knitted to form a fabric. Color is applied by either dyeing or printing. Finally, a finishing technique, usually chemical, is applied to improve the performance and provide fabric characteristics that are suitable for the end use and desirable to the customer.

Fibers

The various fibers used and the methods by which these fibers are put together define the differences among fabrics. Fibers are either natural or manufactured. Natural fibers include cotton from the cotton plant, flax that is processed into linen, wool from sheep, and silk from the silkworm. Manufactured fibers are not found in nature and are produced using different combinations of chemicals. Manufactured fibers include acrylic, nylon, polyester, rayon, and spandex.

Fibers possess certain basic properties or characteristics. A designer must understand these properties to determine if the fabric made from these fibers is suitable for a specific design. The fiber content in a fabric will change the performance and drapability qualities of the fabric. Fabrics can be made entirely of the same fiber or by blending or combining different fibers. This is done when no single fiber possesses all of the properties required to make the most desirable fabric. For example, one of cotton's unfavorable features is that it wrinkles easily. However, if polyester, which possesses excellent wrinkle resistance, and cotton are combined, the fabric will wrinkle less and still maintain the most favorable properties of cotton, such as its absorbency and softness.

A major development of the 1990s is the production of microfibers. These are manufactured fibers that are thinner than a human hair or a strand of silk. Because fabrics produced from microfibers are very soft and drapable, nylon or polyester fibers can, for example, be produced to look and feel like silk.

It is not only the properties of a fiber that determine the fundamental properties of a fabric. Other components, such as yarns, fabric construction, colorization, and finish, also govern how the fabric will ultimately perform. If a property of any component is changed, then the properties of the fabric will change.

Fabric Construction

Although several construction methods are used, the two basic methods of producing fabrics—weaving and knitting—are the most pertinent for this discussion. Woven fabrics are made by interlacing yarns; knitted fabrics are made by interlooping yarns. Different methods of interlacing and interlooping yarns, variations in fiber content and yarn character influence the fabric structure.

Aside from the traditional fabrics used for foundation garments and swimwear, yarns that stretch when pulled and bounce back into shape, are being used for woven and knitted garment. These yarns provide increased comfort, shape retention, and wrinkle resistance when sitting, bending, and stooping, or when engaged in active sports or work activities.

Woven Fabrics

Woven fabrics are formed by interlacing yarns in a *plain weave, twill weave,* or *satin weave.* Some common woven fabrics are cotton, linen, denim, poplin, broadcloth, gingham, sharkskin, corduroy, wool, chambray, and rayon gabardine. An important characteristic of all woven fabrics is that they fray at the cut edge. The looser the weave, the more the cut edge frays. Loosely woven fabrics are usually less durable. When testing the straightness of the cut ends, the crosswise and lengthwise yarns should run at right angles.

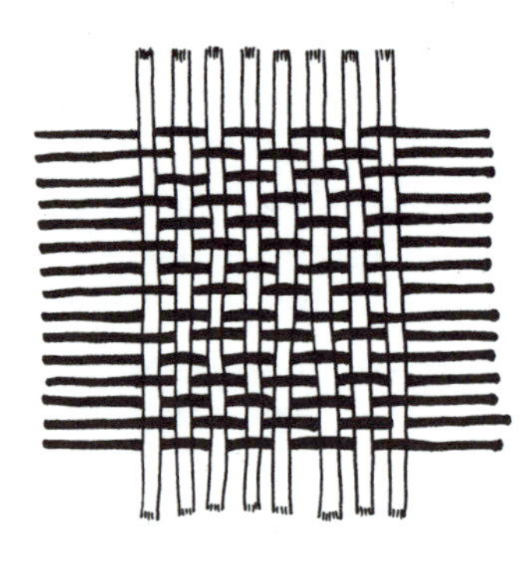

Plain Weave Each thread passes over and under each of the threads going in the opposite direction.

Twill Weave The fabric has diagonal lines. Yarns cross at least two yarns before going under one or more yarns.

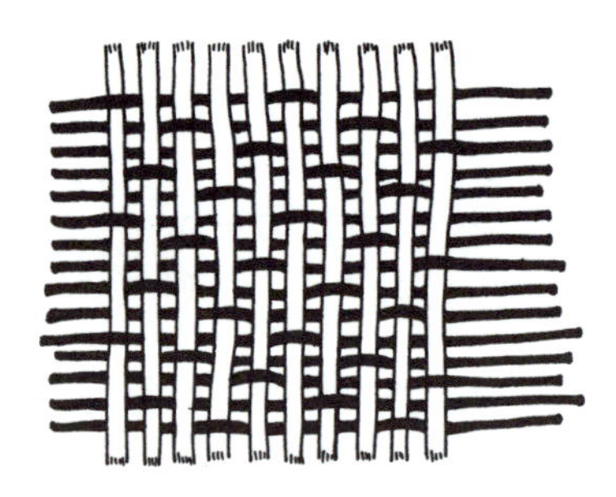

Satin Weave Thread goes over one and under several yarns to create greater luster on the right side of the fabric.

Knitted Fabrics

Knitted fabrics are formed by interlooping yarns. The most common knits are flat jersey knits, purl knits, and rib knits (better known as weft knits.) These knits stretch more in width than in length. Double knits are also weft knits; they are firmer, heavier, have less stretch and more resilience than single knits. Tricot and raschel knits are well-known warp knits. These warp knits have less stretch than weft knits and tend to be run resistant.

The most common characteristic of a knitted fabric is its capacity to change its dimensions by stretching. The amount and direction (one-way or two-way) of stretch varies according to the knitting process. New stretch yarns, manufactured fibers, and double-knit construction have helped to develop and produce knit fabrics that retain their comfort, shape, and size. Stretch fabrics are developed by means of textured yarns, spandex fiber yarns, or chemical treatment of cotton or wool fibers.

Single Knit One set of needles is used to form loops across the fabric width.

Double Knit Two sets of needles are used to give both sides of the fabric a similar appearance.

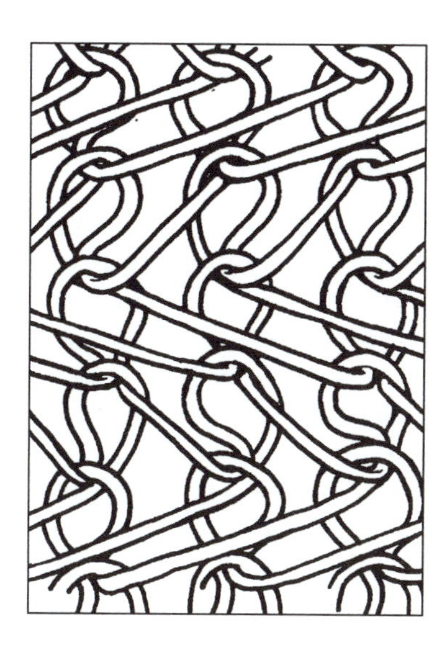

Tricot Knit Several loops are formed in a lengthwise direction.

Understanding Grainline and Crossgrain

Draping skills are acquired with patience and practice. Practice *smoothing* the fabric over the dress form with a light and skillful touch of the hand. Avoid stretching the fabric. The fabric must be premeasured and have correct grainline and crossgrain drawn on the fabric piece.

Lengthwise Grain (Straight of Grain)

The **lengthwise grain** of the fabric is always parallel to the selvage of the fabric goods and is also sometimes referred as the **warp.** The selvage is the firmly woven edge running the length of the fabric on both sides. Strongest threads run in the lengthwise direction and have the least stretch.

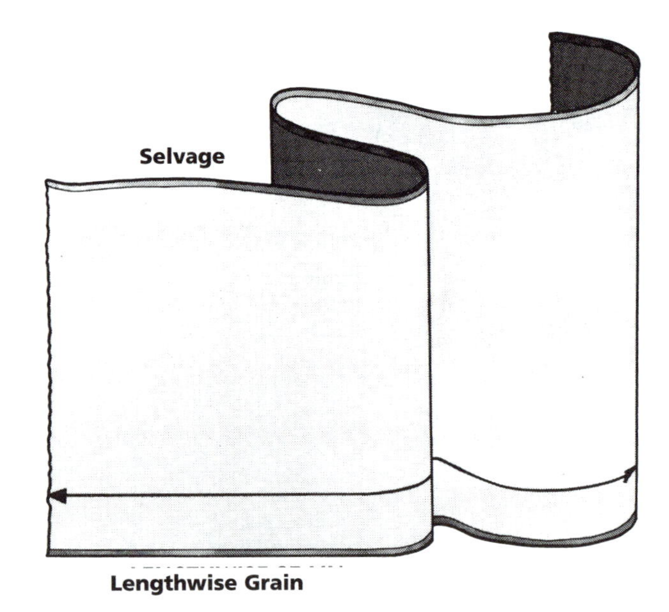

Crosswise Grain

The **crossgrain** is easily recognized as the weave that runs perpendicular to the lengthwise grain of the goods from selvage to selvage. These crossgrain yarns are sometimes referred to as the "filling" yarns and are better known as the **weft**. The crossgrain has slightly more give than the straight of the grain in fabrics. When draping, the crosswise grain usually lies parallel to the floor.

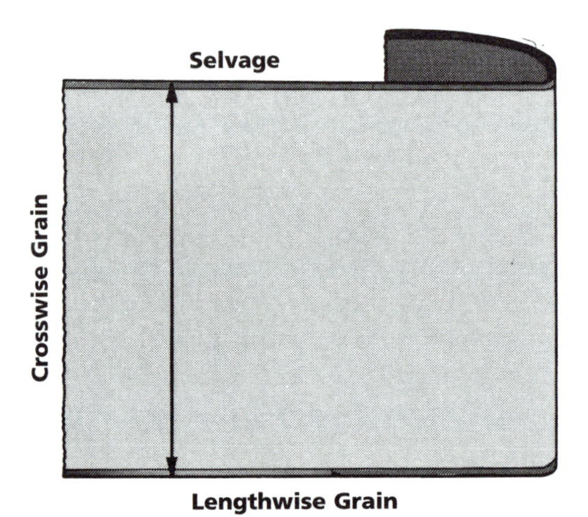

True Bias

To find **true bias** easily, fold the grain of the goods to the crossgrain of the goods to create a perfect 45 degree foldline. Bias fabric always gives and stretches a great deal more than the grain or crossgrain of the goods. Bias is used when a design requires draping contours over the body without using darts.

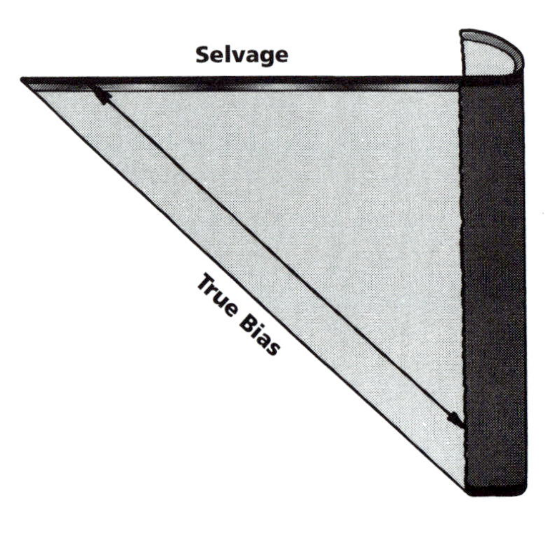

Maintaining Balance (Plumb Theory)

Maintaining balance means that the garment hangs correctly. All garments have a definite relationship with the figure that enables them to hang straight up and down and be parallel to the floor. The garment will twist, drag, or pull when worn if the pieces are not on the correct grainlines and crossgrains. Therefore, when draping any foundation pattern, **aligning the grainline exactly** on the center front of the bodice and **aligning the crossgrain exactly** parallel to the floor (at the bust level for bodices and at hip level for skirts) is critical. This is sometimes known as "plumb theory." Visually, a garment that has incorrect balancing lines will have a hem that is higher or lower in the front than in the back.

After the fabric has been properly aligned on the dress form, the designer may arrange the fabric in any position, radiating from the apex. As darts, tucks, style lines, graceful folds, or gathers are created for each particular design, the grainline and crossgrain should be carefully maintained. This grainline and crossgrain alignment allows the designer to maintain the correct balance between the front and back of the garment.

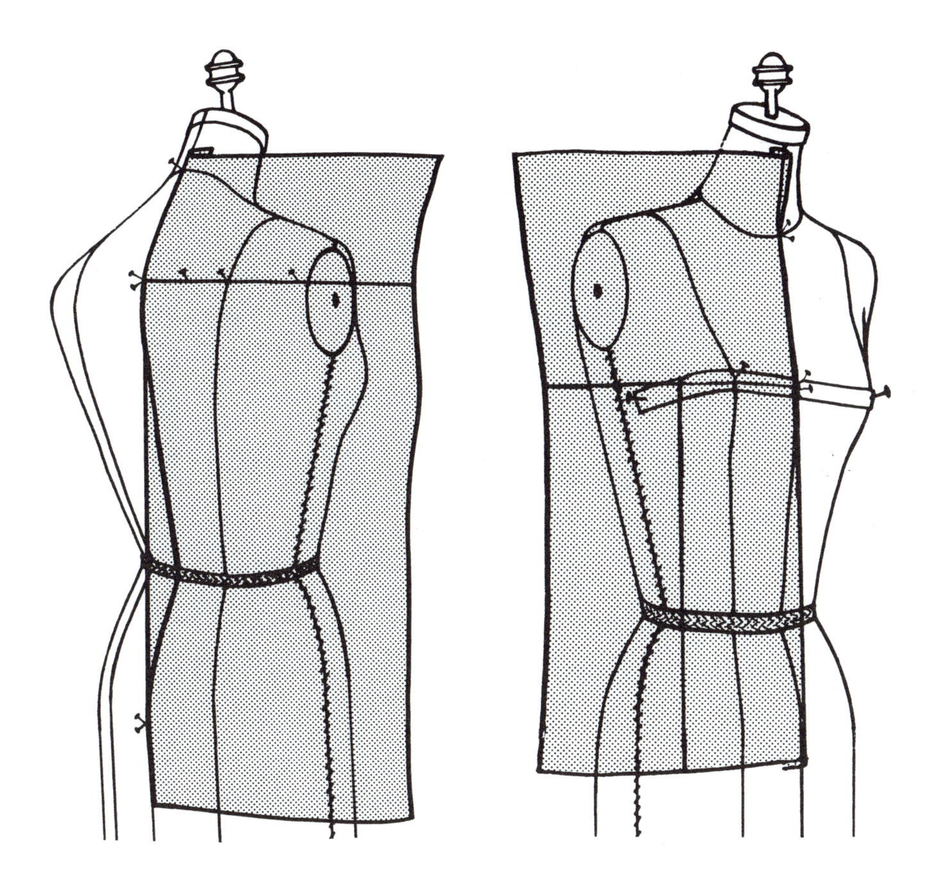

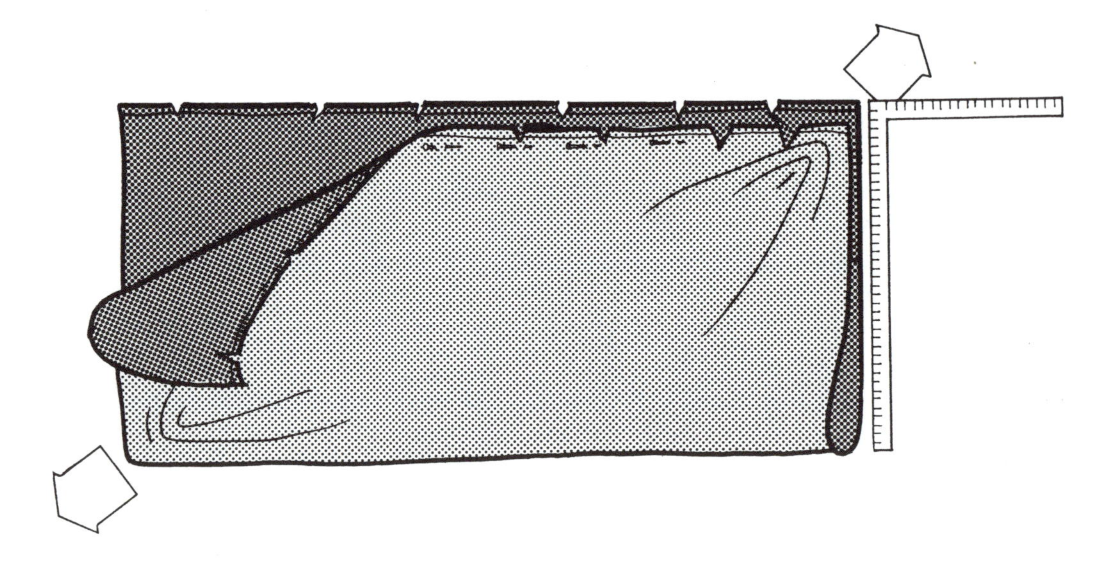

Blocking

Before beginning the draping process, check the fabric to determine if the lengthwise and crosswise threads have distorted from a 90 degree alignment. Blocking is the process of ensuring that the lengthwise and crossgrain threads are at right angles to each other. If the threads of the fabric are not at perfect right angles, the fabric must be realigned or put on grain by blocking.

Fabric grain can be straightened (or "blocked") by folding the fabric from selvage to selvage. Clip the selvage about every two inches to relax the lengthwise grain. Pin all the fabric edges together (excluding the folded side). Gently pull on the true bias for a few moments. Repeat this stretching process a few inches away until the fabric is straight and the crossgrain threads are at a 90 degree angle from the lengthwise threads.

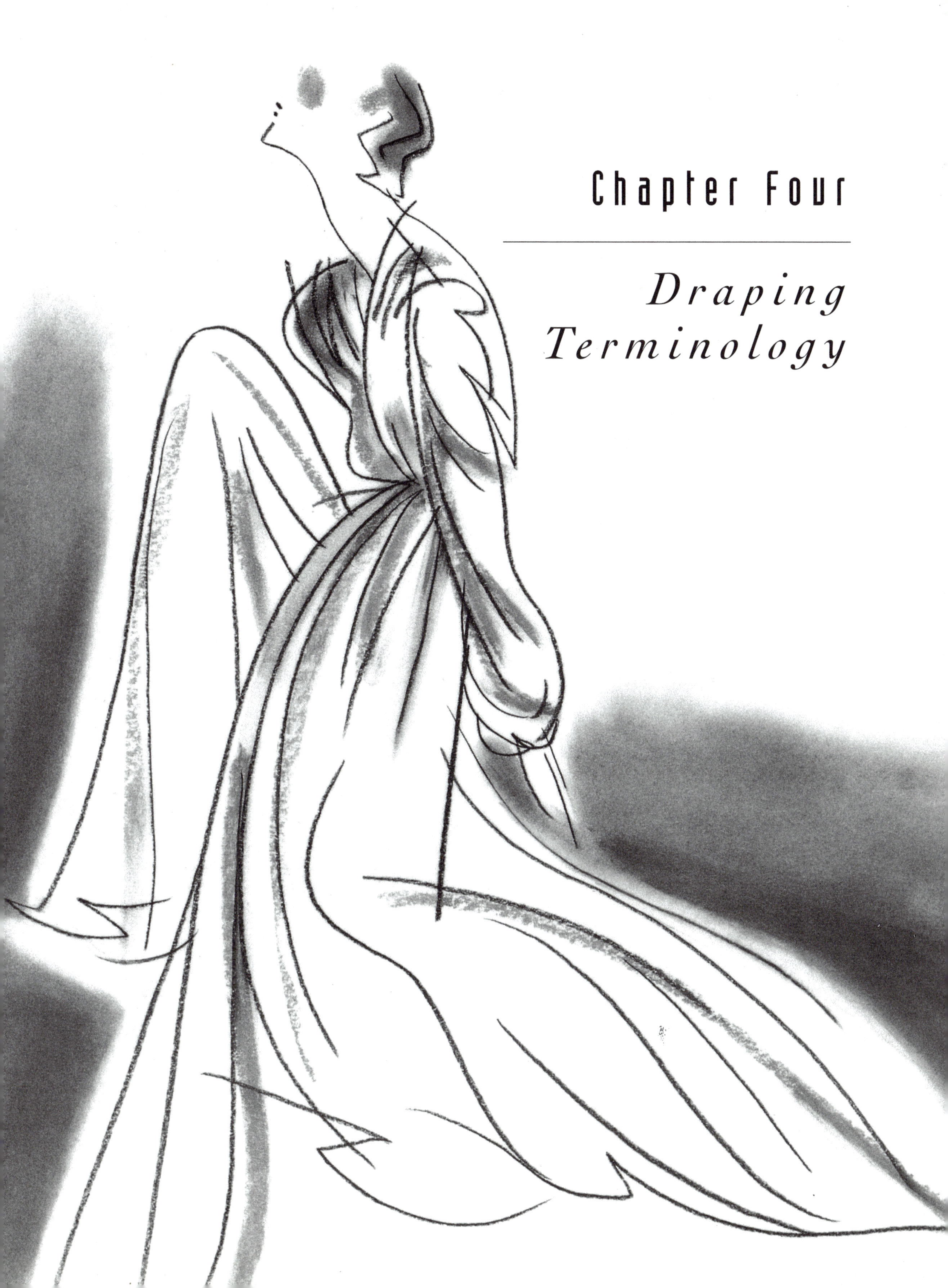

Chapter Four

Draping Terminology

Notching Theory

Notches are the "road signs" that inform an operator which garment piece sews to which piece. Each notch is noted by a pencil marking on the finished drape. Notches help to identify where pattern pieces should be matched. If the garment is properly notched, the operator can easily sew together a garment design quickly and correctly. Therefore, it is important that a patternmaker understands why and where to place notches on a pattern.

Many times a student has difficulty learning where notches are to be placed on a drape or a complete pattern. Here are some basic rules and guidelines that a beginner may follow to help guide the placement of notches.

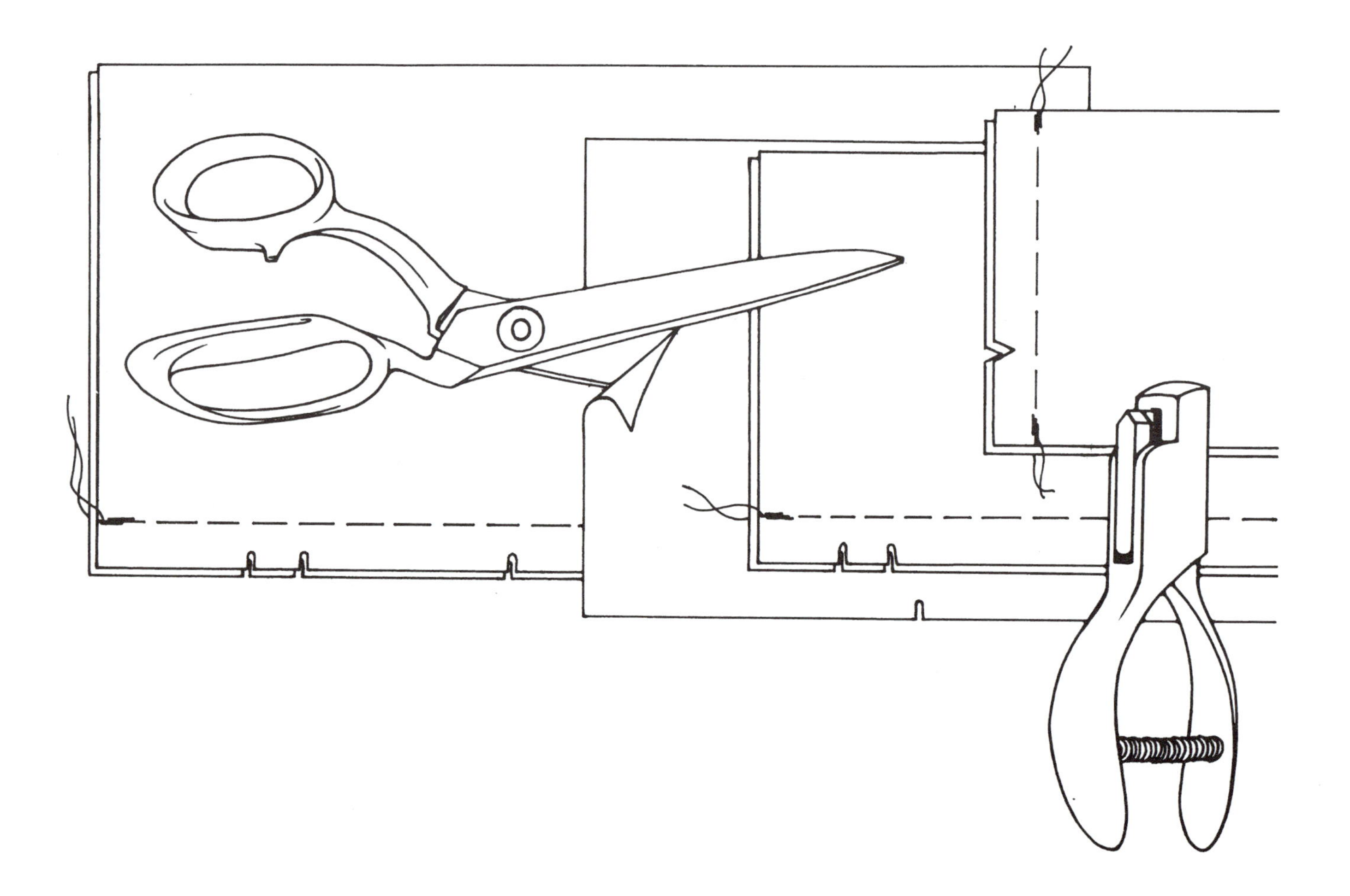

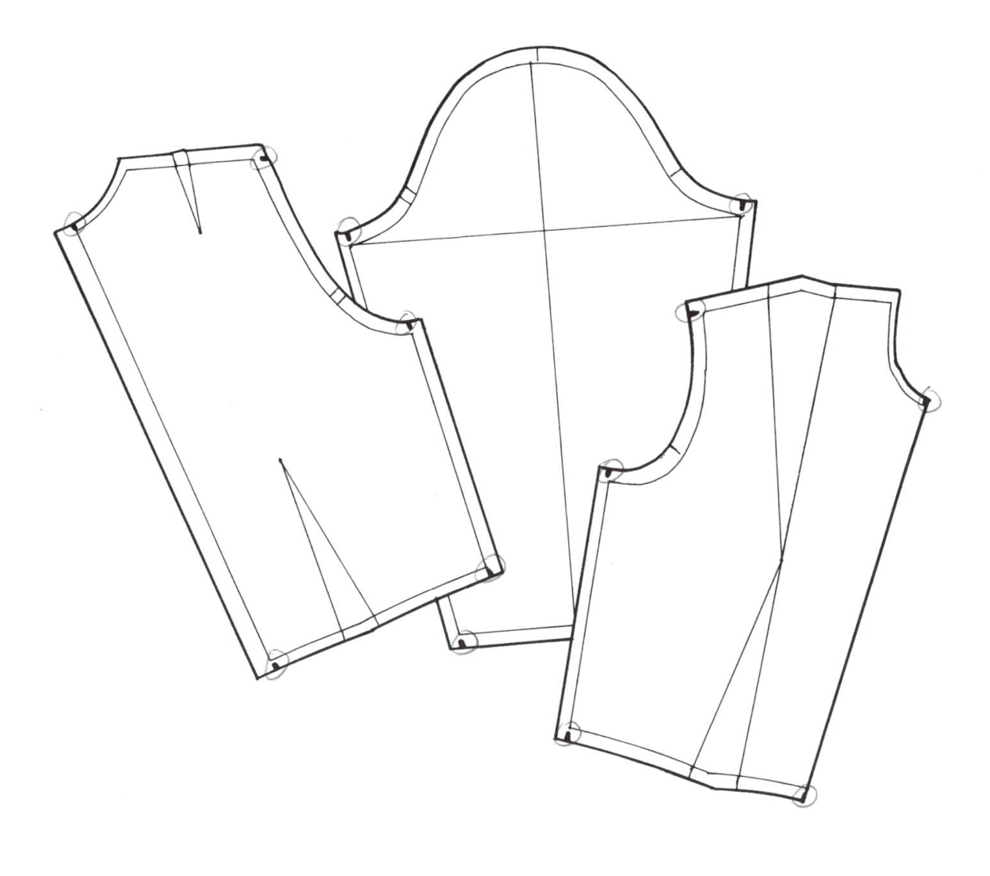

Seam Allowance Notches

Manufacturers save money by having as few notches as possible within the finished pattern. To achieve fewer notches, do not notch the seam allowances of the pattern. Because sewing operators always know how much seam allowances are within the garment, this is readily accepted.

Notching Guidelines

The following rules and guidelines will help the patternmaker correctly place a sufficient number of notches to enable the operator to sew together the garment.

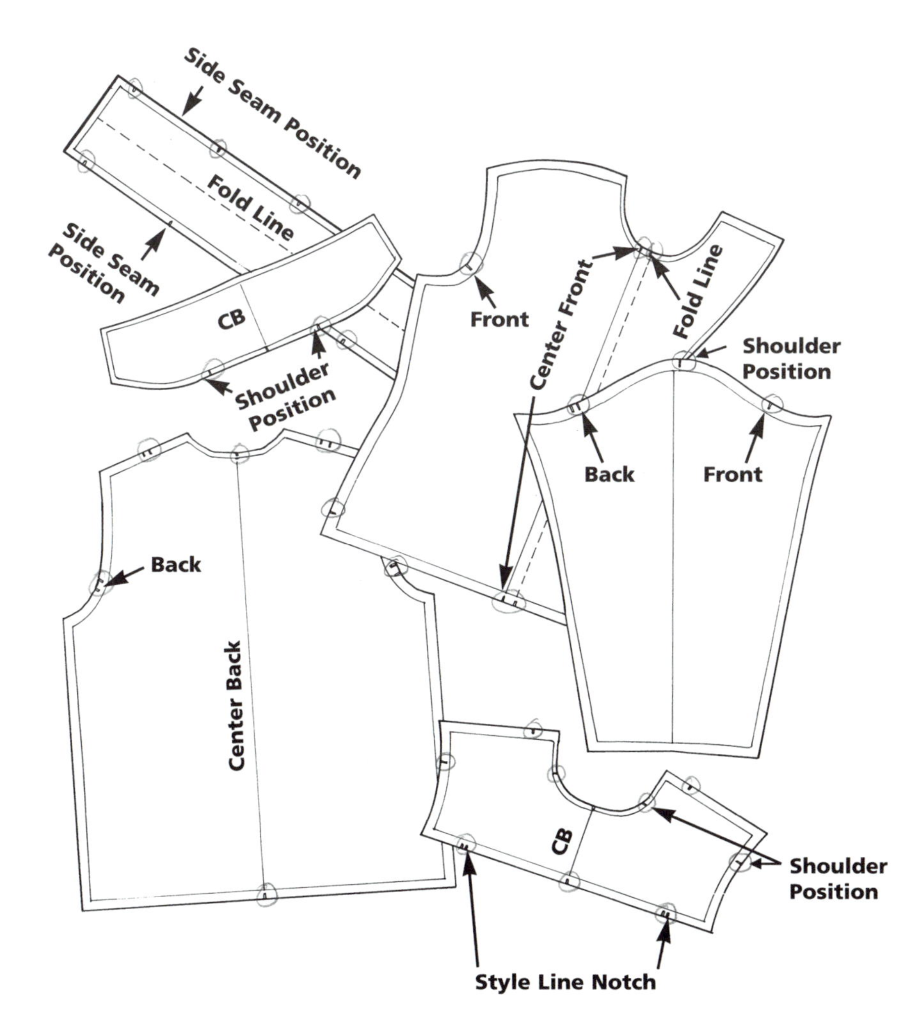

Always Notch

Center front positions All center front locations of blouses, bodices, skirts, and pants should be notched.

Center back positions All center back locations of blouses, bodices, skirts, pants, and collars should be notched.

Shoulder positions All shoulder positions of collars, sleeves, and yokes should be notched.

Side seam positions All side seam positions of waistbands should be notched.

All foldlines Hems, pleats, darts, and foldlines of attached facings are common areas where foldline notches are necessary.

Identify front pattern pieces Single notch.

Identify back pattern pieces Double notch.

NOTE: When pattern pieces look very similar and both have a center fold, the center fold notches will identify all front positions with a **single notch** and the center back position with a **double notch.** A typical garment needing this type of notching is a pull-on blouse, an elastic waist skirt, or a top and under collar.

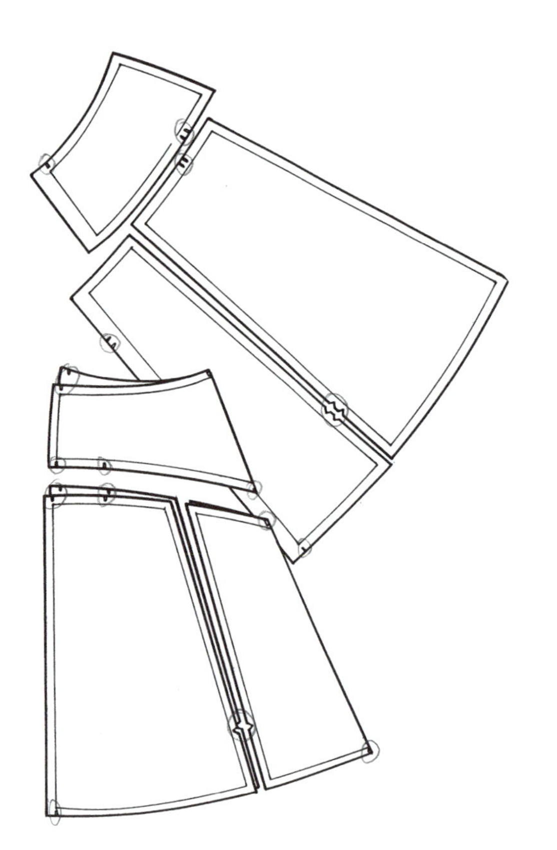

Guidelines for Notching Stylelines

After fully understanding which positions always need to be notched, the patternmaker must apply the following guidelines to accurately and correctly notch all stylelines.

- **A notch must match a notch or seamline.**
- **Notch the pattern so it can be identified as front or back.**
- **Do not center the notches in a styleline.**
- **Do not allow the pattern pieces to flip.**
- **All style lines must be notched so they say "sew me to me."**

Notes

Glossary of Draping Terms

The following is a useful source of terms relating to draping garments. These terms should be helpful to the educator as well as the student and design room professional in order to offer a quick reference to achieve a desired draping technique. Each term is defined to offer a quick understanding of the facts.

Apex The highest point of a bust on a dress form or live model. In draping, the apex is a reference point for establishing the crossgrain position on the front bodice muslin.

Balance The matching of grains and adjacent pattern sections. When trueing, lines on patterns should correspond with lines and measurements on the figure. All patterns have a definite relationship with the figure that enables the garment to hang straight up and down (plumb) and be parallel to the floor. The garment will twist, drag, or pull when worn if the pieces are not on the correct grainlines and crossgrains.

Armhole Balance This allows a set-in-sleeve to hang slightly forward and follow the curvature of the arm. To achieve this balance, the back armhole should measure 1/2-inch larger than the front armhole and have a "horseshoe shape." This extra 1/2-inch back armhole distance also keeps the back bodice distance extended to the front shoulder seam, keeping the shoulder blade level at a perfect crossgrain.

Pants Crotch Seam Balance The back crotch measurement should measure 2-inches longer than the front crotch. This will prevent pants from pulling or sagging.

Pant Leg Seam The back pant leg at the ankle/hem should measure at least 1-inch more than the front leg ankle. This 1-inch difference allows a correct blend into the longer back crotch distance. Otherwise, the legs of the pants will twist and pull.

Perpendicular Line The front bust level of the body, the shoulder blade level on the body, and the hip level on the body should be parallel to the floor. The crossgrains of garments should always be on these lines. Otherwise, the garment will drag and pull downward or upwards.

Plumb Lines The center front of the body and the center back of the body should always be vertical to the floor. Therefore, the grainline of the garment should be parallel to these lines. Otherwise the garment will twist or pull.

Side Seam Balance The front and back side seams should be the same shape and length. In a fitted bodice, side seams and flared skirt side seams should be the same angle off of straight grain. To drape a torso, shift, or fitted skirt, the side seam should be parallel to the center front/back grain.

Waistline Balance The front waist measurement of garments is 1-inch larger than the back waist measurement. This difference allows garments to hang correctly from side seam to side seam.

Bias A line diagonally across the grain of the fabric that offers the greatest stretchability. True bias is at a 45 degree angle.

Blend A technique that helps form a smooth, continuous line or smoothly shapes discrepancies of marks or dots made on the muslin drape. Sleeve seams, princess lines, waistlines, and skirt gores are the most common seams needing blending.

Block A technique to shape the fabric by pulling and realigning it on grain while pressing with steam.

Break Point The point of a controlled turn, roll, or flare usually relating to lapels, shawl collars, revere collars, and notched collars.

Center Back A defined place that indicates the exact center of the pattern or garment in relation to the true center back of a figure.

Center Front A defined place that indicates the exact center of the pattern or garment in relation to the true center front of a figure.

Clip A small cut into the seam allowance that extends almost to the stitch line. It is used on curved seams to release strain and help the seam lie flat when turned, as in necklines, or in corners of squared seams, as in collars, facings, and necklines.

Concave Curve An inside curved seam forming an inward arc, as in armholes and necklines.

Convex Curve An outward curved seam forming a rounded curve, as on the outer edge of scallops, cap lets, peter pan collars, and shawl collars.

Crease Folding and finger pressing the fabric along the grain or structural line.

Crossmarks A mark or set of marks placed on a drape or pattern to indicate the point at which corresponding pieces or garment sections (style lines, shoulder, yokes, collars, front, or back) are to be matched, shirred, or joined.

Crotch Seam The curved seam that is formed at the point where pant legs meet.

Cut in One Two or more pattern sections that are cut as one piece, such as an attached front facing with the bodice or blouse front, or a sleeve with a bodice.

Dart To take up excess fabric of a specified width and taper it to nothing at one or both ends. Used to aid in fitting the garment over the body curves.

Dart Legs The stitch line on both sides of the dart.

Dots A pencil mark placed on a draped muslin or fabric to record the seam lines or style lines. Used as guide mark for trueing.

Ease The even distribution of slight fullness when one section of a seam is joined to a slightly shorter section without forming gathers or tucks. Used to shape set-in sleeves, princess seams, and other areas.

Ease Allowance The amount of excess fabric added to the draped pattern to make garments more comfortable and allow for easier movement.

Fabric Excess The amount of extra fabric manipulated into designated areas (such as shoulder, waist, side bust) to help create body shape and garment style lines.

Fold A fabric ply that doubles back on itself, thereby forming an underlay to create darts, pleats, tucks, or attached facings.

Gather To draw up fabric fullness on a line of stitching.

Grain See Chapter 3, page 16.

Guide Lines on Muslin Directional lines and markings that indicate the grain, crossgrain, center front, center back, shoulder blade, bust level, apex, hip level, and side seam. These lines are drawn on the prepared muslin to facilitate correct draping.

Master Pattern Basic pattern made from specific measurements that is used as a template for tracing rather than to cutting. It may be used to develop other patterns.

Match To bring notches or other construction markings on two pieces together.

Muslin Shell A basic sample garment made from muslin fabric as an aid during the styling and fitting processes.

Notch See Notching Theory, pages 20–22.

Panels A premeasured piece of muslin used to drape a specific design. These premeasured pieces are usually 4 to 10 inches larger than the finished length and width of the pattern piece. If a piece is too large, the weight of the fabric panel may cause an inaccurate drape.

Pivot The shifting or moving of a pattern from a marked position toward a designated guide line.

Ply One layer of fabric when laying out fabric to be cut. (Pl: Plies)

Princess Panel The area of the dress form that extends from the princess seam to the armhole and side seams.

Seam Allowance The amount of fabric allowed for seams in joining together sections of a garment. Seam allowances must be added to any edge that is to be joined to another. The width of the seam allowance depends on the location of the seam and the price range of the manufacturer.

Collars, Facings and Necklines, Armholes, and Other Curves These elements require seam allowances ranging from 1/4 to 1/2 inch. This allowance saves time in trimming these areas after sewing the seam.

Stitched Seam Garments that require a specially stitched seam, such as those made of knit fabrics or sleepwear, require seam allowances of from 1/4 to 1/2 inch.

Traditional Seam Allowances Elements such as shoulder seams, style lines, and side seams require an additional 1/2 to 1 inch seam allowance.

Zipped Seams These seams, which require zippers and are used for fitting and/or alterations, require a 1-inch seam allowance.

Seam Two or more edges of fabric are held together and sewn using a variety of stitches. Seams should be well constructed and appropriate for the fabric, the type of garment, and the location on the garment.

Selvage The narrow, firmly woven finished edge along both lengthwise edges of the fabric that does not ravel.

Shirr A technique to gather up fabric on the stitch line where fullness in the garment is desired. Shirring is sometimes thought of as multiple rows of gathers.

Side Seam A defined place on a pattern or garment that indicates the point at which the front and back of a garment is sewn together.

Slash A straight cut (longer than a clip) from the outer edge of the fabric into the style line of the garment. A slash is made to relieve tension in the muslin, which allows the drape to fit around the curves of the body.

Stitch Line The line designated for stitching the seam, generally 5/8", 1/2", or 1/4" from the cut edge of patterns.

Style Lines Any seam line other than shoulder seams, armhole seams, or side seams. A style line usually runs from one point of a garment to another point. For example, a yoke runs from side seam to side seam; a shoulder princess seam runs from shoulder seam to waistline seam.

Squared Line A straight line drawn perpendicular from another line. An L-square ruler is usually used to create a perfect perpendicular line.

Transferring The process of pinning and tracing all the fabric markings onto the pattern paper. Some designers prefer to transfer and true up muslin drapes on the dotted paper.

Trueing The process of blending the markings, dots, and cross marks made during the draping process. Trueing establishes continuous seams, style lines, darts, or dart variations. Some designers prefer to transfer and true up muslin drapes on the dotted paper. Others prefer to true up directly onto muslin. See pages 40–49 for instructions on the process of trueing.

Trim (Cut) To cut away excess fabric and make the seam narrower after it has been stitched. Also, to remove or eliminate bulk and excess fabric in corners at any point before turning.

Underlay The underside of a draped design that is made when establishing darts, pleats, and extensions.

Vanishing Point The tapered, finished point of a dart.

Part Two

Basic Foundation Patterns

When a manufacturer develops a new clothing line, one of the first requirements is a set of foundation patterns (blocks). These foundation patterns, which should match the proportion, size, and fit of the target customers, are created by draping fabric onto a professional dress form. Because of the importance of these patterns, sufficient time should be allowed to drape, fit, readjust, and refit before a finished set of patterns is prepared.

This unit illustrates various draping methods to create the foundation patterns for the basic bodice, skirt, and shift. Understanding the many uses and application of these foundation patterns is an important key to good design theory. These foundation patterns provide the designer and manufacturer with a constant fit and silhouette, ease allowance, armhole size, waistline measurement, and desired length. Correct use of these foundation patterns will help save valuable time in both fittings and patternmaking. Once the basic skills have been mastered, other designs will be easier to develop.

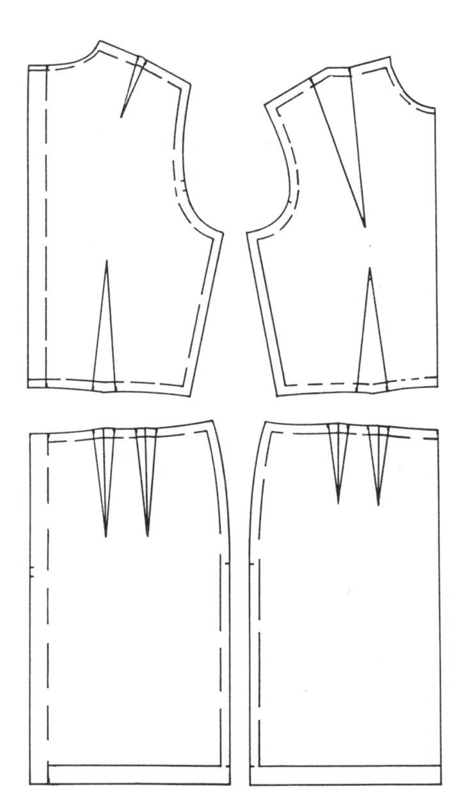

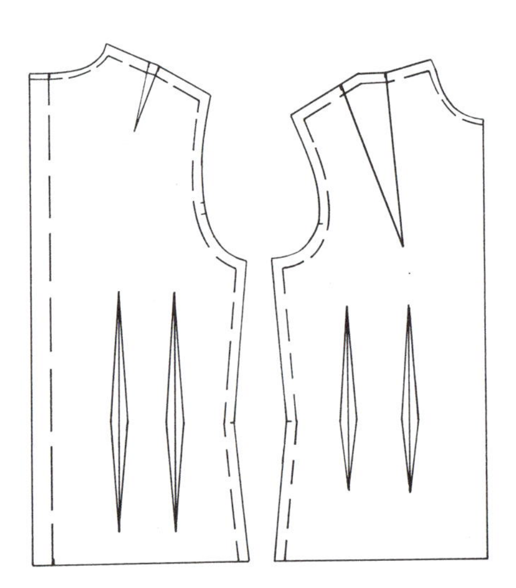

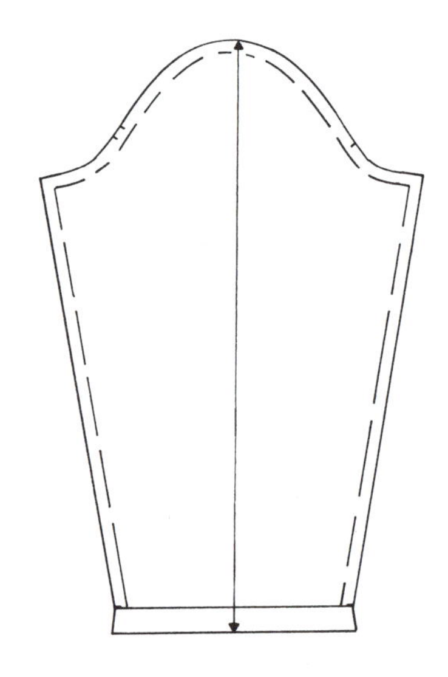

The **basic bodice and skirt slopers** are the most common foundation patterns used to create a three-dimensional design from a flat pattern. These slopers are used to develop other foundation patterns. Darts, tucks, style lines, or gathers can also be created by readjusting the dart areas of these foundation patterns.

The **shift/torso bodice sloper** is a hip-length bodice with a shoulder or side bust dart and sometimes with waistline fisheye darts. This versatile foundation pattern is used to design blouses or dresses that require a fitted armhole. It is also used to make flat pattern designs, which have no waist fitting seams, with a straight-tapered, or flared side seam fit. Dart areas on these foundation patterns can also be converted into tucks, style lines, or gathers.

For the sake of time, the **basic sleeve sloper** is created using the pattern drafting method. However, this design would not be complete unless it was checked for balance, fit, and hang directly on the dress form. See pages 392-394 for a pattern for a sleeve form and instructions to prepare the arm. The chapters include details on how to transfer the finished drapes into complete patterns.

Chapter Five

Basic Bodice

Objectives

By studying the various draping steps in this chapter, the designer should be able to accomplish the following:

- Recognize grain and crossgrain of fabric in relationship to the bust level line, shoulder blade level, and direction and placement of darts.
- Take a flat piece of fabric and make it fit the curves of the body.
- Manipulate and shape a flat piece of fabric to create darts.
- Develop the correct amount of ease allowance, armhole size, waistline shape, measurement, and balance.
- Check and analyze the results of the draping process in order to analyze the fit, hang, balance, proportion, and true up.

Basic Bodice

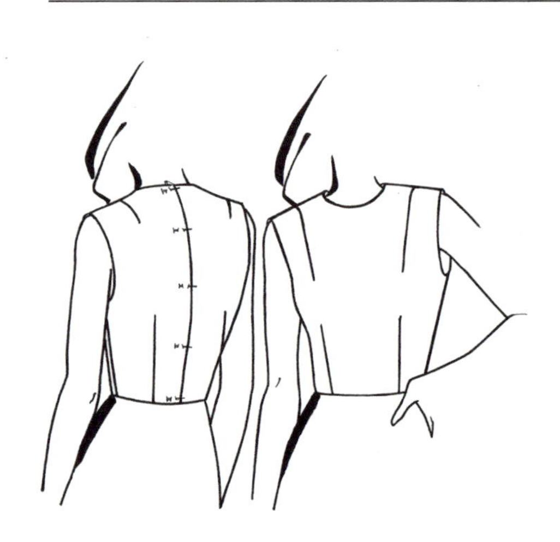

A front and back basic bodice uses darts to control a fitted waist seam. Darts are the key to the fit of a woman's individual figure. Designs emphasizing a fitted silhouette may be achieved when using this darted, waist seam basic pattern.

The basic block pattern is also used to make other basic patterns or garment designs. It is important, therefore, to drape carefully and accurately.

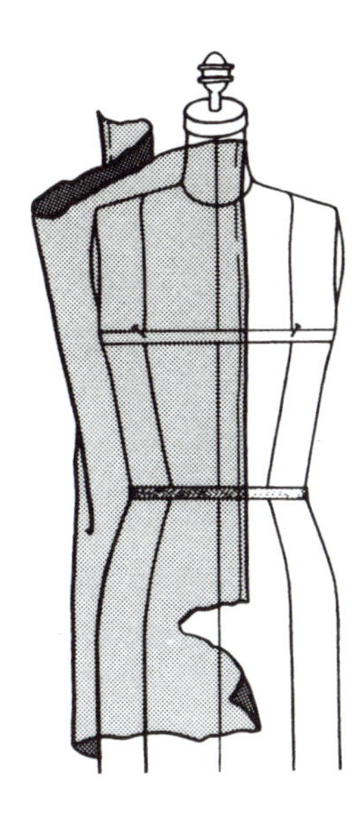

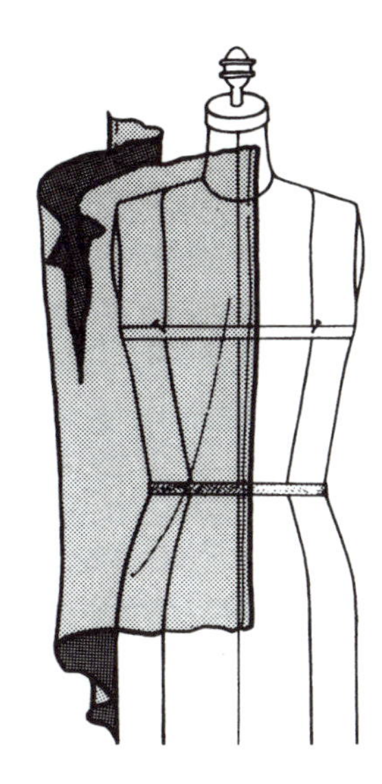

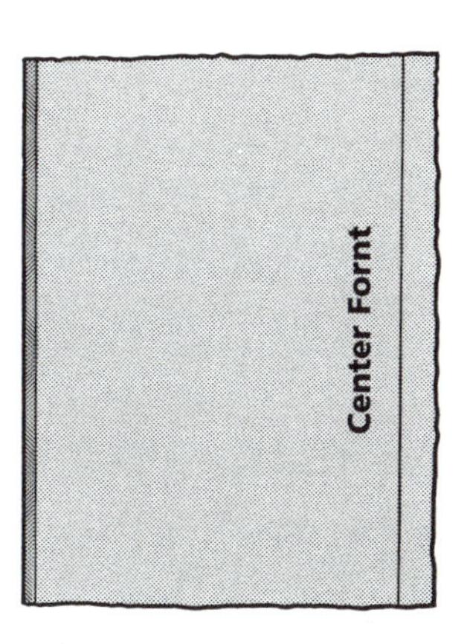

1 **Measure the length for the front bodice** along the straight of grain from the neckband to the waist and add 5 inches.

Snip and tear the fabric at this length.

2 **Measure the width for the front bodice** along the cross-grain from the center front of the dress form to the side seam at the bust level and add 5 inches.

Snip and tear the fabric at this width; then block and press the fabric.

3 **Draw the center front grainline** 1 inch from the torn edge and press under.

Note: The selvage is to your left hand and the torn edge is to your right hand.

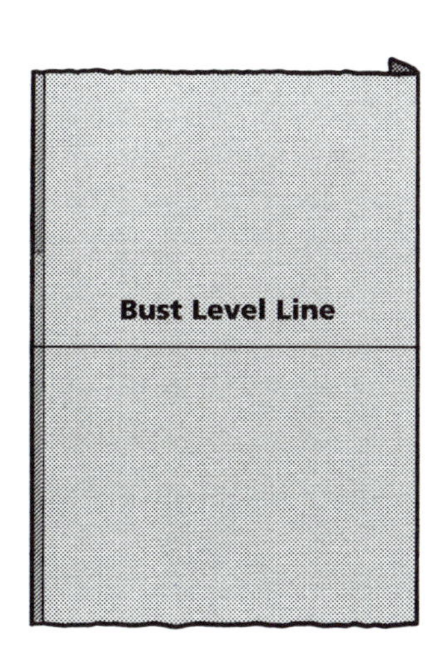

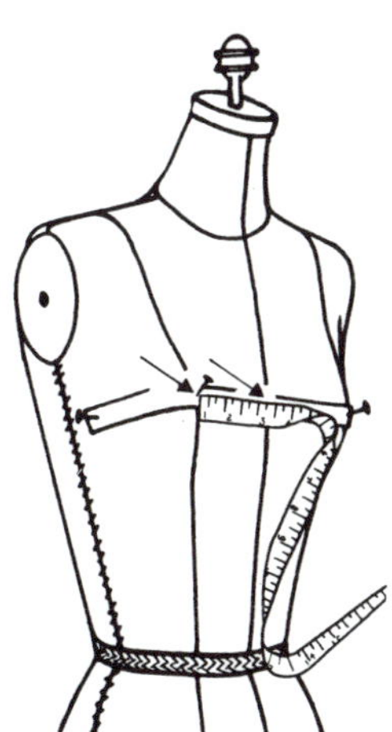

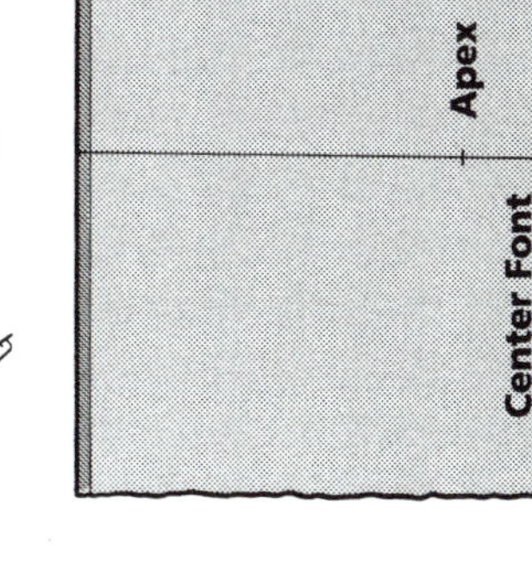

4 **Draw a perfect crossgrain line that will represent the BUST LEVEL LINE.** With an L-square ruler, draw a perfect crossgrain line in the center of the fabric panel.

5 **a. Measure the apex** on the dress form the distance from the center front to the apex.

b. Measure and crossmark the apex this distance on the bust level of the fabric.

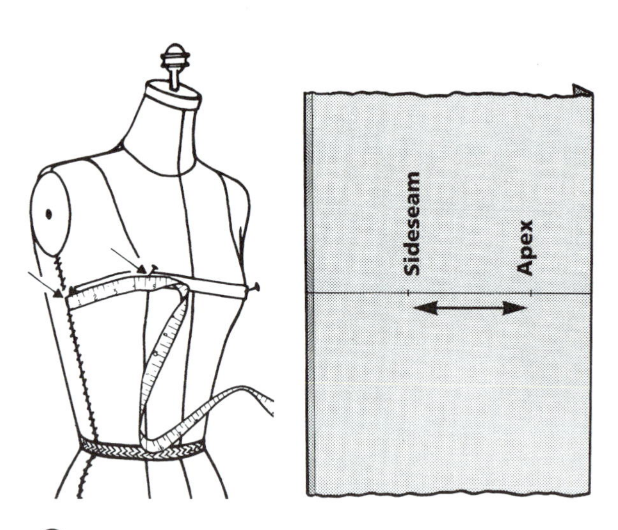

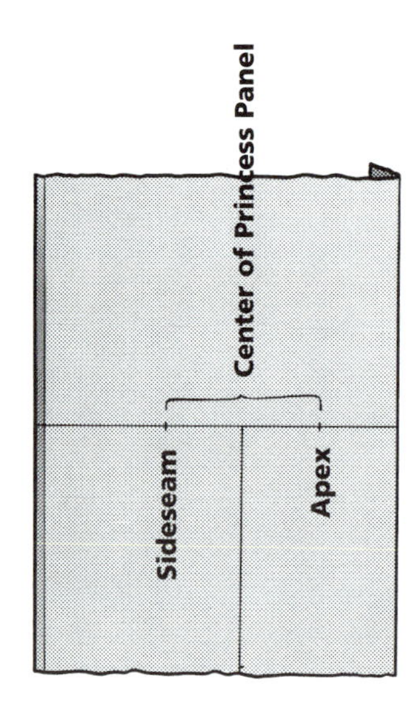

6 **a. Measure from the apex to the side seam** at the bust level on the dress form and add 1/8 inch ease.

b. Measure and crossmark this side seam distance on the bust level of the fabric.

7 **a. Draw the center of the princess panel line.** Divide in half the distance from the apex to the side seam at the bust level.

b. Draw a line parallel to the center front grainline at this divided position, squaring down from the bust level, using an L-square ruler.

Notes

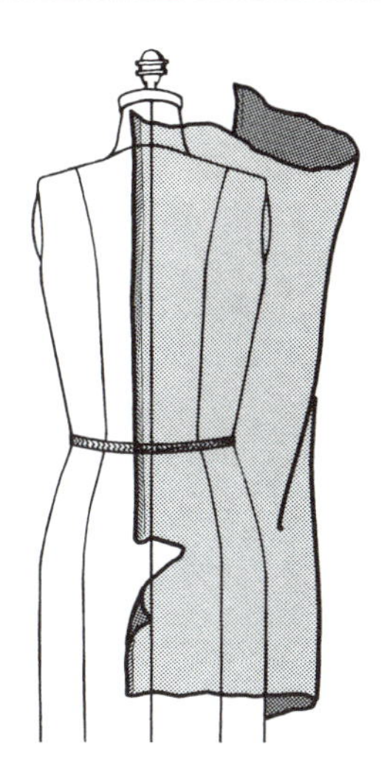

1 **Measure length for the back bodice** along the straight of grain from the neckband to the waist and add 5 inches.

Snip and tear the fabric at this length.

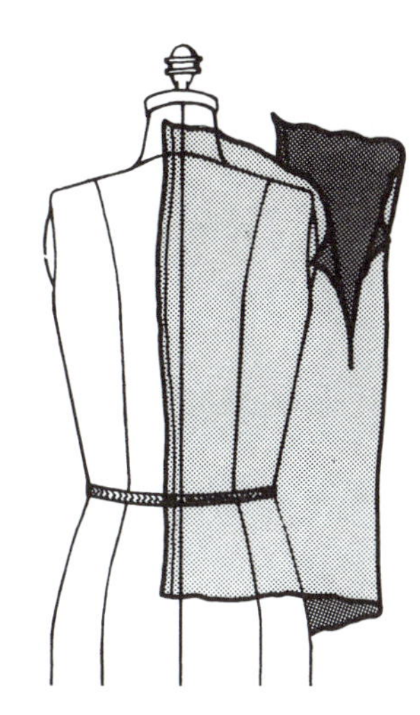

2 **Measure the width for the back bodice** along the cross-grain from the center back seam to the side seam at the underarm, and add 5 inches.

Snip and tear the fabric at this width.

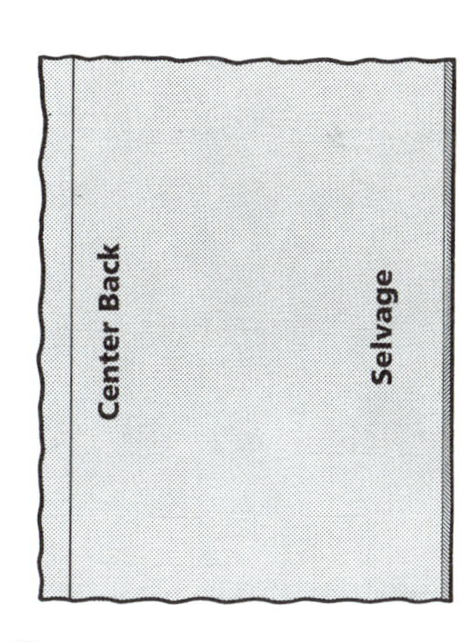

3 **Draw the center back grain-line** 1 inch from the torn edge, and press under.

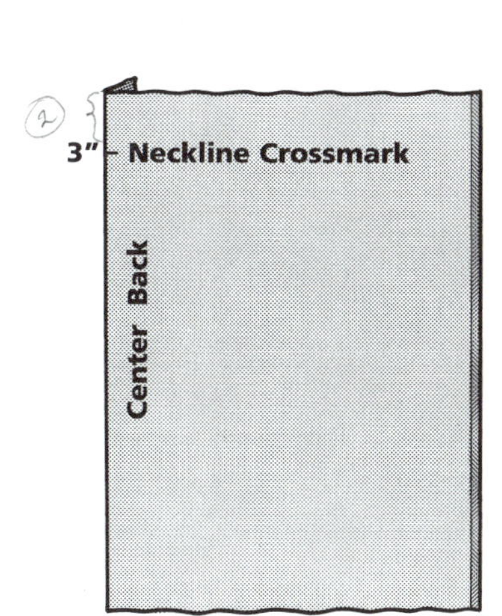

4 **Crossmark the center back neckline position** 3 inches below the top of the fabric on the center back grainline.

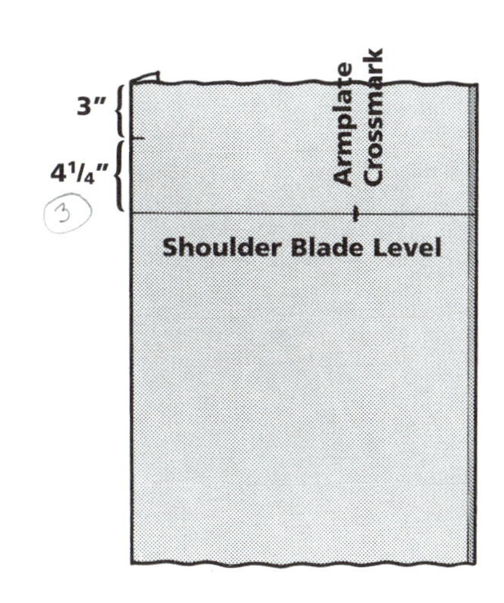

5 **Draw the shoulder blade level line.**

a. Measure down 4 1/4 inches from the back neckline mark.

b. Draw a perfect crossgrain line, using an L-square ruler at this 4 1/4-inch position.

NOTE: This 4 1/4-inch measurement represents one fourth of the distance from center back neck to waist for a size 8 or 10.

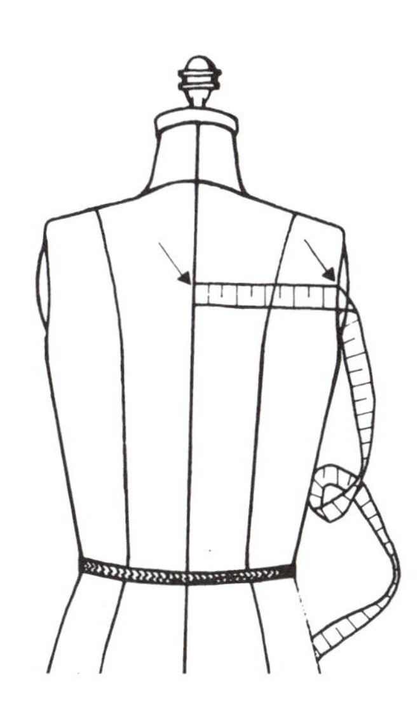

6 **a. Measure the distance from C.B. to the armplate** at the shoulder blade level of the dress form.

b. Crossmark this back shoulder distance on the fabric at the shoulder blade level line.

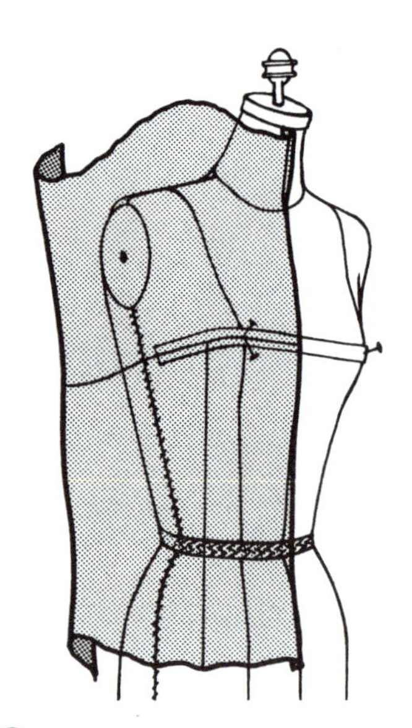

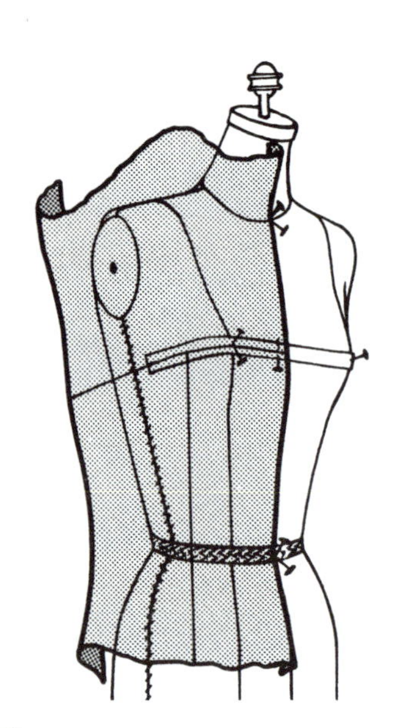

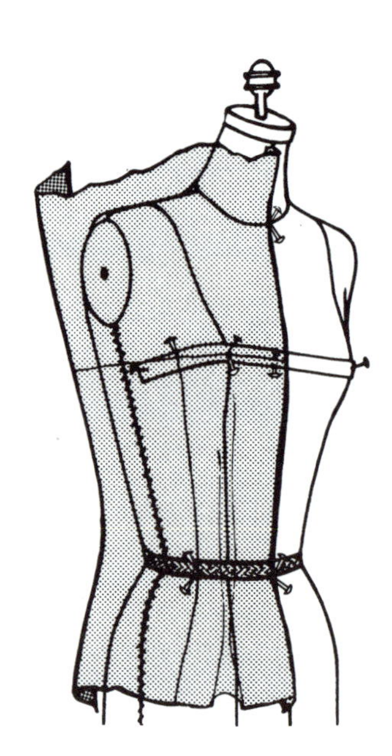

1 **Pin the apex mark** on the fabric to the apex position on the dress form.

2 **Pin the center front grainline fold** of the fabric to the center front position of the dress form.

Anchor pins at C.F. neck and C.F. waist. An additional pin may be needed at the bust level tape.

3 **a. Put a pin on the center of the princess panel position at the waistline** on the dress form and use it as a guide for the following steps.

b. Pin the center of the princess panel line of the fabric exactly in the center of the princess panel of the dress form.

c. Anchor pins at the waistline and the crossgrain.

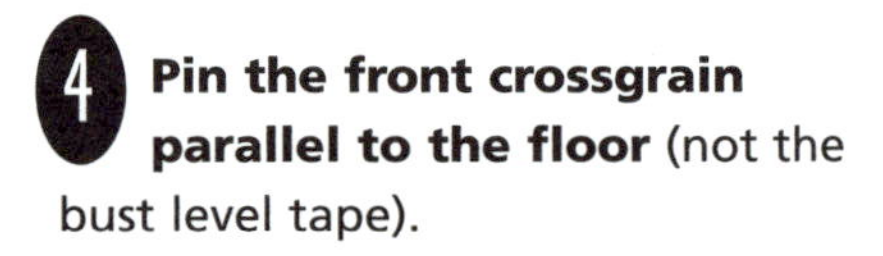

4 **Pin the front crossgrain parallel to the floor** (not the bust level tape).

NOTE: The reason for centering the princess panel line is to verify that the crossgrain line is perfectly aligned. Check that the lengthwise grain is parallel to the C.F. and the crossgrain is parallel to the floor.

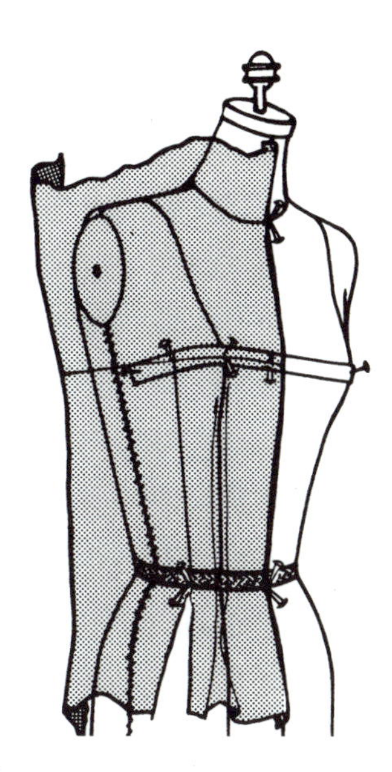

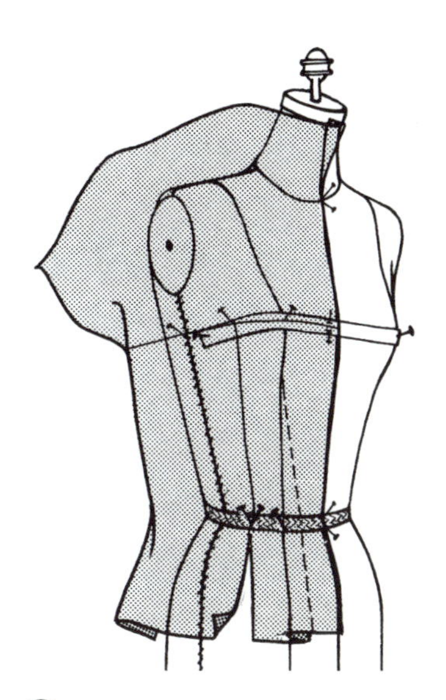

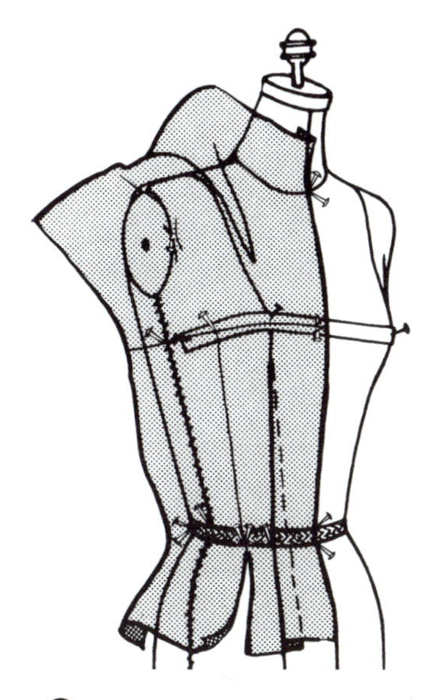

5 **Clip the waistline fabric at the center of the princess panel** from the bottom edge up to the waist seam tape.

NOTE: Overclipping the waistline will result in a tight waistline fit and the lack of necessary ease. See pages 47–48 for correct finished ease.

6 **Pin and drape the front waist dart.** The excess fabric which falls between the center of the princess panel and the center front waist position will become the front waist dart. Be careful not to overstretch the waistline or the rib cage area.

a. Crossmark the princess seam at the waistline. Smooth the fabric from C.F. to the princess seam at the waistline and crossmark. Crease the fabric at the waistline/princess seam crossmark.

b. Pin the excess fabric on the princess seam. The excess fabric is creased at the princess seam crossmark and folded toward the center front. Taper the dart to nothing toward the bust apex.

7 **Smooth and drape the remainder of the waistline.** Smooth the fabric across the waist tape until the fabric passes the side seam. Pin at the side seam/waist corner. Leave a 1/8 inch pinch at the waistline. Also, do not mold the rib cage area.

8 **Pin and drape the side seam and the beginning of the shoulder.**

a. Smooth the excess fabric past the side seam. Be careful not to pull or mold the fabric across the rib cage area.

b. Smooth the fabric up and over the dress form armplate to the shoulder. Create a 1/4"–1/4" pinch at the screw level (middle at ridge) of the armhole. This ensures that the armhole does not become too tight. Pin in place. Leave all excess fabric in the shoulder area.

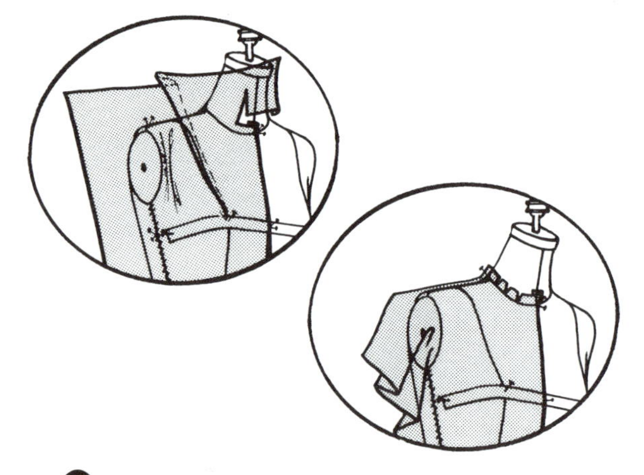

9 **Drape the front neckline.** Trim and clip the neckline at intervals. Smooth the excess fabric around the neck area.

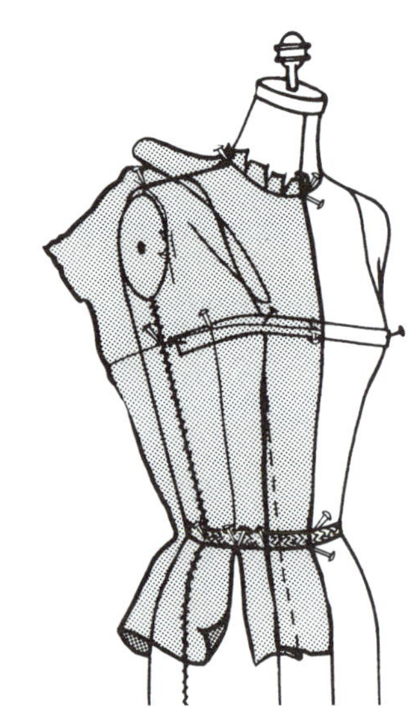

10 **Drape and smooth the fabric over the shoulder/neckline** seam of the dress form to a point just past the princess seam. Pin in place. Crossmark the princess seam and the shoulder.

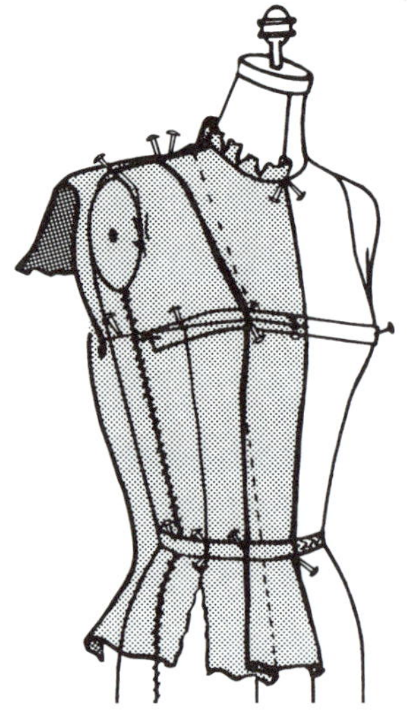

11 **Drape the front shoulder dart.** The excess fabric that falls between the shoulder/neckline and the shoulder/armhole area will become the amount of excess fabric in the shoulder dart. The larger the bust, the larger the dart, the smaller the bust, the smaller the dart.

a. Crease the fabric at the shoulder/princess seam crossmark.

b. Pin the excess fabric on the princess seam. The excess fabric is folded at the princess seam crossmark and folded toward the center front neck. Taper the dart to nothing toward the bust apex.

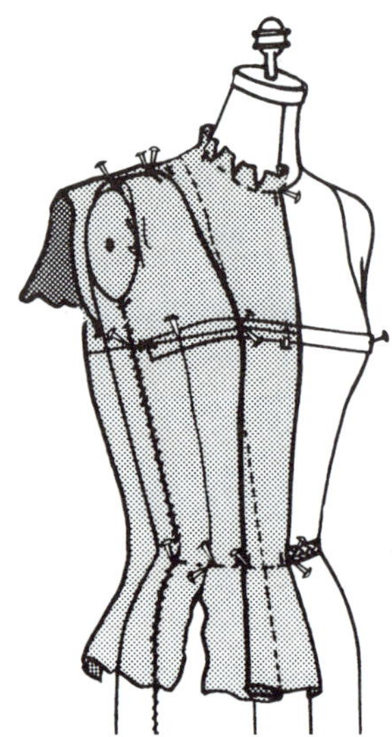

12 **Mark all key areas** of the dress form to the fabric.

Neckline
Crossmark at C.F. neck and at neckline/shoulder corner. Lightly mark remainder of neckline.

Shoulder Seam and Shoulder Dart
Lightly mark shoulder seam, crossmark shoulder dart, and shoulder ridge corner.

Armplate
a. Top at shoulder seam ridge.
b. Middle at screw level.
c. Crossmark bottom at side seam.

Side seam
Lightly mark.

Waistline and Waist Dart
Crossmark at C.F. waist, at side seam waist, and both sides of the dart.

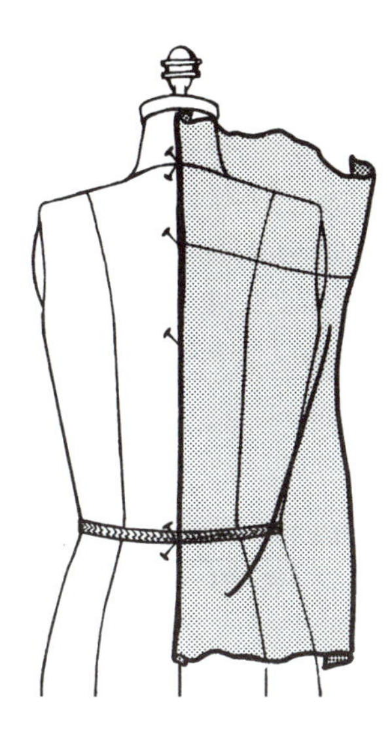

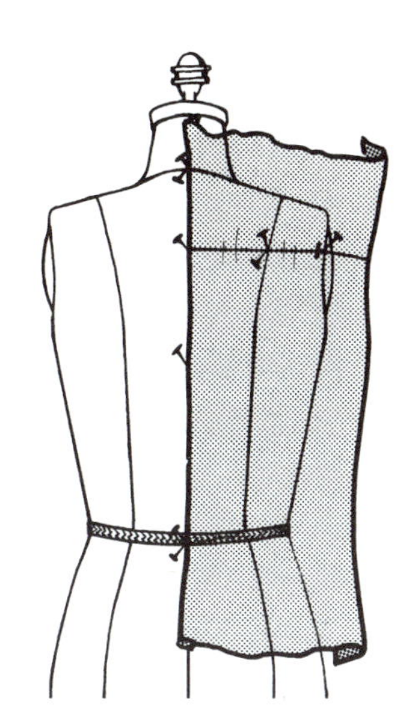

1 Pin the center back grainline fold of the fabric to the center back position on the dress form.

2 Align the neckline position mark of the fabric to the center back neck position on the dress form.

3 Pin and drape the back crossgrain line of the fabric to the shoulder blade level on the dress form. Pin the armplate crossmark 1/4 inch away from the plate (at the armhole ridge). Distribute the excess ease along the shoulder blade level.

NOTE: This line is correctly draped when the drape hangs freely and evenly without any drag or pulled down look. Also, the lower edge of the drape should hang parallel to the floor.

4 Pin and drape in the back waistline dart 7-inches long by 1 1/4-inches wide, as follows:

a. Smooth the fabric toward the side seam until the fabric passes the princess seam. Place a crossmark at the princess/waist seam.

b. Measure and crossmark the waistline 1 1/4 inches toward the side seam from the princess seam/waist crossmark.

c. Measure and crossmark 7 inches up at the middle of the dart, remaining parallel to center back (on grain). Refer to the illustration.

d. Fold the back waistline dart in place. At the waistline, fold the princess seam crossmark to the 1 1/4-inch crossmark. Taper the dart to nothing at the 7-inch mark.

NOTE: The waist dart increases or decreases in width and length as sizes get larger or smaller from a standard size 8 or 10.

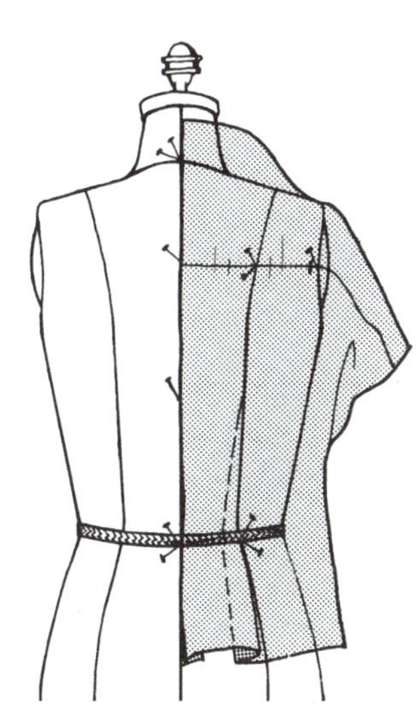

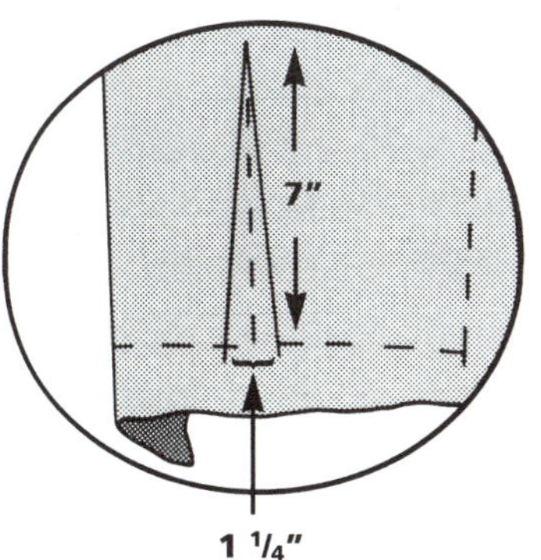

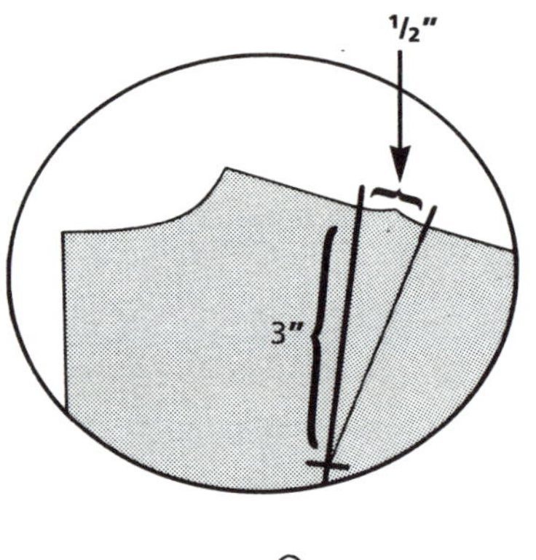

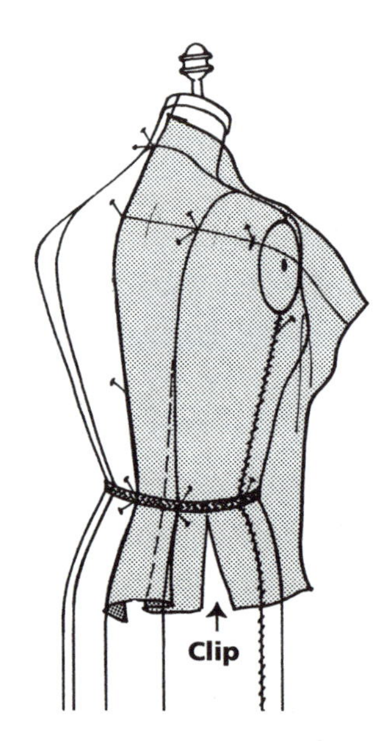

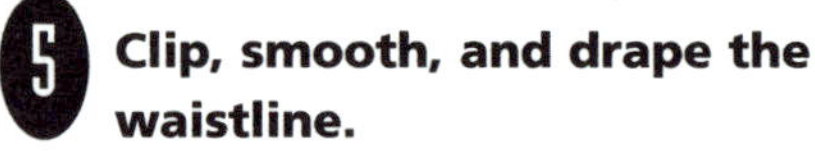

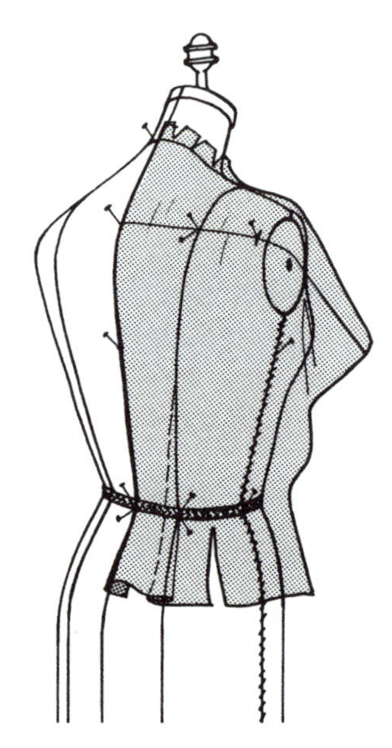

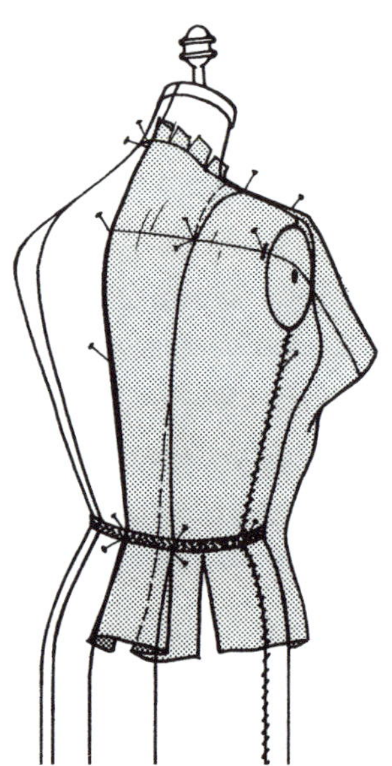

5 Clip, smooth, and drape the waistline.

a. Clip the waistline fabric at the center of the princess panel up to the bottom of the waist seam tape.

NOTE: Overclipping the waistline will result in a tight waistline fit and the lack of necessary ease.

b. Smooth the fabric across the waist tape until the fabric passes the side seam. Pin at the side seam/waist corner.

6 Drape the back side seam. Smooth the fabric past the side seam and flat over the dress form. Be careful not to mold or distort the back rib cage area. Pin in place.

7 Clip, smooth, and drape the back neckline.

a. Carefully trim the excess fabric around the neck area, clipping at intervals.

b. Smooth the fabric over the shoulder/neckline area of the dress form and pin in place.

8 Drape in the back shoulder dart, 3 inches long by 1/2-inch wide as follows:

a. Smooth the fabric over the shoulder seam, starting at the neckline to the princess seam and crossmark.

b. Measure toward the armhole 1/2 inch from the princess seam at the shoulder (width of back shoulder dart), and crossmark.

c. Measure down 3 inches on the princess seam from the shoulder seam, and crossmark.

d. Fold the back shoulder dart in place. Fold the fabric from the princess seam crossmark to the 1/2-inch crossmark. Taper the dart to nothing at the 3-inch crossmark.

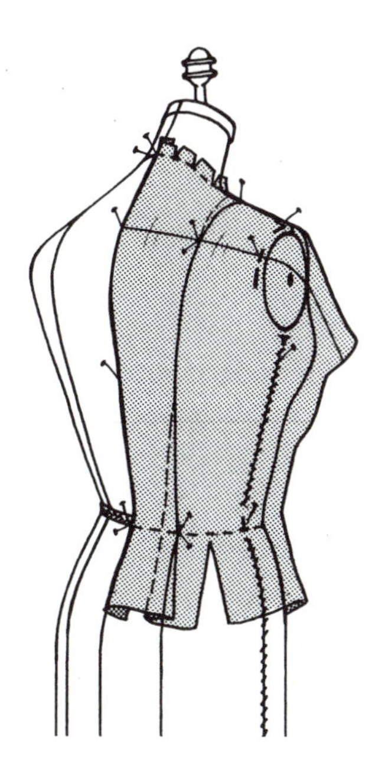

9 Mark all key areas of the dress form to the fabric.

Neckline
Crossmark at C.B. neck and at neckline/shoulder corner. Lightly mark remainder of neckline.

Shoulder Seam and Shoulder Dart
Lightly mark shoulder seam and crossmark shoulder dart and shoulder ridge corner.

Armplate
a. Top at shoulder seam ridge.
b. Middle at screw level.
c. Bottom at the side seam crossmark.

Side Seam
Lightly mark.

Waistline and Waist Dart
Crossmark at C.B. waist, at side seam waist, and both sides of the dart.

Notes

Trueing Basic Bodice Drape

Some designers prefer to transfer and true up muslin drapes on the dotted paper. Others prefer to true-up directly onto muslin. This author recognizes that there is more than one way of creating a design. Illustrations of steps 2 through 10 are examples of the trueing process on the actual muslin drape.

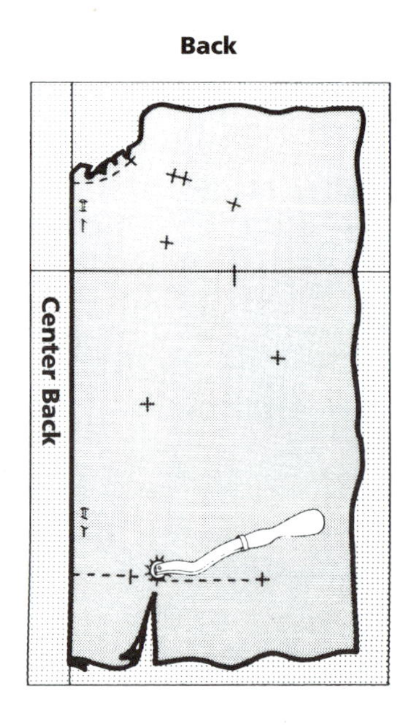

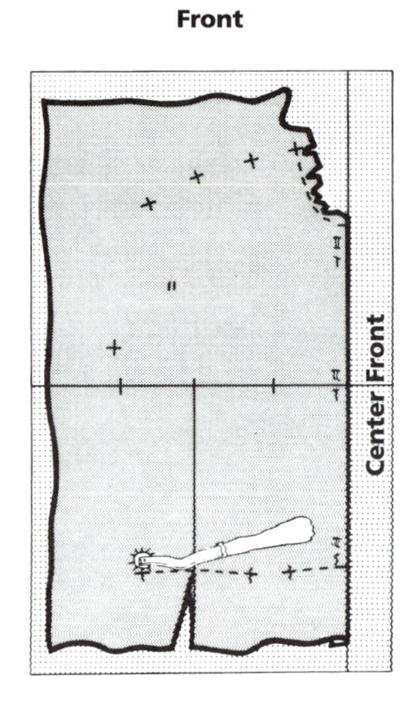

1 Remove the fabric from the dress form and lay it flat on the table. If you are planning to true up the fabric onto paper complete the following steps:

a. Draw in the straight of grain and crossgrain on the pattern paper. Place the fabric on top of the paper, matching the straight of grain and crossgrain.

b. Transfer all the fabric markings, using a trace wheel.

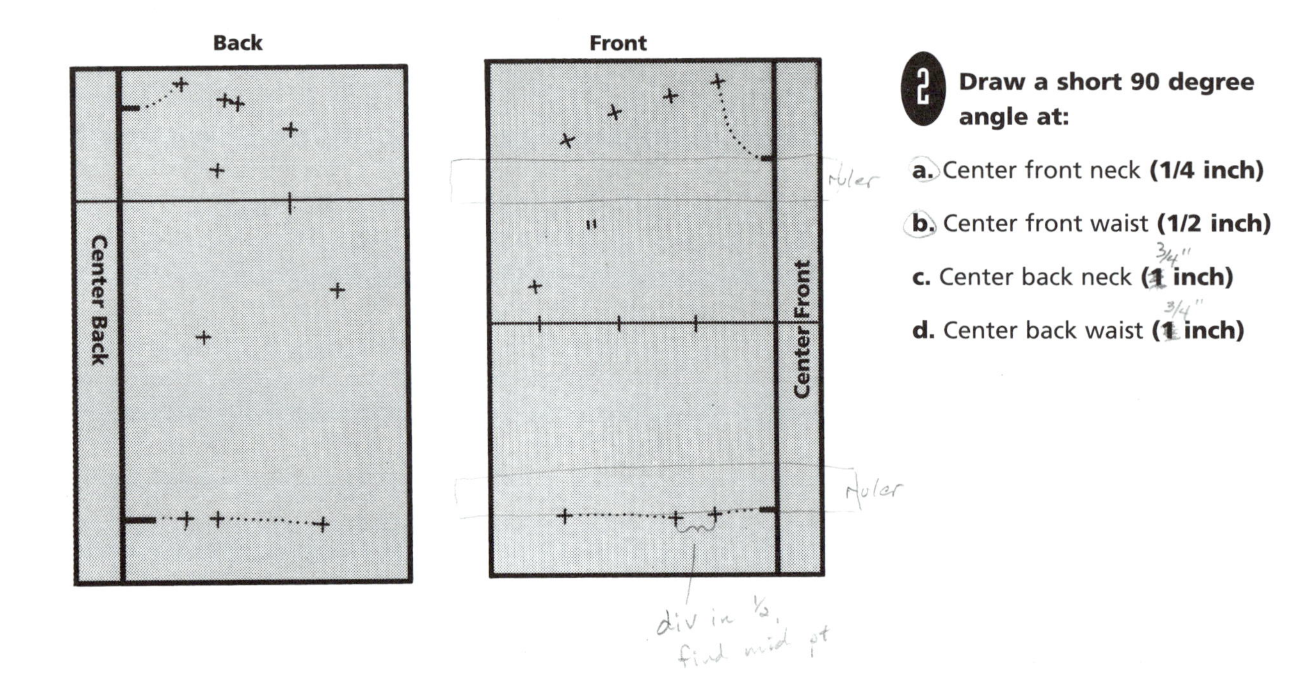

2 Draw a short 90 degree angle at:

a. Center front neck **(1/4 inch)**

b. Center front waist **(1/2 inch)**

c. Center back neck **(1 inch)**

d. Center back waist **(1 inch)**

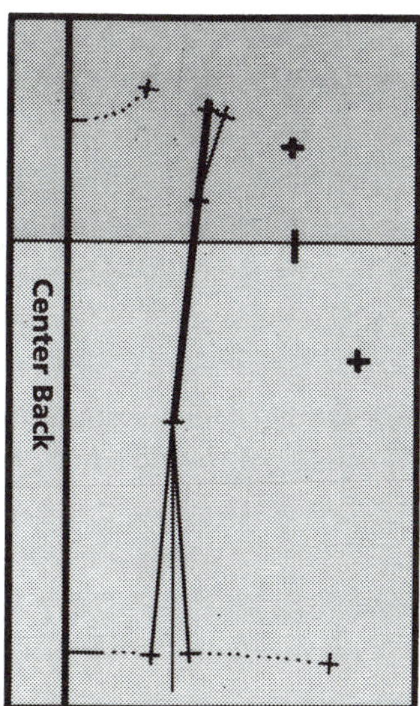

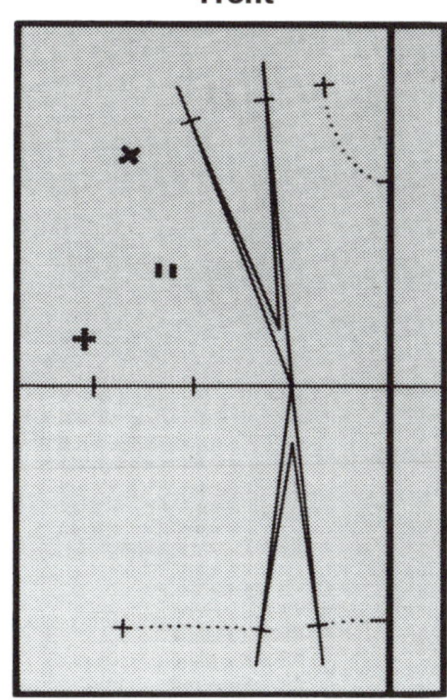

3 **Draw in the four darts** using a straight ruler.

a. **Front waist dart** Locate the center of the dart at the waistline crossmarks. At this center position, extend a grainline to the apex. If necessary, recenter the dart until it is on grain. Draw the dart legs 1 inch from the apex through the waist dart crossmarks. The center of the dart should be on the grain.

b. Front shoulder dart 1 inch from the apex through the shoulder dart crossmarks.

c. Back waist dart Locate the center of the dart at the waistline crossmarks. At this center position, extend a grainline the length of the dart (new vanishing point). Draw lines from the vanishing point (point of the dart) through waist dart crossmarks.

d. Back shoulder dart Vanishing point of back waist dart through shoulder dart crossmarks nearest the neckline. This line will not be exactly on the original princess markings. Measure down 3 inches on the vanishing point line and connect the other shoulder dart crossmark.

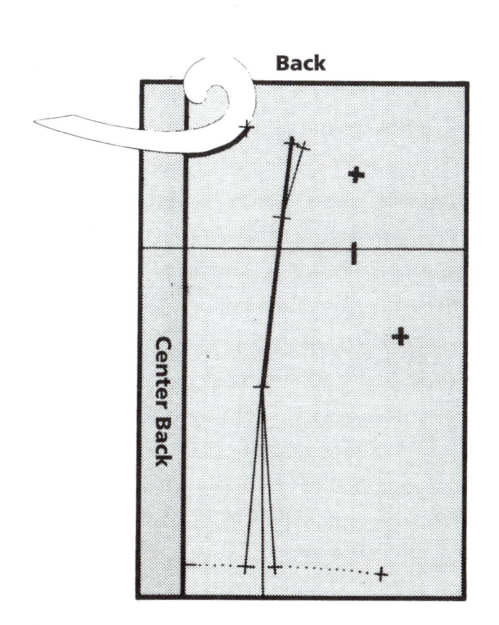

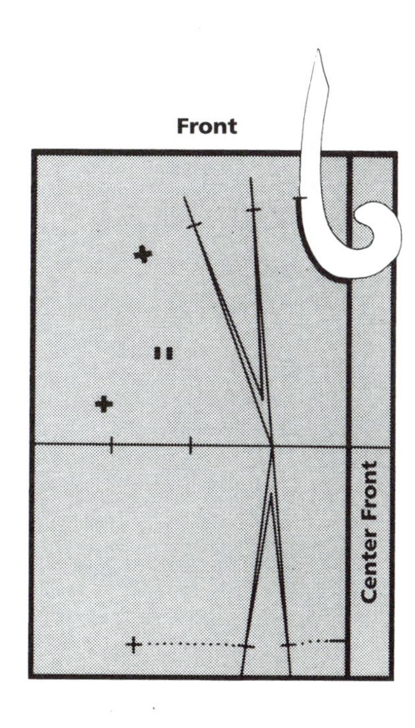

4 **Draw in the front and back necklines** using a french curve ruler, as illustrated. Be sure to blend lines smoothly into the 90 degree angle at center front and center back necklines. Connect the crossmarks at the shoulder seam.

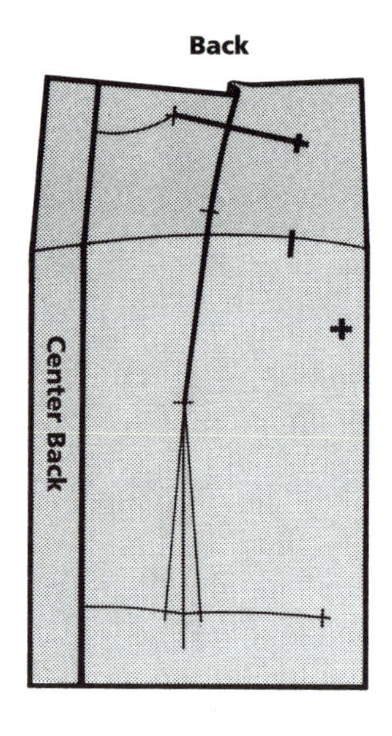

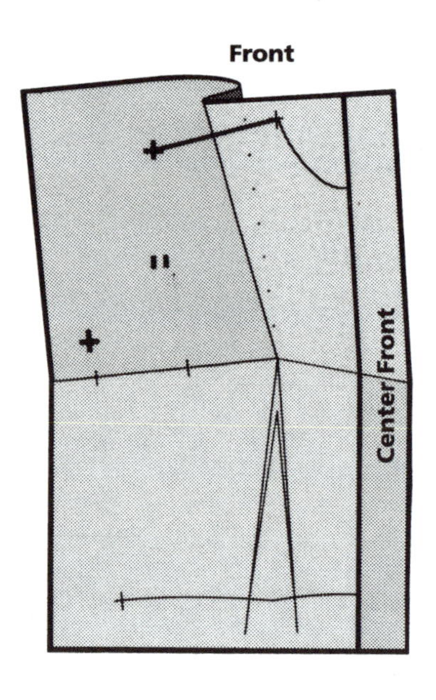

5 Draw in the front and and back shoulder seams. Fold the shoulder darts into position. Using a straight ruler, blend from the shoulder neck corner to the shoulder ridge corner in one continuous line.

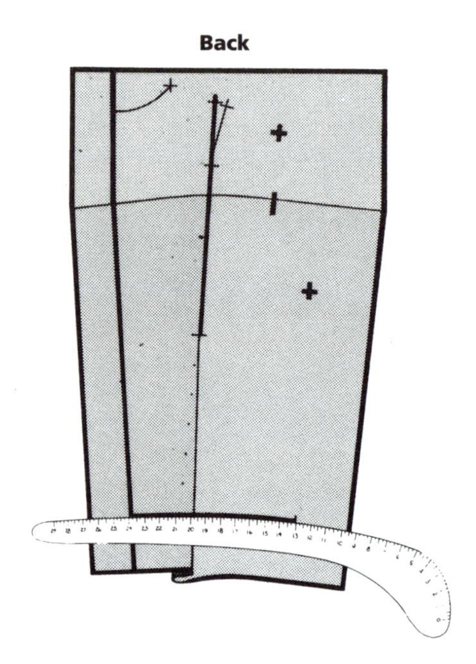

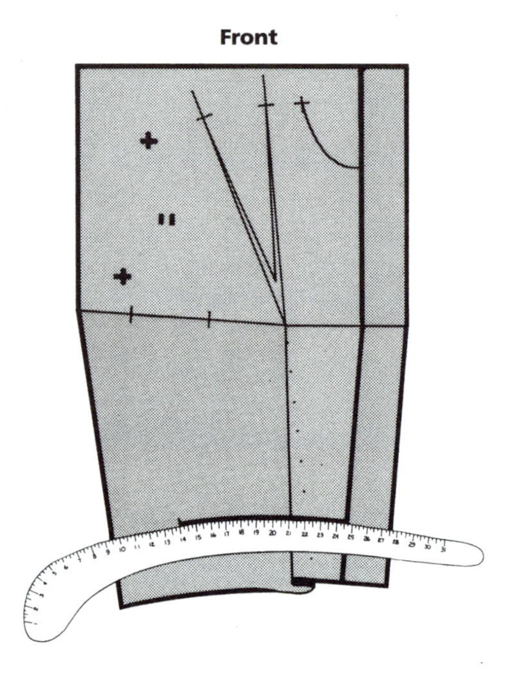

6 Draw in the front and back waistline. Fold the waist dart closed. Using a hip curve ruler, blend the waistline smoothly from center front and the side seam. Then blend the waistline from center back to the side seam.

7 Check the waistline curve. Pin the trued side seams together. The waistline should be drawn in one continuous, smooth line. If this is not the case, the drape is probably incorrect.

Sometimes a slight readjustment is needed to get a smooth continuous curve. This is done by lowering the side seam/waist corner 1/4 inch. If this does not solve the problem, check the drape for accuracy by redraping and rechecking all draping steps.

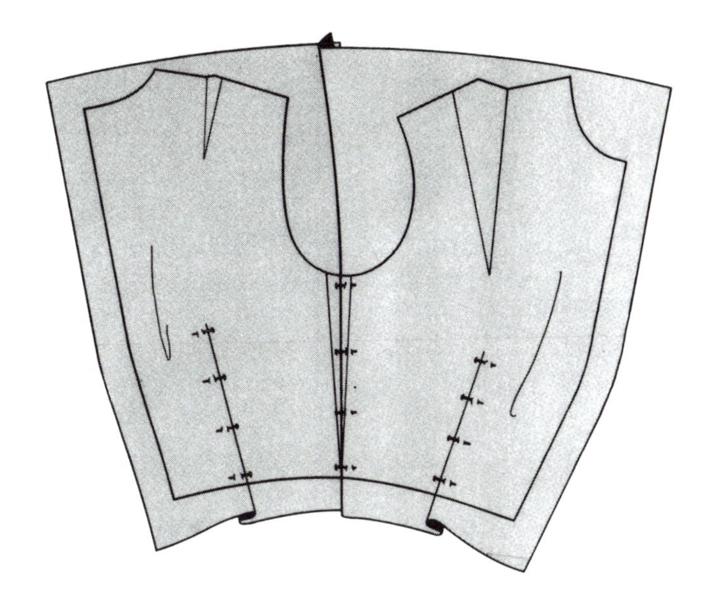

8 Check the front to back waistline distance (waistline balance).

a. Measure from center front to the side seam.

b. Measure from center back to the side seam.

The front waistline should be 1/2 inch longer than the back measurement. If this is not the case, readjust the side seam at the waistline by adding and subtracting the difference.

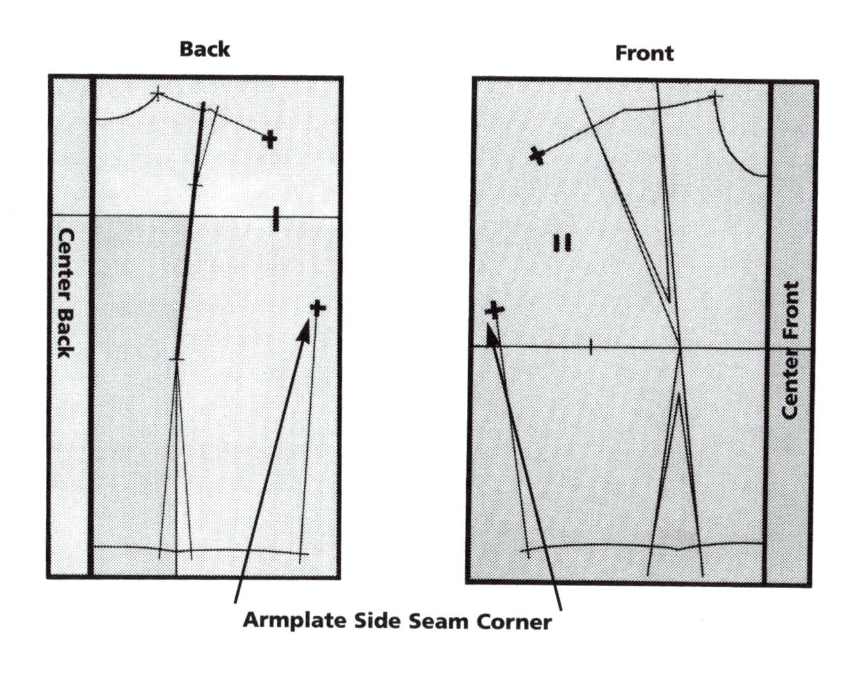

9 Draw in the front and back side seam positions. Using a straight ruler, connect the crossmark at the armplate/side seam to the side seam/waist crossmark.

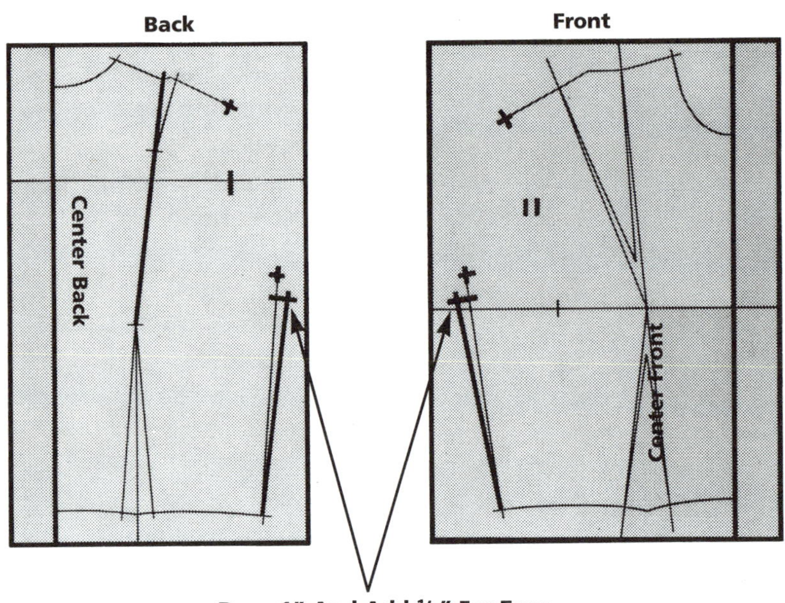

Add side seam ease.

a. Drop the front and back side seams 1 inch. At the underarm/side seam position, drop and crossmark the side seam 1 inch from the armplate/side seam crossmarks.

b. Add 1/2 inch body ease to the front and back side seam/armhole corner, and crossmark.

c. Draw in a new side seam for both the front and back. Connect the 1 inch crossmark with the 1/2 ease crossmark and draw in a new side seam. Connect them to the original side waist corners.

NOTE: The front and back side seams should be the same angle off of straight grain (balanced). If this is not the case, there has been a draping error.

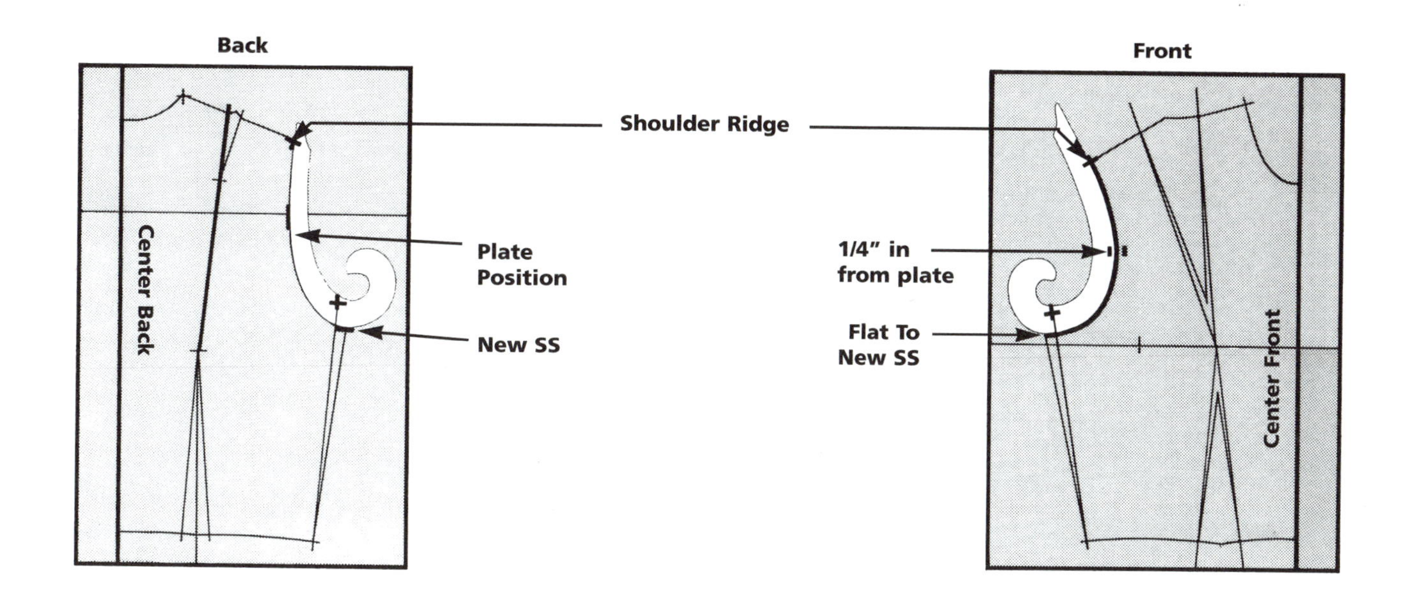

11 **Draw in the back bodice armhole.** Using a french curve, connect the following positions and place the ruler down as illustrated.

a. Shoulder back ridge corner.

b. Plate position at the screw level. Square and draw in a line 1 1/4 inches down from the shoulder blade back crossmark position.

c. The new side seam, at the 1-inch drop position.

The back armhole line should blend parallel to the grain at the screw level armhole mark. The french curved ruler blends at a slight angle at the side seam underarm position. Only the front blends in flat at this position.

12 **Draw in the front bodice armhole.** Using a french curve, connect the following positions and place the ruler down as illustrated.

a. Shoulder ridge corner.

b. 1/4 inch toward center front from the front plate position at the screw level.

c. The first side seam at the 1-inch drop position. Be sure this front armhole line blends in flat for 1/2 inch at the underarm position.

13 **Add seam allowances** to all seams and trim excess fabric.

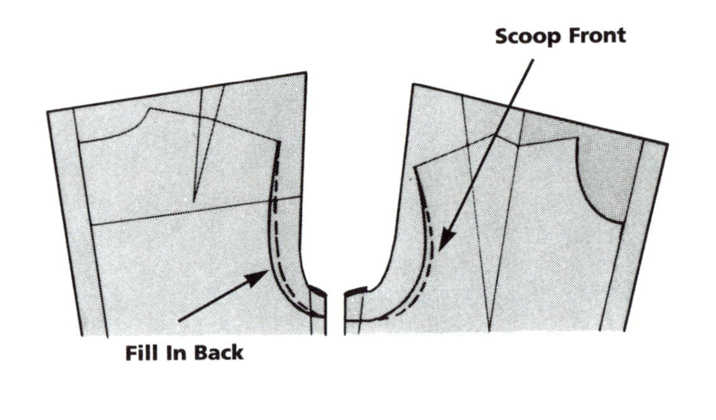

OR

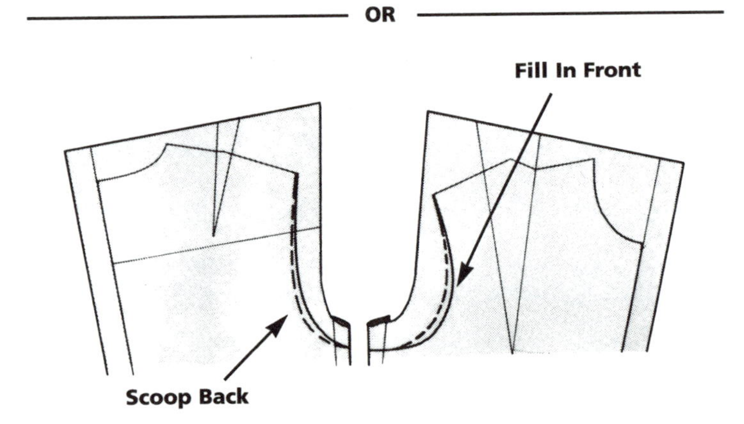

Balancing the Armhole

a. Measure front and back armhole. The front armhole should measure 1/2 inch shorter than the back armhole.

b. Correct front and back armhole. To make the front or back armhole longer: Reshape the front armhole by removing 1/4 inch at the middle of the armhole, shaping back to its original corners at the top and bottom.

To make the front and back armhole shorter: Add 1/4 inch at the mid/armhole area, and again, reshape to its original corners at the top and bottom.

NOTE: If the armhole does not balance by removing or adding 1/4 inch, an error was probably made while trueing or draping the armhole.

Notes

Pin and Check Final Proof of Bodice Drape

After completing and trueing up the fabric drape, pin the finished design together. All pins should be perpendicular to the seamlines. This design drape usually represents one half of the design and is placed on the right side of the dress form. Pin the front drape to the back drape, matching shoulder and side seams very carefully.

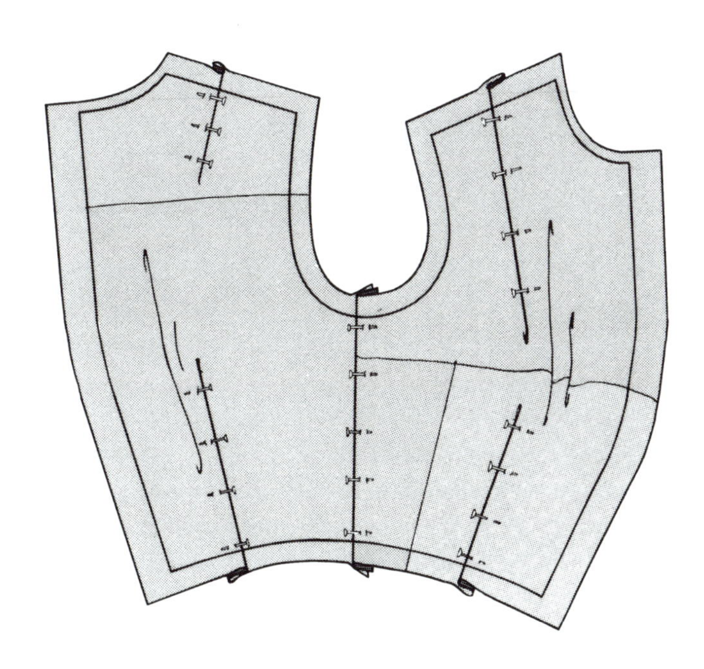

Checklist

A careful check of the finished drape serves several purposes. It may show inaccuracies or errors in the fit. A well-fitted garment looks comfortable, is proportioned naturally to the figure, with the amount of ease that is consistent with current fashion and garment style. Check the ease amounts and balance; then analyze the design concept against the list below. Any changes or corrections can be made at this time.

Evidence of LACK OF EASE:

- Bodice is drawing across the bust or shoulder blade level.
- Waistline may be too tight.
- Bodice molds tightly to the body.
- Side seam pulls or twists away from the side seam of the dress form.

Evidence of EXCESS EASE:

- Shoulder seams appear too long.
- Folds or gapping form across the chest.
- Folds or gapping form into the neckline.
- Folds or gapping excess form at the armhole.

CORRECT AMOUNT OF EASE:

- 1/2 inch pick up ease at the side seam/armhole intersection.
- 1/8 to 1/4 inch ease across the front chest area without pulling the front armhole.
- 1/8 to 1/4 inch ease across the back shoulder blade level without pulling the back armhole.
- 1/4 inch ease at each quarter of the waist.
- Draped side seams align with the dress form side seam.
- Side seams drape together without pulling, twisting, or distorting.

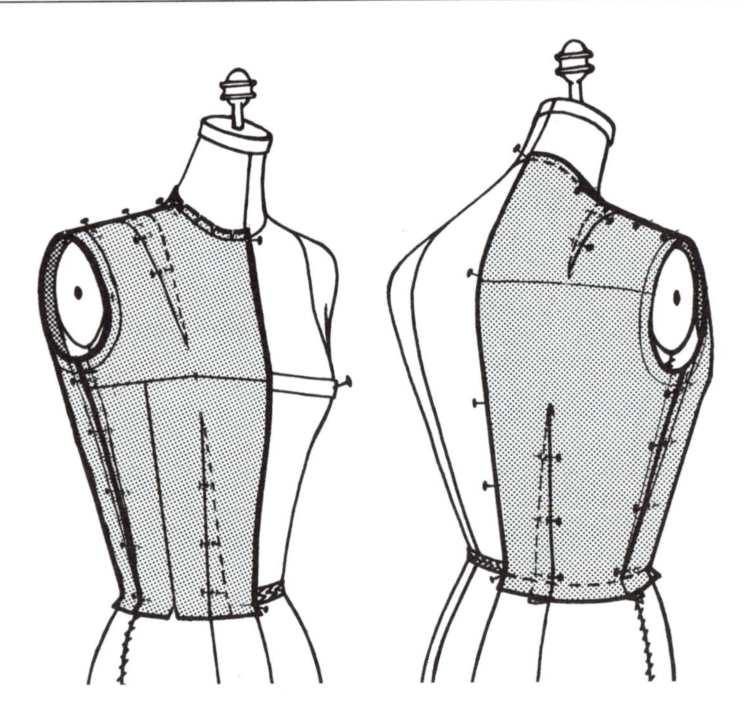

CORRECT BALANCE AND PROPORTION:

- Front and back grainlines hang straight and are perpendicular to the floor.
- Front and back crossgrains are perfectly level to the floor.
- Bodice front darts are pinned in properly:

  1 inch from the apex (vanishing point) to the shoulder crossmarks.

  1 inch from the apex (vanishing point) to the waistline crossmarks.
- All darts are folded in the correct direction (toward the center).
- Shoulder seams match correctly.
- Side seams match and are the same length.
- The drape hangs freely on all seamlines, without any pulling or twisting.
- The armhole shape is correct. The armhole at the side seam is dropped the required amount from the plate and resembles a "horseshoe shape."
- All trued lines are smooth and clean, with the correct amount of seam allowances.
- The overall look of the drape is neat and pressed.

NOTE: If the drape does not hang properly, unpin all joining seams and redrape the front and back independently. Being careful not to pull, stretch, or hold the fabric.

Sewing a Final Muslin Proof

It is advisable to sew together a complete muslin sample of the basic bodice and skirt. (The skirt drape is shown on page 64.) This muslin sample enables the designer to check the fit, balance, and hang of the two pieces as one unit.

Once they are proven accurate, use them as basic patterns for the development of a variety of styles.

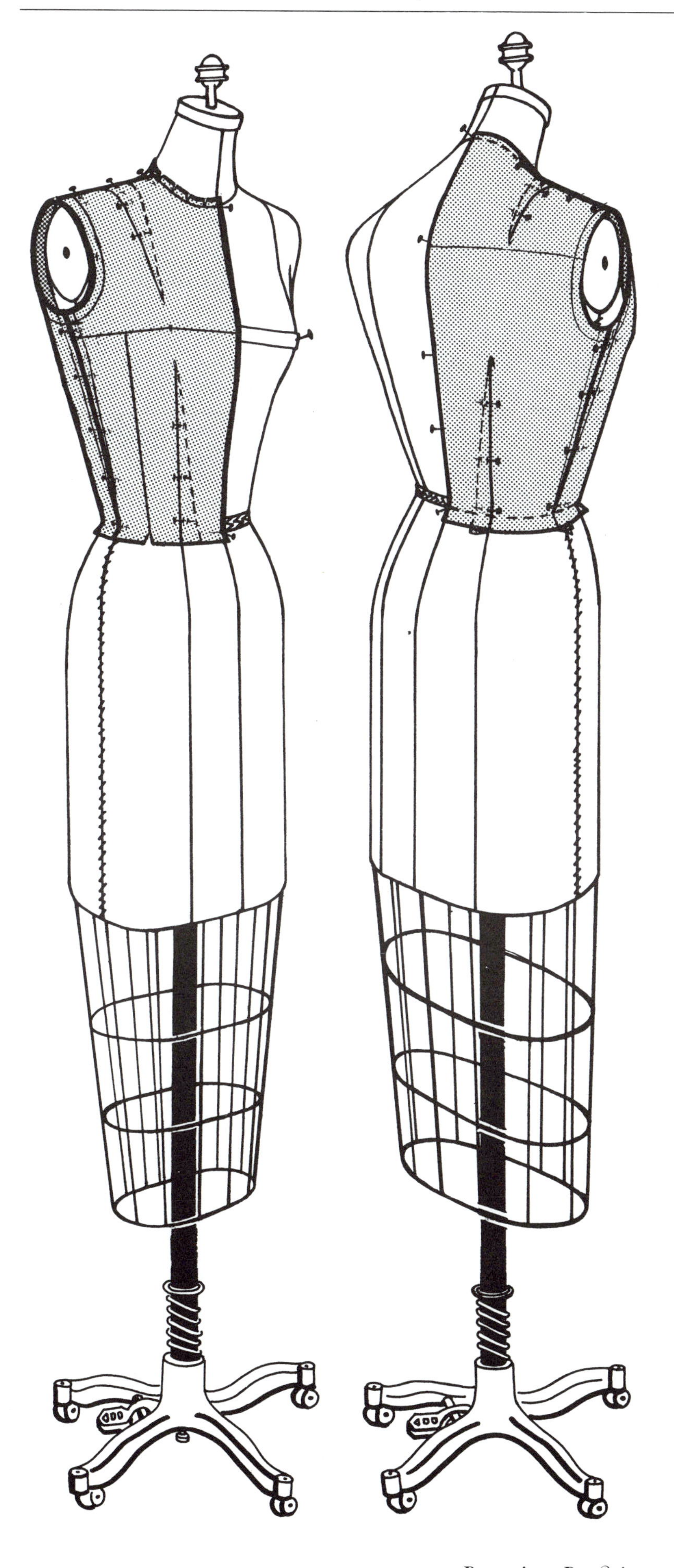

Evaluation Guidelines

To help the student or an instructor have a guidesheet to check their projects, the following chart has been made.

Fabric Preparation

☐ Length and width are premeasured correctly.

☐ Grainline, crossgrain, and all other necessary lines are drawn in correctly.

Drape

☐ **Hang** The grainline and crossgrain are in the correct direction for the design. The design drape is not twisting or pulling.

☐ **Fit** Allows for the proper ease needed for the design. (See page 47 for the proper ease allowance.)

☐ **Proportion** The drape is in the same proportion as the sketch.

☐ **Design Features** Follows such design features of the sketch as number of pleats, amount of fullness, correct collar, correct sleeve, correct button extension, and number of buttons.

☐ **Trued up correctly** Allows for the correct amount of seam allowances; all lines are smooth and clean.

☐ **Pinned Correctly** All pins are at right angles to the style lines.

☐ **Overall Look** The design drape is finished and pressed.

Chapter Six

Basic Skirt

Objectives

By studying the various draping steps in this chapter, the designer should be able to accomplish the following:

- Recognize the grain and crossgrain of a fabric in relation to the hipline of a pattern.
- Take a flat piece of fabric and make it fit the curves of the body.
- Check and analyze the results of the draping process for proper ease, fit, and hang.
- Transfer the drape onto paper and true up the basic skirt pattern.
- Drape and shape a fitted waistline with two darts and straight side seams.
- Develop a one-dart waistline skirt and a shirred waistline skirt from the two-dart basic skirt.

Basic Skirt

The basic straight skirt is a fitted skirt with seams parallel to the dress form. Two darts are fitted into the waistline seam to shape the hips and form the waistline. The darts bring in the excess fabric at the waist position.

This skirt is considered the most important of all skirt drapes because of its versatility in creating many different patterns. The designs created from the basic straight skirt must have a use for the waistline darts. This means that the waistline darts need to be converted into gathers, tucks, styled pleats, yokes, style lines, or simply kept as darts.

Basic Skirt—Preparing the Dress Form

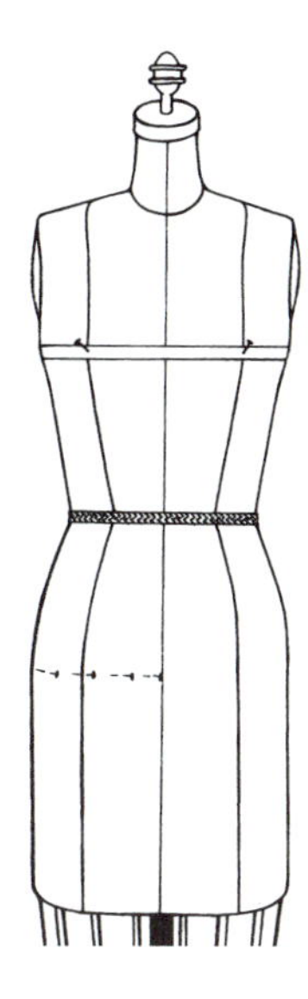

1 Establish the hip level on the dress form. Measure down 7 inches from the waistline on the center front of the dress form. This is the hip level.

2 Place twill tape (or measuring tape) parallel to the floor at this position. Place pins on the dress form at this hip level and remove the tape.

Basic Front & Back Skirt—Preparing the Fabric

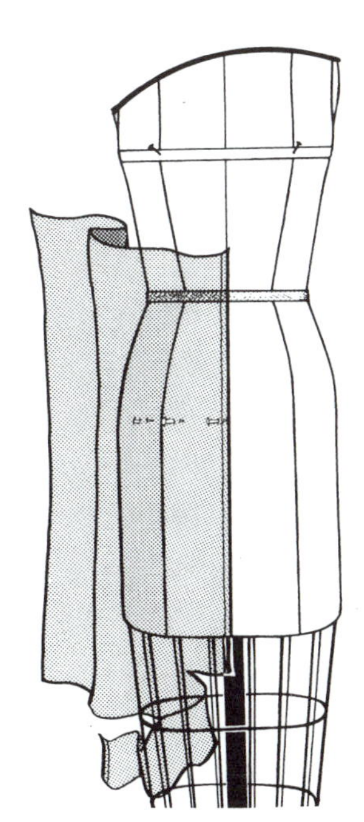

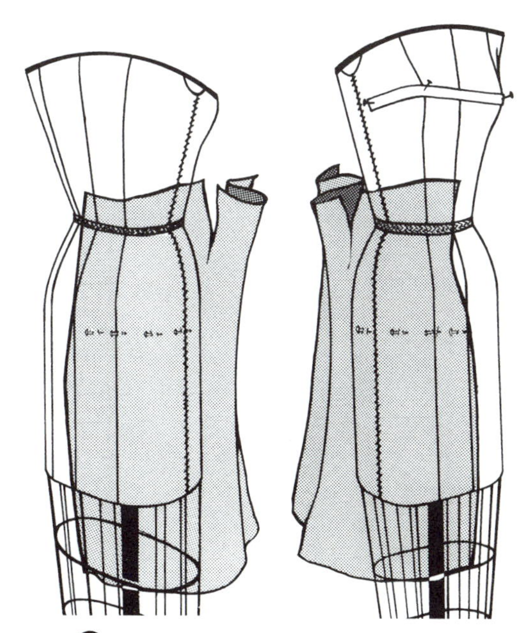

1 Measure the length (along the straight of grain) for the front and back skirt from 2 inches above the waist to the bottom of the dress form. Add 4 inches. Snip and tear the fabric at this length.

2 Measure the width (along the crossgrain) for the front and back skirt at the hip level from center of the dress form to the side seam. Add 3 inches. Snip and tear the fabric at this width.

3 **Draw the center front and center back grainlines** on the fabric 1 inch from the torn edge, and press under.

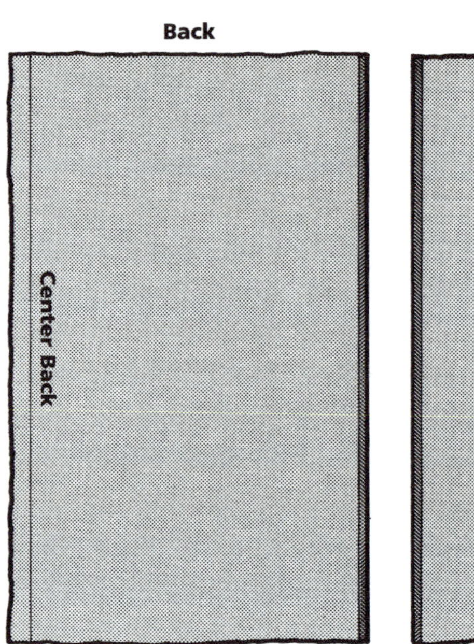

4 **Mark the center front waist position.** Measure down 2 inches from the top of the fabric at the center front fold. Pencil in a waistline mark at this position.

5 **Draw the crossgrains for the front and back skirt.**

a. On the skirt front, measure down 7 inches from the waistline mark. Using an L-square ruler, draw the perfect crossgrain on the skirt front.

b. On the skirt back, measure down 9 inches (on the center back grainline) from the top of the fabric. Using an L-square ruler, draw the perfect crossgrain on the skirt back.

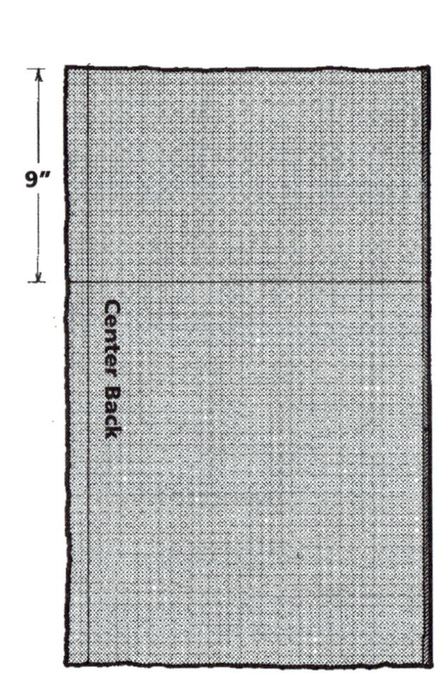

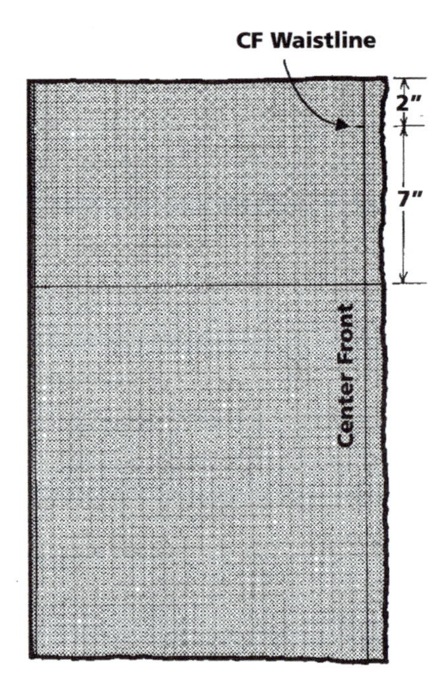

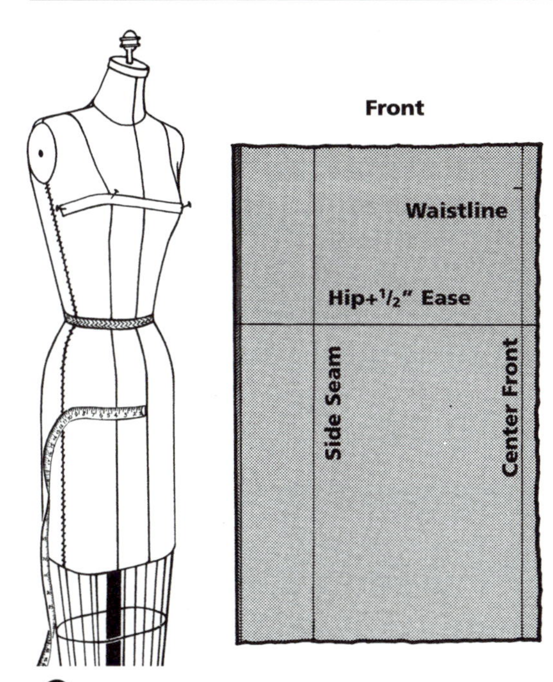

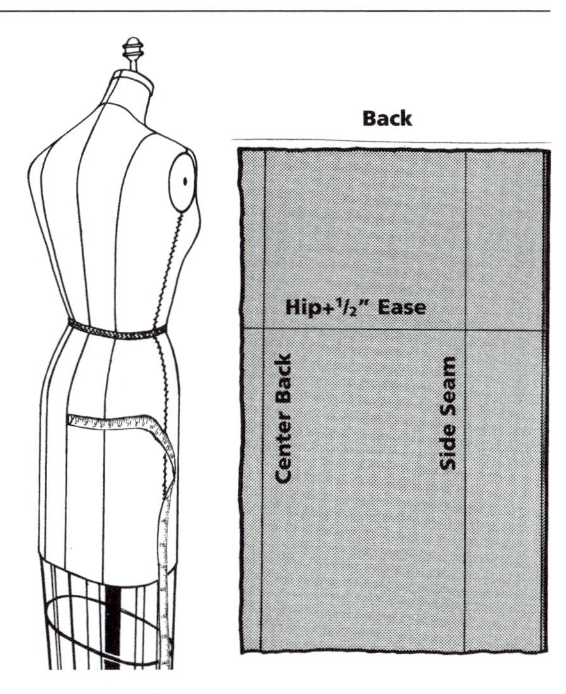

6 **Determine the front side seam.** Measure from C.F. to the side seam (at the hip level), and add 1/2 inch for ease. Transfer this measurement to the fabric. Using this mark, draw a side seam perfectly parallel to the C.F. grainline.

7 **Determine the back side seam.** Measure from C.B. to the side seam (at the hip level), and add 1/2 inch for ease. Transfer this measurement to the fabric. Using this mark, draw a side seam perfectly parallel to the C.B. grainline.

8 **Draw a secondary side seam line.** Measure 3/4 inch toward center front/back from the side seam on both the front and back skirts. This line will be used to help drape in the waistline.

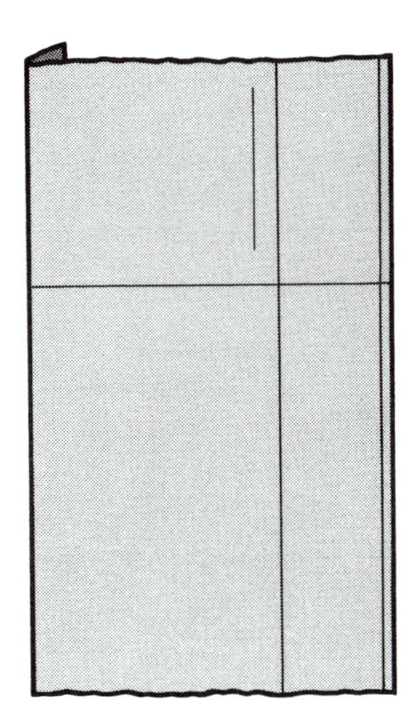

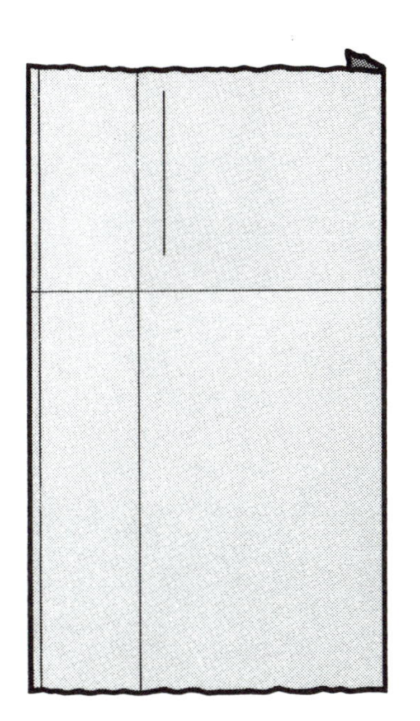

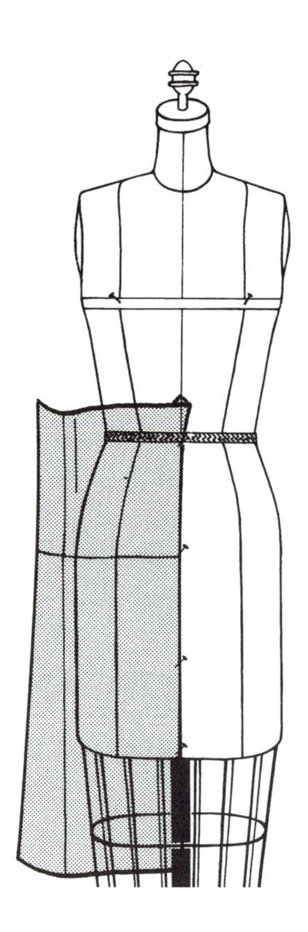

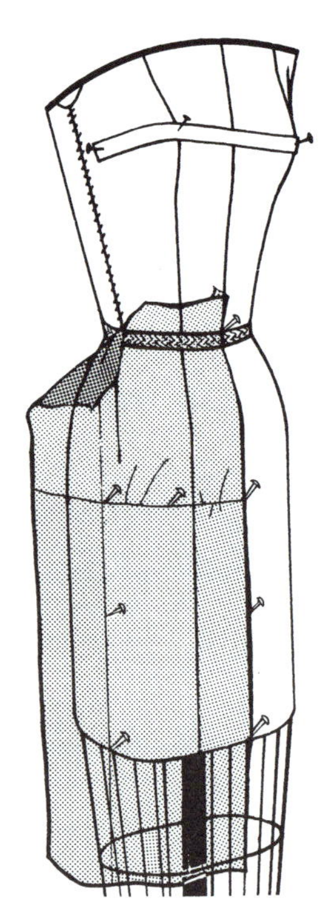

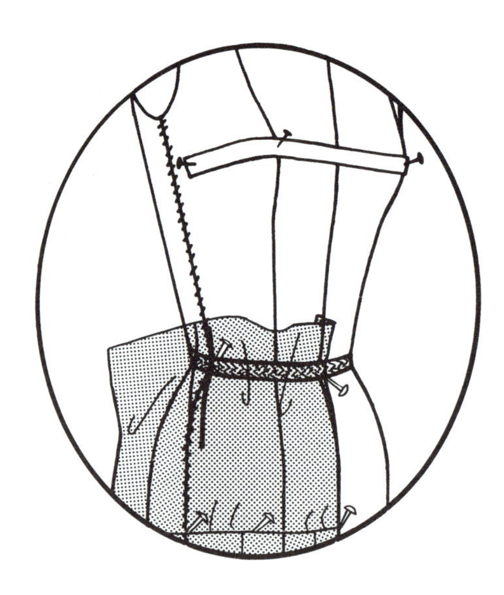

1 **Pin the center front grainline** fold of the fabric on the center front position of the dress form, matching the crossgrain of the fabric to the hip level line on the dress form.

2 **Smooth and pin the crossgrain** of the fabric (evenly distributing the ease) across the dress form to the side seam.

Be sure the fabric crossgrain is parallel to the floor. The side seam of the skirt drape should fall exactly on the side seam of the dress form when the crossgrain is placed perfectly.

3 **Pin the side seam** (below the hip level) to the dress form.

4 **Pin the front 3/4-inch line** to the side seam/waist corner of the dress form.

NOTE: When this side seam/waist corner is draped correctly, a slight gap will occur automatically at the side seam above the hip level.

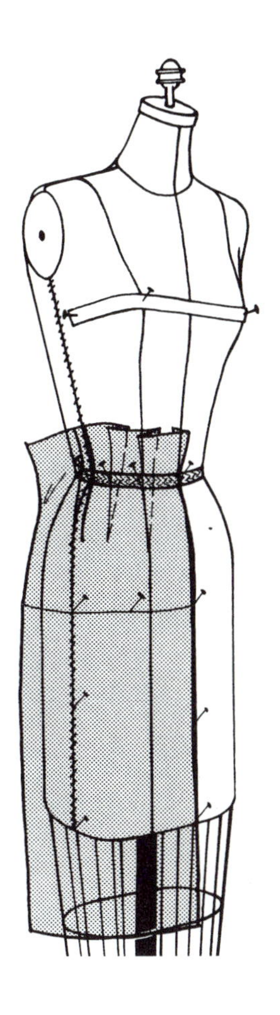

5 Drape in two darts at the front waistline. The excess fabric that falls between center front of the dress form and the pinned 3/4-inch mark on side seam will become the front waist darts.

a. Drape in the first dart (one half of the excess fabric) on the princess seam.

1. Crossmark the princess seam at the waistline. Smooth the fabric from the center front to the princess seam. Crossmark and crease the fabric at the princess seam/waist.

2. Pin the excess fabric on the princess seam. The excess fabric is folded at the princess seam crossmark and folded toward center front. Taper the dart to nothing down toward the hipline.

b. Drape in the second dart (the remaining half of the excess fabric).

1. Measure over on the waistline 1 1/4 inches from the first dart. Place a waistline crossmark at this position. Crossmark and crease the fabric at the waistline crossmark.

2. Pin and drape the excess fabric on the waistline crossmark. The remaining amount of excess fabric is creased at the second crossmark and folded toward center front. Taper the dart to nothing down toward the hipline.

Notes

Basic Back Skirt—Draping Steps

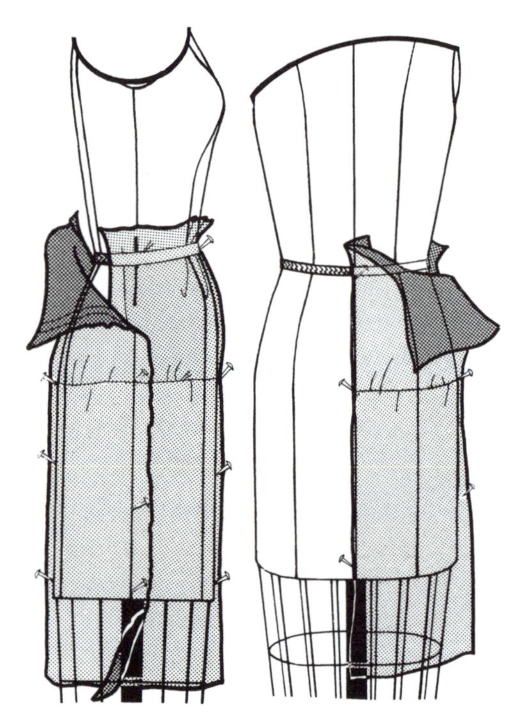

1 Match the back side seam at the hip level to the front side seam at the hip level. The side seams should match and be perfectly parallel to each other.

2 Smooth and pin the cross-grain of the fabric (evenly distributing the ease) across the dress form.

3 Pin the center back grainline fold of the fabric to the center back seam of the dress form.

4 Drape and pin the back 3/4-inch line of the fabric to the side seam/waist corner of the dress form.

NOTE: When this side seam/waist corner is draped correctly, a slight gap will occur automatically on the side seam above the hip level.

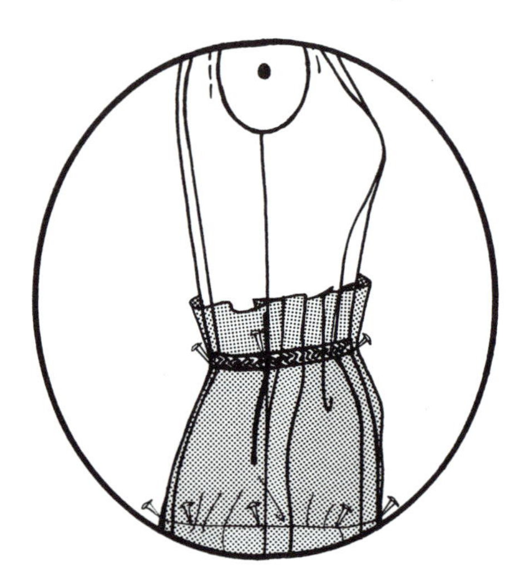

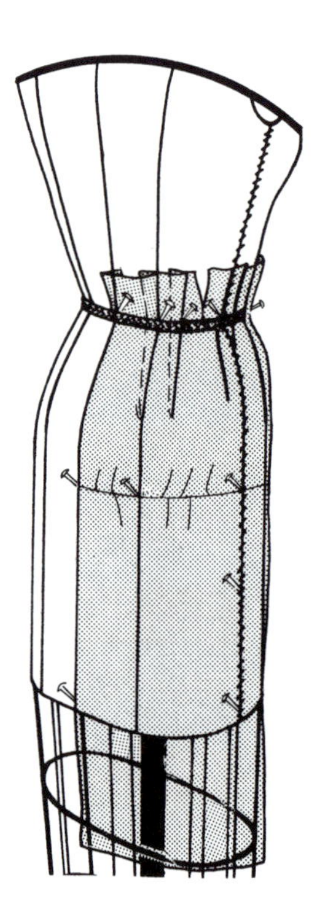

5 Drape in two darts at the back waistline. The excess fabric that falls between center back of the dress form and the pinned 3/4-inch mark on the side seam will become the back waist darts.

a. Drape the first dart (one half of the excess fabric) on the princess seam.

1. Crossmark the princess seam at the waistline. Smooth the fabric from the center back to the princess seam. Crossmark and crease the fabric at the princess seam/waist.

2. Pin the excess fabric on the princess seam. The excess fabric is folded at the princess seam crossmark and folded toward center back. Taper the dart to nothing down toward the hipline.

b. Drape in the second dart (the remaining half of the excess fabric).

1. Measure over on the waistline 1 1/4 inches from the first dart. Place a waistline crossmark at this position. Crossmark and crease the fabric at the waistline crossmark.

2. Pin and drape the excess fabric on the waistline crossmark. The remaining amount of excess fabric is creased at the second crossmark and folded toward center back. Taper the dart to nothing down toward the hipline.

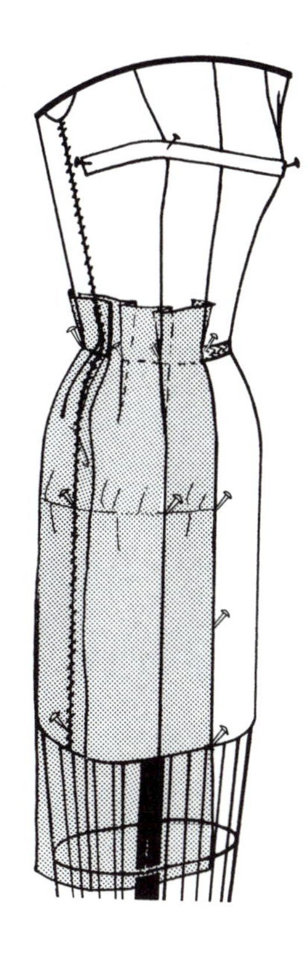

6 **Mark all key areas** of the dress form.

Waistline front and back.

Darts front and back.

Notes

Trueing Basic Skirt Drape

1 Remove the fabric from the dress form and lay it flat on the table. If you are planning to true up the fabric onto paper, complete the following steps.

a. Draw in a straight grainline and the crossgrain at the hip level to match the straight of grain and crossgrain of the fabric on two pieces of paper (one for the skirt front and one for the skirt back).

b. Draw a side seam line. Remeasure the hip and add 1/2 inch ease. Transfer this measurement to the paper. Draw a side seam line at this position parallel to the grainline. (Do this for both the front and back skirts.)

c. Place the fabric drape on top of the paper matching the straight grains and the crossgrain hip levels. The side seamlines should match automatically.

d. Transfer the waistline, darts, and side seam markings onto the paper, using a trace wheel.

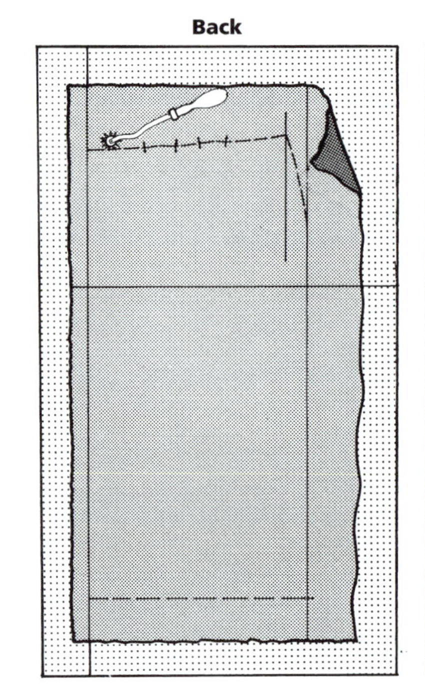

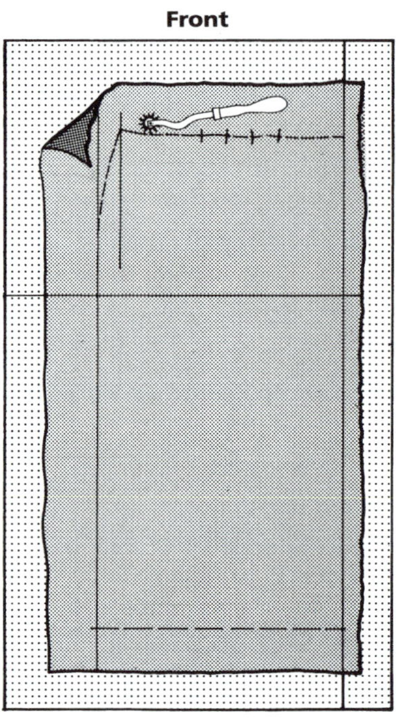

2 **Draw a short 90 degree angle at:**

a. Center front waist **(1/2 inch)**

b. Center back waist **(1 inch)**

3 **Draw the front and back waist darts.**

a. Locate the center of each dart.

b. Draw the center dart line. Using a straight ruler, draw a line for the center of each dart parallel to the grainline. The length of the front darts is 3 1/2 inches. The length of the back darts is 5 1/2 inches. The bottom of each dart line is known as the vanishing point.

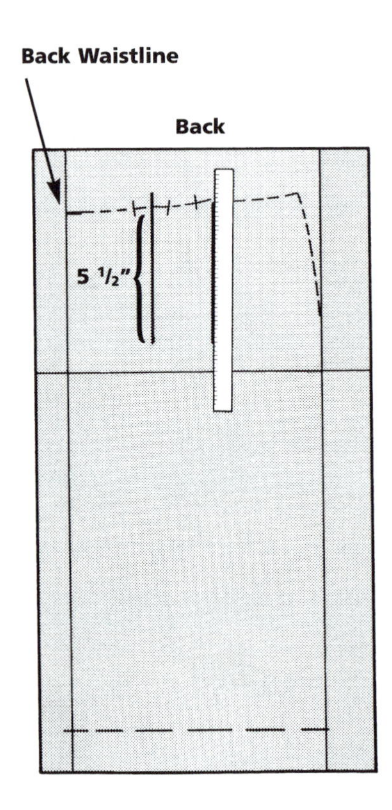

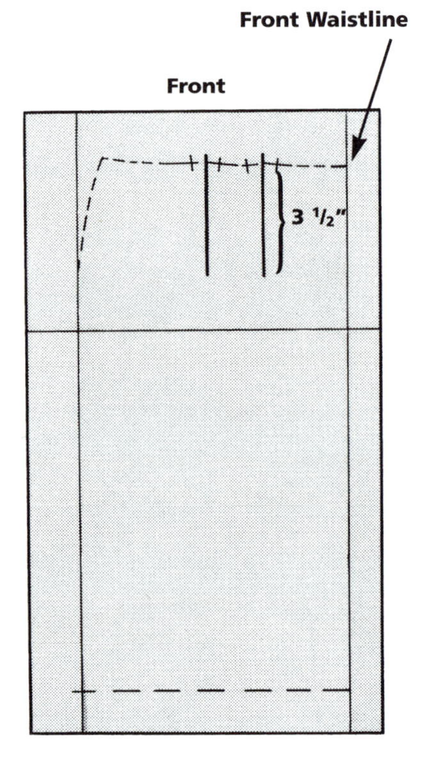

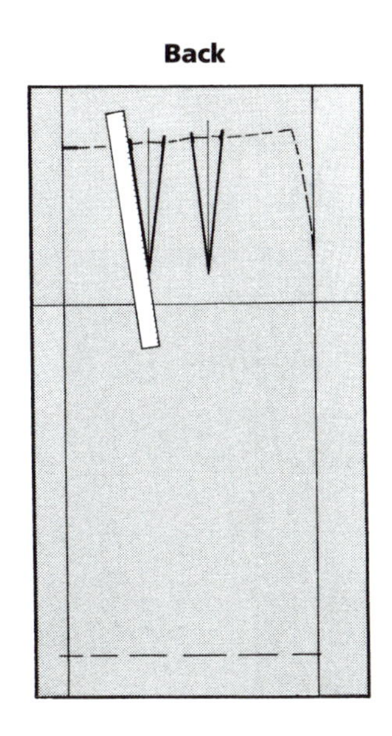

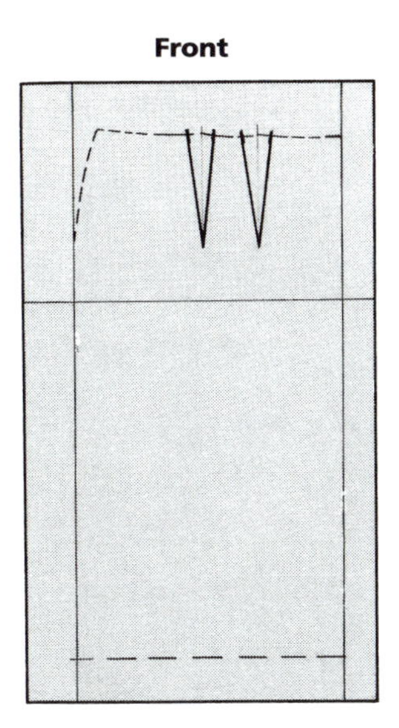

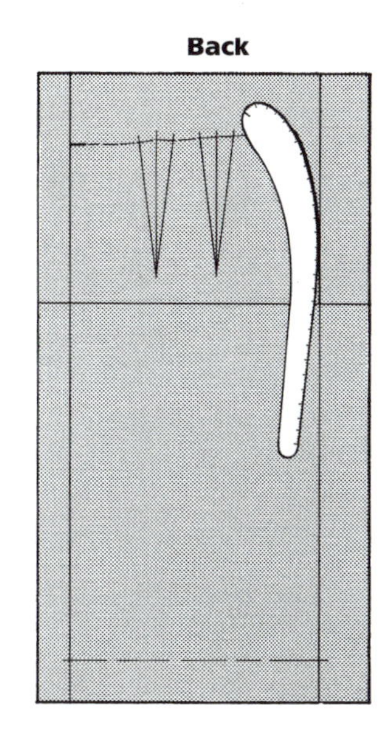

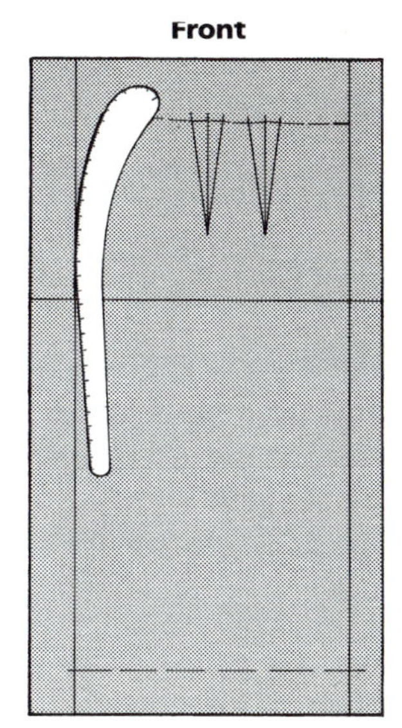

4 Draw in the outer dart legs. Using a straight ruler, draw the outer legs of the darts from the vanishing point to the waistline crossmarks.

5 Draw the side seams. Using a hip curve ruler, place the straight part of this ruler to the side seam/waist corner and the side seam (as illustrated).

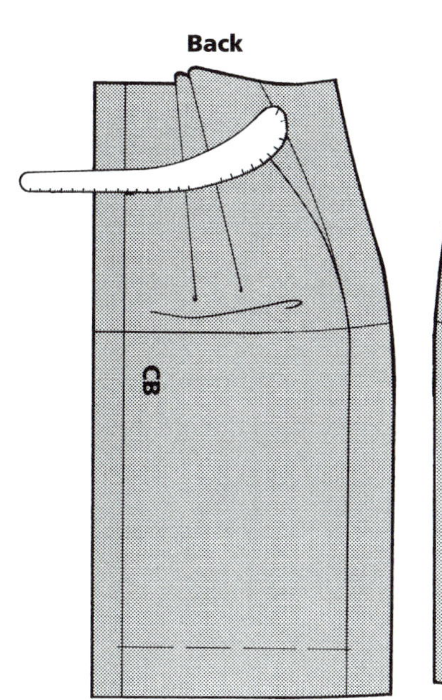

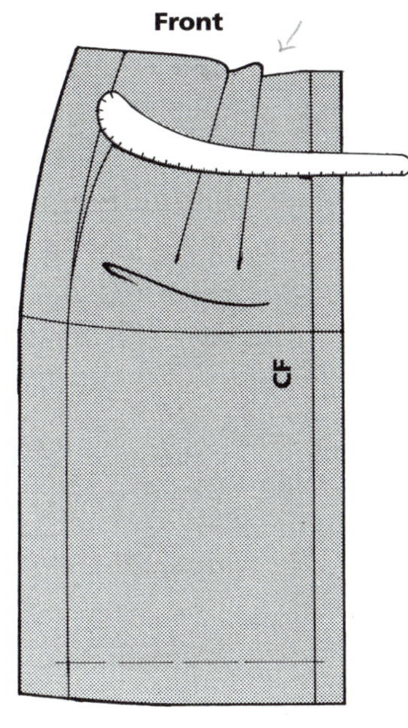

6 Draw the waistline. Fold and pin in the waist darts. With the darts folded in place, use the hip curve ruler and draw the waistline.

Check side seams.

a. Pin the front and back side seams together.

b. Measure the side seams from the hip level to the waistline. These measurements should be the same. If they are not, adjust the back waistline/side seam corner to match the front measurement.

NOTE: If these measurements are more than 5/8 inch off, recheck the drape to create a more accurately draped side seam/waist corner.

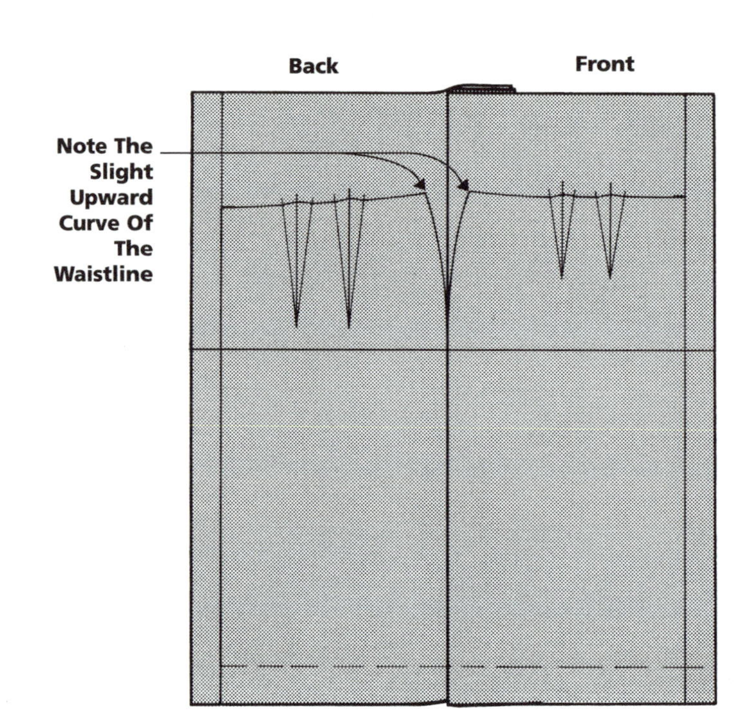

Check the waistline.

a. Pin the front and back skirt side seams to each other. Pin in the darts.

b. Check the waistline shape. This should be a continuous smoother curving line.

c. Match and walk front and back bodice waists to the skirt waists when a bodice is being attached to the skirt. Waistlines should be the same distance when all darts are folded closed.

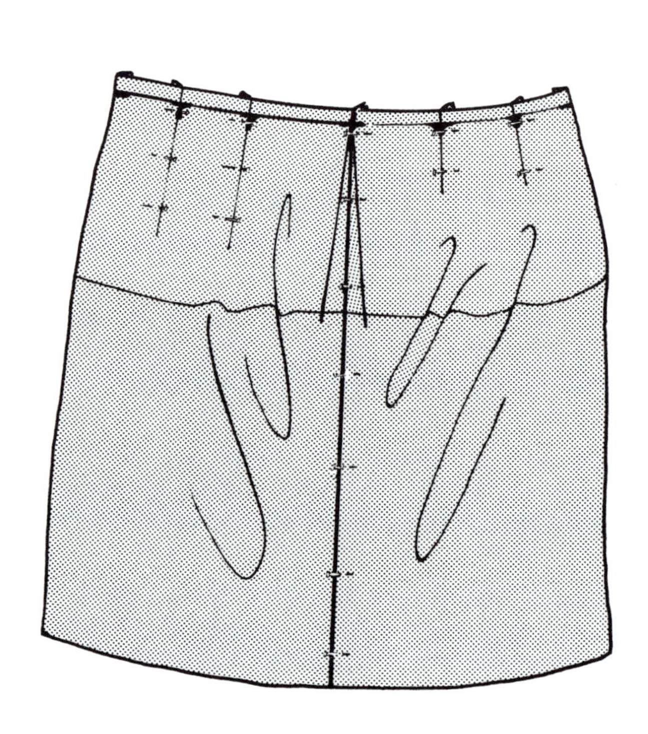

9 **Draw the hemline, with the side seams still pinned.**

a. Measure and crossmark the desired length. Measure from the center back waist down to the desired skirt length.

b. Square a line from center back crossmark, across the skirt to center front of the skirt. This line should be perfectly parallel to the hipline.

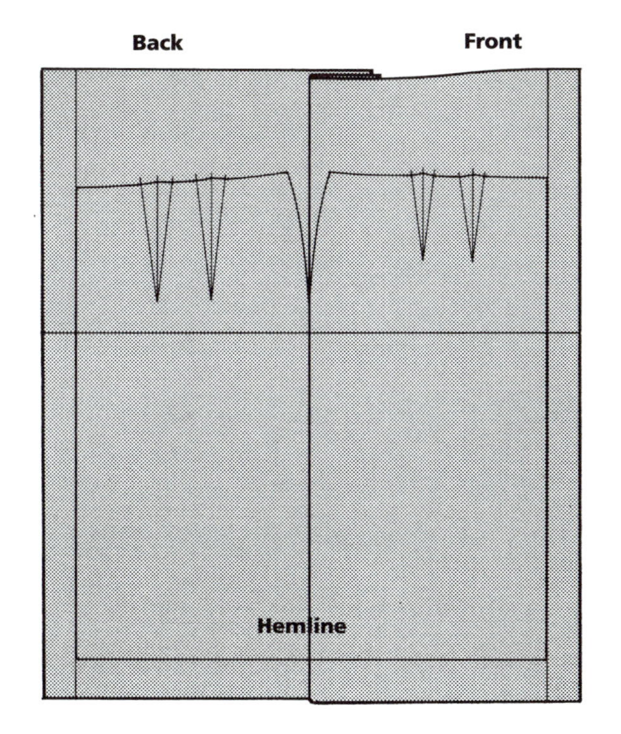

Notes

Pin and Check Final Proof of Skirt Drape

After completing and trueing up the skirt fabric drape, the finished design should be pinned together. This design usually represents one half of the design and is placed on the right side of the dress form. The front drape should be pinned to the back drape, matching the side seams very carefully. All pins should be perpendicular to the seamline.

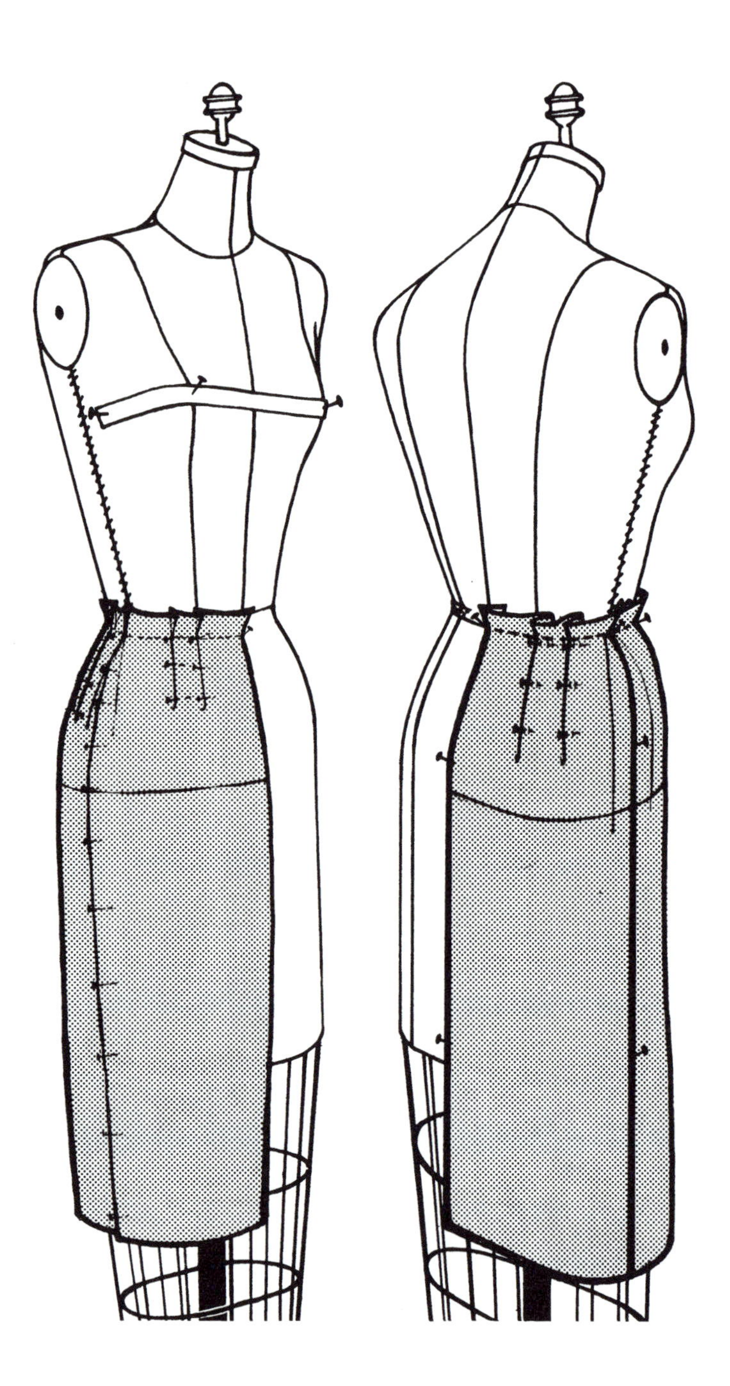

Checklist

A careful check of the finished drape serves several purposes. It may show inaccuracies or errors in the fit. Any changes or corrections can be made at this time.

- Front and back grainlines should be straight.
- Front and back crossgrains should be perfectly level to the floor.
- Hip level ease evenly distributed.
- All trued lines are smooth and clean.
- All trued lines have the correct amount of seam allowances.
- The overall look of the drape is neat and clean.
- Darts are pinned in place to the vanishing points.
- Draped side seams are in alignment with the dress form side seam.
- The drape is correctly balanced. The front of the design is in the front and the back of the design is in the back. It hangs freely on all seamlines.

A basic skirt waistline fullness may also be draped with gathers or a single dart rather than the standard two darts.

Notes

Chapter Seven

Basic Shift

Objectives

By studying the various draping steps in this chapter, the designer should be able to accomplish the following:

- Recognize grain and crossgrain of the fabric in relation to the bust level line, shoulder blade level, direction, and placement of darts, and placement of side seams.
- Take a flat piece of fabric and make it fit the curves of the body.
- Develop a basic shift with the correct amount of ease allowance, armhole size, and side seam balance.
- Drape a side seam and have it hang straight from the bust level line on the front and from the shoulder blade level on the back down to the hem.
- Visualize the basic front and back shift pattern in relation to the figure.
- Check the results of the draping process for proper ease, fit, hang, and proportion.
- Transfer the drape onto paper and true up the basic shift pattern.

Basic Shift

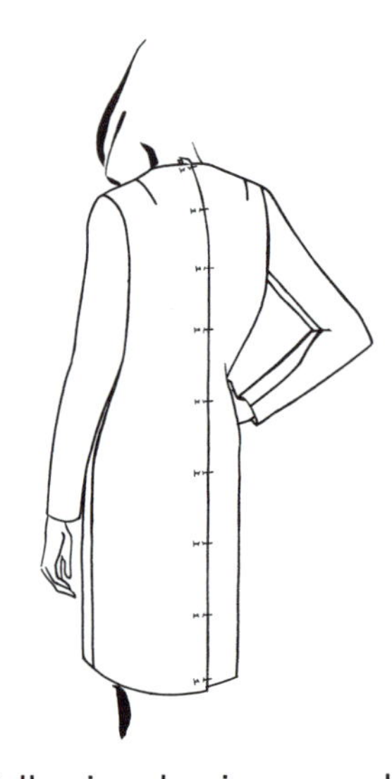

The shift dress is the most basic of all dress styles. The silhouette has a boxy shape without a waist-fitting seam. The side seams hang away from the body and is parallel to center front.

The waist area may be belted, drawn in by using elastic, or slightly fitted by using one or two fisheye darts. Within the silhouette shape, many different styles of pockets, plackets, yokes, necklines, collars, and/or sleeves may be chosen to create the individual style wanted.

The following draping procedures demonstrate how to drape a basic shift dress. Some variations of this traditional design are also included. One can realize the many creative styles and uses for this basic dress design by mastering the following draping procedures.

Basic Front and Back Shift—Preparing the Fabric

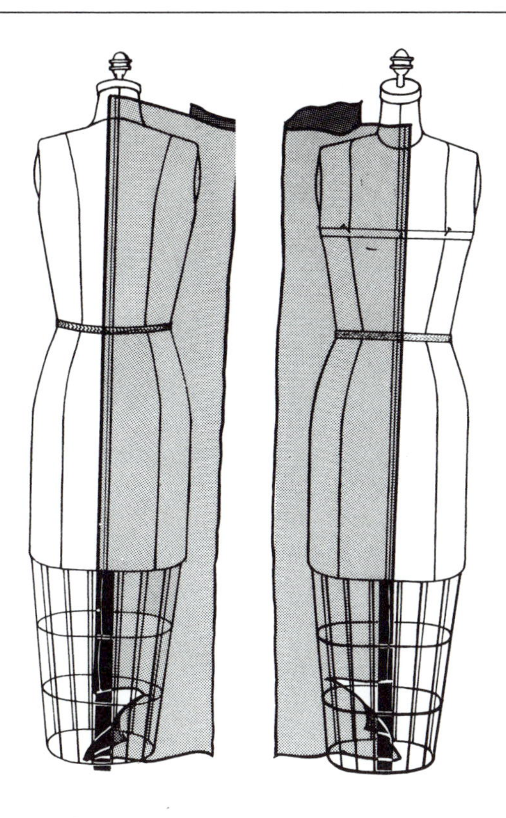

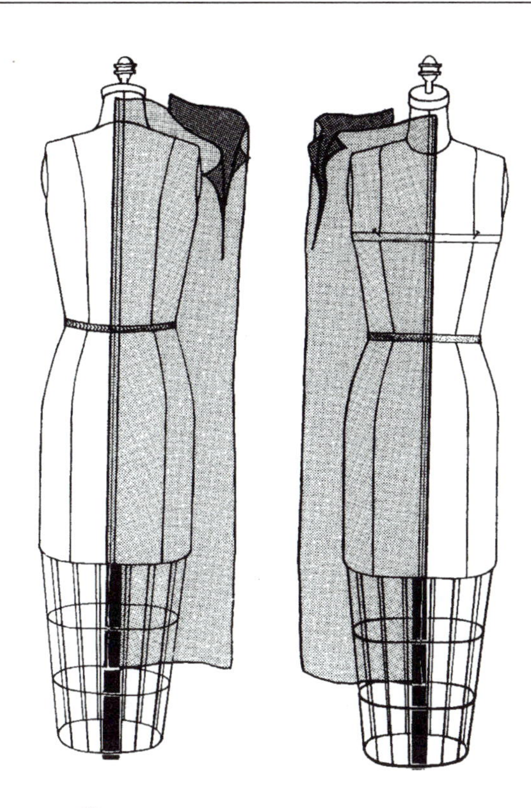

1 Measure the length (along the straight of grain) for the front and back from the neckband to the desired length of the shift dress, and add 3 inches.

Snip and tear the fabric at this length.

2 Measure the width (along the crossgrain) for the front and back from the center front of the dress form to the side seam, and add 5 inches.

Snip and tear the fabric at this width.

3 Draw the center front and center back grainline 1 inch from the torn edge, and press under.

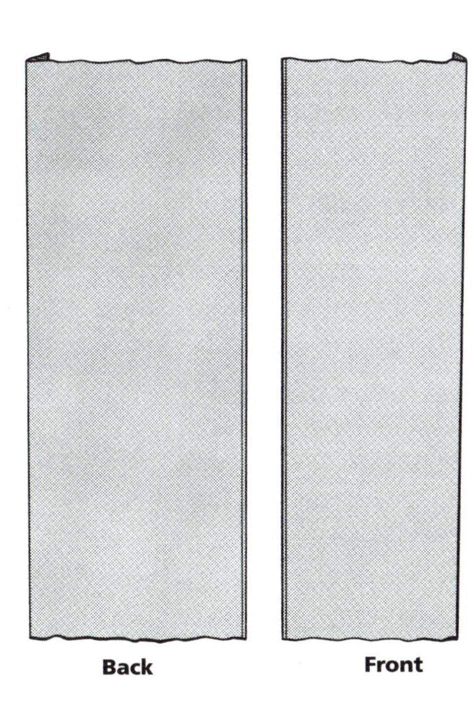

4 Draw two perfect crossgrains on the front fabric piece.

a. Draw in the bust level line. Draw the first crossgrain line 13 inches from the top edge of the fabric.

b. Draw in the hipline. Draw the second crossgrain line 14 inches below the first crossgrain.

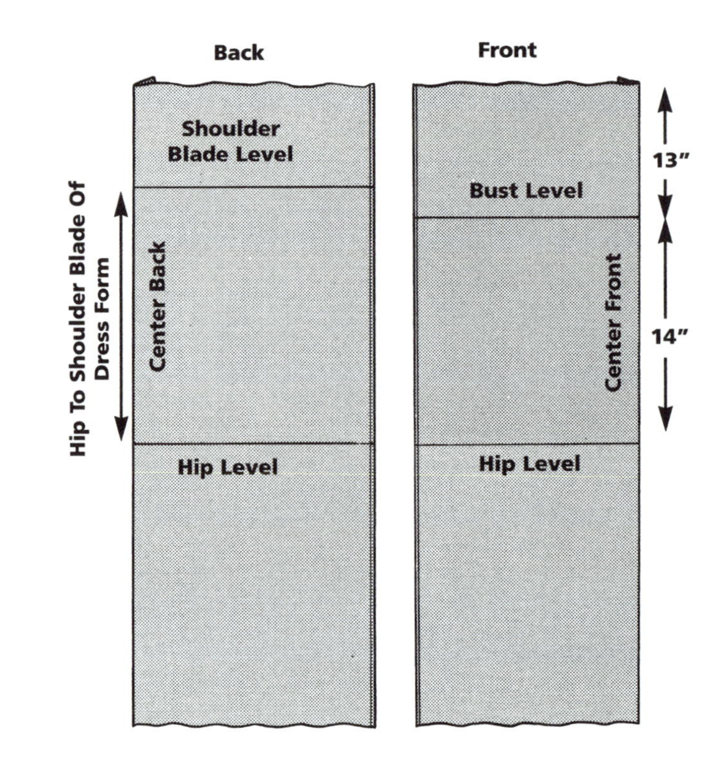

5 Draw two perfect crossgrains on the back fabric piece.

a. Draw in the back hipline. Place the front and back fabric pieces side by side. Draw a crossgrain line on the back piece to match the crossgrain on the front piece.

b. Draw the shoulder blade level line. On the dress form, measure the distance from the hip line to the shoulder blade line. Transfer this measurement to the fabric and draw a crossgrain line at this crossmark.

6 Draw the side seams for the front and back fabric pieces.

a. Measure the dress form at the hip level for the front and back.

1. **Measure from C.F. to the side seam** on the dress form. Add 1/2 inch for ease. Transfer this measurement to the front fabric piece and crossmark.

2. **Measure from C.B. to the side seam** on the dress form. Add 1/2 inch for ease. Transfer this measurement to the back fabric piece and crossmark.

b. Draw the front and back side seam. From this side seam crossmark draw a side seam perfectly parallel to the grainline.

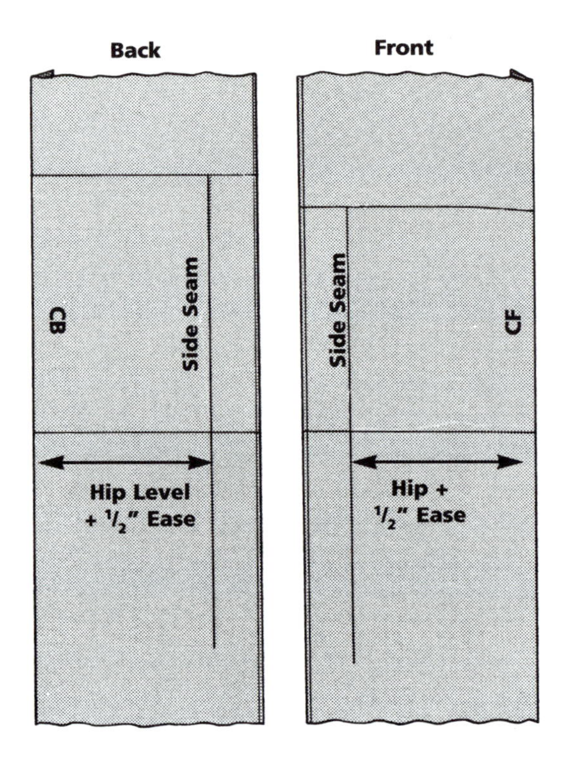

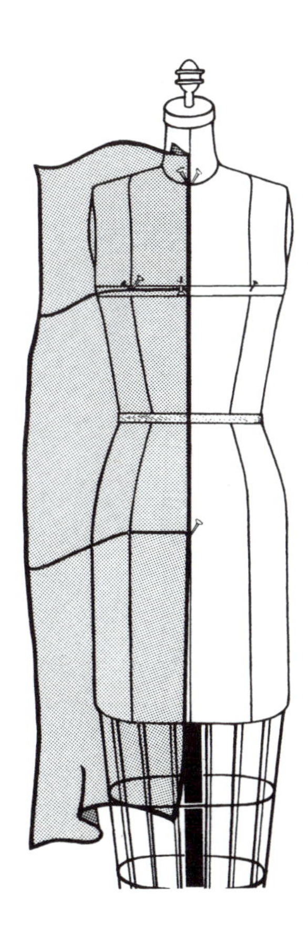

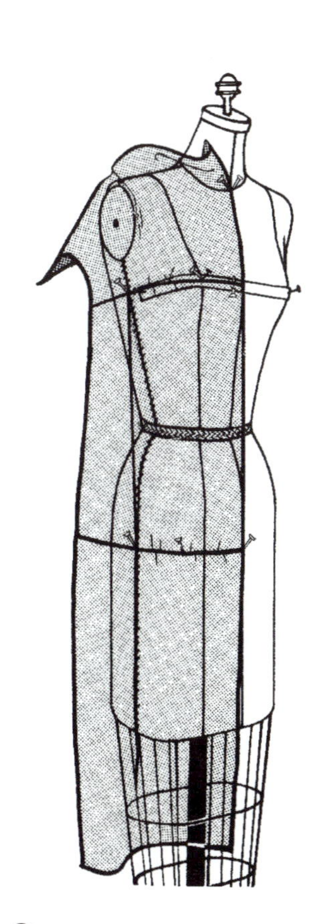

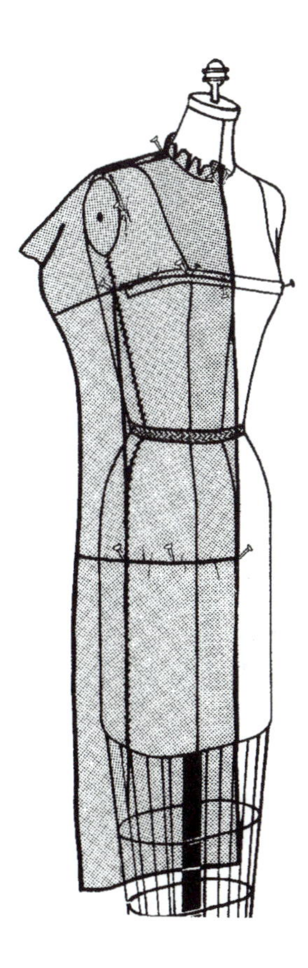

1 Pin the center front grainline fold of the fabric onto the center front position of the dress form.

2 Align the crossgrains at the bust level and at the hip level. Anchor pins at C.F. neck and C.F. hip. An additional pin may be needed at the bust level tape.

3 Pin the front crossgrains and the front side seam. Smooth the fabric across the dress form to the side seam. Pin the side seam. Be sure the fabric crossgrains are parallel to the floor and the side seam is on the side seam of the dress form.

NOTE: Sometimes the dress form tape is crooked and, therefore, the crossgrain should be judged by viewing the crossgrain parallel to the floor.

4 Smooth the fabric up and over the dress form armplate to the shoulder. Create a 1/4"–1/4" pinch at the screw level (middle at ridge) of the armhole. This is to ensure the armhole does not become too tight. Pin in place.

5 Drape the front neckline. Trim excess fabric around the neck and clip at intervals. Continue to smooth and pin the fabric around the neck area.

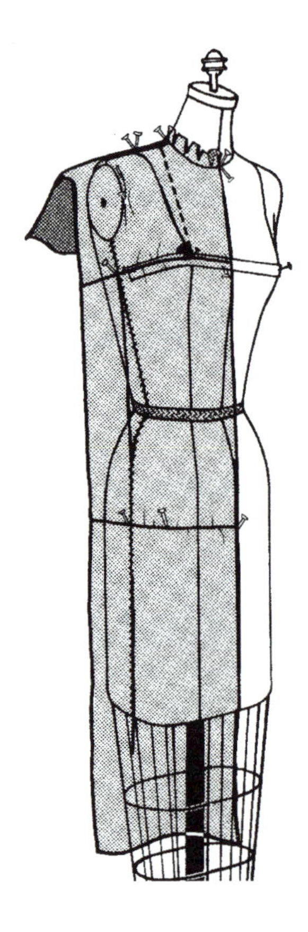

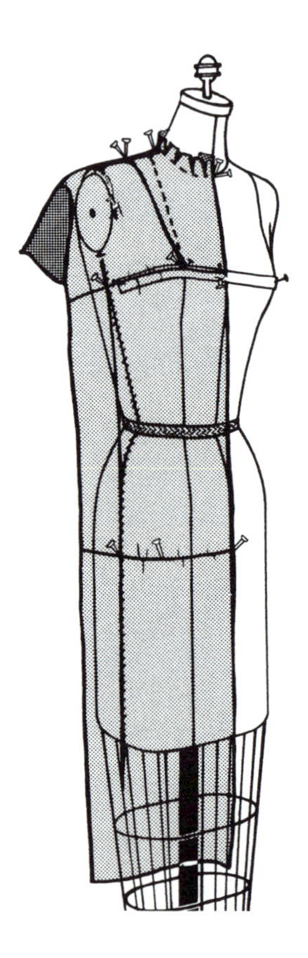

6 **Drape and smooth the fabric over the shoulder/neckline** seam of the dress form to just past the princess seam. Pin in place. Crossmark the princess seam and the shoulder.

7 **Drape the front shoulder dart.** The excess fabric that falls between the shoulder/neckline and the shoulder/armhole area will become the amount of excess fabric in the shoulder dart. The larger the bust, the larger the dart, the smaller the bust, the smaller the dart.

a. Crease the fabric at the shoulder/princess seam crossmark.

b. Pin the excess fabric on the princess seam. The excess fabric is creased at the princess seam crossmark and folded toward center front neck. Taper the dart to nothing toward the bust apex.

8 **Mark all key areas** of the dress form to the fabric.

Neckline Crossmark at C.F. neck and at neckline/shoulder corner. Lightly mark remainder of neckline.

Shoulder Seam and Shoulder Dart Lightly mark shoulder seam, crossmark shoulder dart and shoulder ridge corner.

Armplate
a. Top at shoulder seam ridge.
b. Middle at screw level.
c. Crossmark bottom at side seam.

Side seam Lightly mark

Basic Back Shift—Draping Steps

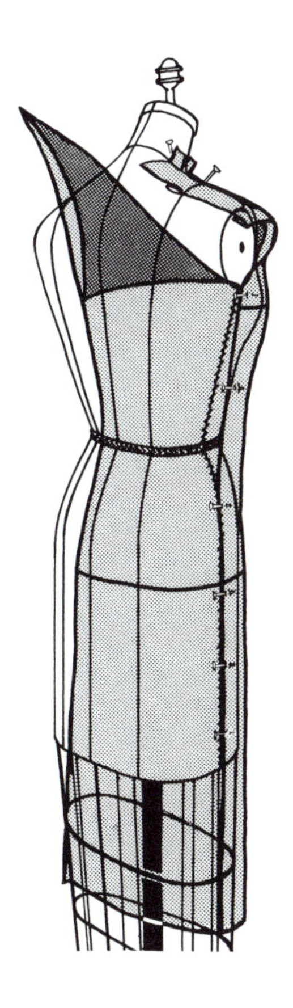

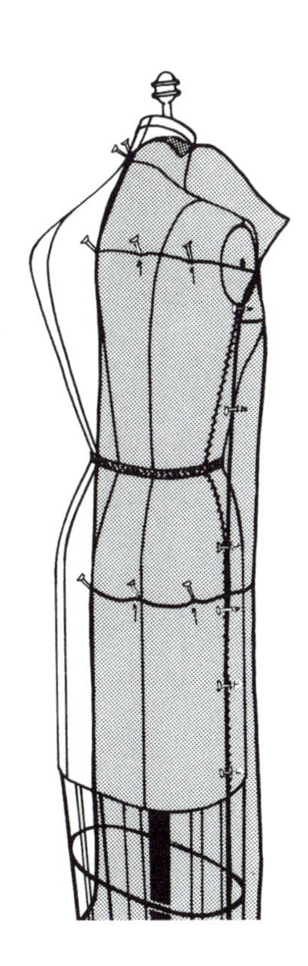

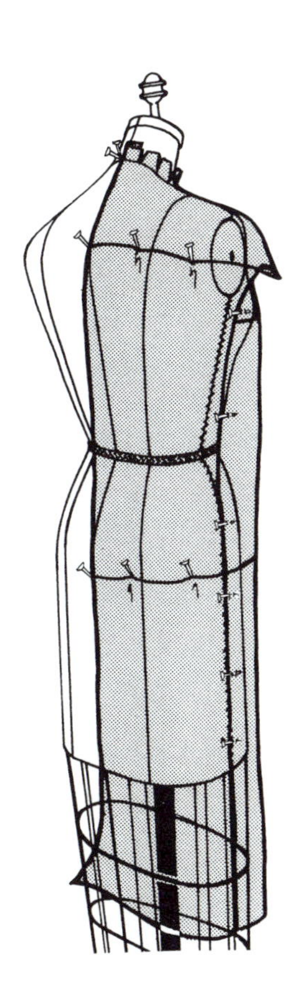

1 Pin the front and back side seams to each other, matching the hip level crossgrains.

2 Pin the center back grainline fold of the fabric to the center back position of the dress form.

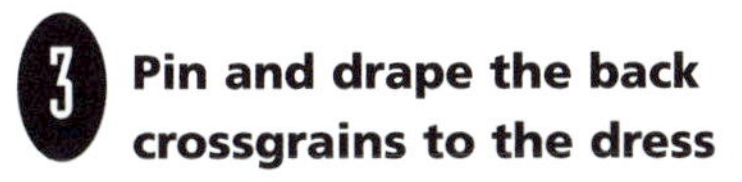

3 Pin and drape the back crossgrains to the dress form. Evenly distribute the ease of both the shoulder blade and the hip level crossgrains. Pin the crossgrains so that they are parallel to the floor.

NOTE: If correctly draped, there should be no drag in the fabric between the two crossgrains.

4 Clip, smooth, and drape the back neckline. Smooth and pin the back neck area into position.

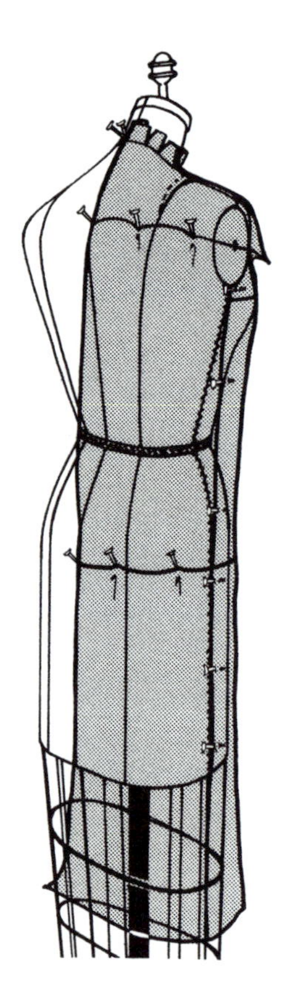

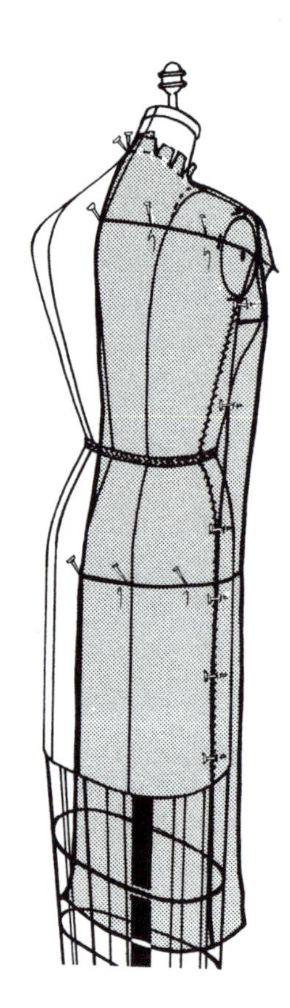

5 **Drape in the back shoulder dart** 3-inches long and 1/2-inch wide as follows.

a. Smooth the fabric over the shoulder seam from the neckline to the princess seam, and crossmark.

b. Measure toward the armhole 1/2 inch from the princess seam at the shoulder, and crossmark.

c. Measure down 3 inches on the princess seam from the shoulder seam.

d. Fold the back shoulder dart in place. Fold the fabric from the princess seam crossmark to the 1/2-inch crossmark. Taper the dart to nothing at the 3-inch crossmark.

6 **Mark all key areas** of the dress form to the fabric.

Back neckline

Shoulder seam and shoulder dart

Armplate
a. Top at shoulder ridge.
b. Middle at screw level.
c. Bottom at side seam.

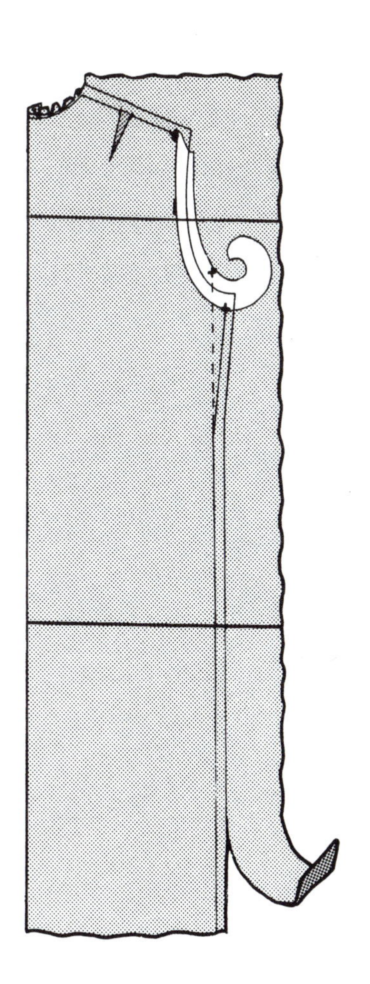

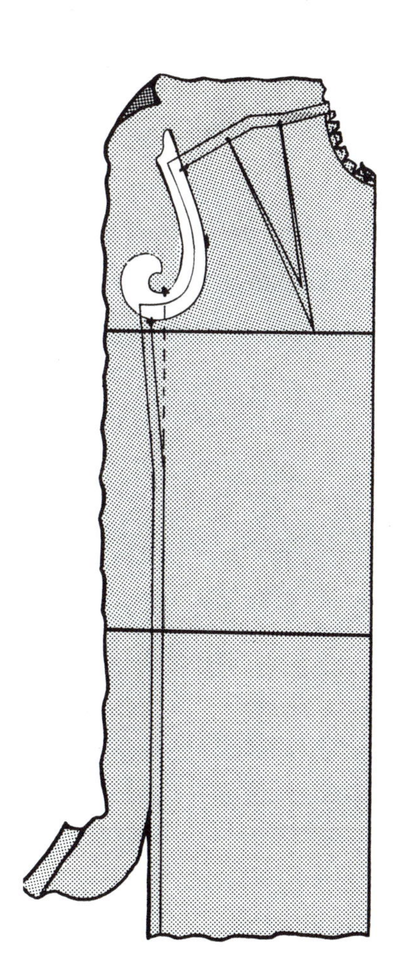

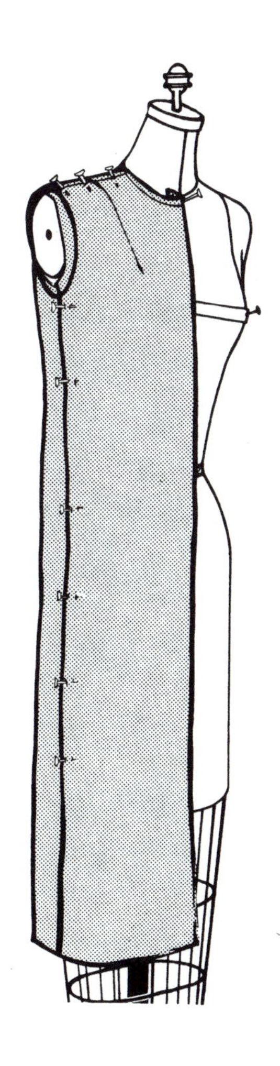

True up the neckline, shoulder, shoulder darts, and the front and back armholes. Remove the fabric drape from the dress form. Add seam allowances and trim excess fabric. Pin darts, side seams, and shoulder seams together.

Return the drape to dress form and check for accuracy, fit, and balance.

Draping the dart into gathers, tucks, or release pleats. The shoulder dart area can be draped into gathers, tucks, or release pleats rather than draping the dart.

The yoke area can also be styled, after which the dart can be converted into gathers, tucks, or release pleats.

Draping the waist area into a more fitted waist. The shift dress can give a more fitted look in the waist area by fitting any number of release pleats or fitting darts. The side seam can be made into any desired fit by simply draping the side seam closer to the body.

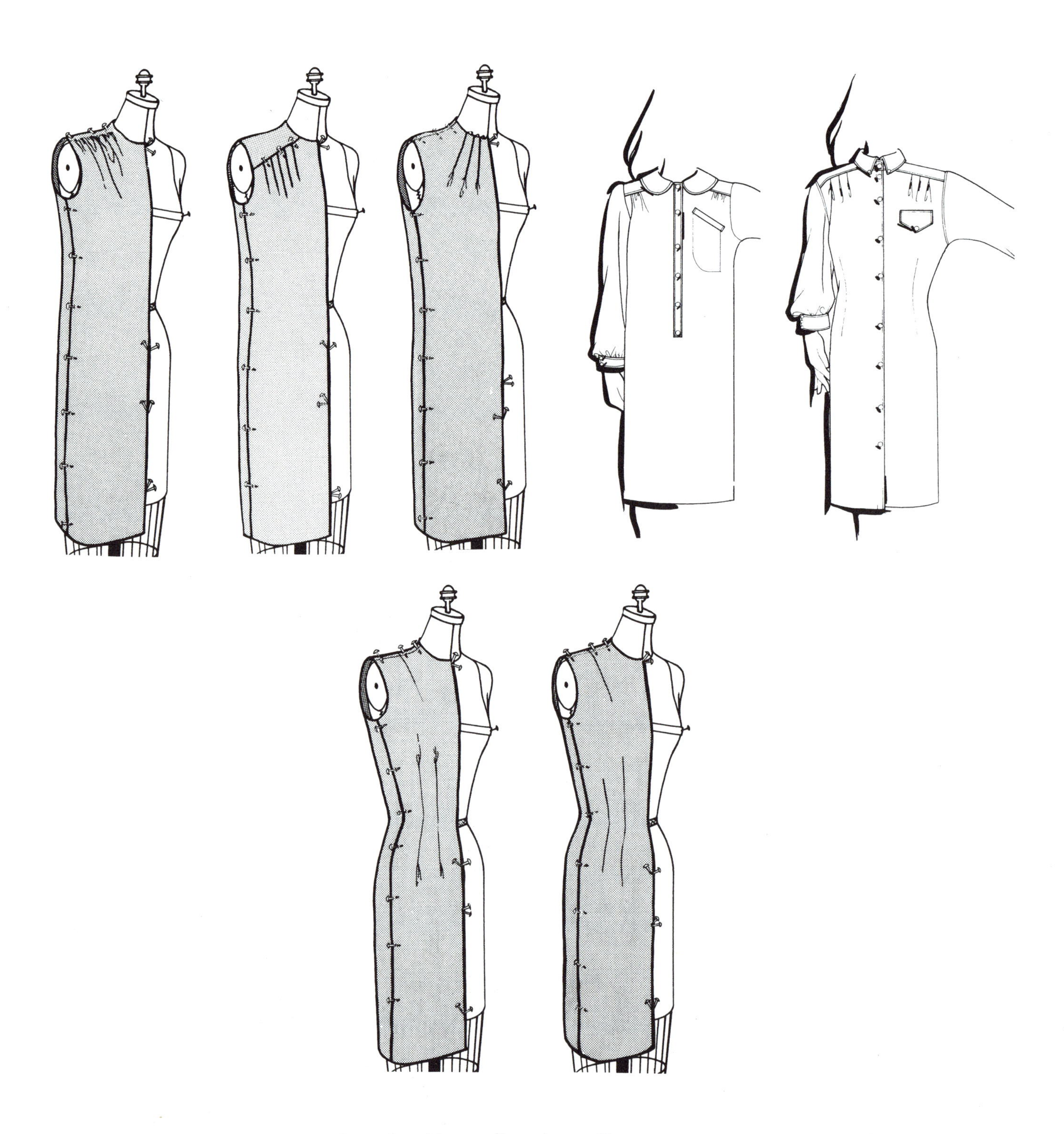

Chapter Eight

Basic Sleeve

Objectives

By studying the various draping steps in this chapter, the designer should be able to accomplish the following:

- Recognize grain and crossgrain of the fabric in relation to the sleeve.
- Take a flat piece of fabric and make it fit the curves of the arm.
- Develop a basic sleeve block with the correct amount of ease allowance, cap size, and measurements.
- Pivot or "walk" the sleeve into the bodice armhole, determine sleeve ease, and place the sleeve cap notches.
- Check the results of the sleeve draft for proper ease, fit, hang, and proportion.
- Adjust sleeve or armhole if any part of the sleeve pattern is incorrect.

Basic Sleeve

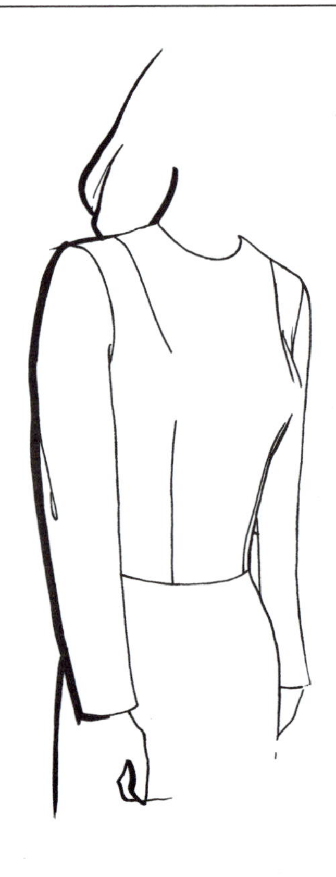

Sleeves are the part of the bodice that covers the arm. A sleeve that is sewn into a traditional armhole of a garment is called a set-in sleeve. This sleeve can be full-length, three quarter length, or elbow length. Various set-in styled sleeves include the basic set-in sleeve, bishop sleeve, puff sleeve, bell sleeve, or cap sleeve. Sleeves can provide a tailored, sportive, or dramatic quality to a garment. To achieve various sleeve styles, it is important to make and understand the "basic" sleeve.

The sleeve can be drafted with a great deal more accuracy than by draping. However, after the draft, the sleeve must be fitted into the armhole of the bodice to check the relationship of the sleeve cap and the armhole, the hang, and the alignment of the grainline.

A basic set-in sleeve must be absolutely accurate to allow the arm to move freely forward or upward and to permit the sleeve to hang properly. The proper amount of cap ease must also be determined.

Basic Sleeve Measurement Chart includes each

Before you draft the Basic Fitted Sleeve, study the following five important measurements.

1. Overarm length (distance from the shoulder to the wrist)

Size	6	8	10	12	14	16	18
Overarm length 3/8" diff	22 3/8"	22 3/4"	23 1/8"	23 1/2"	23 7/8"	24 1/4	24 5/8

2. Underarm length (distance from the underarm armpit to the wrist)

Size	6	8	10	12	14	16	18
Underarm length 1/4" diff	16 1/4"	16 1/2"	16 3/4"	17"	17 1/4"	17 1/2	17 3/4

3. Cap height (remaining distance from the underarm armpit to the shoulder)

Size	6	8	10	12	14	16	18
Cap height 1/8" diff	6 1/8"	6 1/4"	6 3/8"	6 1/2"	6 5/8"	6 3/4	6 7/8

4. Elbow circumference (measurement around the elbow plus 1 inch ease)

Size	6	8	10	12	14	16	18
Elbow circumference 1/2" diff	9 3/4"	10 1/4"	10 3/4"	11 1/4"	11 3/4"	12 1/4"	12 3/4"

5. Bicep circumference (measurement around the upper arm plus 2 inch ease)

Size	6	8	10	12	14	16	18
Bicep circumference 1/2" diff	11 1/2"	12"	12 1/2"	13"	13 1/2"	14"	14 1/2"

1 **Cut a piece of pattern paper** 32-inches long by 24-inches wide. Fold the paper in half lengthwise.

NOTE: One half of the sleeve is drafted. It is then cut on the fold and opened up to make a full sleeve. Minor pattern changes are then made to show the difference between the front and back of the sleeve.

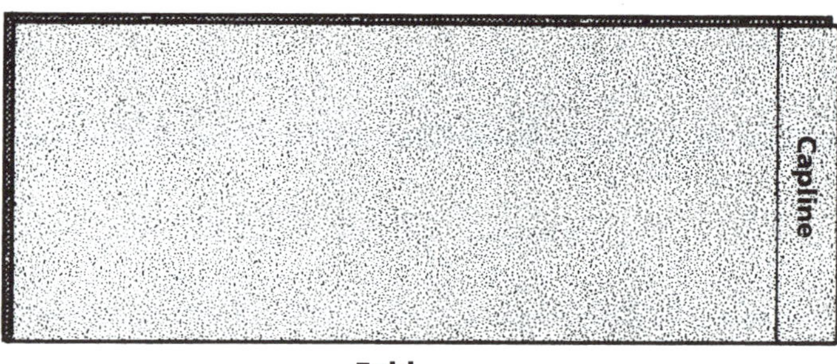

2 **Draw the capline.** With the fold in front of you, draw a perfect crossgrain line 2 inches from the right side of the paper. This is the top of your sleeve, or the capline.

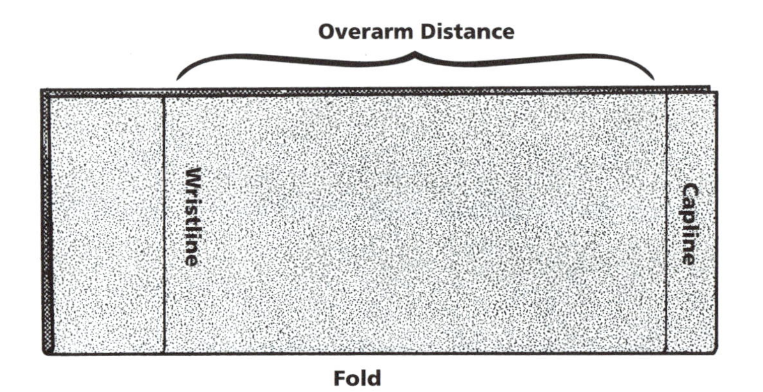

3 **Draw the wrist level line.** With the fold in front of you, measure down from the top of the sleeve (capline) the desired over-arm distance (size 8 is 22 3/4 inches, size 10 is 23 1/8 inches). Using an L-square ruler, draw a perfect crossgrain line up from the fold at this level for the wristline.

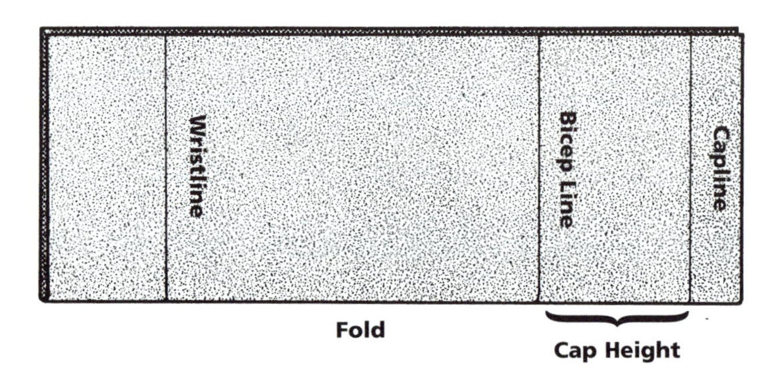

4 **Draw the bicep line.** With the fold in front of you, measure from the top of the sleeve (capline) the desired cap height (size 8 is 6 1/4 inches, size 10 is 6 3/8 inches). Using an L-square ruler, draw a perfect crossgrain line up from the fold at this level for the bicep line.

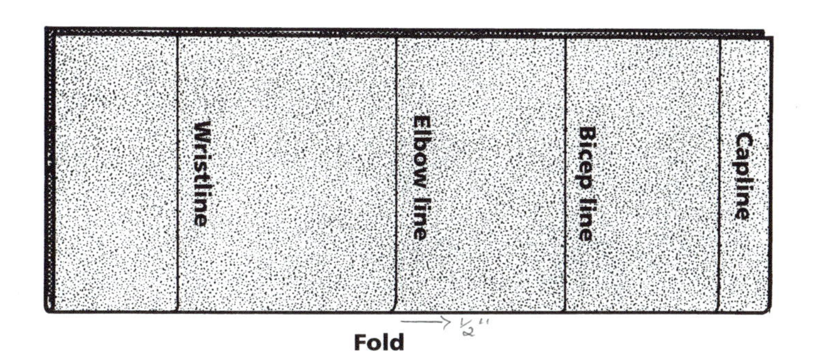

5 **Draw the elbow line.** With the fold in front of you, divide the distance from the bicep line to the wristline in half. Draw in an **elbow line** 1/2 inch above this halfway point.

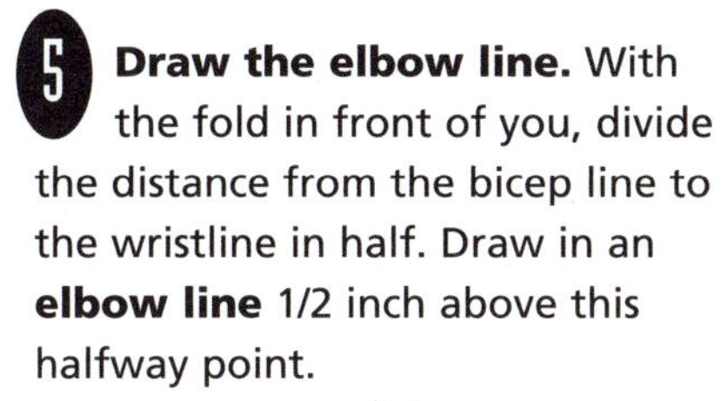

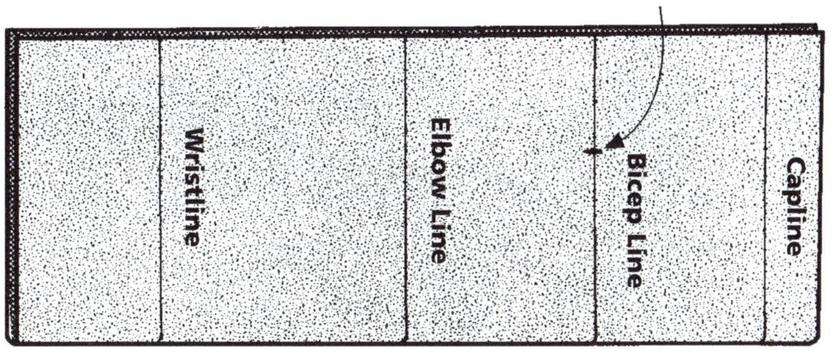

6 **Crossmark one half of the bicep circumference.**

a. Determine the bicep sleeve circumference needed and add the necessary amount of ease. Divide this amount in half (size 8 is 6 inches, size 10 is 6 1/4 inches).

b. Place a crossmark on the bicep line this distance up from the fold of the paper.

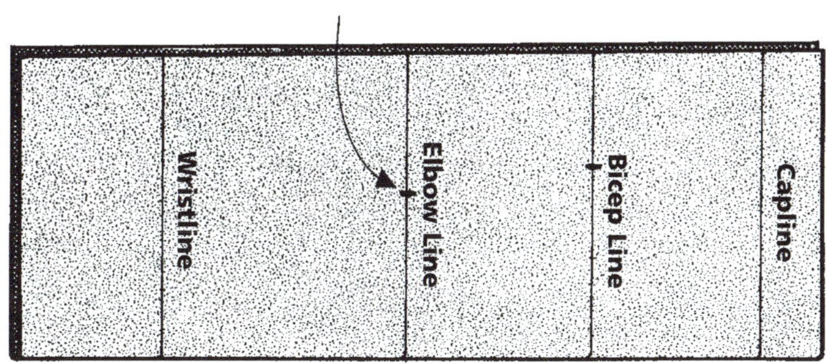

7 **Crossmark one half of the elbow circumference.**

a. Determine the elbow circumference needed and add the necessary amount of ease. Divide this amount in half (size 8 is 5 1/8 inches, size 10 is 5 3/8 inches).

b. Place a crossmark on the elbow line this distance up from the fold of the paper.

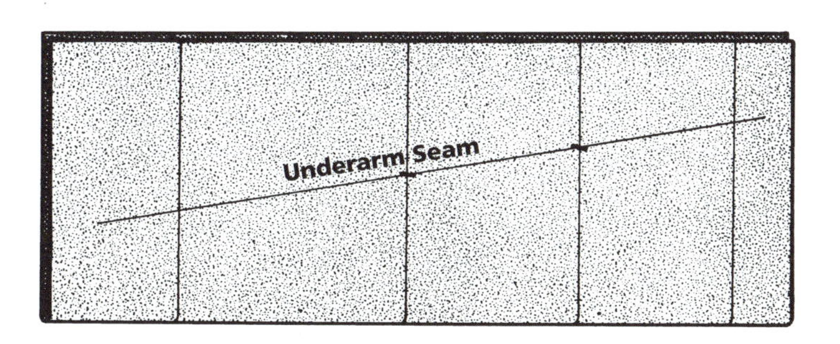

8 **Draw the underarm seamline.** Connect the bicep crossmark and the elbow crossmark. Continue this line straight up until it crosses the top of the sleeve (capline) and down until it crosses the wristline. This line represents the underarm seamline.

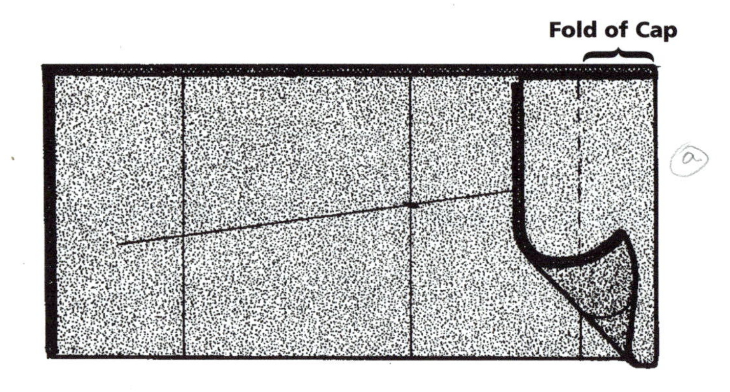

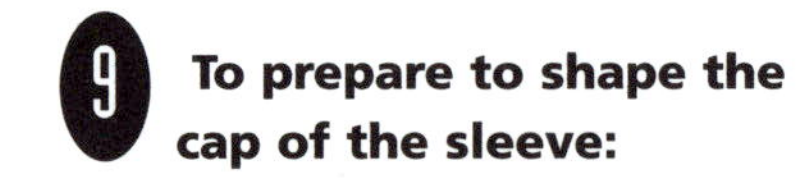

9 To prepare to shape the cap of the sleeve:

a. Fold the cap area in half from the top of the sleeve (capline) to the bicep line.

b. Fold the sleeve in half lengthwise. Place and crease the sleeve foldline to the underarm seamline.

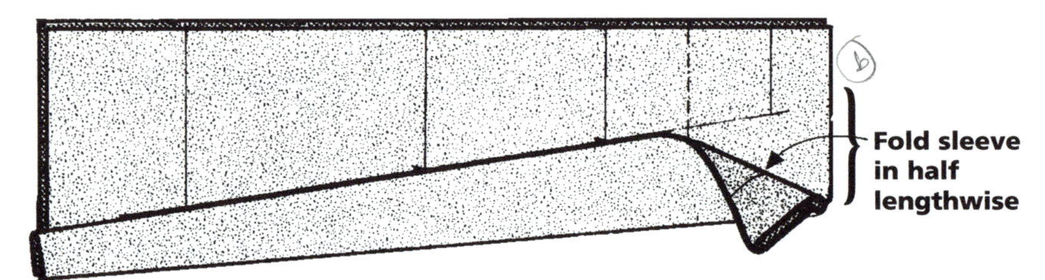

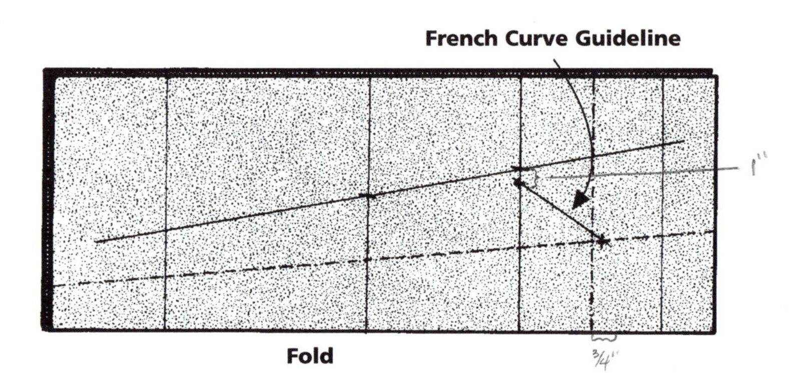

10 Prepare to draw in the cap shape by establishing a guideline for the french curve.

a. Put a crossmark on the bicep line 1 inch in from the underarm seamline.

b. Put a crossmark on the lengthwise fold 3/4 inch above the point at which the folds of the cap height meet.

c. Lightly draw a line to connect these two crossmarks.

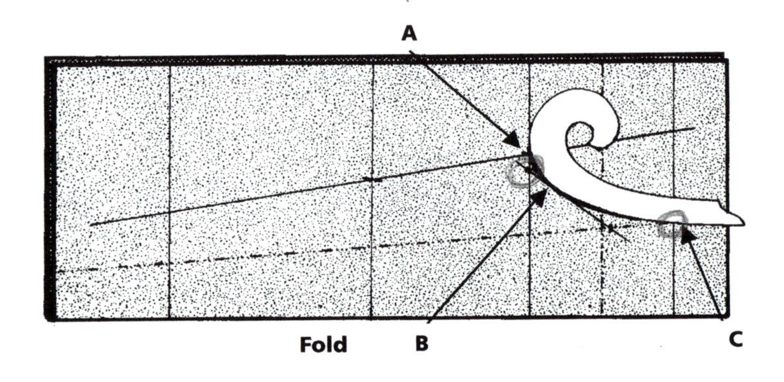

11 Draw the underarm curve of the sleeve cap. Using a french curve and referring to the illustration, connect positions **A** (underarm seam/bicep line corner), **B** (middle of french curve guideline), and **C** (capline at lengthwise foldline).

All three positions must touch the french curve at the same time.

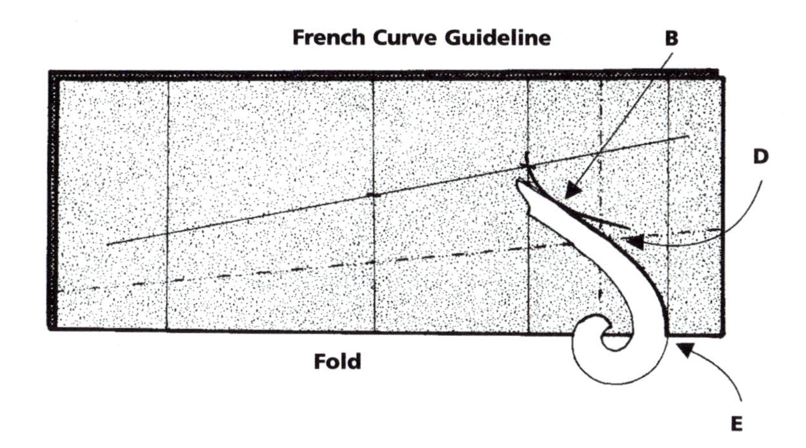

12 **Draw the top portion of the sleeve cap.** Using a french curve and referring to the illustration, **connect positions B** (middle of french curve guideline), **D** (crossmark on lengthwise foldline), and **E** (capline at center sleeve foldline). All three positions must touch the french curve at the same time.

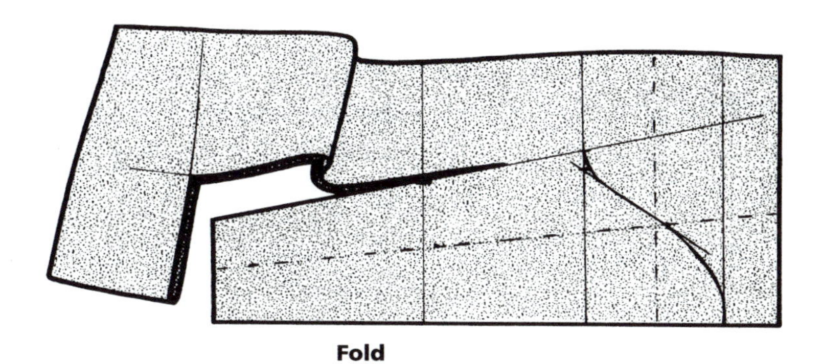

13 **Cut out the entire sleeve.** With the sleeve still folded in half, cut out the sleeve following the newly shaped cap, the underarm seamline, and the wristline.

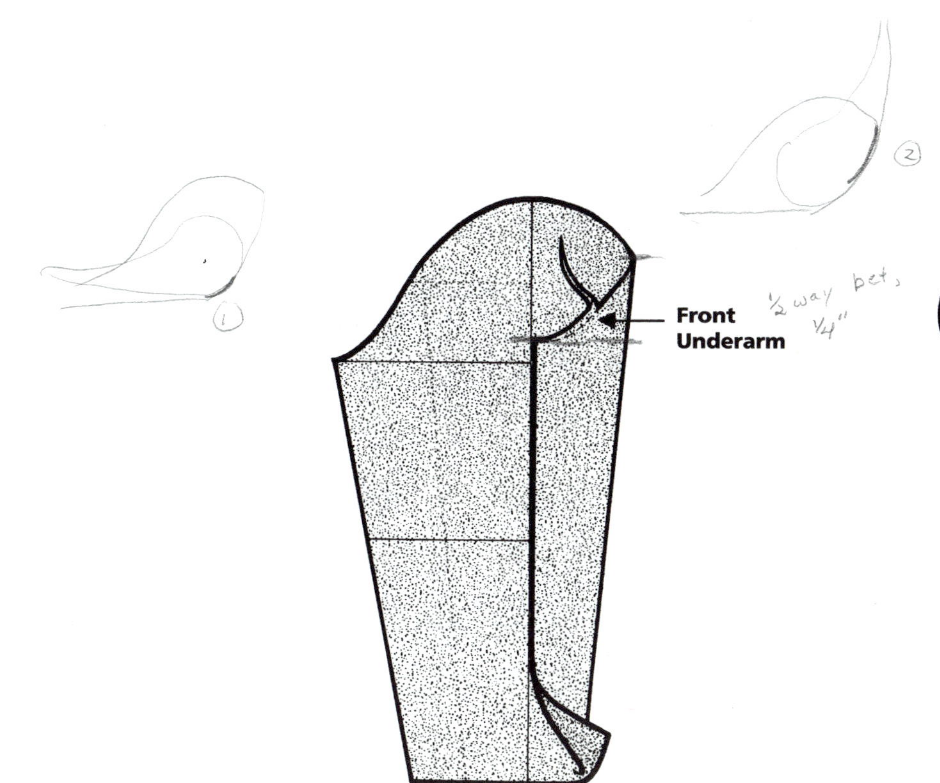

14 **Reshape the front underarm curve.** Open the sleeve draft and fold the unmarked underarm area in half. Remove 1/4 inch to nothing at the middle of this lower curve on the underarm seamline and to nothing at the lengthwise quarter fold. This side represents the front cap/underarm of the sleeve.

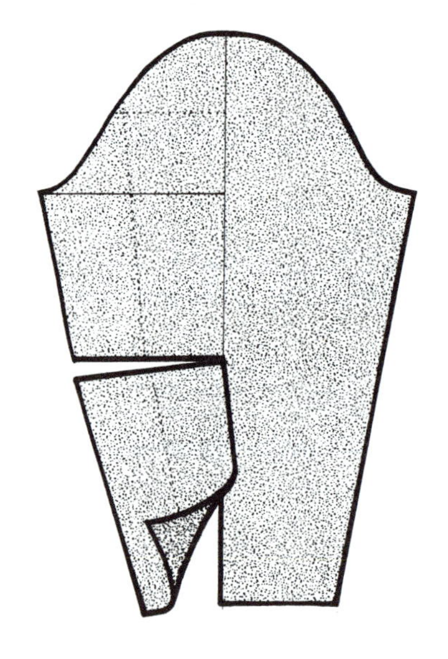

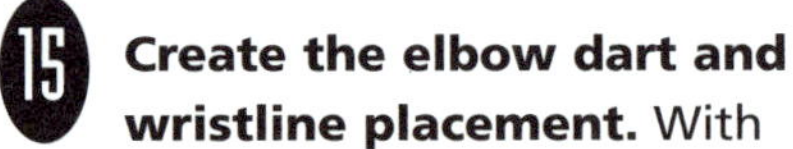

15 **Create the elbow dart and wristline placement.** With the sleeve open, cut on the elbow line to the center foldline of the sleeve. Also cut on the center foldline from the wrist level up to the elbow level. Do not cut through entirely.

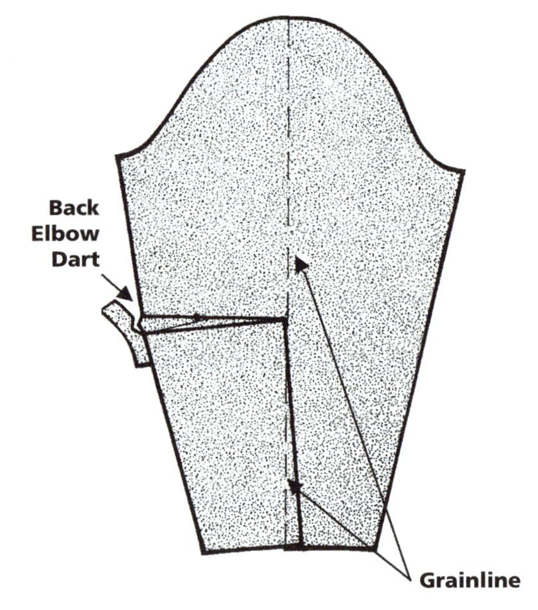

16 **Form the back of the sleeve and the elbow dart** by lapping over the center sleeve line. This will cause an opening at until the elbow line. Lap this center line until the elbow dart area is opened at least 1/2 to 5/8 inch.

Tape a small piece of paper underneath the slashed opening. At this slashed opening, draw the dart 3 1/2 inches long and the width of the opening. Fold the dart closed to determine the shape of the dart, and trim excess paper.

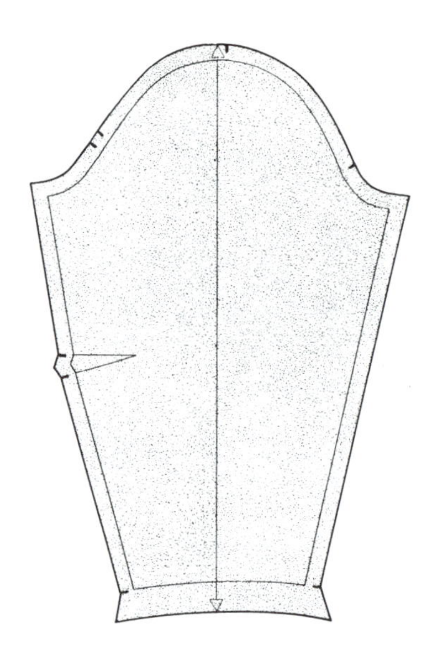

17 **Determine the sleeve cap notches.** Pivot the stitchline of the sleeve cap into the stitchline of the desired armhole. Refer to the pivoting steps on **pages 85–86,** for a clear example of pivoting technique and notch placement.

18 **Add seam allowance to the sleeve.**

Refer to **Walking the Sleeve, pages 85–86,** to **determine the ease amount.** This ease will be "crimped" and evenly distributed from the front (single notch) to the back notches (double notches). The sleeve is now ready for a fitting.

Walking the Sleeve into the Armhole

The silhouette of a sleeve gradually changes from year to year. It may vary from a skimpy short cap to a voluminous puff. It may have a natural shoulder look or a tailored squared look with padded shoulders. In all cases, the sleeve must fit smoothly and yet offer freedom of movement. As a result, each new look must be checked for cap distance, notch placement, and sleeve fit.

To ensure a proper fit, the sleeve must be pivoted to the bodice armhole, matching stitchline to stitchline. This technique is know as "walking the sleeve." Walking a sleeve into an armhole will show if there is enough cap distance, where to match and place the notches, and will determine the amount of ease needed in the cap.

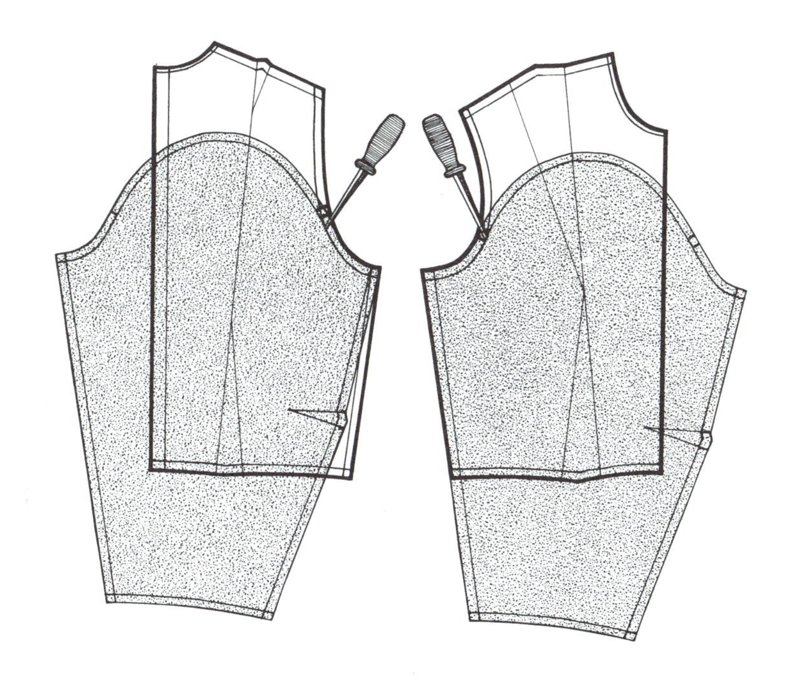

1. **Place the underarm of the sleeve to the underarm of the bodice,** matching the stitchlines and the side seams.

NOTE: The armhole notches for the bodice have already been established.

2. **Pivot the sleeve around the armhole.** Starting at the underarm side seam corner, pivot the sleeve around the armhole until the edges of the sleeve and bodice meet. Use a pencil or an awl at the stitchline of the sleeve to hold the sleeve in place. While walking the sleeve, match and pencil in the front and back armhole notches (one on the front and two on the back).

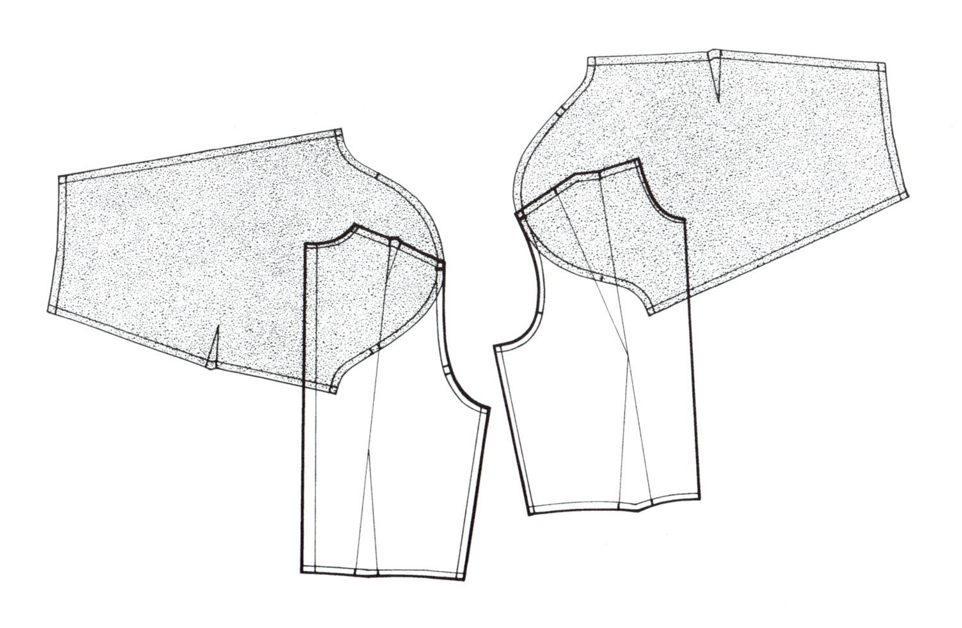

3. **Continue walking the sleeve the remainder of the armhole area.** Move the awl to the point at which the sleeve and the bodice armhole meet. Continue to pivot the sleeve around the bodice armhole, until the edges of the sleeve and bodice meet once again.

4. **Crossmark the shoulder positions.** While walking the sleeve, notch and crossmark on the sleeve cap the front and back bodice shoulder position of the front and back bodice.

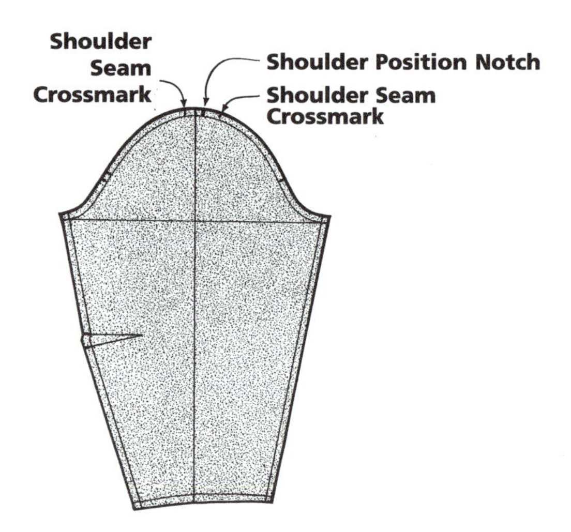

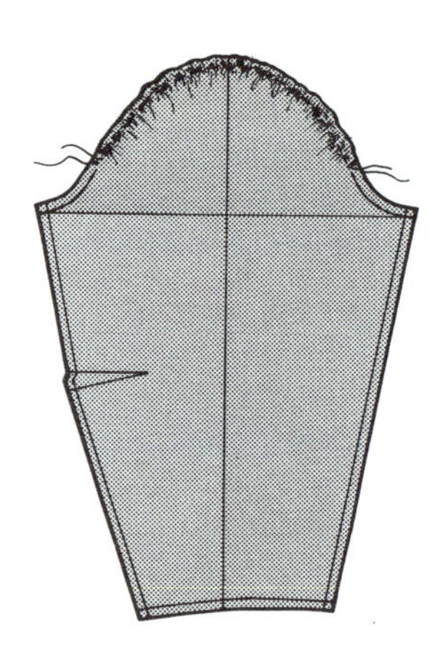

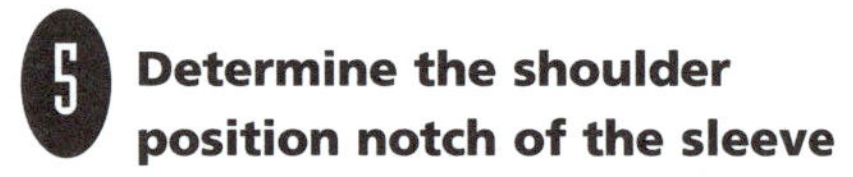

5 Determine the shoulder position notch of the sleeve cap. Divide the distance between the shoulder seam crossmarks in half. This center position is the shoulder notch.

NOTE: If the armhole shape is correct, the notch at the shoulder position will fall 1/4 inch toward the front of the grain. If the notch does not fall close to that position, it can be assumed that the bodice drape and/or the armhole shape is incorrect. (The back armhole should measure 1/2 inch longer than the front armhole.)

6 Determine the amount of sleeve cap ease. The distance between the shoulder position crossmarks is the amount of ease in the sleeve cap. This amount of ease will be evenly distributed or "crimped" into the sleeve from the front underarm notch to the back underarm notches. Crimp (ease in) the sleeve cap from the front notch to the back notches.

Notes

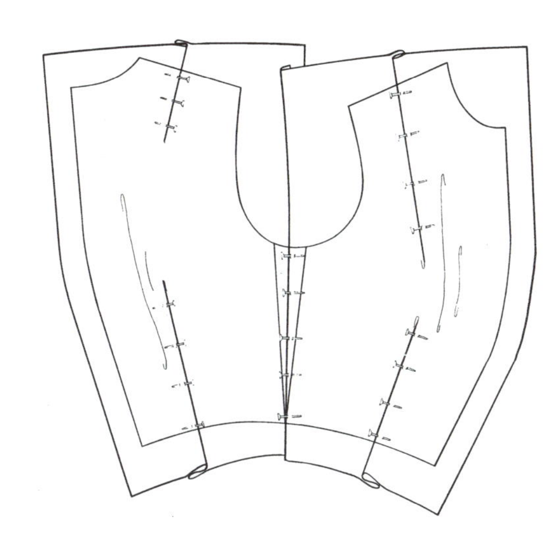

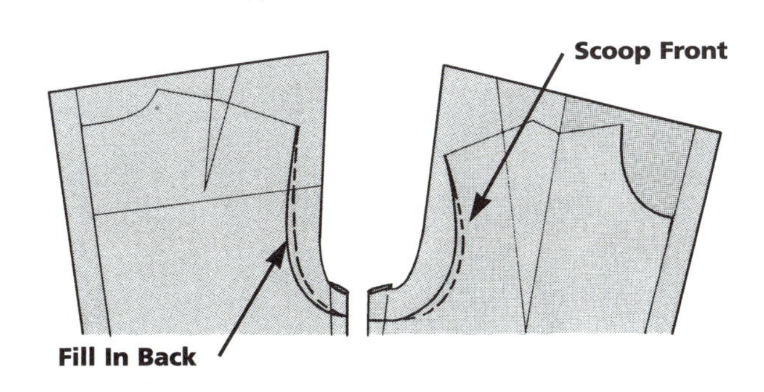

OR

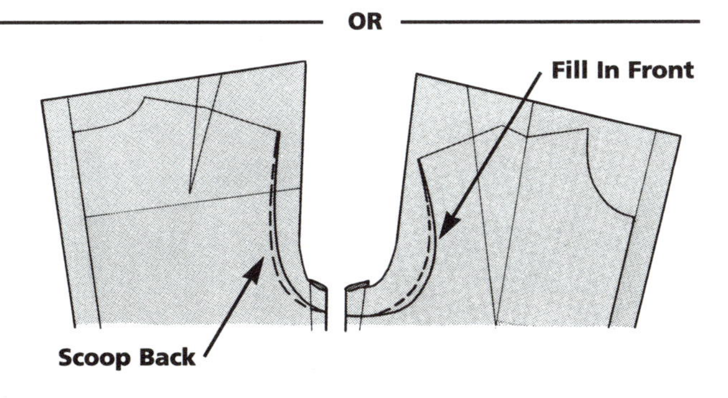

1 Measure front and back armhole The front armhole should measure 1/2 inch shorter than the back armhole.

2 Correct front and back armhole To make the front or back armhole longer: Reshape the front armhole by removing 1/4 inch at the middle of the armhole, shaping back to its original corners at the top and bottom.

To make the front and back armhole shorter: Add 1/4 inch at the mid/armhole area, and again, reshape to its original corners at the top and bottom.

NOTE: If the armhole does not balance by removing or adding 1/4 inch, an error was probably made while trueing or draping the armhole.

Fitting the Basic Sleeve Into the Armhole

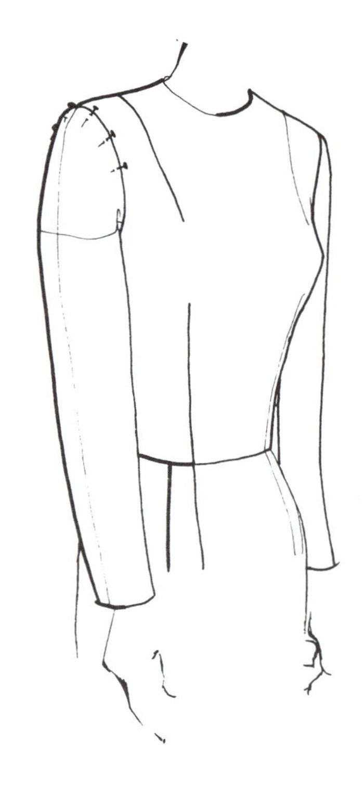

The designer may make pattern adjustments, but still retain the original character of the sleeve. Fitting a sleeve into a garment is essential when a new sleeve has been drafted. The fitting allows the designer to compare the flat pattern dimensions with the hang, movement, proportion, and shape of the actual sleeve.

A properly fitted sleeve will provide the designer with the highest quality garments. Therefore, fittings must be done carefully and accurately.

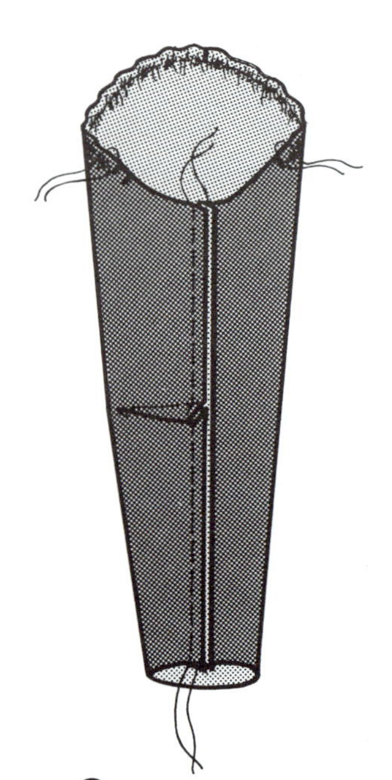

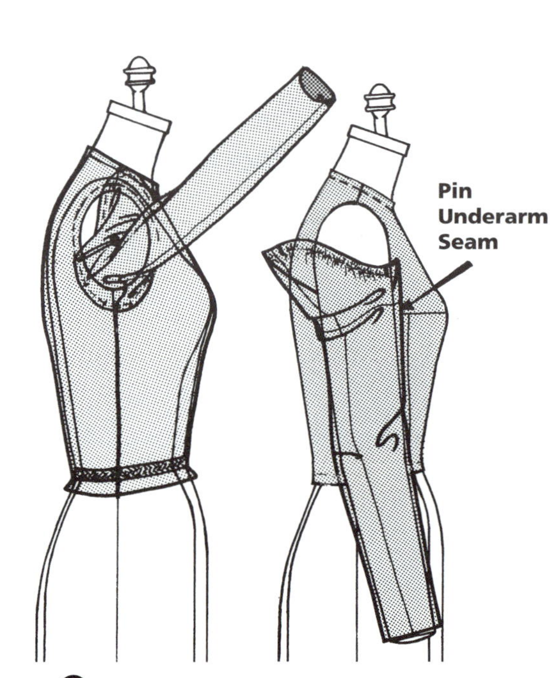

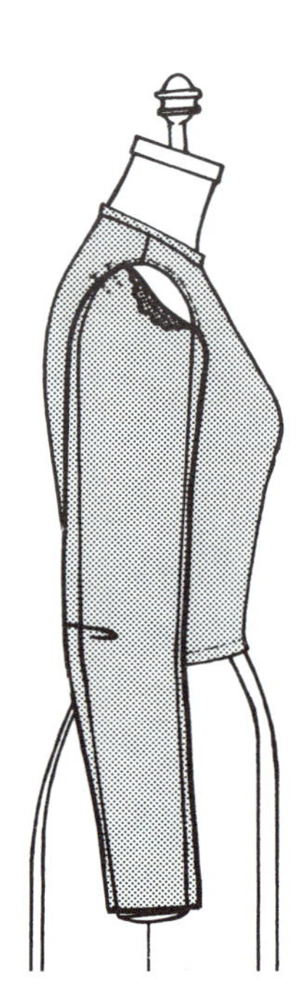

1 Cut, sew, and crimp the basic sleeve. Cut the basic sleeve out of fabric. Sew the elbow dart and the underarm seam. Crimp the sleeve cap from the front notch to the back notches.

2 Pin the underarm seam of the sleeve. Lift the arm to expose the underarm seams and pin the underarm seam of the sleeve to the underarm seam of the bodice armhole. Place the pins parallel to the stitchline, from the front notches down and around to the back notches.

3 Pin the sleeve cap to the remaining portion of the armhole, matching the shoulder notch to the shoulder seam of the bodice and all remaining stitchlines.

Check Final Proof of Sleeve Drape

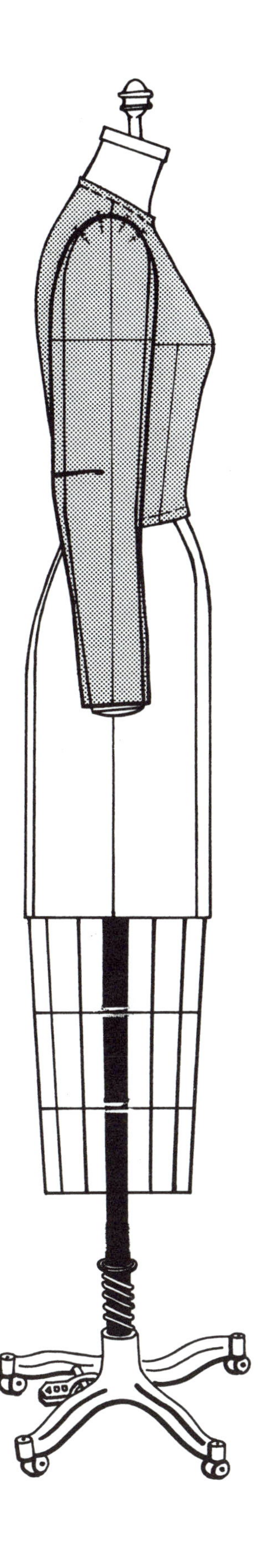

Checklist

Check the sleeve for proper fit and hang.

Grainline Should hang straight and in the middle of the arm. The grainline should fall to the side seam of the dress form.

Crossgrain should be parallel to the floor. It should not pull or sag.

Hang From the elbow level, the sleeve should have a slight forward movement to follow the hang of the human arm.

Ease The sleeve cap should have the correct amount of ease.

NOTE: The amount of ease varies in sleeve styles and among different manufacturers.

Notes for any adjustments.

Adjust and pin the sleeve cap if any of the above areas are slightly off. Draw any changes on draft.

- If the ease amount is too much or too little, check the armhole shape of the bodice.
- If the sleeve swings too far forward or backward, check the armhole shape of the bodice.

  Check sleeve draft for accuracy.
- Position and pin the altered pattern to the original sleeve pattern. Transfer, with a trace wheel, all changes to this pattern and retrue all changes.

NOTE: It would be advisable to make a quick second fitting of the sleeve if there are any changes.

Part Three

Design Variations of the Basic Foundation Patterns

In Parts One and Two, the designer learned to mold and shape fabric on the dress form and to create basic patterns. In Part Three, the designer will learn to use these basic foundation skills to create bodices, skirts, and sleeves. In addition, the design of basic collars and pants, as well as more fashionable variations, is introduced.

Part Three enhances the designer's skills in handling a variety of fabrics. The designs are kept simple and natural while the fabric is draped with the correct amount of ease proportion and is not overworked. Projects explore how to define the style and silhouette over the bust, hip, and waist by emphasizing the use of folds, darts, pleats, and fullness.

Many ideas develop after making a slash to release the excess fabric beyond the normal seam position. Projects illustrating this principle explain the manipulation of draped design. Working with a greater understanding of each method helps the designer recognize the qualities of a well-designed garment.

Chapter Nine

Bodice Variations

Objectives

By studying the various draping steps in this chapter, the designer should be able to accomplish the following:

- Develop creativity and stimulate a variety of bodice designs.
- Mold the fabric and a basic bodice pattern to fit the curves of the body over the bust.
- Manipulate the fabric to create folds, darts, pleats, and fullness radiating from the highest point of the bust.
- Understand how the crossgrain changes when darts are manipulated into different locations.
- Visualize and true up the bodice patterns with shirring and pleats in relationship to the figure, with the correct amount of ease allowance, armhole size, waistline shape, measurement, and balance.
- Check the results of the draping process with regard to fit, hang, balance, proportion, and the true up.

Relocating the Basic Shoulder and Waist Darts

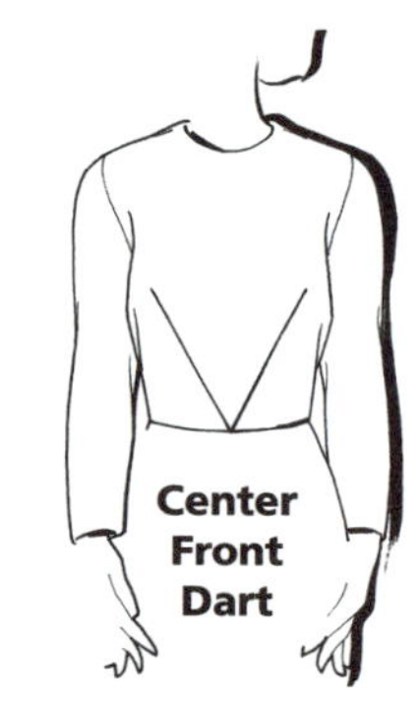

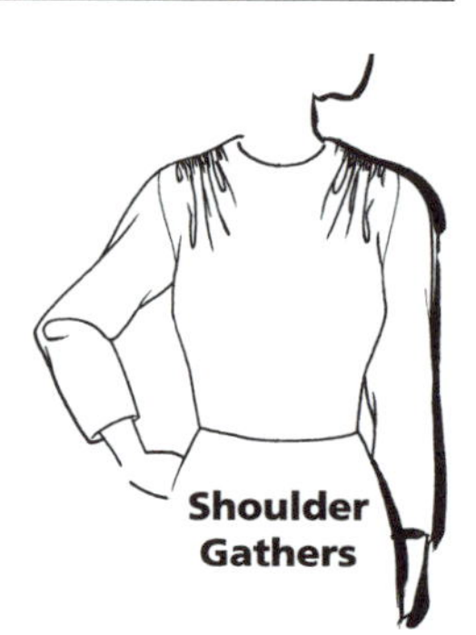

When draping a flat piece of fabric over the curves of the human body, the folds of the fabric radiate from the highest point of the bust. These folds, however, may be arranged in any position radiating from the bust. With a larger body and/or a fuller bust, the fabric excess will be wider, thereby creating wider darts. In contrast, a flat busted figure has less fullness radiating from the apex, thereby resulting in narrower dart excess.

The shoulder and waist darts may be changed from their original locations to anywhere the designer chooses, because they were created by the excess fabric folds radiating from the bust. Thus, these two darts, or the excess fabric, can be combined into one large dart, divided into multiple darts, pleats, or tucks next to one another, or converted into gathers, anywhere on the bodice. These various dart manipulations will create different design details.

Examples of draping techniques that can change the bust fullness into a single dart, gathered fullness, and multiple pleats are given on the following pages. These examples will help a designer learn to value the number of choices available when draping the fabric excess on the body.

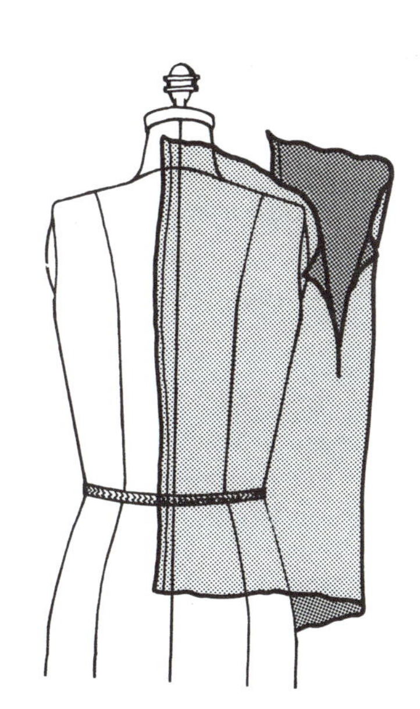

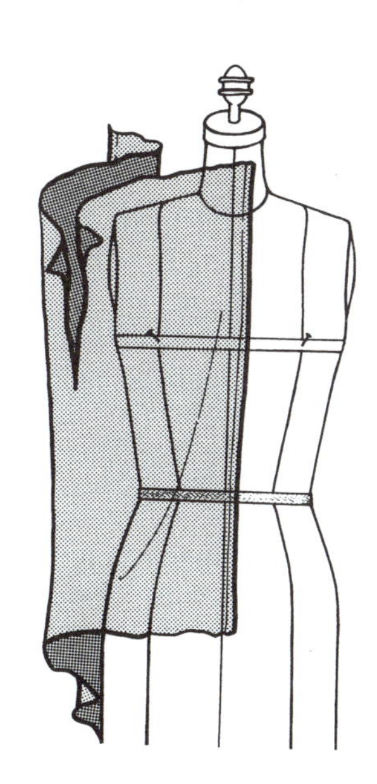

1 **Measure the length for the front and back bodice** along the straight of grain from the neckband to the waist, and add 5 inches.

2 **Measure the width for the front and back bodice** along the crossgrain from the center front of the dress form to the side seam of the bust level, and add 5 inches.

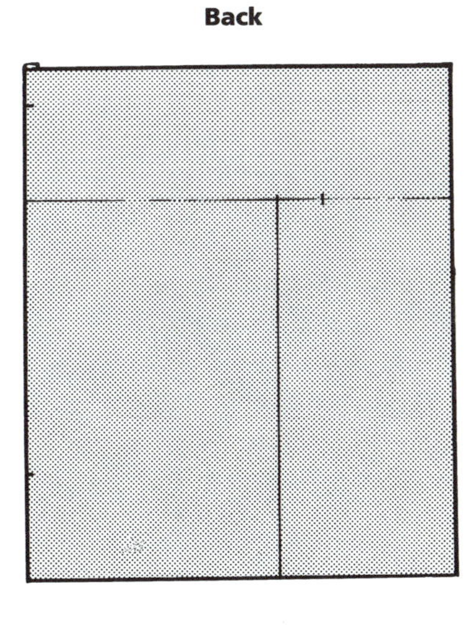

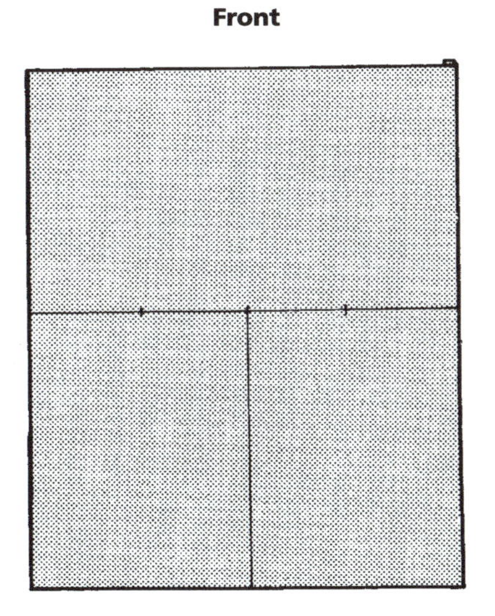

3 **Draw the center front grainline** 1 inch from the torn edge, and press under.

4 **Draw a perfect crossgrain line.** Using an L-square ruler, in the center of the fabric panel, draw a crossgrain line perpendicular to the grainline. This crossgrain line will be referred to as the bust level line.

5 **Measure the dress form** the distance from the center front to the apex.

6 **Measure and crossmark the apex** dress form distance to the bust level line of the fabric.

7 **Measure and draw in the grainline, shoulder blade crossgrain** and plate crossmark for the back fabric piece.

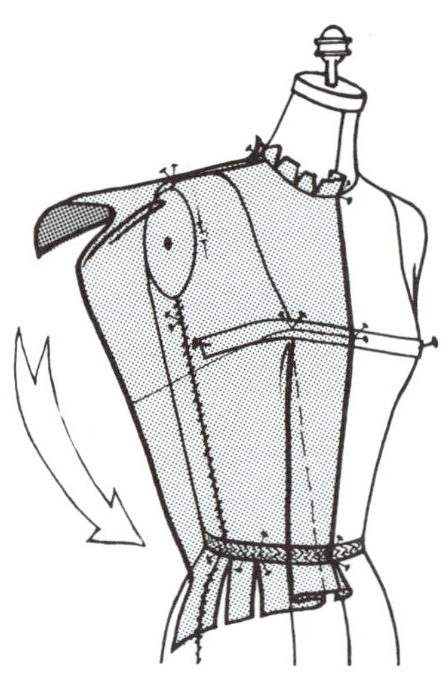

Waist Dart

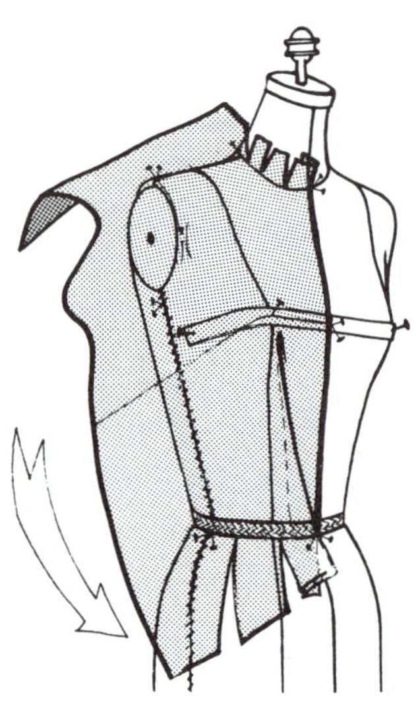

Center Front Waist Dart

1 Pin the apex mark on the fabric to the apex position of the dress form.

2 Pin the center front grainline fold of the fabric to the center front position of the dress form.

Anchor pins at C.F. neck and C.F. waist. An additional pin may be needed at the bust level tape.

3 Drape the neckline by trimming the excess fabric around the neck area and clipping at intervals. Smooth the neckline in place.

4 Drape and pin the shoulder by smoothing the excess fabric across the upper chest area and over the shoulder.

5 Smooth and drape the fabric around the armhole plate, creating a 1/4"–1/4" pinch at the screw level at the armhole ridge. This is to ensure that the armhole does not get too tight.

6 Smooth and drape the fabric past the side seam. The crossgrain will be angling downward (see illustration).

7 Allow all excess fabric to fall into the waistline area below the bust.

8 Clip, smooth, and drape the waistline fabric across the waistline tape.

a. For a single waistline dart, allow all excess fabric to be pinned at the princess seam on the waistline.

b. For a center front/waistline dart, allow all excess fabric to be pinned at the center front/waist area of the dress form.

9 Mark all key areas of the dress form to the fabric.

Neckline Crossmark at C.F. neck and at the neckline/shoulder ridge corner.

Shoulder Seam Lightly mark the shoulder seam and crossmark the shoulder ridge corner.

Armplate

a. Top at shoulder seam ridge.
b. Middle at screw level.
c. Crossmark bottom at the side seam.

Side Seam Lightly mark.

Waistline and Waist dart
Crossmark at C.F. waist, at side seam waist, and both sides of the dart.

TRUE UP

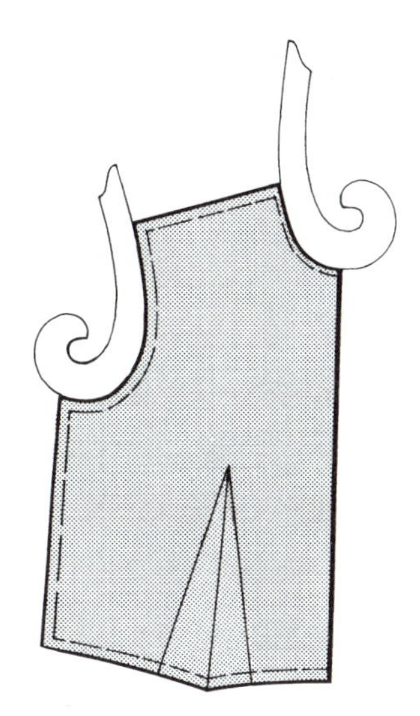

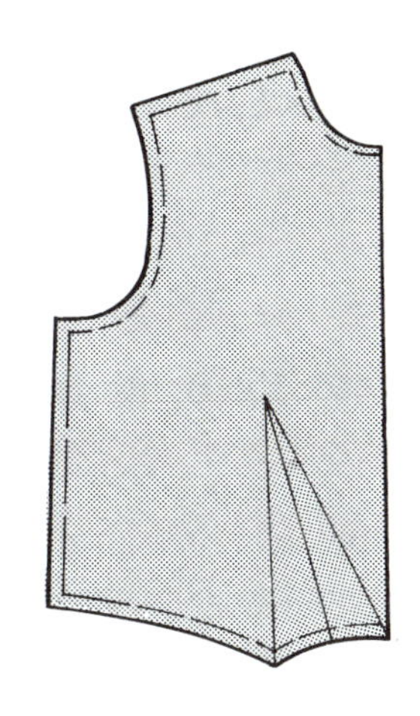

1 **Remove the fabric drape from the dress form.** True up all seams, add seam allowances, and trim excess fabric.

2 **Return the finished drape to the dress form** and check for accuracy, fit, and balance.

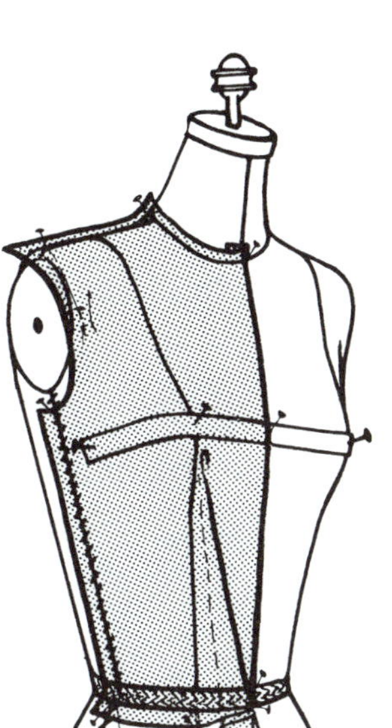

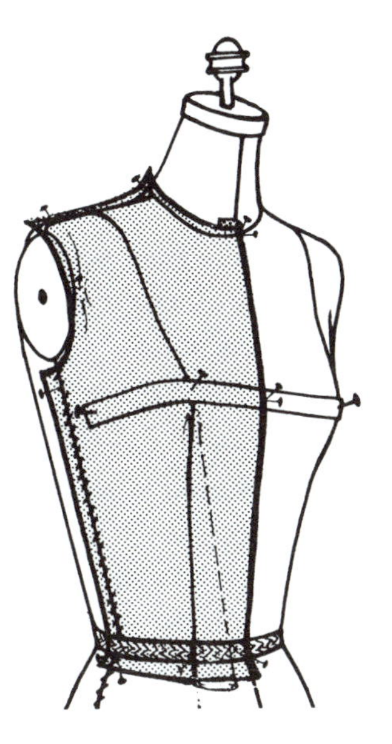

French Dart—Preparing the Fabric

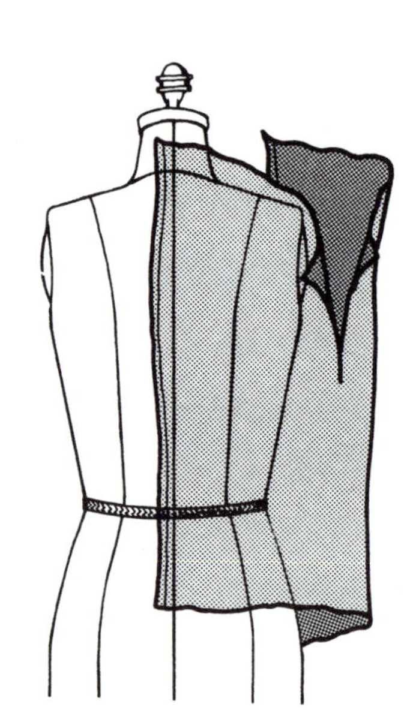

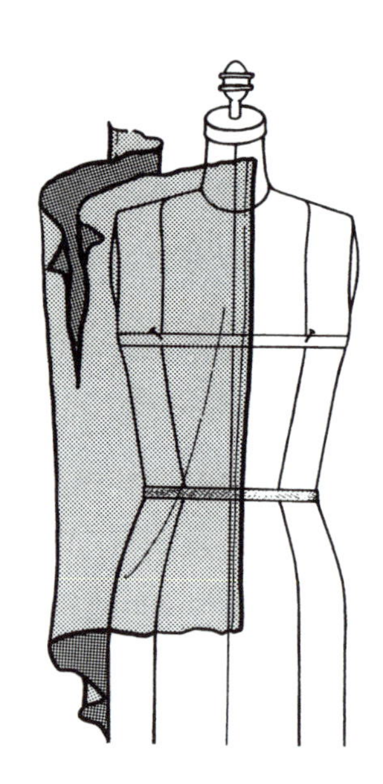

1 **Measure the length for the front and back bodice** along the straight of grain from the neckband to the waist, and add 5 inches.

2 **Measure the width for the front and back bodice** along the crossgrain from the center front of the dress form to the side seam of the bust level, and add 5 inches.

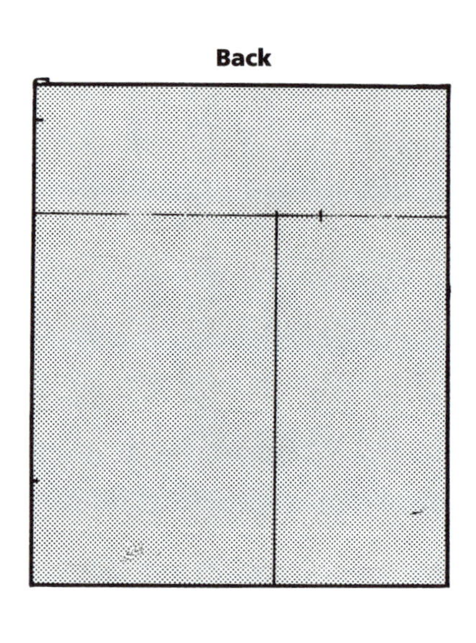

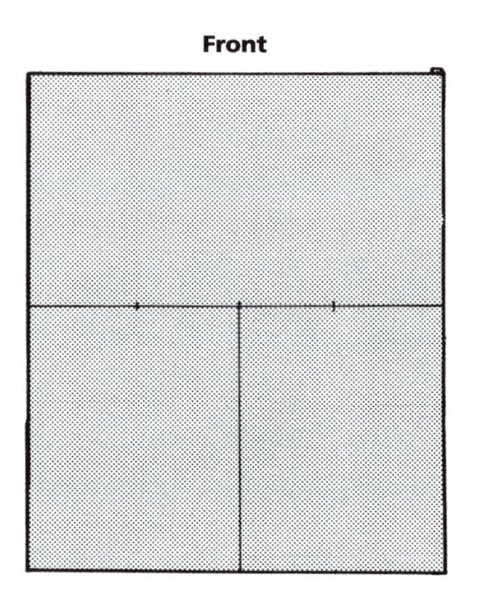

3 **Draw the center front grainline** 1 inch from the torn edge, and press under.

4 **Draw a perfect crossgrain line.** Using an L-square ruler, in the center of the fabric panel, draw a crossgrain line perpendicular to the grainline. This crossgrain line will be referred to as the bust level line.

5 **Measure the dress form** the distance from the center front to the apex.

6 **Measure and crossmark the apex** dress form distance to the bust level line of the fabric.

7 **Measure and draw in the grainline, shoulder blade crossgrain,** and plate crossmark for the back fabric piece.

French Dart—Draping Steps

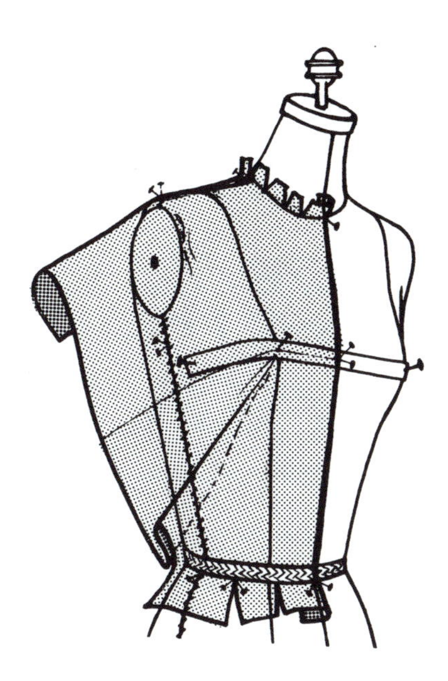

1 **Pin the apex** mark on the fabric to the apex position of the dress form.

2 **Pin the center front grainline fold** of the fabric to the center front position of the dress form.

Anchor pins at C.F. neck and C.F. waist. An additional pin may be needed at the bust level tape.

3 **Drape the neckline** by trimming the excess fabric around the neck area and clipping at intervals. Smooth the neckline in place.

4 **Drape and pin the shoulder** by smoothing the excess fabric across the upper chest area and over the shoulder.

5 **Smooth and drape the fabric around the armhole plate,** creating a 1/4"–1/4" pinch at the screw level at the armhole ridge. This is to ensure that the armhole does not get too tight.

6 **Smooth and drape the fabric to 2 inches above the waistline at the side seam.** The crossgrain will be angling downward (see illustration).

7 **Clip, smooth, and drape the waistline** fabric across the waistline tape. Allow all excess fabric to fall 2 inches above the waistline at the side seam.

8 **For a French dart,** allow all excess fabric to be pinned 2 inches above the waistline at the side seam.

9 **Mark all key areas** of the dress form to the fabric.

Neckline Crossmark at C.F. neck and at the neckline/shoulder ridge corner.

Shoulder Seam Lightly mark the shoulder seam and crossmark the shoulder ridge corner.

Armplate
a. Top at shoulder seam ridge.
b. Middle at screw level.
c. Crossmark bottom at the side seam.

Side Seam and French Dart
Lightly mark the side seam and crossmark both sides of the French dart.

Waistline Crossmark at C.F. waist and at the side seam waist.

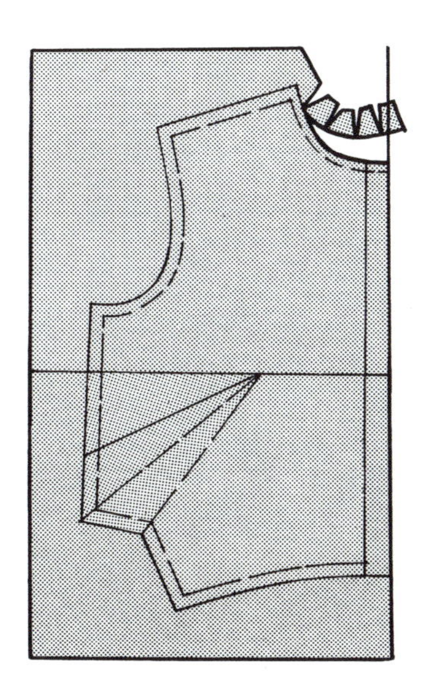

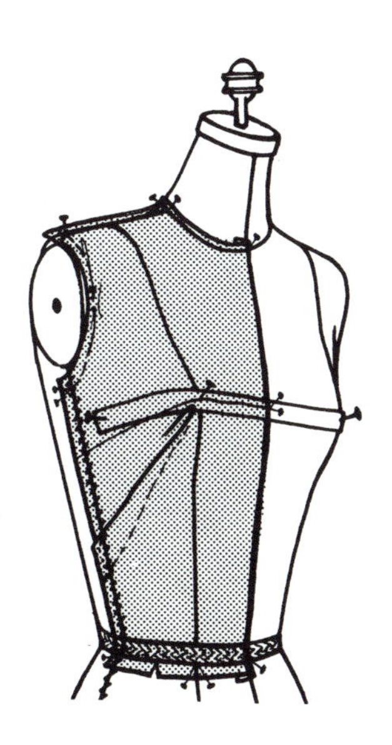

TRUE UP

1 **Remove the fabric drape from the dress form.** True-up all seams, add seam allowances, and trim excess fabric.

2 **Return the finished drape to the dress form** and check for accuracy, fit, and balance.

Converting Dart Excess into Shoulder Gathers — Preparing the Fabric

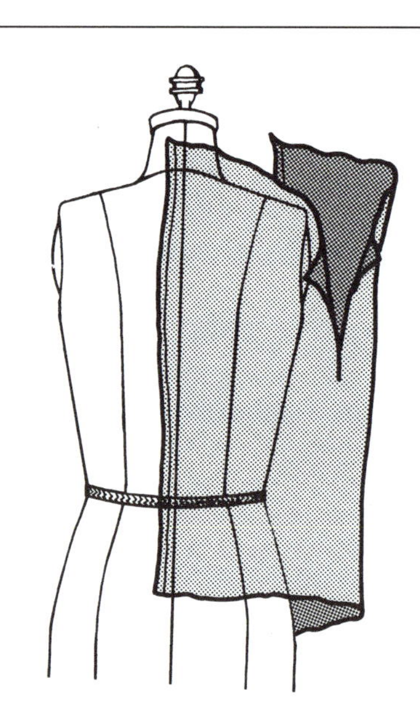

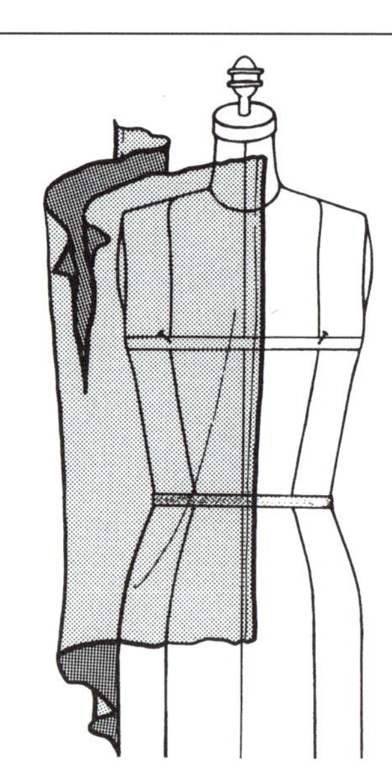

1 **Measure the length for the front and back bodice** along the straight of grain from the neckband to the waist, and add 5 inches.

2 **Measure the width for the front and back bodice** along the crossgrain from the center front of the dress form to the side seam of the bust level, and add 5 inches.

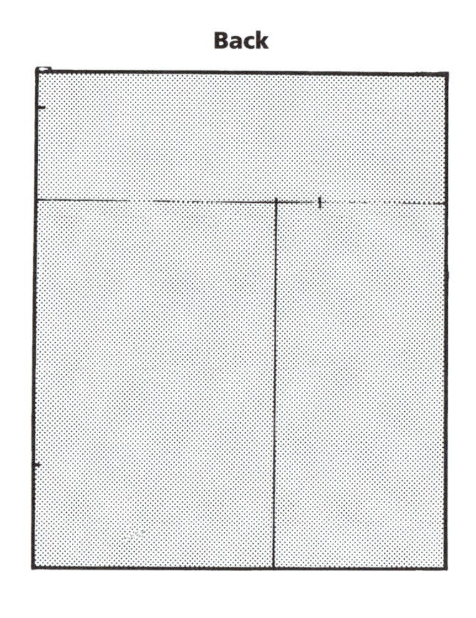

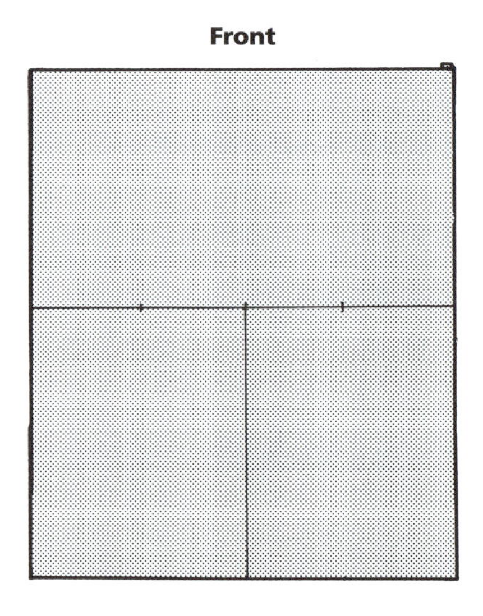

3 **Draw the center front grainline** 1 inch from the torn edge, and press under.

4 **Draw a perfect crossgrain line.** Using an L-square ruler, in the center of the fabric panel, draw a crossgrain line perpendicular to the grainline. This crossgrain line will be referred to as the bust level line.

5 **Measure the dress form** the distance from the center front to the apex.

6 **Measure and crossmark the apex** dress form distance to the bust level line of the fabric.

7 **Measure and draw in the grainline, shoulder blade crossgrain,** and plate crossmark for the back fabric piece.

Converting Dart Excess into Shoulder Gathers — Draping Steps

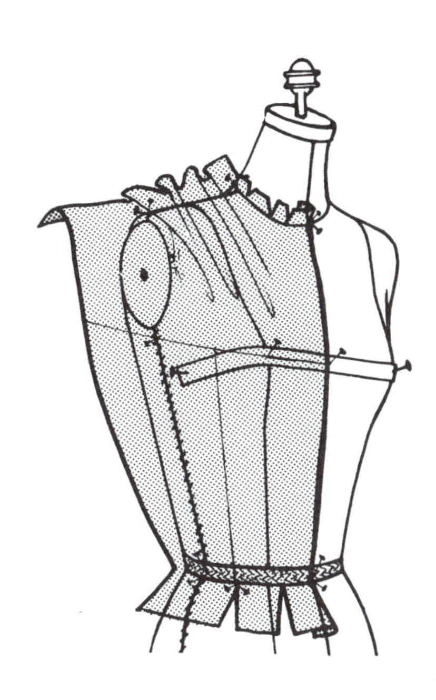

1 **Pin the apex** mark on the fabric to the apex position of the dress form.

2 **Pin the center front grainline fold** of the fabric to the center front position of the dress form.

Anchor pins at C.F. neck and C.F. waist. An additional pin may be needed at the bust level tape.

3 **Drape the neckline** by trimming the excess fabric around the neck area and clipping at intervals. Smooth the neckline in place.

4 **Clip, smooth, and drape the waistline** fabric across the waistline tape. Allow all excess fabric to be moved toward the side seam.

5 **Smooth and drape the fabric past the side seam and up and around the armhole plate.** Smooth the fabric flat over the armhole plate. Create a 1/4"–1/4" pinch at the screw level at the armhole ridge. This is to ensure that the armhole does not become too tight.

6 **Allow the excess fabric to fall into the shoulder area.**

7 **Drape and pin the shoulder fullness.** Divide the excess fabric, creating a gathered effect at the shoulder seam. Pin the fullness at the shoulder.

NOTE: This same process is followed if draping into a shoulder yoke.

8 **Mark all key areas** of the dress form to the fabric.

Neckline Draw in the desired neckline.

Shoulder Seam Lightly mark shoulder seam, shoulder gathers, and crossmark shoulder ridge.

Armplate

a. Top at shoulder seam ridge.
b. Middle at screw level.
c. Crossmark bottom at the side seam.

Side Seam Lightly mark.

Waistline and Waistline Pleats Crossmark at C.F. waist and side seam waist. Lightly mark the remainder of the waistline.

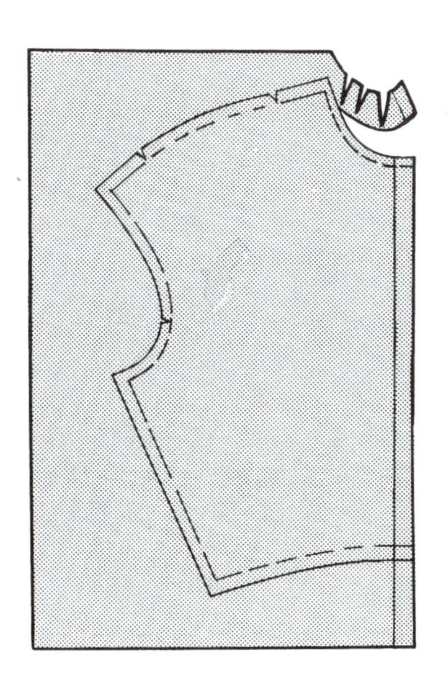

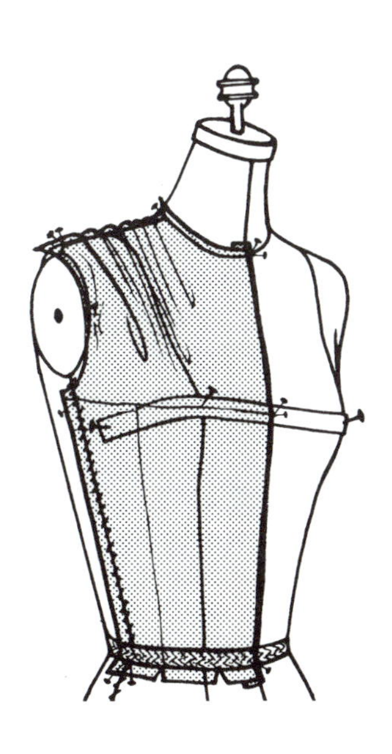

TRUE UP

1 **Remove the fabric drape from the dress form.** True up all seams. Add seam allowances and trim excess fabric.

2 **Return the finished drape to the dress form** and check for accuracy, fit, and balance.

Converting Dart Excess into Center Front Bustline Shirring—Preparing the Fabric

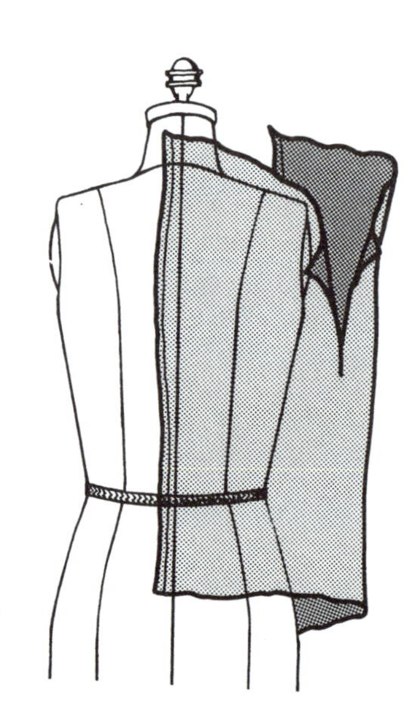

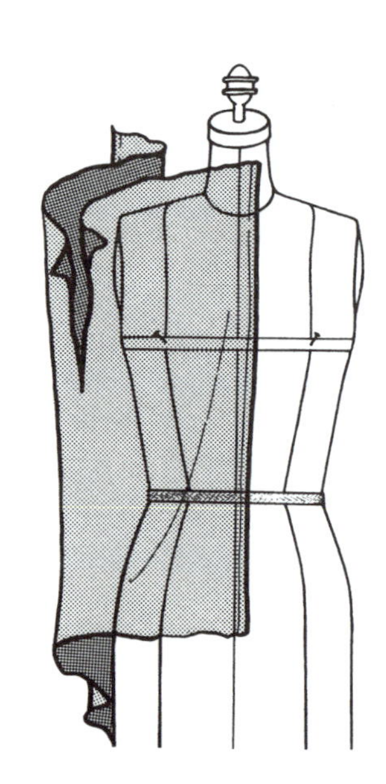

1 **Measure the length for the front and back bodice** along the straight of grain from the neckband to the waist, and add 5 inches.

2 **Measure the width for the front and back bodice** along the crossgrain from the center front of the dress form to the side seam of the bust level, and add 5 inches.

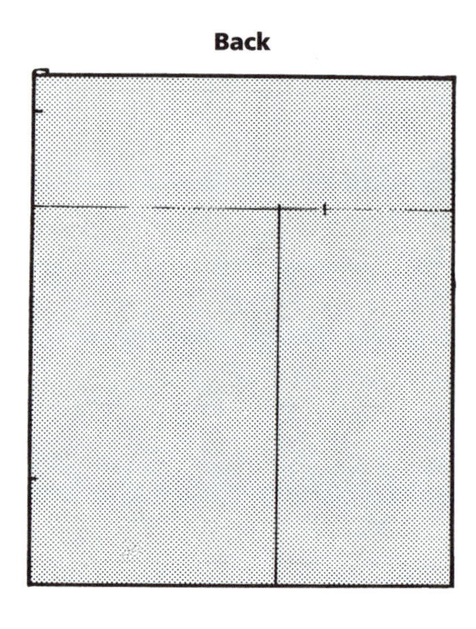

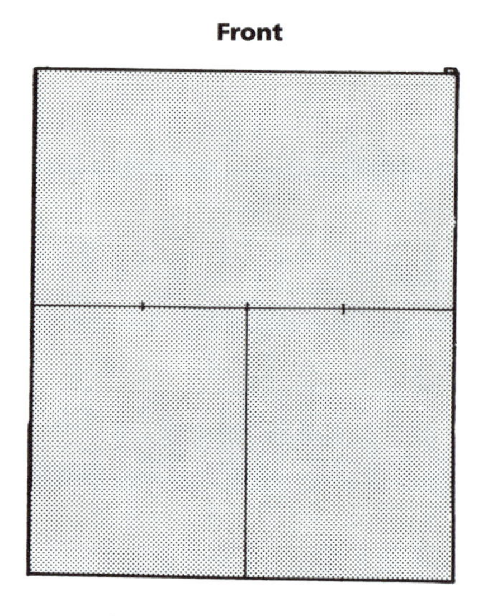

3 **Draw the center of the front grainline** 1 inch from the torn edge, and press under.

4 **Draw a perfect crossgrain line.** Using an L-square ruler, in the center of the fabric panel, draw a crossgrain line perpendicular to the grainline. This crossgrain line will be referred to as the bust level line.

5 **Measure the dress form** the distance from the center front to the apex.

6 **Measure and crossmark the apex** dress form distance to the bust level line of the fabric.

7 **Measure and draw in the grainline,** shoulder blade crossgrain, and plate crossmark for the back fabric piece.

Converting Dart Excess into Center Front Bustline Shirring —Draping Steps

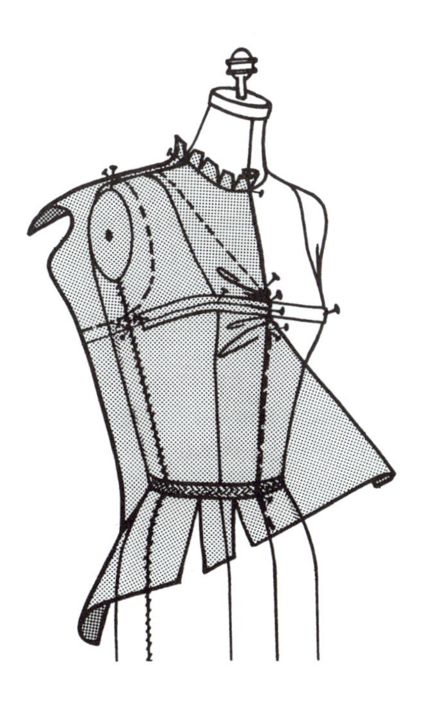

1 **Pin the apex** mark on the fabric to the apex position of the dress form.

2 **Pin the center front grainline fold** of the fabric to the center front position of the dress form.

Anchor pins at C.F. neck and C.F. waist. An additional pin may be needed at the bust level tape.

3 **Drape the neckline** by trimming the excess fabric around the neck area and clipping at intervals. Smooth the neckline in place.

4 **Drape and pin the shoulder** by smoothing the excess fabric across the upper chest area and over the shoulder.

5 **Smooth and drape the fabric around the armhole plate,** creating a 1/4"–1/4" pinch at the screw level at the armhole ridge. This is to ensure that the armhole does not become too tight.

6 **Smooth and drape the fabric past the side seam.** The crossgrain will be angling downward (see illustration). Allow all excess fabric to fall into the waistline area below the bust.

7 **Clip, smooth, and drape the waistline** fabric across the waistline tape. Allow all excess fabric to be moved to center front bustline area.

8 **Evenly distribute and pin all excess fabric** at the bustline area.

9 **Draw in the desired neckline.** Usually a design with shirring at the center front bust, the neckline is lowered (see example).

10 **Mark all key areas** of the dress form to the fabric.

Center Front and Center Front Bust Lightly mark the center front line of the dress form and where the gathered fullness is at center front.

Neckline Draw in the desired neckline.

Shoulder Seam Lightly mark shoulder seam, crossmark shoulder ridge.

Armplate
a. Top at shoulder seam ridge.
b. Middle at screw level.
c. Crossmark bottom at the side seam.

Side Seam Lightly mark.

Waistline Crossmark at C.F. waist, side seam waist, and lightly mark the entire waistline.

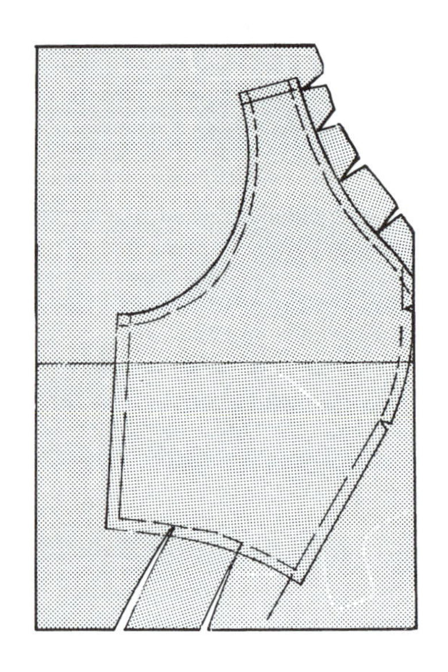

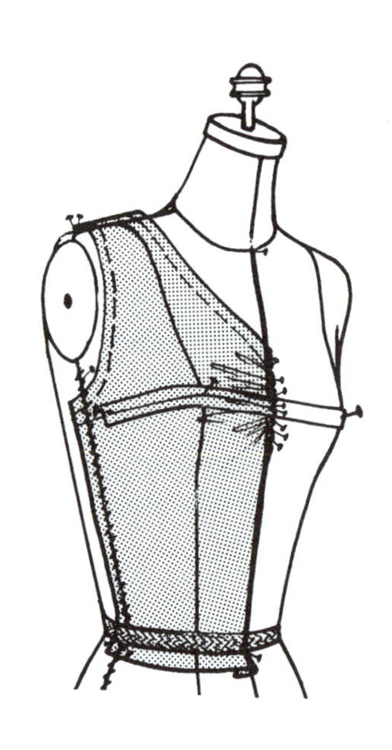

TRUE UP

1. **Remove the fabric drape from the dress form.** True up all seams. Add seam allowances and trim excess fabric.

2. **Return the finished drape to the dress form** and check for accuracy, fit, and balance.

Notes

Chapter Ten

Dartless Shapes

Objectives

By studying the various draping steps in this chapter, the designer should be able to accomplish the following:

- Develop creativity and stimulate a variety of dartless shapes.
- Recognize grain and crossgrain of fabric in relation to the bust level on the front, shoulder blade level on the back, and side seams for a dartless shape.
- Drape a dartless shape with straight side seams and the correct amount of ease allowance, armhole size, and side seam balance.
- Visualize the front and back dartless shape in relation to the figure.
- Have the dartless shape hang straight from the bust level line in the front and shoulder blade level in the back to the hem.
- Visualize and true up the dartless patterns with the correct amount of ease allowance, armhole size, waistline shape, measurement, and balance.
- Check the results of the draping process for a dartless shape with regard to fit, hang, balance, proportion, and the true up.

Dartless Shapes

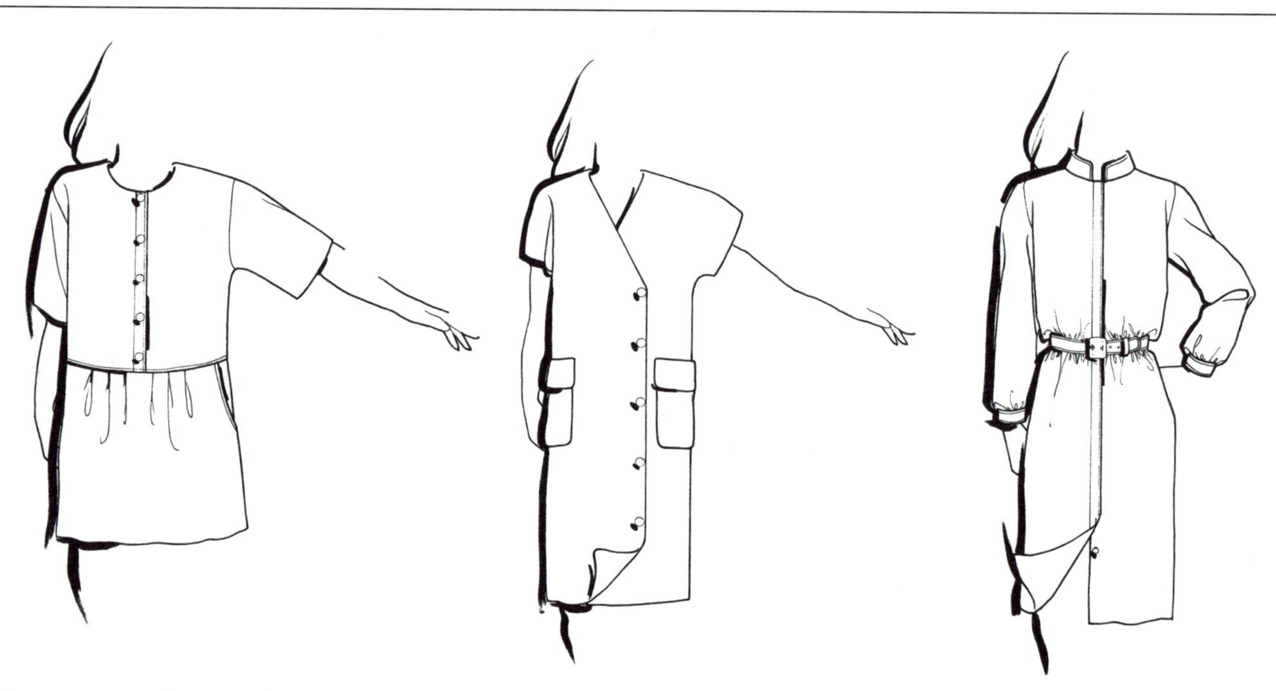

The newest and most influential silhouettes in fashion are the dartless shapes. These shapes are the dartless blouse, the dartless shirt, and the dartless kimono.

Couture designers often prefer to drape dartless designs to ensure fit and balance as each design is created. Illustrated here are the draping steps for creating these basic dartless designs. With these guidelines, a designer will be able to create traditional to wildly outrageous dartless shapes as the fashions change.

Dartless Shirt/Blouse

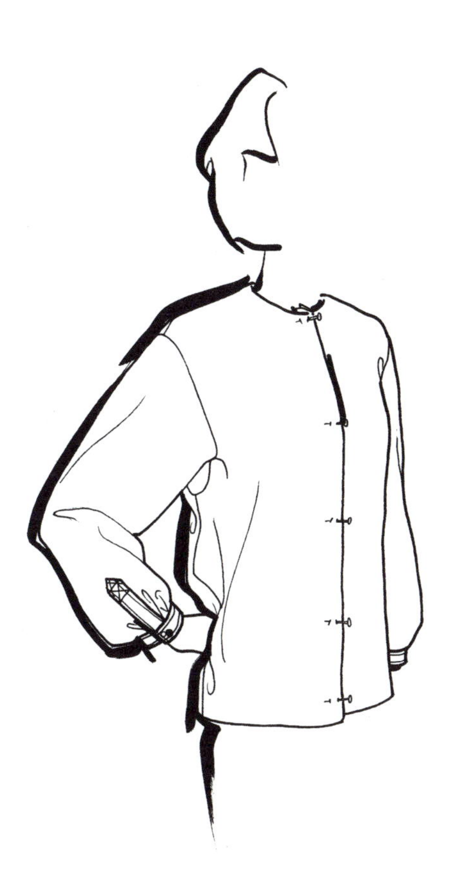

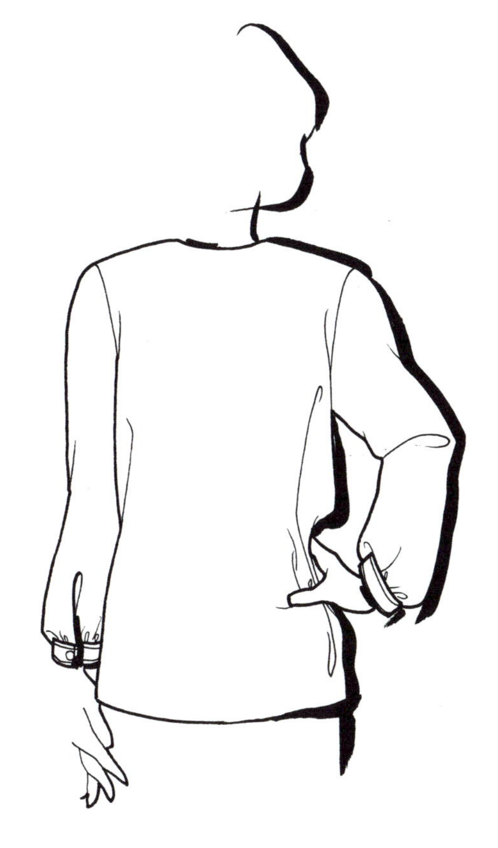

Basic Dartless Shirt Front

Basic Dartless Blouse Front

Basic Dartless Blouse Back

The dartless shirt or blouse is a torsolength bodice without darts or a fitted waist seam. This drape may be used as the basic foundation pattern in designing shirts, blouses, or dresses that require no fitted dart area.

Many dartless designs require a set-in sleeve, which gives more of a blouse look. However, because of the dartless fit, it is necessary for the sleeve to fit into a traditional armhole. This requires a capped sleeve with a slightly lifted bicep line. This additional lift creates a longer underarm length, allowing the sleeve to move more freely up and down as well as forwards or backwards without pulling. This lowered or "exaggerated" armhole sleeve is discussed on pages 208–212 of Chapter 14.

In other circumstances, the dartless design requires a dropped shoulder and a lowered side seam to accommodate a shirt sleeve. Many manufacturers prefer to use a shirt sleeve, rather than a kimono variation, because the sleeve allows greater movement for the customer. The shirt sleeve is discussed on pages 203–207 of Chapter 14.

The dartless blouse/shirt sloper is a hip-length bodice without darts that has a dropped shoulder armhole. This sloper is used to make dartless flat pattern designs for easy-fitting blouses, shirts, and dresses. Pin tucks, pleats, and style lines can be created by readjusting areas of this foundation pattern.

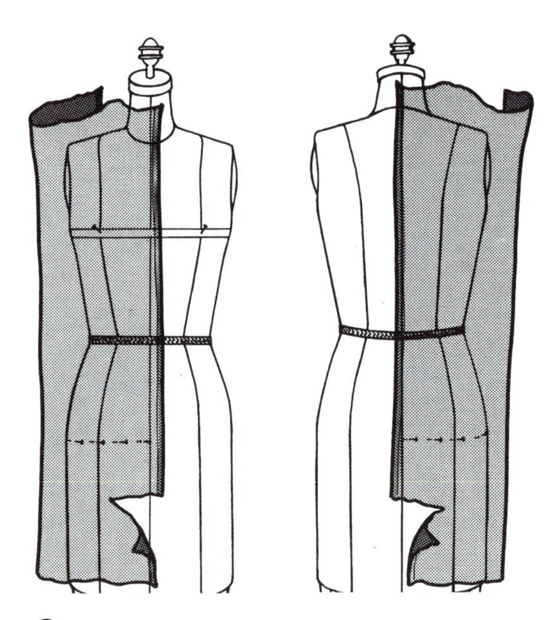

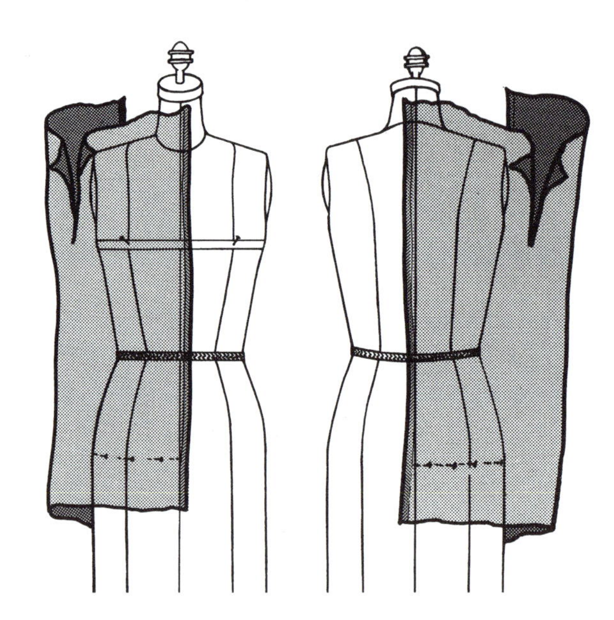

1 **Measure the length** (along the straight of grain) for both the front and back from the neck-band to the hip level, and add 5 inches.

Snip and tear the fabric at this length.

2 **Measure the width** (along the crossgrain) for both the front and back from the center of the dress form to the side seam, and add 4 inches.

Snip and tear the fabric at this width.

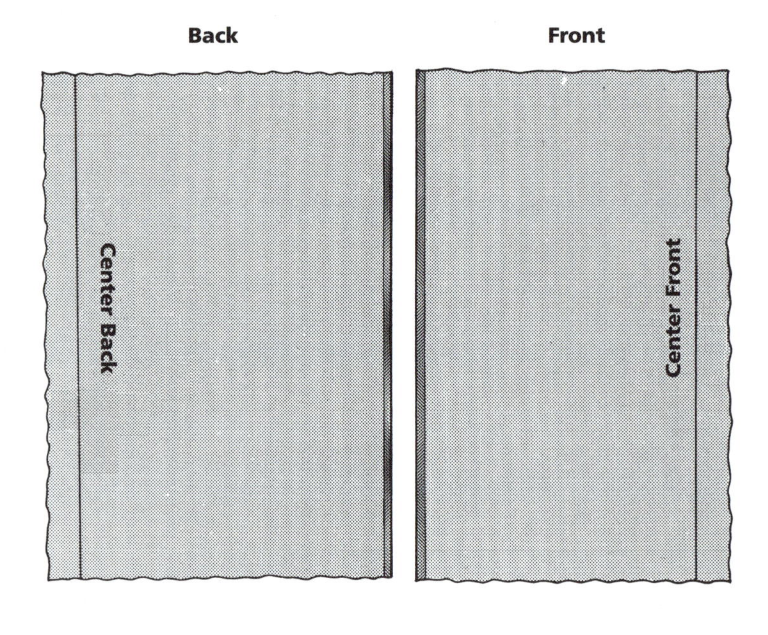

3 **Draw the center front and center back grainlines** 1 inch from the torn edge, and press under.

Press under at center front and center back.

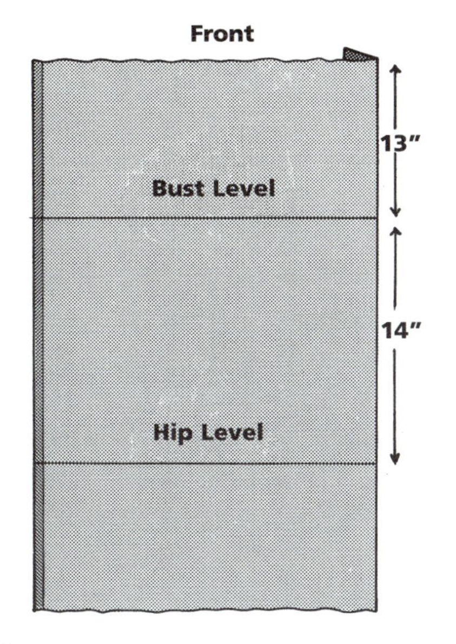

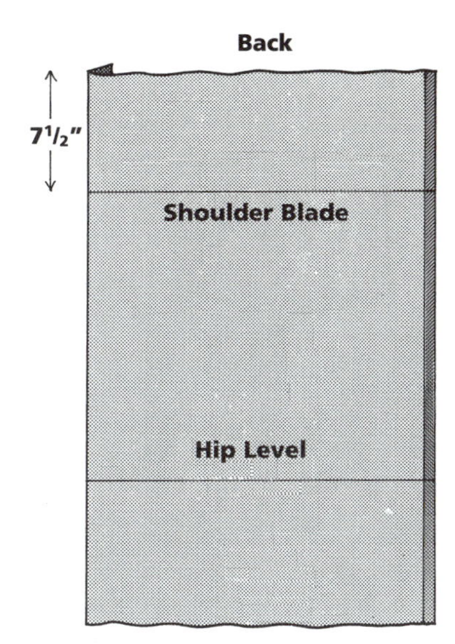

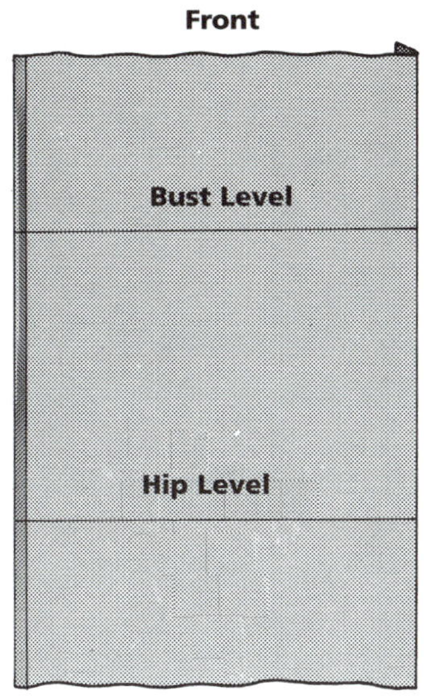

4 On the front fabric piece, draw in two crossgrains.

a. Draw the bust level line. Draw the first crossgrain line **13 inches** from the top edge of the front fabric piece.

b. Draw in the hipline. Draw the second crossgrain line **14 inches** from the first crossgrain line. This indicates the hip level line. On some dress forms this measurement may change slightly.

5 On the back fabric piece draw in two crossgrains.

a. **Draw in the shoulder blade level line.** Draw the first crossgrain line **7 1/2 inches** from the top edge of the back fabric piece.

b. Draw in the hip level line. Place the front and back fabric pieces side by side. Draw in a crossgrain line on the back piece to match the crossgrain on the front piece at the hip level.

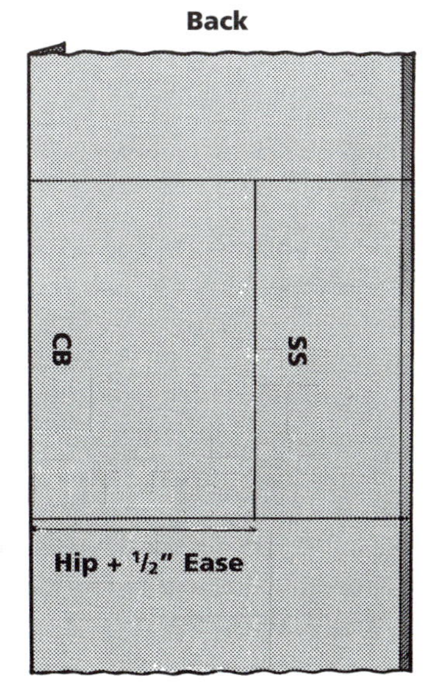

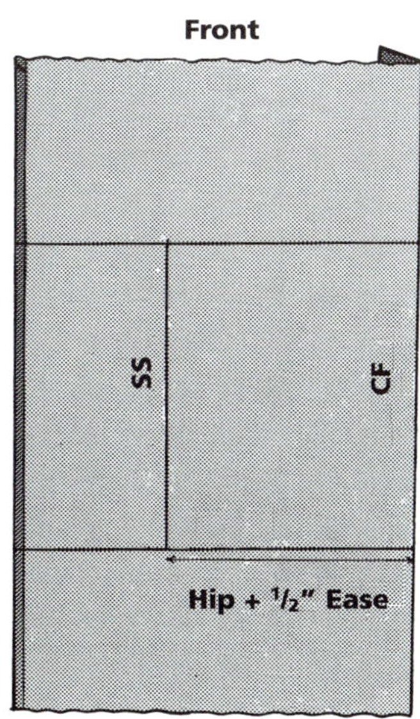

6 Draw in the side seams for the front and back fabric pieces.

a. Measure the dress form at the hip level for the front and back.

1. Measure from C.F. to the side seam on the dress form, and add 1/2 inch for ease. Transfer this measurement to the front fabric piece, and crossmark.

2. Measure from C.B. to the side seam on the dress form, and add 1/2 inch for ease. Transfer this measurement to the back fabric piece, and crossmark.

b. Draw the front and back side seam. From the side seam crossmarks, draw a side seam perfectly parallel to the center grainline.

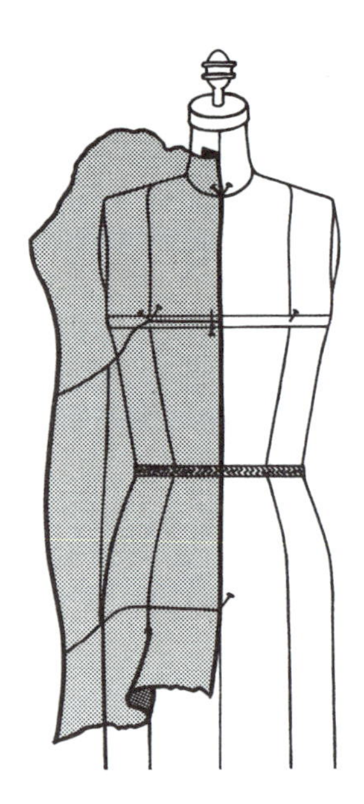

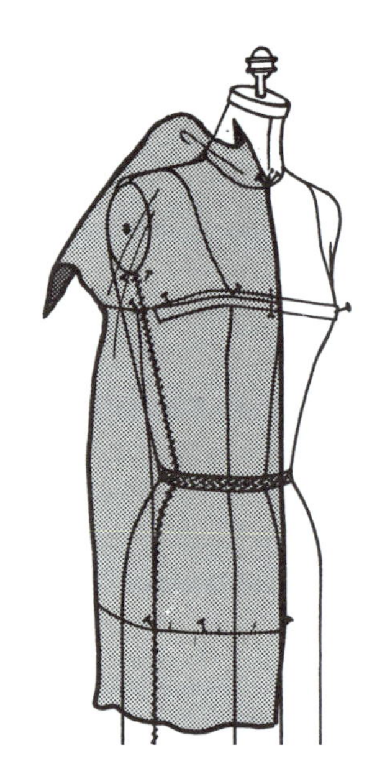

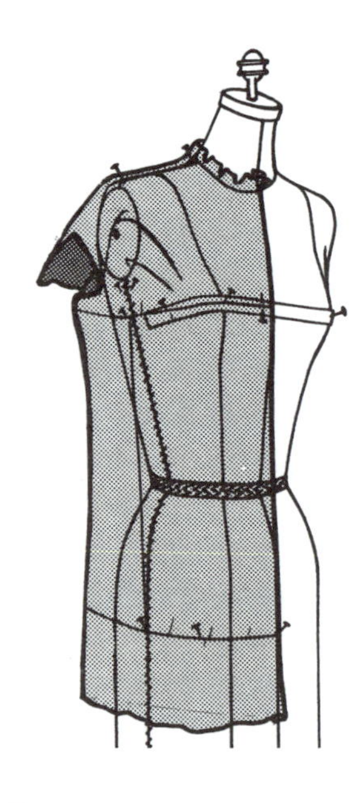

1 **Pin the center front grainline** fold of the fabric on the center front position of the dress form. Be sure to align the crossgrain on the bust level of the dress form.

Anchor pins at C.F. neck and C.F. hip. An additional pin may be needed at the bust level tape.

2 **Smooth and pin the crossgrains** of the fabric across the dress form to the side seam. Distribute the 1/2 inch ease evenly across the dress form.

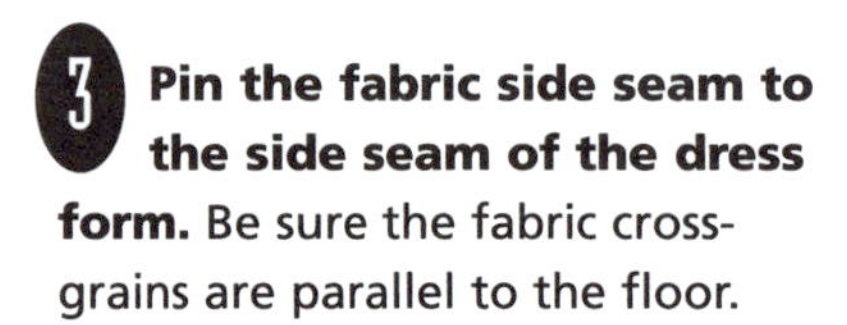

3 **Pin the fabric side seam to the side seam of the dress form.** Be sure the fabric crossgrains are parallel to the floor.

4 **Pin the shoulder/neck area.** Trim and clip the excess fabric around the neck area. Smooth the fabric flat over the shoulder/neck area.

5 **Drape and smooth the fabric over the shoulder/armhole** area of the dress form, and pin in place.

All excess fabric will fall over the armplate area at this time.

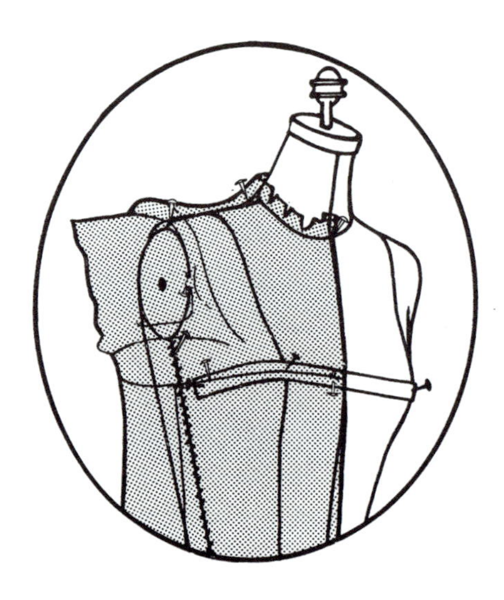

6 **Distribute armhole fullness.**

a. Divide in half all excess fabric over the armhole at the middle of the armhole ridge area.

b. Gently push a slight amount of fabric toward the body in the middle of the armhole ridge area.

c. Pin the armhole ridge area, keeping the excess fabric evenly distributed.

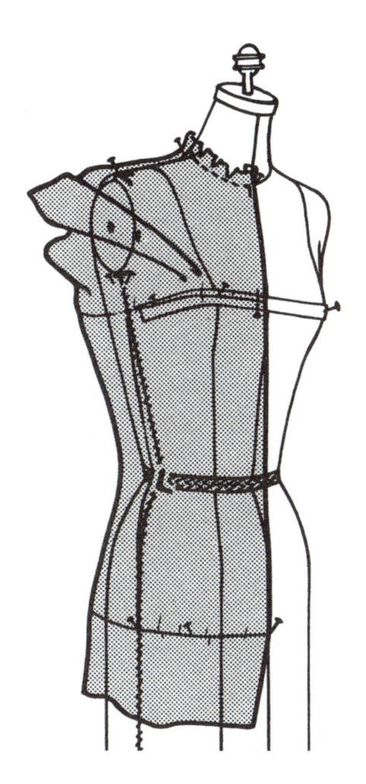

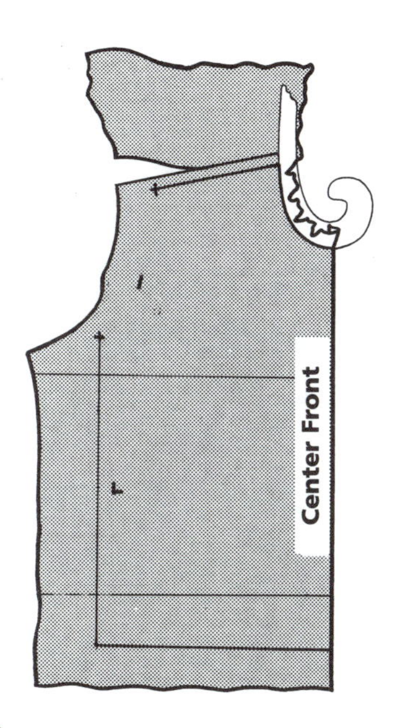

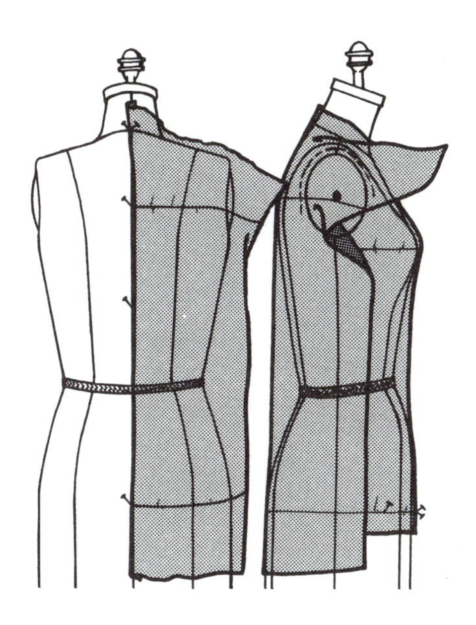

7 **Mark key areas** of dress form on fabric.

Neckline Lightly crossmark.

Shoulder Seam Lightly crossmark.

Armplate
a. Top at shoulder ridge.
b. Middle of the armhole: Crossmark middle of armhole ridge fullness.
c. Bottom at side seam.

Side Seam: Crossmark at the waistline.

8 **True up the neckline and shoulder seams.** Add seam allowances to the front fabric drape, the neckline, and the shoulder. Trim the excess fabric.

Extend the lower edge of the drape to the desired length of the design.

Place the front drape back on the dress form.

9 **Pin the center back grainline** fold of the fabric to the center back position of the dress form.

10 **Match the back hip level crossgrain to the front hip level crossgrain** at the side seams.

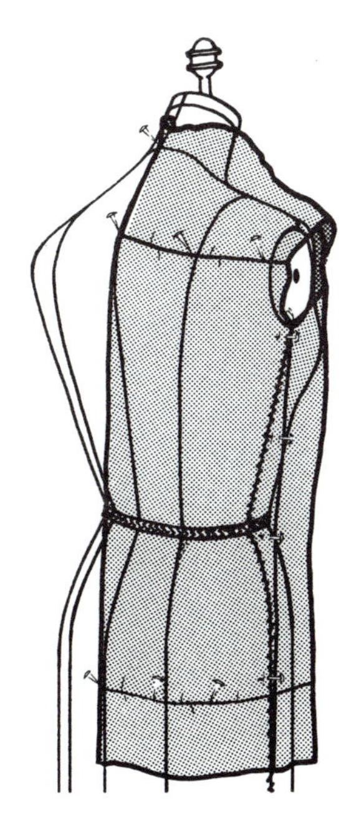

11 **Pin the back crossgrains** to the dress form, evenly distributing the 1/2inch ease.

12 **Match and pin the back side seam to the front side seam.** Be sure the hip level crossgrains are still matching and the fabric is not distorted. The front and back fabric pieces should be hanging plumb.

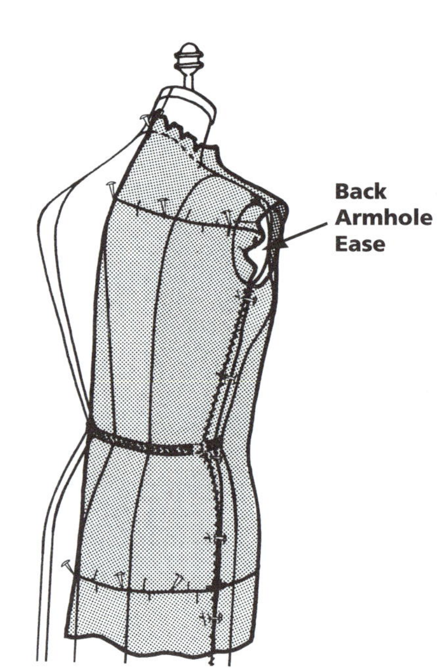

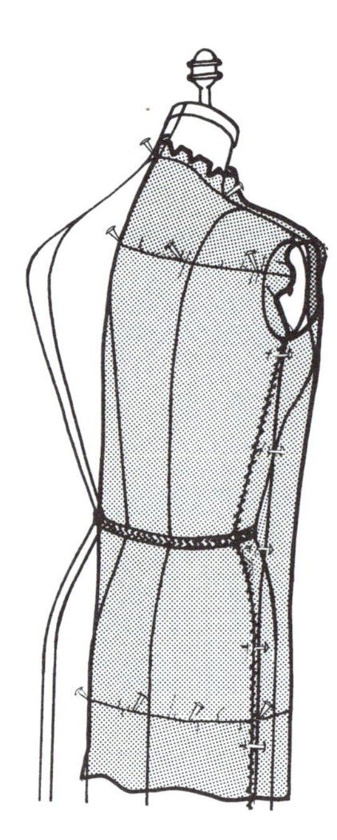

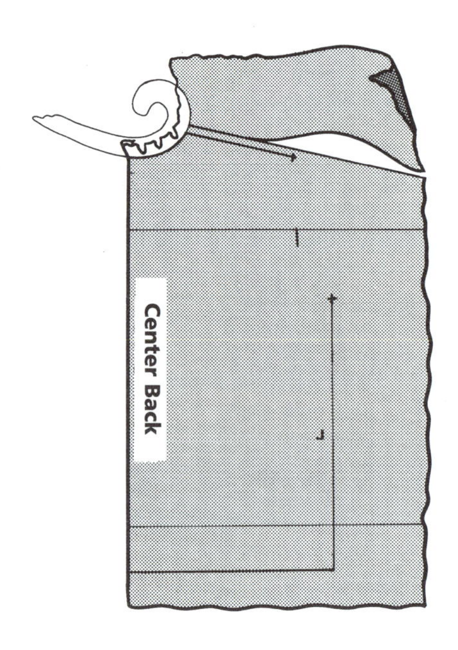

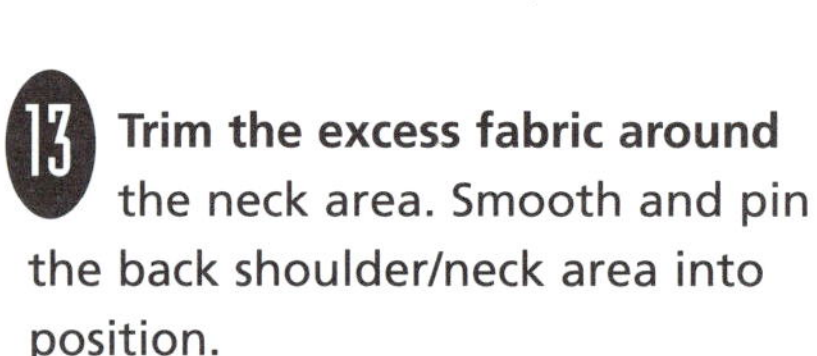

13 **Trim the excess fabric around** the neck area. Smooth and pin the back shoulder/neck area into position.

NOTE: The back armhole area will show a definite amount of ease about halfway from the shoulder seam to the shoulder blade level crossgrain. Leave this ease in the armhole.

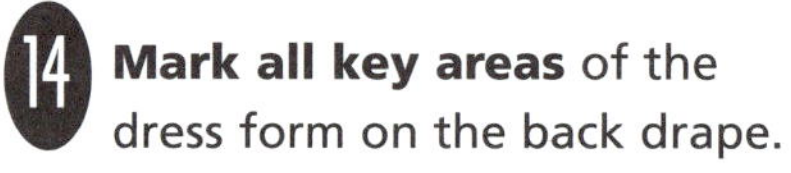

14 **Mark all key areas** of the dress form on the back drape.

Neckline

Shoulder

Armplate

a. Top at shoulder ridge.
b. Middle at screw level.
c. Bottom at side seam.

Side Seam: Crossmark at the waistline

15 **True up the back necklines and shoulder seams.** Remove the back drape from the dress form. Add seam allowances to the back neckline and shoulders. Trim excess fabric.

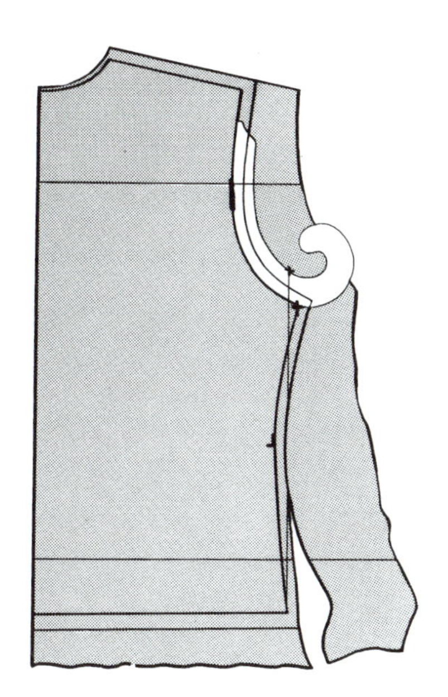

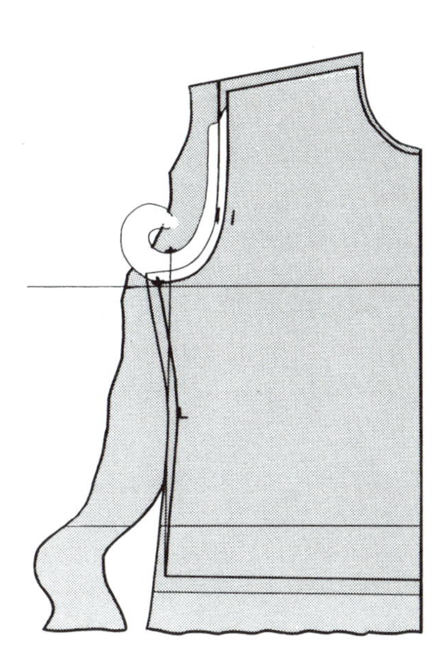

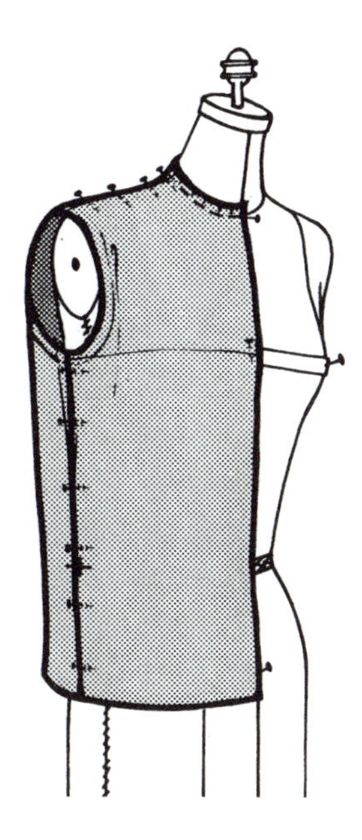

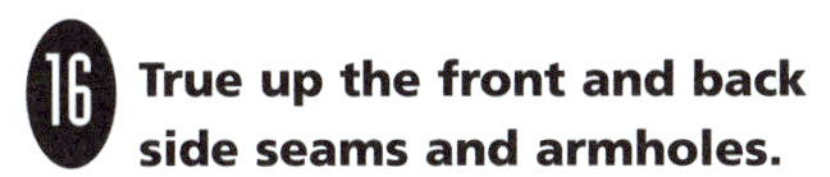

16 True up the front and back side seams and armholes.

a. Drop the armhole/side seam position 2 inches from the side seam plate mark.

b. Add 5/8-inch body ease to the side seam. Connect these new crossmarks and draw in a new side seam with a skirt curved ruler.

c. Draw the armhole, using a french curve. Shape as illustrated. Remember, when the side seams are pinned together, the armhole should be in the shape of a horseshoe.

17 Check and complete the front and back armhole distance.

a. Measure the front and back armholes. The back armhole should measure 1/2 inch more than the front armhole (correct armhole balance).

b. If the armholes do not measure correctly, scoop out the back armhole a bit (1/4 inch) and straighten or fill in the front armhole (1/4 inch).

c. Add seam allowances to all remaining areas and trim excess fabric.

NOTE: Refer to **Sleeves,** pages 197–220, for an appropriate sleeve design.

18 Pin the front and back drapes together. Return the drape to the dress form. Check for balance and fit. If necessary, make corrections.

NOTE: The fabric at the front armhole area will appear slightly folded (for all dartless drapes).

Dartless Shirt Look

Many times a man's shirt look is desired. Therefore, a few changes in the shoulder and armhole/side seam areas are necessary to create the more enlarged armhole fit and casual look.

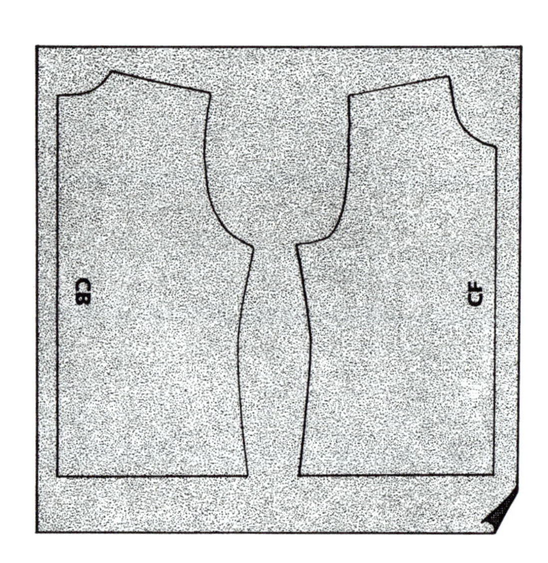

1 **Trace the dartless shirt/blouse pattern** onto pattern paper.

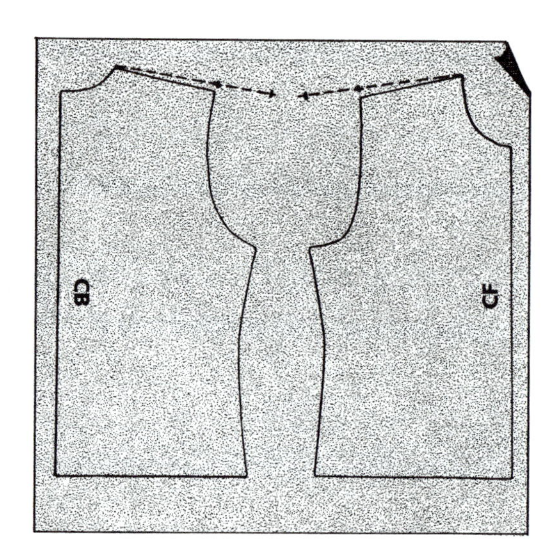

2 **Raise the shoulder 3/4** inch at the original armhole/shoulder corner.

3 **Reshape the shoulder** by drawing a straight line from the shoulder/neck corner to the 3/4-inch mark.

4 **Extend the new shoulder line 3 1/2 inches** from the original armhole/shoulder corner.

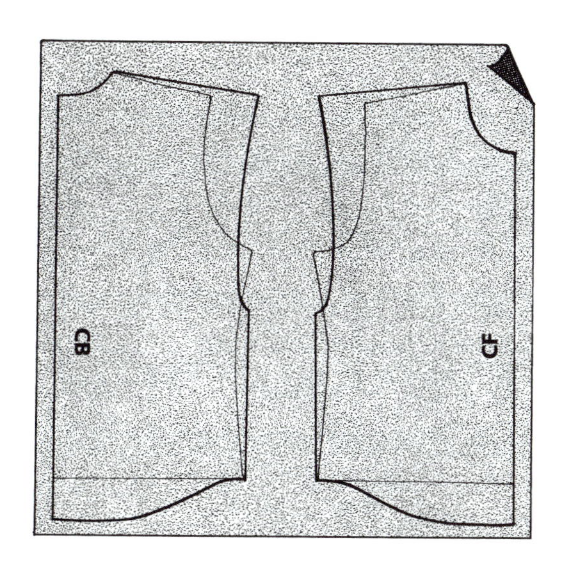

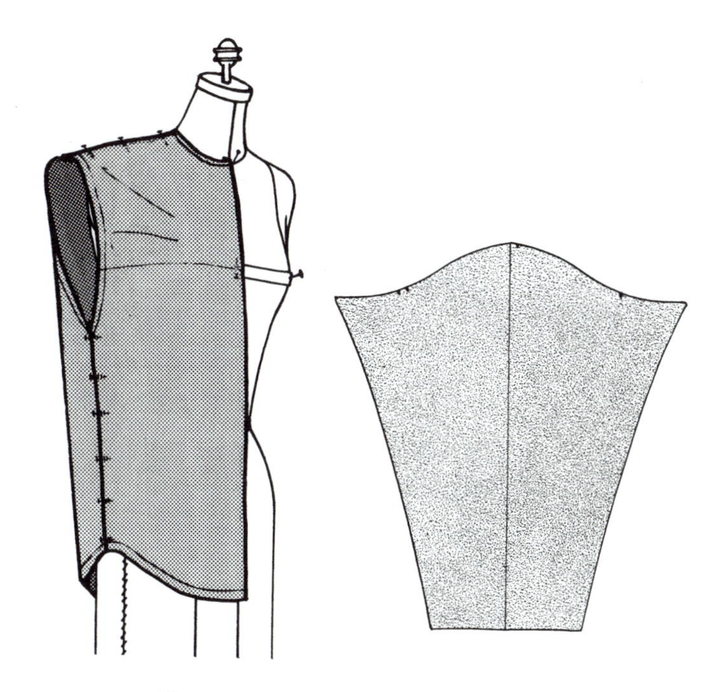

5 **Reshape the armhole/side seam and hem areas.**

a. Lower the armhole/side seam corner 4 inches from the original armhole/side seam corner.

b. Add 1/2-inch ease to the side seam.

c. Draw in a new shirt sleeve armhole. Connect the new shoulder corner to the new side seam corner to create an enlarged armhole. Use a hip curve ruler.

NOTE: The lowered armhole shape no longer has the characteristic horseshoe appearance.

IF DESIRED: Reshape the hem into a "shirttail" look.

6 **Develop the shirt sleeve.** Refer to **Shirt Sleeves, pages 203–207,** to create a correctly lifted sleeve to fit into this newly shaped armhole.

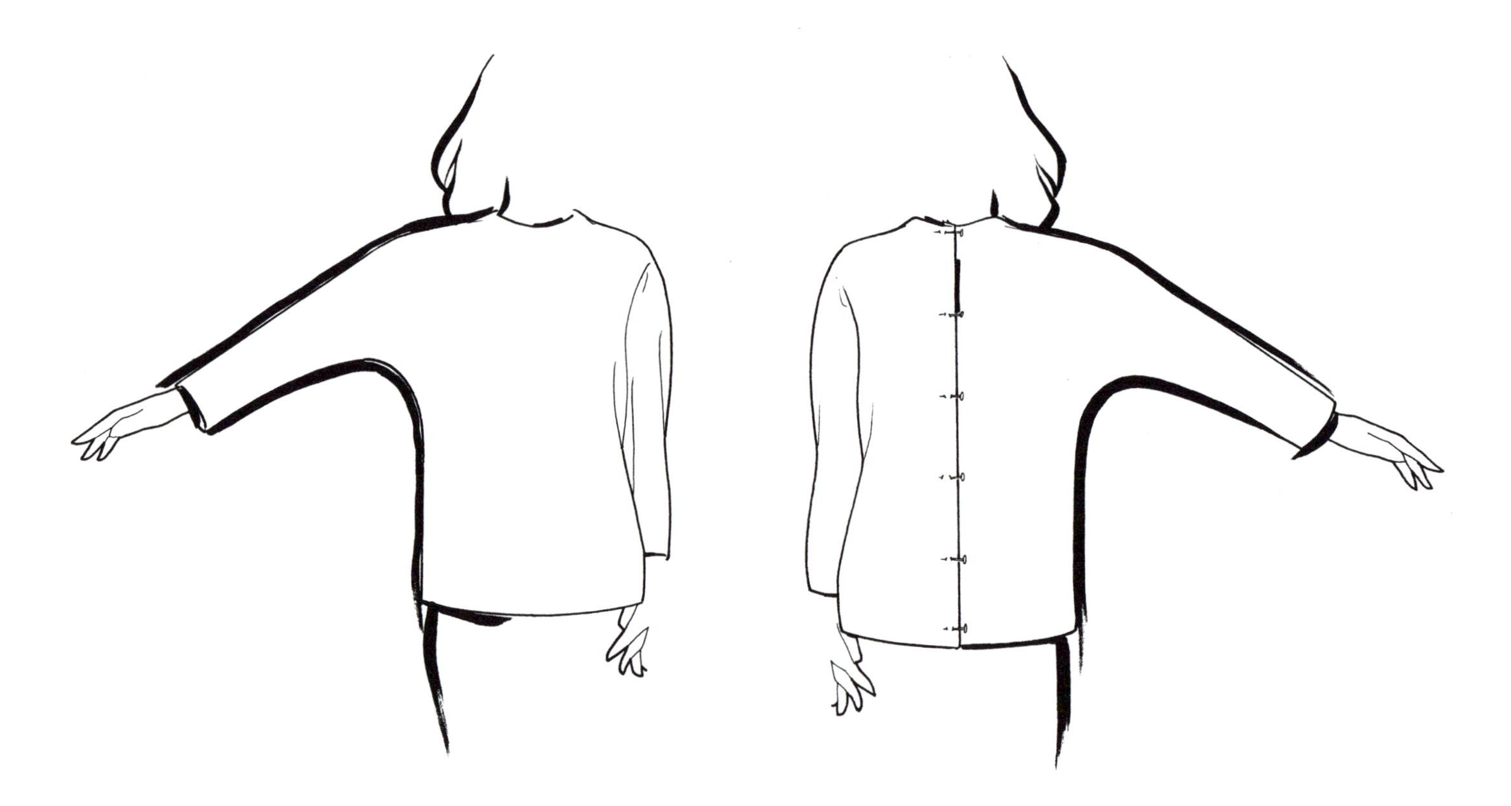

The dartless kimono sleeve design is considered an all-in-one bodice with the sleeve. These sleeve styles are cut in one piece with the dartless front and back blouse. This eliminates the traditional armhole. There is no set-in sleeve and no waistline seam. The silhouette often represents a T-shaped design.

The dartless kimono sloper is a hip-length bodice without darts that has a kimono sleeve. A variety of neckines, sleeve lengths, style lines, and hem lengths can easily be adapted to this design. This sloper is used to make dartless kimono sleeve designs on blouses, shirts, robes, jackets, and dresses.

The kimono is usually rather loose underneath the arm and may have several different design shapes, depending on the effect desired. The shoulder seam helps to give it fit and shape. The front and back bodice are cut in one piece with a shoulder seam and a side seam.

The popularity of this kimono design comes and goes from year to year depending on fashion trends.

Dartless Kimono—Preparing the Fabric

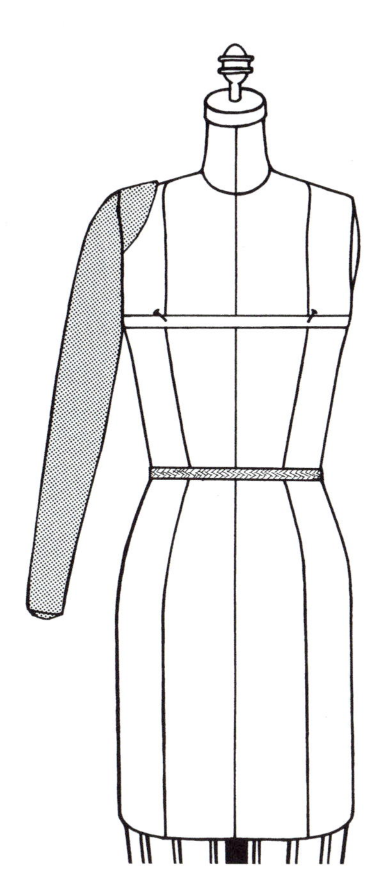

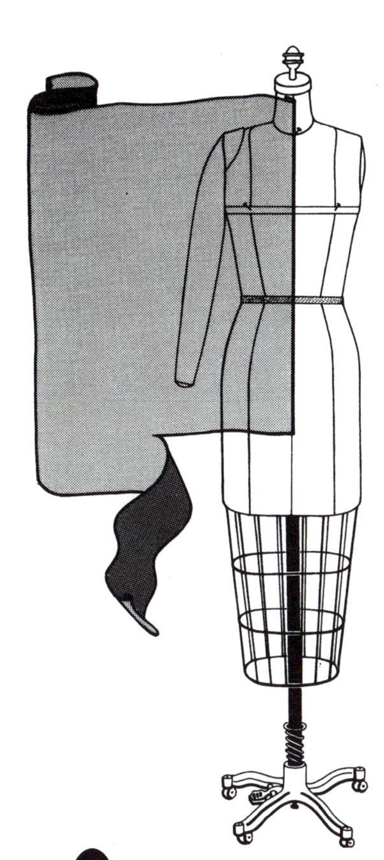

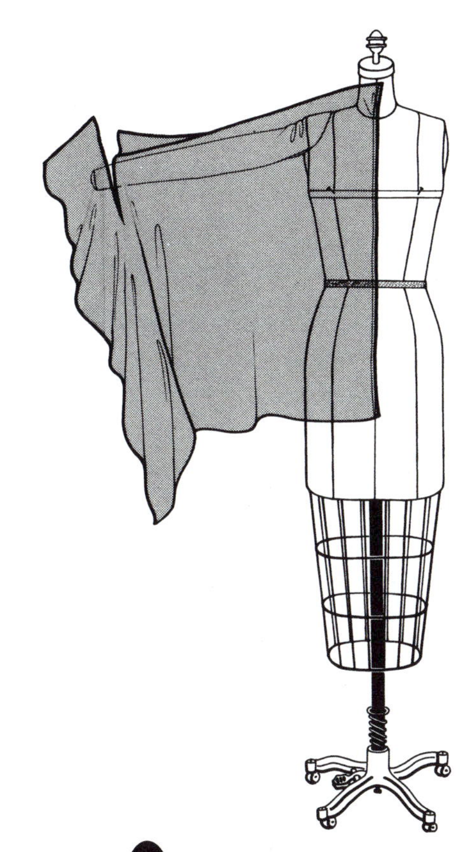

Prepare arm for dress form. For best results in measuring, draping, and fitting a kimono dartless block, prepare and attach the arm to the dress form. Refer to pages 392-394, to prepare this arm for the dress form.

1 Measure the length for the front and back drape along the straight of grain. Measure from the neckband to the hip level and add 5 inches. Snip and tear the fabric at this length.

2 Measure the width for the front and back drape along the crossgrain. Measure from the center of the dress form to the wrist level of the arm. Snip and tear the fabric at this width.

Back

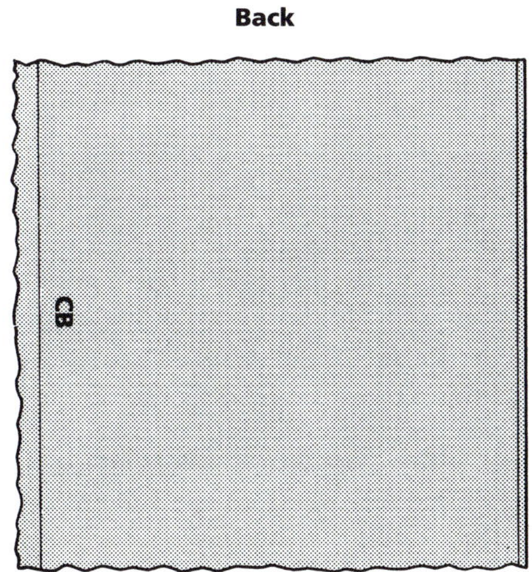

Front

3 Draw the grainlines for the front and back kimono 1 inch from the torn edge, and press under.

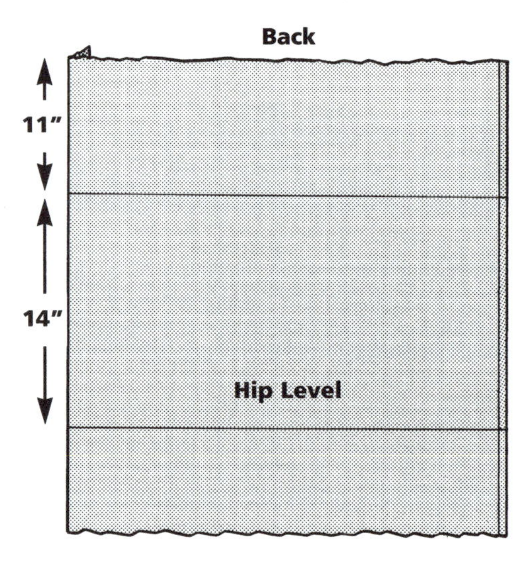

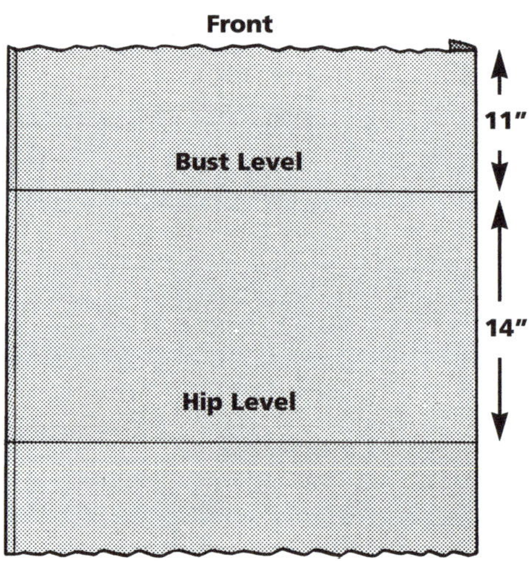

4 Draw two crossgrains for the front and back kimono.

a. Draw the bust level line. Draw the first crossgrain line 11 inches from the top edge of the fabric.

b. Draw in the hipline. Draw the second crossgrain line 14 inches from the first crossgrain line.

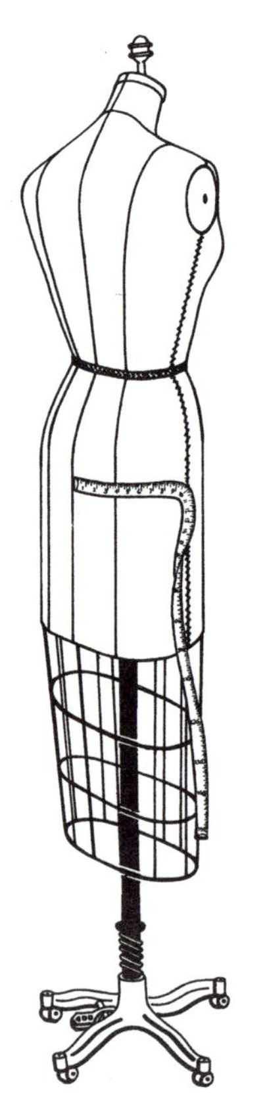

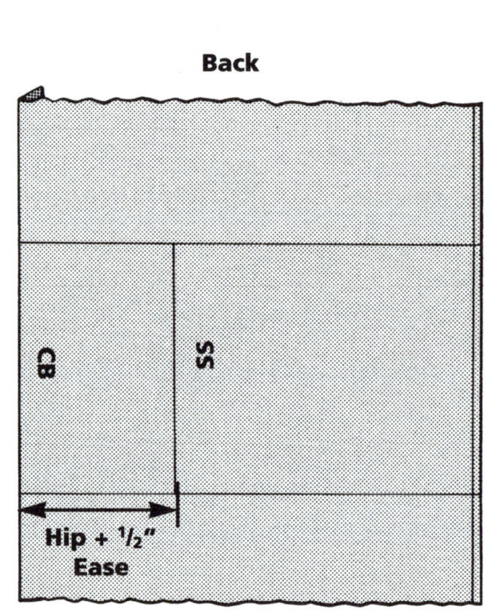

5 Draw the back side seam.

a. Measure the dress form at the hip level from the center back to the side seam, and **add 1/2 inch** for ease.

b. Transfer and crossmark this measurement to the fabric.

c. Draw a back side seam. From the back side seam crossmark, draw a side seam perfectly parallel to the center back grainline.

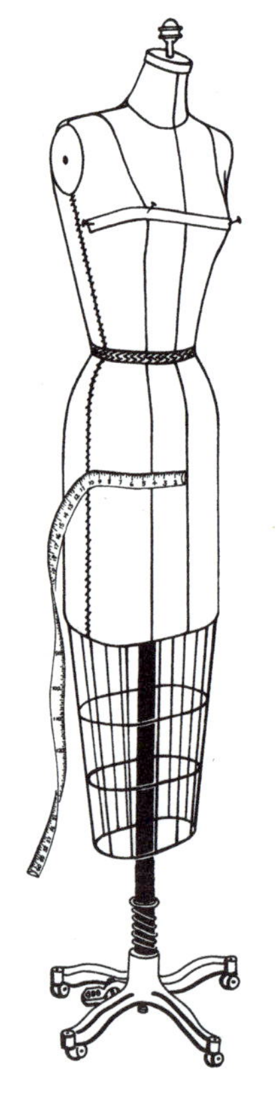

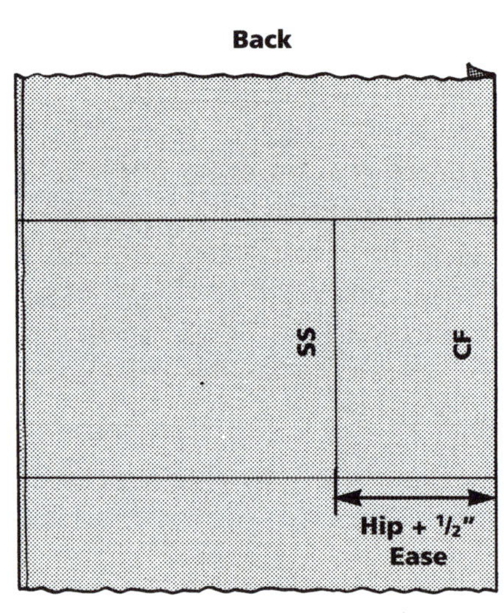

6 Draw in the front side seam.

a. On the dress form at the hip level, measure from center front to the side seam, and **add 1/2 inch** for ease.

b. Transfer and crossmark this measurement to the fabric.

c. Draw the front side seam. From the front side seam crossmark, draw a side seam perfectly parallel to the center front grainline.

Dartless Kimono—Draping Steps

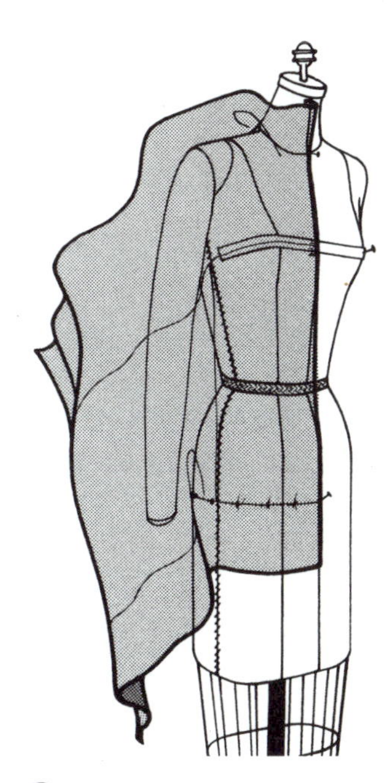

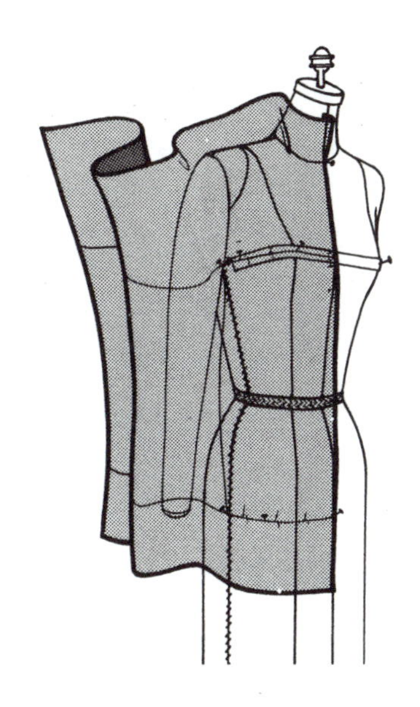

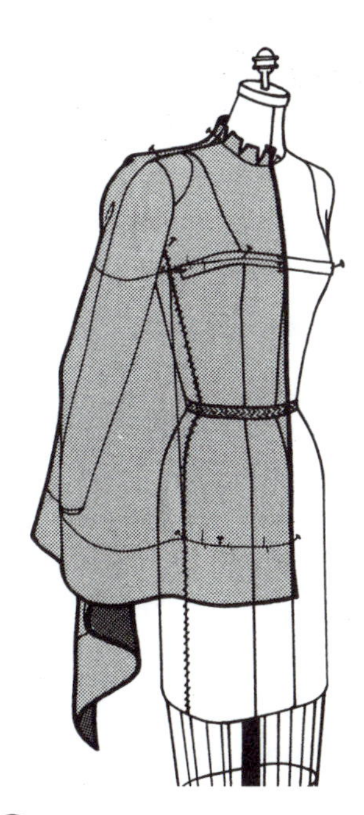

1 Pin the center front grainline fold of the fabric on the center front position of the dress form. Be sure to align the crossgrain at the bust level of the dress form.

Anchor pins at C.F. neck and C.F. hip. An additional pin may be needed at the bust level.

2 Smooth and pin the crossgrains of the fabric across the dress form to the side seam. Distribute the 1/2-inch ease evenly across the dress form.

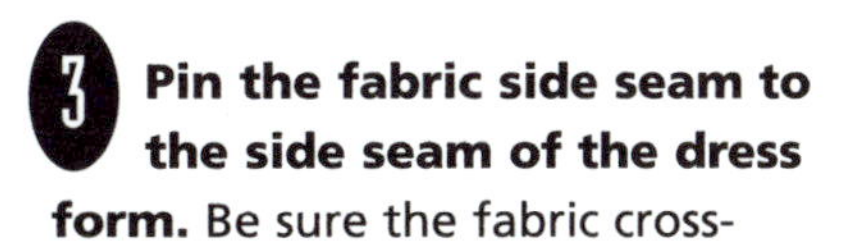

3 Pin the fabric side seam to the side seam of the dress form. Be sure the fabric crossgrains are parallel to the floor.

4 Pin the shoulder/neck area. Trim and clip the excess fabric around the neck area and smooth the fabric flat over the shoulder/neck area.

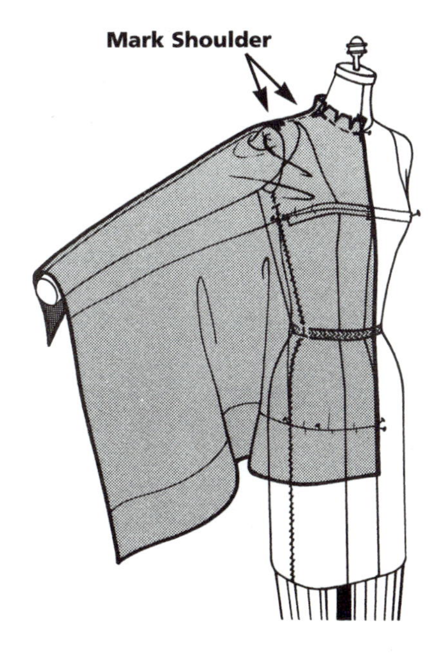

5 Mark the key areas of the dress form on the fabric.

Neckline Lightly mark.

Shoulder Neck Corner Crossmark.

Shoulder Seam to the Ridge Lightly mark.

Side Seam 2 inches below the armplate.

Waistline Crossmark at the side seam.

Remove the fabric drape from the dress form.

6 True up the neckline and side seam, and draw in the kimono sleeve.

a. Raise the shoulder line 1/2 inch at the shoulder ridge.

b. Extend the shoulder line 23 inches from the raised shoulder ridge corner. This raised shoulder line creates a sleeve seam with a higher shoulder slant.

c. Draw a line 8-inches long perpendicular from the shoulder seam, using an L-square ruler.

d. Square the underarm line from the wristline back to the side seam, using an L-square ruler.

e. Measure 1/2 inch toward the center front at the side seam/waistline position. Place a crossmark.

f. Draw in the desired underarm kimono shape from the elbow level to the side seam crossmark.

g. Shape the hip area at the side seam. Blend following the 1/2-inch waistline crossmark back to the original side seam.

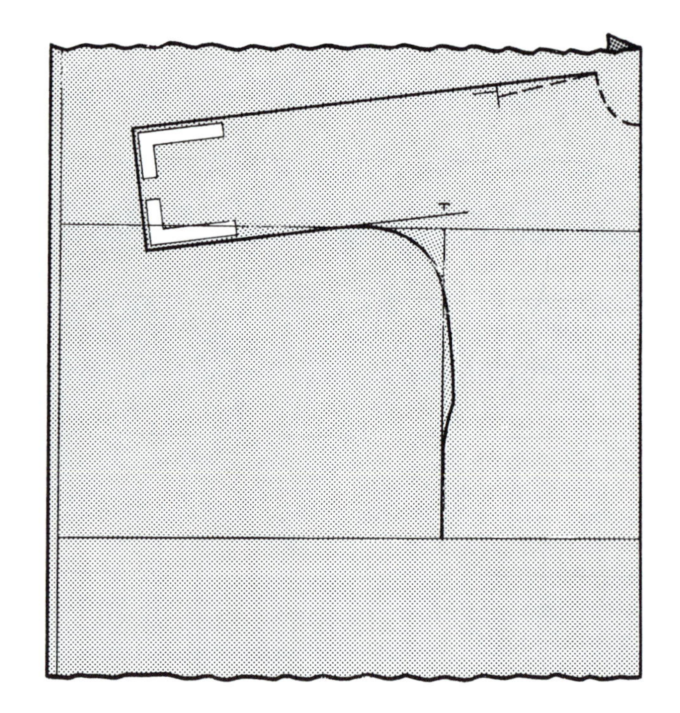

7 Add seam allowances to the front trued up drape. Cut the front drape out.

 **Draft the back kimono drape.**

a. Place the front kimono drape on top of the prepared fabric for the back drape, matching crossgrains.

b. Extend the back center fold grainline 1/2 inch past the front center front fold grainline. Be sure both center grainlines remain parallel.

c. Pin both layers of fabric together, following the front outline drape.

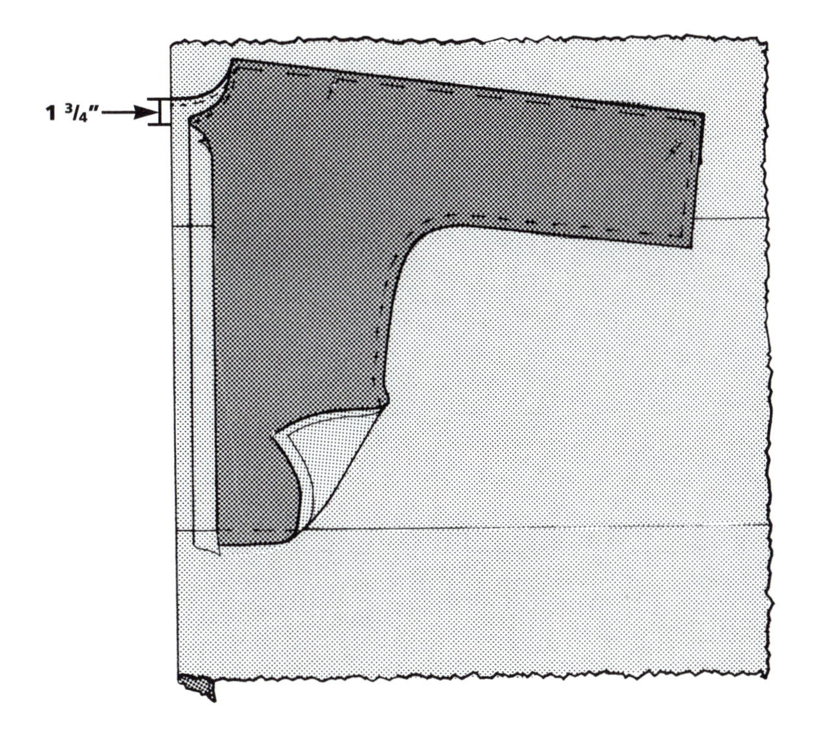

Transfer and draw the back shoulder and back neckline.

a. Mark the back shoulder line. Follow the stitch line of the front shoulder line.

b. Shape the back neckline. Using a french curve, blend from the back shoulder neckline corner to the center back grainline. Referring to the illustration, notice that the back neckline is about 1 3/4 inches higher than the front neckline.

c. Draw in the beginning of the wrist line.

d. Draw in all seam allowance to these lines.

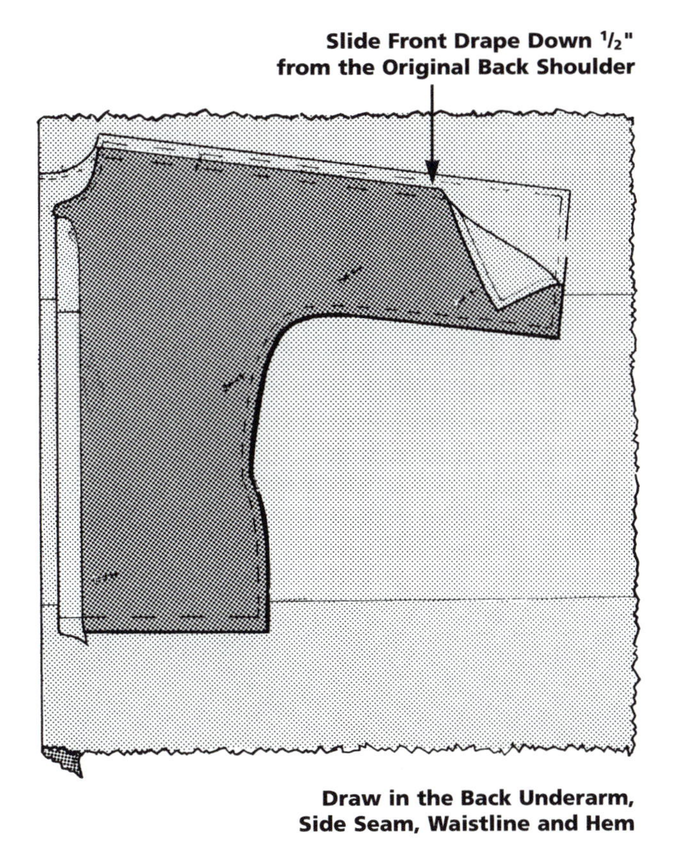

Draw in the Back Underarm, Side Seam, Waistline and Hem

Finish transferring the front seams to the back.

a. Remove all pins and slide the front drape down 1/2 inch from the shoulder. Keep the center back and center front parallel with the back remaining extended out 1/2 inch past center back.

b. Repin the front trued up lines—underarm/side seam, wrist, and hem.

c. Draw in the back underarm/side seam line, wrist line, and hem, following the stitch line of the front.

NOTE: This allows the back shoulder line to extend 1/2 inch more than the front. This maintains body balance.

11 True all seams, add seam allowances, and trim excess fabric.

 **Check the fit of the kimono drape.**

a. Pin the front and back kimono together. Return the drape to the dress form. Place anchor pins along the center front and center back seams. Recheck and mark if necessary. Retrue when off the dress form.

b. Check the hang of this drape.

1. The front and back drapes are plumb (no twists).

2. Side seams align with the dress form side seams.

3. Shoulder seams lay on the shoulder seam of the dress form.

NOTE: If the drape hangs incorrectly, this usually indicates that the shoulder and the back neck area need to be adjusted. This may result in a slightly larger back sleeve width.

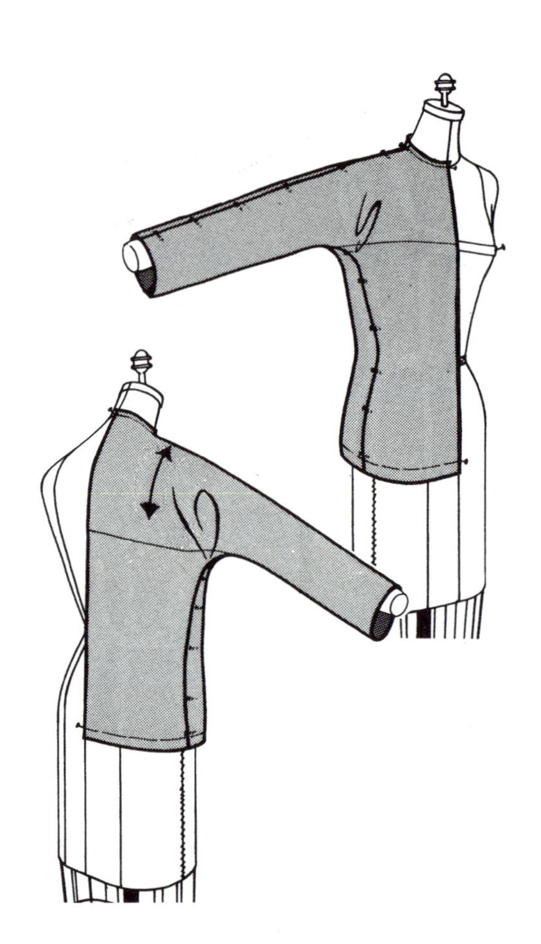

Variation to Achieve Extra Lift

Slash the underarm area of the sleeve up to the shoulder-ridge position. Pivot the sleeve up and blend in new shoulder and underarm lines.

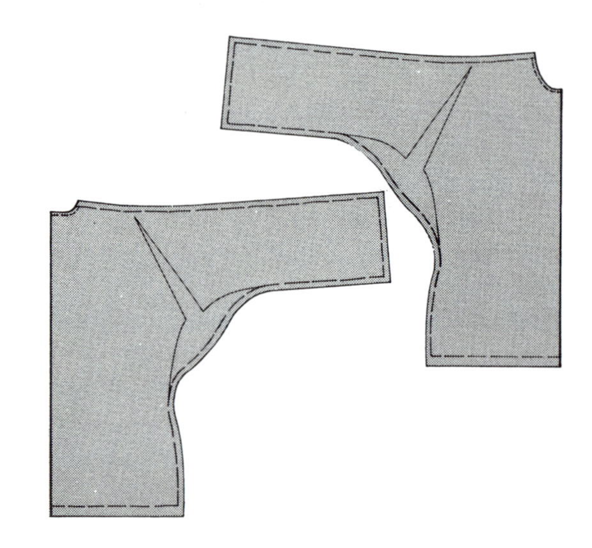

Chapter Eleven

Princess Shapes

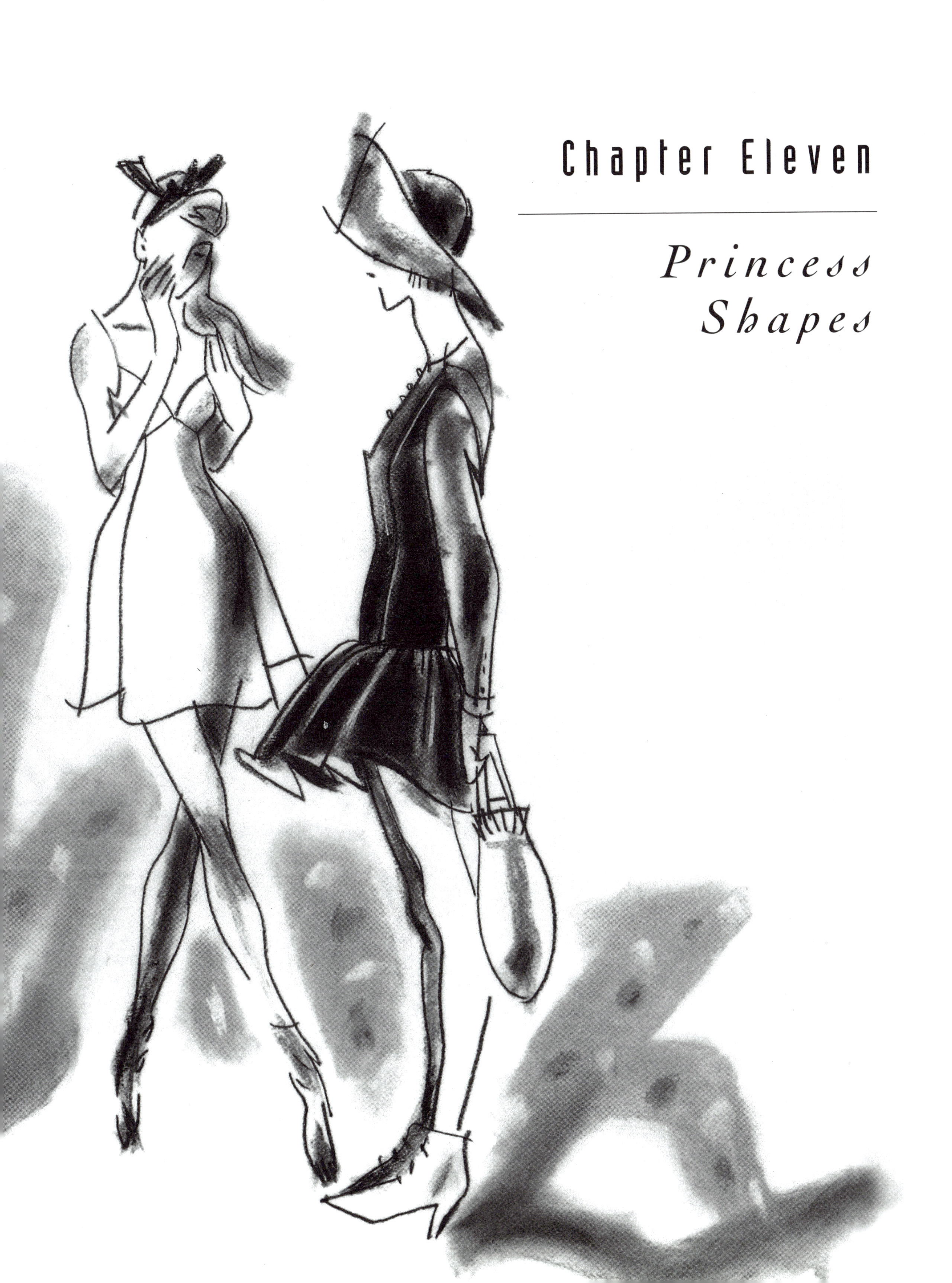

Objectives

By studying the various draping steps in this chapter, the designer should be able to accomplish the following:

- Develop creativity and stimulate a variety of princess shapes.
- Recognize grain and crossgrain of fabric in relation to the bust level on the front, shoulder blade level on the back, and side seams for a princess shape.
- Drape a flat piece of fabric to fit the curves of the body over the bust. Shape the contour of the princess panels into a fitted waist seam or into a seam that is not fitted at the waist but has the correct amount of ease allowance.
- Add flare to the princess panels for a princess slip dress.
- Visualize the front and back princess panels in relation to the figure.
- True up the front and back princess panels with the correct amount of ease allowance, armhole size, waistline shape, measurement, and balance.
- Check the results of the draping process for a princess shape with regard to fit, hang, balance, proportion, and the true up.

Princess Bodice

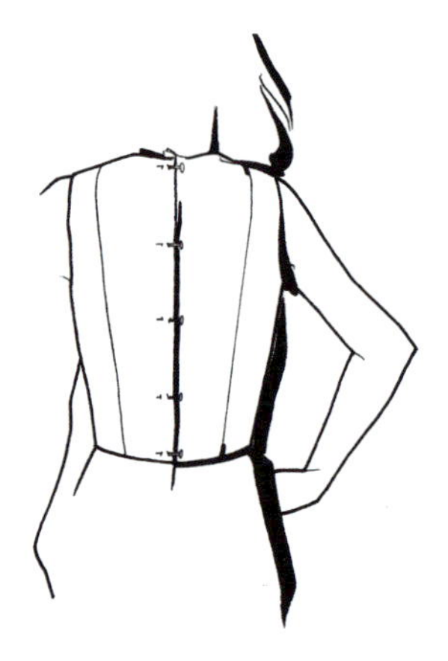

A fitted waist bodice with vertical seams, rather than darts, is known as the princess bodice. These vertical seams divide the bodice into separate panels. When these seams are sewn together, they represent the same shape as the basic bodice, but with vertical seams.

Typically, a princess bodice is a close fitting waist design with an unbroken style line that usually extends from the shoulder or armhole to the waistline. This style line almost always crosses over the midpoint of the bustline (apex) and replaces the need for darts. A princess bodice back should always be designed similarly to the chosen front princess bodice.

There are many variations to a princess style. Illustrated here are examples of some typically fashioned princess bodices.

Princess Bodice—Preparing the Fabric

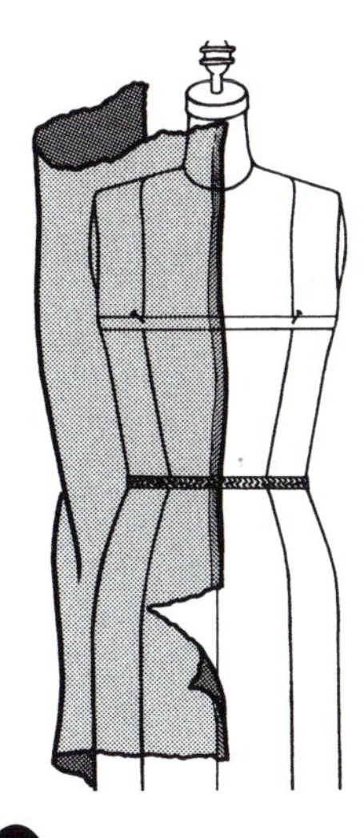

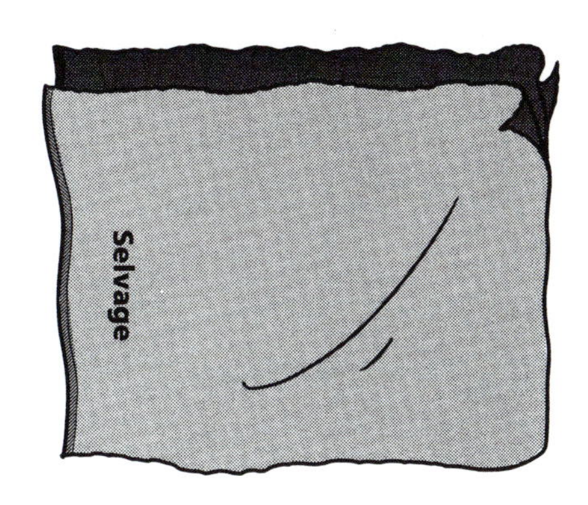

1 **Measure the length** for the front and back panels (along the straight of grain) from the neckband to the waist, and add 5 inches.

Snip and tear the fabric at this length.

2 **Divide the fabric piece in half.** Fold the fabric from selvage to selvage. Snip and tear the fabric piece in half lengthwise.

Use one piece for the front panels and the other piece for the back panels.

3 **Measure the width for the center front panel** (along the crossgrain) from the center front of the dress form to 4 inches past the apex. Using one of the fabric pieces prepared in step 2, snip and tear the fabric at this width.

Use the remaining front fabric piece for the side front panel.

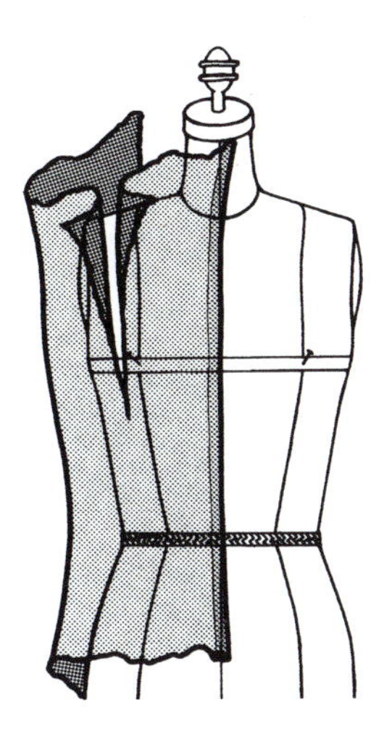

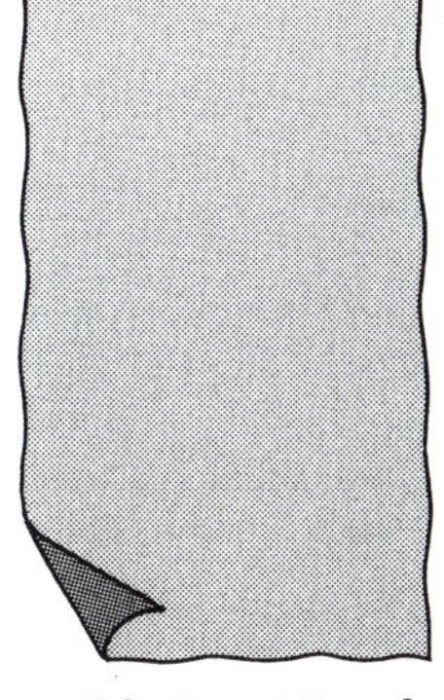

Side Front Panel

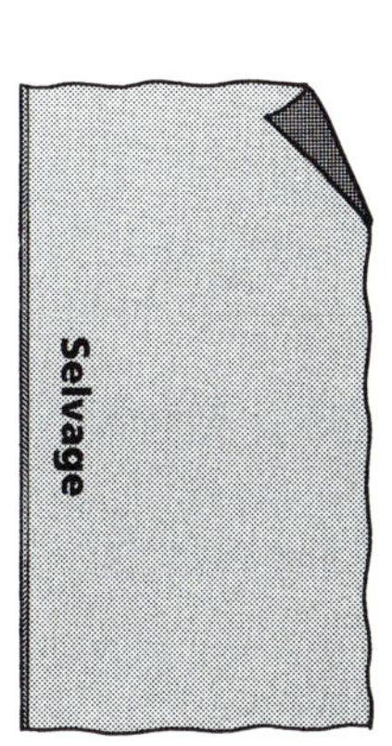

Front Panel

4 **Measure the width for the center back panel.** Measure from the center back of the dress form to the back princess seam at the shoulder blade level, and add 4 inches.

Using the other fabric piece prepared in step 2, snip and tear the fabric this width.

Use the remaining back fabric piece for the side back panel.

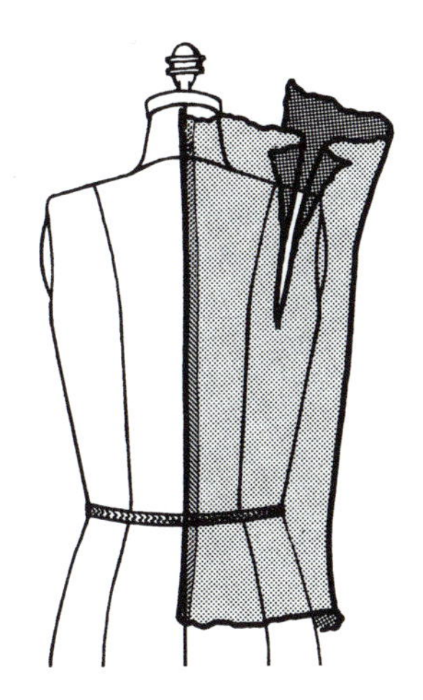

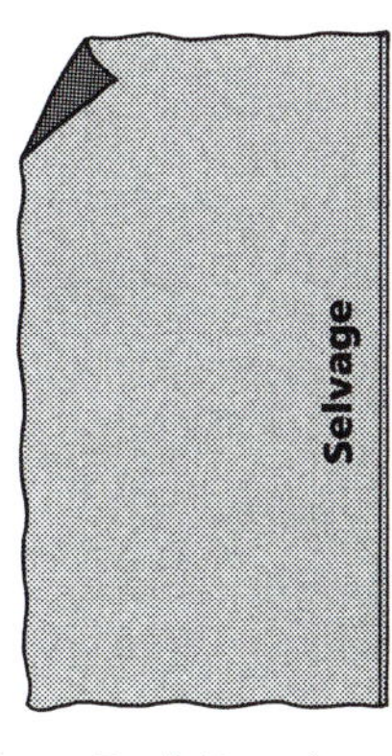

Back Panel

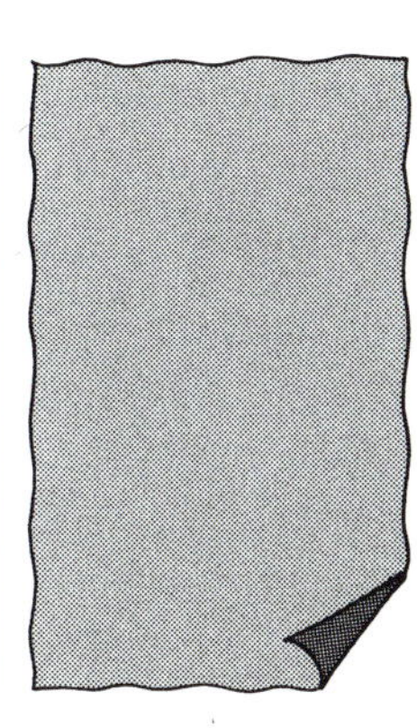

Side Back Panel

5 **Draw in the grainlines on the front panels.**

a. Draw the grainline for the center front panel 1 inch from the torn edge, and press under.

b. Draw the grainline for the side front panel at the center of the fabric piece.

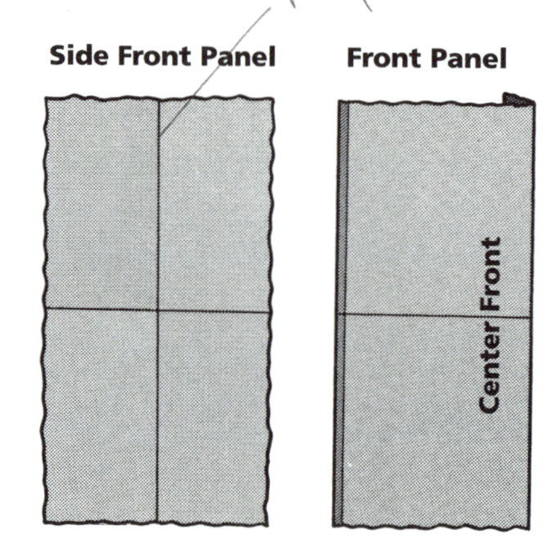

6 **Draw the crossgrain lines** for the front and side front panels in the center of both panels (crosswise).

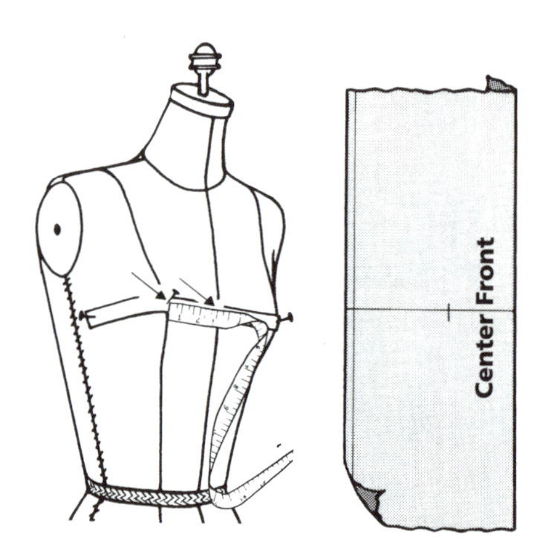

7 **Crossmark the apex.**

a. Measure the dress form from center front to the apex.

b. Crossmark the apex this distance on the center front panel on the crossgrain line.

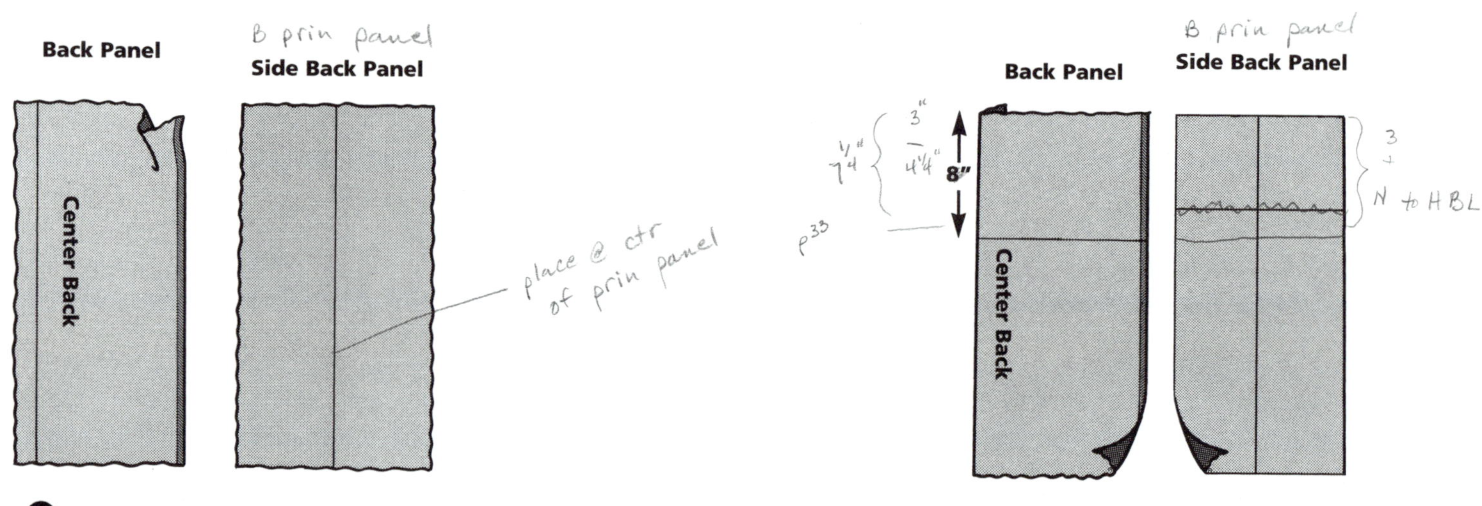

8 **Draw in the grainlines on the back panels.**

a. Draw the grainline for the center back panel 1 inch from the torn edge. Press under.

b. Draw the grainline for the side back panel in the center of the fabric piece (lengthwise).

9 **Draw the crossgrain line** for both back panels 8 inches from the top of the fabric edge.

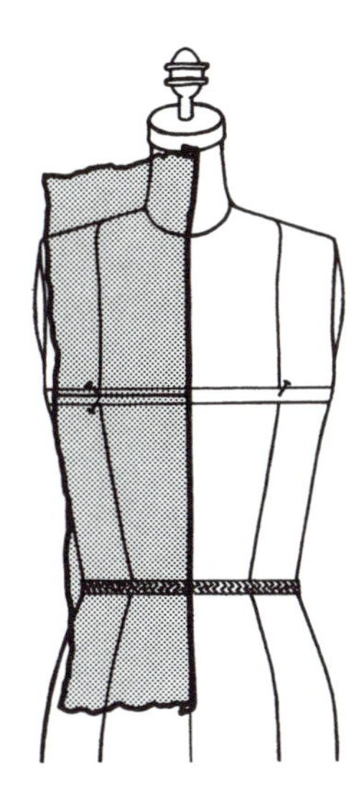

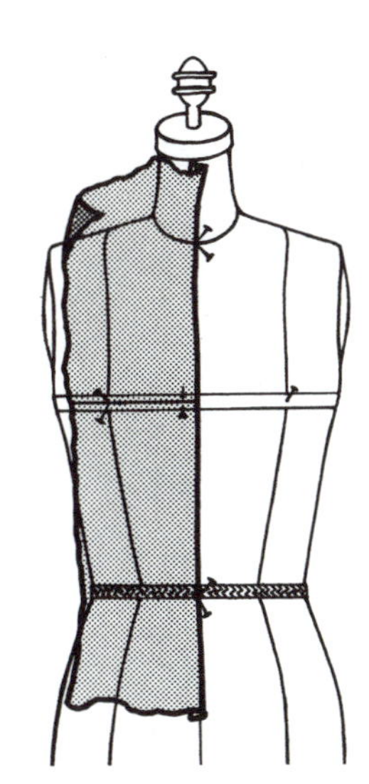

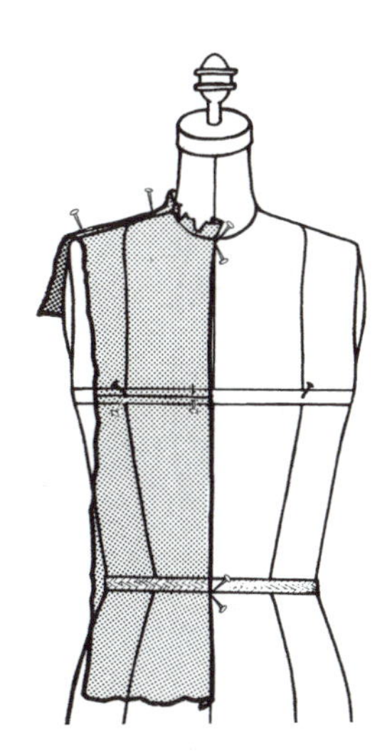

1 **Pin the apex** crossmark on the fabric to the apex position on the dress form.

2 **Pin the center front grainline** fold of the fabric to the center position of the dress form.

Anchor pins at C.F. neck and C.F. waist. An additional pin may be needed at the bust level tape.

3 **Drape the neckline** by trimming the excess fabric around the neck area and clipping at intervals. Smooth the neckline in place.

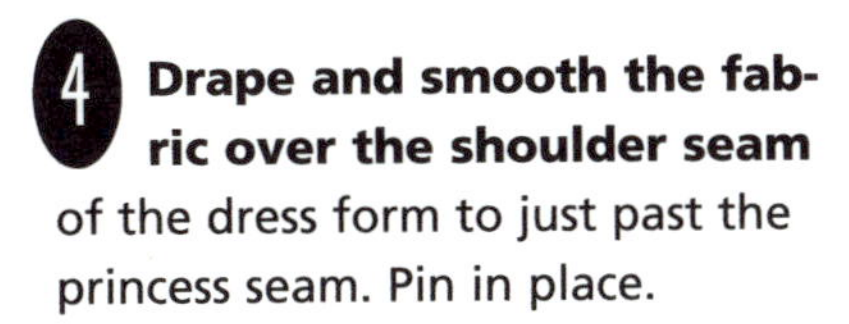

4 **Drape and smooth the fabric over the shoulder seam** of the dress form to just past the princess seam. Pin in place.

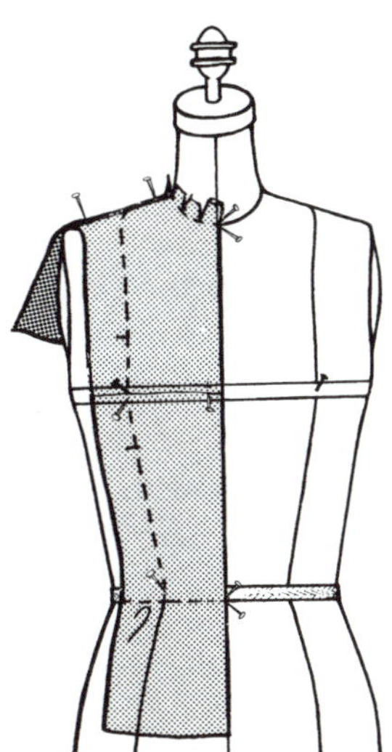

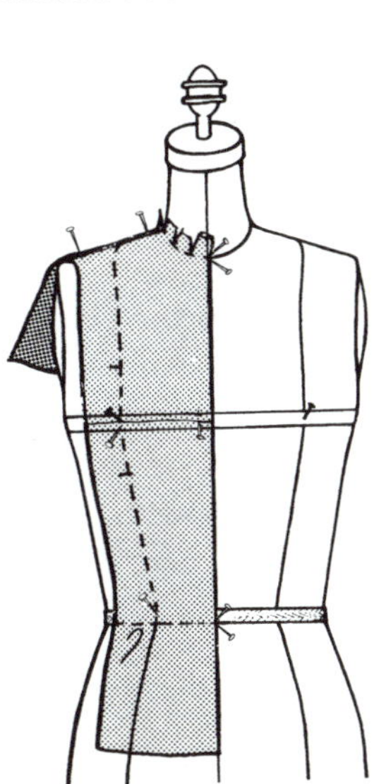

5 **Drape and smooth the waistline** across the waistline tape from center front to just past the princess seam. Pin in place.

6 **Mark all key areas** of the dress form on the center front panel.

Neckline Lightly mark.

Shoulder Seam Lightly mark.

Waistline Lightly mark

Princess Seam and Style Line Crossmarks 2 inches above and below apex

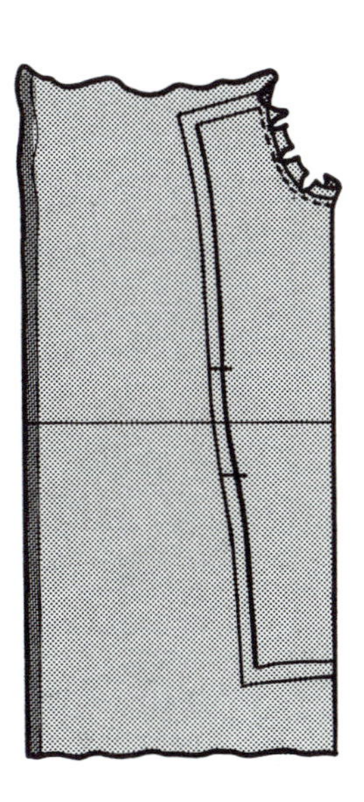

7 **True up center front panel.** Add seam allowances and trim all excess fabric. Place panel back on the dress form.

Side Front Princess Panel—Draping Steps

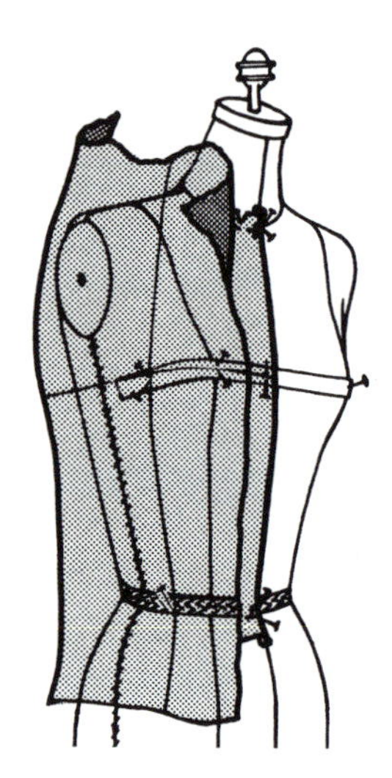

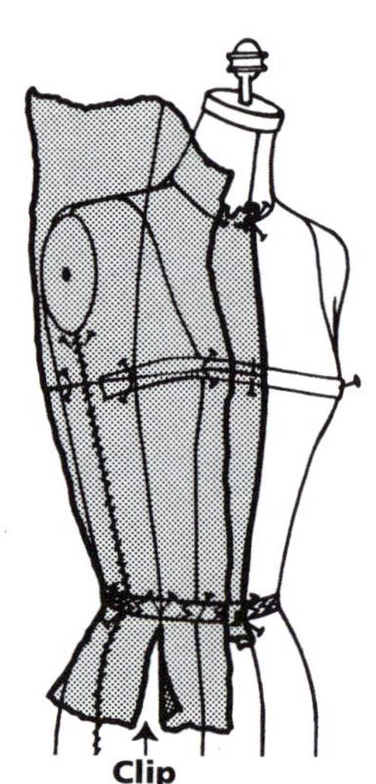

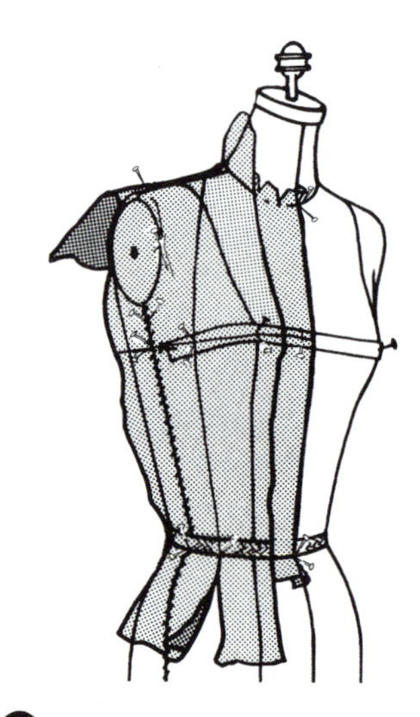

1 **Pin the grainline of the side front panel** to the center of the front princess panel on the dress form.

2 **Match the crossgrain of the side front panel to the crossgrain of the center front panel.** Anchor pins on the crossgrain at the bust level. Place another anchor pin on the straight of grain at the waistline.

3 **Clip the waistline** at the center of the front princess panel up to the bottom of the waist seam tape.

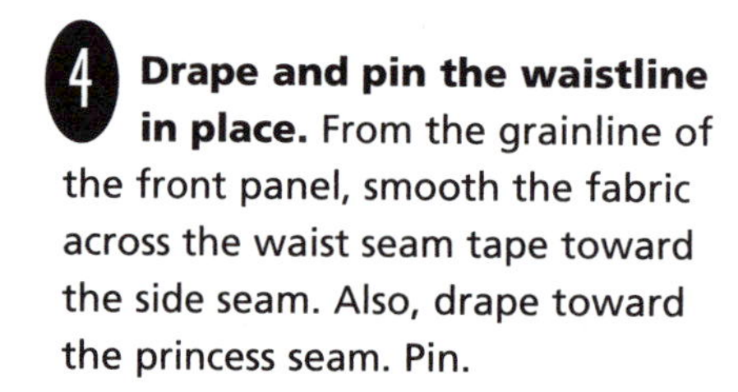

4 **Drape and pin the waistline in place.** From the grainline of the front panel, smooth the fabric across the waist seam tape toward the side seam. Also, drape toward the princess seam. Pin.

5 **Smooth and pin the side seam in place.** From the grainline of the side front panel, smooth the fabric past the side seam of the dress form. Do not allow the grainline to slip out of position. Pin the side seam in place.

6 **Continue to smooth the fabric flat over the armplate.** Create a 1/4"–1/4" pinch at the mid-armhole area ridge.

7 **Drape the shoulder** by carefully smoothing the excess fabric above the bust level up and over the shoulder of the dress form.

NOTE: The grainline will angle toward the neckline above the bust level.

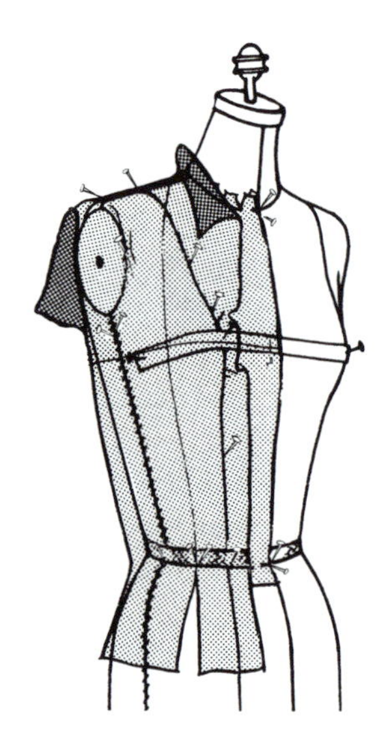

8 **Smooth and pin the princess seam in place.** From the grainline of the side front panel, smooth the fabric over the princess seam betweeen the crossmarks.

NOTE: Excess fabric will drape over the bust level area creating ease at the princess seam between the crossmarks.

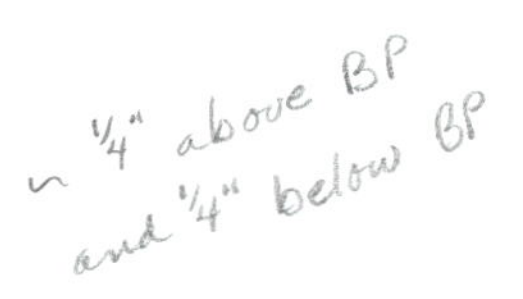

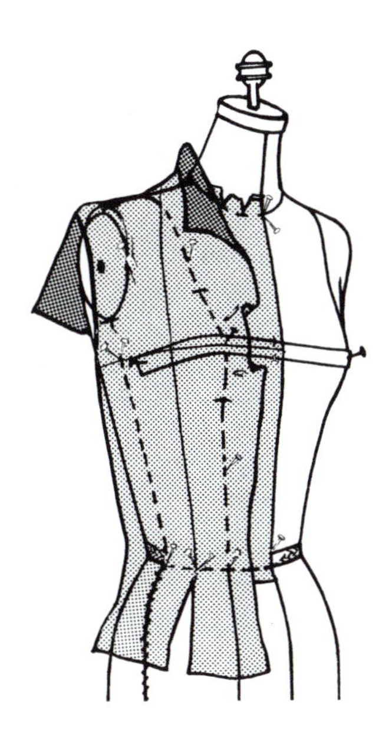

9 **Mark all key areas** of the dress form on the side front panel.

Princess Seam and Style Line Crossmarks match to center front panel crossmarks.

Armplate
a. Shoulder seam at ridge.
b. Middle of plate at screw level (1/4"–1/4" pinch).
c. Bottom of plate at side seam.

Shoulder Seam
Side Seam
Waistline

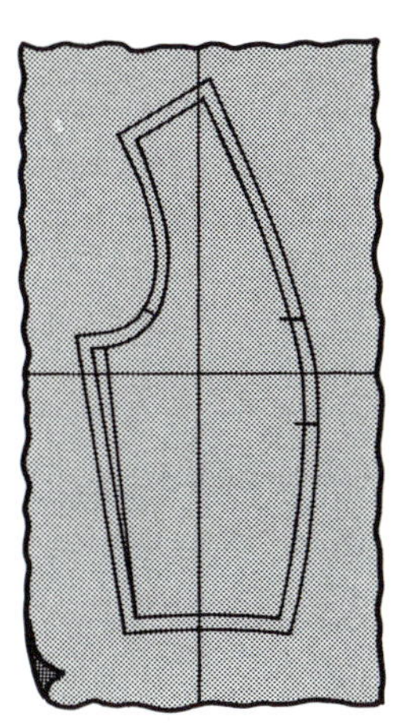

10 **True up all the lines.** Remove the side front panel from the dress form and true up all the lines. Add seam allowances and the front armhole notch.

Trim excess fabric. Pin to front panel. Place the drape on the dress form to check seams, crossmarks, fit, and balance.

Center Back Princess Panel—*Draping Steps*

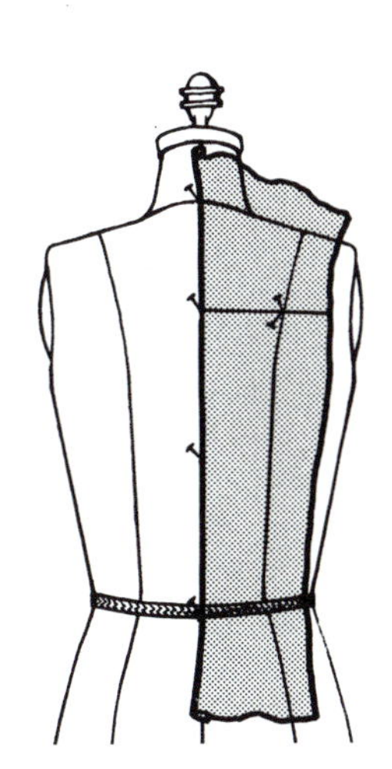

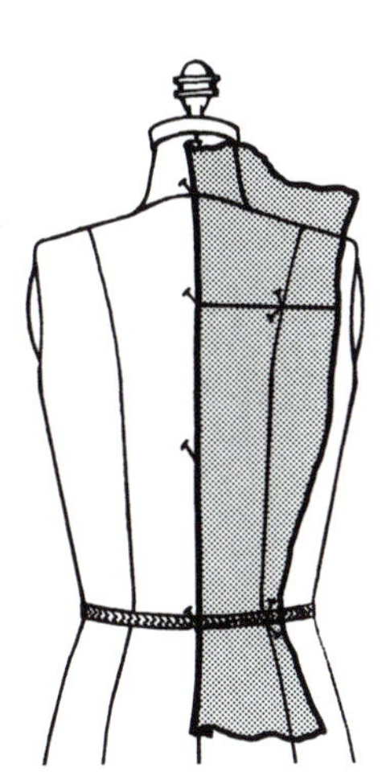

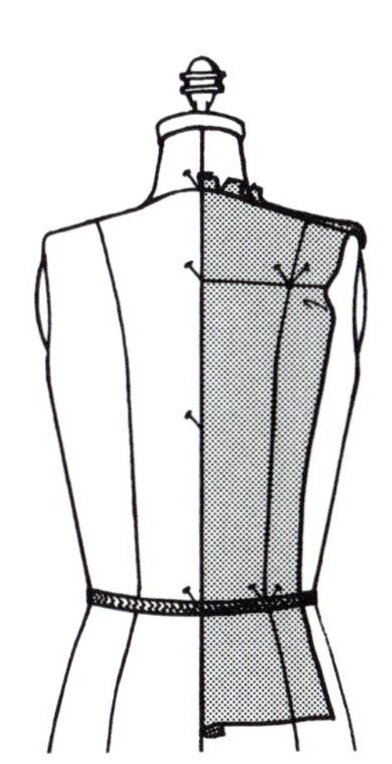

1 **Pin the center back grainline** fold of the fabric to the center back position of the dress form.

2 **Align and pin the cross-grain** of the fabric to the shoulder blade level of the dress form.

3 **Drape and smooth the back waistline** from center back to just past the princess seam. Pin the waistline in place.

4 **Drape and smooth the back neckline.** Carefully trim the excess fabric around the neck area and clip at intervals. Smooth the fabric around the neckline.

5 **Smooth the fabric over the shoulder** of the dress form and pin in place.

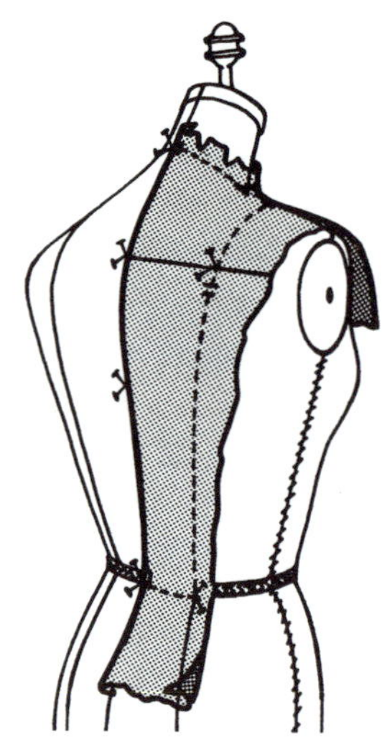

6 **Mark all key areas** of the dress form on the center back panel.

Neckline
Waistline
Shoulder Seam

Back Princess Seam and Style Line Crossmarks double crossmarks are used in the back.

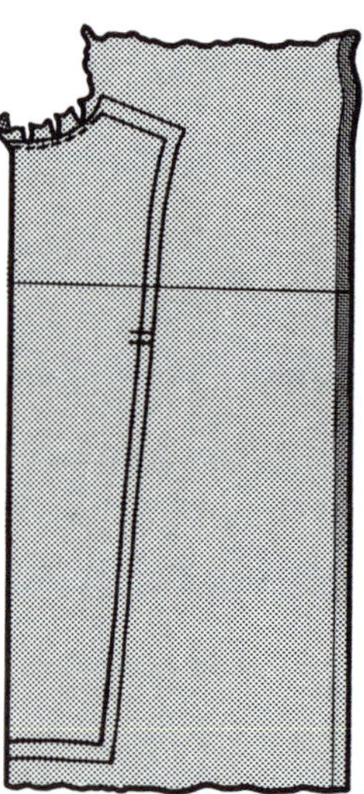

7 **True up all lines.** Remove the center back panel drape from the dress form. True up all lines, add seam allowances, and trim all excess fabric. Place this center back panel drape on the dress form.

Side Back Princess Panel—Draping Steps

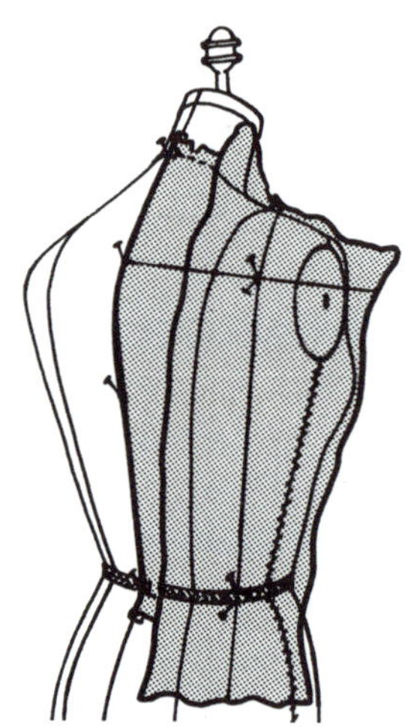

1 **Pin the grainline of the side back panel** to the center of the back princess panel on the dress form.

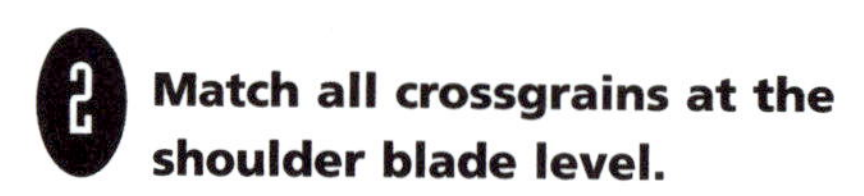

2 **Match all crossgrains at the shoulder blade level.**

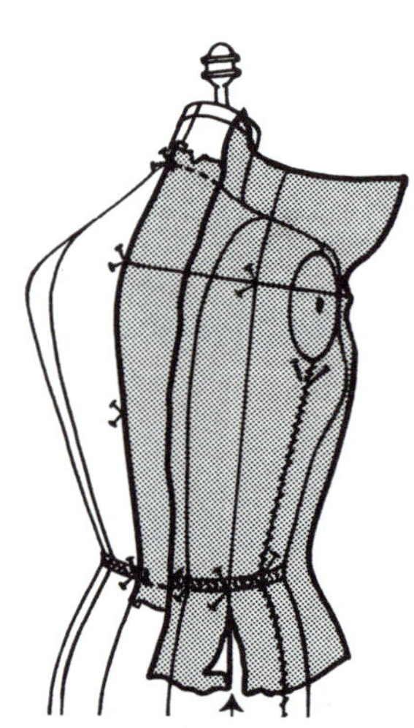

3 **Clip the waistline at the side back panel** up to the bottom of the waist seam tape.

4 **Drape and pin the waistline in place.** From the grainline of the back panel, smooth the fabric across the waist seam tape toward the side seam. Also, drape toward the princess seam.

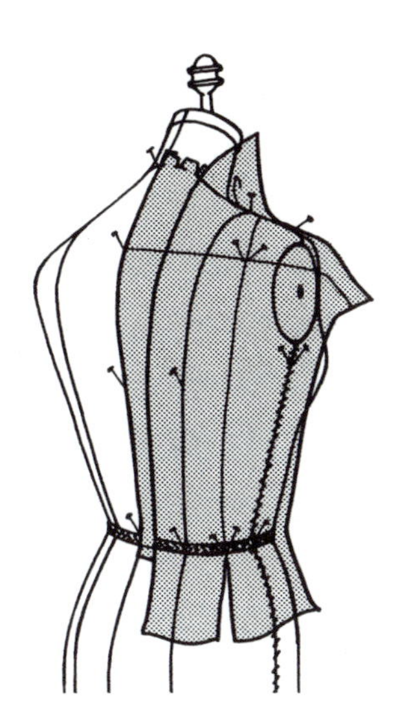

5 **Drape the shoulder** by smoothing the excess fabric from above the shoulder blade level up and over the shoulder seam of the dress form.

NOTE: The grainline will be angled toward the neckline (over the crossgrain).

6 **Smooth and pin the side seam in place.** From the grainline of the side back panel, smooth the fabric past the side seam of the dress form. Do not allow the grainline to slip out of position. Pin the side seam in place.

7 **Drape and pin the princess seam in place.** From the grainline of the side back panel, smooth the fabric past the princess seam of dress form. Do not allow the grainline to slip out of position. Pin the princess seam.

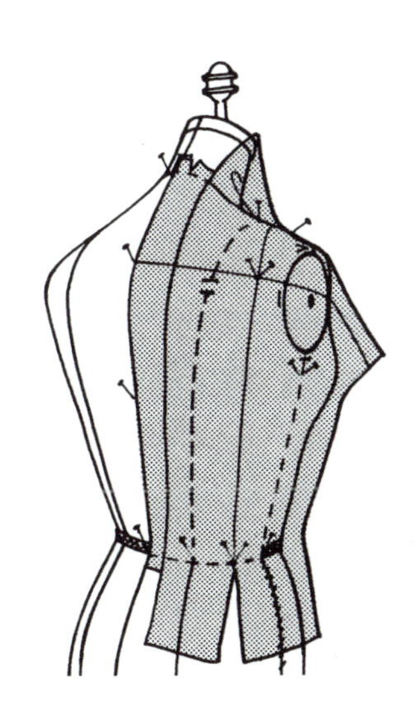

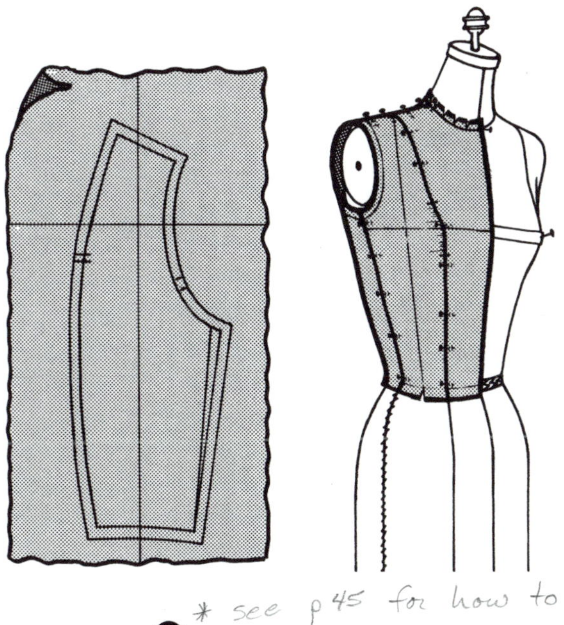

8 **Mark all key areas** of the dress form on the side back panel.

Princess Seam and Style Line Crossmarks match to center back panel double crossmarks.

Armplate
a. Shoulder seam at ridge.
b. Middle of plate at screw level.
c. Bottom of plate at side seam.

Shoulder Seam

Side Seam

Waistline

* see p45 for how to

9 **True up all lines.** Remove the drape from the dress form. True up all lines, add seam allowances and back armhole notches, and trim all excess fabric. Pin the entire garment together and place the drape on the dress form. Check for accuracy, fit, and hang.

Torso Princess Bodice

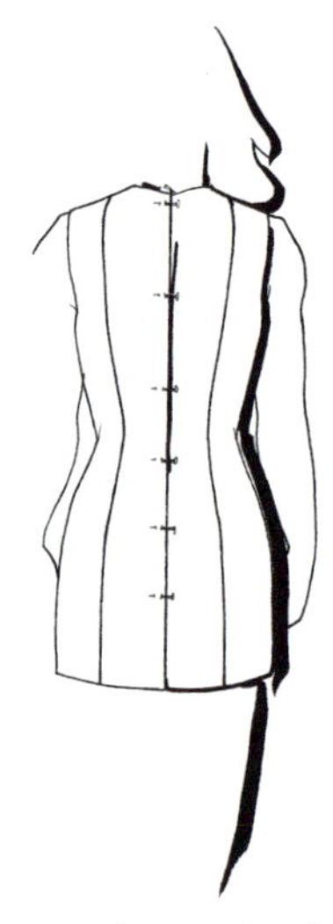

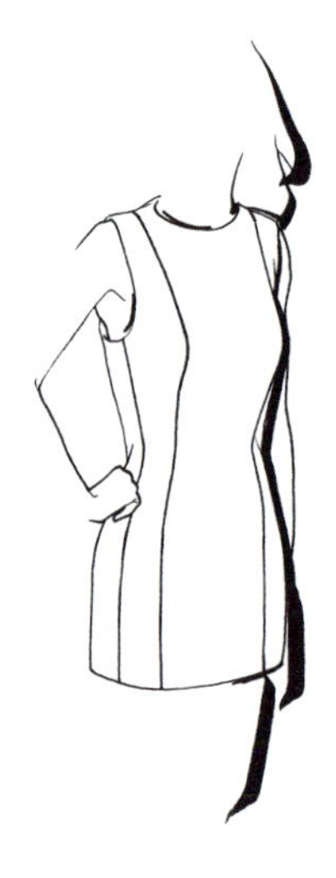

A torso princess bodice is styled with vertical seams rather than darts. This divides the bodice front and back into two panels. It also has no waist fitting seam, allowing for long vertical slimming lines. Once sewn, the princess bodice represents the same shape as the basic torso bodice, or dress, but with vertical seams.

The torso princess drape offers versatility to an important classic and creates a crisp, longer, and slimmer look. Fashionable tops for suits, dresses, or sportswear separates may be designed in this length and shape. Many designers prefer to use this classic pattern to create a sensational body fit and look.

Torso Princess Bodice—Preparing the Fabric

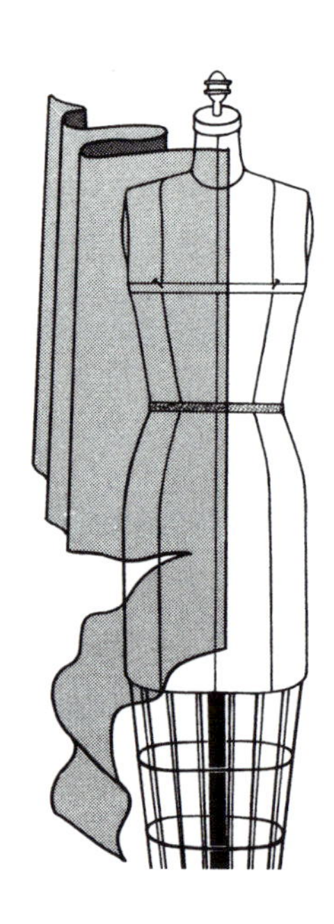

1 Measure the length for the front and back panels (along the straight of grain) from the neckband to the hip area, and add 5 inches. Snip and tear the fabric at this length.

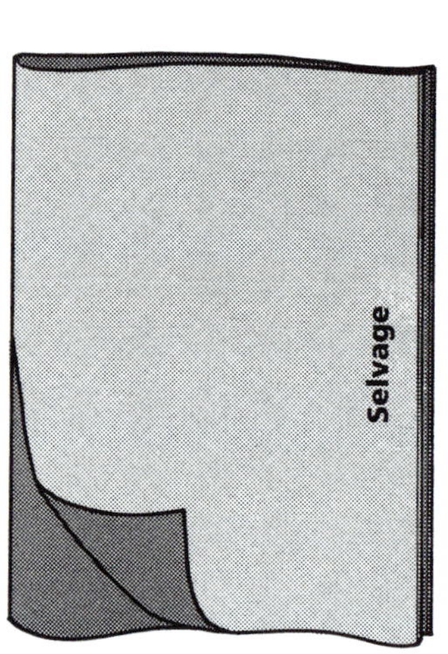

2 Divide the fabric piece in half. Fold the fabric from selvage to selvage. Snip and tear the fabric piece in half lengthwise.

Use one piece for the front panels and the other piece for the back panels.

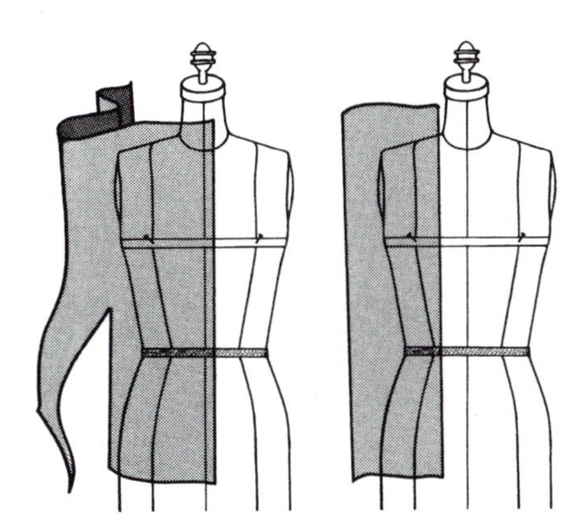

3 **Measure the width for the center front panel** (along the crossgrain) from the center front of the dress form to 5 inches past the apex. Using one of the fabric pieces prepared in Step 2, snip and tear the fabric at this width.

Use the remaining fabric piece for the side front panel.

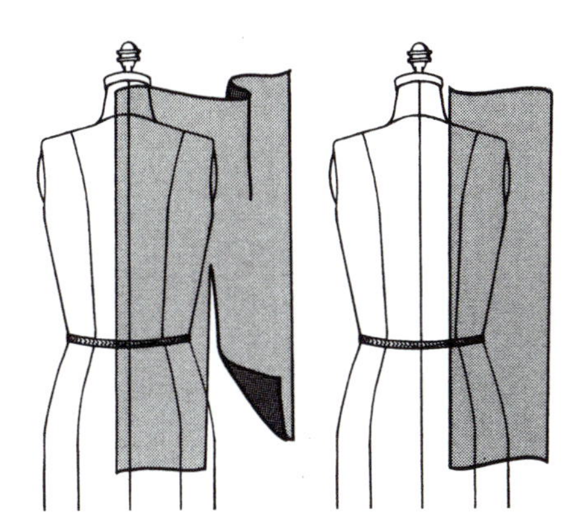

4 **Measure the width for the center back panel** from the center back of the dress form to the back princess seam at the shoulder blade level, and add 5 inches. Using the other fabric piece, snip and tear the fabric at this width.

Use the remaining back panel piece for the side back panel.

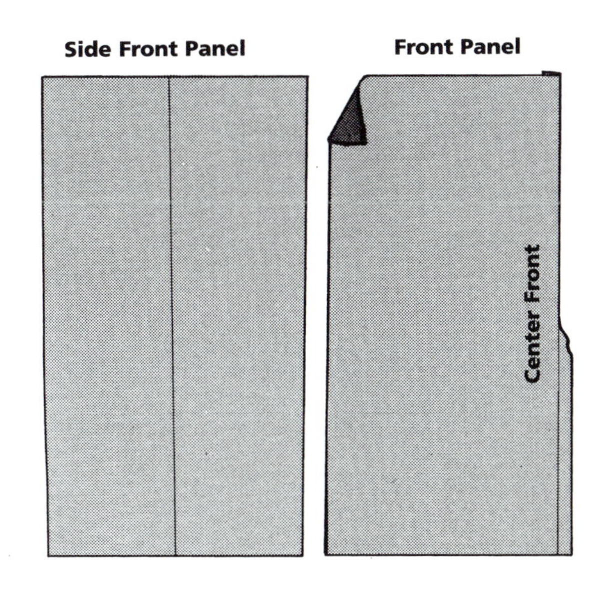

5 **Draw the grainline for the center front panel** 1 inch from the torn edge, and press under.

6 **Draw the grainline for the side front panel** in the center of the fabric piece.

7 Draw the crossgrain lines for the front and side front panels 12 inches from the top edge of the fabric.

8 Crossmark the apex.

a. **Measure the dress form** from center front to the apex.

b. **Crossmark the apex** this distance on the center front panel on the crossgrain line.

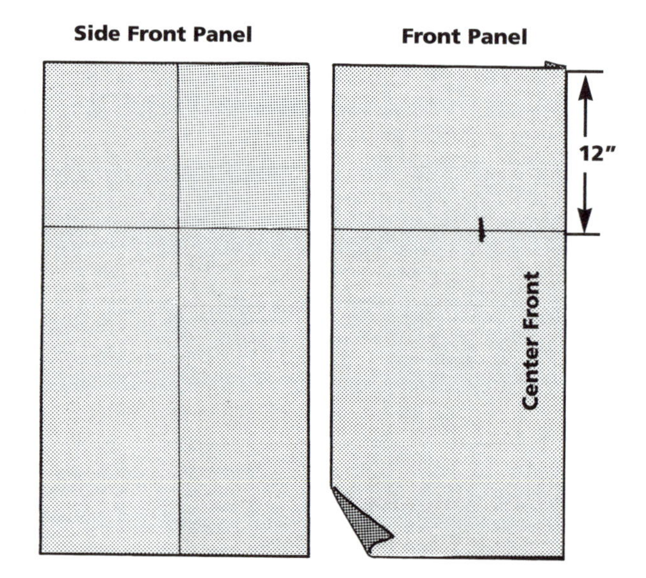

9 Draw the grainline for the center back panel 1 inch from the torn edge, and press under.

10 Draw the grainline for the side back panel in the center of the fabric piece.

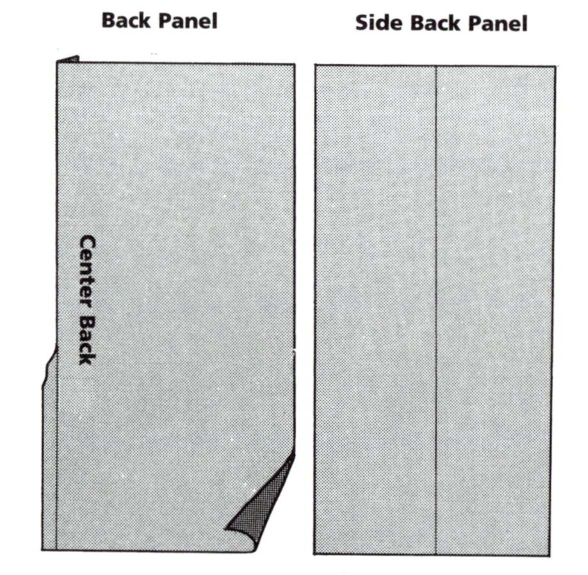

11 Draw the crossgrain lines for both back panels 8 inches from the top edge of the fabric.

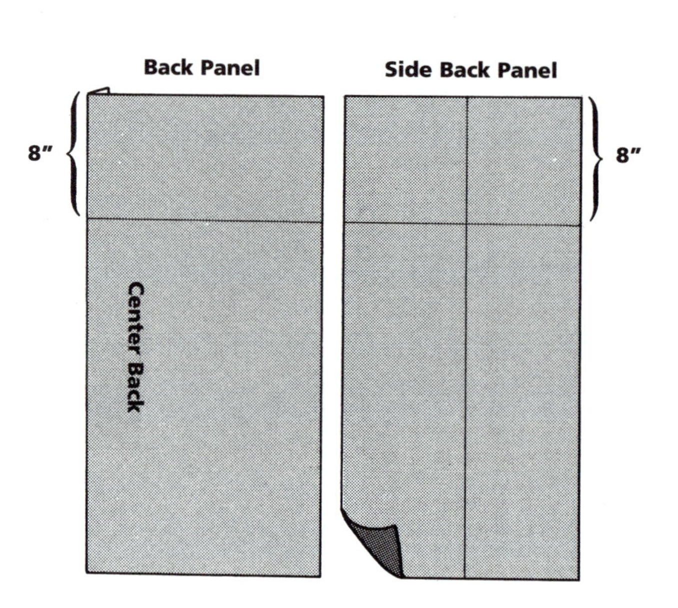

Center Front Princess Panel—Draping Steps

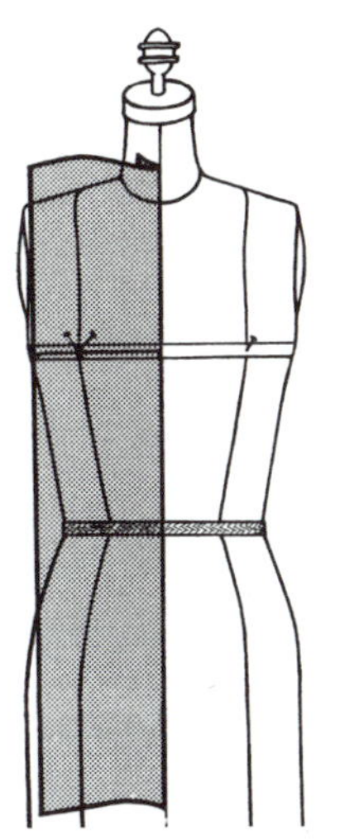

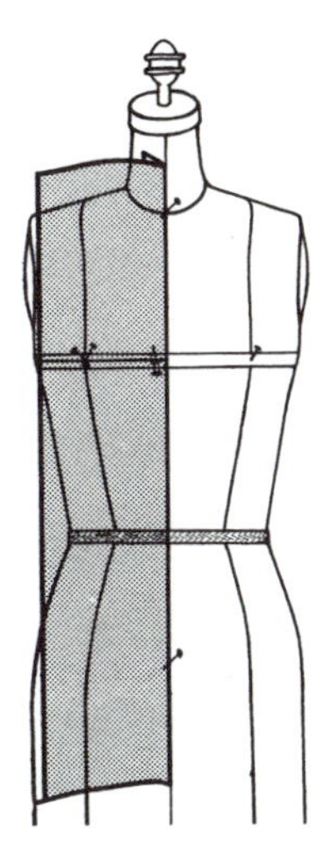

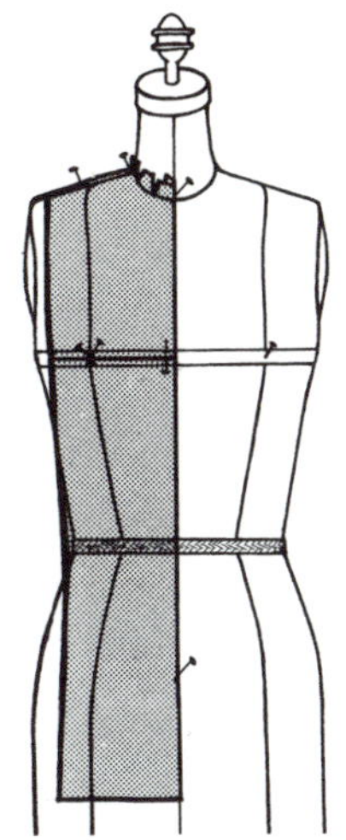

1 **Pin the apex** crossmark on the fabric to the apex position on the dress form.

2 **Pin the center front grain-line** fold of the fabric on the center position of the dress form.

Anchor pins at C.F. neck and C.F. hip. An additional pin may be needed at the bust level tape.

3 **Drape the front neckline** by trimming the excess fabric around the neck area and clipping at intervals. Smooth the neckline in place.

4 **Drape and smooth the fabric over the shoulder seam** of the dress form to just past the princess seam. Pin in place.

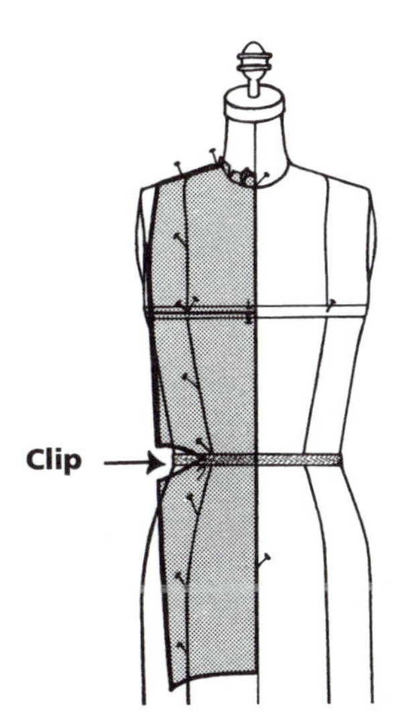

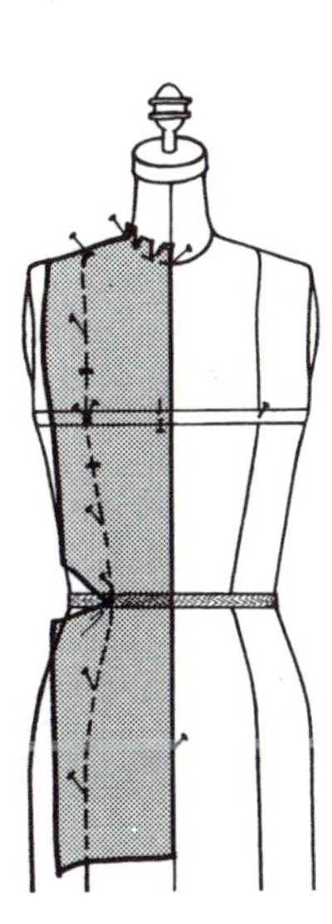

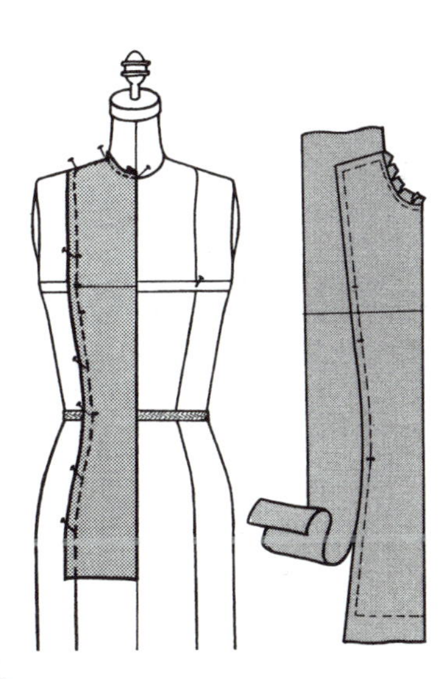

5 **Clip the waistline at the princess seam.**

6 **Drape the princess seam.** Smooth the fabric from center front to just past the princess seam. Pin the princess seam.

NOTE: The fabric at the waistline will be smooth, but not snug.

7 **Mark all key areas** of the dress form on the center front panel.

Neckline

Shoulder Seam

Princess Seam

Style Line Crossmarks Crossmark 2 inches above and below apex.

Hem

8 **True up the center front panel.** Add seam allowances and trim all excess fabric. Place panel back on the dress form.

Side Front Princess Panel—Draping Steps

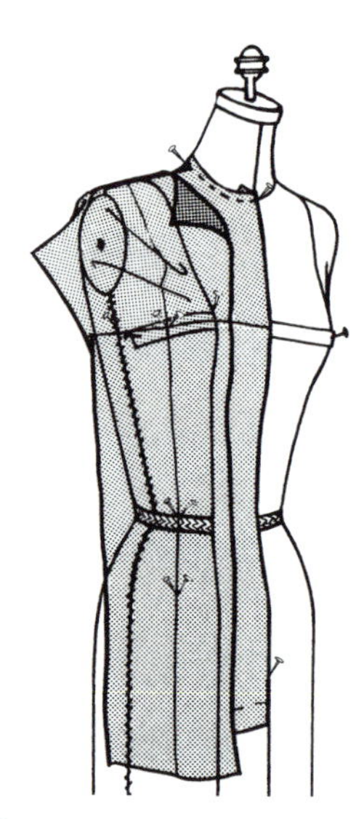

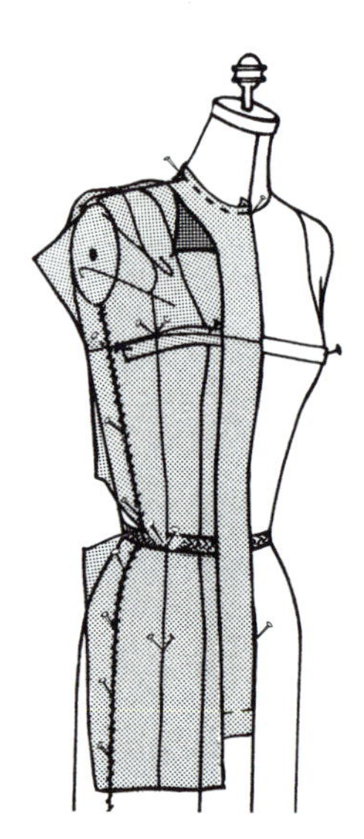

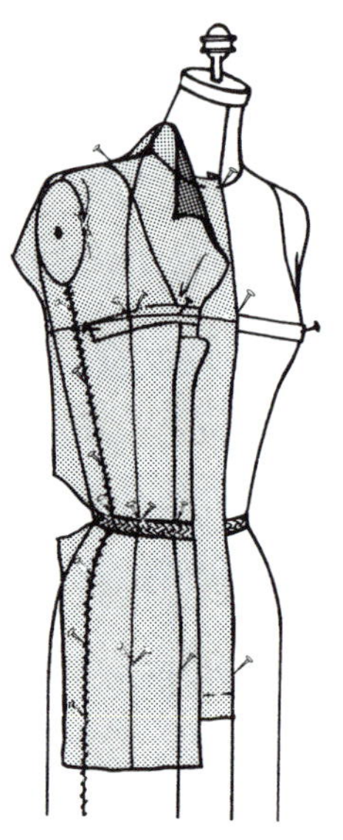

1 Pin the grainline of the side front panel to the center of the princess panel on the dress form.

2 Match the crossgrain of the side front panel to the crossgrain of the center front panel. Anchor pins on the cross-grain at the bust level. Place another pin on the straight of grain at the waistline and the hipline.

3 Clip the waistline at the side seam.

4 Smooth and pin the side seam in place. From the grainline of the side front panel, smooth the fabric past the side seam of the dress form. Pin the side seam in place.

5 Continue to smooth the fabric flat over the arm-plate. Leave the 1/4"–1/4" pinch at the mid-armhole area ridge.

6 Drape the shoulder by carefully smoothing the excess fabric above the bust level up and over the shoulder of the dress form.

NOTE: The grainline will angle toward the neckline above the bust level.

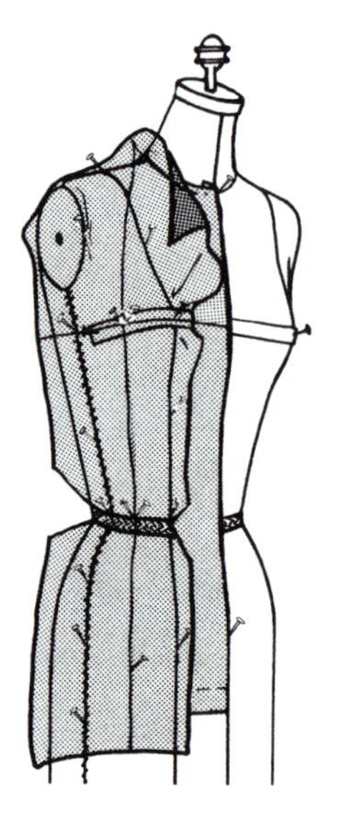

7 Clip the waistline at the princess seam.

8 Smooth and pin the princess seam in place. From the grainline of the side front panel, smooth the fabric past the princess seam of the dress form. Pin in place.

NOTE: Excess fabric will drape over the bust level area creating ease at the princess seam between the crossmarks.

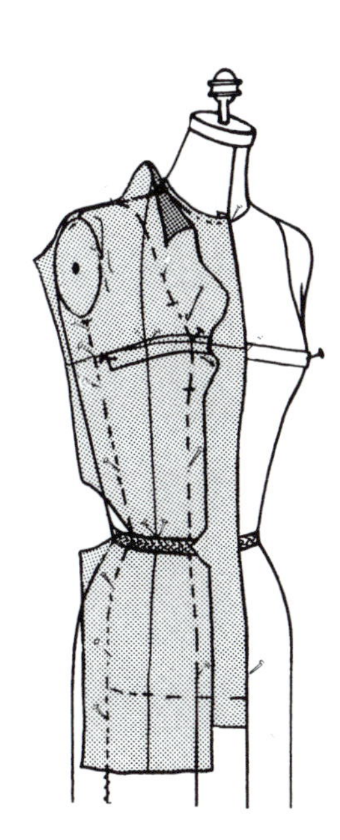

9 **Mark key areas** of the dress form on the side front panel.

Princess Seam
Style Line Crossmarks Match to center front panel crossmarks.

Armplate
a. Shoulder seam at ridge.
b. Middle of plate at screw level (1/4″–1/4″ pinch).
c. Bottom of plate at side seam.

Shoulder Seam

Side Seam

Hem

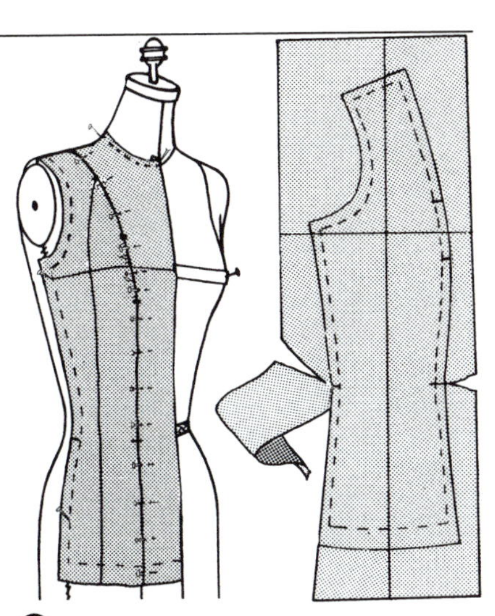

10 **True up all the lines.** Remove the side front panel from the dress form. True up all the lines and add seam allowances.

Trim all excess fabric. Pin the front panel to the side front panel. Place the drape on the dress form to check seams, crossmarks, fit, and balance.

Center Back Princess Panel—*Draping Steps*

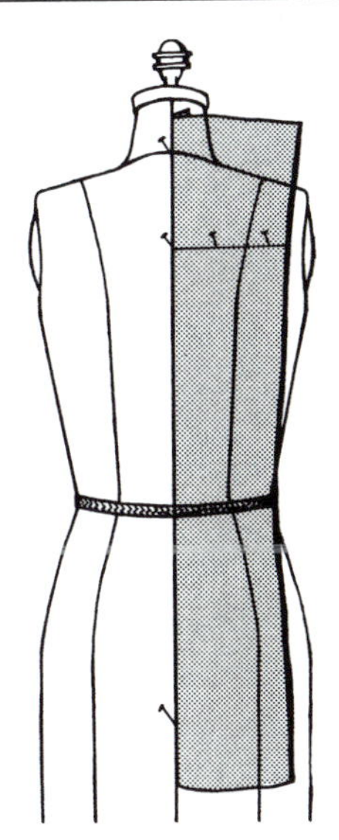

1 **Pin the center back grainline** fold of the fabric to the center back position of the dress form.

2 **Align and pin the crossgrain** of the fabric to the shoulder blade level of the dress form.

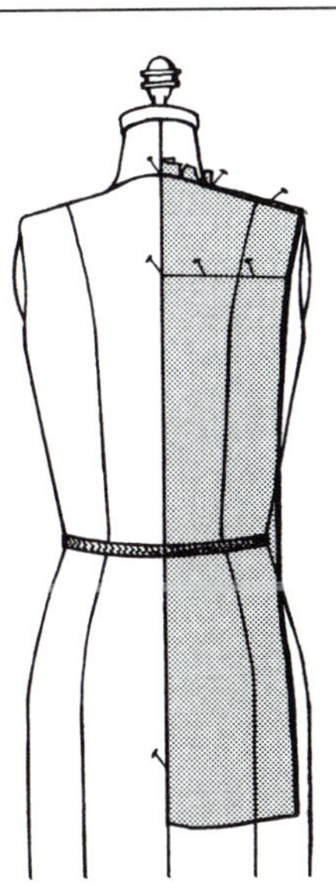

3 **Drape and smooth the back neckline** by carefully trimming the excess fabric around the neck area and clipping at intervals.

4 **Continue to drape and smooth the shoulder** over the shoulder of the dress form. Pin in place.

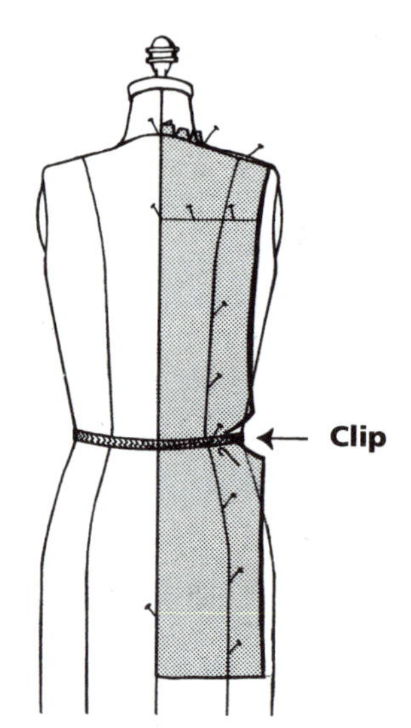

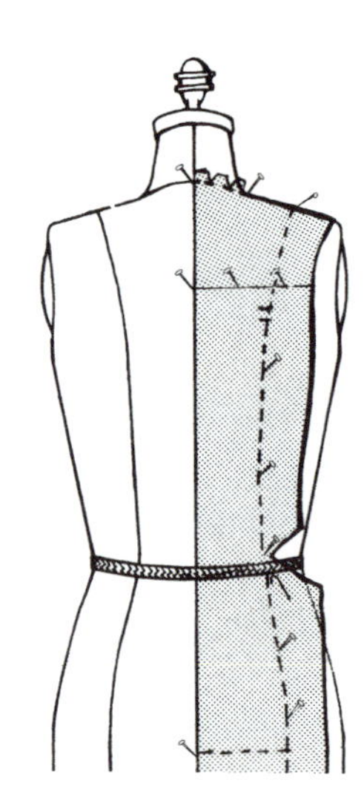

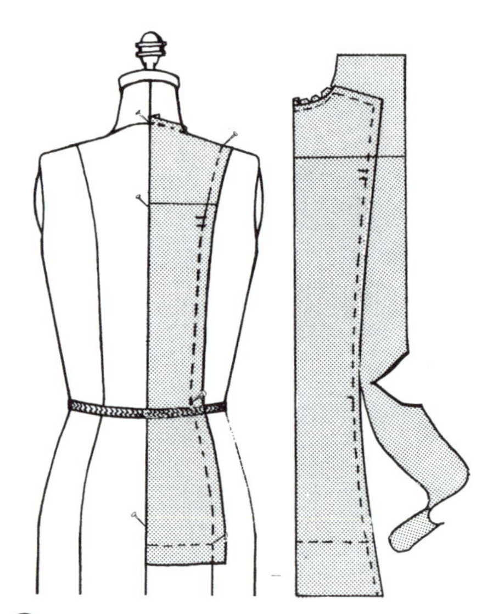

5 **Clip the waistline at the princess seam.**

6 **Drape the princess seam.** Smooth the fabric across the dress form from center back to just past the princess seam. Pin in place.

NOTE: The waist area will drape smoothly, but will not be snug tight.

7 **Mark all key areas** of the dress form on the center back panel.

Neckline

Shoulder Seam

Back Princess Seam

Style Line Notches A double notch is used in the back.

Hem

8 **True up all lines.** Remove the center back panel drape from the dress form. True up all lines, add seam allowances, and trim all excess fabric. Place the drape back on the dress form.

Side Back Princess Panel—Draping Steps

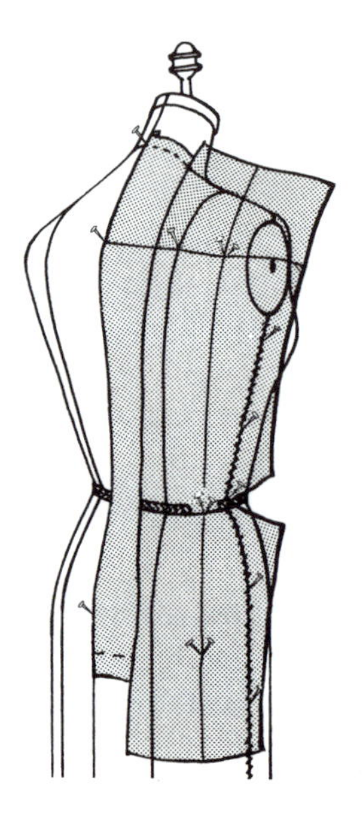

1 **Pin the grainline of the side back panel** to the center of the back princess panel on the dress form.

2 **Match all crossgrains at the shoulder blade level.**

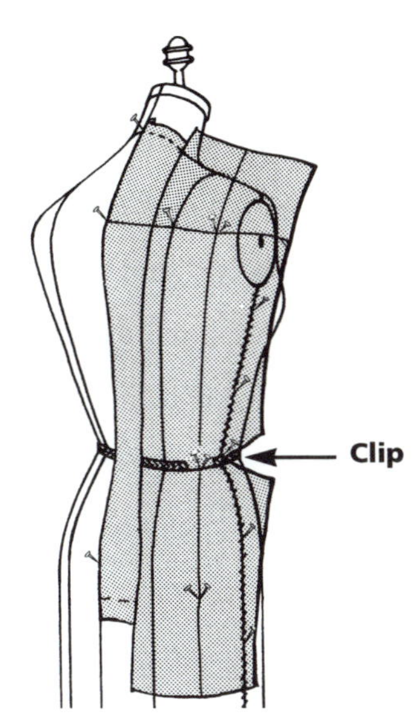

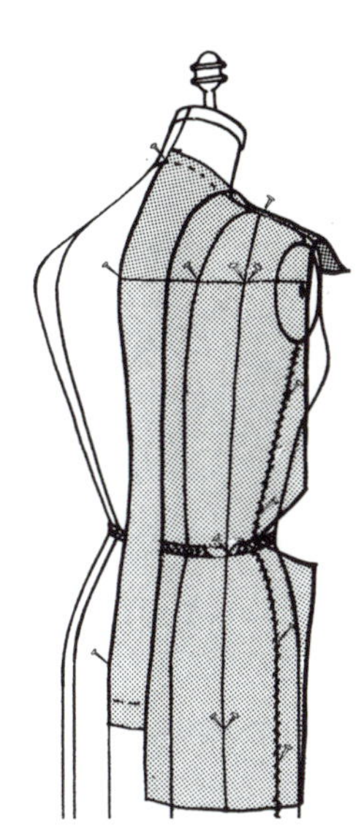

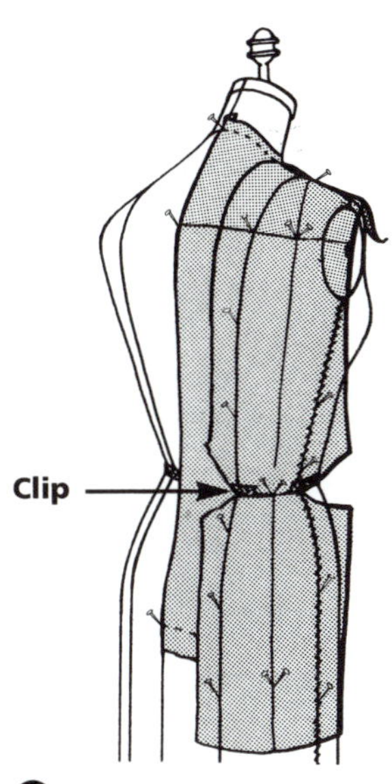

3 **Clip the waistline at the side seam.**

4 **Smooth and pin the side seam in place.** From the grainline of the side back panel, smooth the fabric past the side seam of the dress form. Pin the side seam in place.

5 **Drape the shoulder** by smoothing the excess fabric from above the shoulder blade level up and over the shoulder seam of the dress form.

NOTE: The grainline will be angled toward the neckline (above the crossgrain).

6 **Clip the waistline at the princess seam** of the side back panel.

7 **Smooth and pin the back princess seam in place.** From the grainline of the side back panel, smooth the fabric past the princess seam of the dress form. Do not allow the grainline to slip out of position. Pin the princess seam in place.

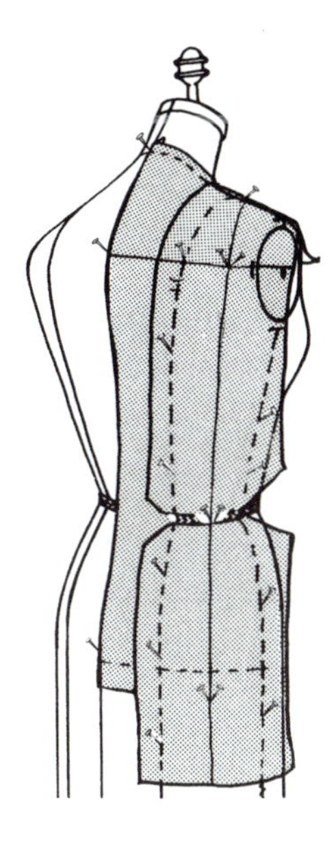

8 **Mark all key areas of the dress form on the side back panel.**

Princess Seam and Style Line Crossmarks Match to center back panel double crossmarks.

Armplate

a. Shoulder seam at ridge.

b. Middle of plate at screw level.

c. Bottom of plate at side seam.

Shoulder Seam

Side Seam

Hem

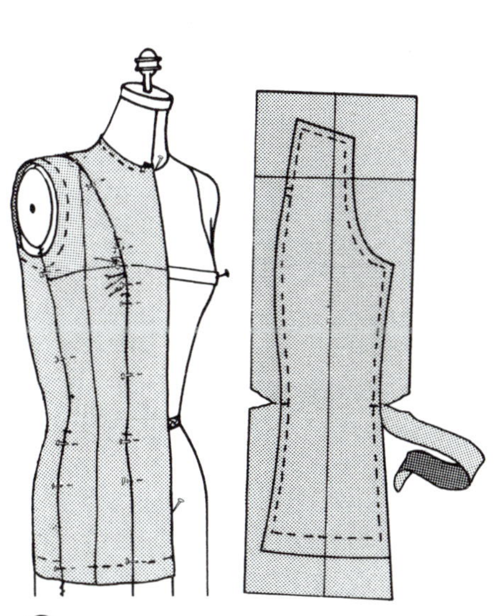

9 **True up all lines.** Remove the drape from the dress form. True up all lines, add seam allowances, and trim all excess fabric.

Pin the entire garment together and place the drape on the dress form. Check for accuracy, fit, and hang.

Princess Slip Dress

The princess slip dress is a sleeveless styled dress with a neckline beginning above the bust. It is held in place with thin spaghetti straps. The slip dress is styled with vertical seams that divide the dress front and back into two panels. The princess slip dress has no waist fitting seam, allowing for long vertical slimming lines. An additional "flare" amount is draped into the dress panels from the waist area to the hemline. The slip dress is usually made of soft fabric which gives the dress a feathery, flowing appearance.

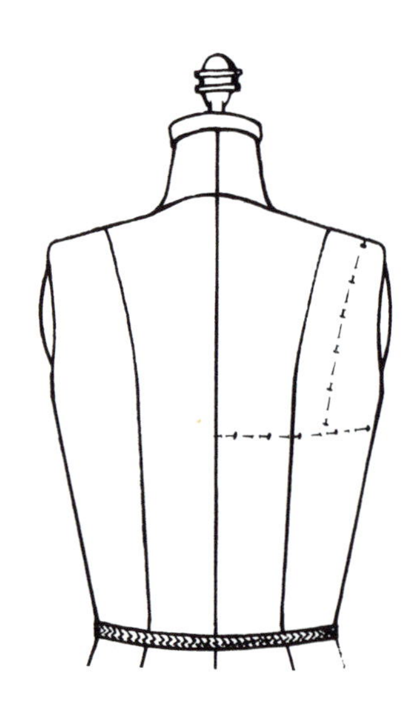

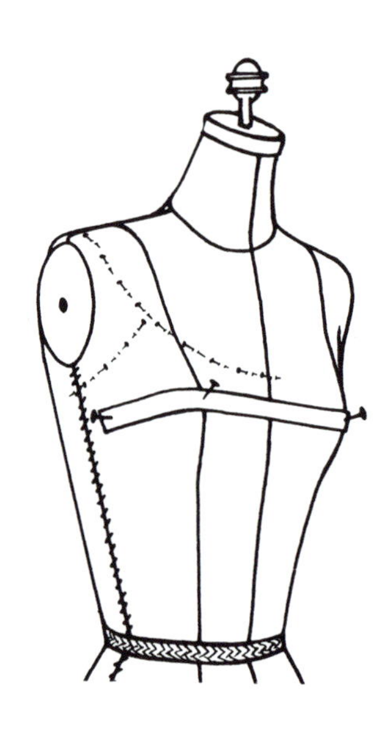

Prepare the dress form.

Place pins on the dress form at the desired bustline.

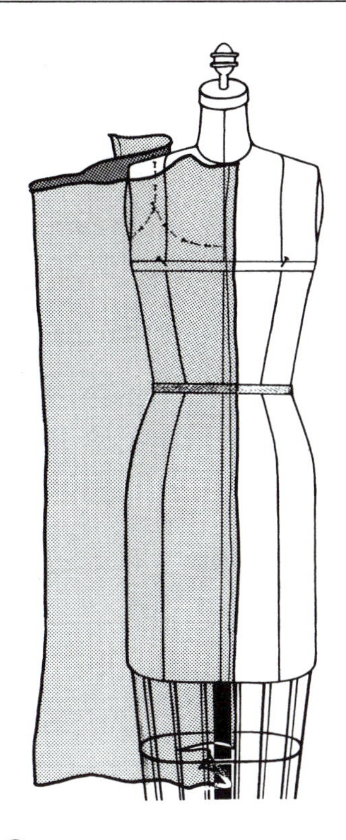

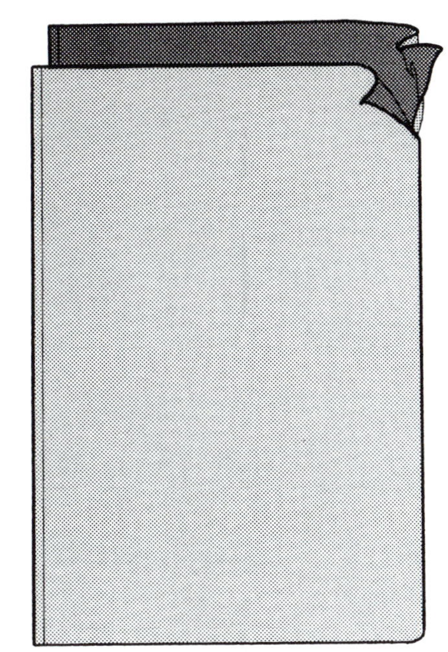

Front Panels

1 Measure the length for the front and back panels (along the straight of grain) from the neckband to the desired length and add 5 inches. Snip and tear the fabric at this length.

2 Divide the fabric piece in half. Fold the fabric from selvage to selvage, snip and tear the fabric piece in half lengthwise.

Use one piece for the front panels and the other piece for the back panels.

3 Measure the width for the center front panel (along the crossgrain) from the center front of the dress form to the front princess seam at the apex, and add 5 inches. Snip and tear the fabric this width.

Use the remaining fabric piece for the side front panel.

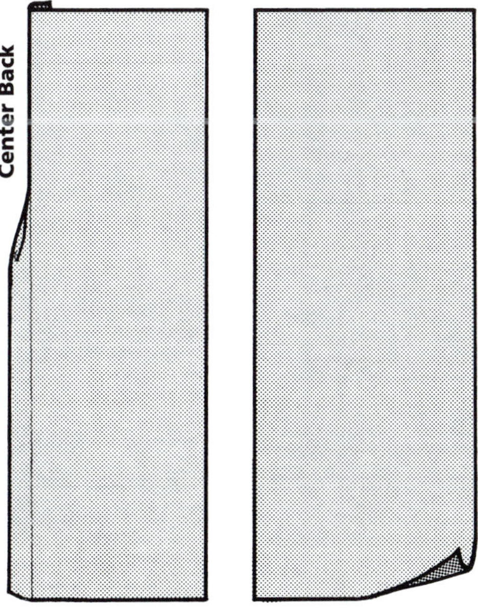

Back Panels

4 Measure the width for the center back panel from the center back of the dress form to the back princess seam at the shoulder blade level, and add 5 inches. Using the other fabric piece, snip and tear the fabric this width.

Use the remaining back panel piece for the side back panel.

5 **Draw in the fabric grainlines.**

a. Draw the grainline for the center front and center back panels 1 inch from the torn edge. Press under.

b. Draw the grainline for the side front and side back panels in the center of the fabric pieces.

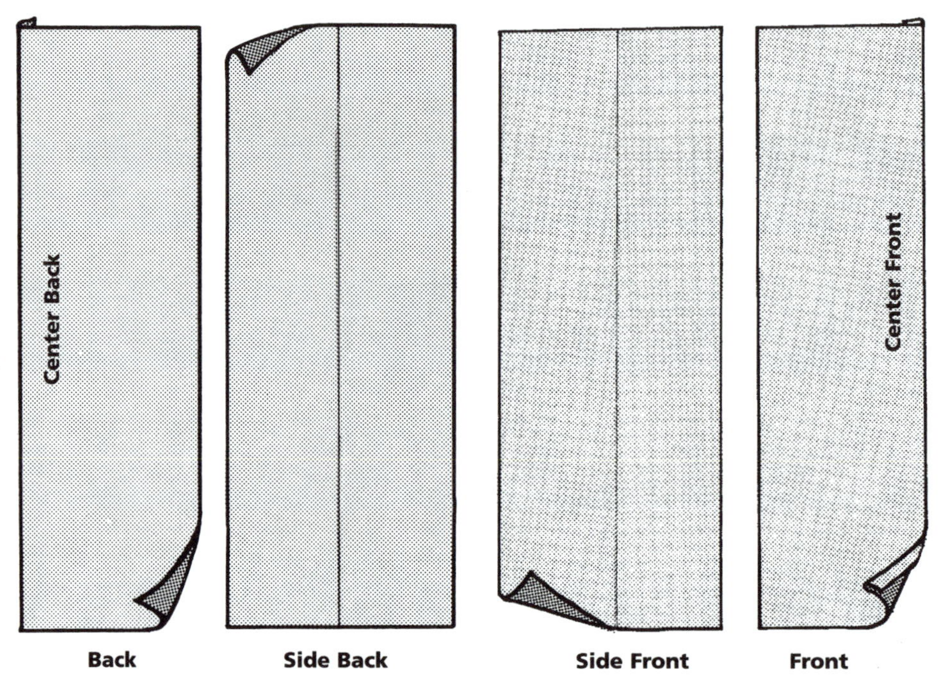

Notes

Center Front Princess Panel—Draping Steps

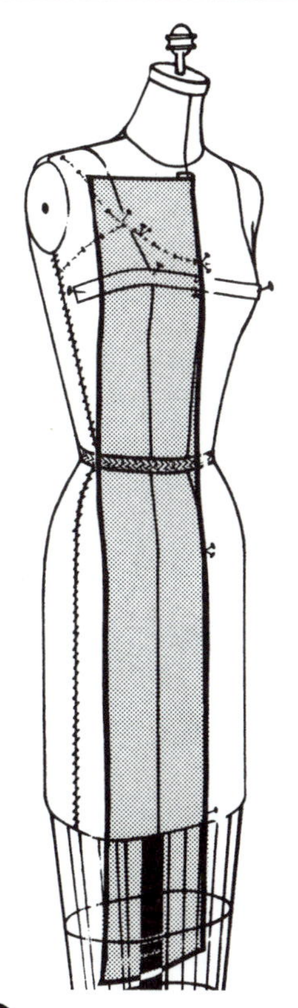

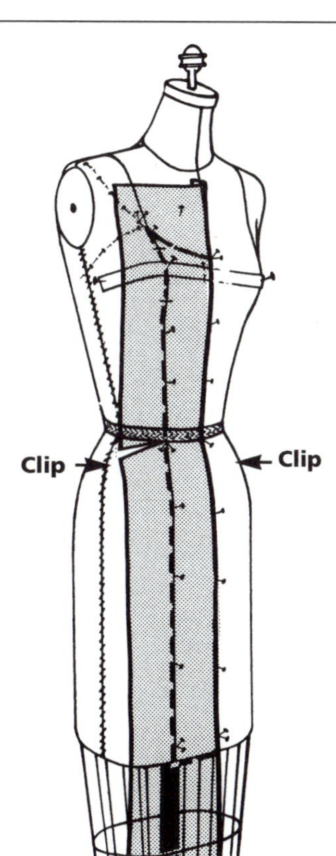

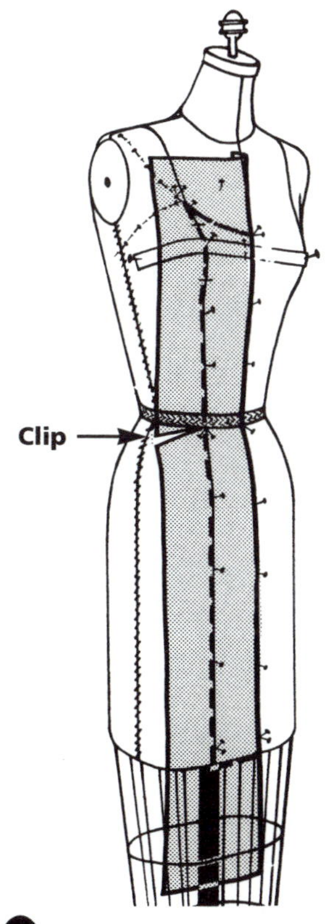

1 **Pin the center front grainline** fold of the fabric to the center position of the dress form. The fabric piece should extend at least 3 inches above the front styled neckline.

2 **Clip the waistline at the princess seam.**

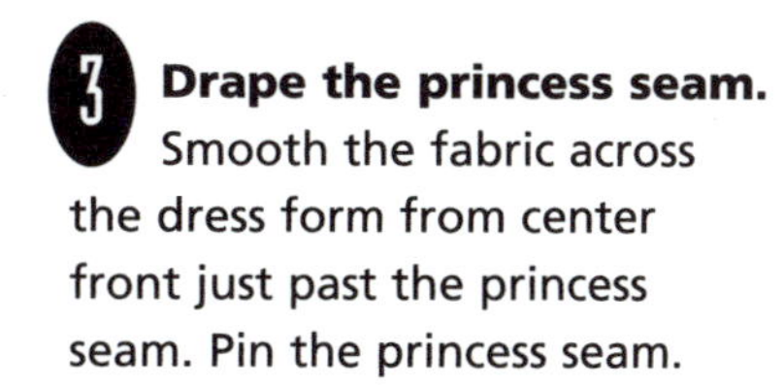

3 **Drape the princess seam.** Smooth the fabric across the dress form from center front just past the princess seam. Pin the princess seam.

NOTE: The fabric at the waistline will be smooth, but not snug tight.

4 **Mark all key areas** of the dress form on the center front panel.

Bustline Styled Neckline

Princess Seam

Style Line Notches Crossmarks 2 inches above and below apex.

Hem Follow the bottom of the dress form or a rung.

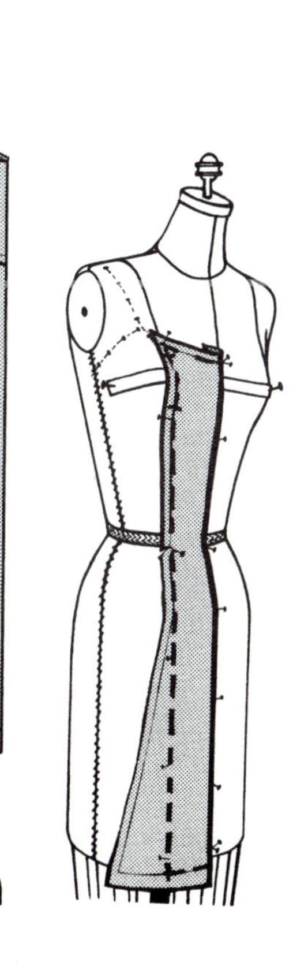

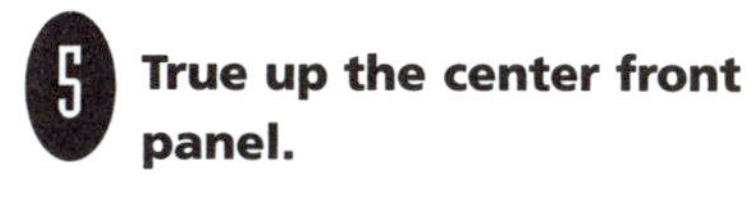

5 **True up the center front panel.**

Add the amount of flare desired at the hemline of the princess seam. Blend this flare into the waistline at the princess seam.

Add seam allowances and trim all excess fabric. Place panel back on the dress form.

Side Front Princess Panel—Draping Steps

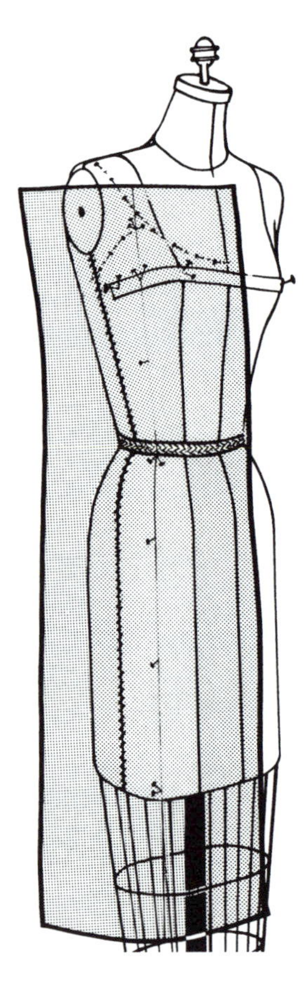

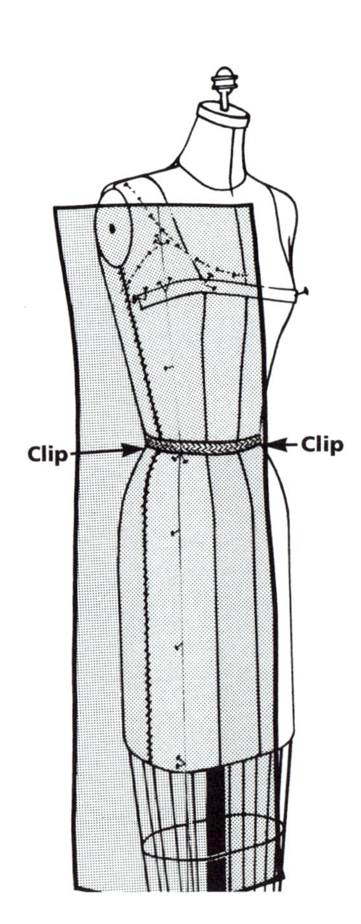

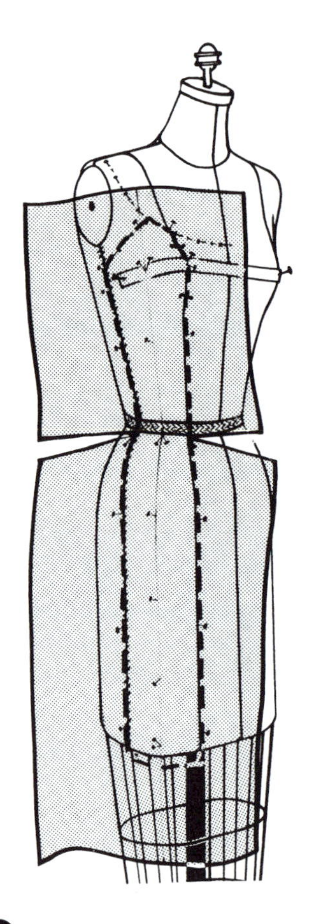

1 Pin the grainline of the side front panel to the center of the princess panel on the dress form. The fabric piece should extend at least 3 inches above the styled neckline.

2 Clip the waistline at the side seam.

3 Smooth and pin the side seam in place. From the grainline of the side front panel, smooth the fabric past the side seam of the dress form. Pin the side seam in place.

4 Clip the waistline at the princess seam.

5 Smooth and pin the princess seam in place. From the grainline of the side front panel, smooth the fabric past the princess seam of the dress form. Pin in place.

NOTE: The excess fabric will drape over the bust level area creating ease at the princess seam between the notches.

6 Mark all key areas of the dress form on the side front panel.

Princess Seam

Style Line Notches Match to center front panel notches.

Bustline Styled Neckline

Side Seam

Hem

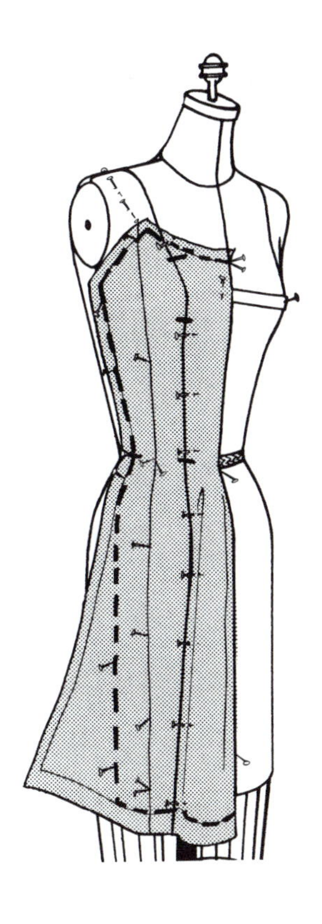

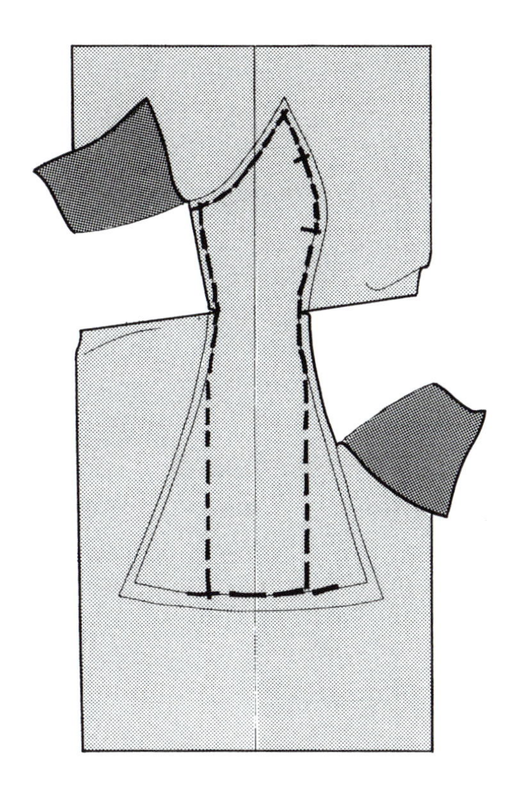

7 **True up all lines.** Remove the side front panel from the dress form and true up all the lines. Add the amount of flare desired at the hemline of the princess seam and the side seam. Blend this flare into the waistline.

Add seam allowances and trim all excess fabric. Pin the front panel to the side front panel. Place the drape on the dress form to check seams, notches, and balance.

Center Back Princess Panel—*Draping Steps*

1 **Pin the center back grainline** fold of the fabric to the center back position of the dress form. The back panel should extend at least 3 inches above the back styled neckline.

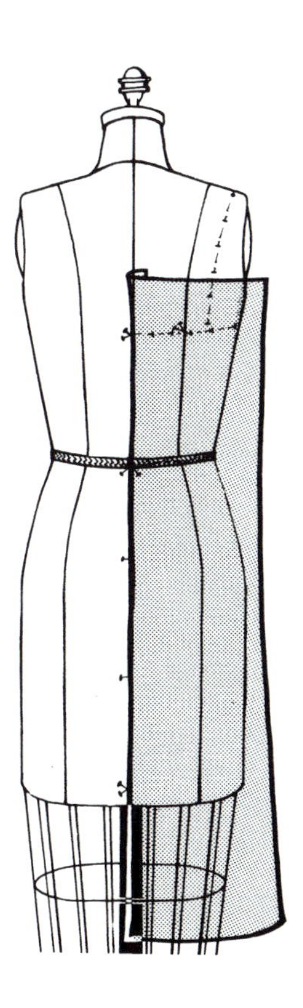

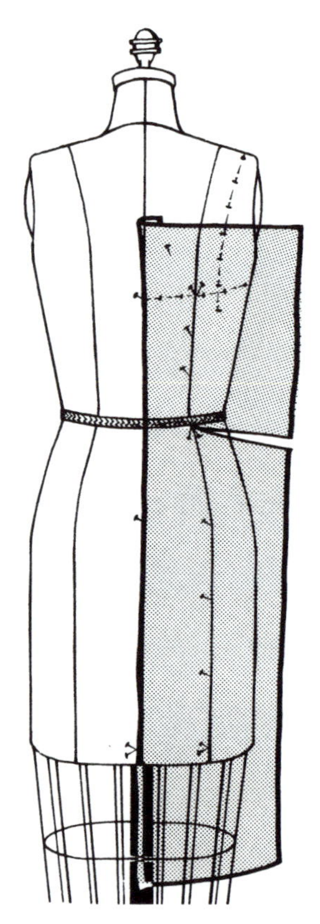

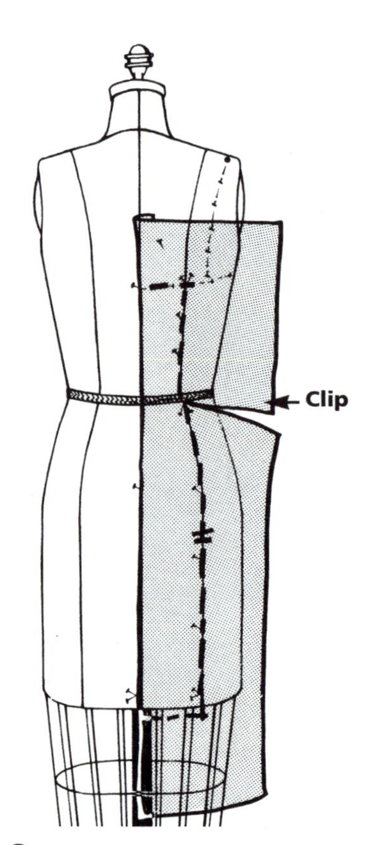

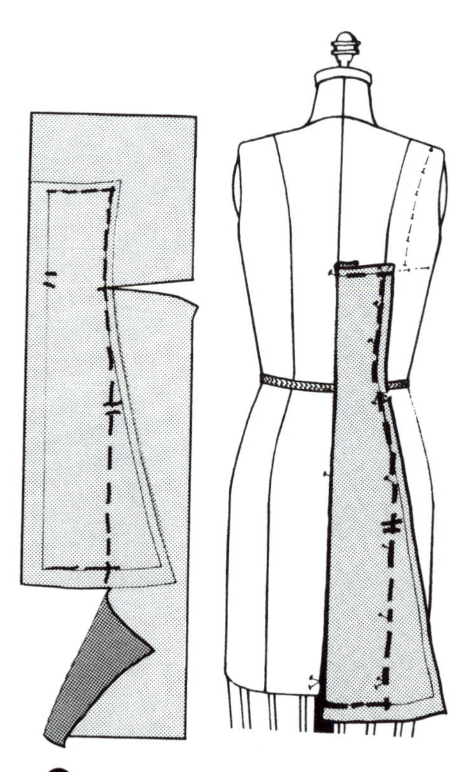

2 **Clip the waistline at the princess seam.**

3 **Drape the princess seam.** Smooth the fabric across the dress form from center back to just past the princess seam. Pin in place.

NOTE: The waist area will drape smoothly, but will not be snug.

4 **Mark all key areas** of the dress form on the center back panel.

Bustline Styled Neckline

Back Princess Seam

Style Line Notches A double notch is used in the back.

Hem

5 **True up all lines.** Remove the center back panel drape from the dress form and true up all lines. Add the amount of flare desired at the hemline of the princess seam. Blend this flare into the waistline at the princess seam.

Add seam allowances and trim all excess fabric. Place the drape back on the dress form.

Side Back Princess Panel—Draping Steps

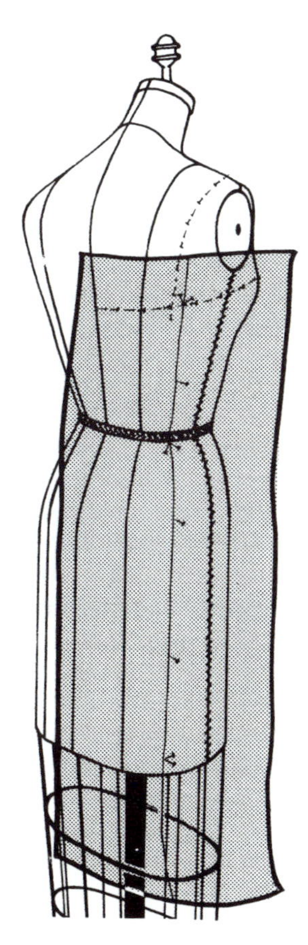

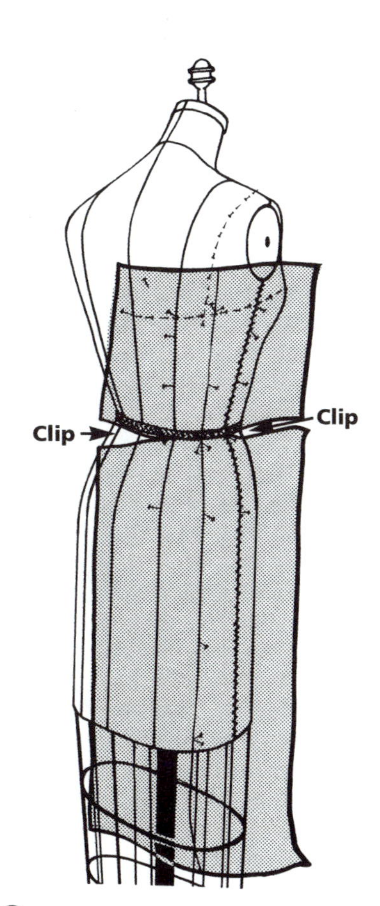

1 **Pin the grainline of the side back panel** to the center of the back princess panel on the dress form.

2 **Clip the waistline at the side seam.**

3 **Smooth and pin the side seam in place.** From the grainline of the side back panel, smooth the fabric past the side seam of the dress form. Pin the side seam in place.

4 **Clip the waistline at the princess seam.**

5 **Smooth and pin the back princess seam in place.** From the grainline of the side back panel, smooth the fabric past the princess seam of the dress form. Do not allow the grainline to slip out of position. Pin the princess seam in place.

6 **Mark all key areas** of the dress form on the side back panel.

Princess Seam

Styleline Notches Match to center back panel double notches.

Bustline Styled Neckline

Side Seam

Hem

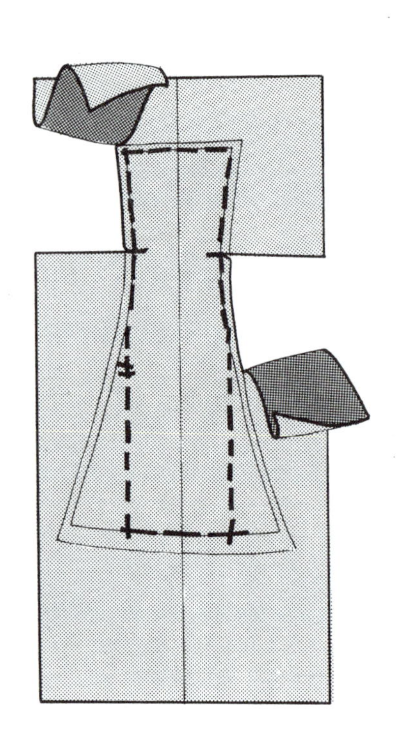

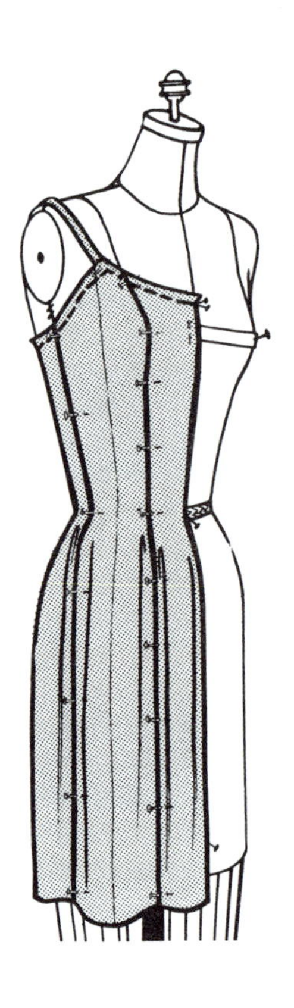

7 **True up all lines.** Remove the drape from the dress form and true up all lines. Add the amount of flare desired at the hemline of the princess seam and the side seam. Blend this flare into the waistline.

Add seam allowances and trim all excess fabric. Pin the entire garment together and place the drape on the dress form. Check for accuracy, fit, and hang.

Notes

Chapter Twelve

Skirts

Objectives

By studying the various draping steps in this chapter, the designer should be able to accomplish the following:

- Recognize grain and crossgrain of fabric in relation to the hip level line of front and back skirt variations.
- Design and drape variations for flared, dirndl, peg, and circular skirt styles.
- Drape a flat piece of fabric into a fitted waistline without darts and create flares falling from the upper hip of the body.
- Drape a flat piece of fabric and draw in fullness into a waistline with pleats and fullness.
- Drape a flat piece of fabric and shape multiple flares which fall from the fitted dartless waistline into multiple flares at the lower edge of the hemline.
- Check and balance the front and back side seams on all skirt variations.
- True up and visualize the front and back skirt pieces in relation to the figure.
- Check the results of the draping process for the skirt back and make necessary changes.

Flared Skirt

The flared skirt is fitted in at the waist and hip area with flares falling from the bottom of the hip. The waistline seam has a distinctive semicircular curve. When the waistline curve is sewn into a straight waistband or waistline, the lower section flows evenly and smoothly over the hip.

The traditional flared skirt does not have a center front seam. However, it does have side seams and a center back seam. This skirt is also called an A-Line skirt.

Manufacturers use the flared (A-Line) skirt as a block or sloper. The designs created from the flared skirt have a definite A-Line or circular silhouette. Style lines, waistbands, a variety of pockets, and different hem lengths can easily be adapted to create a combination of designs. The length of the skirt is dictated by the season and, of course, the occasion and purpose of the design.

It is important to drape a flared skirt in the same fabric quality required by the finished design.

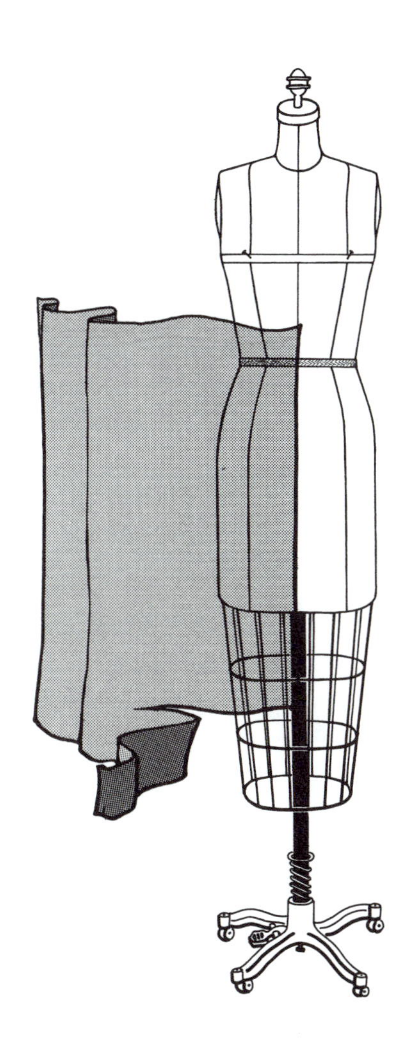

1 Measure the length (along the straight of grain) for both the front and back skirt from 5 inches above the waist tape to the desired length of the design.

Snip and tear the fabric at this length.

2 Divide the fabric piece in half. Fold the fabric from selvage to selvage. Snip and tear the piece in half lengthwise.

One piece will be used for the skirt front and the other piece will be used for the skirt back.

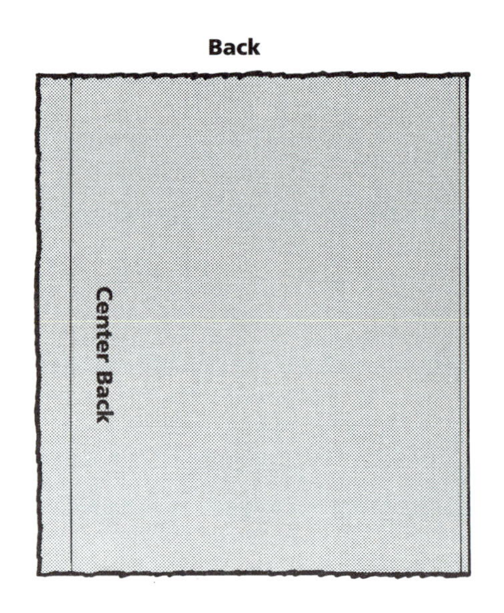

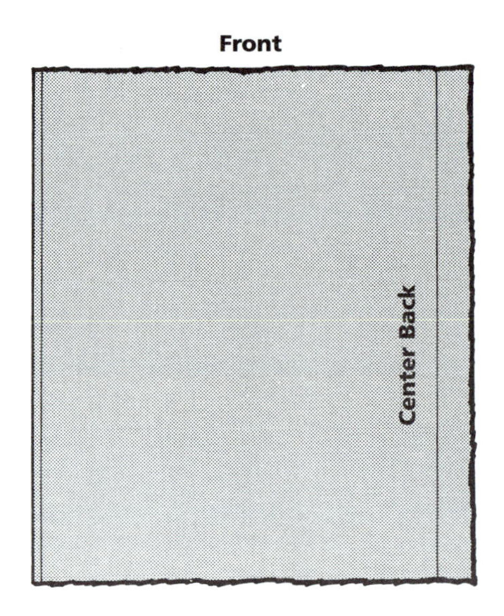

3 **Draw the center front and center back grainlines** on the fabric 1 inch from the torn edge, and press under.

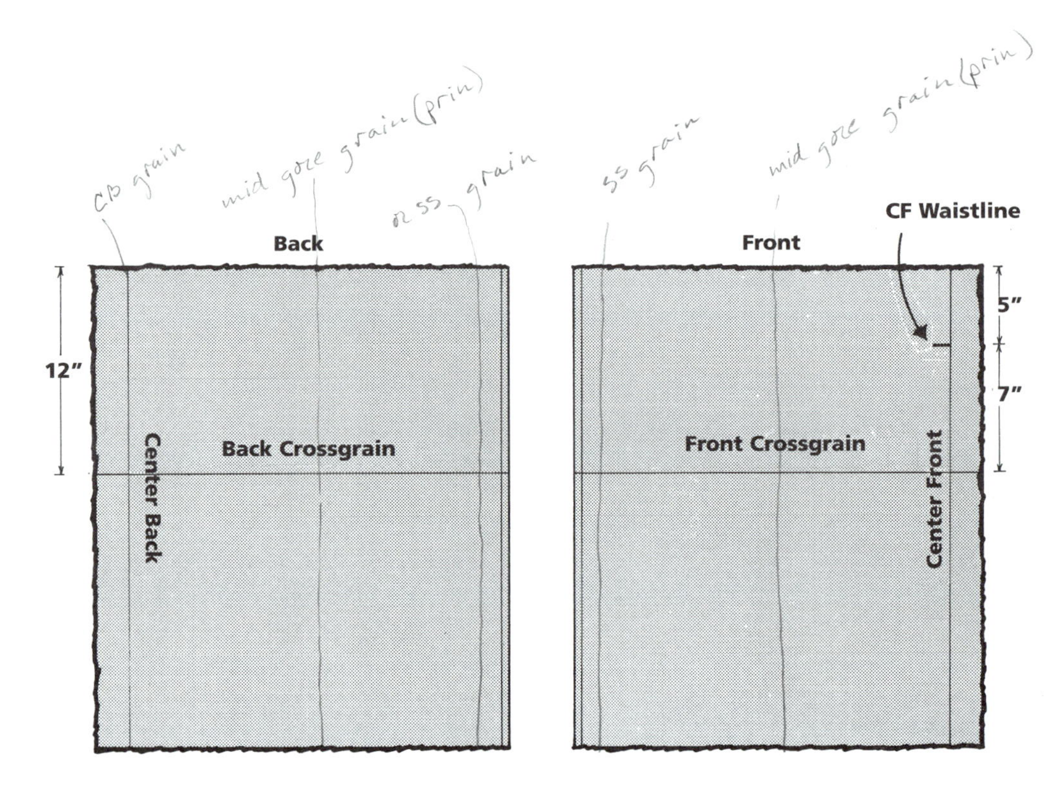

4 **Crossmark the waistline.** Measure down 5 inches from the top of the fabric (on the grainline). Pencil in a waistline mark.

5 **Draw a perfect crossgrain at the hip level on both the front and back skirts.**

a. On the skirt front, measure down **7 inches** from the waistline mark. Draw a perfect front crossgrain at this level.

b. On the skirt back, measure down **12 inches** (on the grainline) from the top edge of the fabric. Draw a perfect back crossgrain at this level.

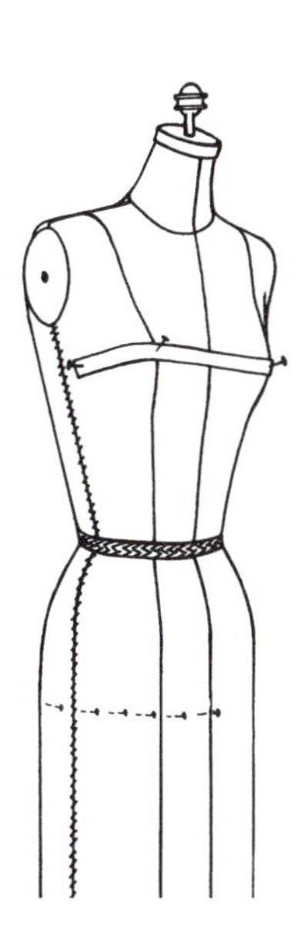

Prepare the dress form.

Pin, or use style tape, at the front and back hip level line.

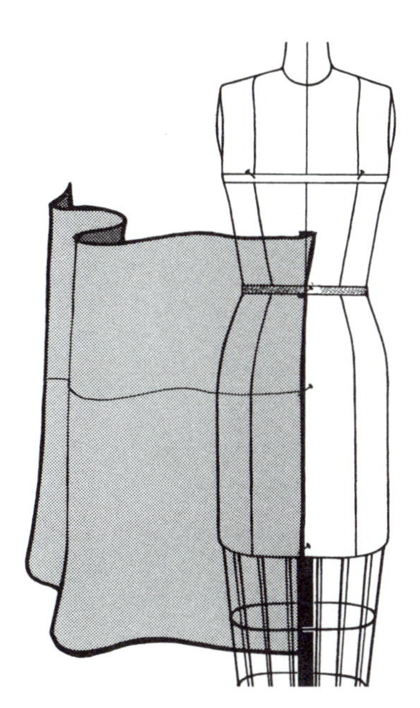

1 Pin the center front grainline fold of the fabric to the center front position of the dress form.

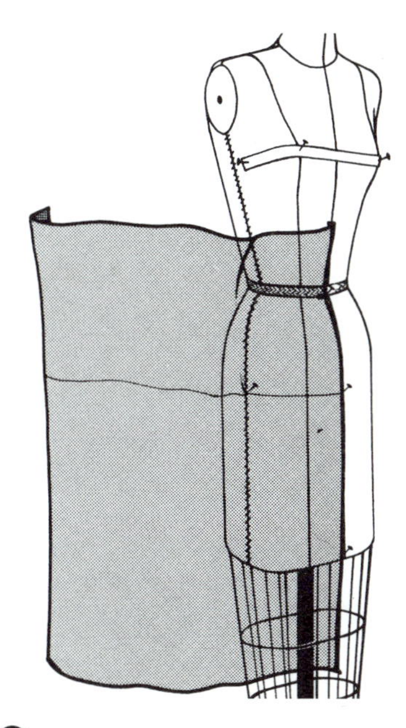

2 Smooth and pin the crossgrain of the fabric at the hip level of the dress form to the side seam. Anchor a pin at the side seam/hip level.

3 Drape the waistline of the front panel. Clip the fabric from the top edge down to the waistline and trim excess fabric. Smooth the fabric over the dress form at the waistline from the center front over to the side seam. Pin at the side seam/waist corner.

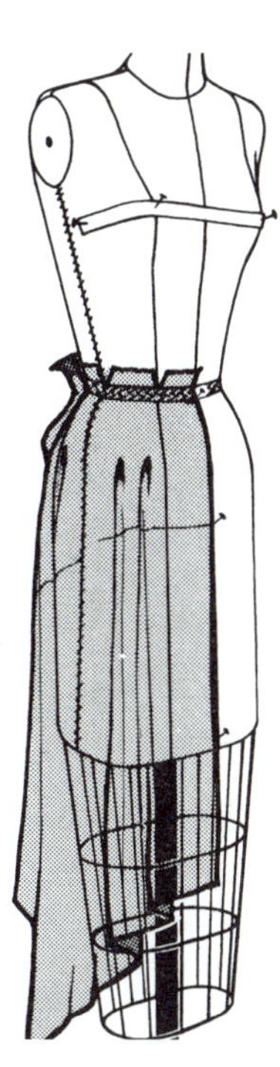

4 Remove the pin at the side seam/hip and allow the drape to fall freely.

NOTE: Two skirt flares will fall from the hip level.

5 Mark all key areas.

Waistline Front

Side Seam

Hem Follow the bottom of the dress form or rung.

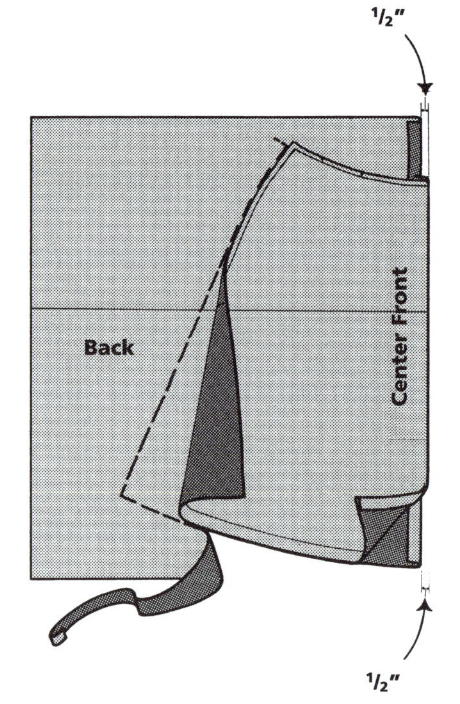

6 True up the front drape. Remove the fabric drape from the dress form. True up the front drape, add seam allowances, and trim all excess fabric.

7 Draft back skirt drape.

a. Place the skirt front drape on top of the back fabric prepared for the skirt back drape, matching crossgrains.

b. Extend the front grainline fold 1/2 inch past the back grainline fold. Be sure both center grainlines remain parallel. This distance allows for the difference between the back waistline amount and the front waistline amount.

c. Pin both layers of fabric together.

d. Draw the back skirt stitchlines. Follow the same markings as the skirt front (side seam, hem, and temporary waistline).

NOTE: The back waistline will be redone when a final fit is checked. This is because the front and back waistline shape are slightly different.

8 Check the fit and balance of the flared skirt drape.

a. Pin together the front and back side seams. Place this drape on the dress form.

b. Double check the hang of this drape. Pin center front and center back waists. Adjust the back waistline until the skirt hangs properly.

- Side seams of drape fall on side seams of dress form.
- The front and back drapes hang correctly (no twists or sags from the waistline).
- Center back waistline is lower than the trued up waistline of the back drape.

NOTE: If the drape does not hang correctly, this usually indicates that the center back at the waistline should be dropped (approximately 1/4 to 1/2 inch).

c. Pencil in a new back waist shape.

Flared Six Gore Skirt

The flared six gore skirt has vertical seams that divide the basic straight skirt into equal or nonequal panels. This added seam divides the skirt into six gores that are fitted at the waistline and flare out at the hemline. These seams provide the designer with a place to add additional flare, pleats, or decorative stitching.

This classic can be made in a variety of fabrics with a variety of waistbands and pocket details. Its length varies with the season.

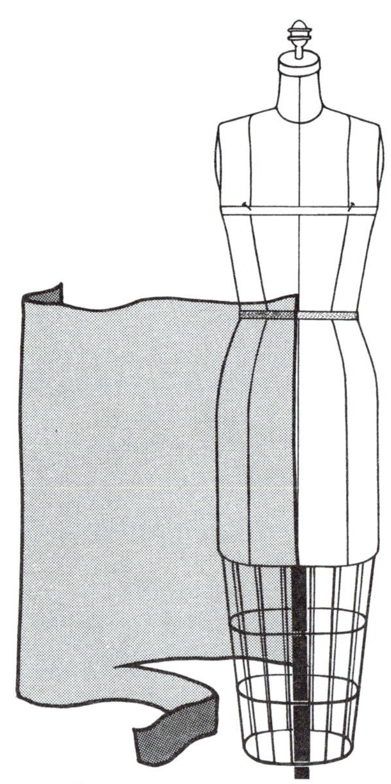

1 **Measure the length** (along the straight of grain) 2 inches above the waist to the desired length of the skirt. Snip and tear the fabric at this length.

2 **Divide the fabric piece in half lengthwise.** Fold fabric from selvage to selvage. Snip and tear fabric piece in half lengthwise.

One piece will be used for the front panels and the other piece will be used for the back panels.

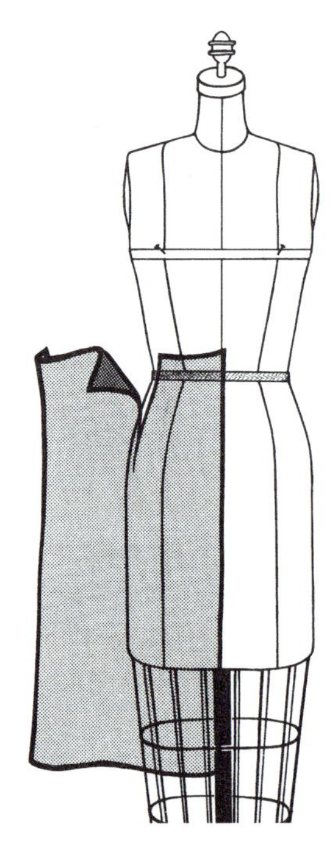

3 **Measure the width for center front panel** (along the crossgrain) from the center front of the dress form to the widest part of the princess seam. Add 4 inches to this width. Snip and tear the fabric at this width.

Use remaining fabric piece for the side front panel.

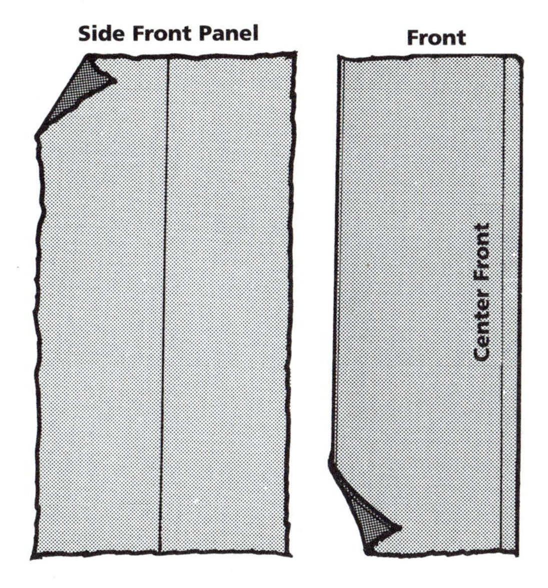

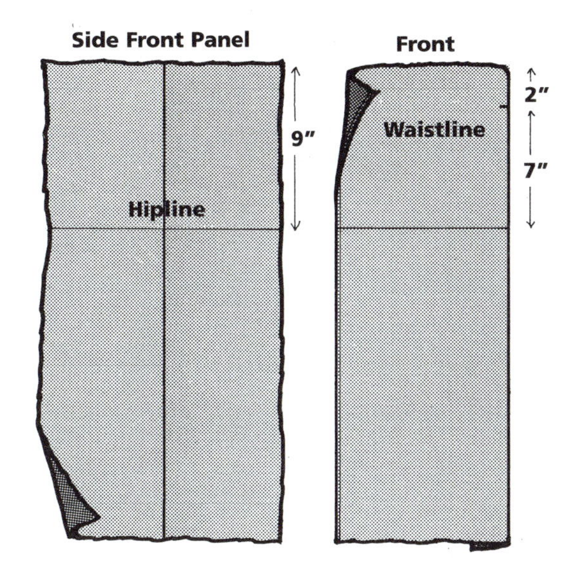

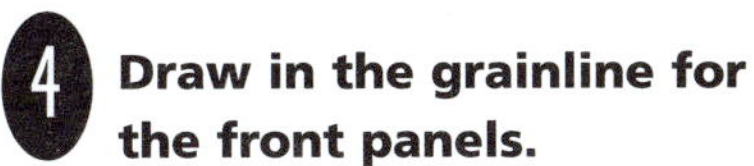

4 Draw in the grainline for the front panels.

a. Draw the grainline for the C.F. panel 1 inch from the torn edge. Press under.

b. Draw the grainline for the side front panel at the center of the fabric piece.

5 Draw a waistline mark. On the center front panel, measure down 2 inches from top edge of the fabric, and draw a waistline mark.

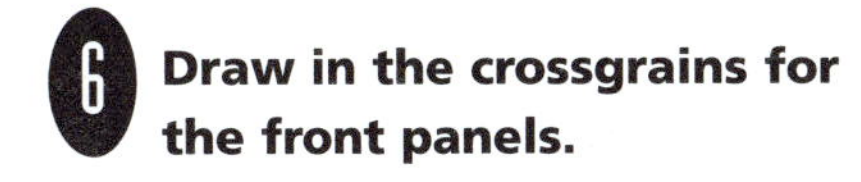

6 Draw in the crossgrains for the front panels.

a. From the waistline mark, measure down another **7 inches** and draw a perfect crossgrain line at this level.

b. On the side front panel, measure down **9 inches** and draw a perfect crossgrain line.

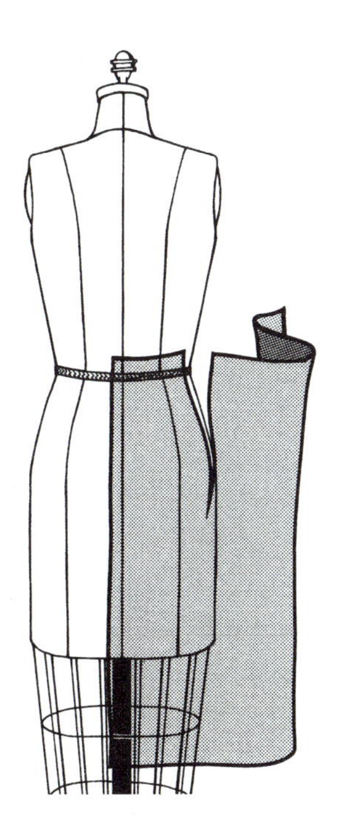

7 Measure the width for the center back panel (along the crossgrain). Measure from center back of the dress form to the widest part of the back princess seam. Add 4 inches to this width. Snip and tear the fabric at this width.

Use remaining fabric piece for the side back panel.

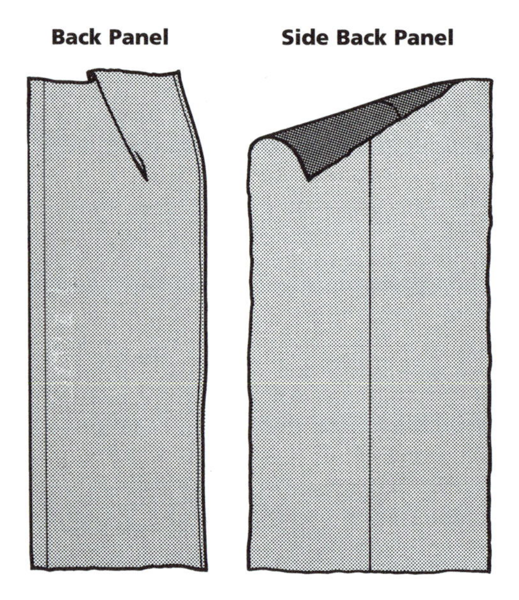

8 **Draw the grainline for the center back panel** 1 inch from the torn edge, and press under.

9 **Draw the grainline for the side back panel** at the center of the fabric piece.

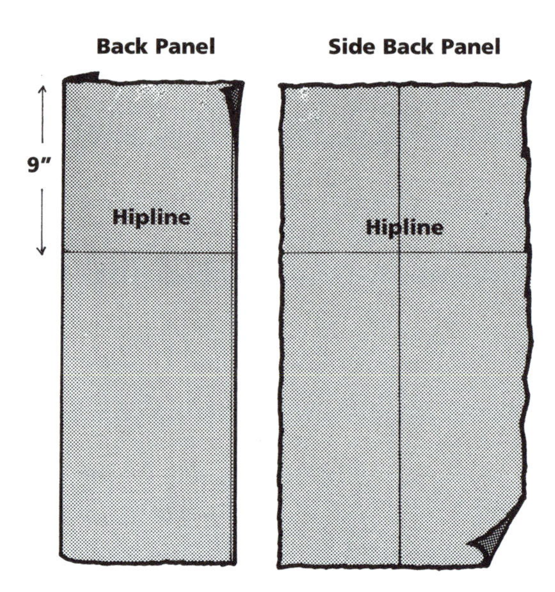

10 **Draw the crossgrain lines of the back panels** 9 inches from the top edge of both back panels.

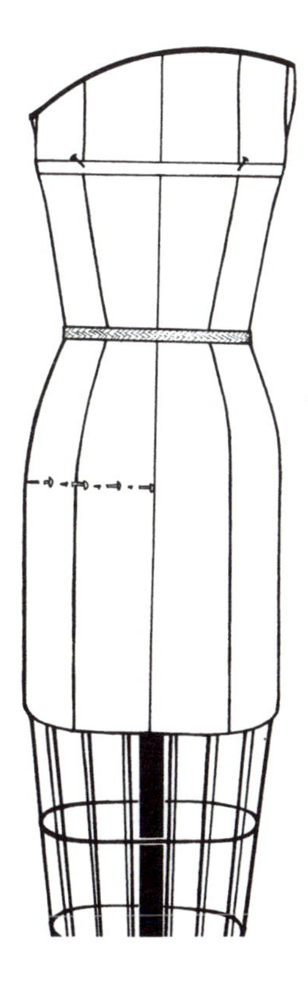

Prepare the dress form.

Pin, or use style tape, at the front and back hip level line.

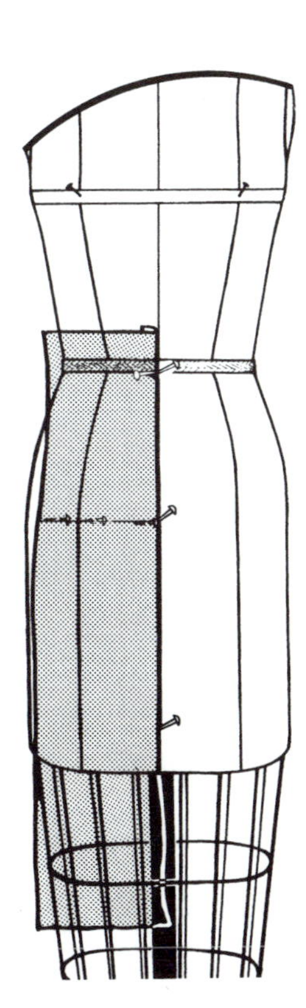

1 Pin the center front grainline fold of the fabric on the center front position of the dress form.

2 Align the fabric crossgrain to the hip level line on the dress form. Pin both the center front and the crossgrain.

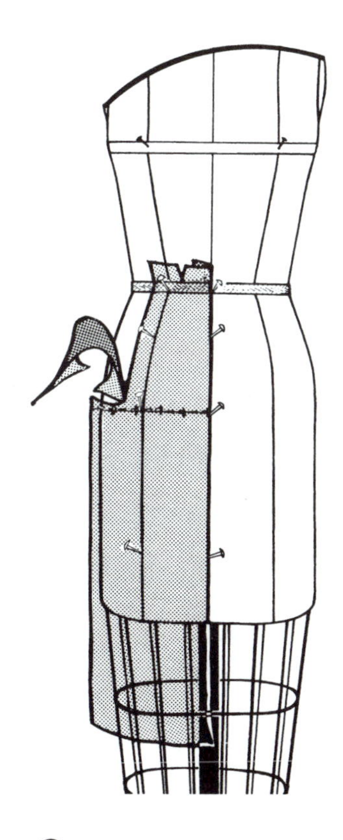

3 Drape the waistline and the princess seam of the center front panel.

a. Carefully trim and clip the fabric from the top edge down to the waistline. Smooth the fabric over the dress form waist tape just past the princess seam. Pin in place.

b. Drape the front princess seam. Smooth the fabric over the entire princess seam of the dress form from the waistline down to the bottom of the dress form. Trim the fabric at the princess seam down to the hip level.

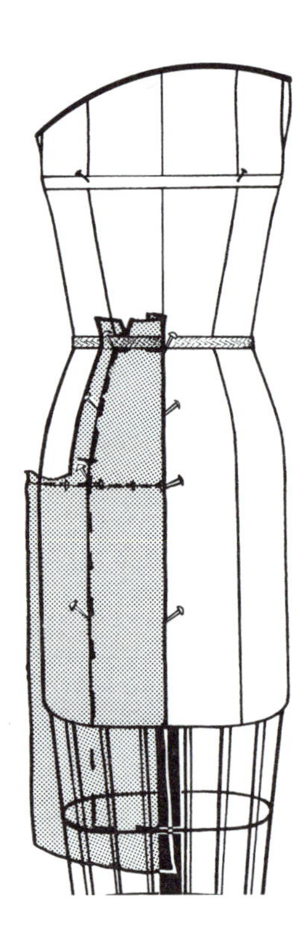

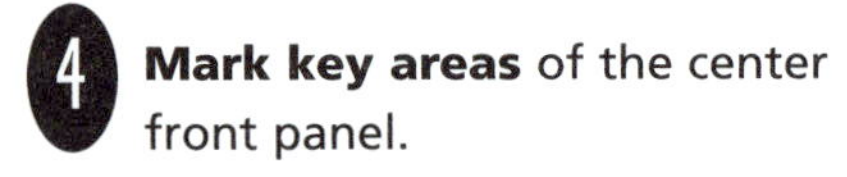

4 **Mark key areas** of the center front panel.

Waistline Lightly mark C.F. to the princess seam.

Princess Seam Lightly mark waistline to bottom.

Style Line Notch Mark just above crossgrain.

Hem

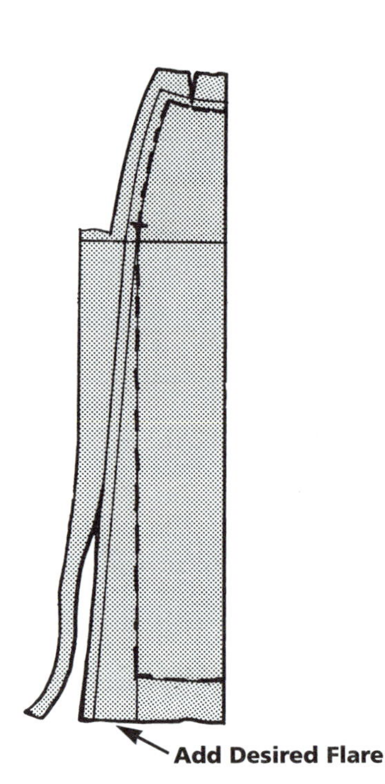

5 **True up all lines.**

a. Remove the center front panel drape from the dress form. True up all lines.

b. Add desired flare at hemline. This amount is usually 1 inch to 2 inches, depending on the length and style of skirt. Blend this additional flare into the princess seamline just above or just below the crossgrain.

c. Add seam allowances and trim all excess fabric.

6 **Pin the grainline of the side front panel** to the center of the princess panel on the dress form.

7 **Match the crossgrain of the side front panel** to the hip level line. Pin the crossgrain at this level.

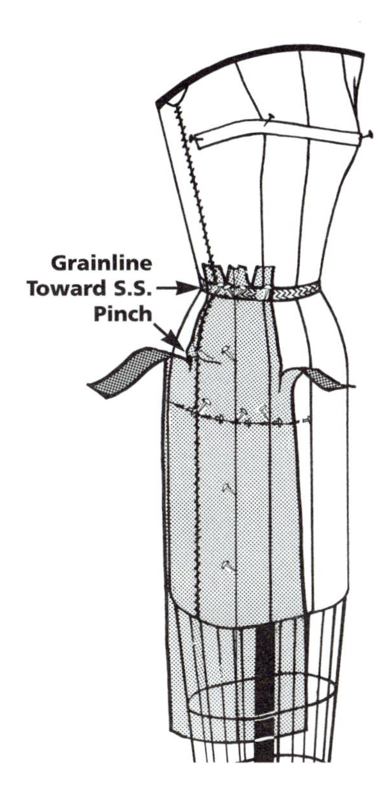

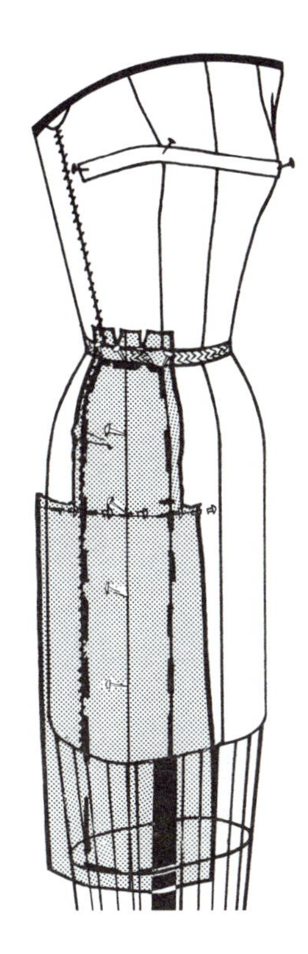

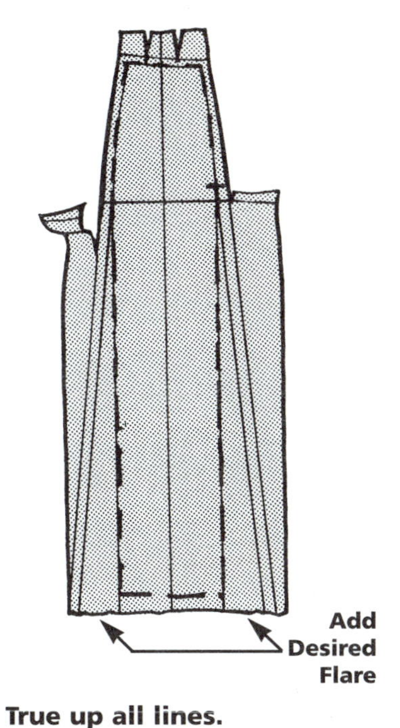

8 Drape the waistline, princess seam, and side seam of the side front panel.

a. Clip the fabric from the top edge down to the waistline. Smooth the waistline from the grainline toward the seam.

b. Smooth the princess seam from the grainline to past the princess seam of the dress form from the waistline down to the bottom of the dress form. Trim the fabric at the princess seam down to the hipline.

c. Smooth the side seam from the grainline to past the side seam over the hip. Trim excess fabric from the waistline down to the hipline.

NOTE: It may be necessary to allow the grainline, at the waistline, to fall about 1/2 inch toward the side seam. This will allow the side panel to be smooth over the princess seam and creates a pinch at the side seam. (See illustration)

9 Mark key areas of the side front panel.

Waistline Lightly mark from princess seam to side seam.

Princess Seam Lightly mark from the waistline to the bottom.

Style Line Notch Mark just above crossgrain to match front notch.

Hem

10 True up all lines.

a. Remove the side front panel drape from the dress form. True up all lines.

b. Add desired flare at the hemline. This amount will match the amount used for the center front panel. Blend this additional flare into the princess seamline and the side seamline. Be sure to blend this amount smoothly just above or just below the crossgrain.

c. Add seam allowances and trim excess fabric.

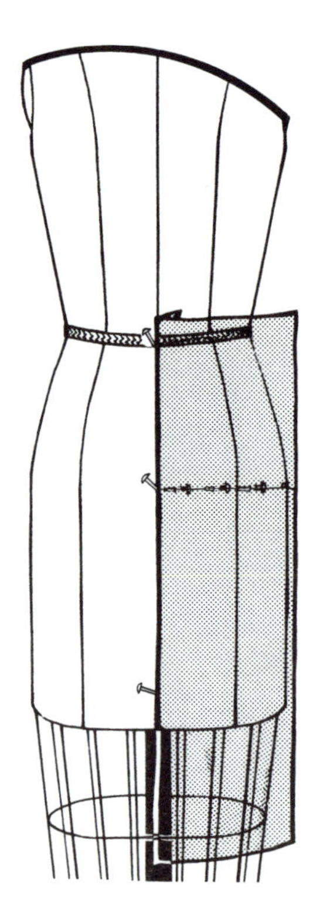

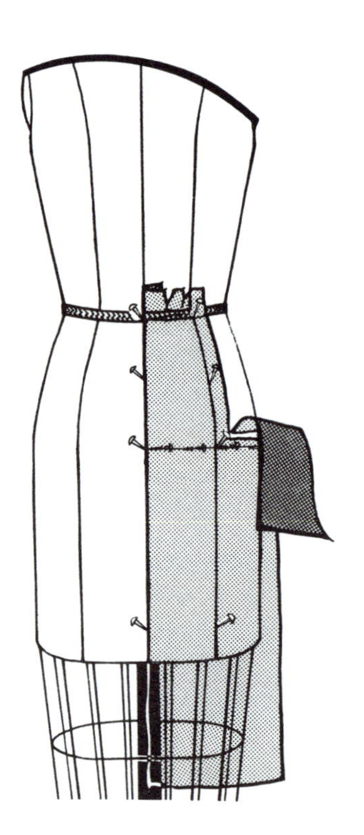

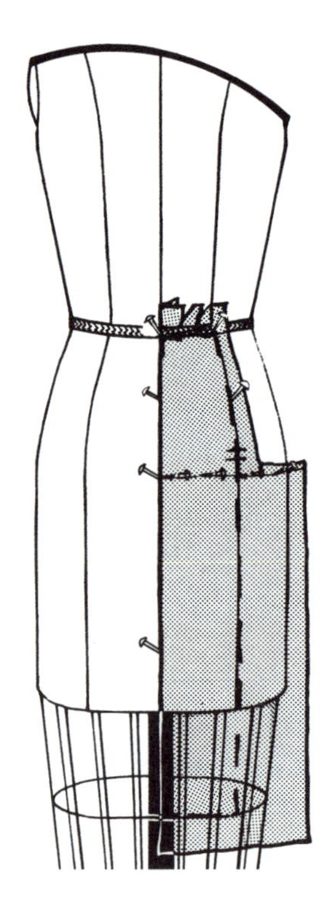

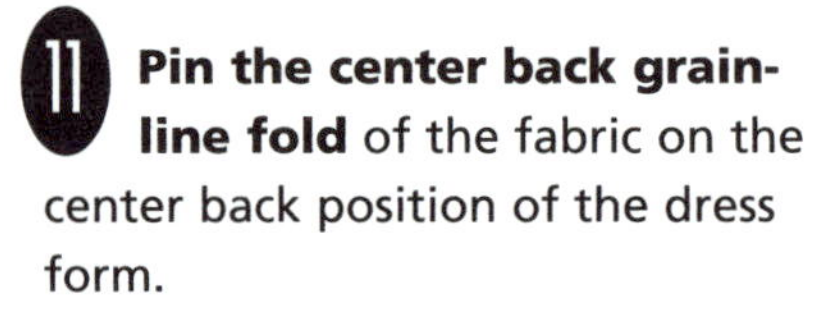

11 **Pin the center back grainline fold** of the fabric on the center back position of the dress form.

12 **Match the crossgrain to the hip level line.** Pin both the center back and the crossgrain.

13 **Drape the waistline of the center back panel.** Carefully trim and clip the fabric from the top edge down to the waistline. Smooth the fabric over the dress form waist tape just past the princess seam. Pin waistline in place.

14 **Drape the back princess seam.** Smooth the fabric over the entire princess seam of the dress form from the waistline down to the bottom of the dress form. Trim the fabric at the princess seam down to the hipline.

15 **Mark key areas** of the center back panel.

Waistline Lightly mark from C.B. to the princess seam.

Princess Seam Lightly mark from the waist down to bottom.

Style Line Notches Mark double notch just above hipline.

Hem

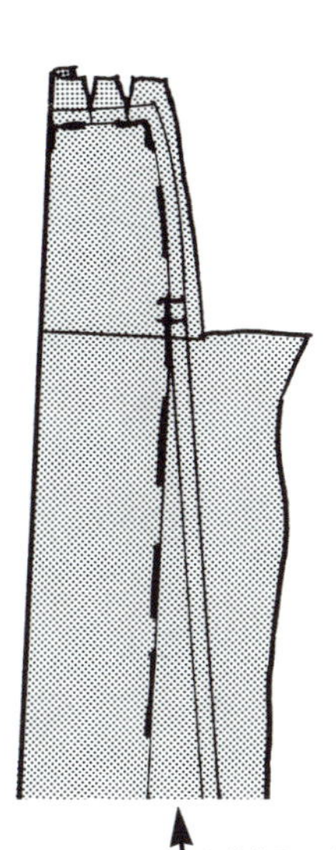

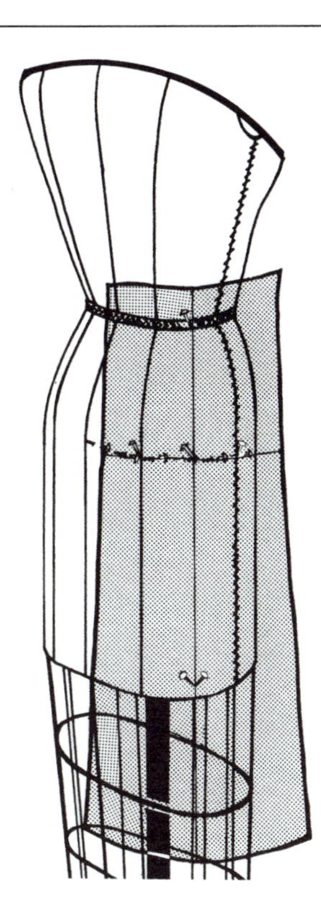

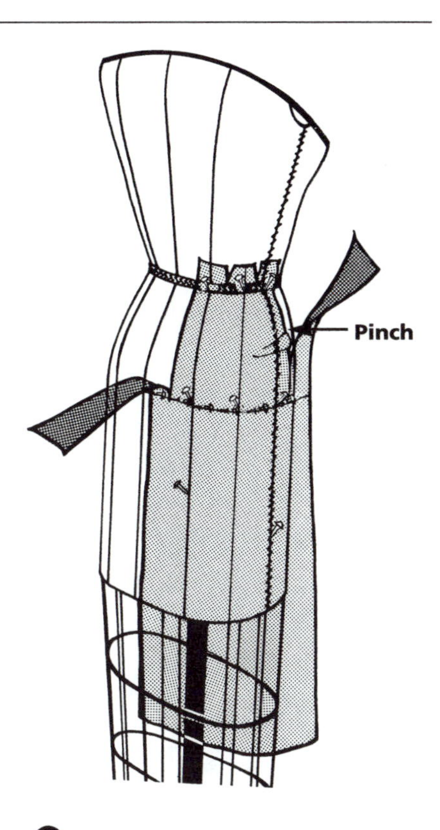

16 True up all lines.

a. Remove the center back panel drape from the dress form. True up all lines.

b. Add desired flare at the hemline. This amount is usually a bit less than the amount of flare added on the front panels. Smooth and blend this additional flare into the princess seam just above or just below the crossgrain.

c. Add seam allowances and trim excess fabric.

17 Pin the grainline of the side back panel to the center of the back princess panel on the dress form.

18 Match the crossgrain of the side back panel to the hip level line. Pin the crossgrain at this level.

19 Drape the waistline. Clip the fabric from the top edge down to the waistline. Smooth the waistline from the grainline toward the seam.

20 Smooth and drape the princess seam from the grainline to past the princess seam of the dress form from the waistline down to the bottom of the dress form. Trim the fabric at the princess seam down to the hipline.

21 Drape and smooth the side seam from the grainline to past the side seam over the hip. Trim excess fabric from the waistline down to the hipline.

NOTE: It may be necessary to allow the grainline, at the waistline, to fall about 1/2 inch toward the side seam. This will allow the side panel to be smooth over the princess seam and creates a pinch at the side seam. (See illustration)

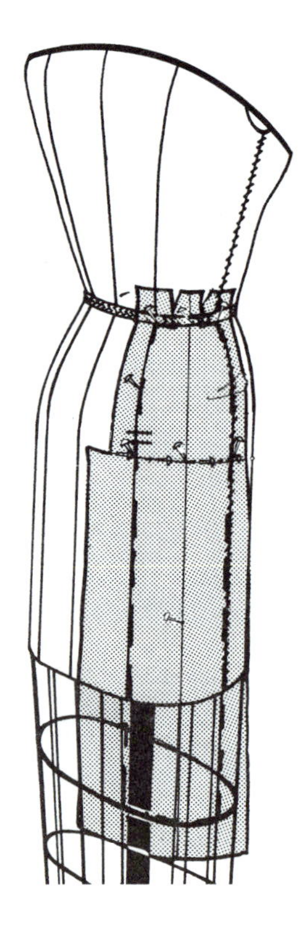

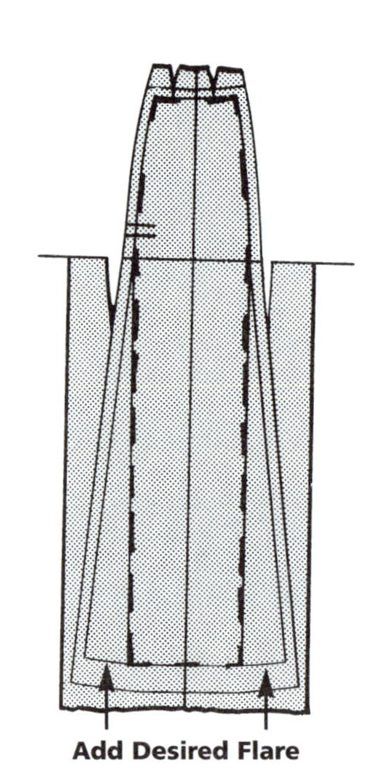

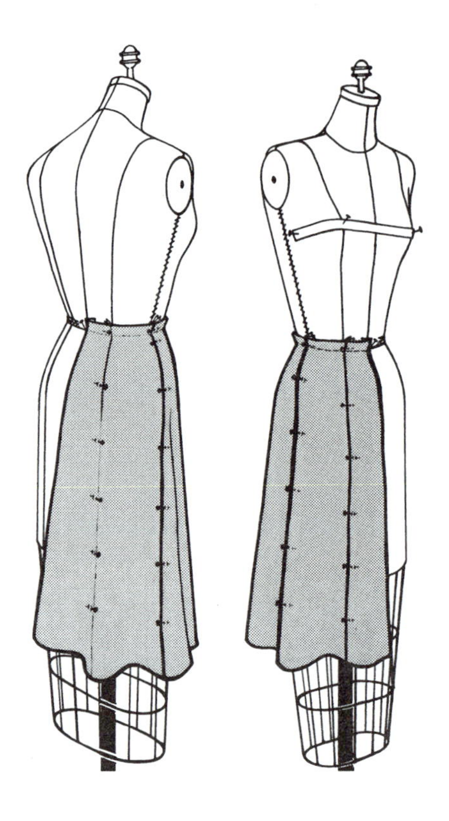

Mark key areas of the side back panel.

Waistline Lightly mark from side seam to princess seam.

Princess Seam Lightly mark from waistline to bottom.

Side Seam Lightly mark entire side seam.

Style Line Notch Mark double notch to match back panel.

Hem

23 **True up all lines.**

a. Remove the side back panel from the dress form. True up all lines.

b. Add desired flare at the hemline. This amount will match the amount used for the center back panel. Blend this additional flare into the princess seamline and the side seam. Be sure to blend this amount smoothly just above or just below the crossgrain, whichever creates the smoother line.

c. Add seam allowances and trim excess fabric.

NOTE: A perfectly balanced skirt has 1/2 inch less flare in the back hemline to balance to the 1/2 inch less in the waistline.

24 Pin and place the entire drape on the dress form. Check for accuracy.

These pleated skirts maintain the same vertical seams as the six gore skirts, which are fitted at the waistline and flare out at the hemline.

Kick Pleat

The gore skirt with kick pleats, however, has vertical seams with an added underpleat extension in the gore. The length and width of a kick pleat depends on the design. A typical pleat is narrower at the top and wider at the hemline.

Box Pleat

The box pleat has the same vertical seams as the kick pleat and the same underpleat extension. However, it has an additional underpiece that is sewn into the pleat extension areas of the skirt.

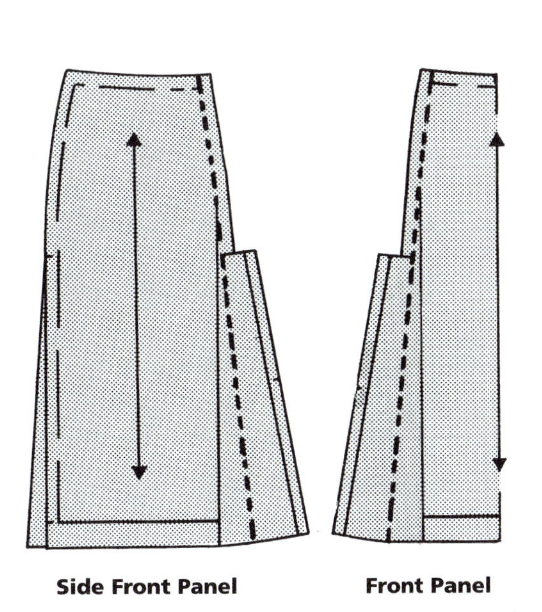

NOTE: Illustrated is a pleat placed on the 3seamline of the gore. The pleat is drawn in from the hip level to the hemline.

When pinning to check for fit and proportion, place the correct sides of the gore panel together. Pin the gore from the top of the waistline, across the top of the pleat, and down to the hemline. After the skirt is pinned, the pleat extension may be pressed to one side. The upper portion of the pleat will then be held in place with decorative topstitching.

Gore Skirt with Kick Pleats and Box Pleats

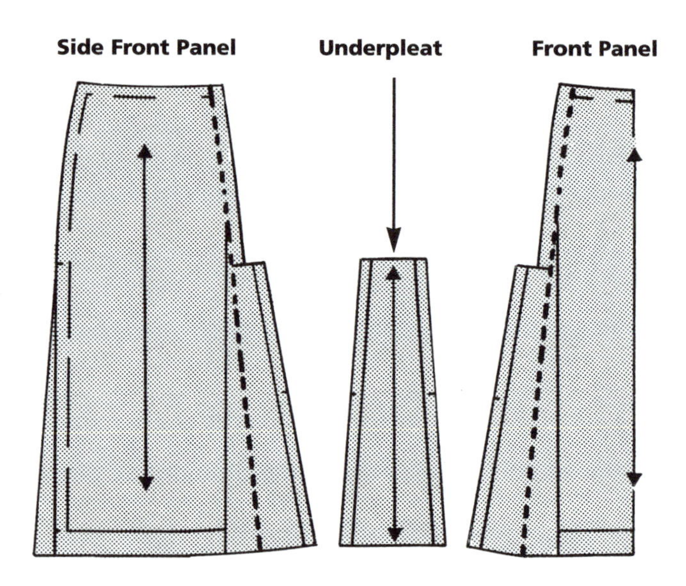

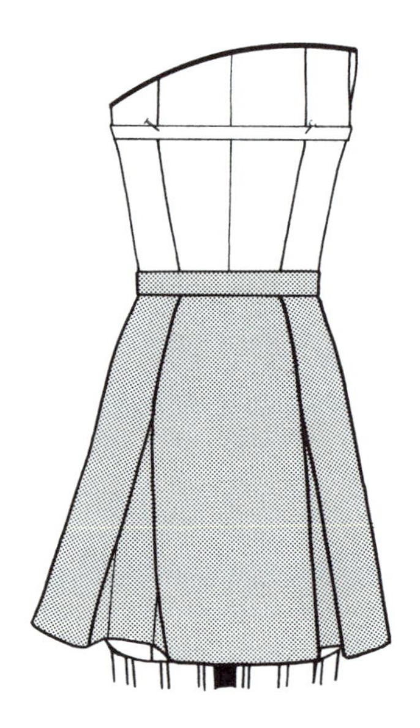

When pinning to check for fit and proportion, pin the additional underpiece to each side of the pleat extension. Then, pin the gore from the top of the waistline down to the pleat. Press each pleat extension back toward the panel and to the center of the underpiece.

These classic pleated skirts can be made in a variety of fabrics with different waistbands and pocket details. Their length varies with the season.

Notes

Dirndl Skirt

The dirndl (or gathered) skirt is a rectangular fabric piece gathered and sewn into a fitted waistline or yoke. The amount of fullness and the lengths may vary.

This is a good lesson for learning to draw in fullness and maintain grainlines.

This skirt offers a fresh and carefree look for many design concepts. The variety of fabrics, pockets, flounces, and trims available can update, accentuate, and enhance the design.

Dirndl Skirt*—Preparing the Fabric*

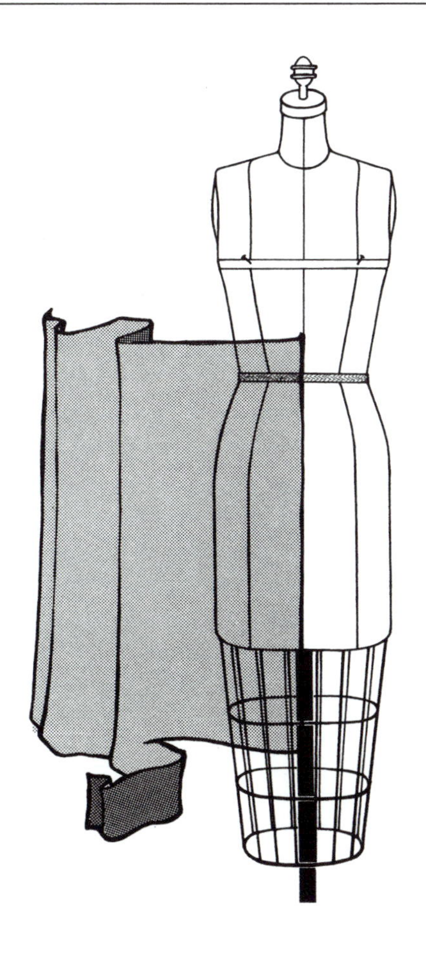

1 **Measure the length** along the straight of grain. Measure for the desired length of the front and back skirt, and add 4 inches. Snip and tear the fabric at this length.

2 **Divide the fabric piece in half.** Fold the fabric from selvage to selvage in half. Snip and tear the fabric at this width.

3 Draw the grainlines for the front and back skirts 1 inch from the torn edge. Press under.

4 Draw in the front and back hipline.

a. Measure down 11 inches from the top edge of the fabric.

b. Draw in a perfect crossgrain at this position. This should be done for the front and back skirts.

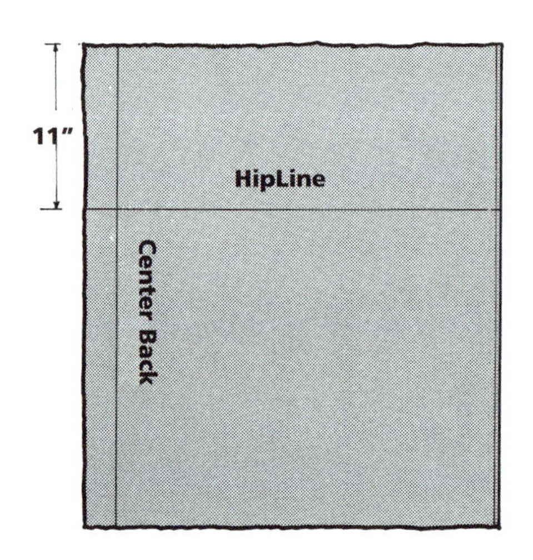

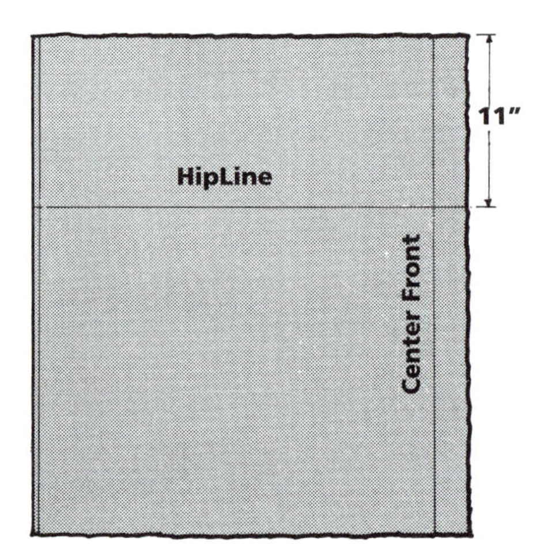

5 Draw a side seam 2 inches from the selvage side of the fabric parallel to the center grainline.

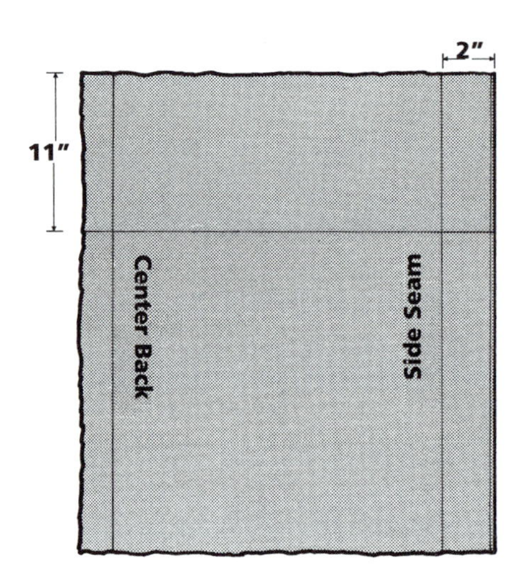

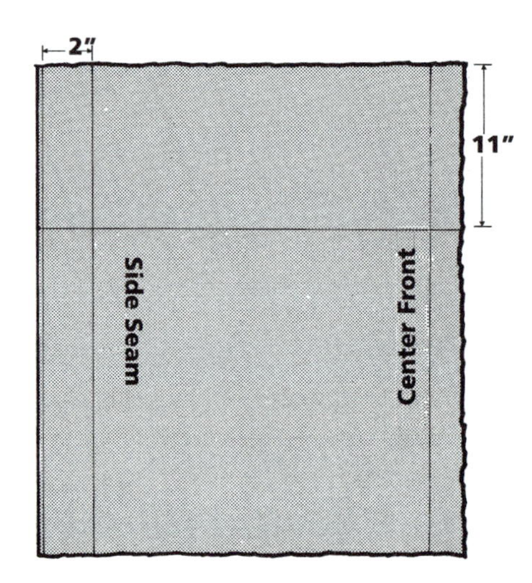

Dirndl Skirt—Draping Steps

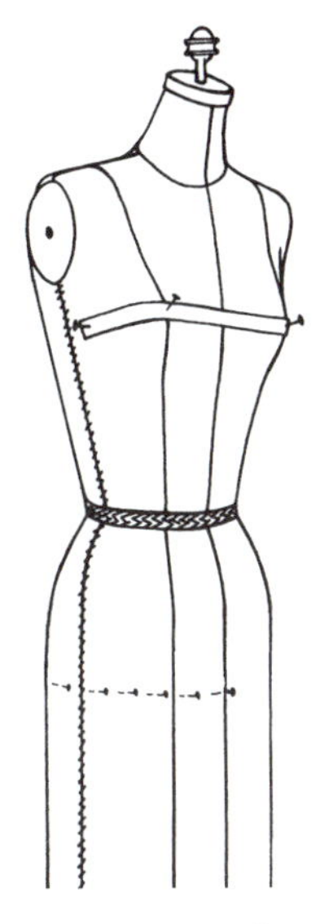

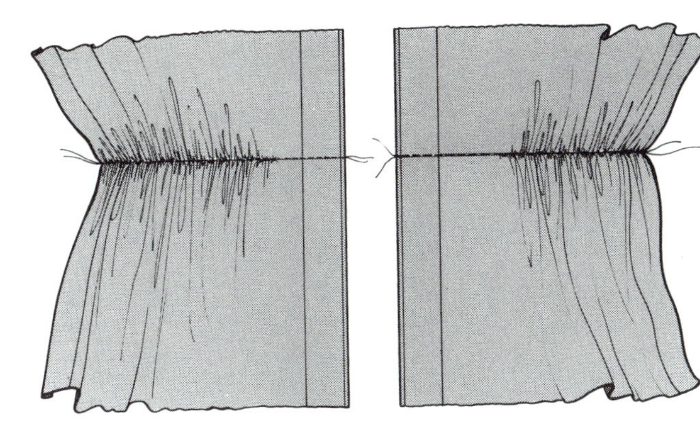

Prepare the dress form.

Measure down 7 inches on the center front of the dress form. Place a tape parallel to the floor at this hip level from center front to center back. Place pins on the dress form at this level and remove the tape.

1 Gather the fabric on the crossgrain line for both the front and back. Bring in the fullness to the amount of the hip measurement.

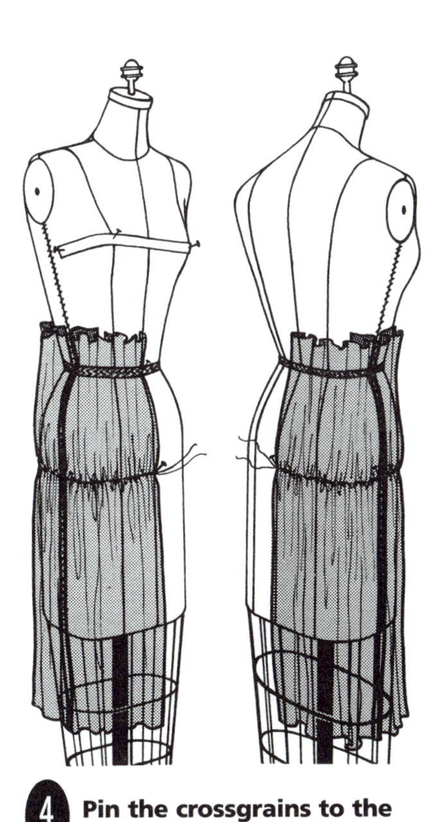

2 Pin the center front and back grainline folds of the fabric pieces on the center positions of the dress form.

3 Align the crossgrain at the hip level.

4 Pin the crossgrains to the hip level of the dress form. Evenly distribute the gathered fabric across the dress form to the side seam at the hip level. Be sure the fabric crossgrains are parallel to the floor and the side seams match.

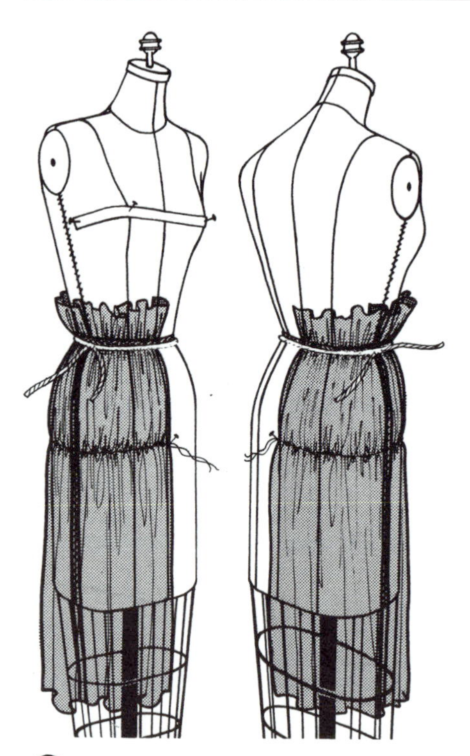

5 Gather the fullness at the waistline. Draw in the fullness at the waistline with a piece of twill tape. Evenly distribute the gathers.

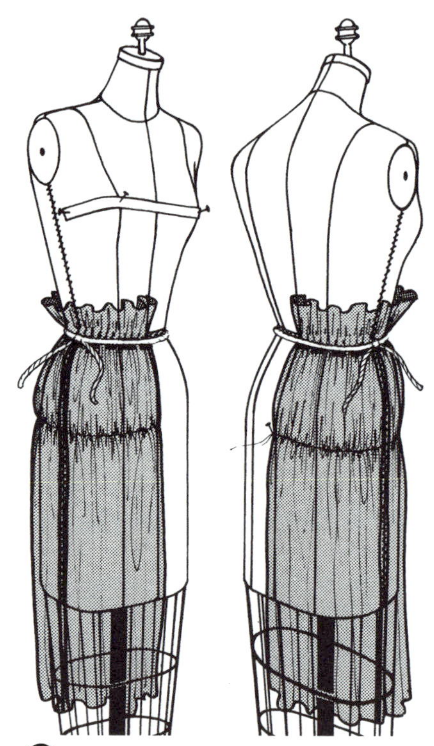

6 Mark key areas.

Waistline

Hem Lightly mark the bottom of the dress form or a rung. The hem should be parallel to the floor.

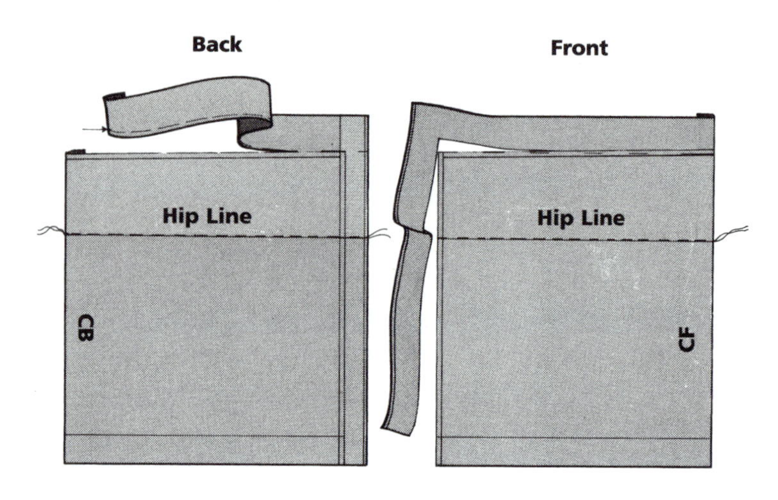

7 True up the drape. Remove the fabric from the dress form, true up the drape, and add seam allowances.

8 Pin the front and back pieces together and place on the dress form to check for accuracy. Make all necessary corrections.

Peg Skirt

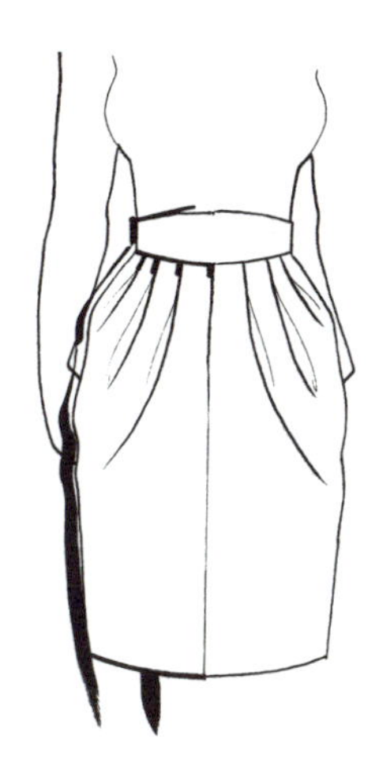

The peg skirt is easily recognized by its billowing fullness over the hip area. This fullness is formed by draping deep folds, which are drawn into the waistline. At the same time, the lower edge is drawn back into the body allowing enough movement with ease and freedom. This skirt is also known as the hobble skirt.

A beautifully draped peg skirt depends largely on the skill of the designer because the waistline details have to be skillfully placed into position to create the hip fullness. This skirt, which is flattering and quite feminine, is usually draped out of soft, pliable fabrics.

Peg Skirt—Preparing the Fabric

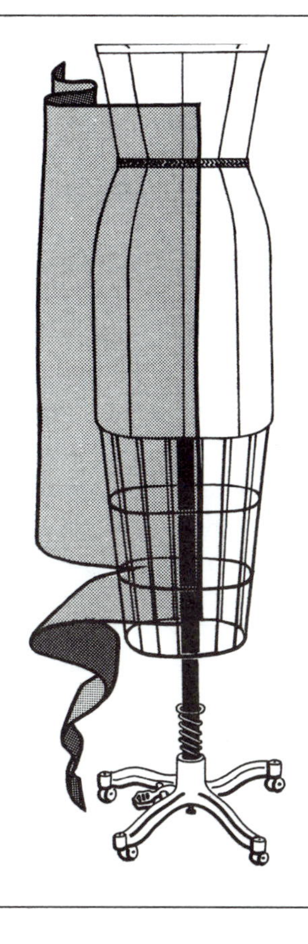

1 **Measure the length** along the straight of grain of the desired skirt and add 6 inches. Snip and tear the fabric at this length.

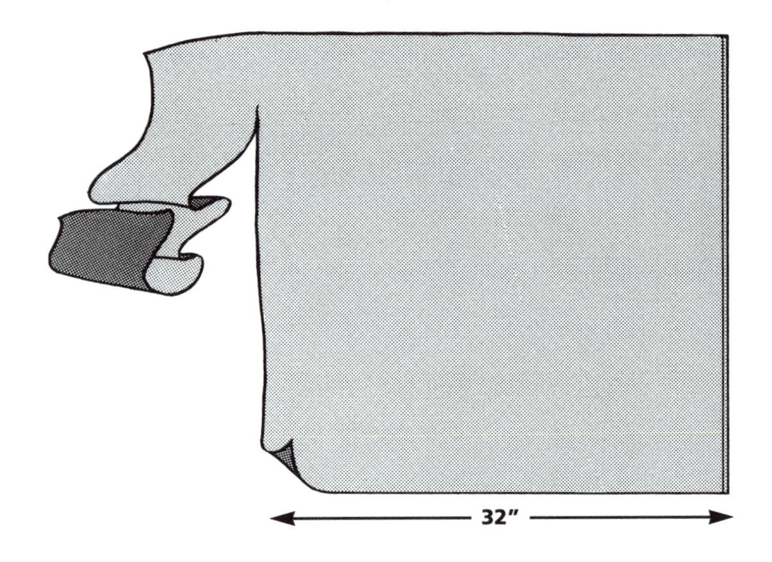

2 **Measure the width** along the crossgrain 32 inches to determine the width of the fabric. Snip and tear the fabric at this width.

NOTE: When the drape is completed, there will be a seam at the center front and a seam at center back. **However,** there will be no side seam.

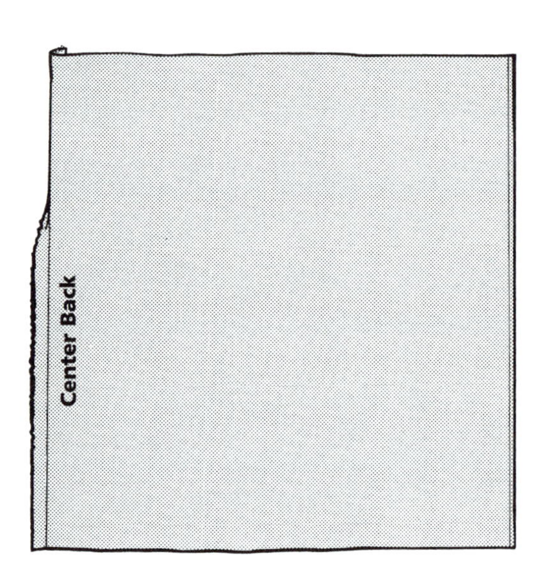

3 **Draw the center back grainline** parallel to the grainline on the left side of the fabric, and press under.

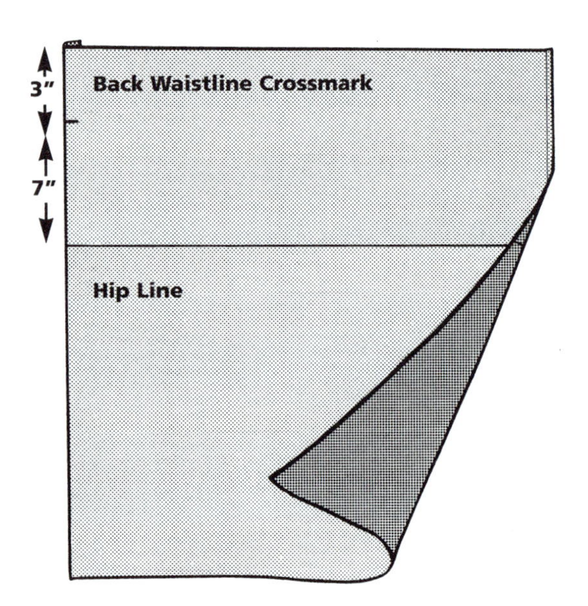

4 **Mark the center back waist position.** From the top edge of the fabric, measure down 3 inches on the center back grainline. Draw a waistline mark.

5 **Draw in the hipline.** On the center back grainline, measure down 7 inches from the waistline mark. Draw a perfect crossgrain.

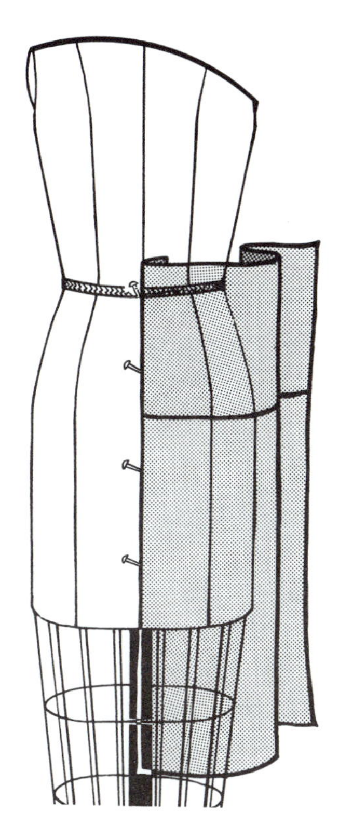

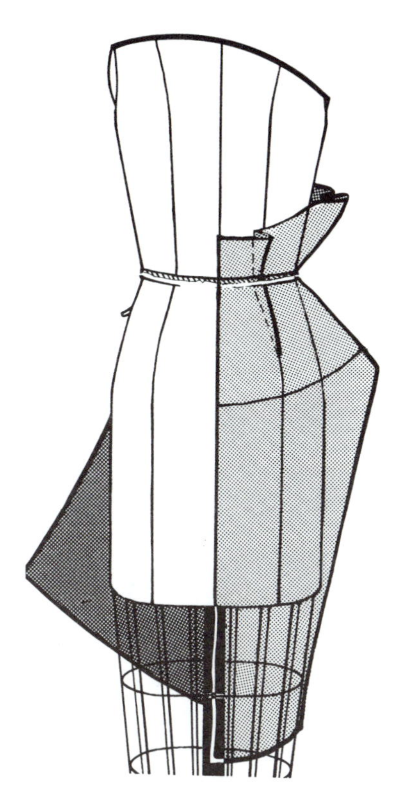

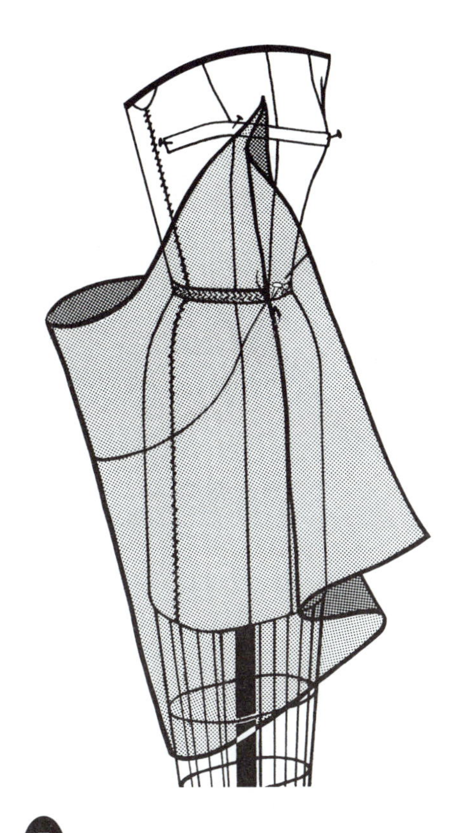

1 **Pin the center back grainline** fold of the fabric to the center back position of the dress form.

2 **Drape the back waistline and back waist dart.** Smooth the fabric across the back waist seam tape to the princess seam. Drape a 1-inch deep back waist dart.

3 **Drape the crossgrain to center front.** Using the hipline on the fabric as a guide, lift and hold the fabric. Draw it into the center front/waist position. Pin the hipline at the center front waistline of the dress form. The grainline will angle in a bias direction.

NOTE: This lifting process will maintain greater fullness at the waist level and minimum fullness at the hem level. However, enough fullness at the hem level must be allowed for walking ease.

If the skirt front is draped on a true bias, maximum waistline fullness is achieved. However, if the center front is draped on a partial bias line, less fullness is created at the waistline.

Both methods are acceptable draping procedures.

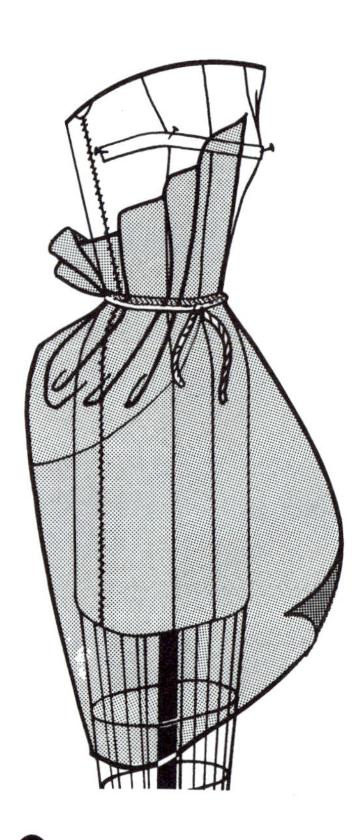

4 Gather the fullness at the waistline. With a piece of twill tape, tie the fabric at the waistline. Evenly distribute the gathers.

5 Pleat the desired number of pleats at the waistline. At the same time, push down slightly on each pleat to help billow the fabric at the hip level. Also, slightly pull up the center front bias waist position.

NOTE: Pushing down and maintaining gathers (instead of pleats) will give a style variation to this very dramatic skirt. The number of pleats or darts and the amount of fullness desired is up to the individual designer.

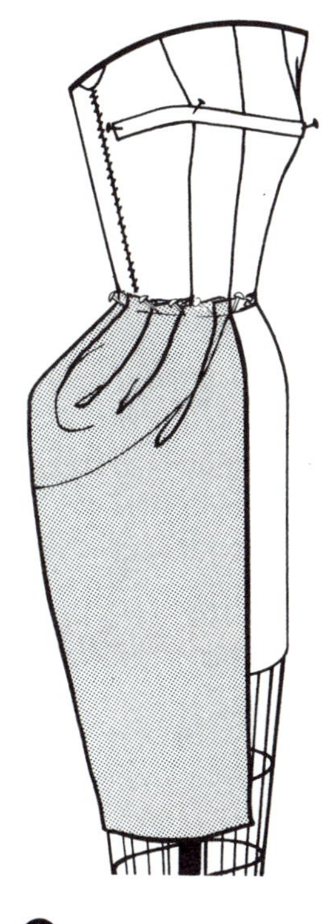

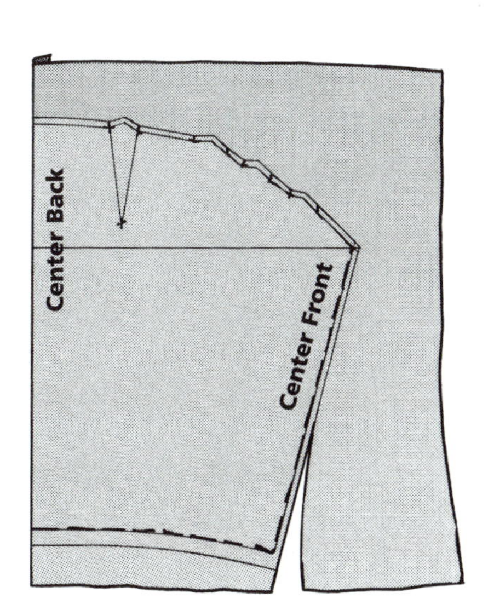

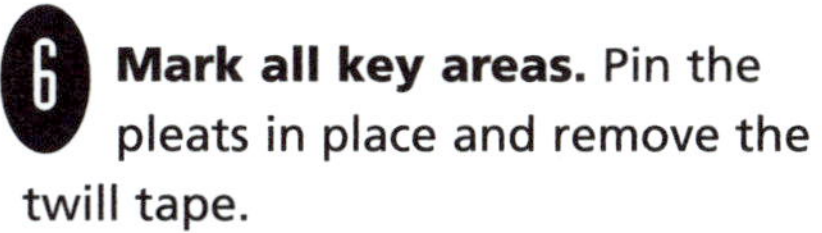

6 **Mark all key areas.** Pin the pleats in place and remove the twill tape.

Waistline
Pleats
Hem

7 **True up the drape.** Remove the fabric from the dress form. True up the drape, add seam allowances, and trim excess fabric. Pin in the pleats and place drape back on the dress form. Check for accuracy, making all necessary corrections.

Circular Skirt

The circular skirt has a fitted waist seam with an exaggerated circular curve in the waistline. When this waistline is sewn into a straight waistband, multiple flares of fullness fall into the hemline, thereby creating a multiple flared skirt silhouette. The lower edge may have any amount of sweep desired, depending on the amount of fullness draped into the waist. It may also be designed in any length. For example, a short circular skirt may be used to design a skating or ballet costume, whereas a longer softer design may be more suitable for an evening dress.

Circular Skirt—Preparing the Fabric

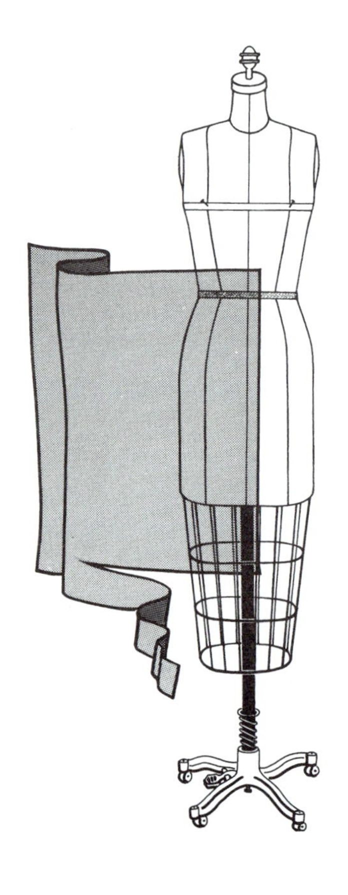

1 **Measure the length** along the straight of grain. Measure for the front and back skirt 5 inches above the waist tape to the desired length of the design.

Snip and tear the fabric at this length.

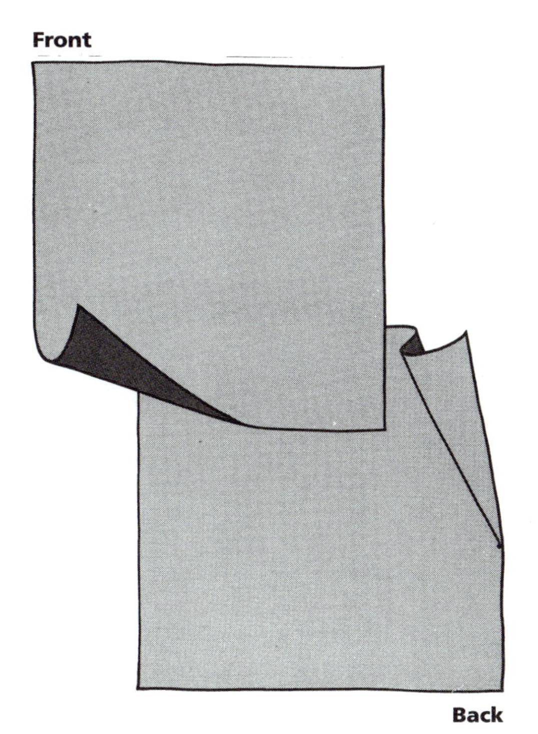

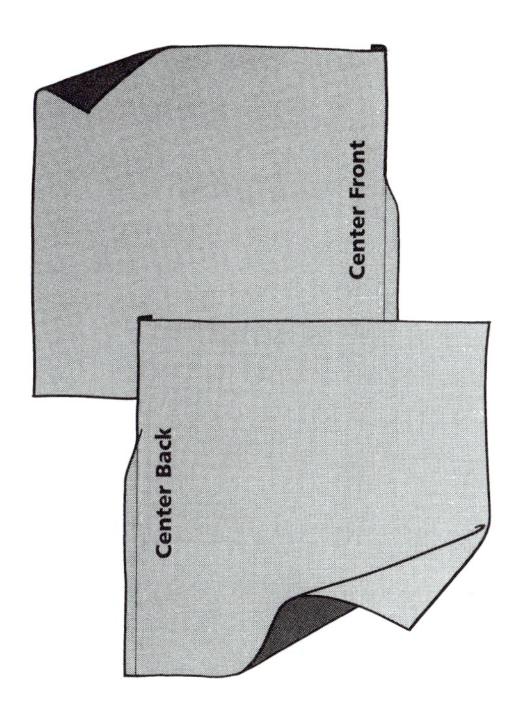

2 **Measure the width** along the crossgrain. Measure the same measurement as the desired length for the front and back skirt. This makes a perfect square.

3 **Draw grainlines for the center front and center back** skirt 1 inch from the torn edge, and press under.

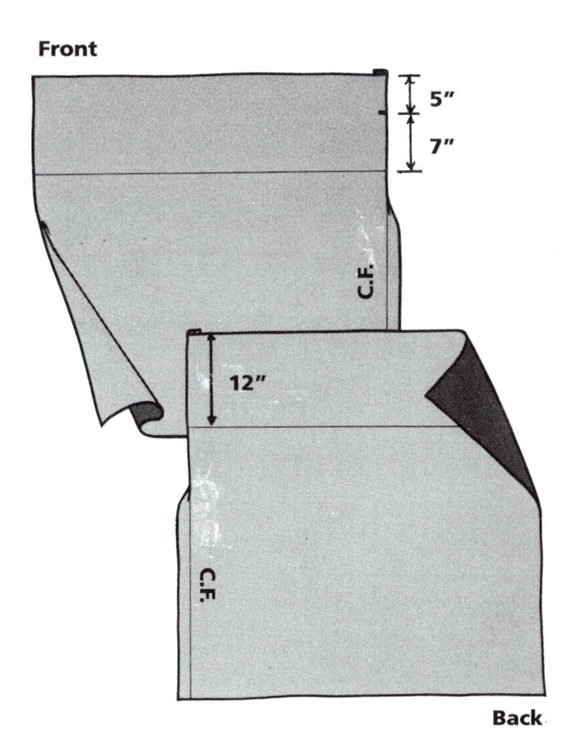

4 **Mark the center front/waist position.** Measure down 5 inches from the top edge of the fabric on the grainline. Draw a waistline mark.

5 **Draw the front and back crossgrains.**

a. On the front fabric piece, measure down **7 inches** from the waistline mark. Draw a perfect front crossgrain at this hip level.

b. On the back fabric piece, measure down **12 inches** on the grainline from the top edge of the fabric. Draw a perfect back crossgrain at this hip level.

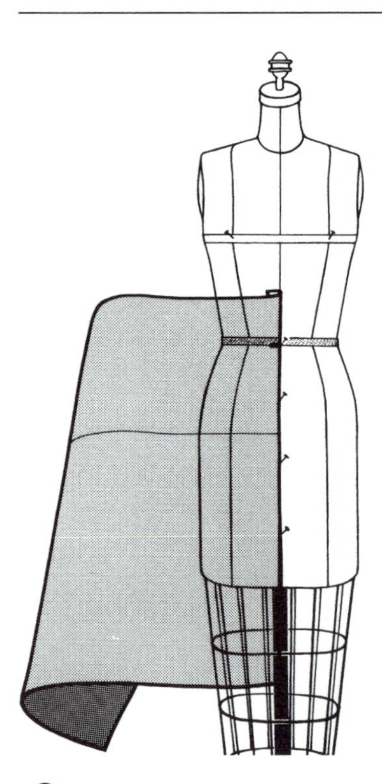

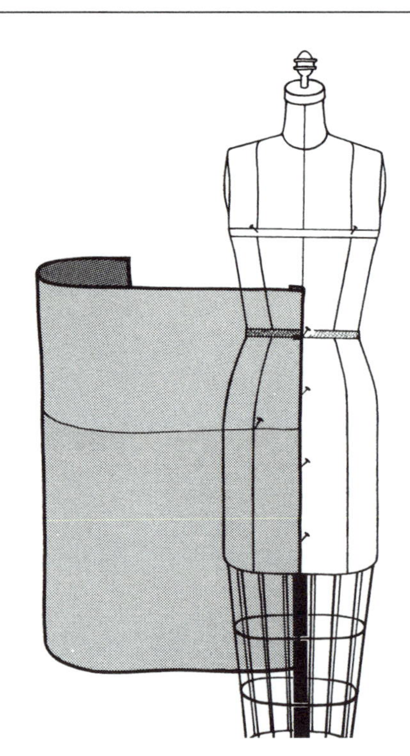

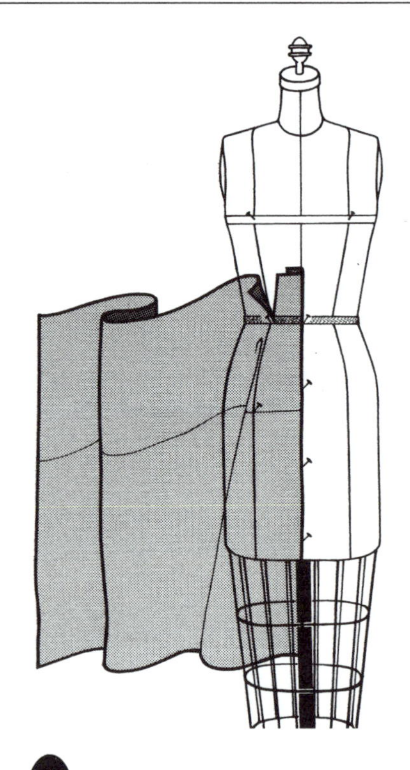

1 **Pin the center front grainline fold** of the fabric at the center front position of the dress form.

2 **Align the waistline mark** on the fabric to the center front waistline position of the dress form.

3 **Drape the crossgrain to the princess seam.** Following the hip level of the dress form, smooth and drape the crossgrain to the princess seam. Anchor a pin at this position.

4 **Drape the front waistline to the princess seam.**

a. Clip the fabric from the top edge down to the waistline.

b. Smooth and drape the fabric at the waistline to the princess seam.

c. Anchor a pin on the waistline at the princess seam.

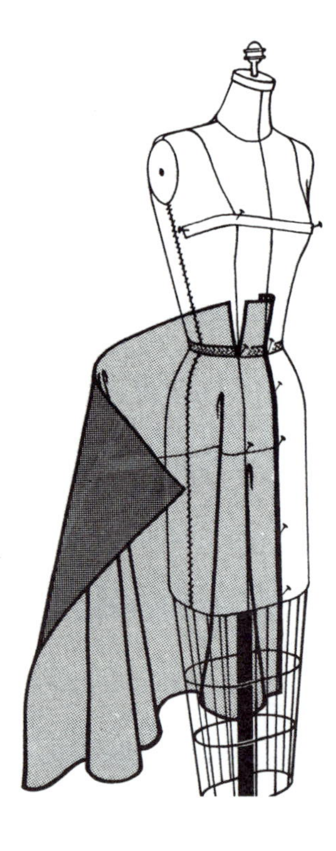

5 **Drape the first skirt flare.** Pivot the fabric downward from the waistline at the princess area, forming a nice flowing flare.

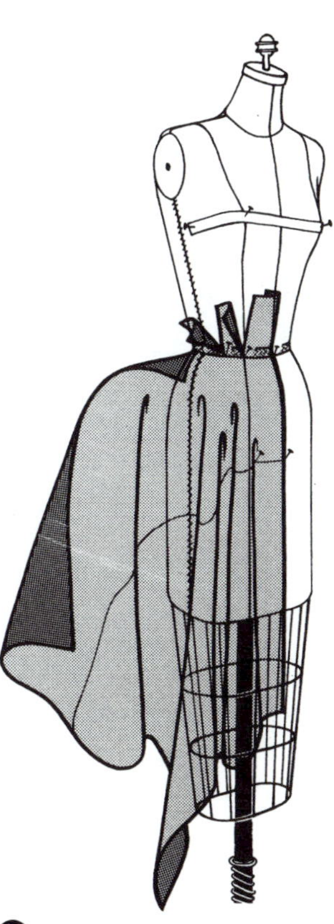

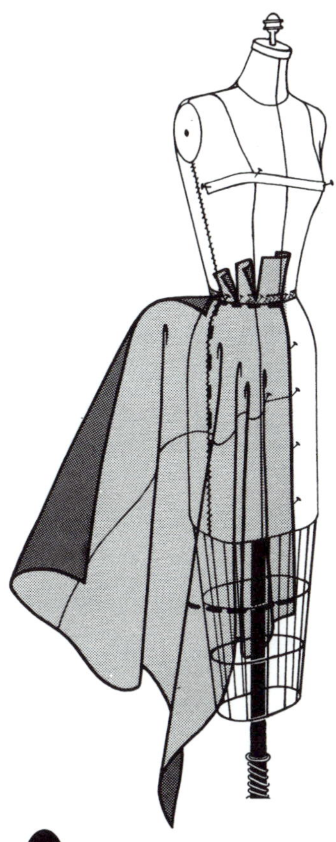

6 **Clip, pivot, pin, and drape the second flare** about 1 inch from the first flare, at the waistline. Smooth the fabric downward and toward the side seam.

7 **Continue to clip, pivot, and pin the waistline where each flare is desired.**

8 **Mark key areas.**

Waistline

Side Seam

Hem Follow the bottom of the dress form cage.

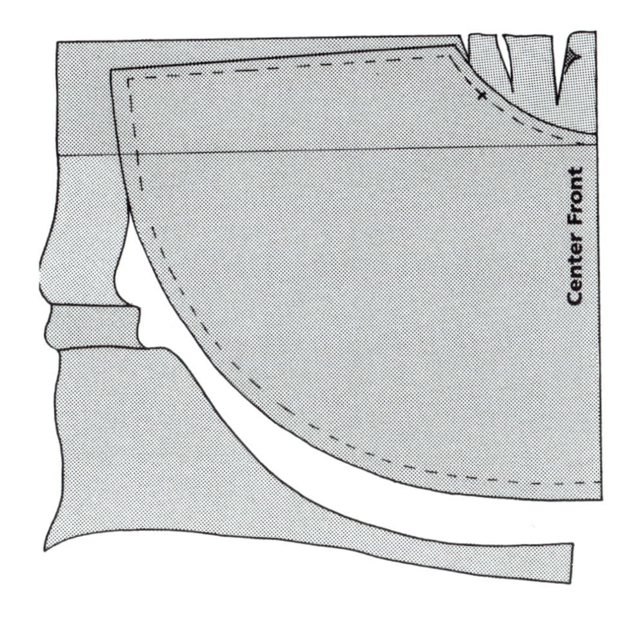

9 **True up the front drape.** Remove the fabric drape from the dress form. True up the front drape, add seam allowances, and trim the excess fabric.

10 Place the front skirt drape on top of the prepared fabric for the back drape.

a. Match the crossgrains of the front and back skirt. At the same time, place the center fold grainlines parallel, allowing the front to extend 1/2 inch over the back grainline. Keep the grainlines parallel. This distance allows for the difference between the back waistline amount and the front waistline amount.

b. Draw the skirt back stitch lines. Follow the same markings as the skirt front (temporary waistline, side seam, and hem).

NOTE: The back waistline will be redone when the final fit is checked. This is because the front and back waistline shapes are slightly different.

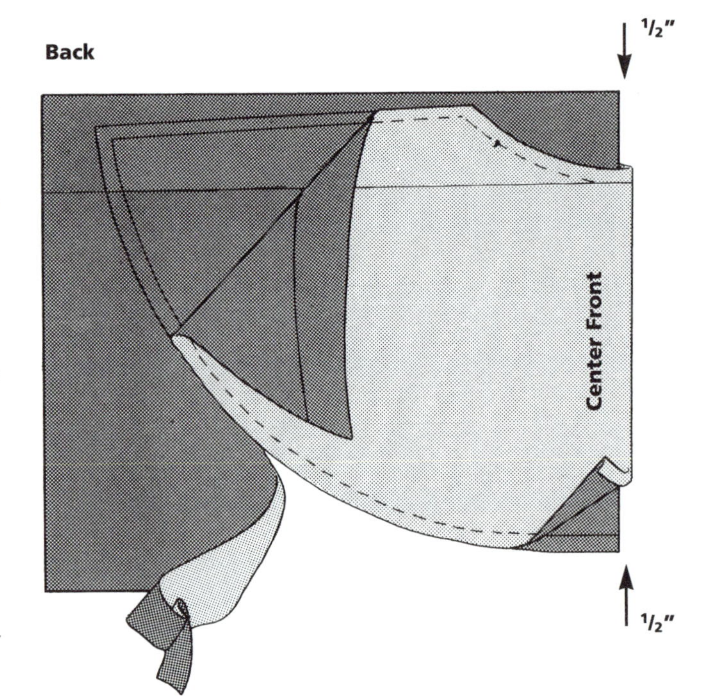

11 Check the fit and balance of the circular skirt. Pin the fabric pieces together at the front and back side seams. Place this drape back on the dress form. Adjust the back waistline until the skirt hangs properly and the side seams are in alignment with the side seams on the dress form. Pin center front and center back waists.

Bias Circular Skirt

As one drapes a bias fabric into a circular skirt, the bias quality of the fabric provides inherent stretchability. The features of a bias fabric include:

- The designer creates the amount of fullness.
- Each "flare" must be draped with the same amount of fullness. This allows for the same degree of stretch in the hemline.
- The front and back drapes do not need the same amount of fullness, but many they are the same.
- The shape of the waistline is controlled by the amount of fullness; the front and back waistlines will not always be symmetrical.
- The waistlines will definitely be a different shape; the back will be deeper and more rounded.
- The natural balance, side seam to side seam, is still achieved.
- Center front and center back will not always be on perfect bias. This depends on the amount of fullness draped into the skirt.
- The hemlines will show a minimum of fall out, or even no fall out, when draped and sewn.

Bias Circular Skirt—Preparing the Fabric

1 **Measure the length** desired for a front and back skirt. Measure the length along the straight of grain from the waistline to the desired length, and add 12 inches. Snip and tear the fabric at this length.

2 **Use the entire width of the fabric pieces for the front and back circular skirt drape.**

3 **Draw the grainline** from the front and back skirt fabric pieces 1 inch from the selvage.

4 **Draw the crossgrain** for the front and back skirt fabric pieces 10 inches from the top of the fabric edge. Draw the crossgrain halfway across the fabric piece.

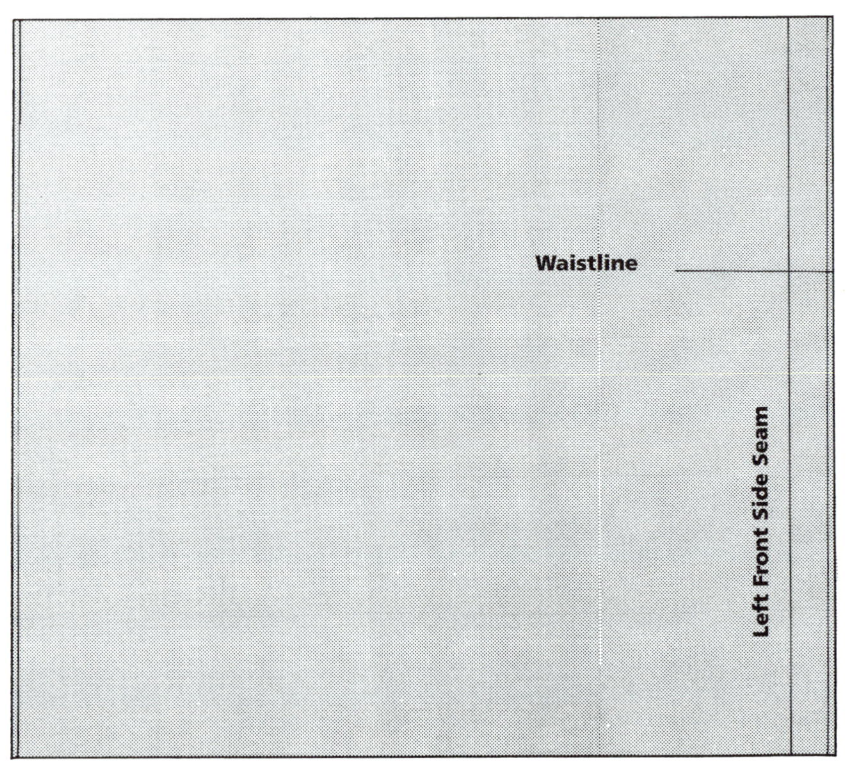

Front Skirt

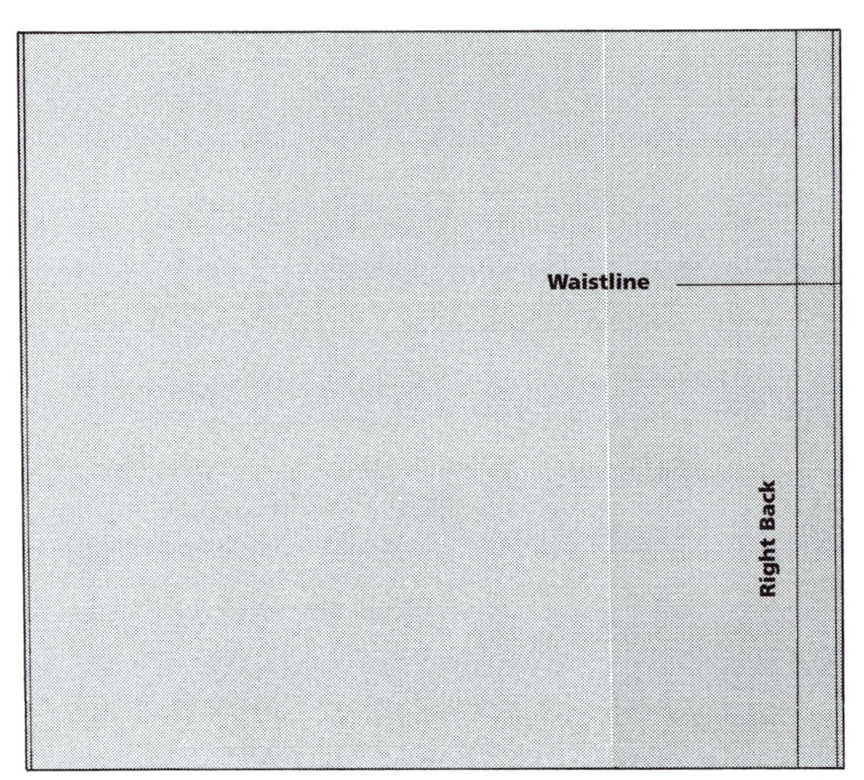

Back Skirt

Bias Circular Front Skirt—Draping Steps

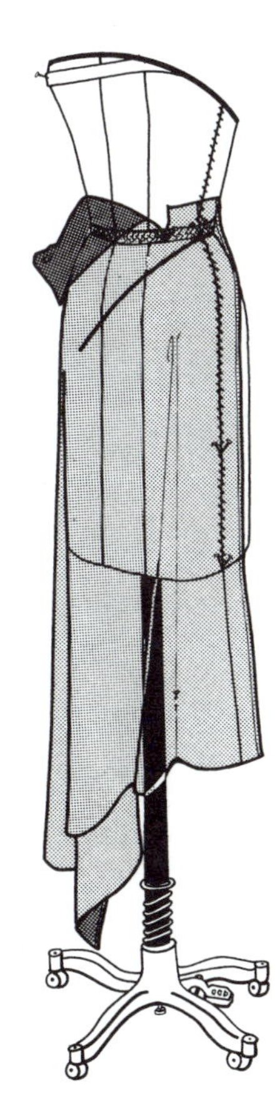

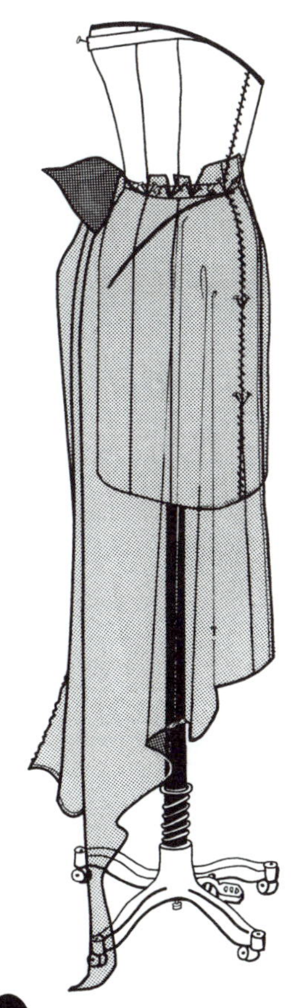

1 **Pin the grainline** to the side seam of the left side of the dress form.

2 **Align and drape the crossgrain** on the waistline of the left side seam of the dress form. Pin at the side seam.

3 Allow the fabric to hang smoothly and evenly across the front of the dress form.

4 **Trim, smooth, pin, and clip the waistline for the first flare.**

a. Approximately 2 inches from the side seam, trim the fabric from the top edge down to the waistline.

b. Smooth and drape the fabric at the waistline to approximately 2 inches from the side seam.

c. Clip the fabric from the top edge down to the waistline.

5 **Drape the first skirt flare.** Pivot the fabric downward from the waistline pin, forming a nice flowing flare. Place another pin on the bottom of the flare to hold it in place.

NOTE: Each flare must have the same amount of fullness to maintain a balanced hemline.

6 **Trim, smooth, pin, and clip the waistline for the second flare.**

a. Smooth and drape the front waistline about 1 1/2 inches from the first flare. Anchor another pin at this waistline position.

b. Trim, pin, and clip the fabric at the new waistline location.

c. Pivot the drape the second flare downward from the waistline at the second waistline pin.

Form the same amount of flare as was in the first flare.

7 **Continue to smooth, trim, pin, clip, and pivot** the waistline where each flare is desired till the entire front skirt is draped.

8 **Mark key areas** from the dress form to the fabric.

Waistline

Side Seam

Hem Follow the bottom of the dress form as a guide.

Bias Circular Back Skirt—Draping Steps

1 **Pin the grainline** to the side seam of the right side of the dress form.

2 **Align and drape the cross-grain** on the waistline of the right side seam of the dress form. Pin at the side seam.

3 **Allow the fabric** to hang smoothly and evenly across the back of the dress form.

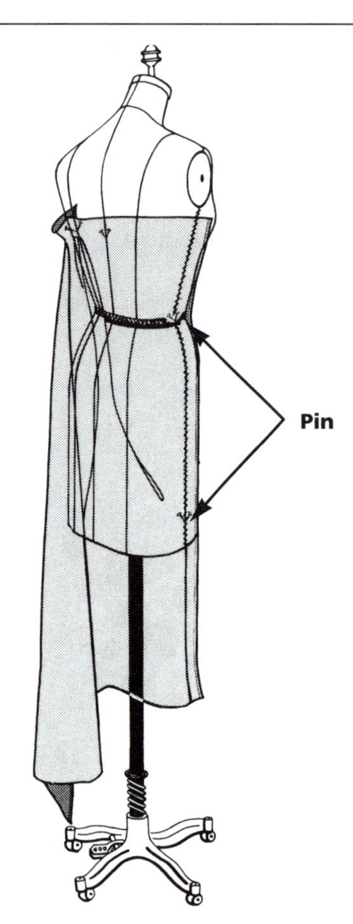

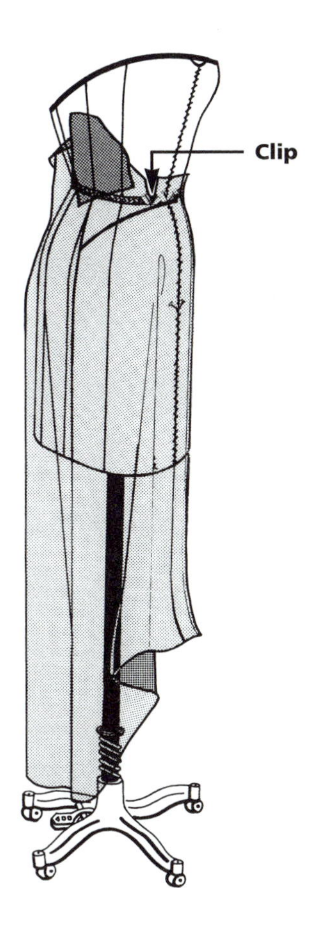

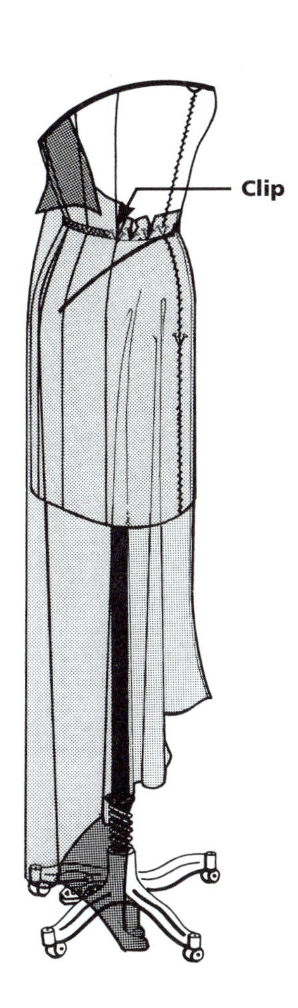

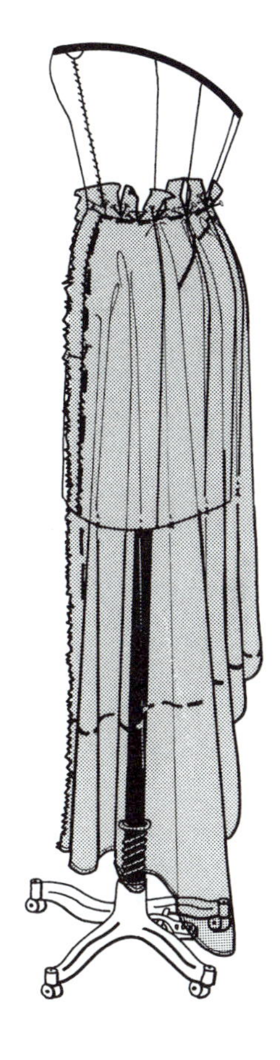

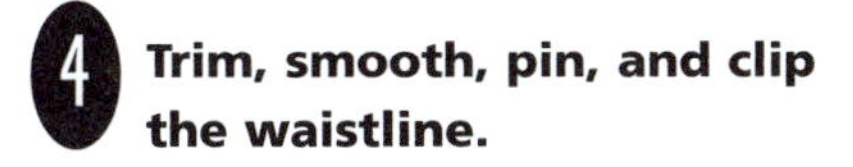

4 Trim, smooth, pin, and clip the waistline.

a. Approximately 2 inches from the side seam, trim the fabric from the top edge down to the waistline.

b. Smooth and drape the fabric at the waistline to approximately 2 inches from the side seam.

c. Clip the fabric from the top edge down to the waistline.

5 Drape the first skirt flare. Pivot the fabric downward from the waistline pin, forming a nice flowing flare. Place another pin on the bottom of the flare to hold it in place.

NOTE: Each flare must have the same amount of fullness to maintain a balanced hemline.

6 Trim, smooth, pin, and clip the waistline for the second flare.

a. Smooth and drape the back waistline approximately 1 inch from the first flare. Anchor another pin at this waistline position.

b. Trim, pin, and clip the fabric at the new waistline location.

c. Pivot the drape the second flare downward from the waistline at the second waistline pin.

Form the same amount of flare as was in the first flare.

7 Continue to smooth, trim, pin, clip, and pivot the waistline where each flare is desired until entire back skirt is draped.

8 Mark key areas from the dress form to the fabric.

Waistline

Side Seam

Hem Follow the bottom of the dress form as a guide.

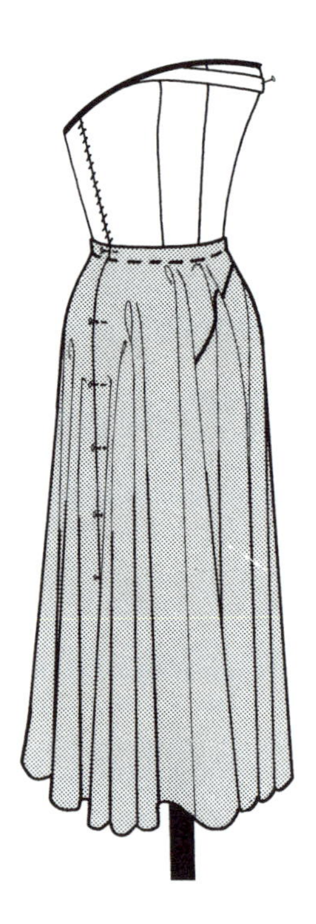

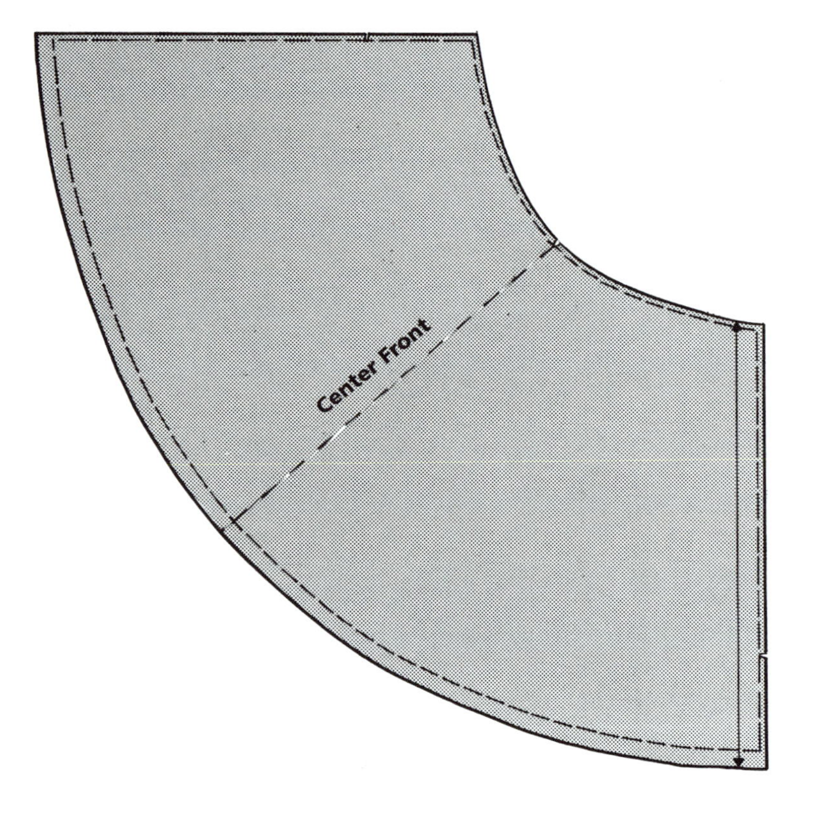

9 True up the front and back skirt drapes. Remove the front and back drapes from the dress form. True up all seams, add seam allowances, and trim excess fabric.

Check the fit and balance. If necessary, make corrections.

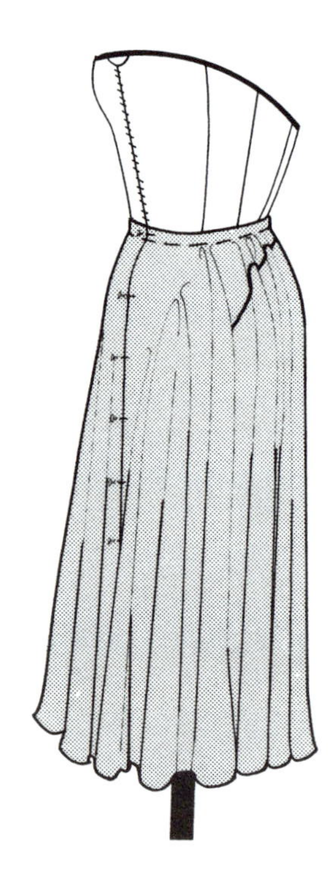

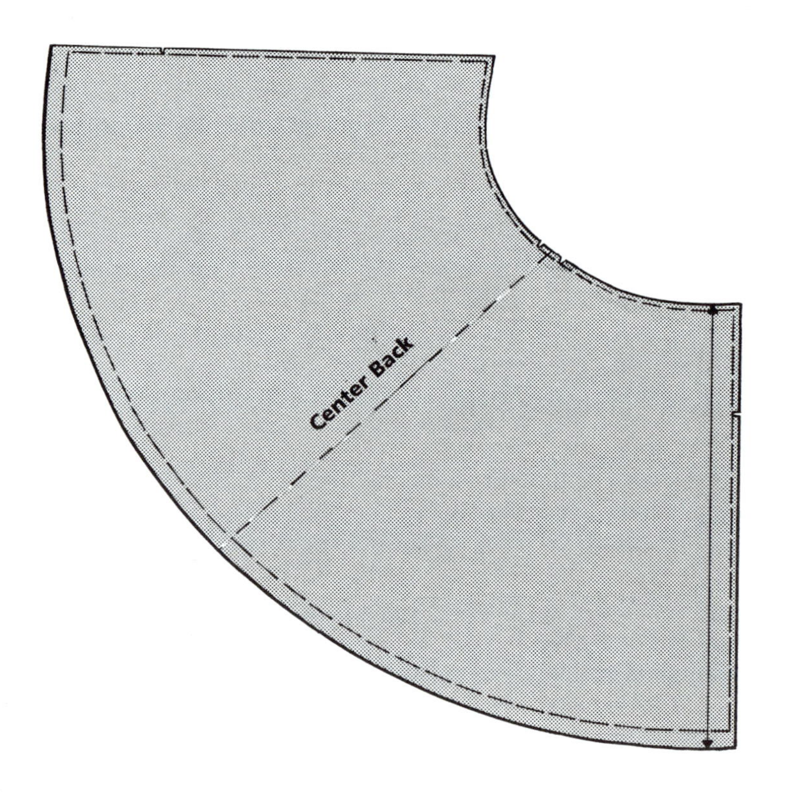

Chapter Thirteen

Pants

Objectives

By studying the various draping steps in this chapter, the designer should be able to accomplish the following:

- Recognize grain and crossgrain of fabric in relation to the hip level and crotch line of pants.
- Drape a flat piece of fabric and shape the front and back crotch seams, allowing for the desired amount of crotch ease.
- Drape a flat piece of fabric and shape the leggings with the desired amount of fullness.
- True up and visualize the front and back pant panels in relation to the figure.
- Check and balance the front and back side seams on all pants variations.

Pants

Pants will always be an important part of the fashion scene. The waist area can be flat and plain, pleated slightly, or full. They can be finished with a waistband, elastic, draw-string, or faced. Pants are seen in many lengths, from very short to just below the ankle. The leg shapes vary from slightly flared to straight or tapered. Careful draping on a pant form will enable the designer to create a wonderful appearance regardless of style or fabric.

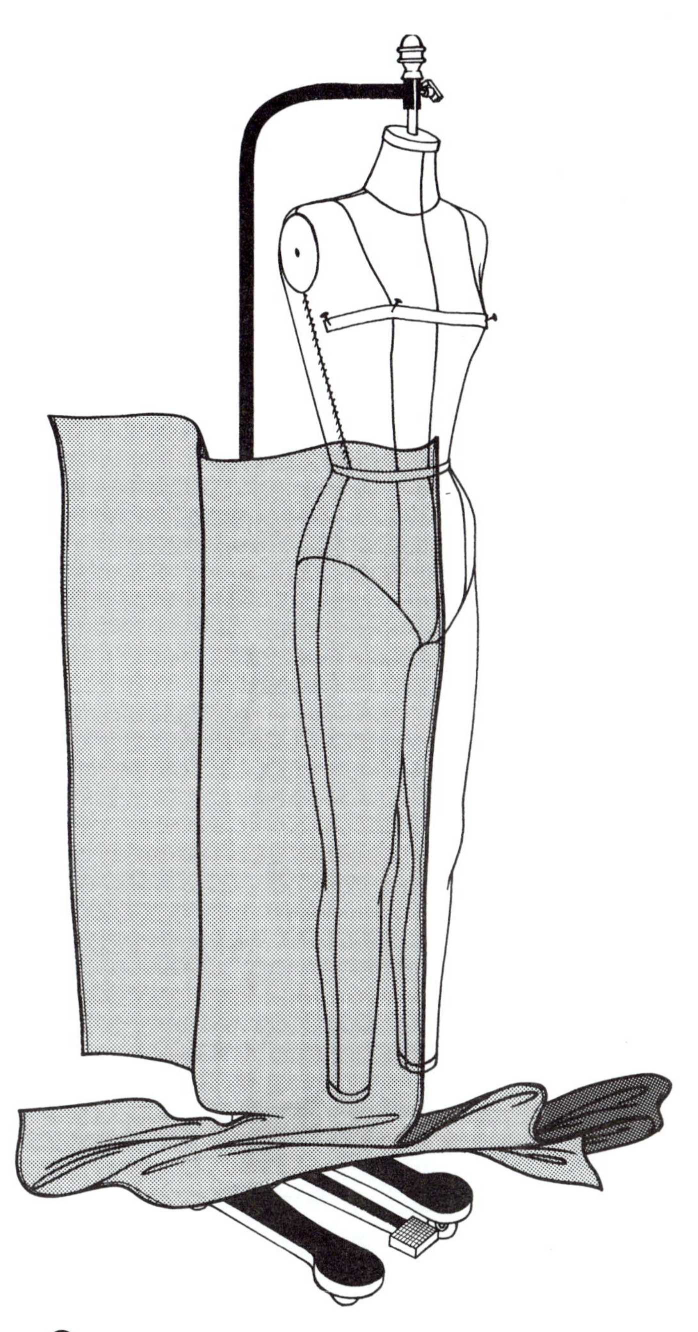

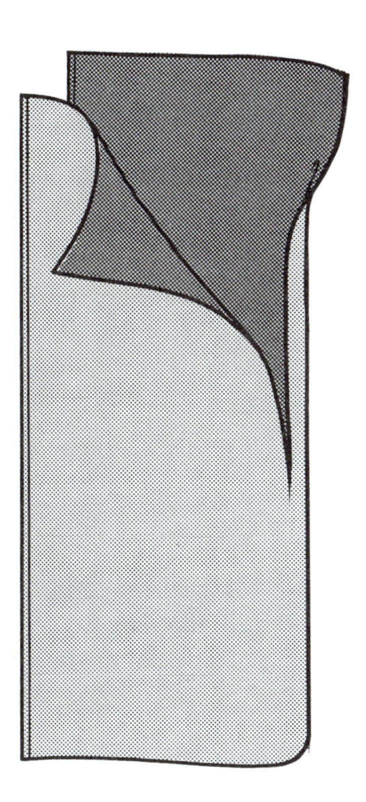

1 **Measure the length** along the straight of grain. Measure from 2 inches above the waist to the desired length (ankle) of the pants.

Snip and tear the fabric at this length.

2 **Fold the fabric piece in half from selvage to selvage.** Snip and tear this piece in half lengthwise.

One piece will be used for the front legging, and the other piece will be used for the back legging.

3 **Draw the grainline for the front and back legging** in the middle of the fabric pieces.

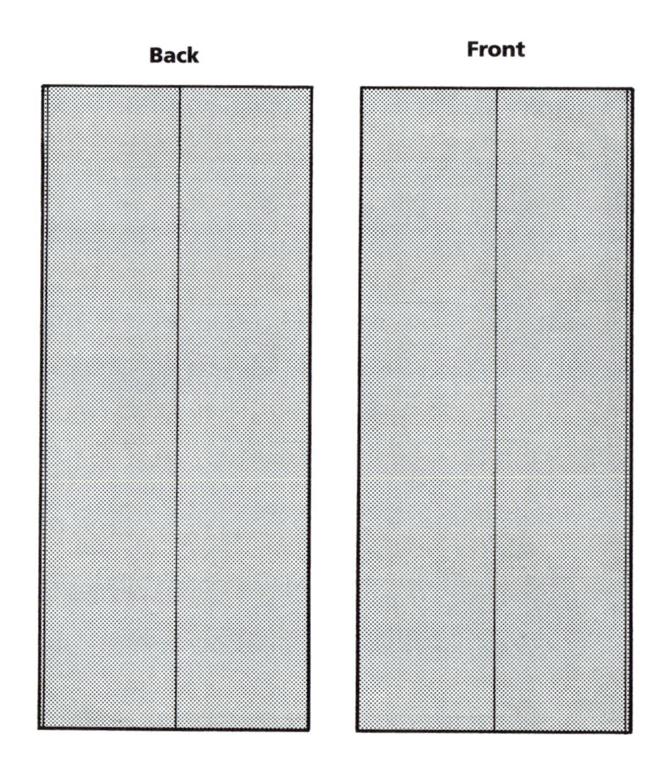

4 **Draw the crossgrain for the front and back legging** 10 inches from the top edge of the fabric pieces.

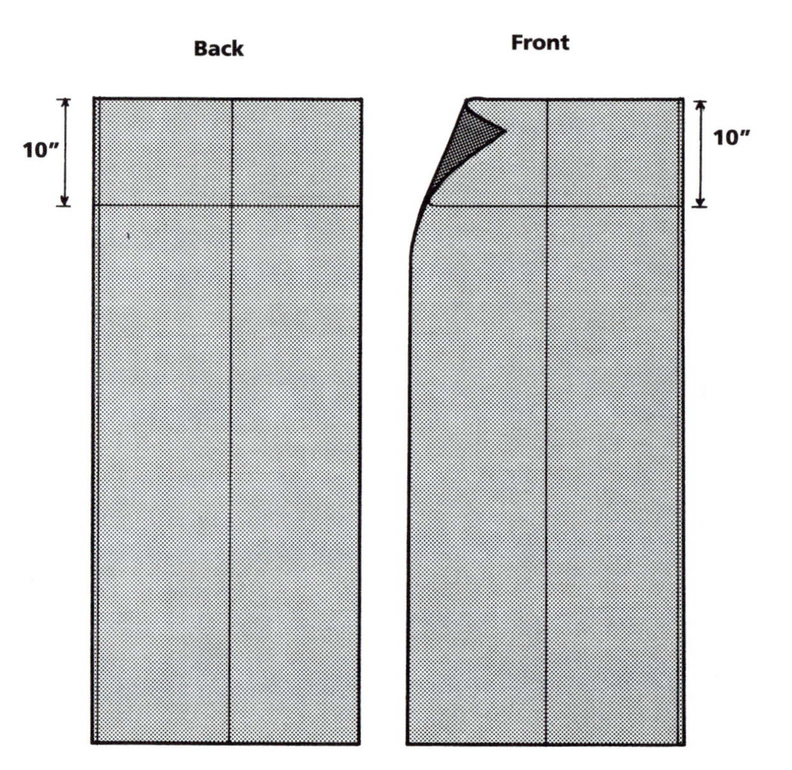

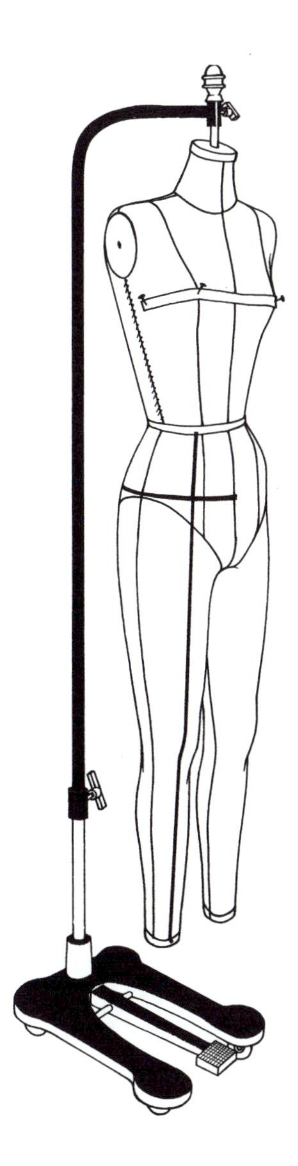

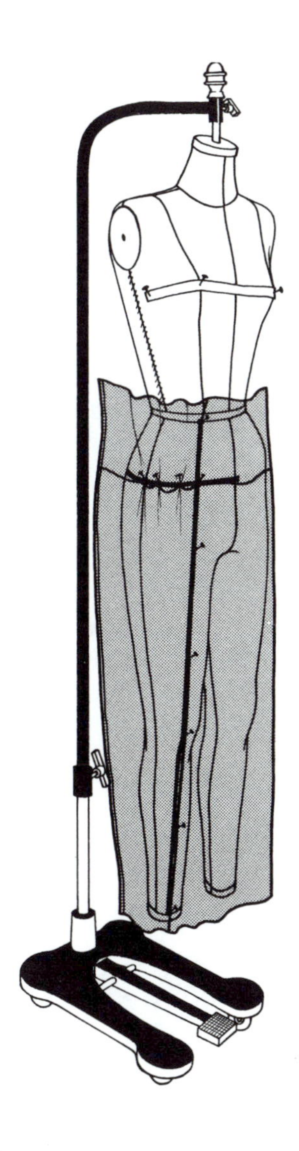

Prepare the pant form.

a. Pin style tape on the pant form at the hip level. This style tape should extend from center front to center back of the form. This hip level tape will represent the crossgrain position of the fabric.

b. Pin another style tape in the center of the front and back leg of the pant form. This style tape will represent the straight of grain position of the fabric.

1 Align and pin the center front grainline and crossgrain of the fabric on the front hip level tape and grainline tape of the dress form. Be sure to allow for ease on the crossgrain.

2 Align and pin the center back grainline and crossgrain of the fabric on the back hip level tape and grainline tape of the dress form. Be sure to allow for ease on the crossgrain. Refer to step 3 for more information about proper amount of ease.

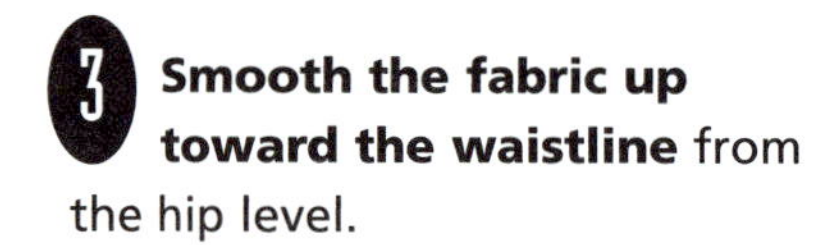

3 **Smooth the fabric up toward the waistline** from the hip level.

4 **Drape in the desired styling of the waistline area** (darts, pleats, release tucks, gathers, etc.).

NOTE: For a fuller waistline area, such as gathers or pleats, much more ease would need to be added on the crossgrain

5 **Trim, clip, and drape the front and back crotch areas,** allowing for the appropriate crotch ease for the desired pant.

6 **Pin and drape the center front and center back seam.** Smooth the fabric up from the crotch to the center waistline area. Keep in mind the desired waistline styling.

7 **Pin the front and back inseams together.** Style the inseam legging and shape the desired width.

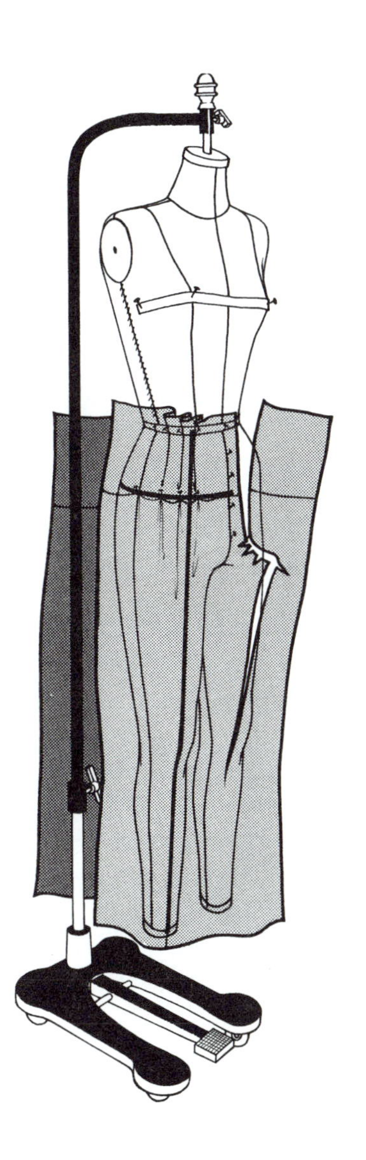

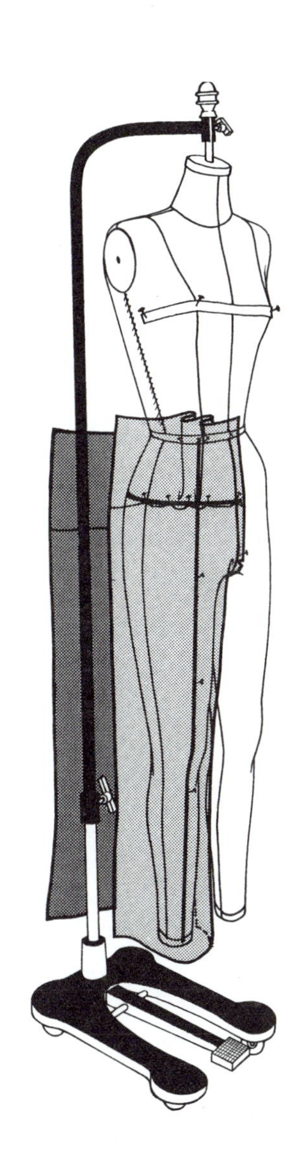

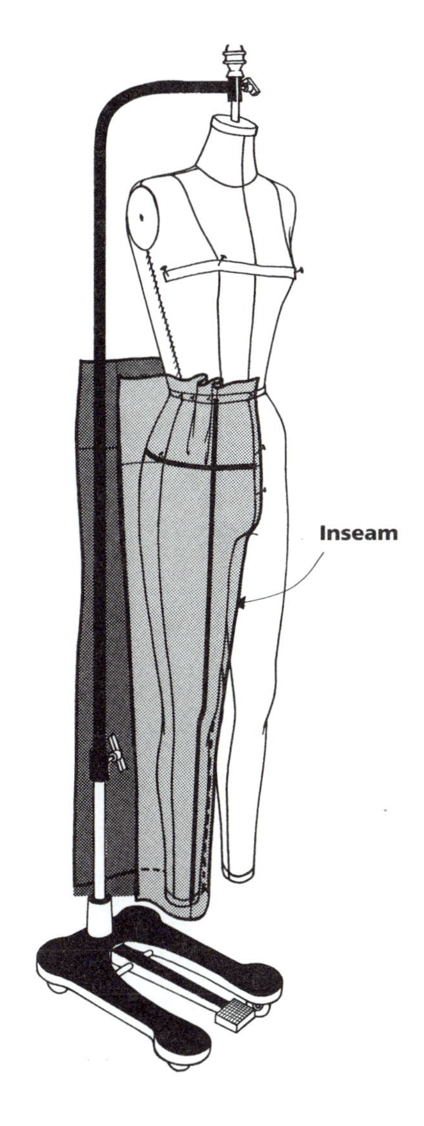

8 **Pin the front and back side seams together** from the hip level up. Complete the desired shaping of the front and back waistline at the side seam.

9 **Pin the front and back side seams** together from the hip level down. Style the side seam legging shape desired from the hip level down.

NOTE: The legging shape should be equal from both sides of the legging grainline.

10 **Mark key areas.**

Waistline and Crossmark Any darts, tucks, or pleats.

Center Front and Center Back Crotch

Front and Back Inseams

Front and Back Side Seams

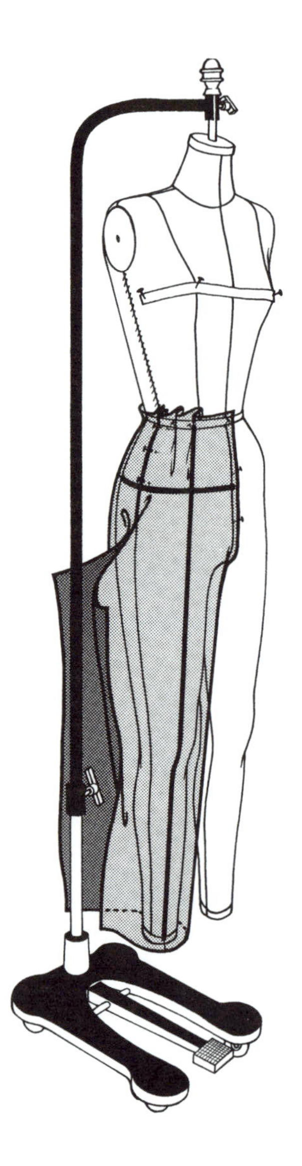

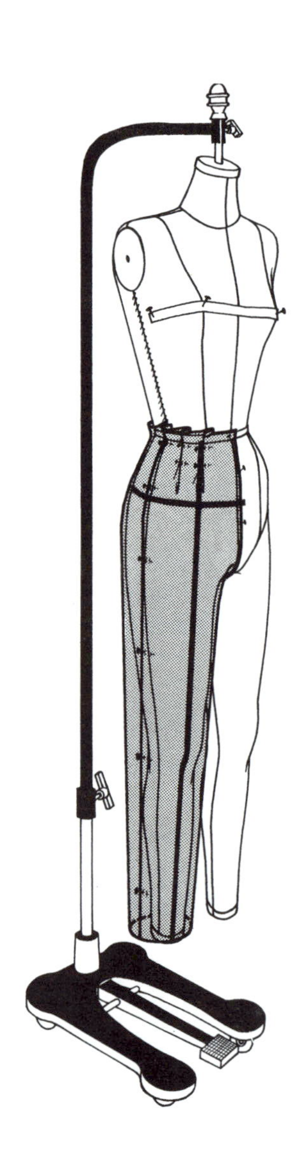

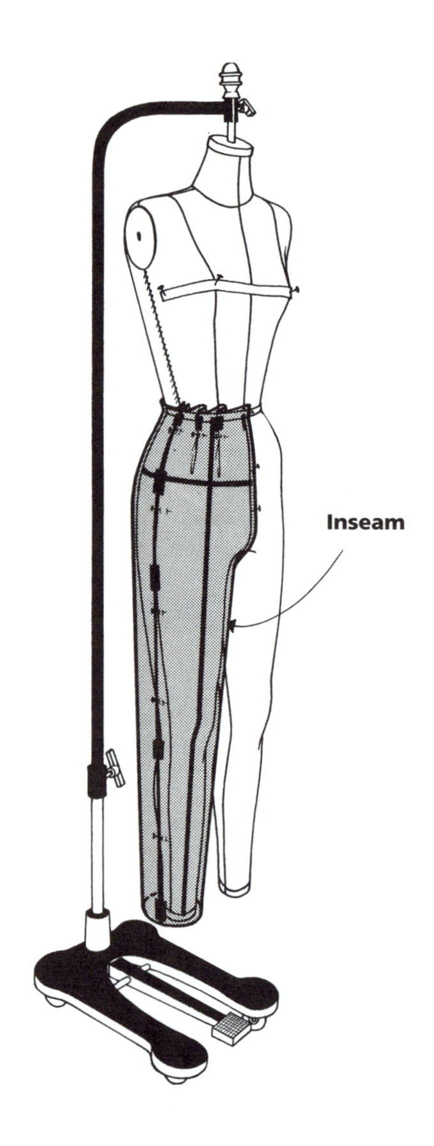

11 **True up all lines.** Remove the front and back pant drape from the pant form. True up all lines, add seam allowances, and trim excess fabric.

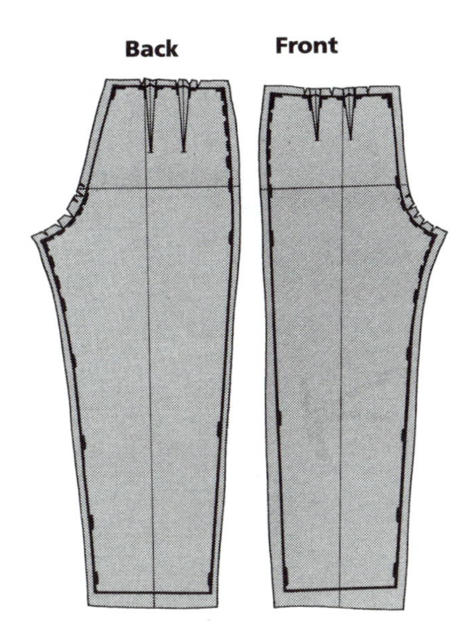

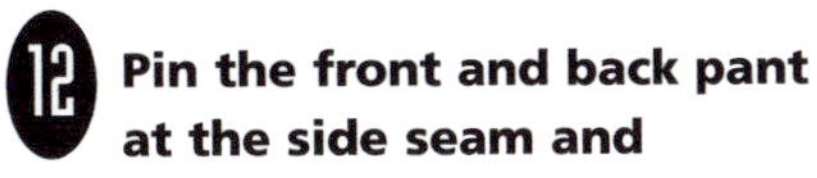

12 **Pin the front and back pant at the side seam and inseams.** Return the fabric drape to the pant form and check for accuracy.

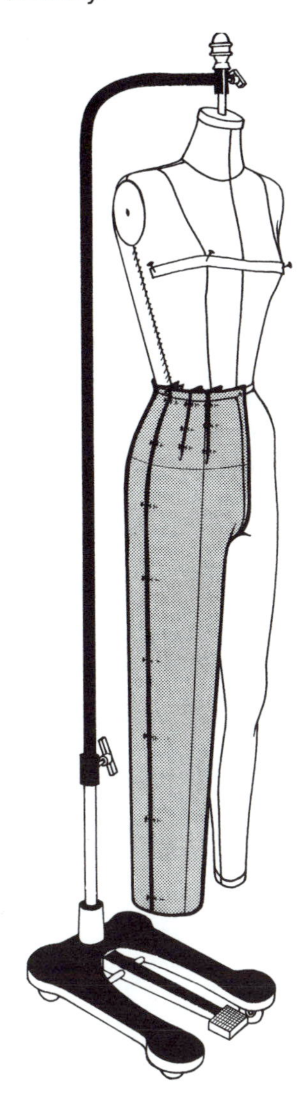

Straight Legged Pants

Drape the legging straight down.

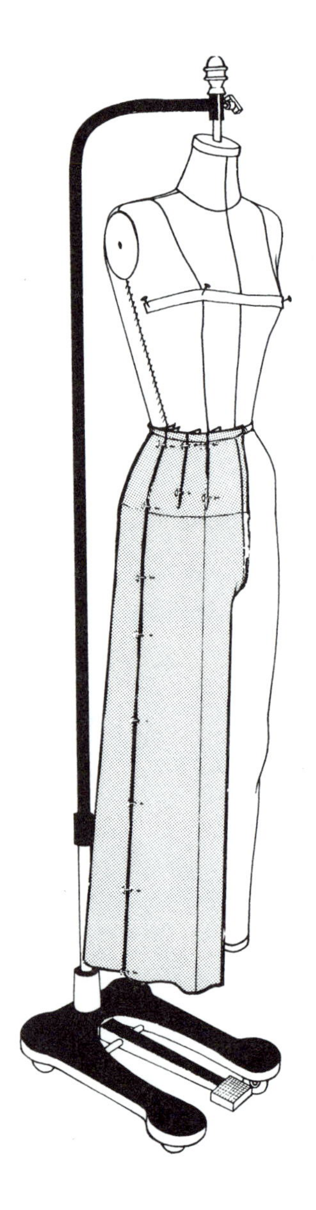

Palazzo Styled Pants Legs

Drape the legging so that it flares out from the inside and side seams. It is also necessary to create a flare that falls from the waistline in the middle of the legging.

Chapter Fourteen

Sleeves

Objectives

By studying the various draping steps in this chapter, the designer should be able to accomplish the following:

- Recognize grain and crossgrain of fabric in relation to the sleeve.
- Adjust the basic sleeve to allow for more arm movement.
- Convert the basic sleeve into an enlarged armhole to be used with coat sleeves.
- Combine and attach the raglan sleeve to a bodice yoke and achieve an easy sleeve movement.
- Pivot or "walk" the sleeve into the bodice armhole, determine sleeve ease, and place the sleeve cap notches.
- Check the adjusted sleeve to be sure it has the correct amount of ease allowance, cap size, and measurements.
- Check the fit, hang, and ease allowance into the desired armhole.
- Make sleeve or armhole adjustments if necessary.

Sleeves

The four projects in this chapter illustrate (1) how the basic sleeve is adjusted to allow more arm movement; (2) how to convert the basic sleeve into a basic shirt sleeve; (3) how to adjust the basic sleeve to accommodate a larger armhole, such as for a coat; and (4) how to design a raglan sleeve for a blouse.

Adjusting a Sleeve for More Arm Movement

A set-in sleeve sometimes needs a longer underarm seam to allow the arm to move more freely up and down or to allow greater ease of movement forward and backward. To achieve an easier movement in a sleeve, draft a new sleeve from the original set-in sleeve, using the following steps.

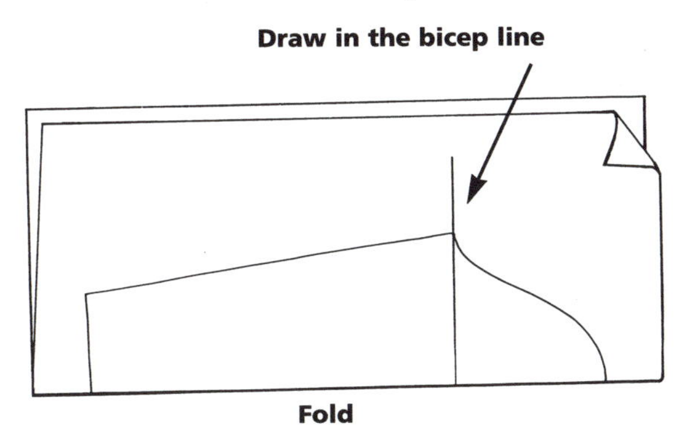

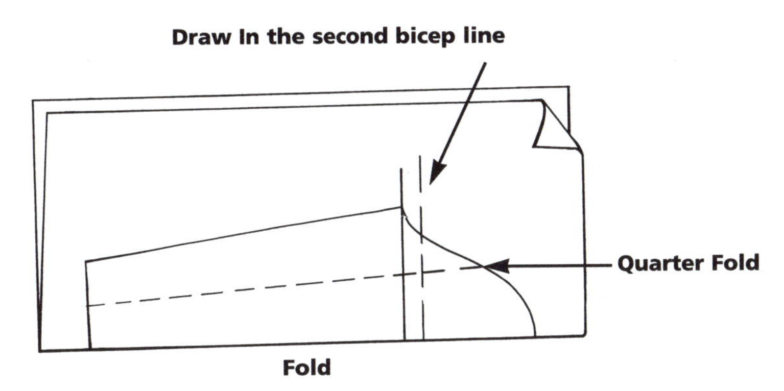

1. **Cut a piece of pattern paper** 32-inches long by 30-inches wide. Fold the paper in half lengthwise.

2. **Place the basic block sleeve (without the elbow dart) on the pattern paper,** matching center of the sleeve (straight of grain) to the paper pattern fold.

3. **Draw in the entire sleeve lightly** from the center of the sleeve cap (fold of paper) around and down to the wristline.

4. **Remove the original sleeve pattern. Draw in the bicep line** on the pattern paper from the center fold of the paper at the bicep level of the drawn in sleeve.

5. **Draw in a new bicep line** 1 inch above the original bicep line on the pattern paper of the new sleeve pattern draft.

6. **Draw in the quarter fold** position of the sleeve (see illustration) of the new sleeve pattern draft.

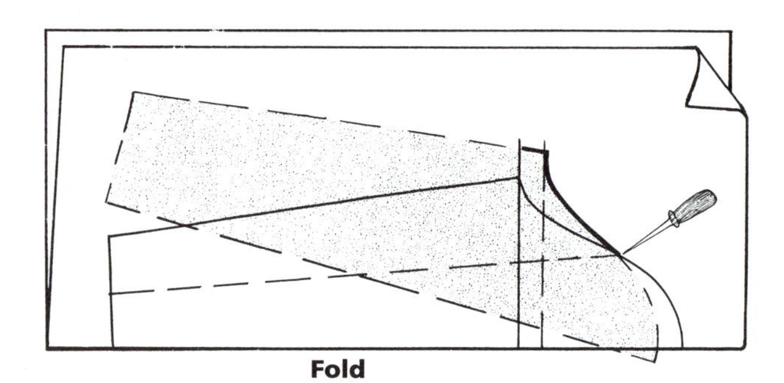

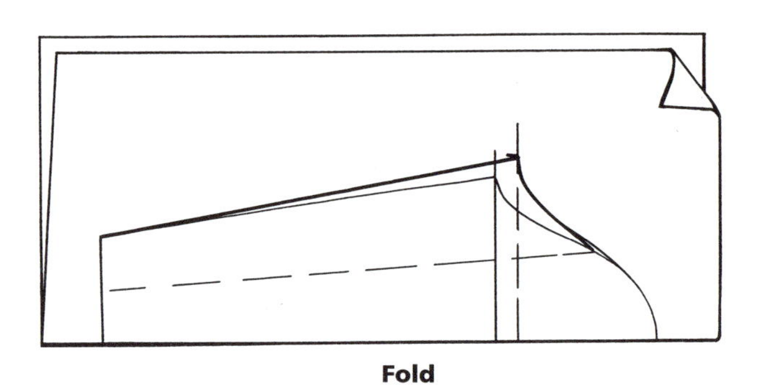

7 Place the original sleeve on top of the paper sleeve draft. Match the center of the sleeve to the paper fold and the original bicep lines.

8 Pivot the sleeve up to the "new bicep line." Using an awl at the quarter fold/cap area, pivot the sleeve underarm up until the side seam/bicep corner touches the "new bicep line."

9 Draw in a new cap line. Using the pattern as a guide, draw from the quarter fold cap area down to the new bicep corner.

10 Draw a new underarm sleeve seam line. Using a straight ruler, connect the new underarm/bicep corner down to the original wristline.

11 Blend the new cap line. Using a curved ruler, blend a new capline. Reshape the underarm seams.

12 Cut out the sleeve pattern.

NOTE: These changes alter the length of the sleeve cap. Therefore, it is important to walk the sleeve into the armhole to determine if the sleeve cap length is too long or too short, and if the sleeve cap has sufficient ease. Step 14 offers directions for adding or subtracting cap distance.

13 **Walk the sleeve cap** into the desired garment armhole (See Basic Sleeve, pivoting instructions, pages 85-86.)

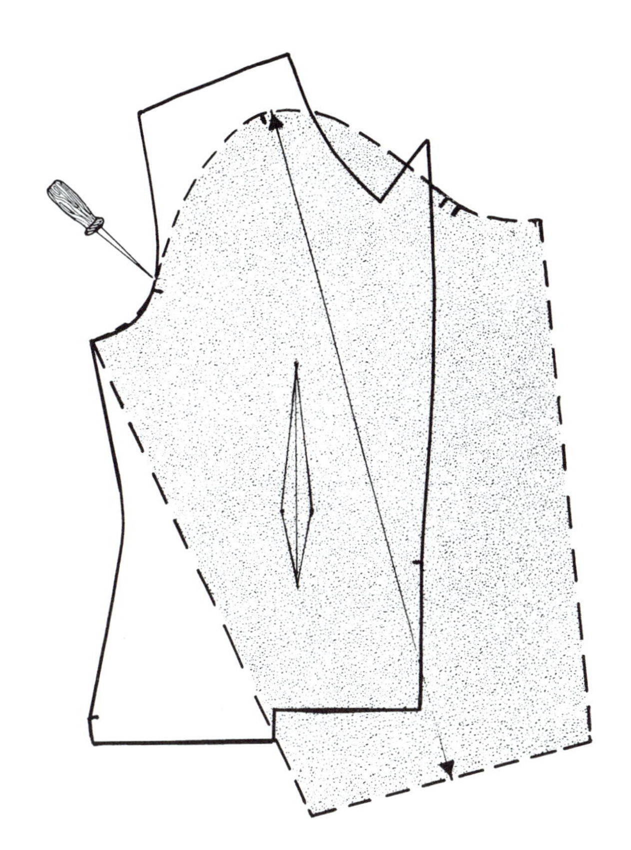

a. Place the underarm of the sleeve to the underarm of the bodice, matching the stitchlines and the side seams.

NOTE: The armhole notches for the bodice have already been established.

b. Pivot the sleeve around the armhole. Use a pencil or an awl at the stitchline of the sleeve to hold the sleeve in place. Starting at the underarm side seam corner, pivot the sleeve around the armhole until the edges of the sleeve and bodice meet.

While walking the sleeve, match and pencil in the front and back armhole notches (one on the front and two on the back).

c. Continue walking the sleeve the remainder of the armhole area. Move the awl to where the sleeve and the bodice armhole meet. Continue to pivot the sleeve around the bodice armhole, until the edges of the sleeve and bodice meet once again.

Repeat this pivoting procedure until the sleeve cap meets at the shoulder/armhole corner.

d. Crossmark the shoulder positions. While walking the sleeve, crossmark on the sleeve cap the front and back bodice shoulder position of the front and back bodice. Note the amount of ease in the sleeve cap.

14 **If the sleeve cap proves to be too long or too short, do the following.**

a. Too short Slash the center of the sleeve and the quarter folds from the top of the sleeve to the wrist level. Open and add the desired amount of cap distance. Divide the other half in half again. Add this amount to both side seam/bicep corners. Blend all new lines.

b. Too long Slash the center of the sleeve and the quarter folds from the top of the sleeve to the wrist level. Close and subtract the desired amount. Divide the other half in half again. Subtract this amount from both side seam/bicep corners. Blend all new lines.

NOTE: A fitted sleeve could require 1 to 1-1/2 inches of ease in the sleeve cap. The fabric, style, and manufacturer are factors in determining the amount of ease required.

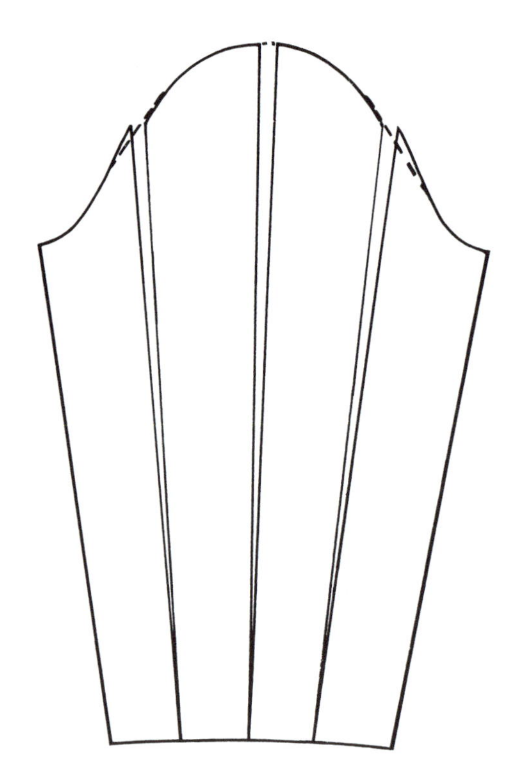

Too short

15 **Repeat fitting steps** as shown earlier in this unit (Fitting the Basic Sleeve, pages 88-89). Also, complete the fitting on a live model to ensure proper arm movement.

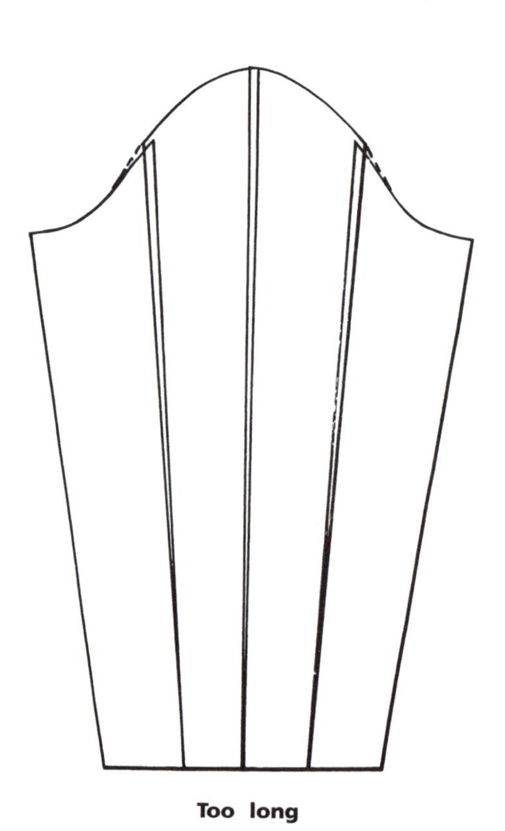

Too long

Shirt Sleeve

The shirt sleeve is a tailored wrist-length sleeve that sets smoothly into an extended shoulder and a dropped armhole with only a minimum amount of ease. To accommodate the extended shoulders, the shirt sleeve has a shallow cap height with a higher than normal bicep level. Because of its generous bicep fit, this sleeve design allows freedom of movement as well as comfort.

1 Prepare sleeve cap, grainline, and crossgrain.

a. Adjust the sleeve cap by using either the basic sleeve or the adjusted basic sleeve. Extend the sleeve cap amount out and down to accommodate the amount the sleeve armhole was extended for the longer armhole measurement of the shirt.

b. Draw a straight of grainline in the center of the sleeve.

c. Draw a new bicep line on the sleeve at the new bicep level.

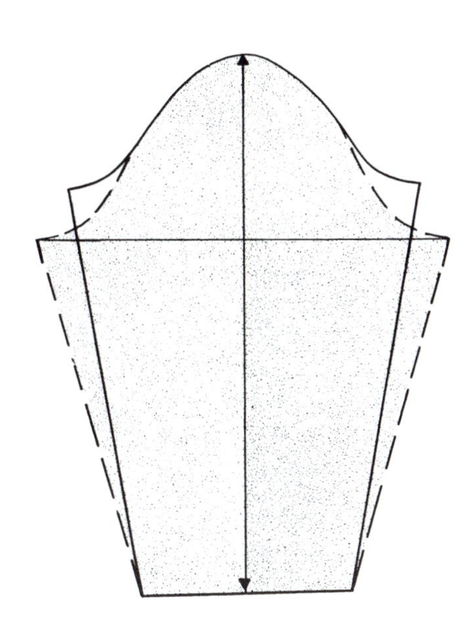

2 **Cut a piece of pattern paper** 32-inches long by 30-inches wide. Fold the paper in half lengthwise.

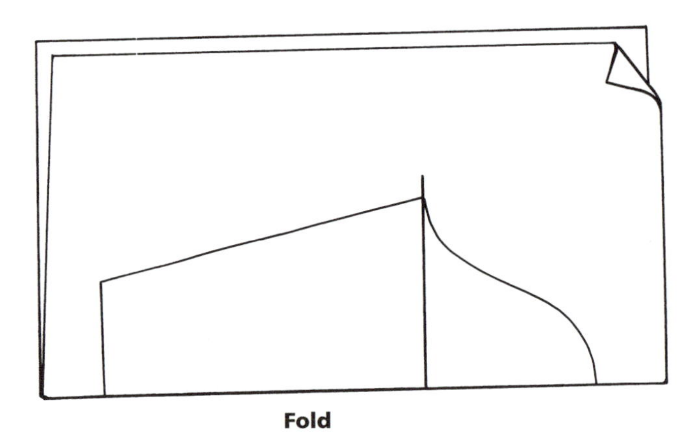

3 **Place the newly adjusted sleeve on top of the pattern paper,** matching the center of the sleeve (straight of grain) to the paper pattern fold.

4 **Draw in the entire sleeve lightly** from the center of the sleeve cap (fold of paper) around and down to the wristline.

5 **Remove the original sleeve** pattern from the new sleeve draft.

6 **Draw in a bicep line on the pattern paper** from the center fold of the paper at the bicep level of the drawn in sleeve.

7 **Draw in a new bicep line on the new sleeve draft.** Measure down 3 1/2 inches from the traced sleeve cap. At this position, draw in a new bicep line.

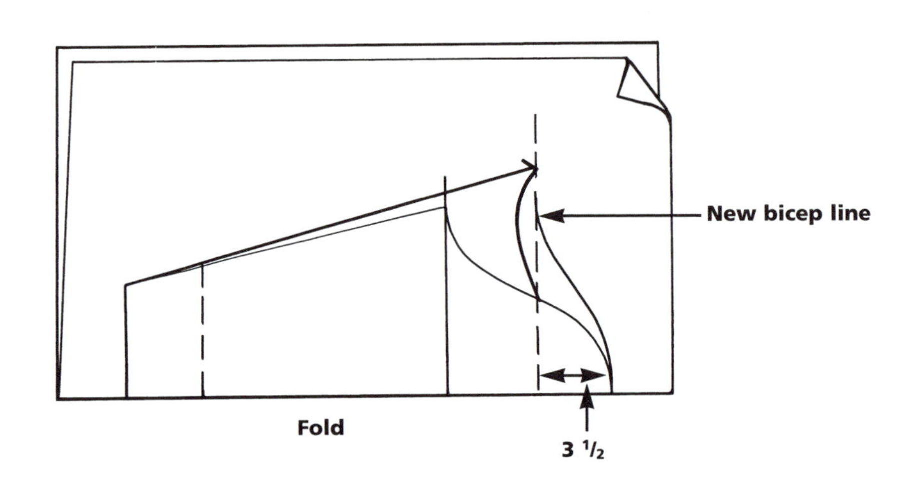

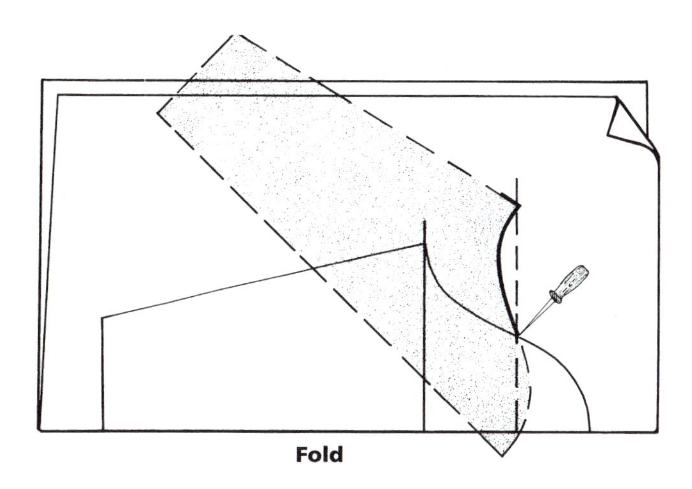

8 Place the original adjusted sleeve back onto the paper. Match the center of the sleeve to the paper fold draft and the original bicep lines.

9 Pivot the sleeve up to the new bicep line. Using an awl at the quarter fold/cap, pivot the sleeve underarm up until the side seam/bicep corner touches the new bicep line.

10 Draw in a new cap line. Using the pattern as a guide, draw from the quarter fold cap area down to the new bicep corner. Remove the original sleeve from the draft.

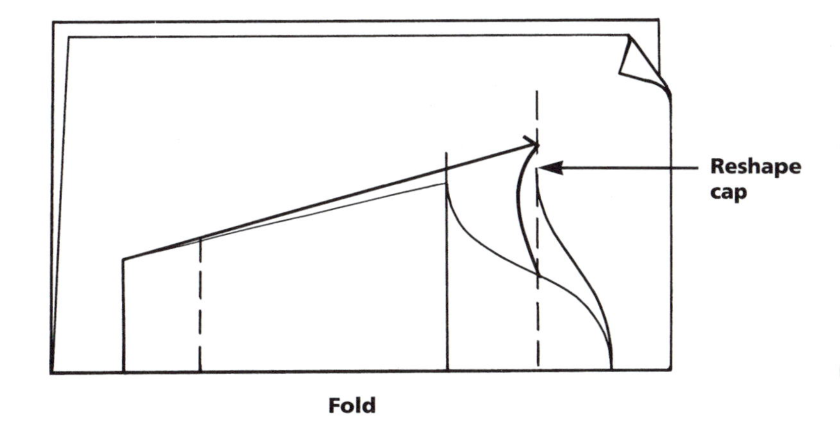

11 Draw a new underarm sleeve seam line. Using a straight ruler, connect the new underarm/bicep corner down to the original wristline.

12 Blend the new cap line. Using a curved ruler, blend a new sleeve cap stitchline. The sleeve cap should be a clean, smooth "lazy S shape."

13 Cut the sleeve pattern out.

NOTE:

a. These changes alter the length of the sleeve cap. Therefore, it is important to "walk" the sleeve into the armhole to determine if the sleeve cap length is long enough or too short, and if the sleeve cap has sufficient ease. Step 15 offers directions for adding or subtracting cap distance.

b. Most shirt sleeves require only **1/2-inch ease** in the sleeve cap.

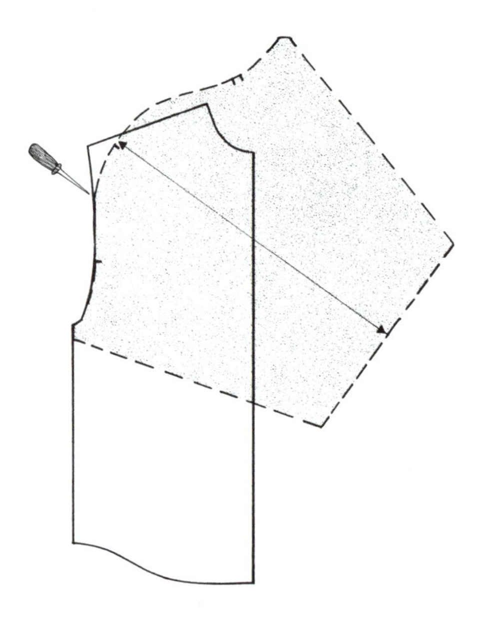

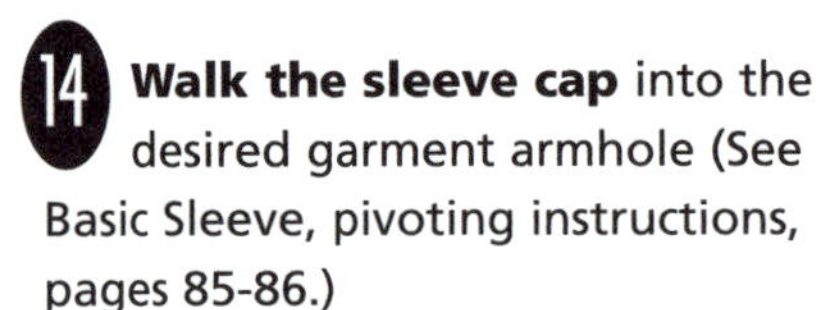

14 **Walk the sleeve cap** into the desired garment armhole (See Basic Sleeve, pivoting instructions, pages 85-86.)

a. Place the underarm of the sleeve to the underarm of the bodice, matching the stitchlines and the side seams.

NOTE: The armhole notches for the bodice have already been established.

b. Pivot the sleeve around the armhole. Use a pencil or an awl at the stitchline of the sleeve to hold the sleeve in place. Starting at the underarm side seam corner, pivot the sleeve around the armhole until the edges of the sleeve and bodice meet.

While walking the sleeve, match and pencil in the front and back armhole notches (one on the front and two on the back).

c. Continue walking the sleeve the remainder of the armhole area. Move the awl to where the sleeve and the bodice armhole meet. Continue to pivot the sleeve around the bodice armhole, until the edges of the sleeve and bodice meet once again.

Repeat this pivoting procedure until the sleeve cap meets at the shoulder/armhole corner.

d. Crossmark the shoulder positions. While walking the sleeve, crossmark on the sleeve cap the front and back bodice shoulder position of the front and back bodice.

NOTE: A shirt sleeve usually requires **1/2-inch ease,** whereas a fitted sleeve could require 1 1/2 inches of ease. The fabric, style, and manufacturer are factors in determining the amount of ease required.

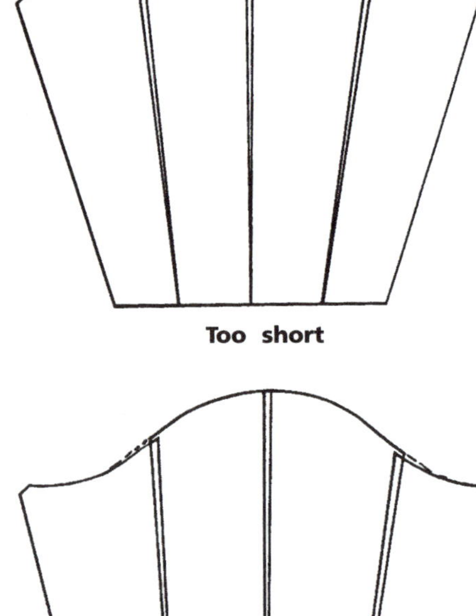

Too short

Too long

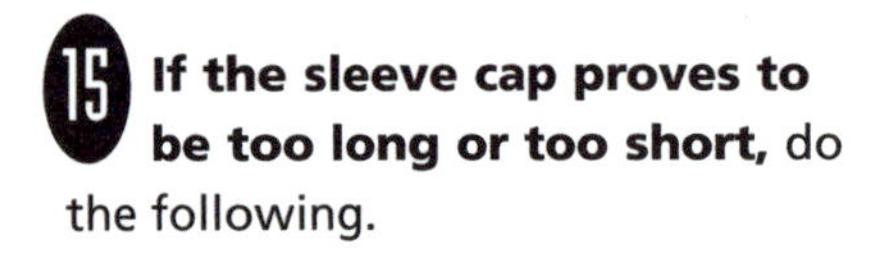

15 **If the sleeve cap proves to be too long or too short,** do the following.

a. Too short Slash the center of the sleeve and the quarter folds open from the top of the sleeve to the wrist level. Open and add desired amount of cap distance. Add this amount to both side seam/bicep corners. Blend all new lines.

b. Too long Slash the center of the sleeve and the quarter folds from the top of the sleeve to the wrist level. Close and subtract the desired amount. Blend all new lines.

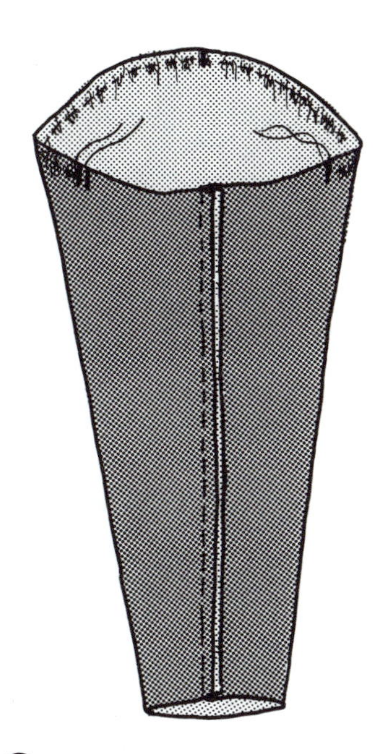

16 **Prepare the sleeve pattern for a fitting.** Cut shirt sleeve out of fabric. Sew the underarm seams together. Crimp the sleeve cap from the front notch to the back notches.

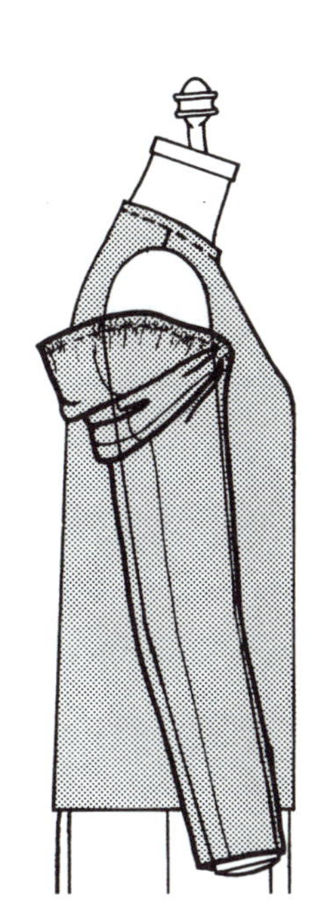

17 **Lift the arm to expose the underarm seams and pin the underarm seam** of the sleeve to the underarm seam of the bodice armhole. Place the pins on the stitchline, from the front notches down and around to the back notches.

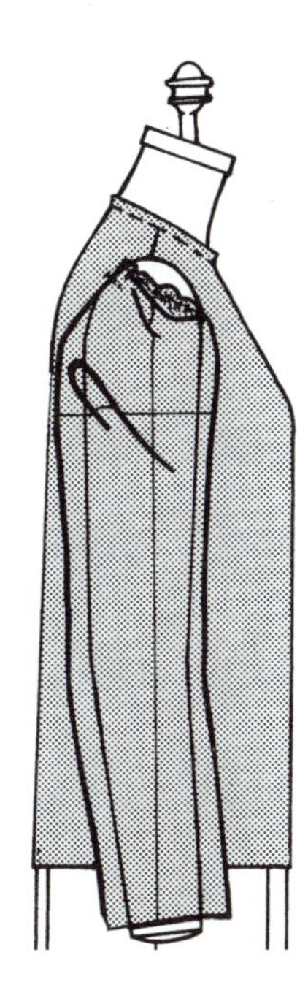

18 **Pin the sleeve cap** to the remaining portion of the armhole, matching the shoulder notch to the shoulder seam of the bodice and all remaining stitchlines.

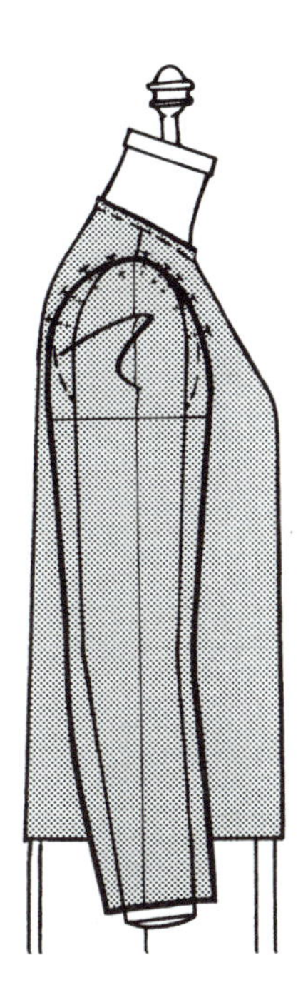

19 **Check the sleeve for accurate fit and hang.** See Fitting the Basic Sleeve, pages 88-89, to check the sleeve for proper fit and any notes on adjustments.

The important feature of the lowered or exaggerated armhole sleeve is that the bicep level and cap height are wider than normal. This allows the sleeve to fit into a lowered armhole on the bodice. The more the bodice armhole is lowered, the more the bicep level should be lifted and extended. This will create greater freedom of movement after the sleeve cap has been enlarged to accommodate the larger armhole.

This type of armhole may be used with a basic sleeve or a shirt sleeve look. For instance, a designer may want a sportswear styling with a sportive and active look. Or, the designer may want an enlarged coat sleeve styling with a higher cap and shoulder padding. The style of garment and the desired cap height will influence the sleeve shape designed.

1 Prepare sleeve cap, grainline, and crossgrain.

a. Adjust the sleeve cap by using the basic sleeve. Extend the cap to accommodate the longer armhole measurement and additional side seam ease.

b. Draw a straight of grainline in the center of the sleeve.

c. Draw a new bicep line on the sleeve at the new bicep level.

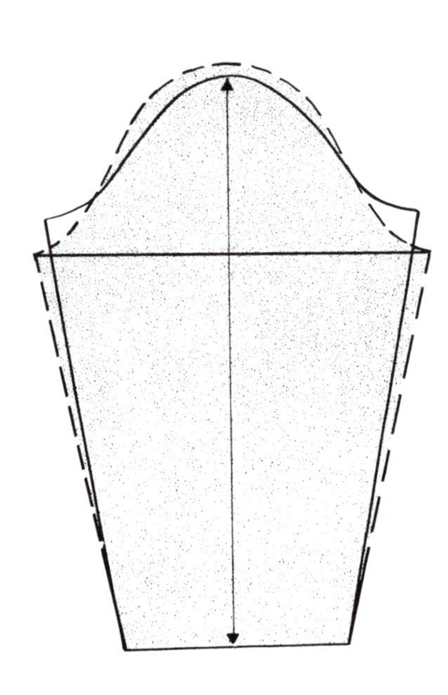

2 **Cut a piece of pattern paper** 32-inches long by 30-inches wide. Fold the paper in half lengthwise.

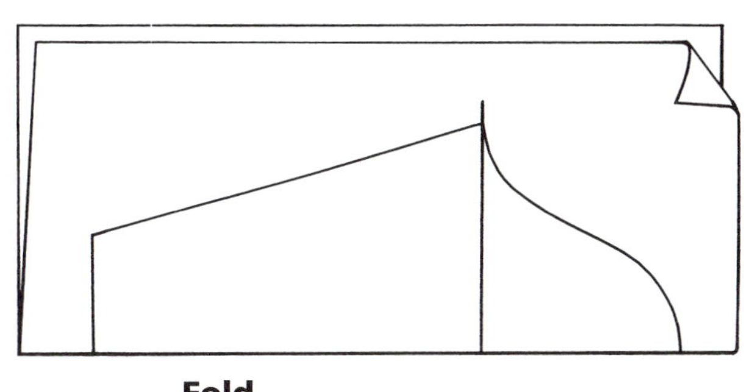

3 **Place the newly adjusted sleeve on top of the pattern paper,** matching the center of the sleeve (straight of grain) to the paper pattern fold.

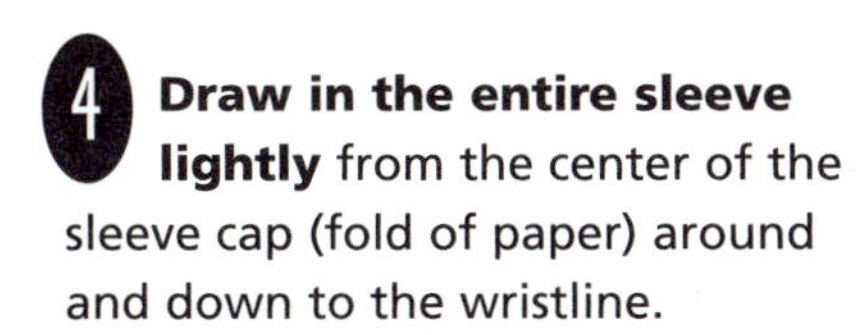

4 **Draw in the entire sleeve lightly** from the center of the sleeve cap (fold of paper) around and down to the wristline.

5 **Remove the original sleeve** pattern from the new sleeve draft.

6 **Draw in a bicep line** on the pattern paper from the center fold of the paper at the bicep level of the drawn in sleeve.

7 **Draw in a new bicep line on the new sleeve draft** 1 1/2 to 2 inches above the original bicep line on the pattern paper.

8 **Draw in the quarter fold position** of the sleeve (see illustration).

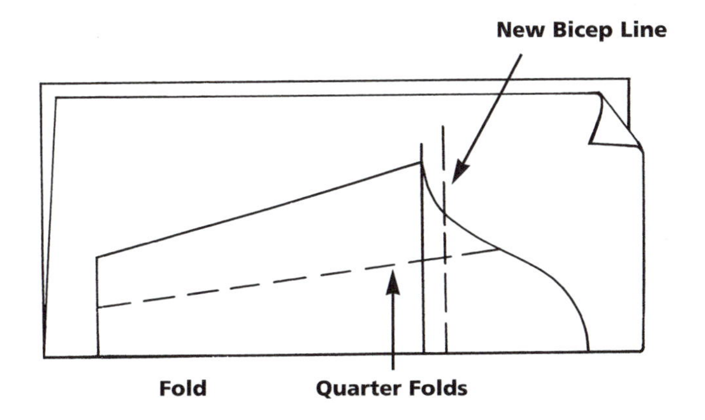

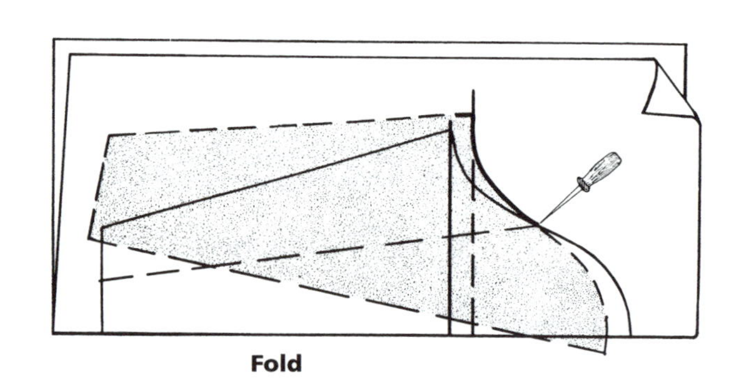

9 Place the newly adjusted sleeve on top of the paper sleeve draft. Match the center of the sleeve to the paper fold and the original bicep lines.

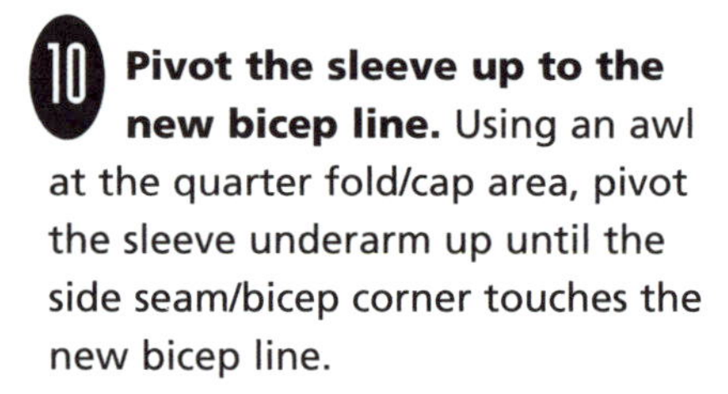

10 Pivot the sleeve up to the new bicep line. Using an awl at the quarter fold/cap area, pivot the sleeve underarm up until the side seam/bicep corner touches the new bicep line.

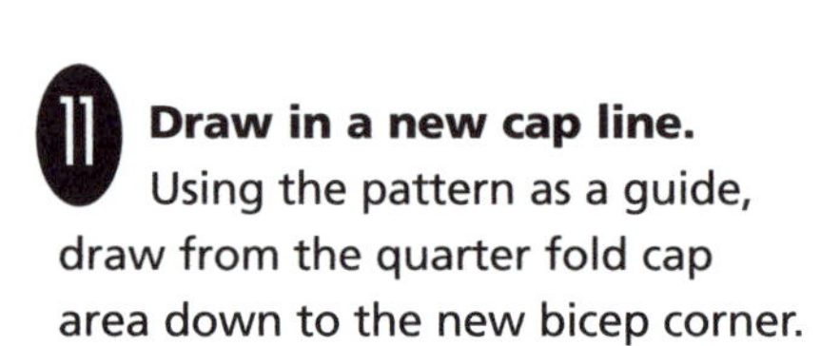

11 Draw in a new cap line. Using the pattern as a guide, draw from the quarter fold cap area down to the new bicep corner.

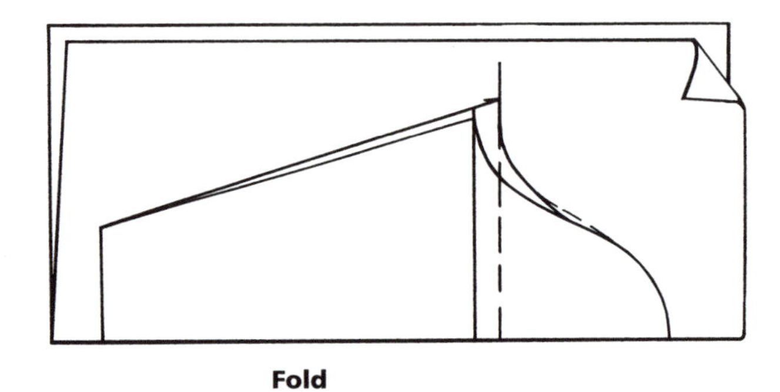

12 Draw a new underarm sleeve seam line. Using a straight ruler, connect the new underarm/bicep corner down to the original wristline.

13 Blend the new cap line. Using a curved ruler, blend a new capline. Reshape the underarm seams.

14 Cut out the sleeve pattern.

NOTE: These changes alter the length of the sleeve cap. Therefore, it is important to walk the sleeve into the armhole to determine if the sleeve cap length is too long or too short, and if the sleeve cap has sufficient ease. Step 16 offers directions for adding or subtracting cap distance.

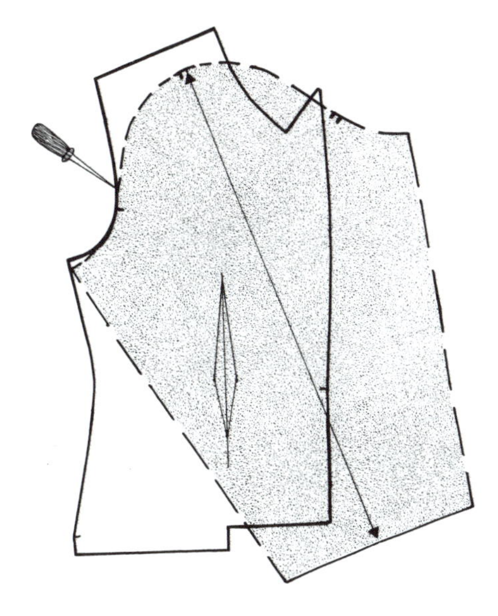

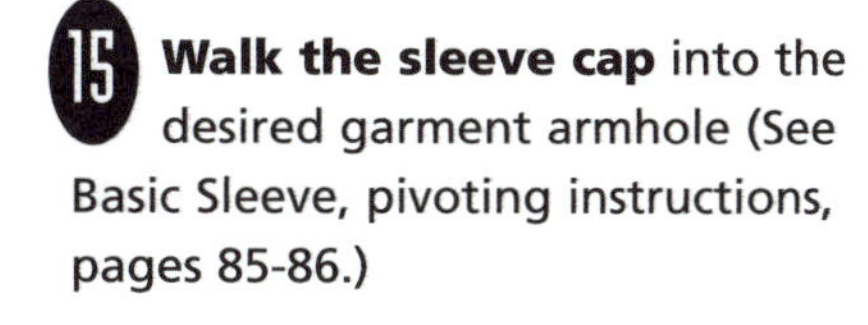

15 **Walk the sleeve cap** into the desired garment armhole (See Basic Sleeve, pivoting instructions, pages 85-86.)

a. Place the underarm of the sleeve to the underarm of the bodice, matching the stitchlines and the side seams.

NOTE: The armhole notches for the bodice have already been established.

b. Pivot the sleeve around the armhole. Use a pencil or an awl at the stitchline of the sleeve to hold the sleeve in place. Starting at the underarm side seam corner, pivot the sleeve around the armhole until the edges of the sleeve and bodice meet.

While walking the sleeve, match and pencil in the front and back armhole notches (one on the front and two on the back).

c. Continue walking the sleeve the remainder of the armhole area. Move the awl to where the sleeve and the bodice armhole meet. Continue to pivot the sleeve around the bodice armhole, until the edges of the sleeve and bodice meet once again.

Repeat this pivoting procedure until the sleeve cap meets at the shoulder/armhole corner.

d. Crossmark the shoulder positions. While walking the sleeve, crossmark on the sleeve cap the front and back bodice shoulder position of the front and back bodice. Note the amount of ease in the sleeve cap

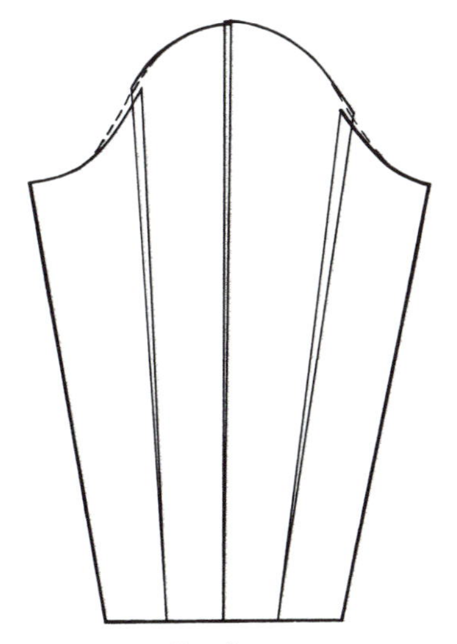

Too long

16 **If the sleeve cap proves to be too long or too short,** do the following.

a. Too short Slash the center of the sleeve and the quarter folds from the top of the sleeve to the wrist level. Open and add the desired amount of cap distance. Divide the other half in half again. Add this amount to both side seam/bicep corners. Blend all new lines.

b. Too long Slash the center of the sleeve and the quarter folds from the top of the sleeve to the wrist level. Close and subtract the desired amount. Divide the other half in half again. Subtract this amount from both side seam/bicep corners. Blend all new lines.

NOTE: A fitted sleeve could require 1 1/4 inches to 2 inches of ease in the sleeve cap. The fabric, style, and manufacturer are factors in determining the amount of ease required.

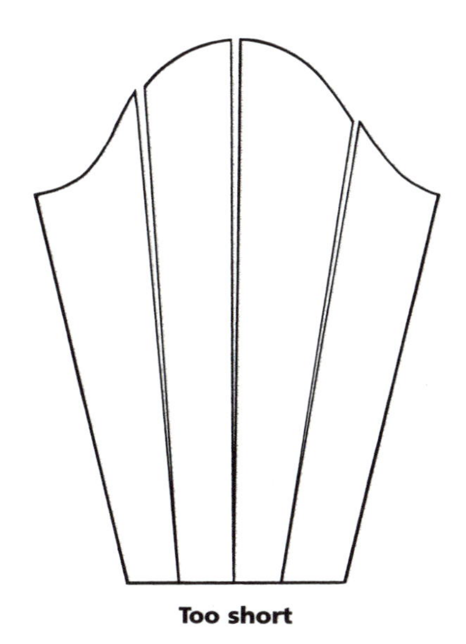

Too short

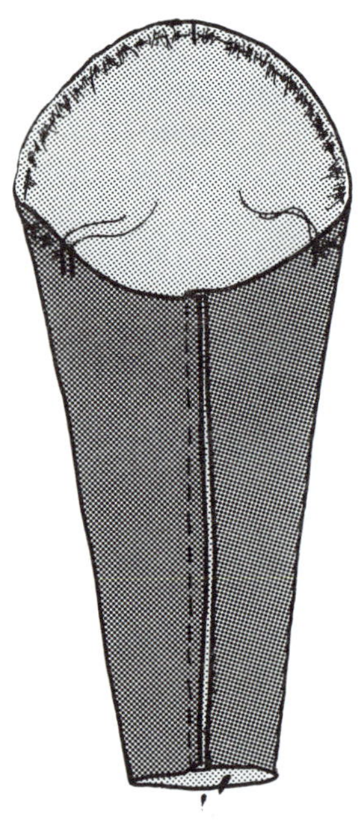

17 Prepare the sleeve pattern for a fitting. Cut the sleeve out of fabric. Sew the underarm seams together. Crimp the sleeve cap from the front notch to the back notches.

NOTE: If an elbow dart is required (usually in the fitted sleeve, but not in the shirt sleeve), draft an elbow dart at this time. Refer to Basic Sleeve, pages 84.

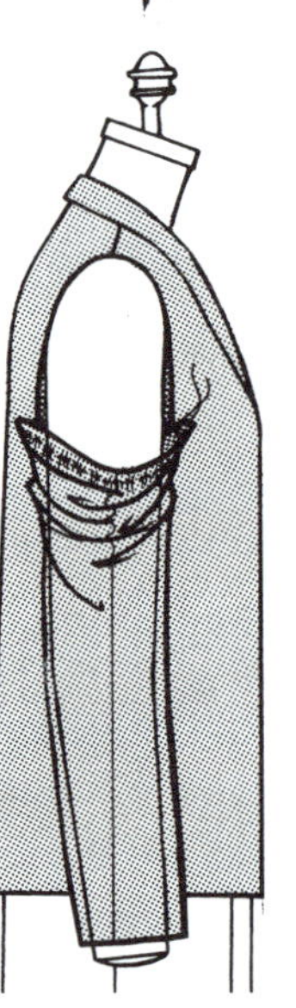

18 Lift the arm to expose the underarm seams and pin the underarm seam of the sleeve to the underarm seam of the bodice armhole. Place the pins on the stitchline, from the front notch down and around to the back notches.

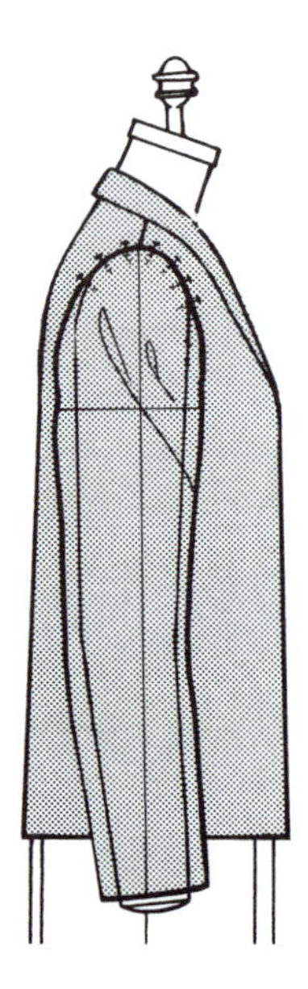

19 Pin the sleeve cap to the remaining portion of the armhole, matching the shoulder notch to the shoulder seam of the bodice and all remaining stitchlines. See Fitting the Basic Sleeve, pages 88-89, to check the sleeve for proper fit and notes on adjustments.

The raglan sleeve has a traditional underarm side seam that extends up to the front and back neckline. The design of the raglan creates a yoke area on the bodice, retaining its original underarm armhole curve in both the bodice and the sleeve. The depth of the armhole is the same as the normal armhole and falls in the same manner as any set-in sleeve. The sleeve is usually cut in two pieces with a shoulder seam.

The sleeve, however, needs a wider bicep line and a longer underarm seam so that the arm can be raised comfortably. Therefore, use Adjusted Sleeve with more Arm Movement (pages 198-202) to drape this raglan style.

If the lower portion of the armhole is deeper than the normal armhole, then use the Exaggerated Lowered Armhole Sleeve, pages 208-212, to drape this raglan style.

Raglan Sleeve —Preparing the Fabric

Prepare the Dress Form

Pin the desired yoke (raglan) seam on the front and back. The yoke line should start at the armplate, just below the screw level, and finish 1 inch below the shoulder at the neckline.

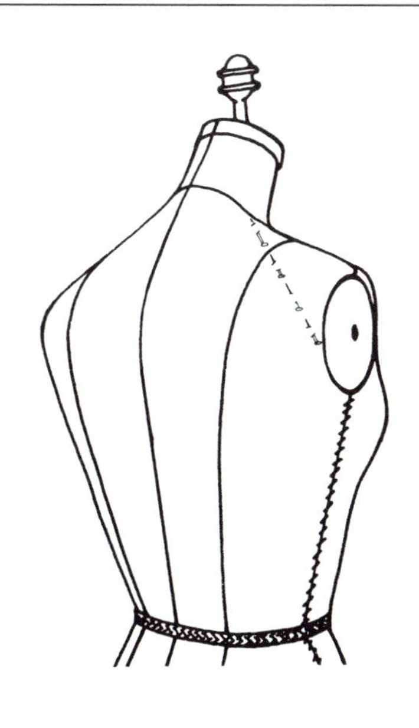

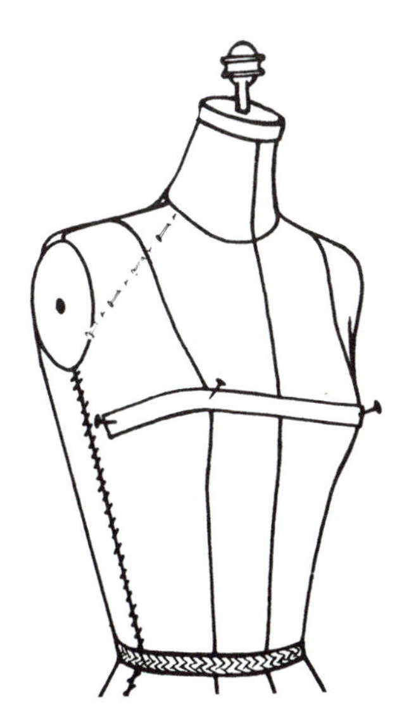

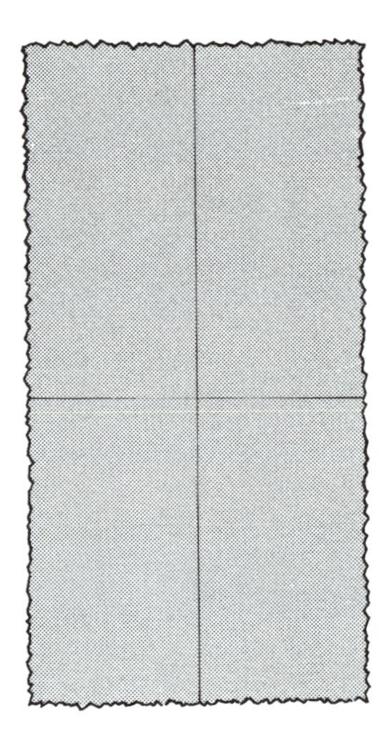

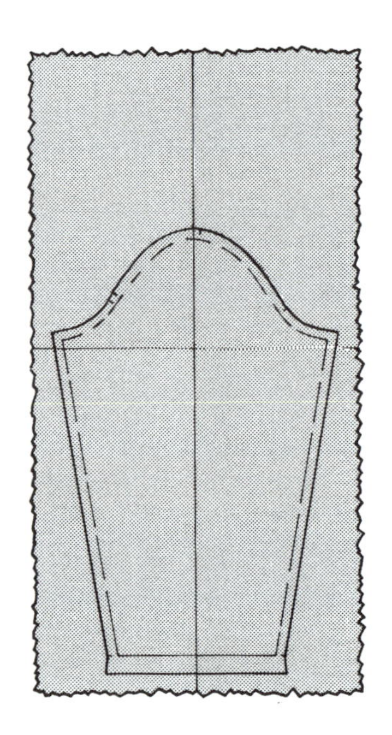

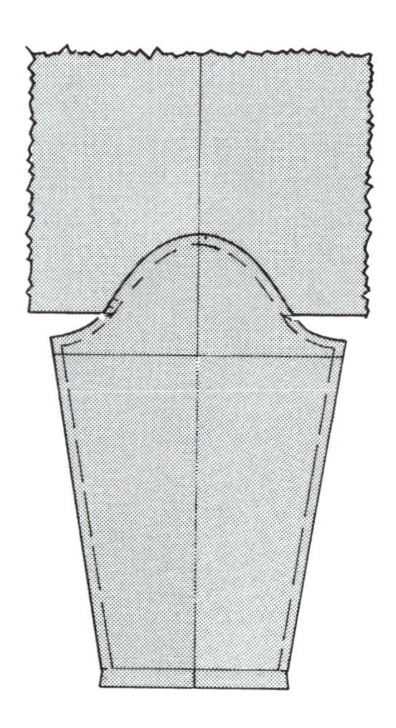

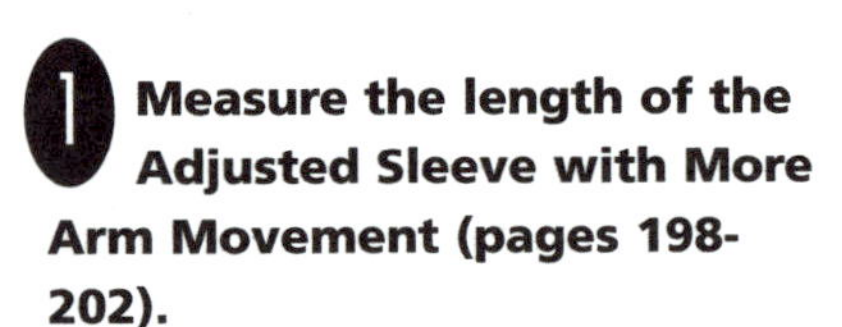

1 Measure the length of the Adjusted Sleeve with More Arm Movement (pages 198-202).

2 Cut a piece of muslin 34-inches long by 30-inches wide.

a. Draw in a grainline in the center of the muslin piece.

b. Draw in a crossgrain (bicep line) on a piece of muslin 16-inches from the top of the muslin piece.

3 Place the Adjusted Sleeve with More Arm Movement, without the elbow dart, on the muslin matching center of the sleeve (straight of grain) to the grainline on the muslin. Align the biceps level line of the sleeve to the crossgrain line.

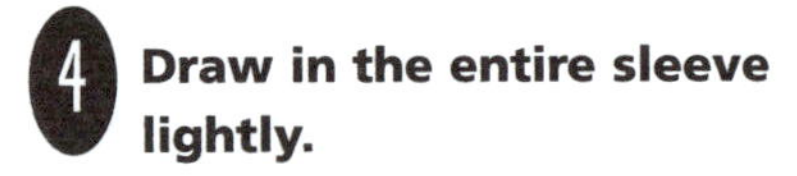

4 Draw in the entire sleeve lightly.

5 Remove the original sleeve pattern.

6 Add seam allowances to the entire sleeve.

7 Cut out the sleeve from the wrist level up to 3 inches of the underarm of the sleeve. Leave the remaining muslin on the cap area of the sleeve.

Raglan Sleeve—Preparing the Bodice Fabric

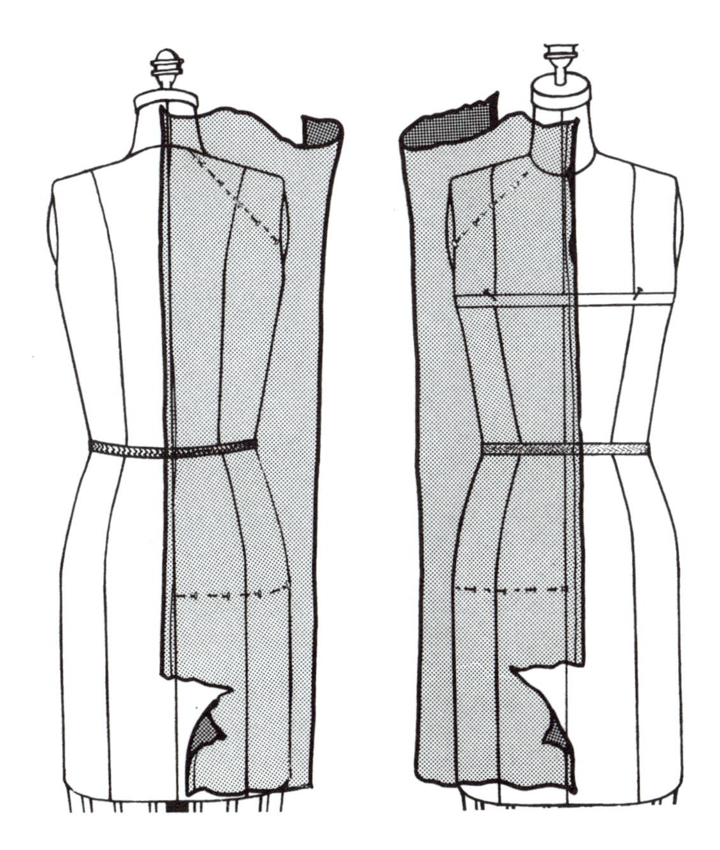

1 **Measure the length** (along the straight of grain) for both the front and back from the neckband to the hip level and add 5 inches.

Snip and tear the fabric this length.

2 **Measure the width** (along the crossgrain) for both the front and back from the center of the dress form to the side seam and add 4 inches.

Snip and tear the fabric this width.

3 **Draw the center front and center back grainlines** 1 inch from the torn edge. Press under.

4 **On the front and back fabric piece, draw in the crossgrains.**

5 **Draw in the side seams for the front and back fabric pieces.** (Refer to Basic Shift, pages 00-00, for more detailed instructions.)

a. Pin the following areas:

- center front bodice
- crossgrains
- fabric side seam to the side seam of the dress form
- shoulder neck area

b. Drape and smooth the fabric over YOKE STYLE LINE area of the dress form. Pin in place.

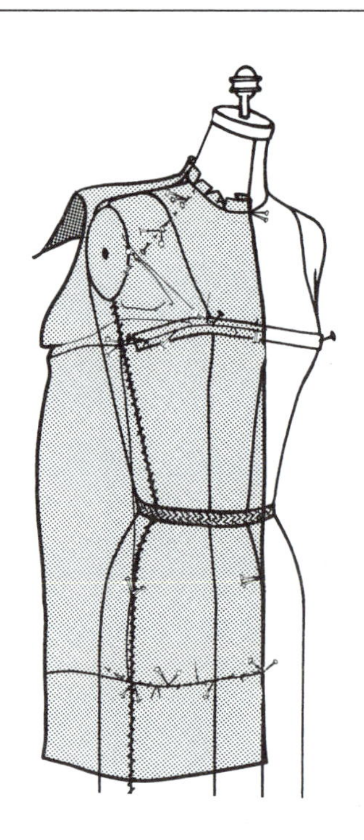

Drape the armhole and the side bust dart.

a. Smooth the fabric over the dress form armplate. Create a 1/4-inch pinch at the screw level (middle at ridge) of the armhole. Allow all excess fabric to fall over the bust level area at this time.

b. Drape the side bust dart. Allow the excess fabric to fall onto the crossgrain and fold in the side bust dart at the bustline level. Fold and pin a side bust dart utilizing the excess fabric on the crossgrain bust level line.

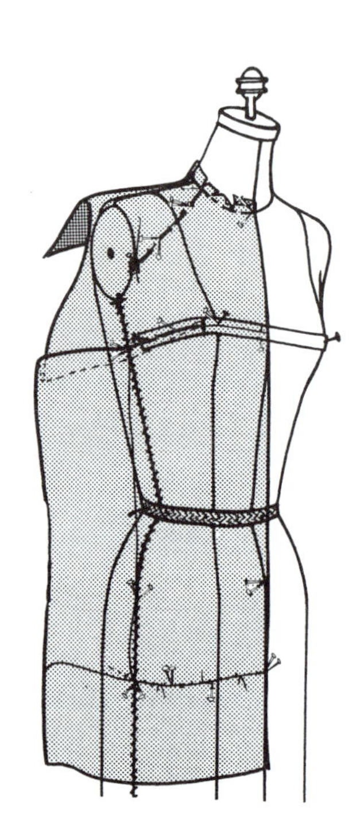

Mark key areas of the front dress form on the fabric:

Neckline Lightly crossmark.

Front yoke style line Lightly crossmark

Side seam at the waistline

Armplate
a. Middle of the armhole
b. Bottom at side seam

4 True up the front bodice, add seam allowances, and place the drape on the dress form.

NOTE: To blend raglan style line: If a smooth continuous line is desired from the mid-armhole area into the yoke style line, it will be necessary to blend these two points.

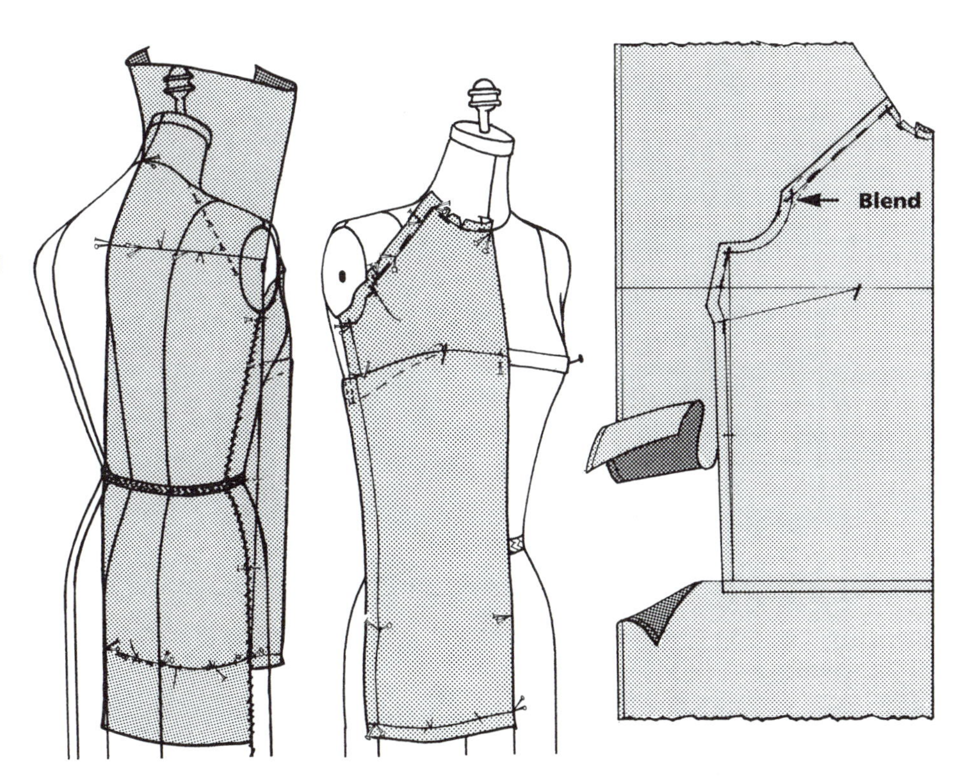

5 Fold the back side seam under and pin the back side seam to the front side seam. The seam allowance of the front will be toward the back.

6 Match the back hip level crossgrain to the front hip level crossgrain at the side seams.

7 Pin the center back grainline fold of the fabric to the center back position of the dress form. Be sure the hip level crossgrains are still matching and the fabric is not distorted. The front and back fabric pieces should be hanging plumb.

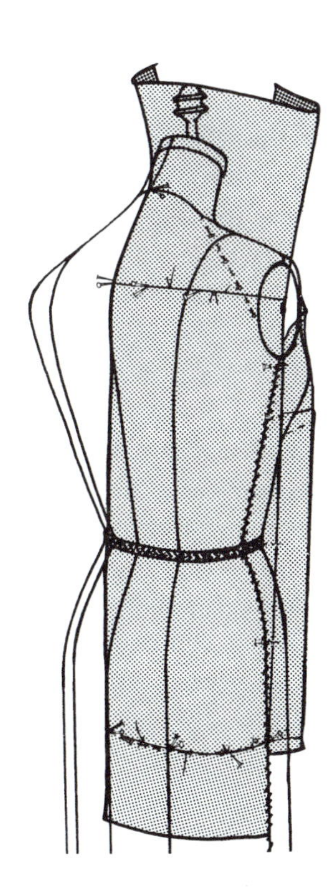

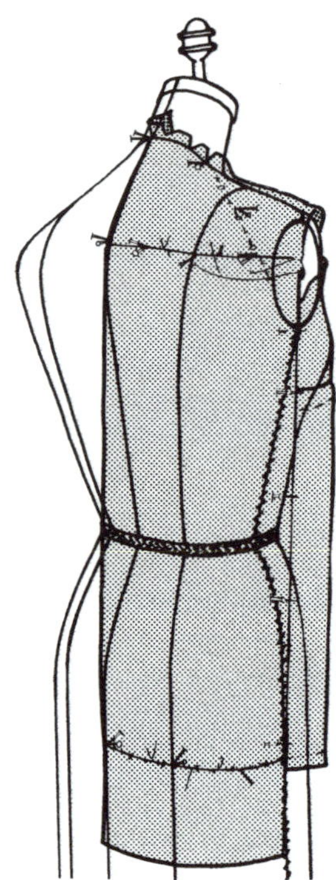

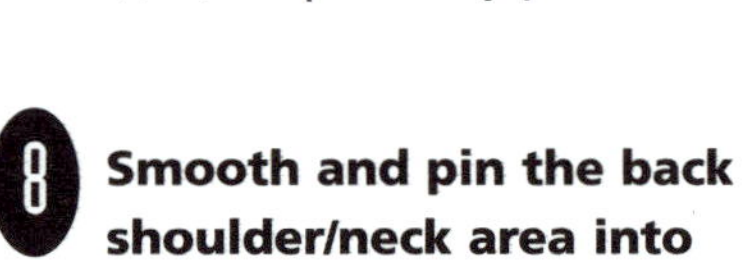

8 Smooth and pin the back shoulder/neck area into position.

NOTE: The back armhole area will show a definite amount of ease about halfway from the shoulder seam to the shoulder blade level crossgrain. Leave this ease in the armhole.

9 Drape and smooth the fabric over YOKE STYLE LINE area of the dress form. Pin in place.

10 Mark key areas of the back dress form on the fabric:

Neckline Lightly crossmark.

Back yoke style line Lightly crossmark

Side seam at the waistline

Armplate
a. Middle of the armhole - crossmark middle of armhole ridge fullness
b. Bottom at side seam

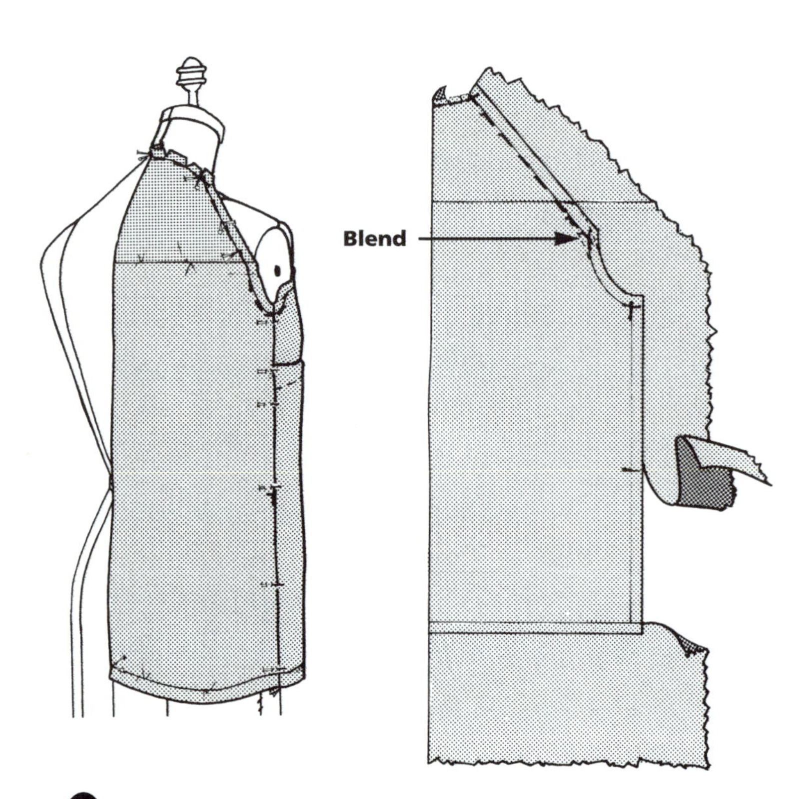

11 True up all seams. Remove the front and back drape from the dress form and true up all seams. Add seam allowances: 1/4 inch at the back neckline; 1/2 inch to all other seams.

NOTE: **To blend raglan style line:** If a smooth continuous line is desired from the mid-armhole area into the yoke style line, it will be necessary to blend these two points.

12 Return the drape to the dress form and check for accuracy, fit, and balance. The drape should fit smoothly around the neckline without gaping or stretching. Also, the entire bodice drape should fit all areas of the dress form correctly.

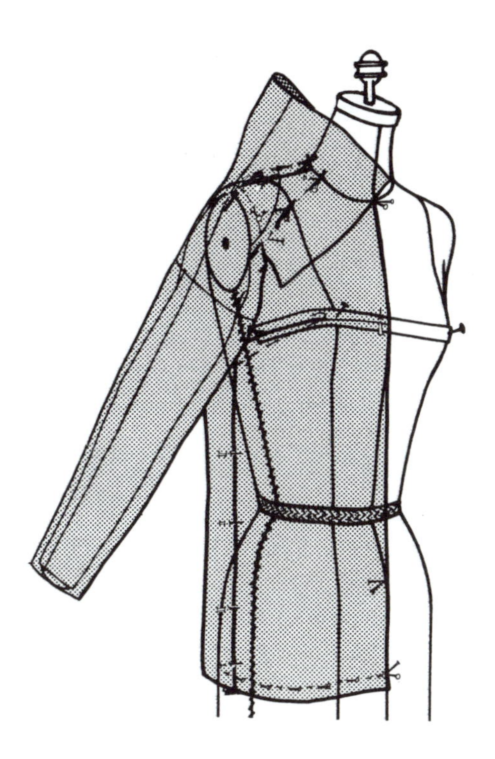

Prepare the dress form.

Attach the arm to the dress form.

1. **Pin the underarm seam of the sleeve together.**

2. **Place the sleeve over the arm on the dress form.** Align the sleeve grainline in the center of the arm and toward the shoulder seam of the dress form.

3. **Hold the arm out from the dress form and pin** the underarm section of the sleeve cap into the lower armhole of the bodice.

4. **Drape the sleeve into the front and back style lines** of the garment desired.

a. Smooth the front cap area of the sleeve toward the neckline and pin along all style line seams.

b. Smooth the back cap area of the sleeve toward the neckline and pin along all style line seams.

5. **Smooth the front and back shoulder seams together.** From the yoke style line, smooth the fabric up to the shoulder seam of the dress form. Excess fabric will be created above the shoulder seam.

NOTE: When the arm is attached to the dress form this will add about a 3/8-inch shoulder excess at the shoulder/ridge intersection.

6. **Mark key areas** of the sleeve on fabric.

Neckline Lightly crossmark

Front yoke style line Lightly crossmark

Back yoke style line Lightly cross-mark

Shoulder seam to ridge

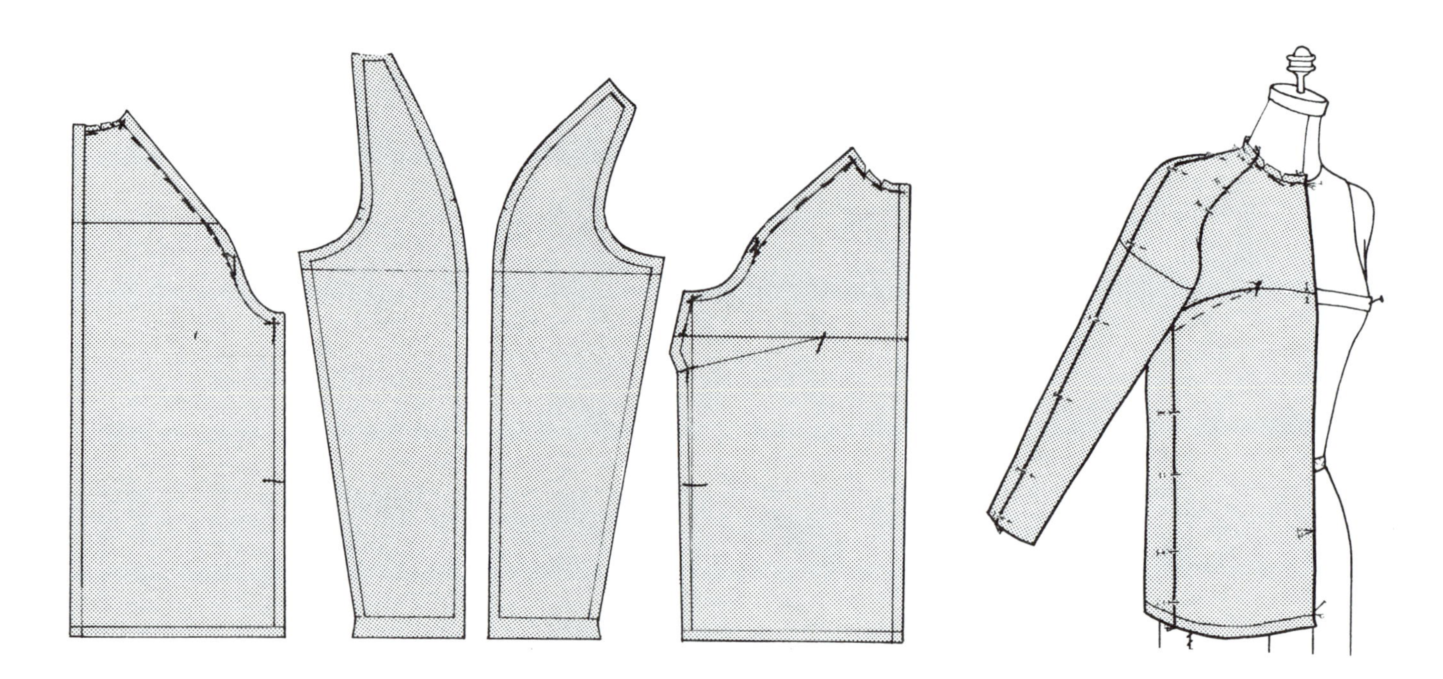

7 **True up all seams.** Remove the sleeve and the front and back drape from the dress form and true up all seams.

a. Separate the front and back sleeve. Cut the sleeve at the grainline. This will make a full shoulder seam, a separate front sleeve, and a back sleeve.

b. Add seam allowances: 1/4 inch at the front and back neckline of the sleeve; 1/2 inch to all other seams.

c. Add 1-inch hem allowance at the bottom of the sleeve.

NOTE: **To blend raglan style line:** If a smooth continuous line is desired from the armhole into the yoke style line, it will be necessary to blend these two points.

Chapter Fifteen

Collars

Objectives

By studying the various draping steps in this chapter, the designer should be able to accomplish the following:

- Recognize grain and crossgrain of fabric in relation to the collar as it is draped into the neckline.
- Drape a flat piece of fabric and fit the crossgrain into the back neckline.
- For a turtleneck collar, drape a piece of fabric cut on the bias into the front and back neckline.
- Drape and shape the collar neckline into the front neckline of the bodice.
- Create a collar stand for convertible and turtleneck collars.
- Shape the outer collar edge in the desired design.
- True up and check the results of the draping process with regard to the finished shape, width, and fit.

Collars

The focal point of a garment is the neckline. Collars frame the face and in most cases are noticed before other details of the garment. It is important, therefore, that a collar is flattering and that effort is spent in carefully draping and trueing the desired collar design.

This chapter describes a variety of collars that encircle the neck edge—some collars lay flat on the shoulders, some collars rise up from the neckline and then fold over onto the shoulders, and some collars stand up from the neck edge. By using correct and skillful draping methods, a designer can create multiple styles from a traditional collar. By changing the shape of the neckline, the designer can control the amount of stand desired for a particular design, thereby creating a flat collar rather than a traditional stand collar, or vice versa. Also, the designer can see the exact width and outside shape necessary to create a perfectly balanced design.

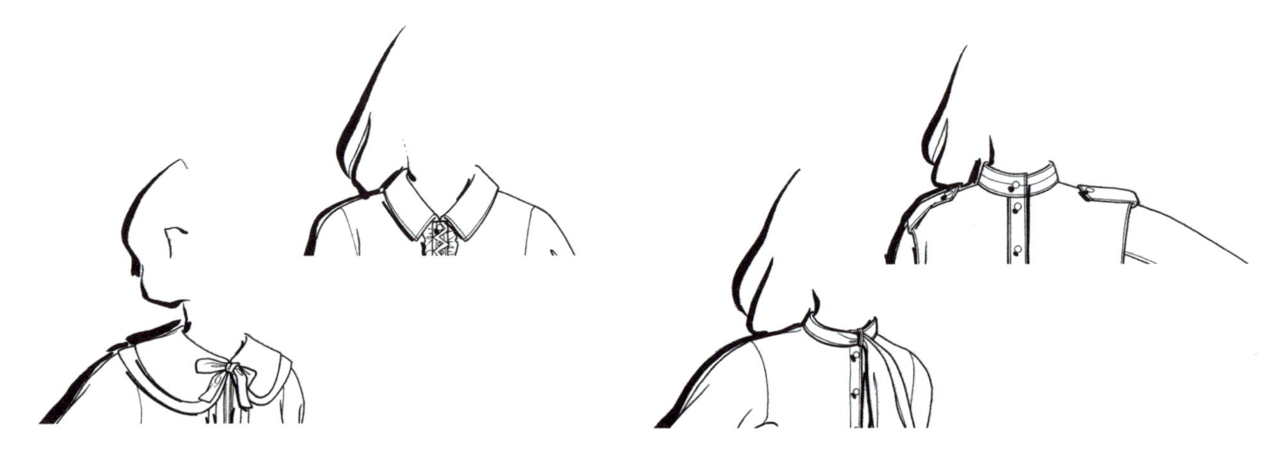

Convertible Collar

The convertible collar is a roll over collar without a separate stand. The outside shape of the collar can be designed in a variety of shapes, usually pointed, and the collar may be worn open or closed against the front neckline. The neck edge of this collar is relatively straight and produces a high standing collar that rolls back onto itself. When the neck edge of the collar has a slight curve, it gives a less pronounced stand when sewn into a garment. A convertible collar works well on almost any neckline, from V-necklines to jewel necklines.

Convertible Collar—Preparing the Fabric

1 **Measure the width** of the desired collar design (along the straight of grain), and add 4 inches.

Illustrated: approximately **6 inches.**

2 **Measure the length** of the desired collar design (along the crossgrain) from center back to center front, and add 4 inches. Snip and tear the fabric at this crossgrain length.

Illustrated: approximately **12 inches.**

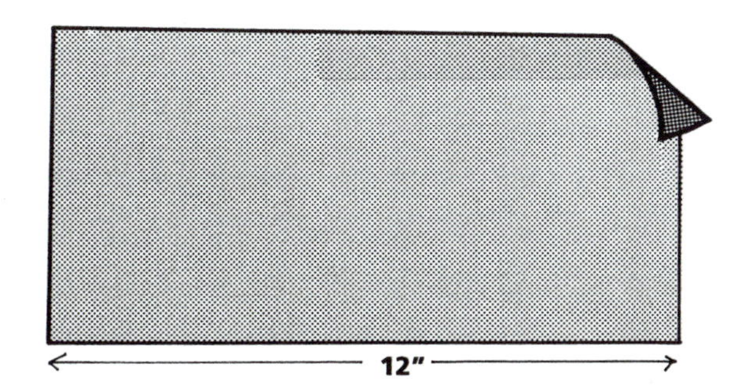

3 **Draw the center back grainline** 1 inch along the torn edge and parallel to the grain of the fabric. Press under.

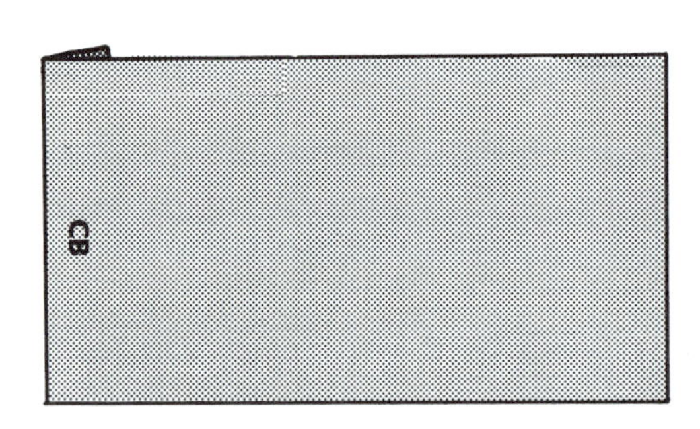

4 **Draw a perfect crossgrain line** 1 inch from the lower edge of the fabric. Use an Lsquare ruler.

5 **Draw a shorter second crossgrain line** 1/2 inch above the first crossgrain line, starting about 3 inches from the grainline fold (see illustration).

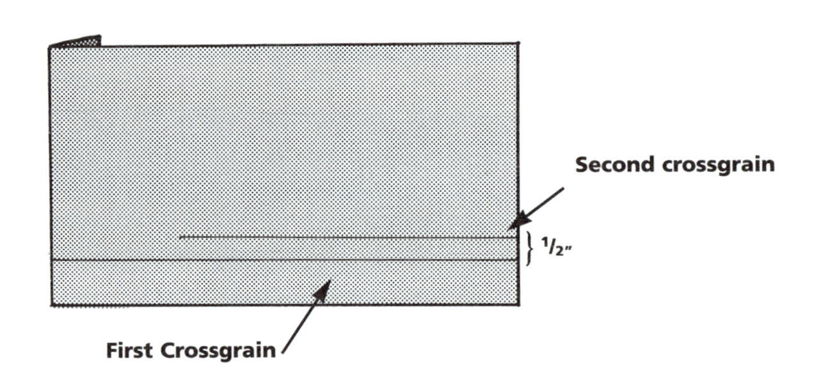

Notes

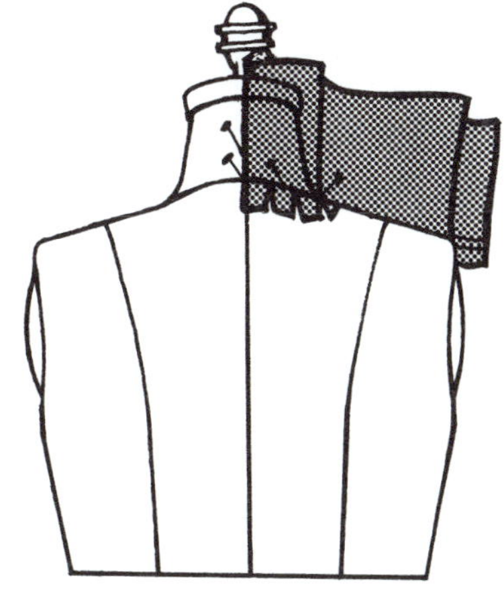

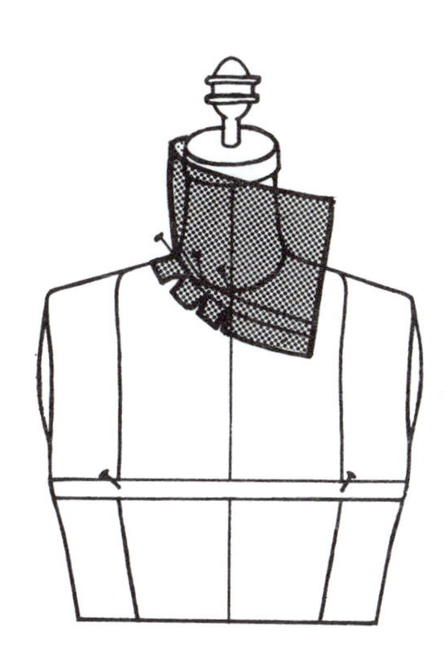

NOTE: Drape convertible collar into the designed neckline of the garment.

1 **Pin the center back grainline** fold of the fabric on the center back neckline position of the dress form.

2 **Align the crossgrain of the fabric** on the neckline of the dress form.

3 **Drape the back neckline.** Clip, smooth, and pin the crossgrain along the neckline from the center back to the shoulder of the dress form.

4 **Drape the front neckline.** Clip, smooth, and pin the crossgrain line from the shoulder to the front neckline of the dress form.

5 **At the same time, allow the second crossgrain to drop** and shape onto the neckline at the center front position of the dress form.

If desired, draw in the neckline at this time.

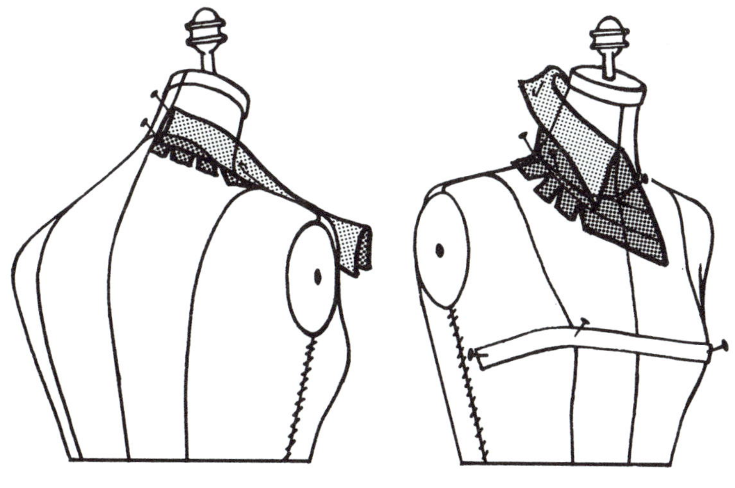

6 **Drape the collar stand.** Anchor a pin on the center back upper fold. This is to ensure that the collar stand does not fall off of the center back and stays perpendicular to the grain. Fold the fabric over on itself (the desired width) at center back. The fold will continue around to the front of the drape, gradually disappearing at center front.

dot Mark N bef working top part

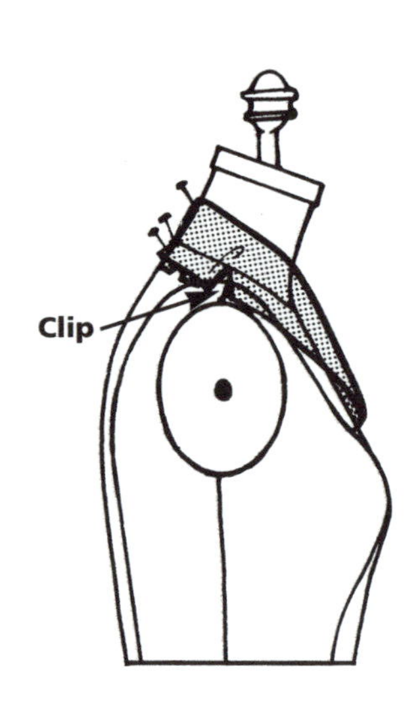

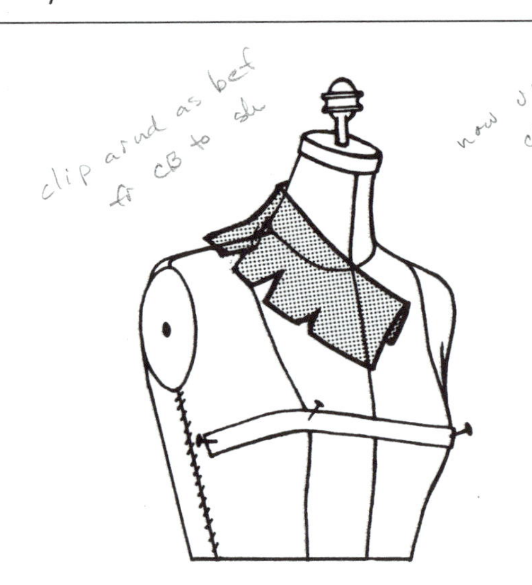

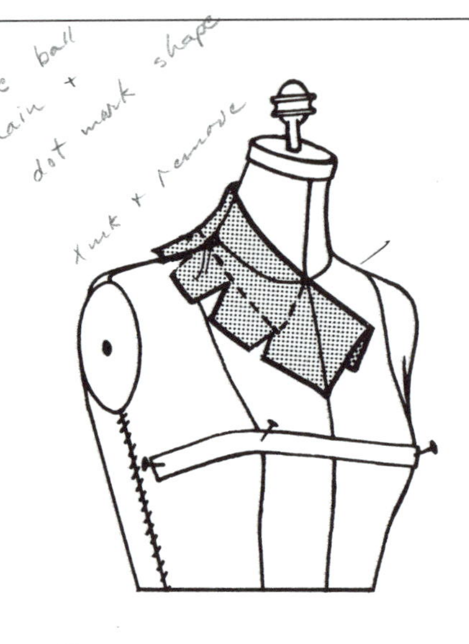

7 Clip the collar, at the shoulder. To allow the collar to lay down easily, clip from the outer raw edge up to the desired width of the collar. After clipping, place another pin at the center back, just below the neckline.

8 Trim and clip the fabric up to the desired collar width and shape. The collar will automatically lay over the shoulder and drape flat at center front point.

9 Draw the desired outer edge styling. Starting at center front neck, continue to draw the desired width, finishing at center back.

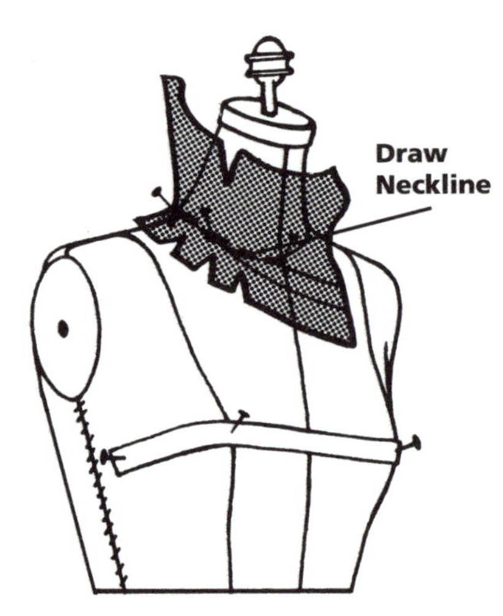

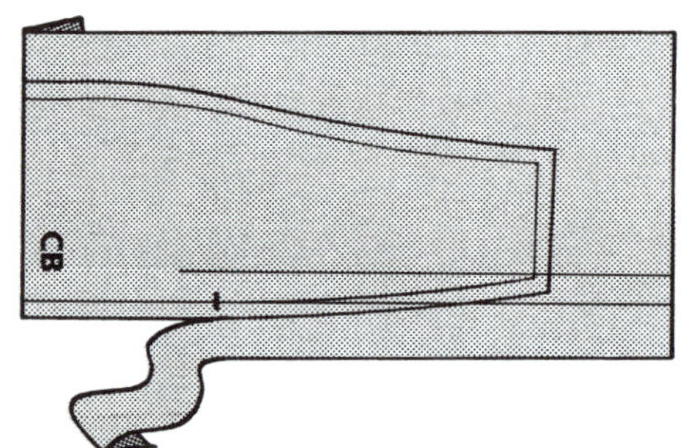

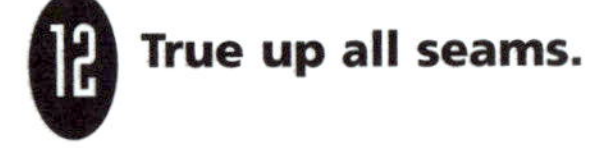

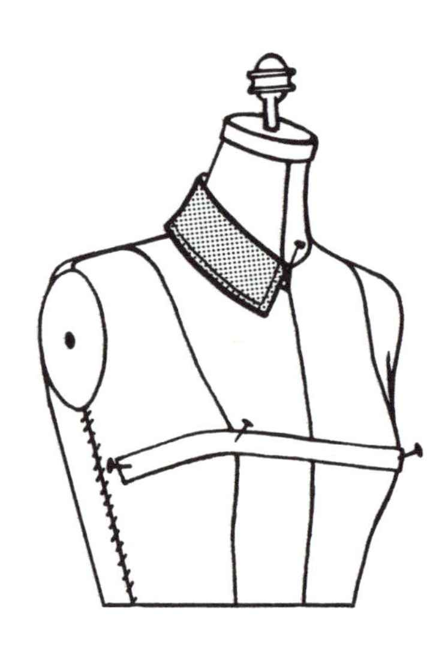

10 Draw the neckline. Flip the collar up and draw the front neckline from the shoulder to center front.

11 Crossmark a shoulder position notch.

12 True up all seams.

a. Remove the collar from the dress form and true up all lines. Add 1/4 inch.

b. Transfer the collar shape to the other side of muslin.

c. Add 1/4-inch seam allowance around the collar edges and trim excess fabric.

13 Check the collar fit and outside shape. Return the trued collar to the dress form and check for accuracy, fit, shape, and balance. The drape should fit smoothly around the neckline without gapping or stretching.

Mandarin Collar

The mandarin collar is generally a narrow, standing collar that curves around the neck smoothly. The width of the collar and how closely it is draped to the neckline will create many different designs. It can be stiff and close to the neck for a military effect; it can be a soft loose band for a more casual look; or it can be made with its opening in the back creating a narrow standing band type of collar. Also, a tie collar can be developed by adding long tie strips at the center front ends.

Mandarin Collar Preparing the Fabric

1. **Measure the width of the desired collar,** and add 2 inches. Snip and tear the fabric at this width.

   Illustrated: approximately 4 inches.

2. **Measure the neck area** from center back to center front, and add 4 inches. Snip and tear the fabric (along the crossgrain) at this length.

   Illustrated: approximately 12 inches.

12"

3 **Draw the center back grainline** 1 inch along the torn edge and parallel to the grain of the fabric. Press under.

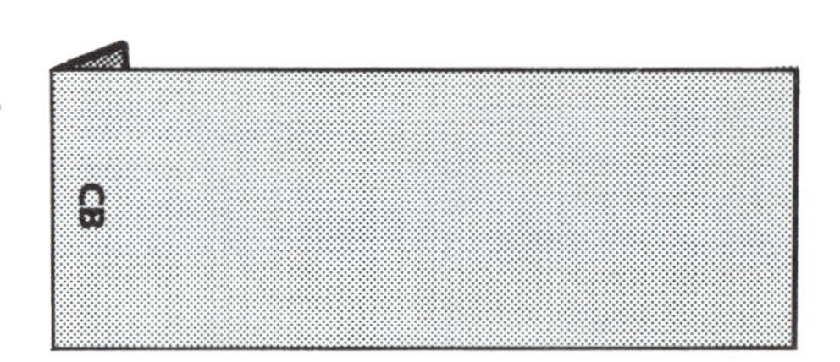

4 **Draw a perfect crossgrain line** 1 inch from the lower edge of the fabric.

5 **Draw a second crossgrain line** 1/2 inch above the first crossgrain line, starting about 3 inches from the grainline fold (see illustration).

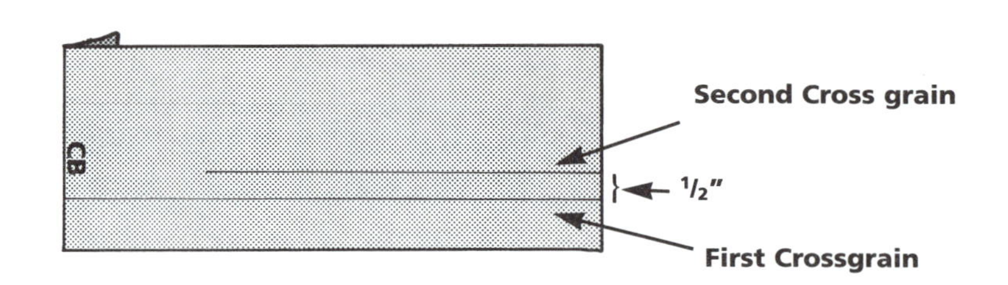

Notes

Mandarin Collar—Draping Steps

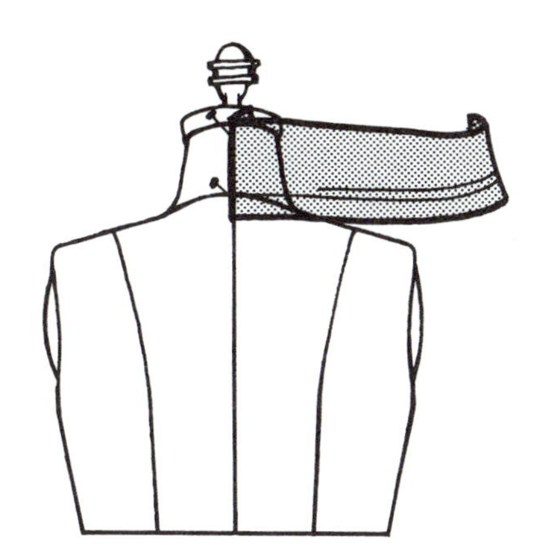

NOTE: Drape mandarin collar into the designed neckline of the garment.

drape same as convertible w/o folding down

1 **Pin the center back grainline** fold of the fabric on the center back position of the dress form neckline.

2 **Align the crossgrain** of the fabric on the neckline of the dress form.

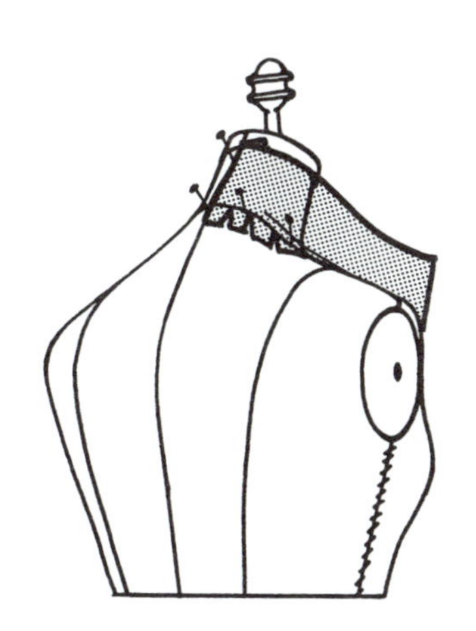

3 **Drape the crossgrain.** Clip, smooth, pin, and drape the crossgrain along the back neckline seam of the dress form from the center back to the shoulder seam.

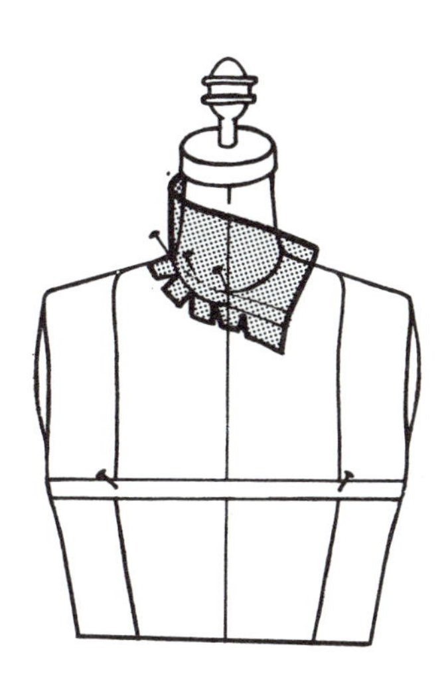

4 **Drape the crossgrain on the neckline** of the dress form to center front. From the shoulder, continue to clip, smooth, pin and drape the crossgrain on the front neckline of the dress form. Allow the second crossgrain to drop and shape onto the neckline at the center front position of the dress form.

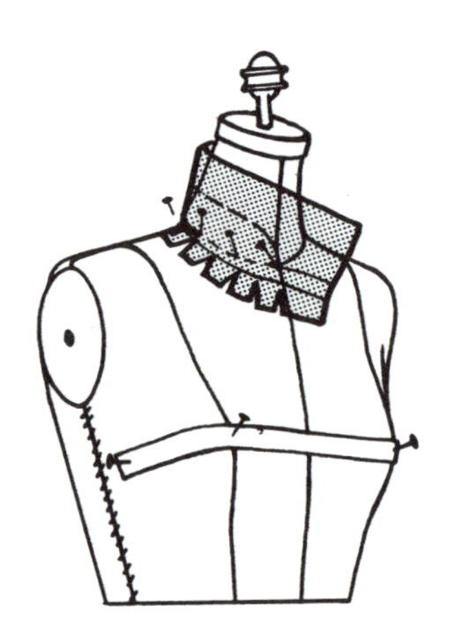

5 **Draw the new front neckline** from the shoulder to center front.

6 **Crossmark a shoulder position notch.**

7 **Draw the desired outer edge styling** from center front neck to center back in the desired width and parallel to the neckline.

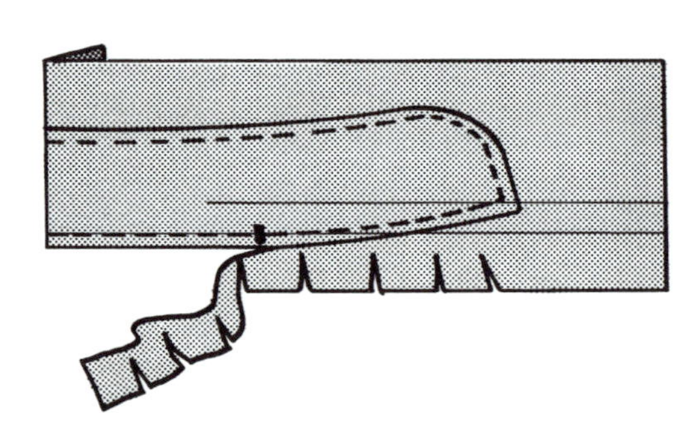

8 **True up all seams.**

a. Remove the collar from the dress form and true up all seams.

b. Add 1/4 inch seam allowance around the outer edges and trim excess fabric. The center back grainline will be placed on the fold of the fabric.

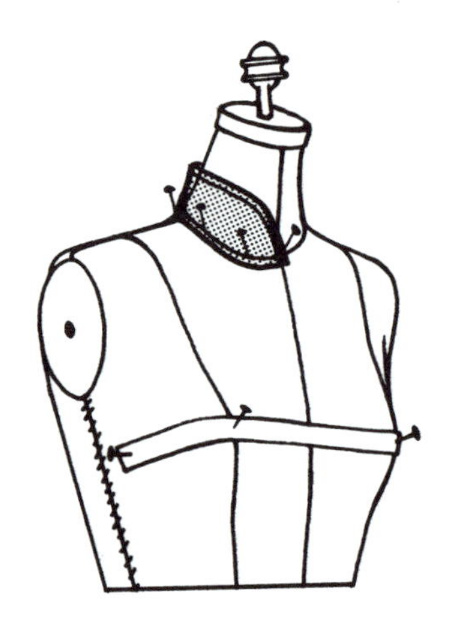

9 **Check the collar fit and outside shape.** Return the trued collar to the dress form and check for accuracy, fit, shape, and balance. The drape should fit smoothly around the neckline without gapping or stretching.

Variation

For a band collar, prepare the fabric drape in the same manner, draping the collar from center front to center back.

Peter Pan Collar

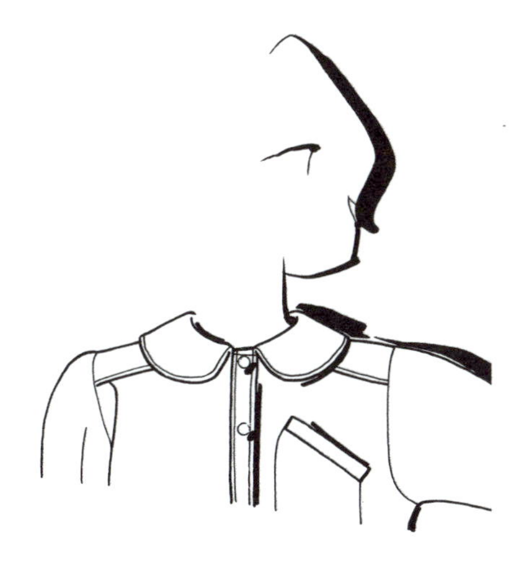

A traditional peter pan collar is a lay down collar that has very little roll because the neck edge is curved similarly to the garment neckline. The round shape and flat drape are recognizable characteristics in a traditional peter pan collar. However, the collar width may vary from very narrow to exceptionally wide, and the outside edge may be shaped in various designs.

The peter pan collar can provide appealing design qualities in such fabrics as fine cottons, laces, open work weaves, or silks.

Peter Pan Collar—Preparing the Fabric

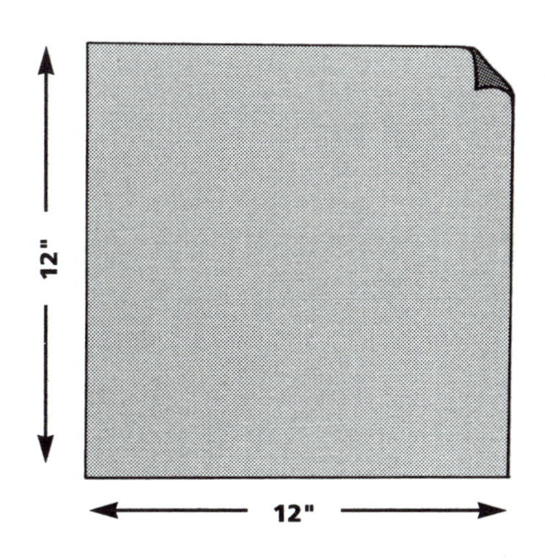

1 **For the length and width of this collar,** measure the desired area and add 9 inches. Cut a perfect square this measurement.

Illustrated: approximately **12-inch square.**

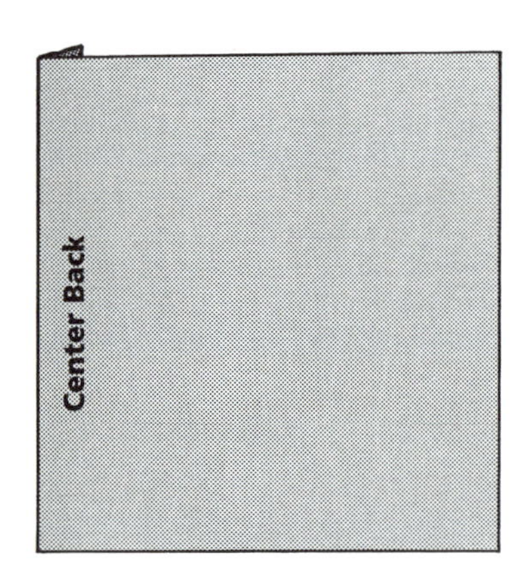

2 **Draw the center back grainline** 1 inch along the torn edge and parallel to the grain of the fabric. Press under.

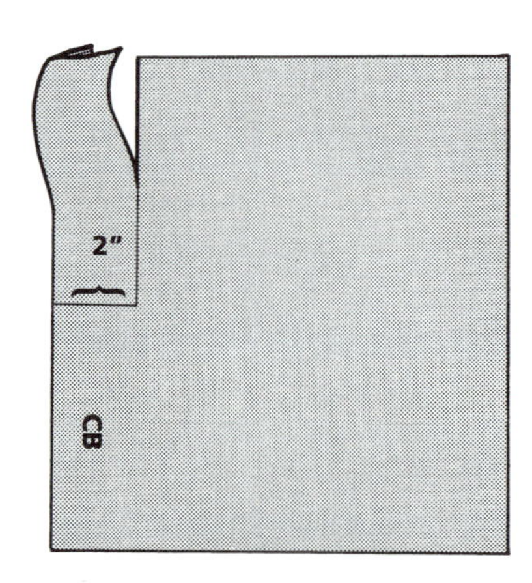

3 **Prepare back neck opening.**

a. **Draw a perfect crossgrain 2-inches long** half the distance from the lower edge of the fabric piece. Draw a perfect crossgrain 2-inches long at this position.

b. **Draw a second grainline** parallel to and 2 inches from the center back grainline.

c. **Cut along the crossgrain line and the second grainline,** and then remove this rectangular piece of fabric.

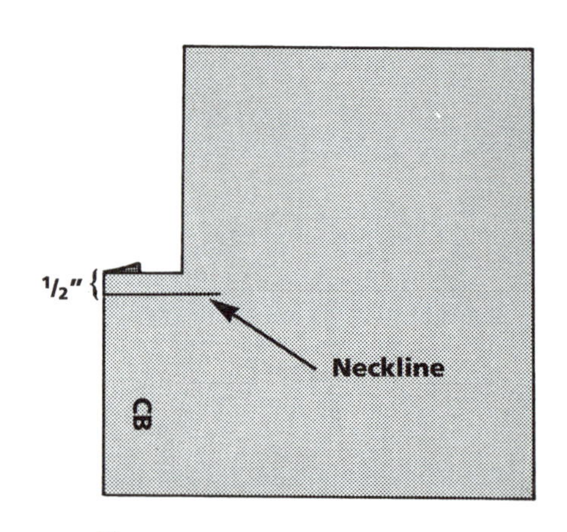

4 **Draw a short crossgrain 1/2 inch below** the cut edge crossgrain. This indicates the center back/neck position.

Notes

Peter Pan Collar—Draping Steps

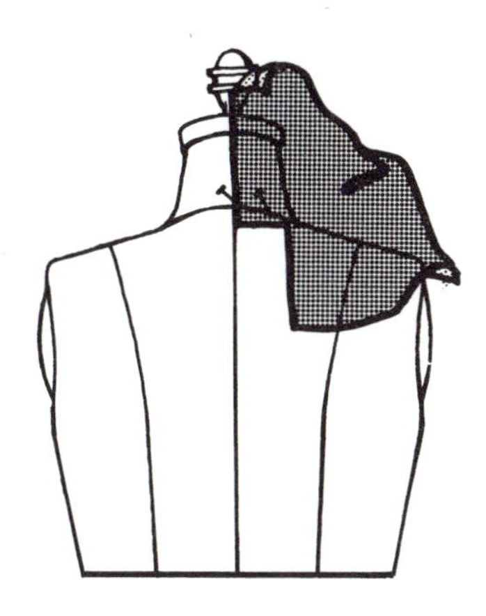

NOTE: Drape peter pan collar into the designed neckline of the garment.

1 **Pin the center back grainline** of the fabric to the center back position of the dress form neckline.

2 **Align the center back neckline position** (1/2-inch-short crossgrain mark) of the fabric on the center back position of the dress form.

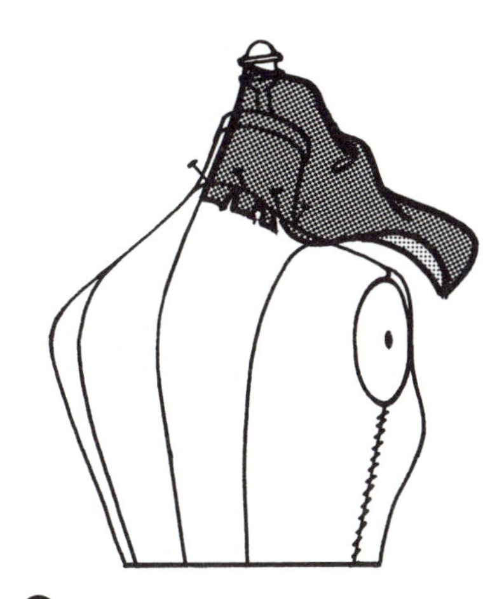

3 **Clip, smooth, and pin the crossgrain along the back neckline** seam of the dress form from the center back to the shoulder seam.

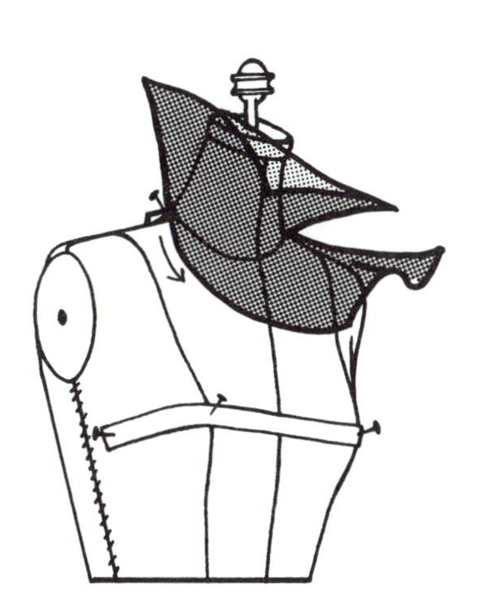

4 **Clip, smooth, and pin the front neckline.**

a. Pivot the lower edge of the fabric piece around the front neckline of the dress form from the shoulder seam of the garment. Keep the fabric flipped up.

b. Clip, smooth, drape, and pin the fabric around the front dress form neckline, finishing at center front position.

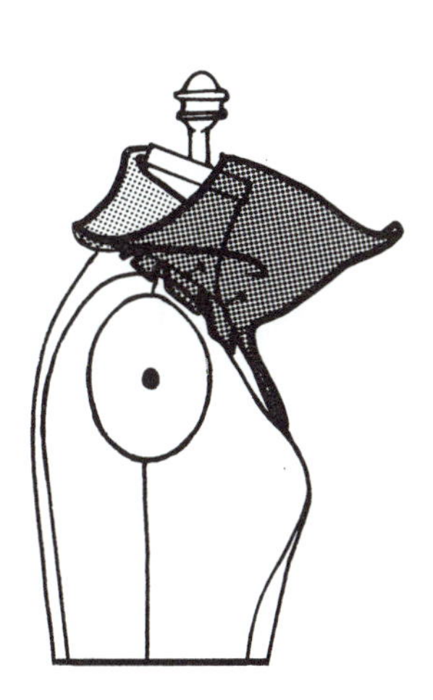

5 **Flip the fabric piece down** over the neckline so the fabric is laying down over the body and shoulder areas.

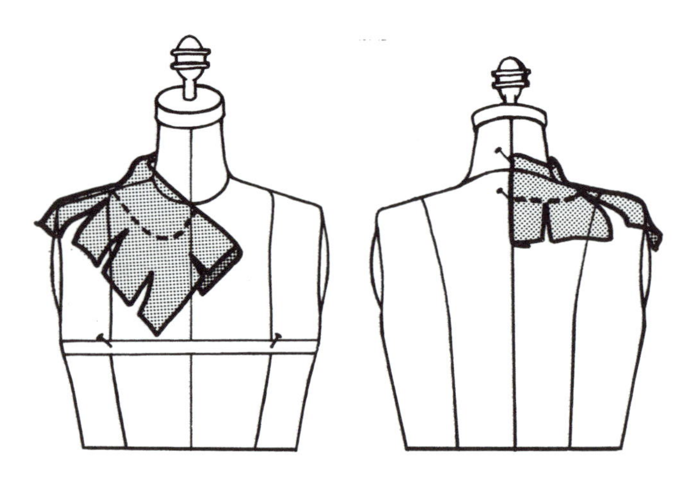

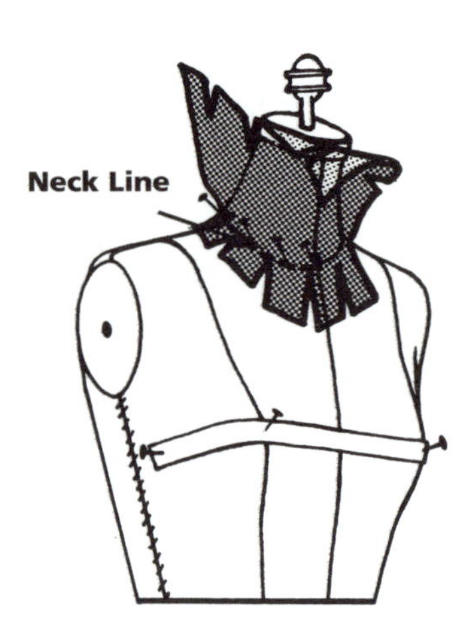

6 **Clip the outer edge of the fabric** up to where the outer edge of the collar may be drawn. This will allow the collar to lay smoothly.

7 **Draw the desired collar style,** starting at the center front neck area of the dress form.

NOTE: It is vital that the center back grainline should remain on the center back of the dress form.

8 **Draw the desired neckline** from the center back to the center front.

9 **Draw a crossmark at the shoulder seam** of the dress form.

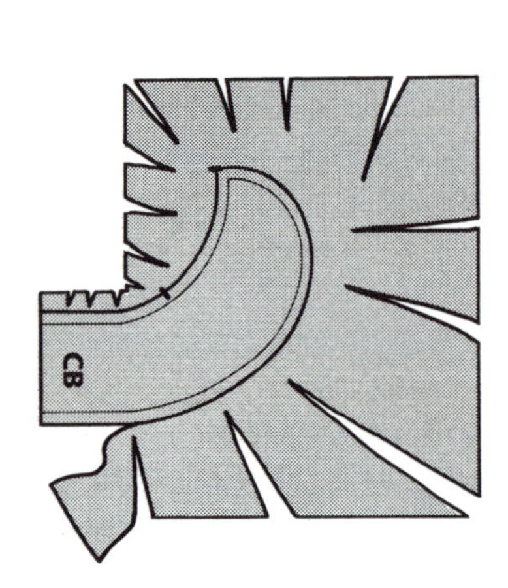

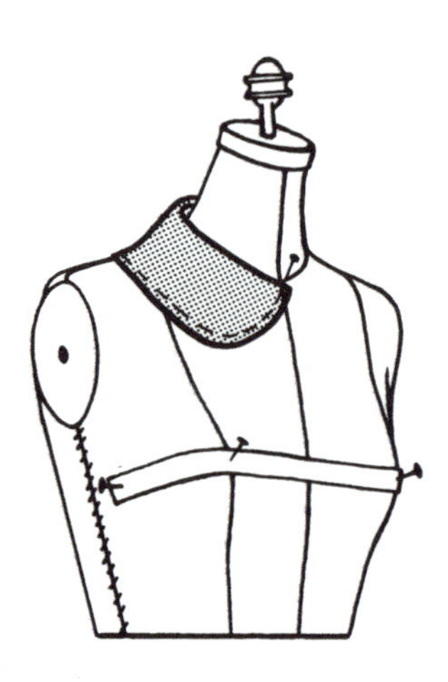

10 **True up all seams.**

a. Remove the collar from the dress form and true up all seams.

b. Add 1/4-inch seam allowance around the outer edges and trim excess fabric.

c. To make a complete collar, place the center back grainline on the fold of the fabric.

11 Return the trued collar to the dress form and check for accuracy, fit, and balance. The drape should fit smoothly around the neckline without gapping or stretching.

Turtleneck Collar

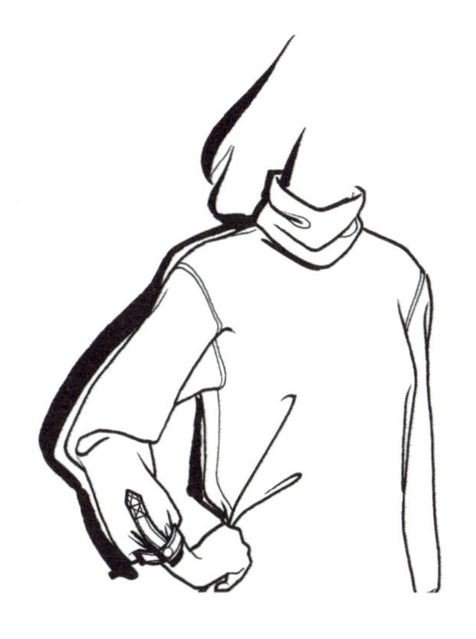

The turtleneck collar is a one-piece standing bias collar rolled over to cover the neckline. This bias turnover effect makes a smooth roll possible and allows the collar to be draped into a high neckline to give a close-to-the-body effect or into a wide lowered neckline to give a cowl-draped effect. The turtleneck-collar serves two design functions; It provides extra warmth for its wear-er and adds a decorative and flat-tering design to the neck edge.

Turtleneck Collar—Preparing the Fabric

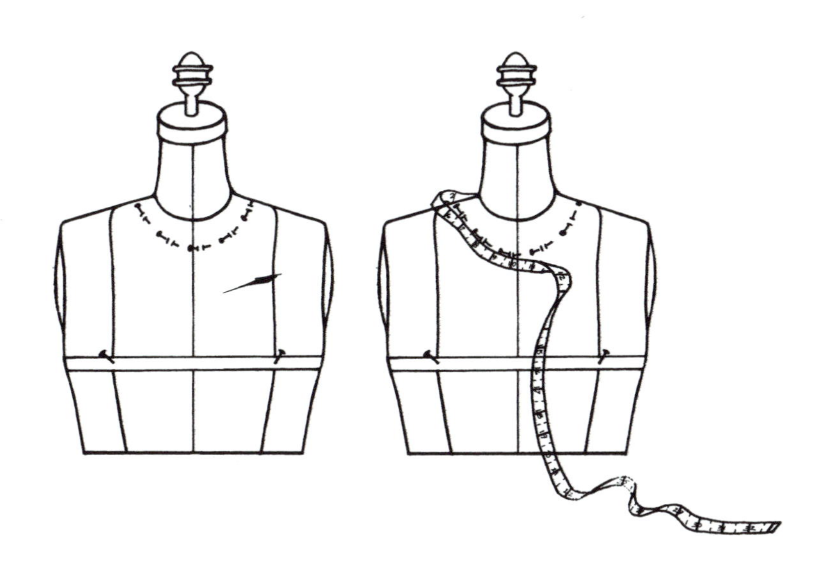

Prepare the dress form.

a. Place pins at the desired neckline on the dress form.

b. Measure the total desired neckline. Remember, the wider and/or lower the neckline, the more exaggerated the turtleneck collar.

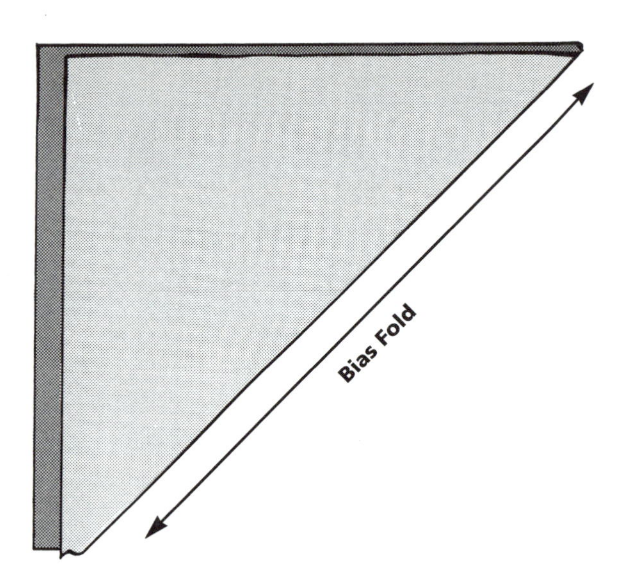

1 **Fold a large piece of fabric** on the bias (30-inch to 40-inch square).

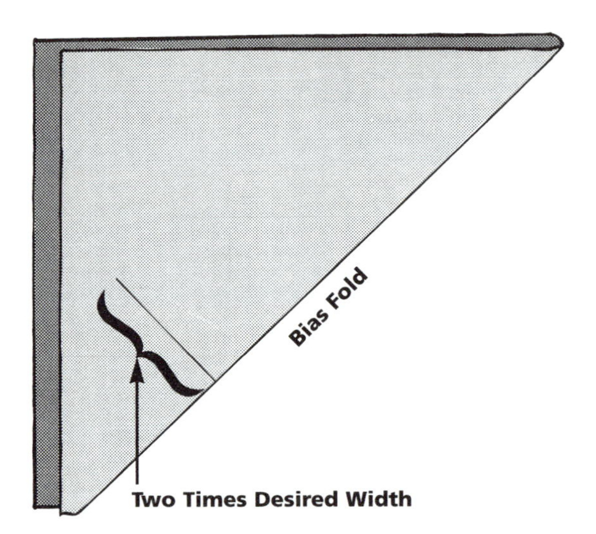

2 **Square a line from the fold** twice the desired width of the collar. Add 1/2 inch. This line should be placed as close to the left end of the fabric as possible.

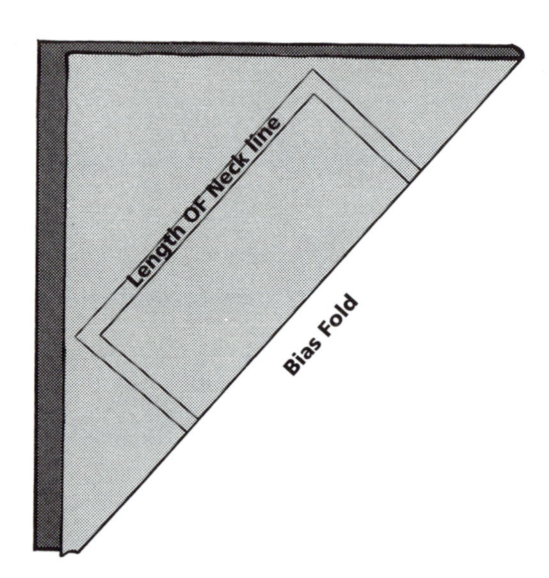

3 **Draw a line parallel to the bias fold** that is the length of the neckline. Start at the line squared from the fold.

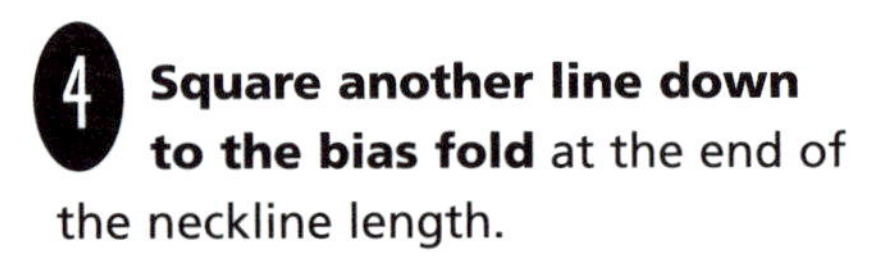

4 **Square another line down to the bias fold** at the end of the neckline length.

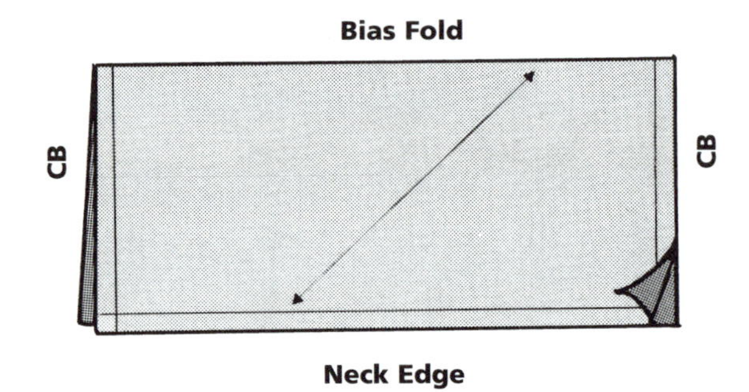

5 **Add seam allowances on all outer lines.** Cut along these lines and remove the excess fabric.

Turtleneck Collar—Draping Steps

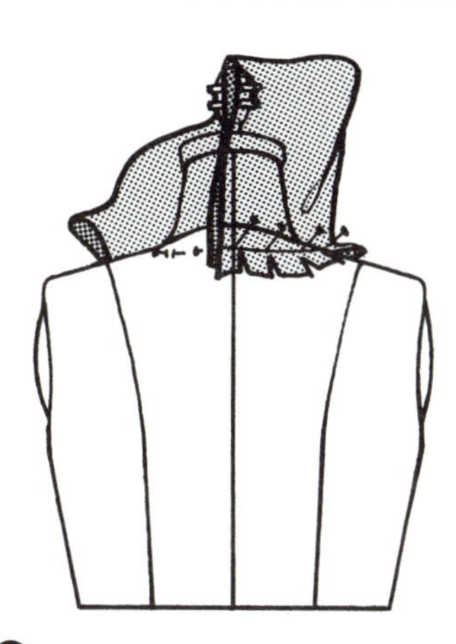

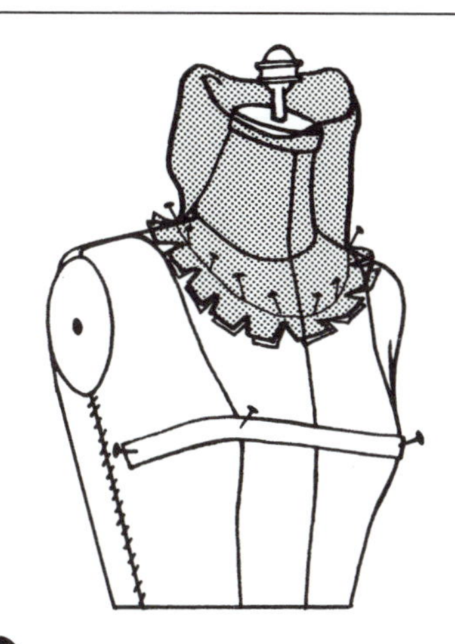

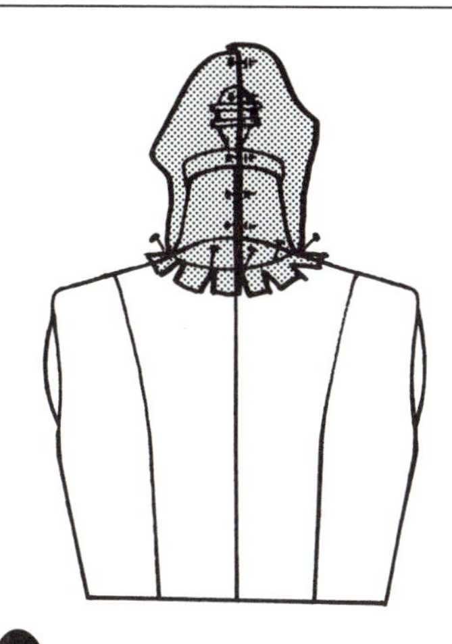

1 **Pin and clip both layers of the fabric along the desired neckline** guideline. Pin the center back guideline to the center back position of the dress form. Keep the fabric folded.

2 **Align the neckline edge** of the fabric on the desired neckline guideline of the dress form.

3 **Pin and clip both layers of the fabric until the entire desired neckline is encircled.** Follow the desired neckline guideline on the dress form.

4 **Match and pin the right and left center back guidelines** from the neck edge up to the fold of the fabric.

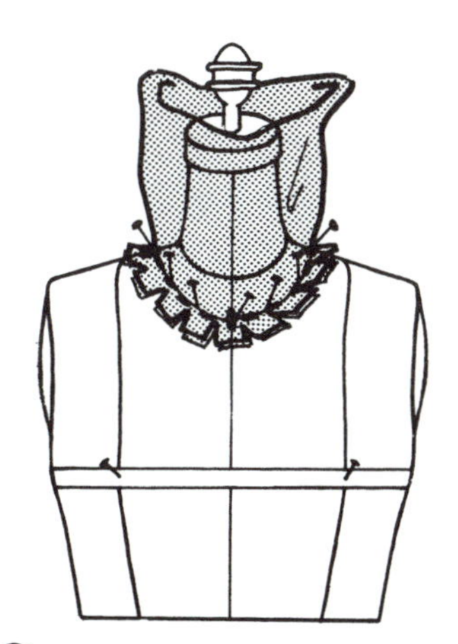

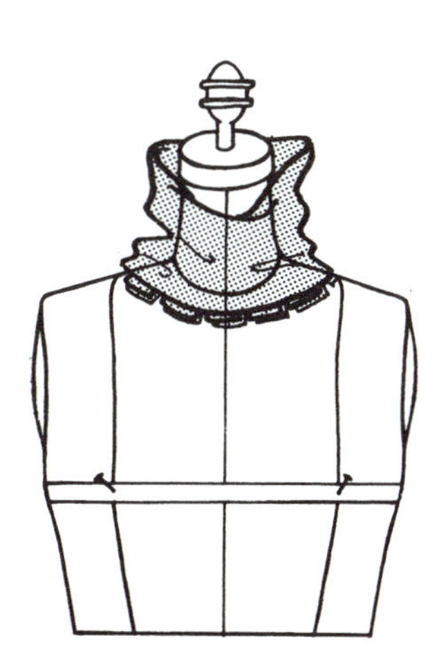

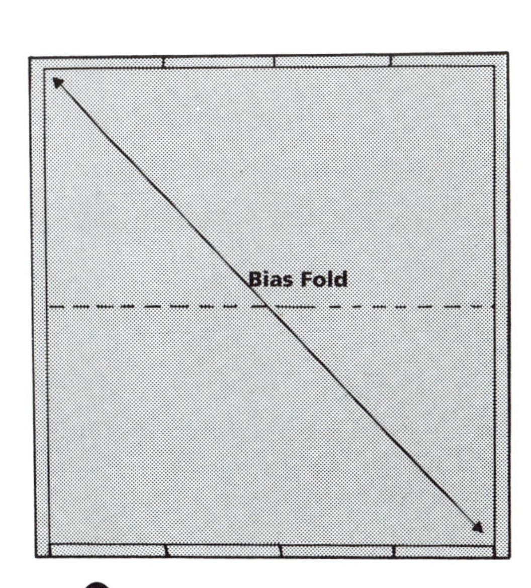

5 **Draw the entire neckline.**

6 **Crossmark the shoulder position notches.**

7 **Fold the bias fold edge of the fabric back over on itself,** covering the neckline.

NOTE: This drape enbles the designer to check the proportion of width and amount of fullness. Lowering and/or raising the neckline will lengthen and/or shorten the amount of fullness. At the same time, adding or shortening the width of the drape will create less or more collar stand.

8 **True up all seams.** Remove the collar from the dress form and true up all seams.

NOTE: The collar will remain on the bias.

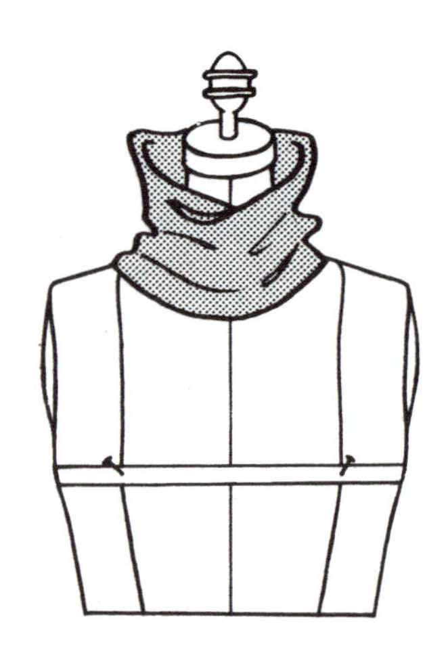

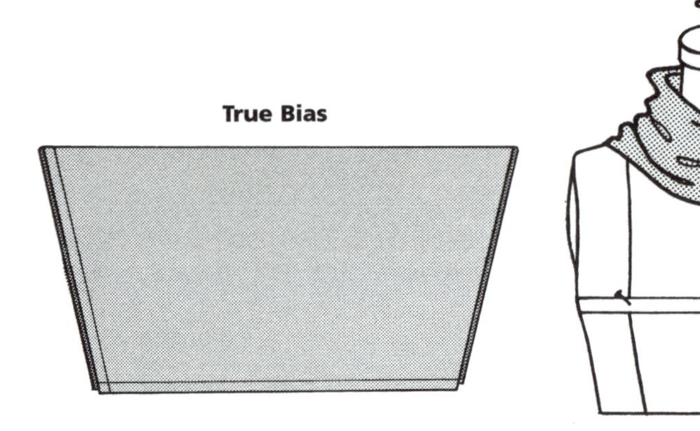

9 **Return the trued collar to the dress form.** Check for accuracy, fit, and balance. The drape should roll and fit smoothly around the neckline.

Variation

For a more draped or cowl effect, prepare the fabric wider at the folded edge. Taper the collar back onto the desired neckline.

Notes

Notched Collar

The notched collar garment has a single- or double-breasted lapel and always has a front opening. The design has an indentation, or "notch," cut out where the collar joins the lapel. The collar is cut separately from the lapel which is similar to a convertible collar. The lapels and collars vary in many shapes, lengths and widths.

The notched collar drapes and finishes into a carefully styled lapel, which is cut in one piece with the front of the garment. The collar, which is cut separately, can be made with either a high back neck stand by draping in a straight back neckline, or a shallow back neck stand by draping a curved back neckline. The notched collar is great for suits, jackets, coats, dresses, or blouses. It provides a tailored, flattering, and custom touch to traditional garments. The notched collar may provide crisp and sharp or soft and rounded shapes to a neckline.

Notched Collar—Preparing the Fabric

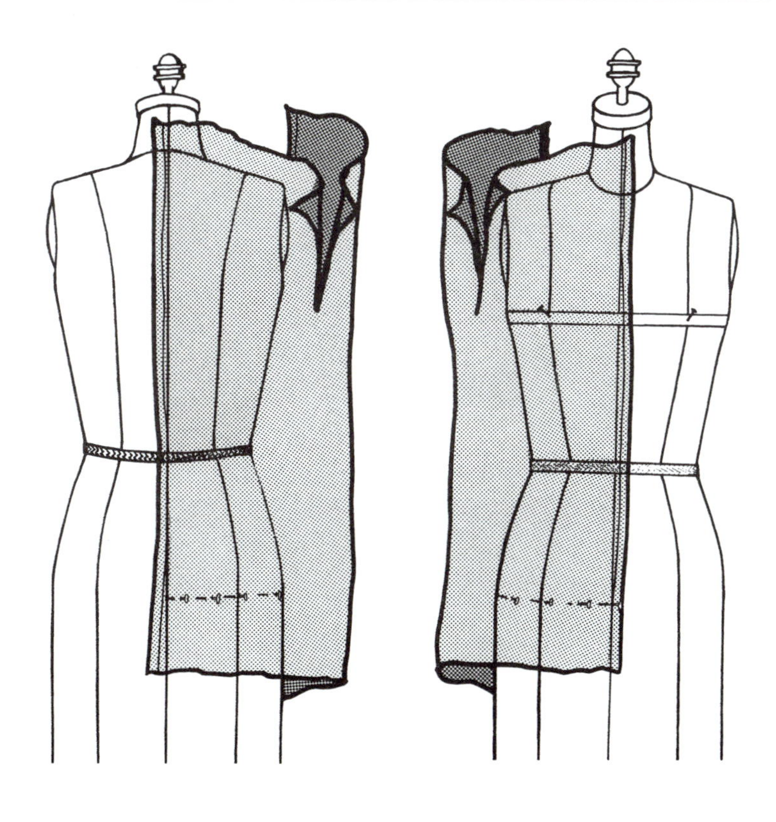

1. **Measure the length** for the front and back bodice (along the straight of grain) from the neckband to the length of the desired garment, and **add 4 inches.** Snip and tear the fabric at this length.

2. **Measure the width** for the front bodice (along the crossgrain) from the center front to the side seam, and **add 9 inches.** Snip and tear the fabric at this width.

3. **Measure the width for the back bodice** (along the crossgrain) from the center back to the side seam, and **add 4 inches.** Snip and tear the fabric at this width.

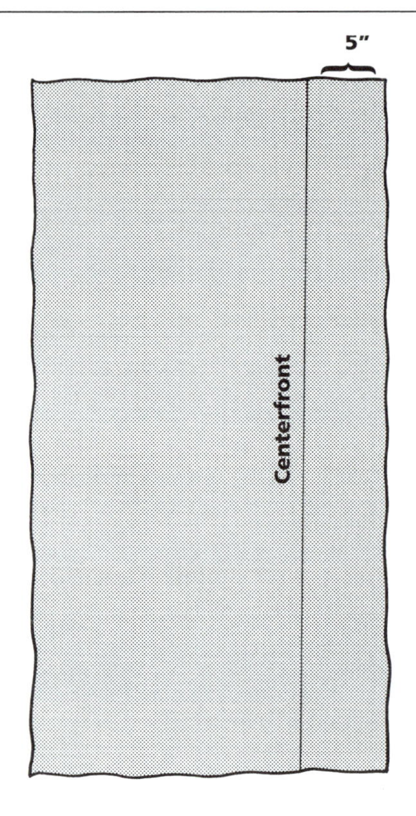

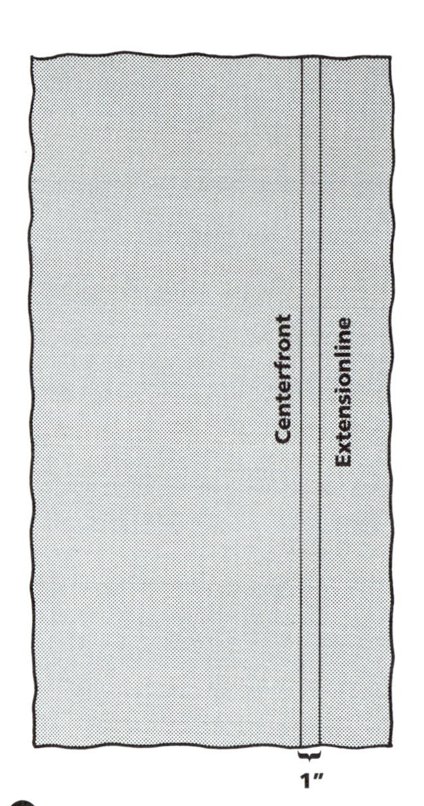

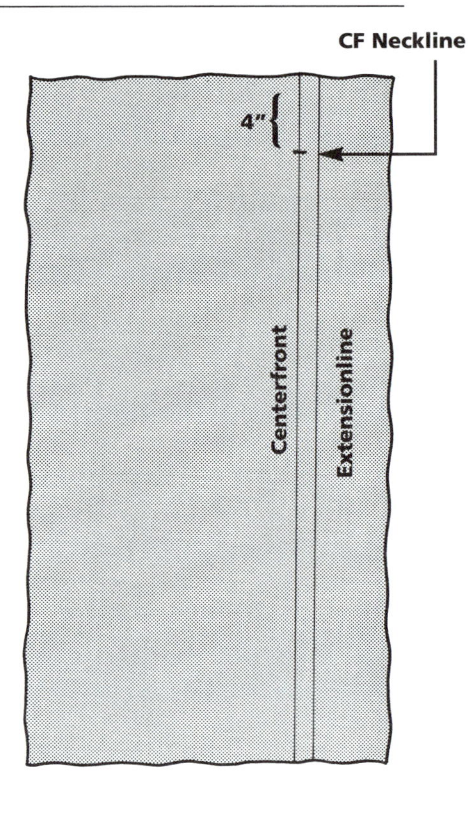

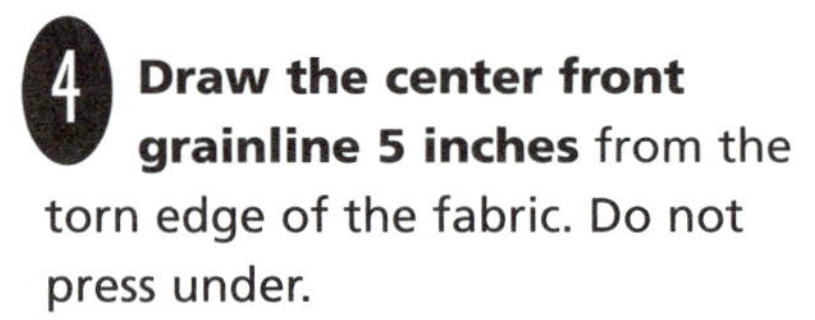

4 **Draw the center front grainline 5 inches** from the torn edge of the fabric. Do not press under.

5 **Draw the desired extension line** toward the torn edge and parallel to the center front grainline. Illustrated: 1 inch.

If a double-breasted design is desired, add 2 to 2 1/2-inches extension amount.

6 **Crossmark a center front neckline position.** Measure down 4 inches from the top edge of the fabric on the center front grainline and crossmark.

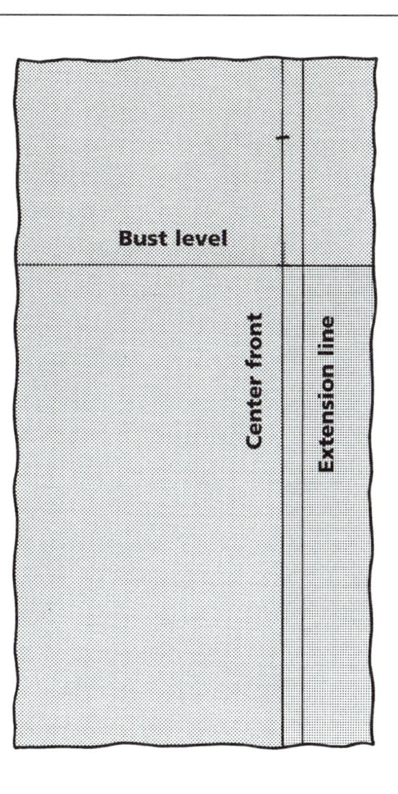

7 Determine the position of the crossgrain line.

a. Measure the distance from the center front neck to the bustline level on the dress form.

b. Measure and crossmark this neckline to bust level distance on the center front line of the fabric.

c. Draw a perfect crossgrain line at the bust level line crossmark, using an Lsquare ruler.

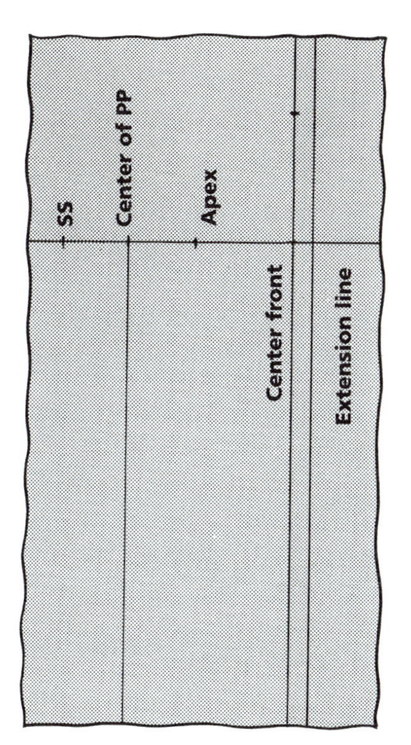

8 Crossmark the apex, the side seam, and the center of the princess panel line on the crossgrain line. If necessary, refer to Basic Bodice, page 29.

9 For a straight jacket, draw in the hip level line, the center front to side seam distance plus 1/2" ease, and the side seam.

Notched Collar—Preparing the Collar

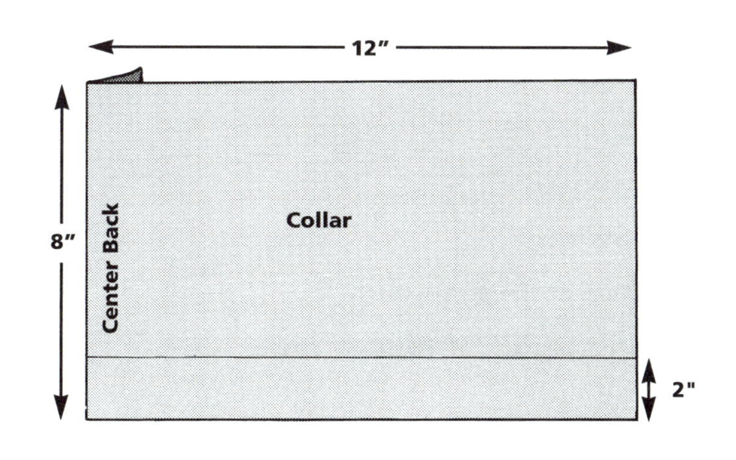

1 Measure the length of the desired collar. This should be approximately 12 inches (crossgrain).

2 Measure the width of the desired collar. And add 4 inches This should be approximately 8 inches (lengthwise grain).

3 Draw a straight of grain 1 inch from the torn edge and parallel to the grain of the fabric, and press under.

4 Draw a crossgrain 2 inches from the lower edge of the fabric piece (see illustration).

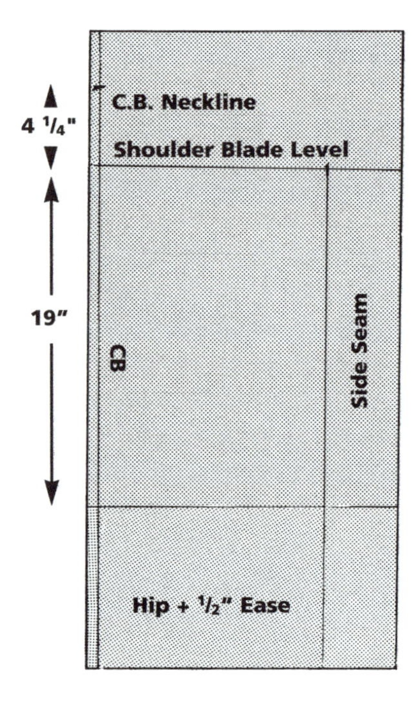

NOTE: Prepare the back fabric piece.

1 Draw in the center back grainline, the back neckline crossmark, the shoulder blade level, the side seam, and the hipline on the fabric piece as illustrated.

Refer to the Basic Shift for more detailed fabric preparation, **pages 69–70.**

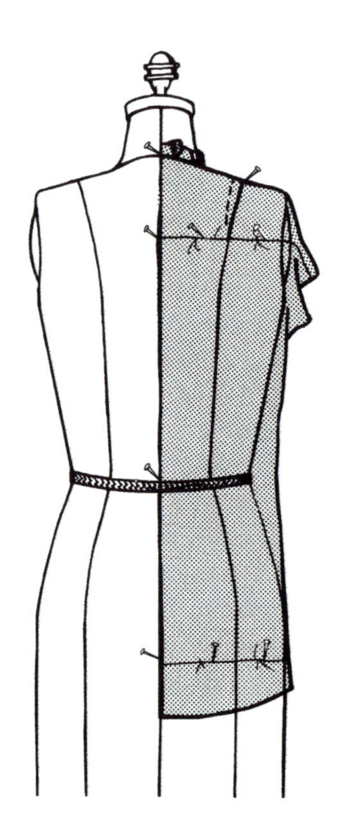

Back Drape

2 Referring to the design sketch, completely drape the back to match the desired design of the front. Refer to the Basic Shift, **pages 71–75,** for more detailed draping steps.

NOTE: The back neck area should be draped to the natural back neckline to accommodate the notched collar. Also, if the jaket has shoulder pads, place a shoulder pad on the dress form before draping

Mark all key areas of the back drape.

Neckline

Shoulder

Shoulder Dart

Armhole Ridge

Armplate at the screw level

Side Seam armhole at the side seam

Hem

True up the back add seam allowances, and return the drape to the dress form to check the fit.

Notched Collar — Front Bodice Draping Steps

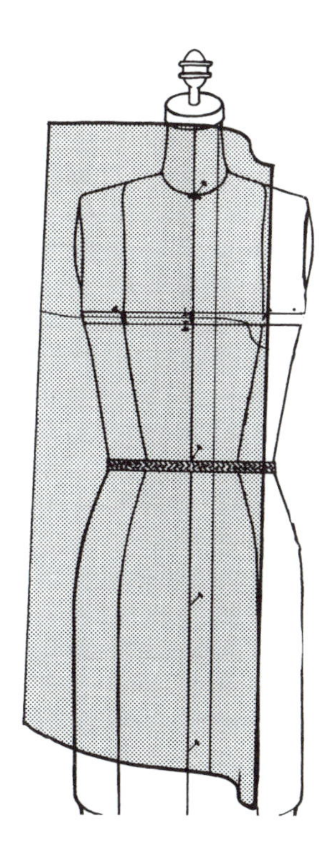

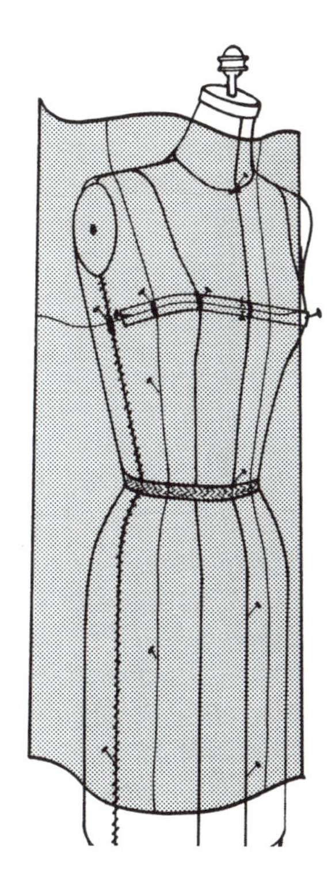

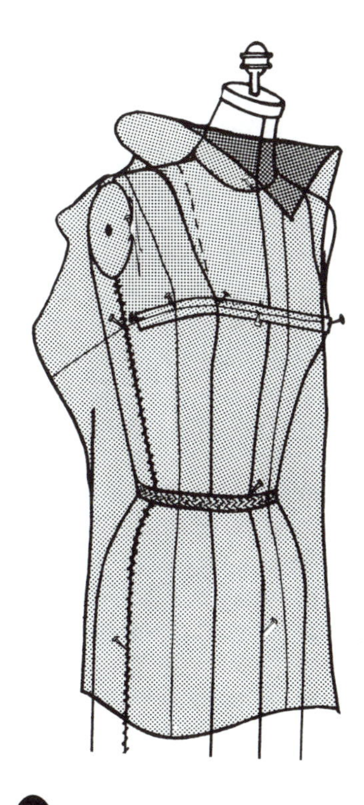

1 Pin the apex crossmark on the fabric to the apex position of the dress form.

2 Smooth and drape the fabric from the apex over to the center front of the dress form.

a. Pin the neckline crossmark to the center front neck of the dress form.

b. Pin the remainder of the center front grainline to the center front of the dress form, from the neckline down.

3 Align and pin the side seam and the center of the princess panel lines to the dress form. Anchor pins at the center of princess panel and on the side seam at the hipline.

4 Align and pin the crossgrain, at the bust level and at the hip level, making sure not to distort or pull the fabric.

5 Pin the side seam and waist area. Remove the pin at the center of the princess panel at the waistline and allow the fabric to hang loosely to the hip (plumb).

NOTE: If a fitted waist seam is desired, clip and smooth in a fitted waistline and waistline dart. Pin the remaining side seam.

6 Smooth the fabric up and over the dress form armplate to the shoulder. Create a 1/4"–1/4" pinch at the screw level (middle at ridge) of the armhole. This is to ensure the armhole does not become too tight. Pin in place.

7 Drape a shoulder dart by keeping the side seam area smooth and flat. Allow all excess fabric to fall on the shoulder princess seam. (This amount varies from one bust size to another.) Fold and pin this excess fabric on the shoulder princess seam of the dress form. The excess fabric is folded toward the center front neck.

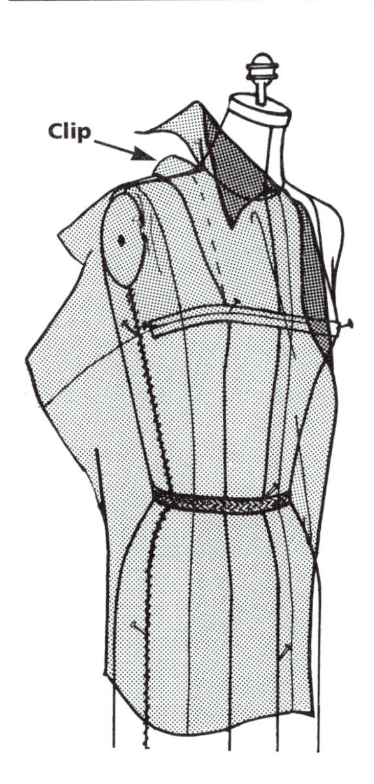

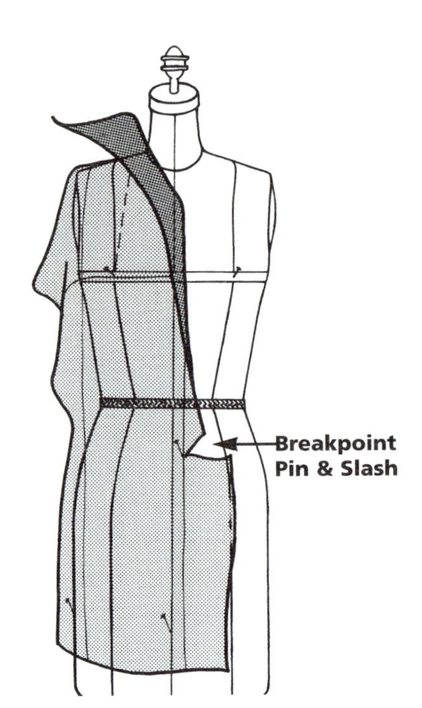

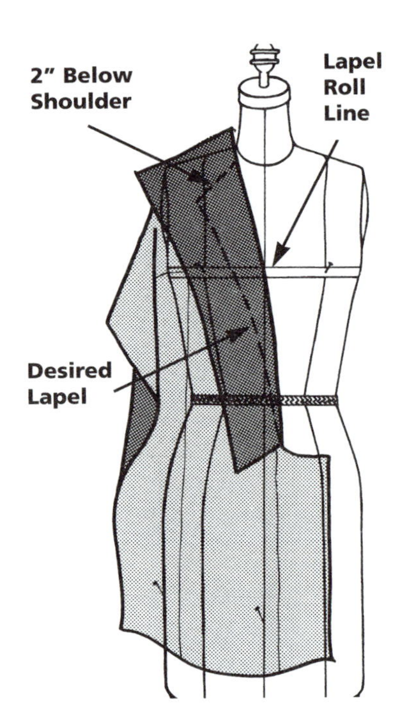

8 Clip the fabric from the back of the shoulder to the neckline/shoulder corner. Anchor a pin in the neckline/shoulder corner.

9 Remove the pins from the center front neck crossmark down to the center front bustline.

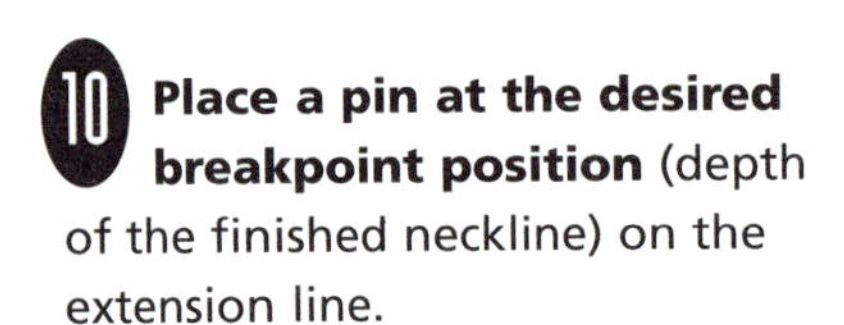

10 Place a pin at the desired breakpoint position (depth of the finished neckline) on the extension line.

11 Pin the grainline and the extension line to the dress form. Pin from the breakpoint position down to the bottom of the drape.

12 Remove center front line pins from the dress form above the breakpoint pin.

13 Slash the fabric at the breakpoint from the outer edge of the fabric into the breakpoint pin.

14 Fold in a lapel roll line by folding back the fabric in the front of the garment. Start at the extension breakpoint pin and finish at the neckline/shoulder pin.

15 Draw the desired lapel shape. Start at the neckline fold about 2 inches below the shoulder (refer to sketch). Finish drawing at the breakpoint on the extension line.

NOTE: The neckline fold above the lapel line is the new front neckline of the jacket.

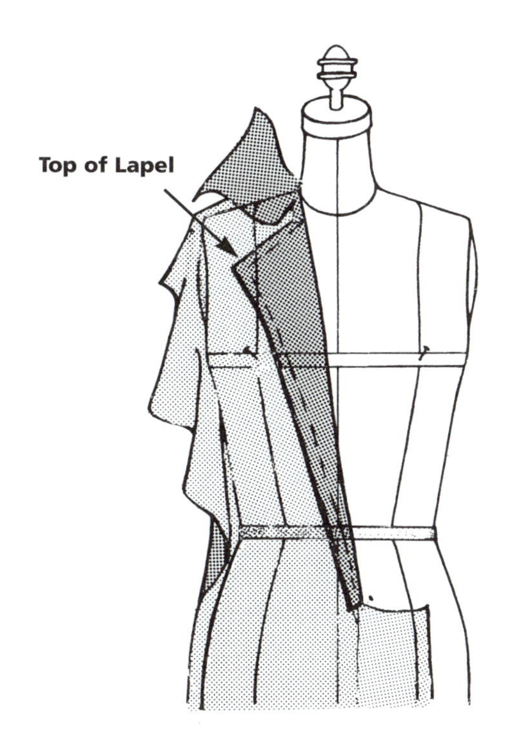

16 **Trim the excess fabric at the top portion of the front neckline and the entire lapel,** leaving 1-inch excess fabric. Clip the fabric where the lapel meets the neckline. Also trim the lapel down to the breakpoint, leaving 1-inch excess fabric.

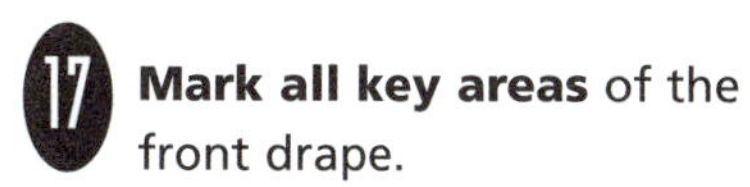

17 **Mark all key areas** of the front drape.

Neckline down to the top of the Lapel

Shoulder
Darts
Armhole
Side Seam
Hem

Notes

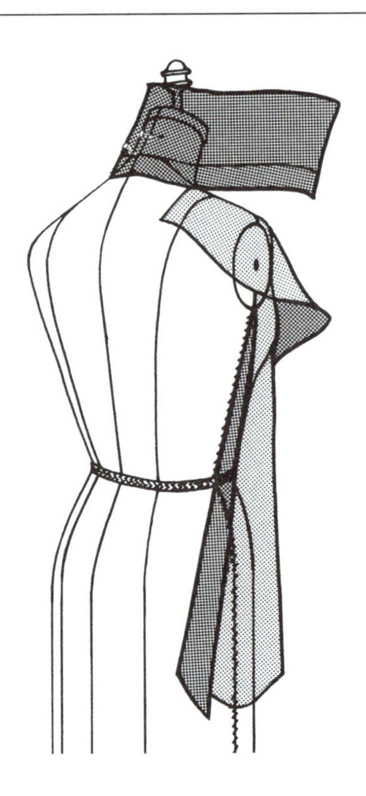

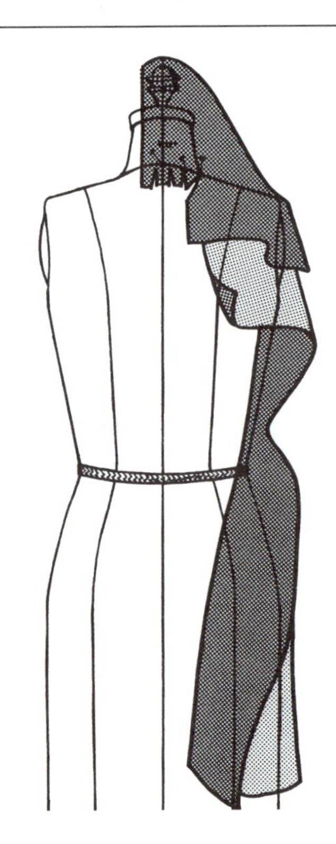

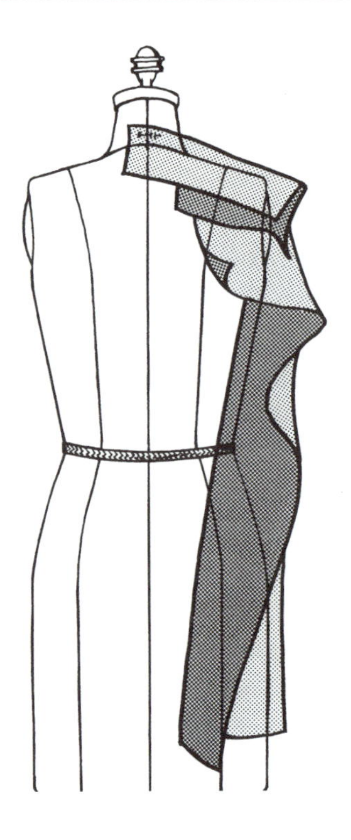

1. **Pin the center back collar grainline** of the fabric on the center back position of the dress form neckline.

2. **Align the collar crossgrain** on the neckline of the dress form.

3. **Clip, smooth, and pin the collar crossgrain** along the back neckline seam of the dress form to the shoulder seam of the dress form. Clip and pin at the neckline/shoulder corner.

4. **Fold the fabric over onto itself to create a collar stand.** Anchor a pin on the center back upper fold at center back neck. (This is to ensure that the collar stand does not fall off of center back and remains perpendicular to the grain.)

   Fold the fabric over onto itself at this upper fold pin.

5. **Trim and clip the back collar outer edge** of the fabric up to the desired width and shape of the collar. By clipping, the collar will lay over the back shoulder area smoothly.

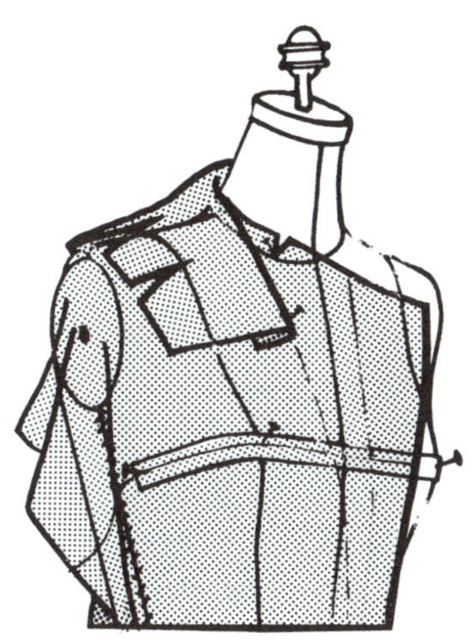

6 Drape the front collar into the roll line of the bodice lapel.

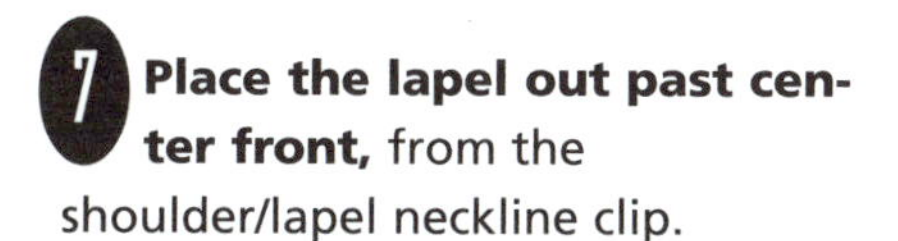

7 Place the lapel out past center front, from the shoulder/lapel neckline clip.

Allow the front of the collar to fold into the same angle as the underneath side of the roll line of the lapel. Adjust the collar till the desired amount of stand in the collar is reached.

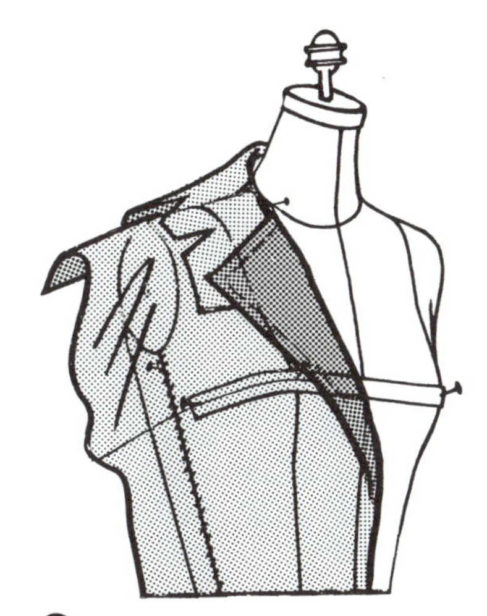

8 Lay the lapel on top of the collar. From the neckline clip, allow the lapel to lay on top of the draped collar.

Roll line will flip back onto garment to make front of collar.

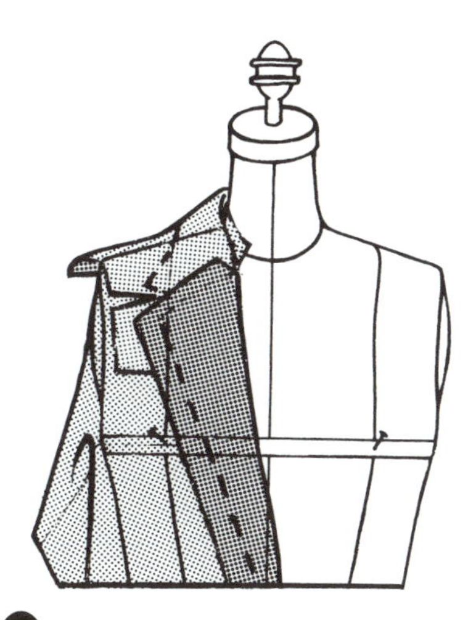

9 Draw in the desired collar style. Start drawing at center back and angling it into the top of the lapel about 1 1/2 inches from the lapel outer edge. Crossmark this position on the lapel with a "lapel neckline notch" (refer to illustration).

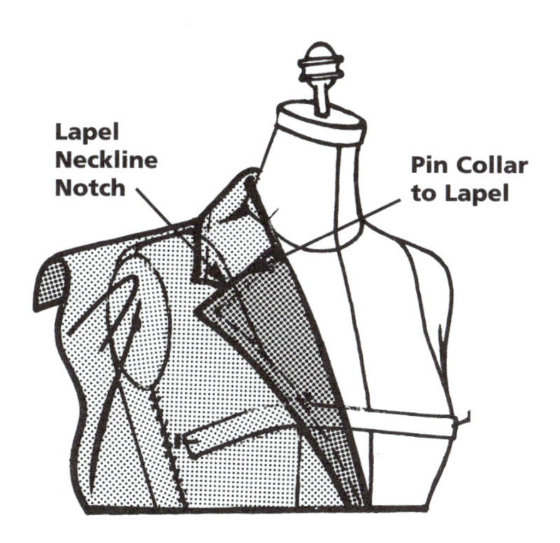

10 Pin the lapel and the collar to each other where the collar and the lapel meet.

Check for desired lapel shape. Reshape if necessary.

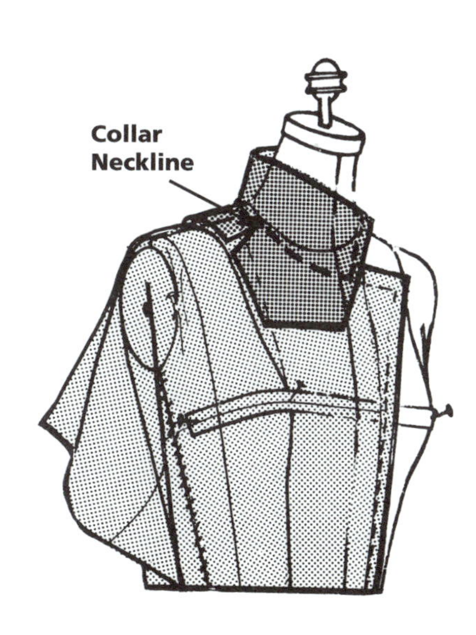

11 Draw in the collar neckline.

a. Turn the collar and lapel up and out.

b. Draw in the back collar neckline from center back of the dress form to the shoulder of the dress form. Mark the shoulder position notch.

c. Using the jacket neckline as the guide, continue to mark the collar front neckline to the "lapel neckline notch."

d. Transfer the "lapel neckline notch" to the collar where the lapel and the collar meet.

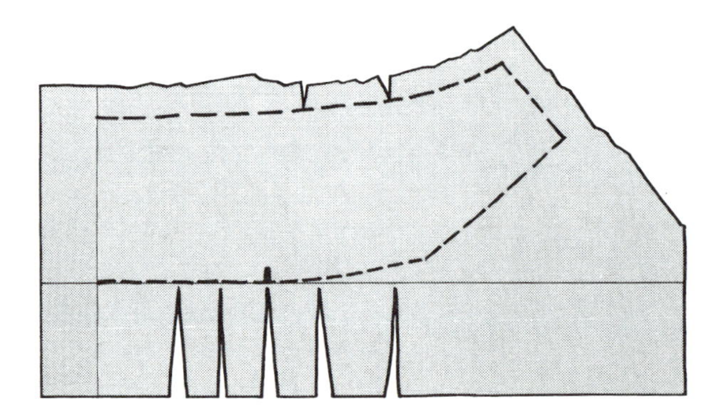

12 True up all collar seams. Remove the collar from the dress form and true up all collar seams. Add 1/4-inch seam allowance around the collar outer edges and trim excess fabric.

NOTE: Usually the center back of the finished top collar is placed on the fold. For an under collar, a center back seam is often used and this collar piece is placed on the bias for an easier roll of this collar.

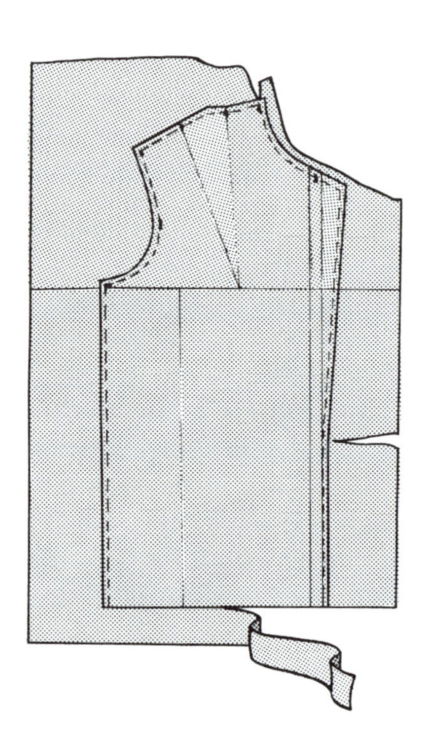

13 True up all bodice seams. Remove the bodice drape from the dress form and true up all bodice seams. Add seam allowances and trim excess fabric.

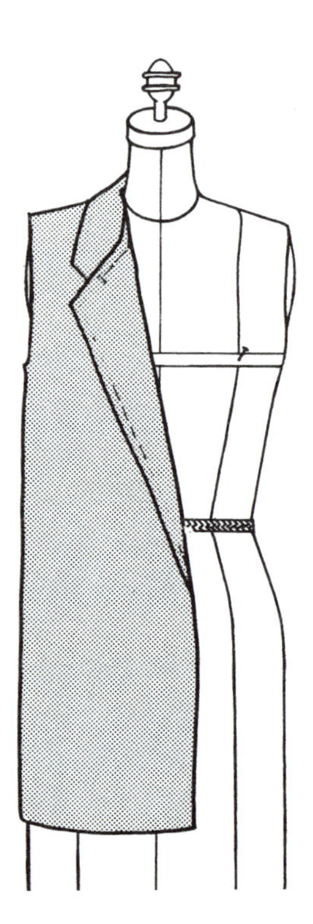

14 Check the garment fit and collar shape. Return the trued collar and garment to the dress form and check for accuracy, fit, and balance. The drape should fit smoothly around the neckline without gapping or stretching.

Shawl Collar

The main characteristic of a shawl collar is that the lapel and upper collar are cut in one piece with the garment. The collar has a center back seam to allow the front of the jacket to stay on straight of grain. The length and width of the collar vary greatly depending upon the intended effect of the styled jacket. The outer shape of the collar may have a curved, scalloped, or notched edge.

The back neck area may be straight for a higher stand or have a slight curve for a little less stand. The back neck shaping allows the collar to roll the amount the designer wants.

The shawl collar works successfully in every sort of neckline from high neck to dramatically low-cut lines. It is important to take great care in draping and styling the selected shape to give a polished and put-together look.

Shawl Collar—Preparing the Fabric

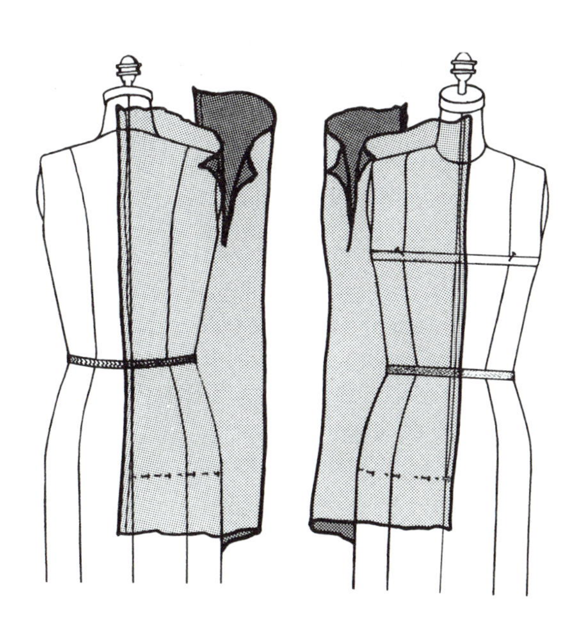

1. **Measure the length** for the front and back drape (along the straight of grain) from the neckband to the length of the desired garment. **Add 10 inches.** Snip and tear the fabric at this length.

2. **Measure the width** for the front and back drape (along the crossgrain) from center front to the side seam. Add 10 inches for the front. **Add 4 inches** for the back. Snip and tear the fabric at this width.

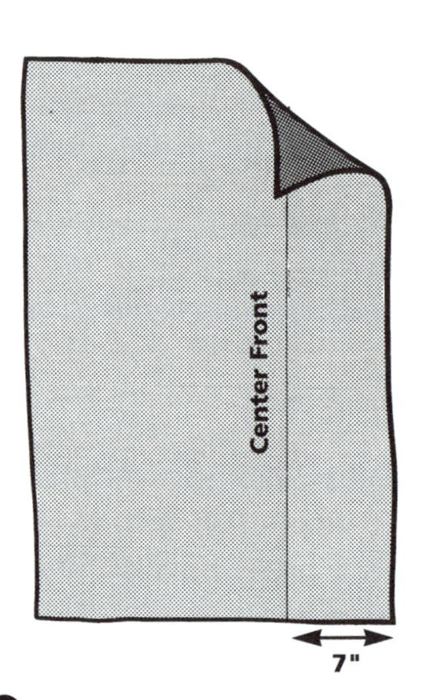

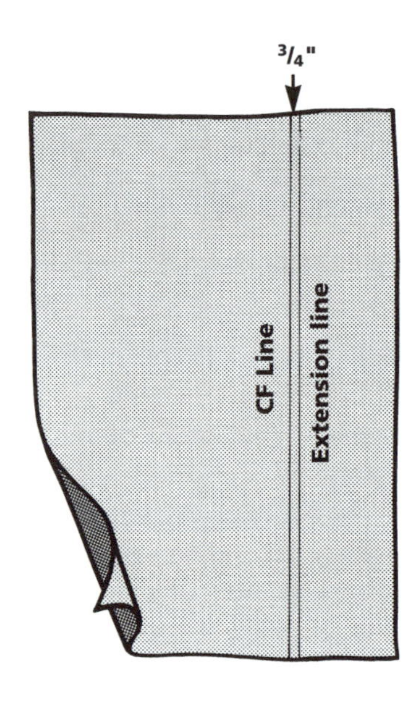

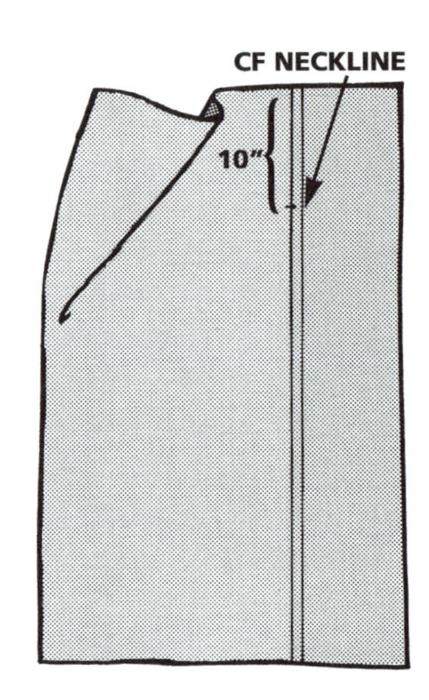

3 Draw the center front grainline 7 inches from the torn edge of the fabric. Do not press under.

4 Draw in the desired extension line toward the torn edge and parallel to the center front grainline. Illustrated: **3/4 inch.**

5 Crossmark the center front neckline position. Measure down 10 inches from the top edge of the fabric on the center front grainline and crossmark.

6 Determine the position of the crossgrain line.

a. Measure the distance from the center front neck to the bustline level on the dress form. This is the neckline to bust level distance.

b. Measure and crossmark the neckline to bust level distance on the center front line of the fabric.

c. Draw a perfect crossgrain line at the bust level line crossmark, using an L-square ruler.

7 Crossmark the apex, the side seam, and the center of the princess panel line on the crossgrain line. If necessary, refer to Basic Bodice, page 29.

8 For a straight jacket, draw in the hipline 14-inches from the bust level line. Draw in a side seam the distance from center front to the side seam and add 1/2-inch for ease. Refer to the Basic Shift, page 67.

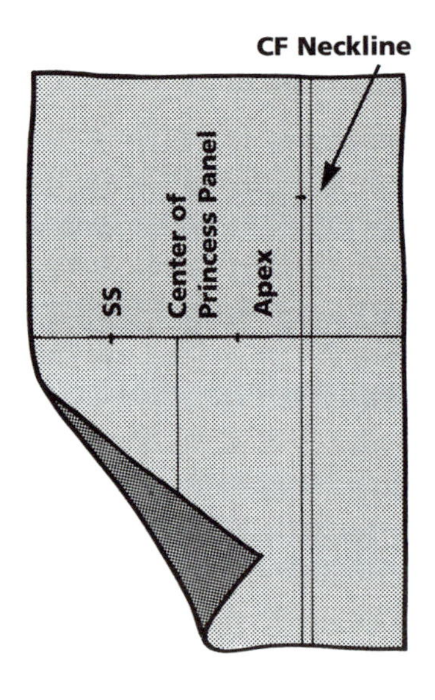

Shawl Collar—Back Bodice Draping Steps

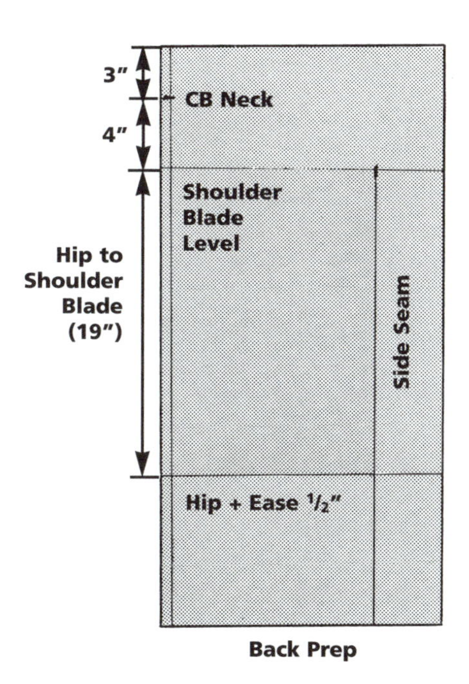

Back Prep

NOTE: Prepare the back fabric piece.

1 Draw in the center back grainline, the back neckline crossmark, the shoulder blade level, the side seam, and the hipline on the fabric piece as illustrated.

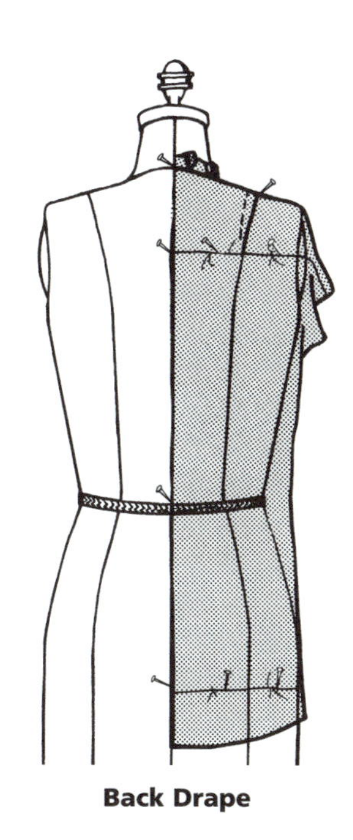
Back Drape

2 Referring to the design sketch, completely drape the back to match the desired design of the front. Refer to the Basic Shift, page 67, for more detailed draping steps.

NOTE: The back neck area should be draped to the natural back neckline to accommodate the notched collar. Also if the jacket has shoulder pads, place a shoulder pad on the dress form before draping.

True up the back, add seam allowances, and return the drape to the dress form.

Mark all key areas of the back drape.

Neckline
Shoulder
Shoulder Dart
Armhole Ridge
Armplate at Screw Level
Armplate at side seam
Side Seam
Hem

Shawl Collar—Front Bodice Draping Steps

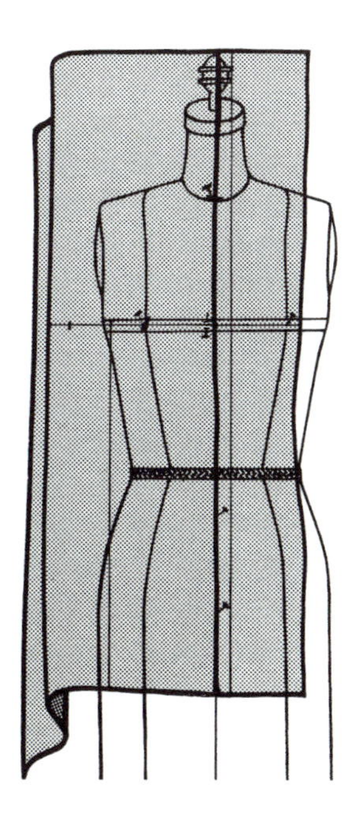

1 **Pin the apex crossmark** on the fabric to the apex position of the dress form.

2 **Smooth and drape the fabric from the apex over to the center front of the dress form.**

a. Pin the neckline crossmark to the center front neck of the dress form.

b. Pin the remainder of the center front grainline to the center front of the dress form, from the neckline down.

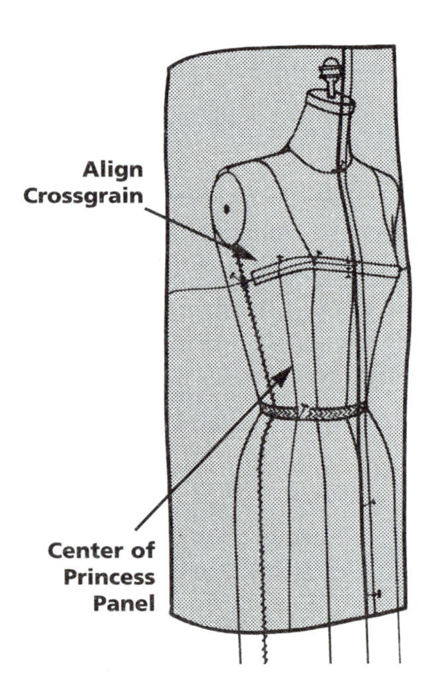

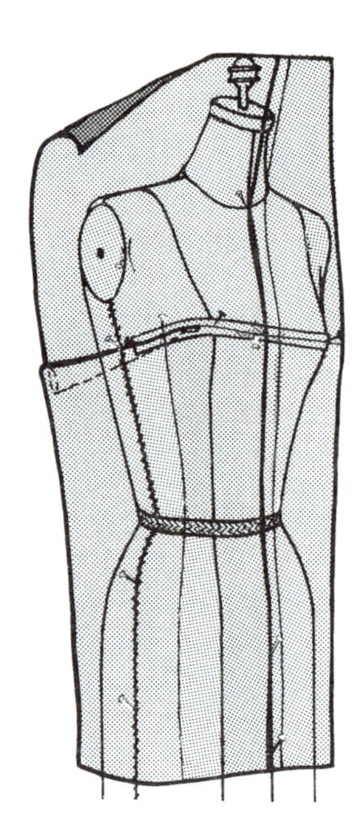

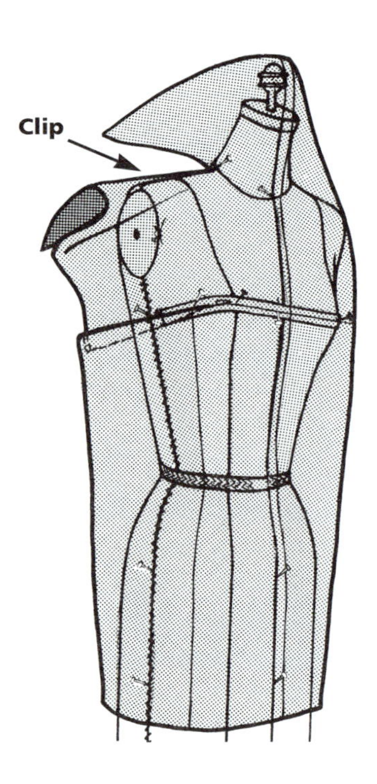

3 **Align and pin the center of the princess panel line** to the dress form. Anchor pins on the side seam of the dress form.

4 **Align and pin the crossgrain,** ad the bust level and the hip level. Make sure not to distort or pull the fabric.

NOTE: The side seam should be perfectly paralled to the center of the princess panel line.

5 **Drape the side bust dart and shoulder area.**

a. Drape the shoulder area by laying the fabric smooth and flat over the shoulder ridge.

b. Smooth the fabric over the dress form armplate. Create a 1/4″–1/4″ pinch at the screw level (middle at ridge) of the armhole. This is to ensure the armhole does not become too tight. Pin in place.

c. Unpin the bust level line and allow the excess fabric to fall below the crossgrain line. Fold the excess fabric up and into the bustline level line. This creates a side bust dart utilizing the excess fabric that is falling below the bust level line.

d. Allow all fabric below the dart and the bustline to hang loosely to the hip (plumb).

6 **Clip the fabric** starting at the back princess area into the neckline/shoulder corner. Anchor a pin in the neckline/shoulder corner.

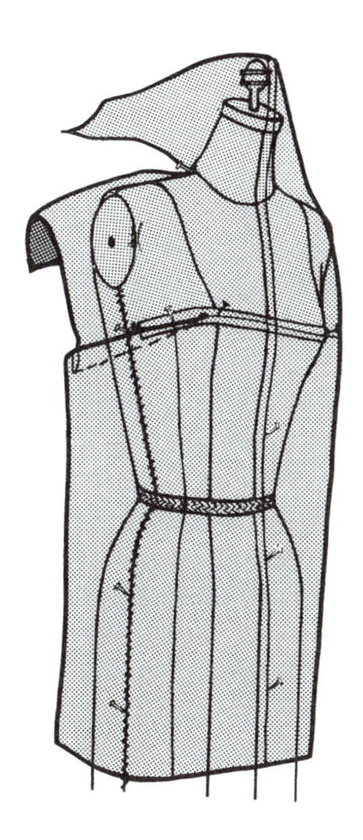

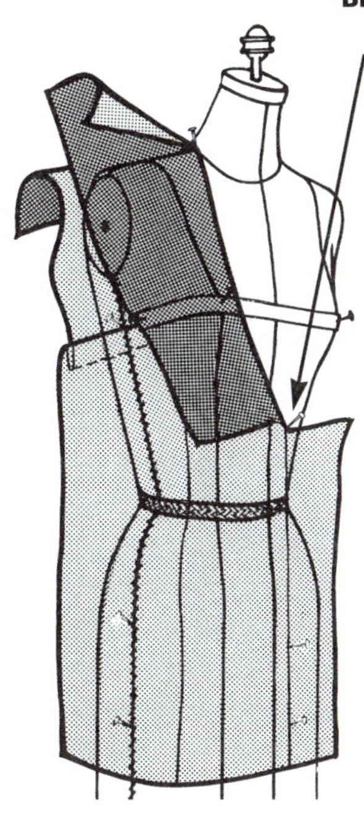

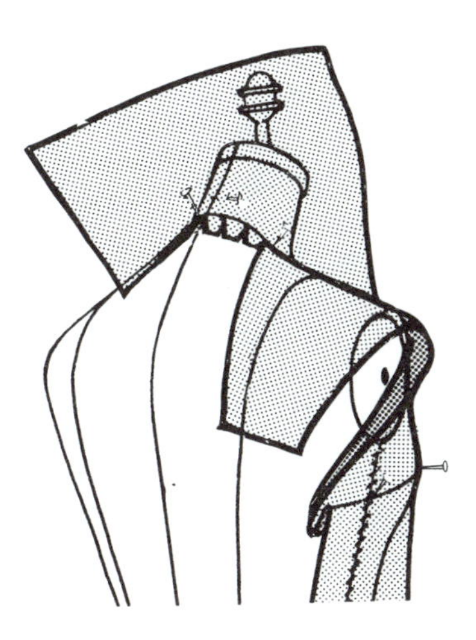

7 Pin breakpoint, grainline, and extension lines.

a. Place a pin at the desired breakpoint position (depth of the finished neckline) on the extension line.

b. Pin the grainline and the extension line to the dress form from this breakpoint position down to the bottom of the drape.

c. Remove the pins above the breakpoint pin.

8 Slash the fabric at the breakpoint from the outer edge of the fabric into the breakpoint pin.

9 Trim the excess fabric from the breakpoint pin down to the bottom of the fabric.

10 Fold in a lapel/collar roll line by turning back the fabric in the front of the garment. Start at the extension breakpoint pin and finish at the neckline/shoulder pin.

11 Clip, pin, smooth, and drape the fabric around the back neckline.

a. Lift the lapel area up, starting from the shoulder/neckline pin.

b. Clip pin and drape the back lapel area around the back neckline of the dress form.

c. Mark the finished neckline.

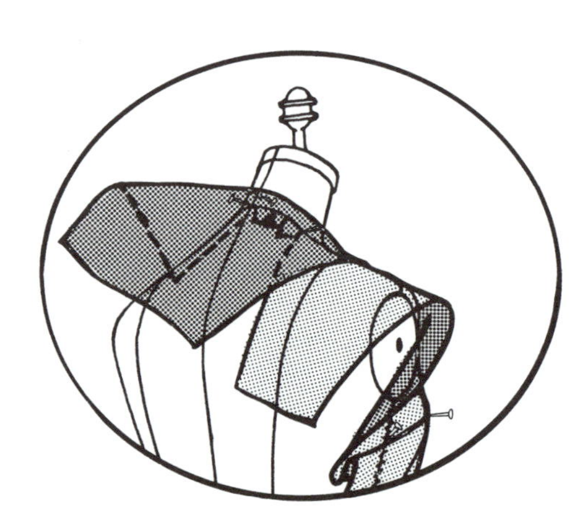

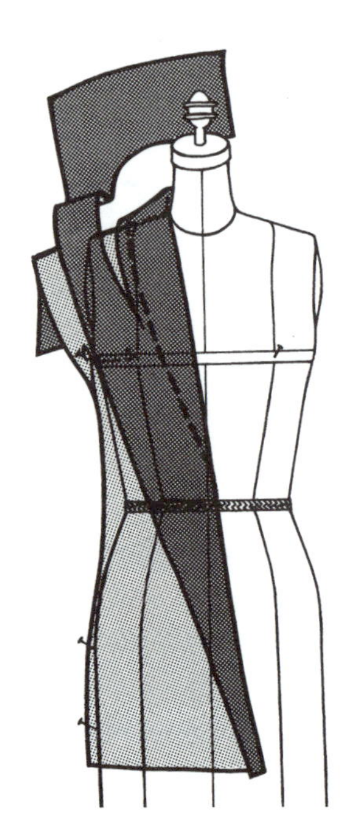

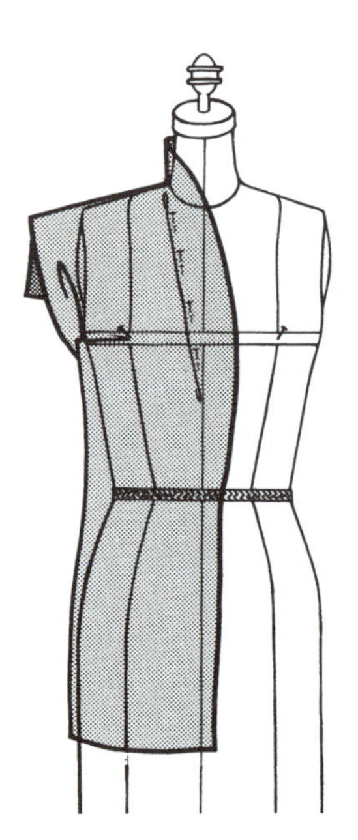

12 **Anchor a pin at center back upper fold**. This is to examine that the collar stand does not fall off of center back. Fold the fabric over this upper fold pin to create a collar stand at center back. Pin in place.

13 **Clip the outer edge** of the fabric up to the desired collar width.

14 **Draw the desired outer edge of the collar,** starting at the breakpoint pin. Finish drawing at the center back of the collar.

15 **Trim excess fabric,** leaving enough for seam allowances.

16 **Drape a fisheye dart.** Flip the collar up and drape a fisheye dart on the roll line of the collar. The dart should start at the neckline/shoulder corner and drape to the center front of the jacket.

NOTE: The fisheye dart allows the roll line to create a slight roll.

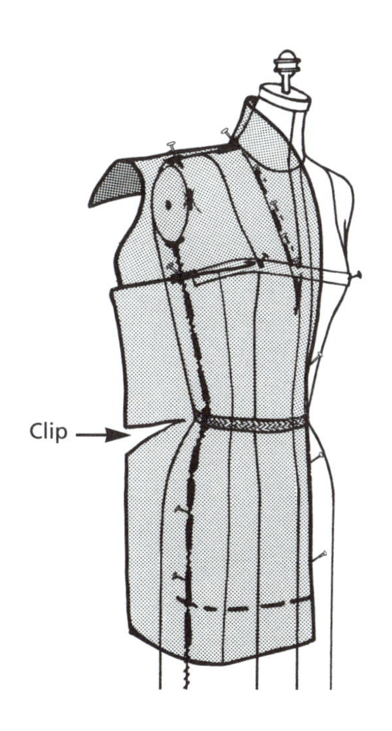

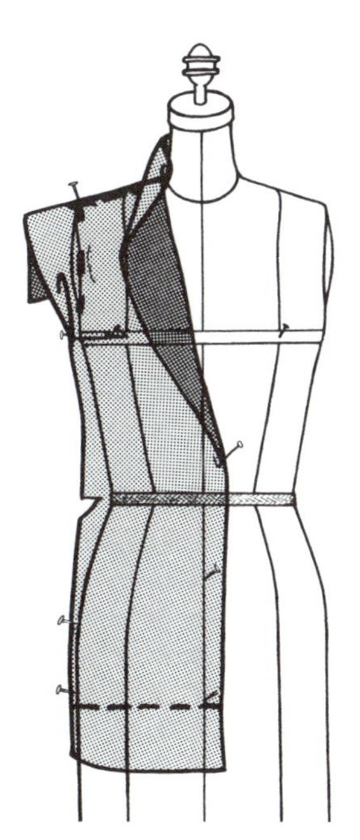

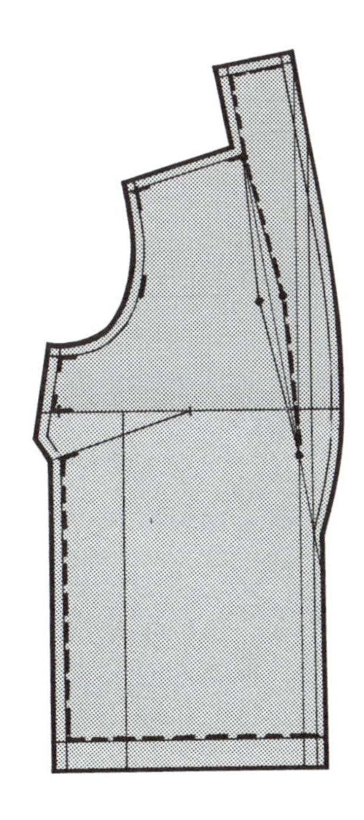

17 **Mark all key areas** of the dress form on the front and back drape.

Shoulders

Fisheye Dart

Armplate

a. Shoulder seam at ridge.
b. Plate at screw level.
c. Plate at underarm/side seam.

Side Seam and Dart

Bottom of Desired Design or Waistline

NOTE: For a more fitted side seam, clip the waist area of the side seam. Drape the side seam closer to the dress form.

18 **True up all seams.** Remove the front and back drape from the dress form and true up all seams. Add 1/4-inch seam allowances at the back neckline and the outer edges of the collar. Add 1/2-inch seam allowance to all other seams.

19 **Check the drape.** Pin the front and back to each other. Return the drape and collar to the dress form and check for accuracy, fit, and balance. The collar should fit smoothly around the neckline without gapping or stretching. Also, the entire bodice drape should fit all areas of the dress form correctly.

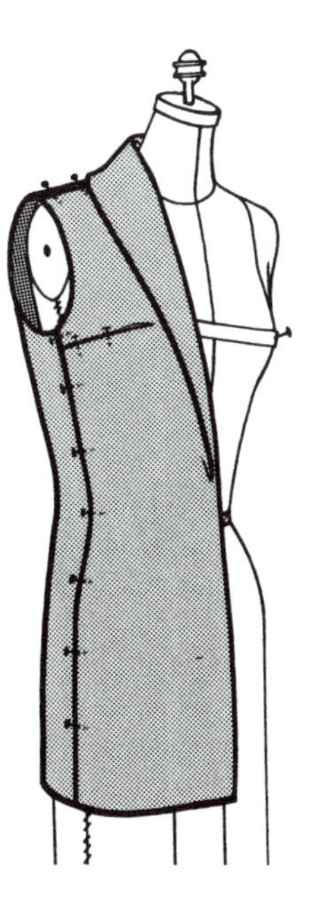

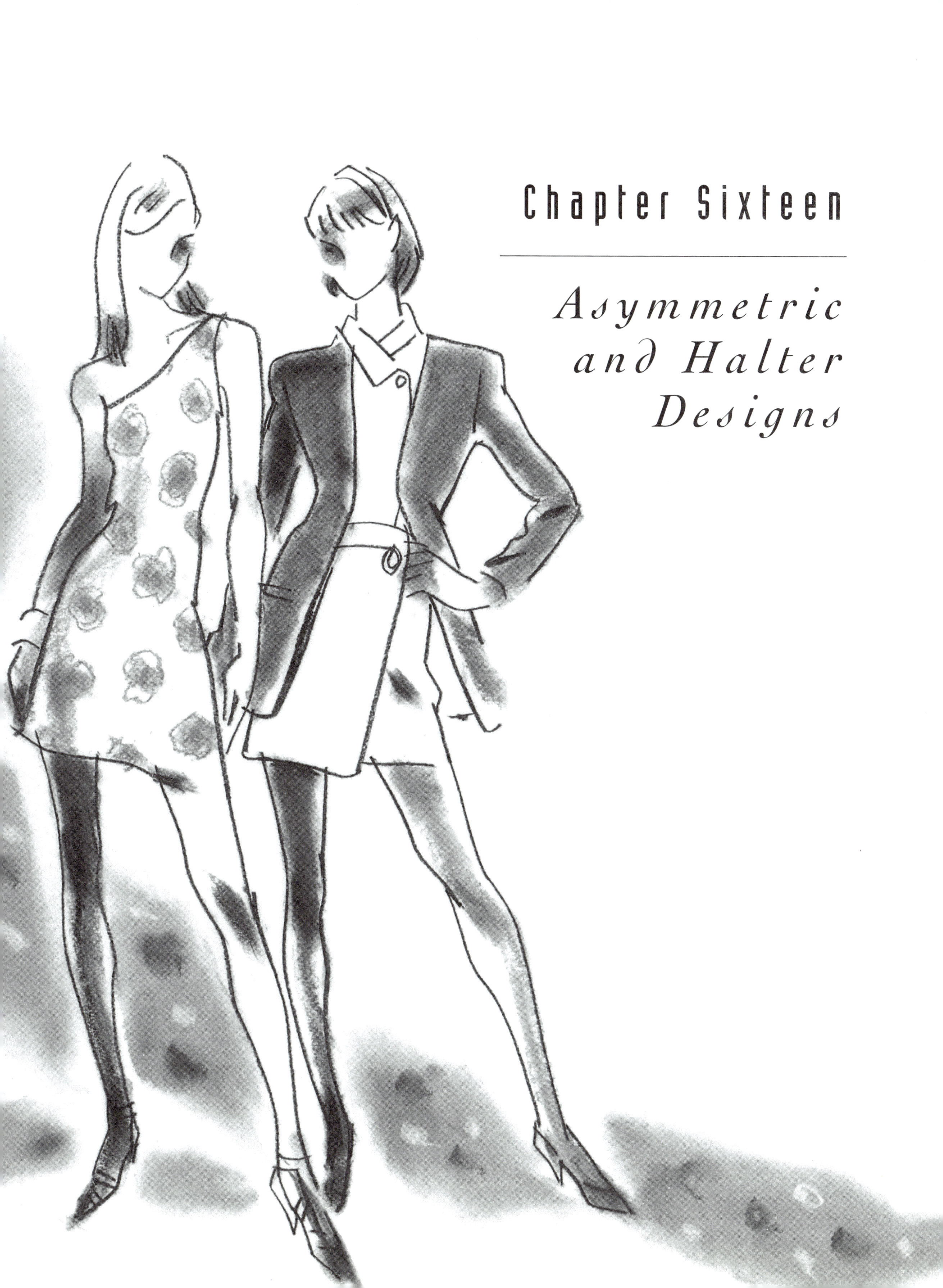

Chapter Sixteen

Asymmetric and Halter Designs

Objectives

By studying the various draping steps in this chapter, the designer should be able to accomplish the following:

- Develop creativity and stimulate a variety of asymmetric and halter designs.
- Recognize grain and crossgrain of fabric in relation to the bust level of the front and back asymmetric designs on the bias position of halter designs.
- Drape a flat piece of fabric into an asymmetric design with an informal balance in which each side of the bodice offers a different silhouette.
- Manipulate the fabric to fit the curves of the body and over the bust, and to shape it into a fitted waistline seam of the asymmetric or halter design.
- Drape soft fabric cut on the bias into fitted asymmetric halter or cowl designs.
- Visualize the front and back asymmetric designs in relation to the figure.
- Check the results of the draping process for an asymmetric design with regard to fit, hang, balance, proportion, and the true up.

Asymmetric and Halter Designs

Skirts, bodice, collars, and dresses may be designed with an asymmetrical feature. An asymmetrical design has an informal balance, with each side of the garment offering a different silhouette. The garments are generally draped to one side which crosses over center front. Many of these designs have vertical or diagonal lines intersecting the waistline. It may have side closings, it may be tied to one side, or it may be sewn closed with a center back zipper opening.

Asymmetric Bodice

The asymmetrical bodice design has an informal balance, with each side offering a different silhouette rather than the traditional balance. Generally, the larger front piece crosses center front with a smaller piece that lays underneath. The asymmetric design may be draped to one side with pleats, darts, or gathers. Many have a side closing or cover only one shoulder.

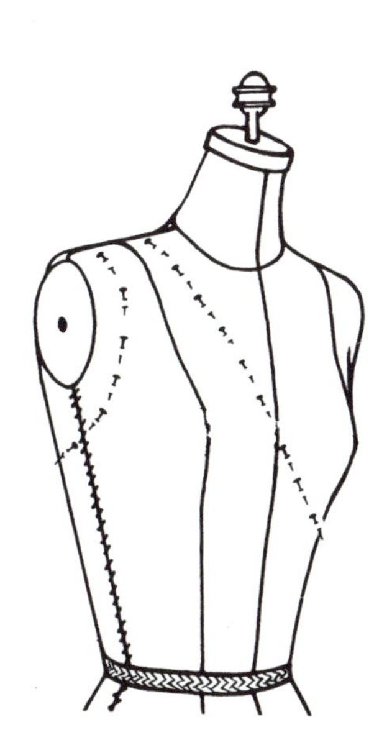

Prepare the dress form.

Remove the bra tape on the dress form. Pin or use style tape indicating the desired neckline and/or armhole shapes.

NOTE: These steps are required for all designs.

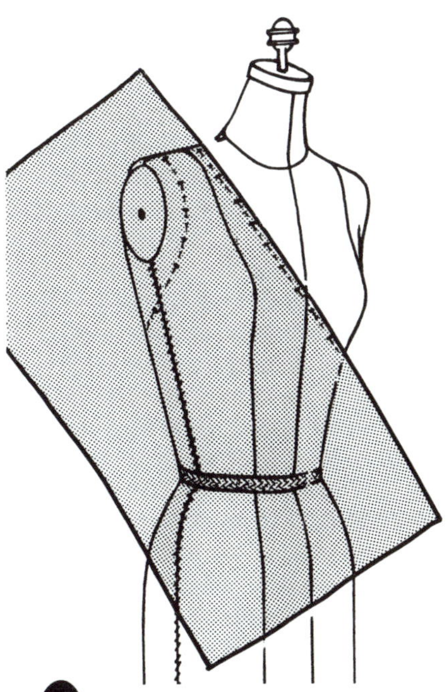

1 Measure the length for the front bodice along the desired neckline from the shoulder to the length of the bodice, and add 10 inches.

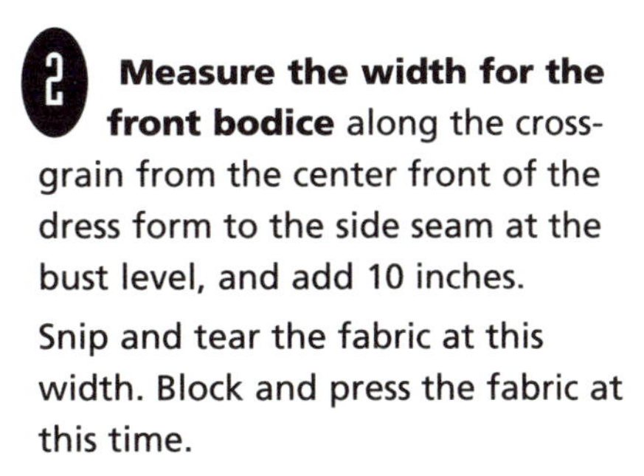

2 Measure the width for the front bodice along the crossgrain from the center front of the dress form to the side seam at the bust level, and add 10 inches.

Snip and tear the fabric at this width. Block and press the fabric at this time.

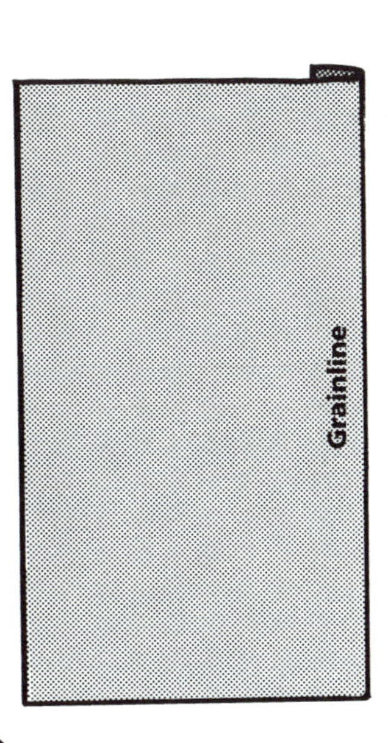

3 Draw a grainline 2 inches from the torn edge. Press under. This grainline will be the neckline edge of the garment design.

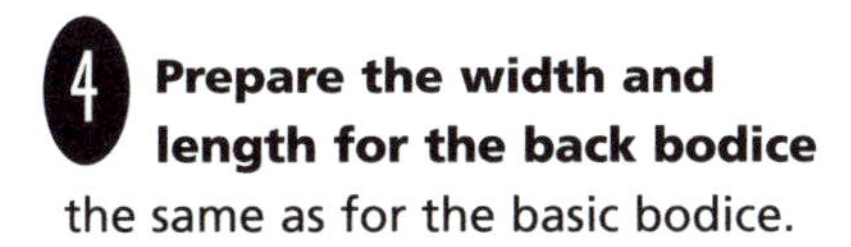

4 Prepare the width and length for the back bodice the same as for the basic bodice.

Asymmetric Bodice—Front Bodice Draping Steps

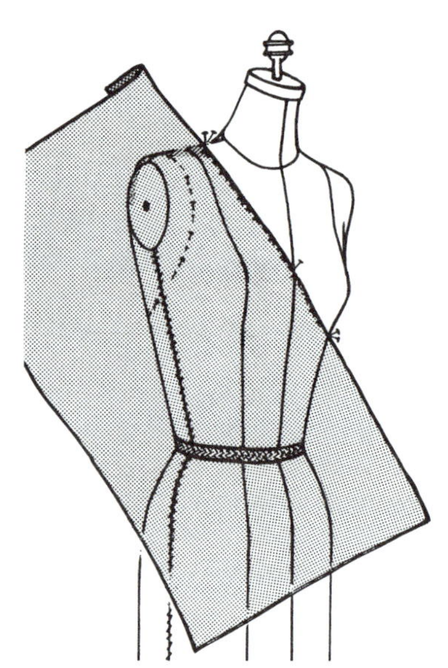

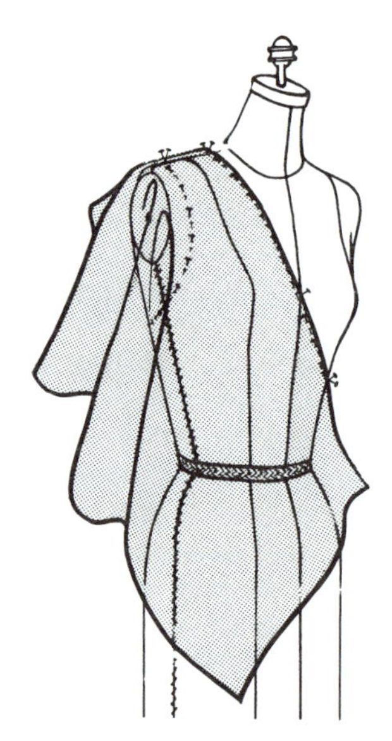

1 Pin the grainline fold of the fabric along the desired neckline. Allow several inches of the fabric to extend beyond the shoulder and several inches past the lowest point of the design. Place pins at the shoulder and the lowest point of the neckline.

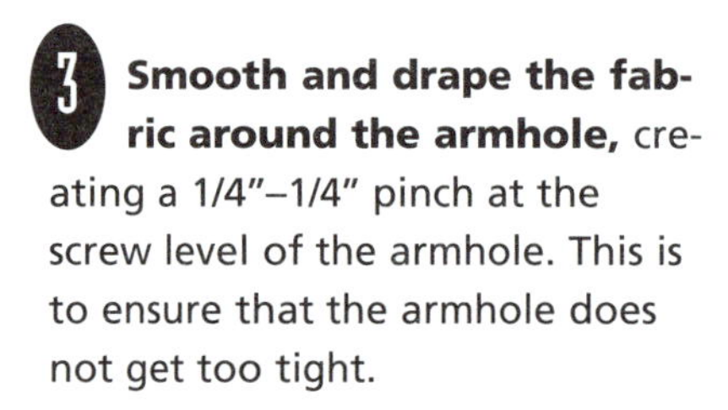

2 Drape and pin the shoulder by smoothing the excess fabric across the upper chest area.

3 Smooth and drape the fabric around the armhole, creating a 1/4"–1/4" pinch at the screw level of the armhole. This is to ensure that the armhole does not get too tight.

4 Smooth and drape the fabric flat over the side seam. All excess fabric will now fall into the waistline area below the bust.

5 Clip, smooth, and drape the waistline fabric across the waist tape. Allow all excess fabric to drape into the styled area of the asymmetric design. Pin excess fabric at this location.

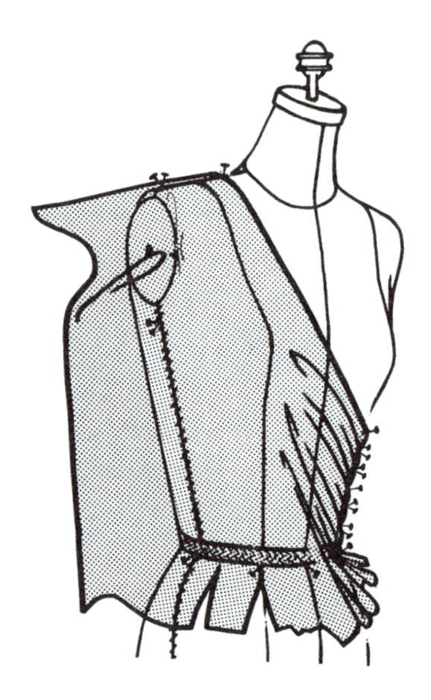

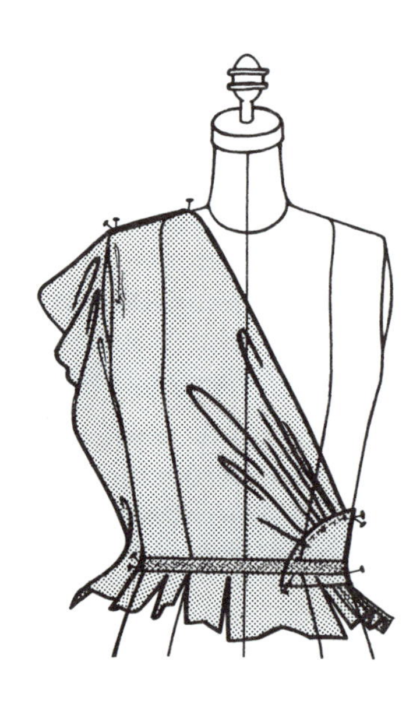

6 Fold, tuck, pleat, or gather in the fullness at the area where the asymmetric design requires the fullness.

Add design features if desired.

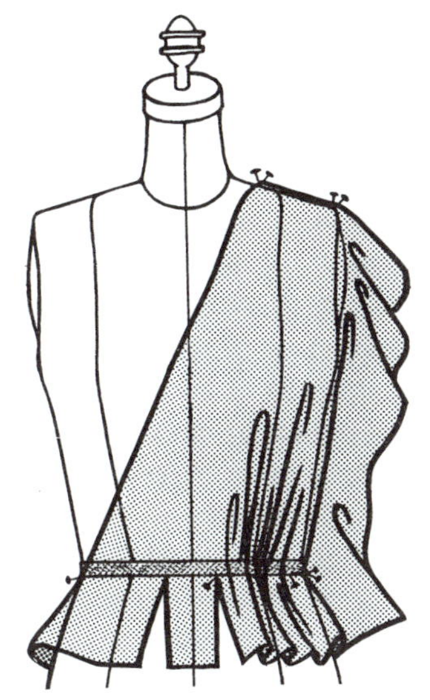

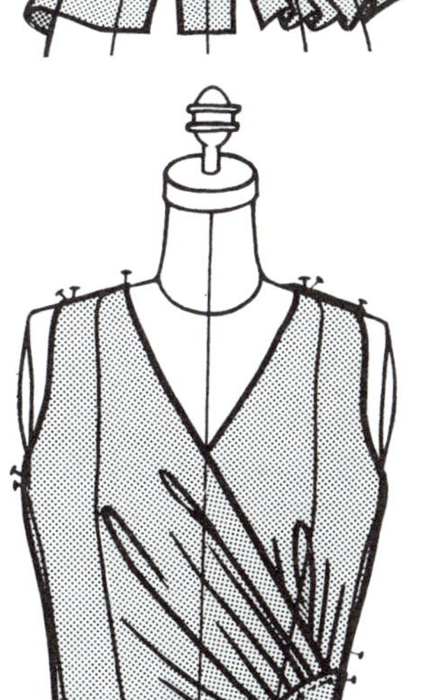

NOTE: These steps apply only if the left side of the design is different from the right side.

1 Pin the grainline fold of the fabric along the desired neckline of the left side.

2 Drape and pin the shoulder.

3 Smooth and drape the fabric around the armhole, creating a 1/4"–1/4" pinch at the screw level of the armhole.

4 Smooth and drape the fabric flat over the side seam. All excess fabric will now fall into the waistline area below the bust.

5 Fold, tuck, pleat or gather in the fullness at the waistline below the bust. Pin excess fabric at this location.

6 Make all key areas of the dress form on the fabric:

Center Front Place a crossmark at C.F. neck and C.F. waist. Mark the entire center front line of the dress form.

Shoulder Seam Lightly mark the shoulder seam and crossmark the shoulder ridge corner.

Armplate
a. Top at shoulder seam ridge.
b. Middle at screw level.
C. Crossmark bottom at side seam.

Side Seam Lightly crossmark.

Waistline Lightly crossmark the entire waist area of the drape.

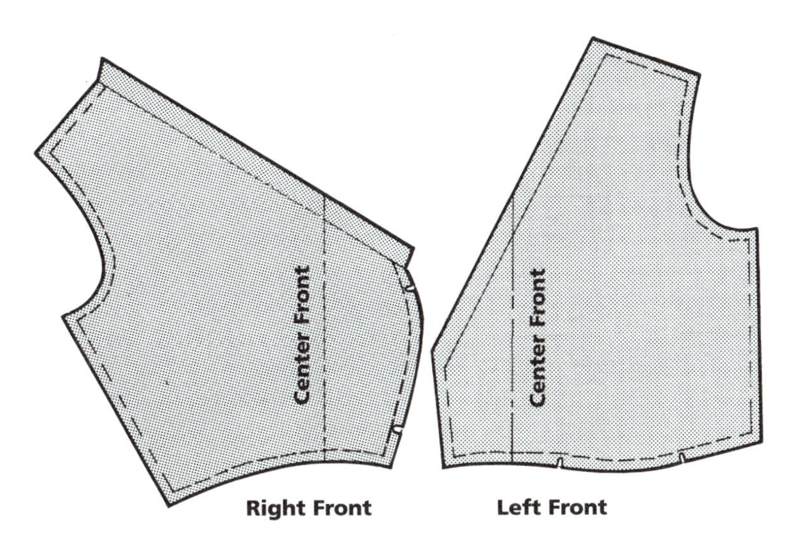

7 True up. Remove the fabric drape from the dress form. True up all seams, add seam allowances, and trim excess fabric. Pin the front drape to the back drape.

8 Return the finished drape to the dress form and check for accuracy, fit, and balance.

Drape the back bodice the same as the basic bodice.

The bias halter is a front fitted sleeveless bodice with a flat or rolled neckline strip extending to the back of the neckline. Generally, the side seam area of the lower bodice extends to the back, which may be tied, attached to a midriff, or sewn to the waist of a skirt

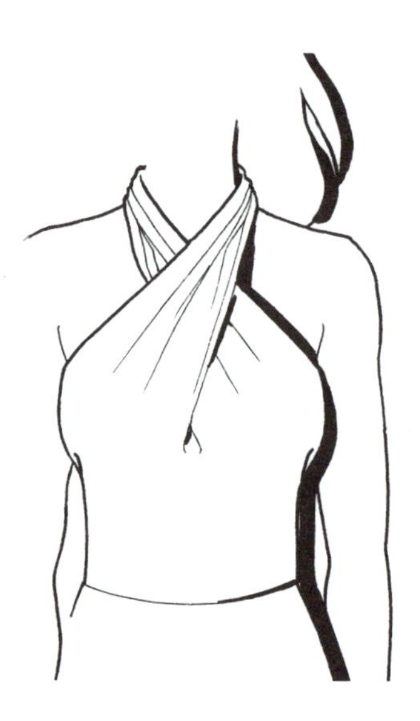

Bias Halter—Preparing the Fabric

1. **Measure and cut a perfect 34-inch square** of fabric which is wide enough for an entire front.

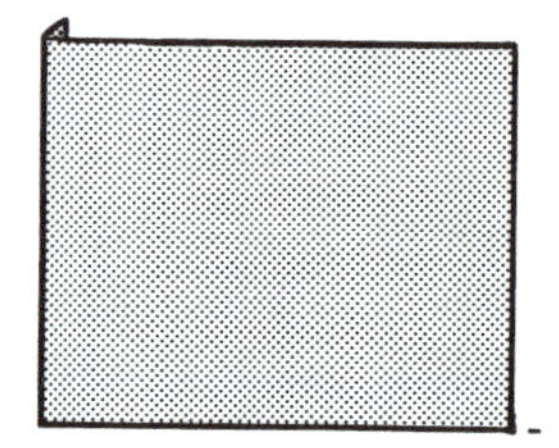

2. **Draw a true bias line** diagonally across the piece of fabric. This bias line will be the center front line of the garment.

3. **Draw a second true bias line** diagonally across the piece of fabric opposite the first bias line. This bias line will represent the bust level line of the garment.

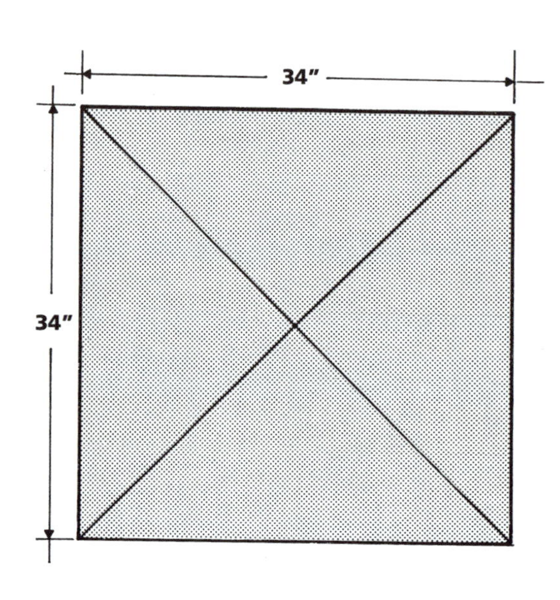

4. **For the back design,** measure the width and length of the back style, and add 3 inches. Snip and tear the fabric at this width and length.

5. **Draw in a grainline for the center back panel** 1 inch from the torn edge, and press under.

Bias Halter—Draping Steps

Prepare the dress form.
Remove the bra tape on the dress form. Pin or use style tape indicating the desired neckline and/or armhole shapes.

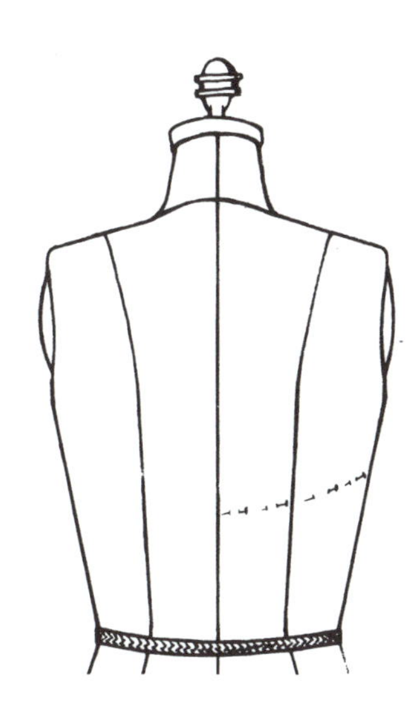

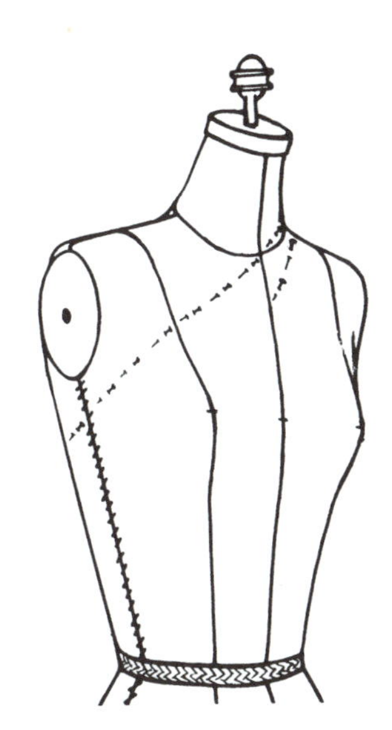

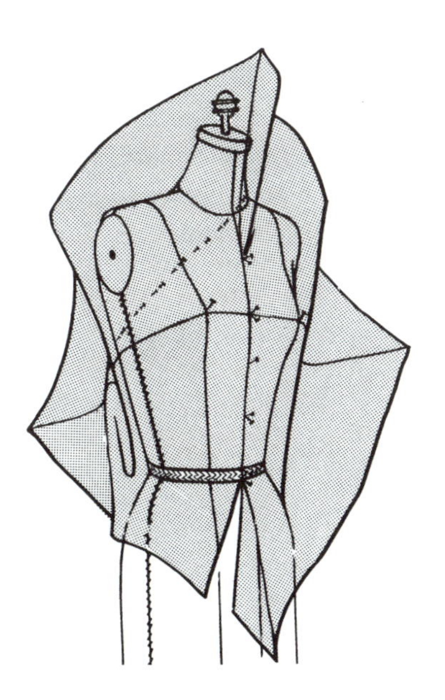

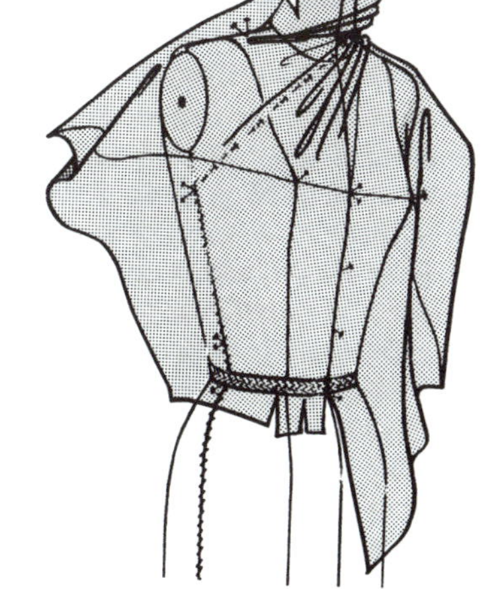

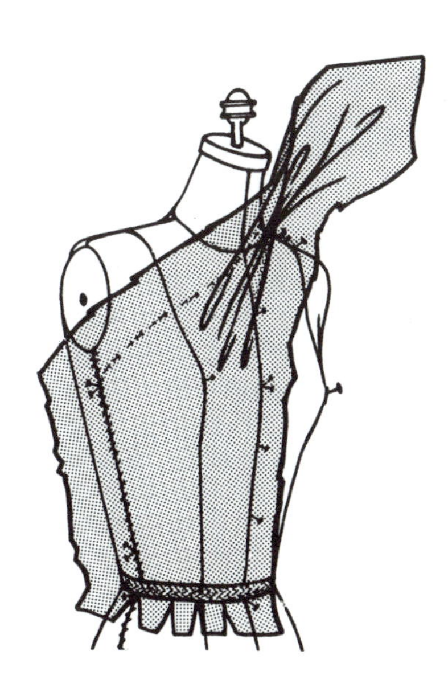

1 Pin and drape the center front bias line on the center front position of the dress form.

2 Align the bias crossgrain on the bust level of the dress form.

3 Trim, clip, and drape the waistline on the right side of the dress form.

4 Smooth and drape the fabric up and across the side seam. All excess fabric will now be falling toward the neckline above the bust level.

NOTE: The direction of the bust level line is now angled upwards.

5 Trim away the fabric at the side seam, around the premarked bare armhole, and around the neck area, leaving a 2-inch excess.

6 Smooth and drape the fabric around the trimmed armhole.

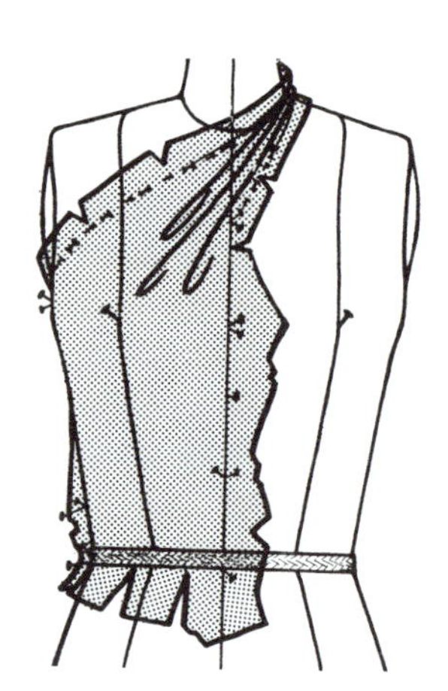

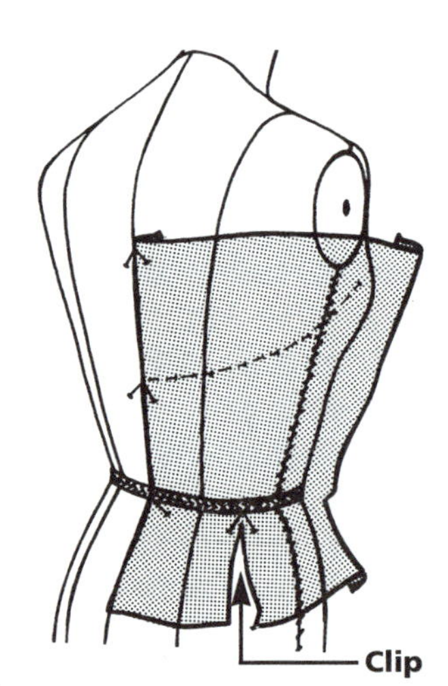

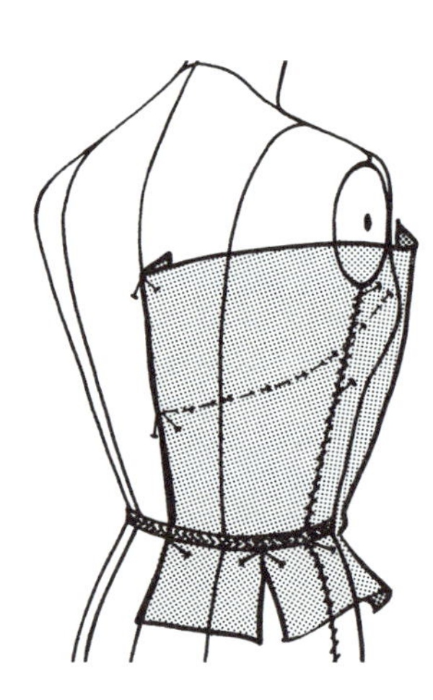

7 **Fold, tuck, pleat, or gather in the fullness around the neckline finishing at the center back neck area.**

8 **Pin the center back grainline fold** of the fabric to the center back position of the dress form. The center back panel should drape at least 2 inches above the chosen style line.

9 **Clip the waistline fabric** of the back bodice up to the bottom of the waist tape of the dress form.

10 **Drape and smooth the waistline** from center back, across the waist tape, toward the side seam.

11 **Drape and smooth the back side seam flat.** Match the side seam of the back bodice to the front side seam of the halter top.

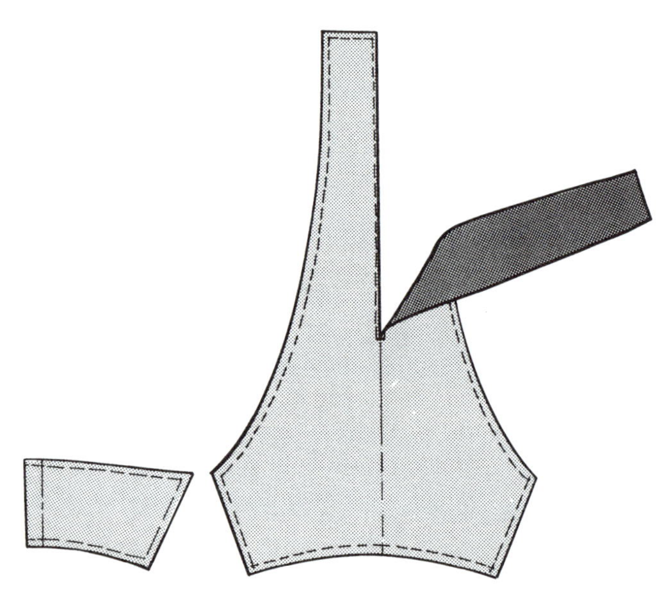

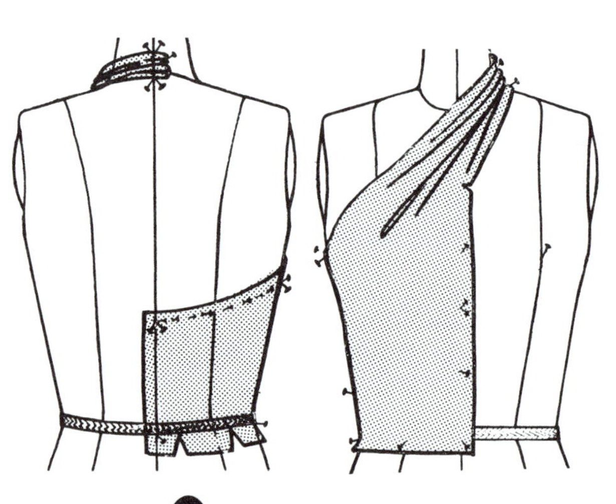

12 **Mark all key areas** of the dress form to the fabric.

Armhole/Neckline Follow the bare shoulder style line up and around the front and back neckline.

Side Seam Lightly crossmark.

Waistline Lightly crossmark the entire waist area of the drape.

13 **True up.** Remove the fabric drape from the dress. True up all seams, add seam allowances, and trim excess fabric. Pin the front drape to the back drape.

Return the finished drape to the dress form and check for accuracy, fit, and balance.

Asymmetric Skirt

A wrap skirt adds a large extension (usually 3 inches) past center front. Two front skirts are draped to give a top lay with some styling detail and an under skirt that usually remains basic. The top extension "wrap" may have addditional styling elements, including various shapes, pleats, ruffles, or fringes.

Asymmetric Skirt—Preparing the Fabric

Fold Fabric in Half—Snip and Tear

1. **Measure the length** (along the straight of grain) for the front and back skirt from 2 inches above the waist to the bottom of the dress form, and add 4 inches. Snip and tear the fabric at this length.

2. **Measure the width for the right and left front panels.** Fold the front fabric piece in half from selvage to selvage. Snip and tear the fabric piece in half length-wise. Use one piece for the right front panel and use the other piece for the left front panel.

3. **Measure the width for the back skirt.** Measure, along the crossgrain, from center back to the side seam at the hip level, and add 3 inches. Snip and tear the fabric at this width.

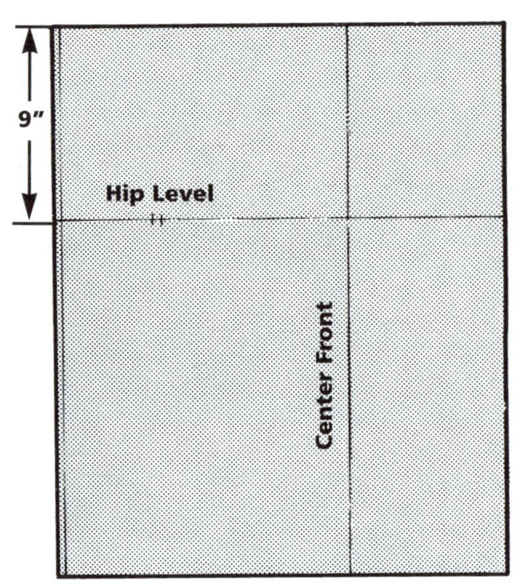

Right Front Skirt

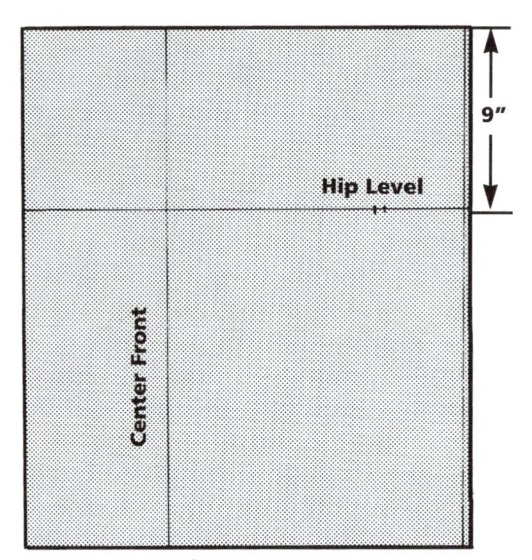

Left Front Skirt

4 Draw the center front grainline on the right and left skirt panels. On the fabric, measure 7 inches from the torn edge.

5 Draw a crossgrain on the right and left skirt panels. Mesure down 9 inches from the top edge of the panel. Using an L-square ruler, draw in the crossgrain on both panels.

6 Draw the side seam for the right and left skirt panels. Measure from center front to the side seam (at the hip level), and add 1/2 inch for ease. Transfer this measurement to the fabric on the hip line. Using this mark, draw a side seam perfectly parallel to the center front grainline from the hip line down.

7 Draw the back grainline, crossgrain, and side seam the same as for the basic back skirt.

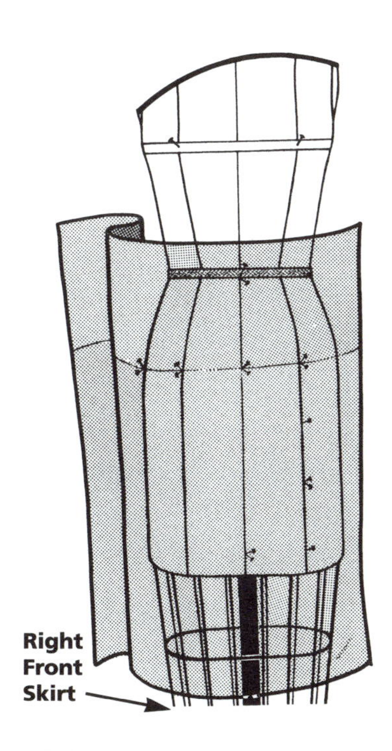

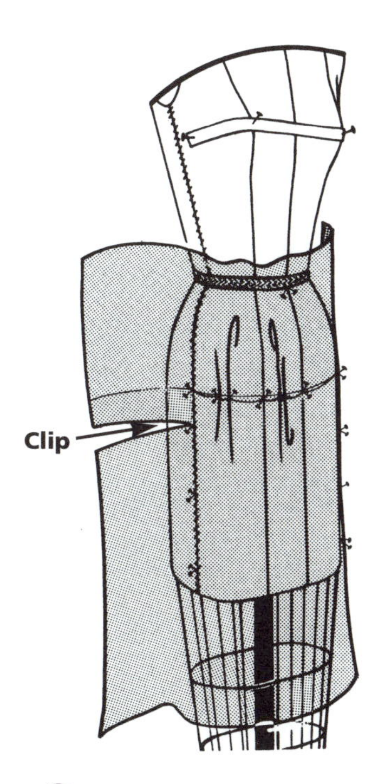

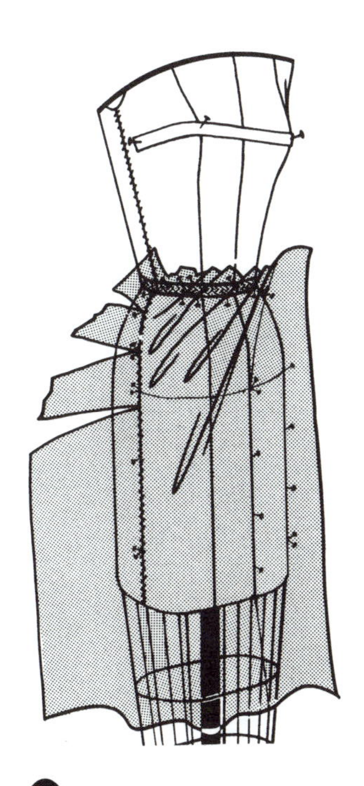

1. **Pin the right center front grainline of the fabric** on the center front position of the dress form, matching the crossgrain of the fabric to the hip level line on the dress form.

2. **Smooth and pin the crossgrain** of the fabric (evenly distributing the ease) across the dress form to the side seam.

3. **Pin the side seam,** from below the hip level, to the dress form.

4. **Clip the fabric** from the outer edge of the fabric into the side seam at the point from which the lowest pleat will radiate. Place a pin on the side seam at this clip.

5. **Fold the first pleat at the waistline.** The first pleat should start at the waistline between center front and the opposite princess panel. It should drape from the waistline to nothing at the pinned side seam.

6. **Continue to clip, pin, fold, and drape the remaining of the desired number of waistline pleats.**

Asymmetric Skirt—Left Front Draping Steps

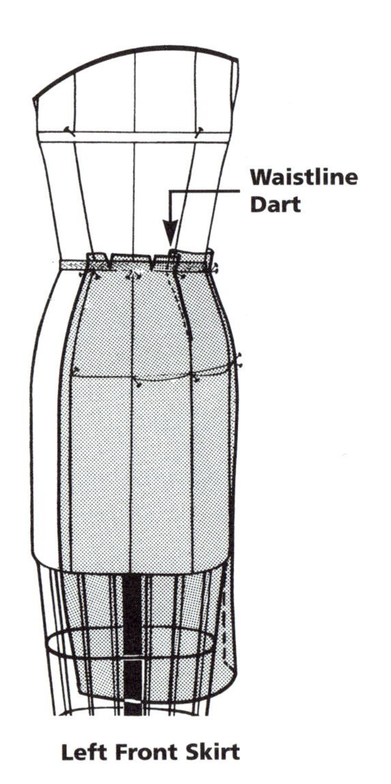

Left Front Skirt

1 **Pin the left center front grainline of the fabric** on the center front position of the dress form, matching the cross-grain of the fabric to the hip level line on the dress form.

2 **Smooth and pin the cross-grain** of the fabric (evenly distributing the ease) across the dress form to the side seam.

3 **Pin the side seam,** from below the hip level, to the dress form.

4 **Drape in one or two waistline darts** and the remainder of the side seam down to the hip level. Smooth the fabric from center front to the princess seam. Crossmark the waistline at the princess seam. Drape in one or two waistline darts.

Entire Back Skirt

5 **Drape the back skirt** the same as the basic back skirt. Match side seam to side seam and crossgrain to crossgrain.

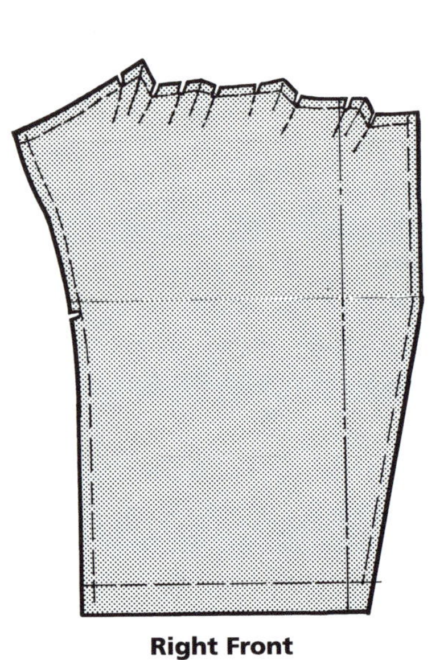

Right Front

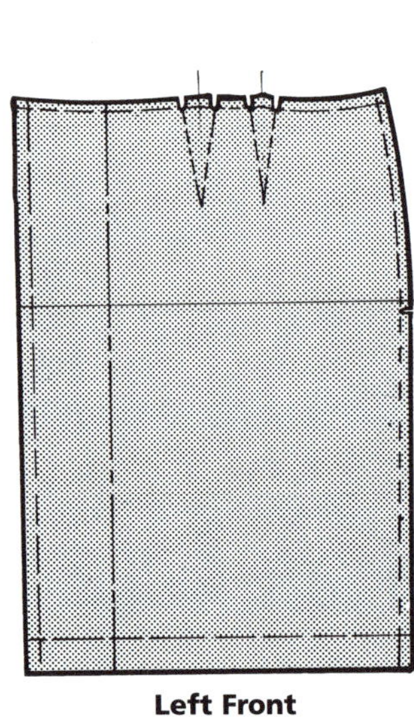

Left Front

6 **Mark all key areas.**

Waistline Front and back.
Darts Left front and back.
Pleats Right front.

7 **True up** Remove the fabric drape from the dress form. True up all seams, add seam allowances, and trim excess fabric.

Return the finished drape to the dress form and check for accuracy, fit, and balance.

Asymmetric Collar

There are many varieties of asymmetrical collar designs and many neckline shapes in which this collar may be draped. This collar typically crosses over the center front. The collar may have a slight roll or may have a high stand at the neck edge, depending on the design desired.

The best results of this collar design are achieved when draped because of the crossover effect. The asymmetrical collar puts pizzazz back into an otherwise simple collar and may turn any neckline into instant fashion.

Asymmetric Collar*—Preparing the Fabric*

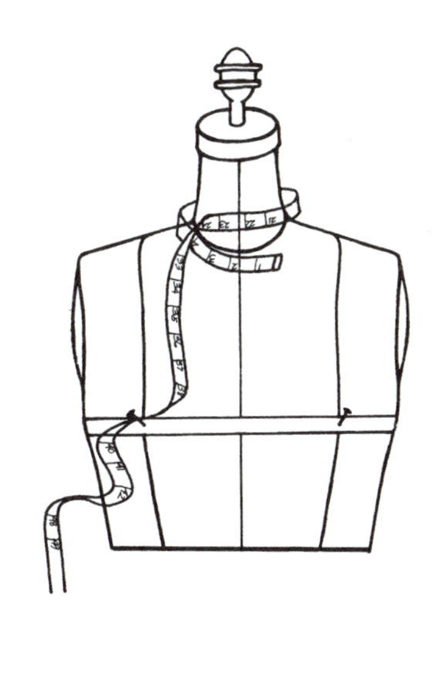

1 **Measure the desired neckline distance** (along the crossgrain) both right and left sides of the dress form for the length of this collar. Snip and tear the fabric at this length.

Illustrated: approximately **20 inches.**

2 **Measure the desired width of the collar** (along the grainline) and double this measurement.

Illustrated: approximately **18 inches.**

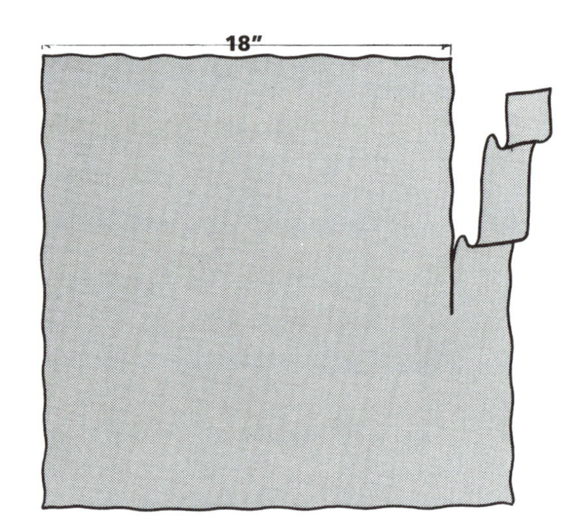

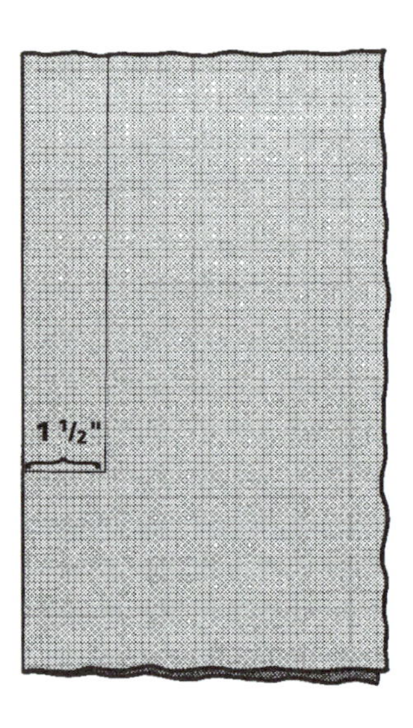

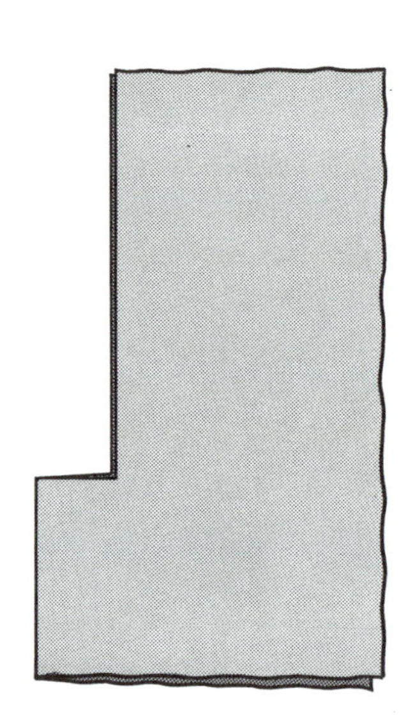

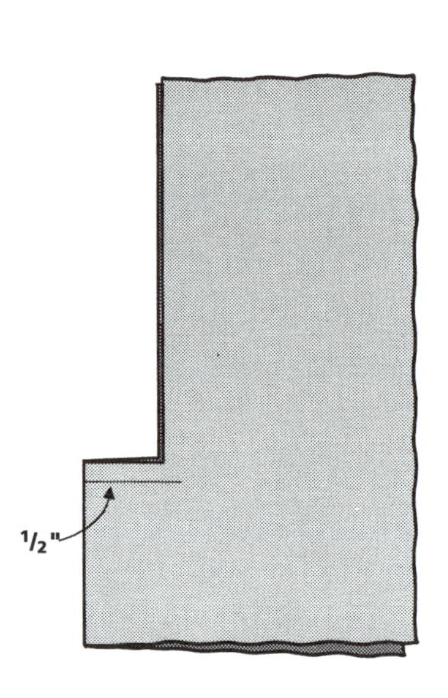

3 **Preparing the back neck opening.**

a. Fold the fabric in half lengthwise, parallel to the grainline.

b. Measure up from the lower edge one third the measurement of the fabric piece. Measure along the foldline.

c. Draw a perfect crossgrain line 1 1/2-inches long.

d. Draw a grainline 1 1/2-inches parallel from the fold of the fabric.

4 **Cut along the crossgrain line and the grainline,** and remove the excess fabric.

5 **Draw a short crossgrain line** 1/2 inch below the cut crossgrain. This indicates the center back/neck position.

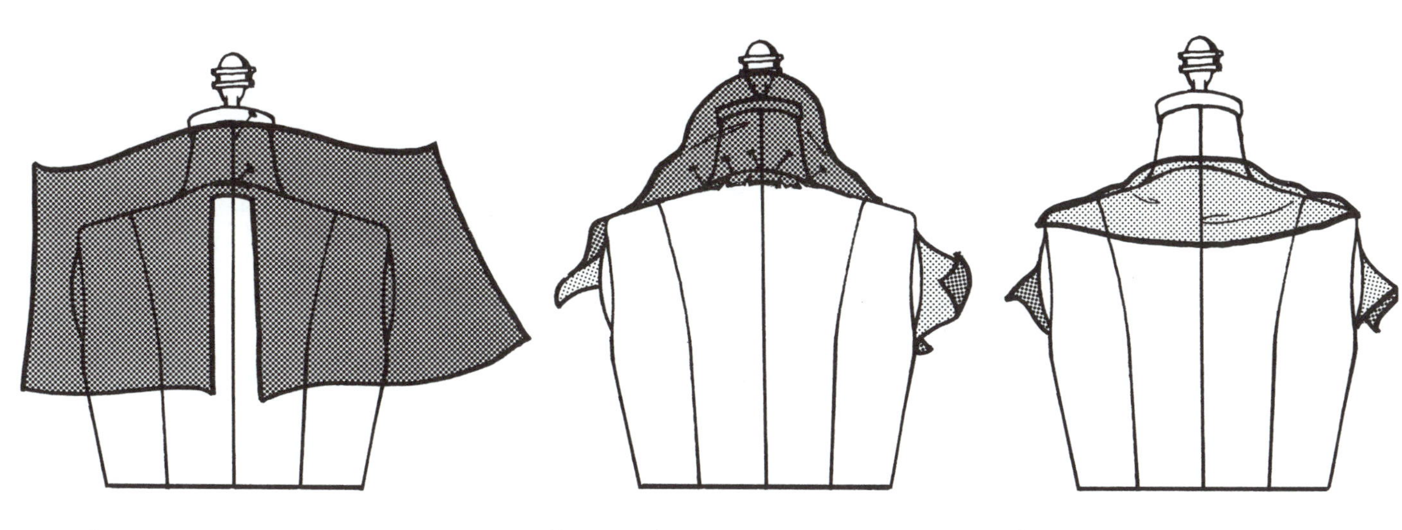

1 Pin the center back grainline of the fabric to the center back position of the dress form neckline. Keep the fabric open and flipped up.

2 Align the center back neckline crossmark on the fabric to the center back neckline on the dress form.

3 Clip, smooth, and pin the entire back neckline from shoulder seam to shoulder seam. Keep the fabric flipped up.

4 Fold the fabric down onto the body and over the back draped neckline. The fabric should be laying smooth and clean.

5 Drape the right front neckline. From the shoulder position, flip the fabric up onto the front neck of the dress form. Drape the desired right front neckline of the collar, passing the center front position, and finishing the desired asymmetrical position.

NOTE: The straighter this front neckline, the more the stand of the collar. Therefore, for less stand, drape the front neckline with a definite curving seam.

6 Flip the fabric of the right front collar so it is laying down over the shoulder and body.

7 Clip the outer edge of the fabric up to the desired collar style to allow the collar to lay smoothly. Draw the desired collar style.

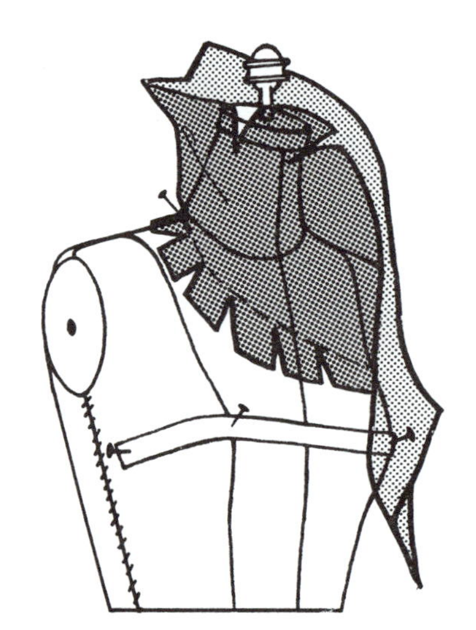

8 Draw the right front collar neckline. With the collar flipped up, draw the right front collar neckline to the center back position.

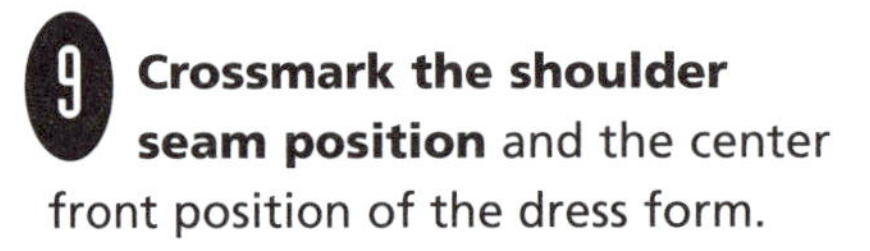

9 Crossmark the shoulder seam position and the center front position of the dress form.

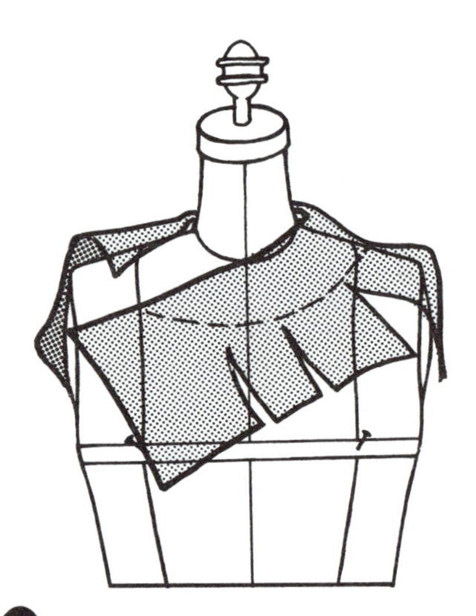

10 Drape the left front collar, following the same draping procedures as the right front collar (Steps 4, 5, and 6). Continue to clip, smooth, and pin the left front neckline from the shoulder seam to past the center front.

11 Draw the entire left neckline. Flip the collar up and draw the entire left neckline.

12 Crossmark the shoulder seam position and the center front position of the dress form.

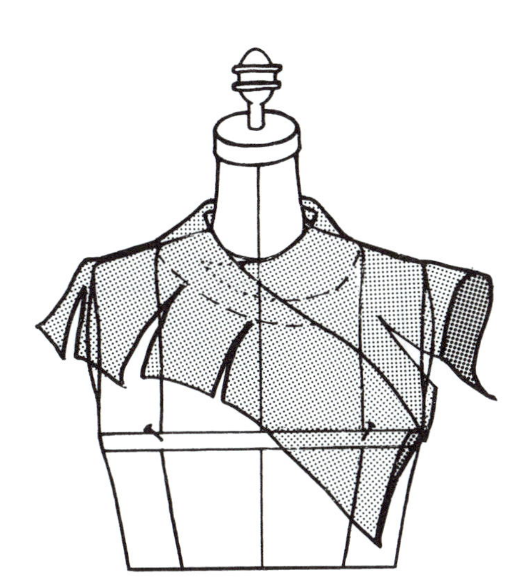

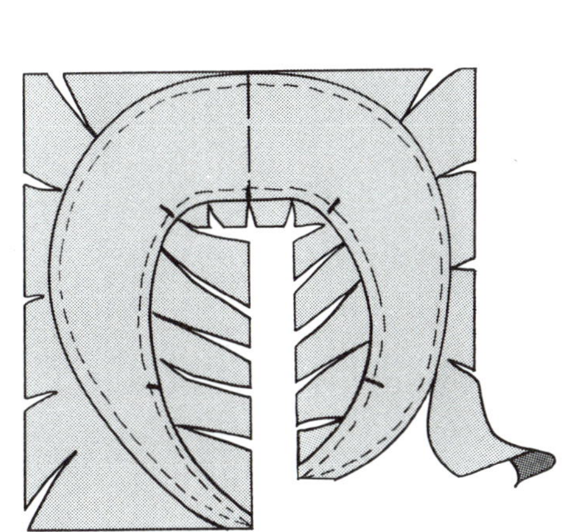

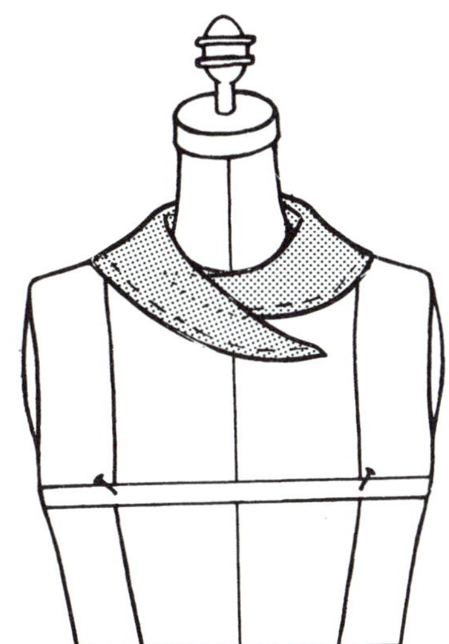

13 **Flip the fabric of the left front collar so it is laying down** over the shoulder and body.

14 **Clip the outer edge of the fabric** up to the desired collar style. This allows the collar to lay down smoothly.

15 **Draw the desired style.**

NOTE: The back collar width should be exactly the same from shoulder seam to shoulder seam.

16 **True up all seams.** Remove the collar from the dress form and true up all seams. Add 1/4inch seam allowance around the outer edge and trim excess fabric. Label the center back grainline on the fold of the the fabric.

17 **Check for accuracy, fit, and balance** by returning the trued collar to the dress form. The drape should fit smoothly around the neckline without gapping or stretching.

Part Four

Advanced Design Variations

After mastering the principles and techniques of draping, the designer will be able to apply this information to designing and creating more unusual and complicated cuts. Those approaching the challenging designs in this section must have experience in the application of basic and intermediate draping styles and sewing skills. Much pleasure and satisfaction can be derived from creating original styles.

Projects show how to emphasize a figure's most pleasing attributes through subtle illusion. Thus, designers learn to achieve a total effect, while still paying attention to the most minute details.

This part discusses bias dresses, sculptured dresses, yoke-styled garments, and knit and halter designs. It explores how fabric, and its various fibers and weaves, reacts differently to each design. Other considerations are draping the cloth against the body on the bias weave and with knit fabric. Although there are step-by-step guidelines for these designs, a great deal of finesse and technique is required to accurately drape these styles.

Chapter Seventeen

Dresses

Objectives

By studying the various draping steps in this chapter, the designer should be able to accomplish the following:

- Manipulate the fabric and learn how to mold and shape the fabric on the dress form.
- Maintain a smooth and easy-flowing design that does not overwork a piece of fabric.
- Explore and define style lines and silhouettes over the bust, hip, and waist to create folds, darts, pleats, and/or fullness.
- Develop creativity and stimulate a variety of ideas.
- Enhance draping skills in handling pliable fabric to define a design and judge what designs are flattering to a particular figure.

Bias-cut Slip Dress

Because of the inherent stretchability of bias fabric, designers such as Donna Karan used it to create new dress styles for the 1990s. The bias-cut slip dress has won approval in the retail market at all levels. It can be slipped on over the head, which makes it easy to get into and out of, and it is comfortable to wear. As designers, you should understand that if bias-cut garments are draped improperly, they will hug the body and every imperfection will be emphasized.

The bias cut slip dress is a sleeveless styled dress with a neckline beginning above the bust. It is held in place with thin spaghetti straps. This dress is cut on the bias of a soft fabric, which results in a closer fit that stretches and conforms to the movements of the body.

The slip dress is an alternative to the bodysuit. It may be worn alone or with a soft cardigan, a tailored blazer, or leggings.

1 **For the length and width** of the dress, measure and cut two perfect 45-inch squares.

2 **Draw a true bias line** diagonally across the pieces of fabric.

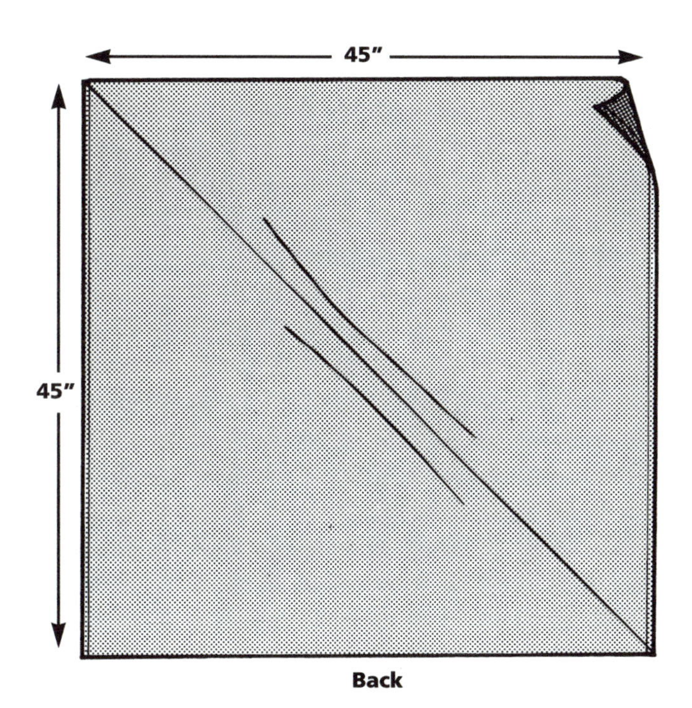

Back

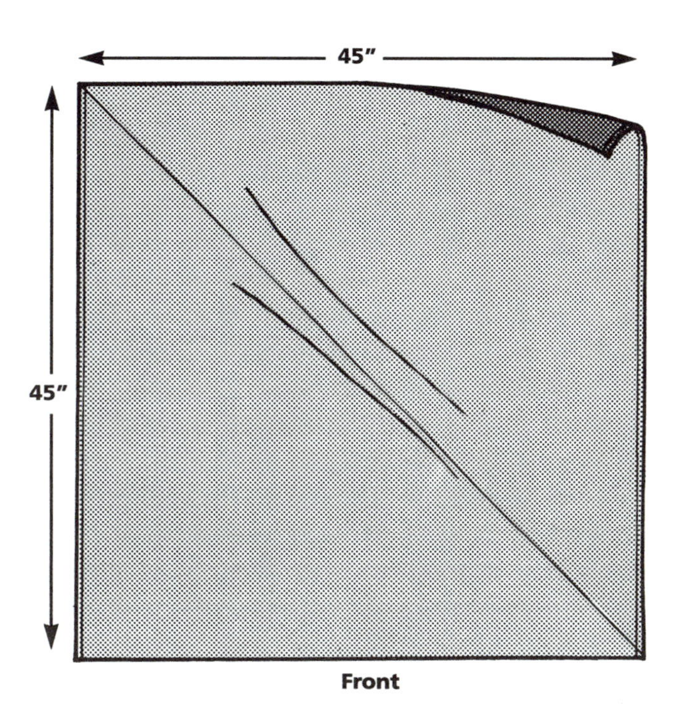

Front

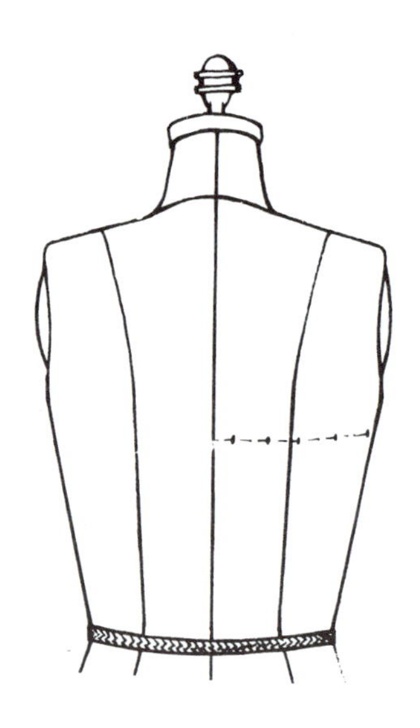

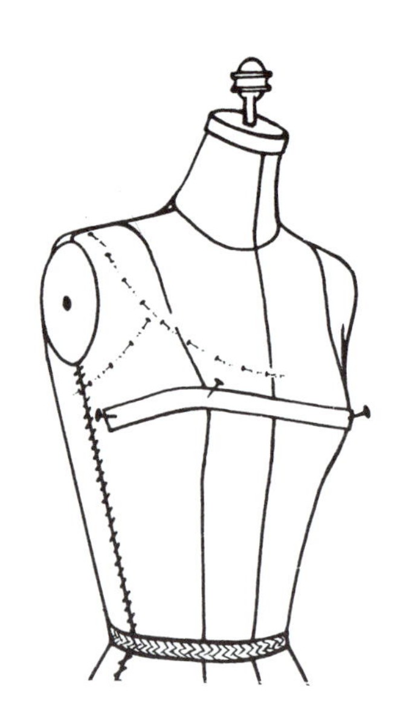

Prepare the dress form.
Place pins on the dress form at the desired bustline. Remove the bust level tape (bra) from the dress form.

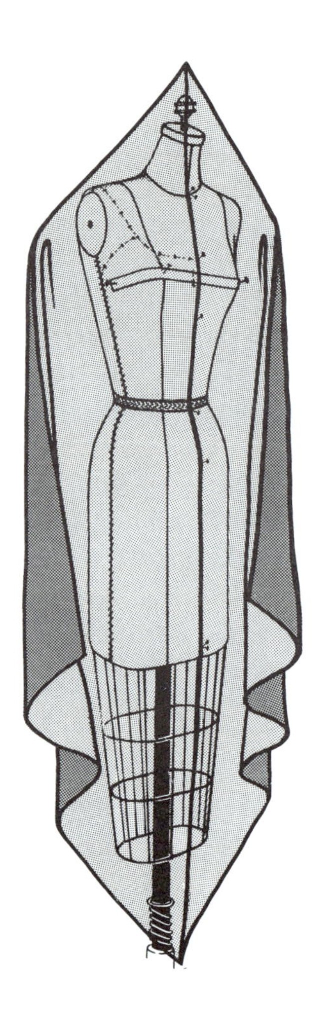

1 **Pin the bias line of the fabric** to the center front position of the dress form. The fabric piece should extend at least 3 inches above the styled bustline.

2 Smooth, clip, and pin the fabric across the neckline style line. Approximately 2 inches from center front, clip the fabric from the top edge down to the neckline style line. Pin the neckline style line seam at the clip.

3 Create a slight flowing flare below the bust. Because the fabric is on the bias and is soft, the bust area can be molded into a close-to-body fit. As this bias drape is molded over the bustline, a slight flare will be created below the bust that extends to the hemline.

4 Smooth, clip, and pin approximately 2 inches from the first clip of the neckline style line. Mold and smooth the remainder of the bust area. Continue to smooth the fabric across the neckline style line seam, over the bust, and toward the side seam.

5 Clip, smooth, and fit the side seam down to the waistline. As the side seam is being fitted, a second slight flare will be created from the hipline in the middle of the princess panel. Drape in the remaining of the side seam below the waistline.

6 Mark all key areas of the dress form of the center front panel.

Front Bustline Style Line Seam

Waistline at Side Seam Place a waistline notch.

Side Seam Lightly mark.

Hem Follow the bottom of the dress form or a rung.

DO NOT REMOVE THE DRAPE FROM THE DRESS FORM

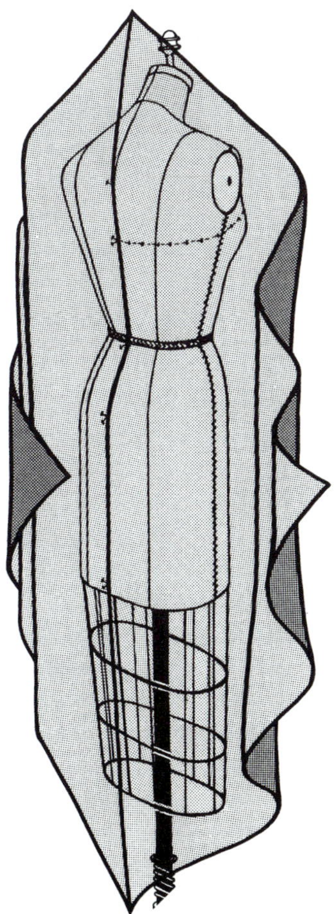

7 Pin the bias line of the fabric to the center back position of the dress form. The fabric piece should extend at least 3 inches above the styled bustline.

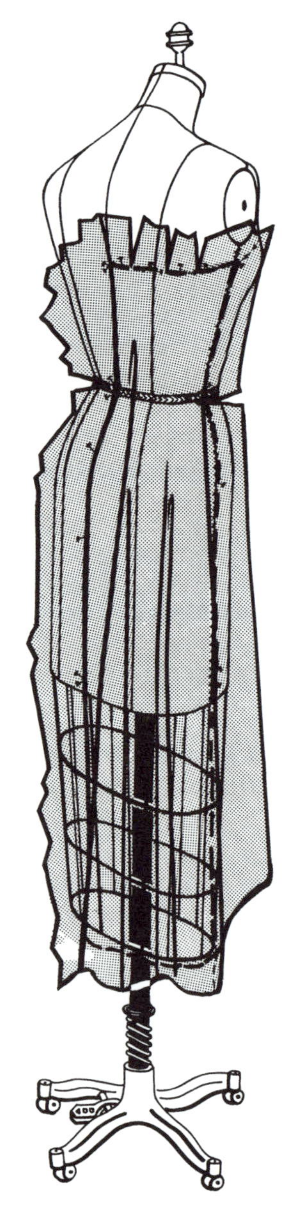

8 Smooth, clip, and pin the fabric across the back neckline style line. Approximately 2 inches from center back, clip the fabric from the top edge down to the back neckline style line. Pin the neckline style line seam at the clip.

9 Create a slight flowing flare below the back neckline style line. As this bias drape is being molded over the back neckline style line, a slight flare will be created at the princess seam that extends to the hemline.

10 Smooth, clip, and pin approximately 2 inches from the first clip of the back neckline style line. Mold and smooth the remainder of the back neckline area. Continue to smooth the fabric across the neckline style line seam toward the side seam.

11 Clip, smooth, and fit the side seam down to the waistline. As the back side seam is being draped, pin it to the front side seam. As the side seam is being fitted, a second slight flare will be created from the hipline in the middle of the princess panel. Drape in the remaining of the side seam below the waistline.

12 Match the back side seam to the front side seam, pinning and fitting the dress until the desired side seam shape is achieved.

13 Mark all key areas of the dress form of the center front panel.

Back Bustline Style Line Seam

Waistline at Side Seam Place a waistline notch.

Side Seam Lightly mark.

Hem Follow the bottom of the dress form or a rung.

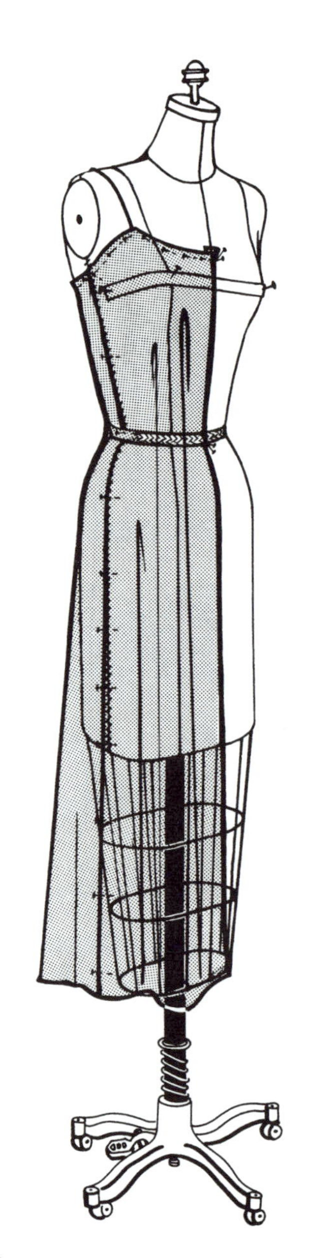

14 Drape and measure the amount of spaghetti strapping needed for this design. Add an inch for seam allowance.

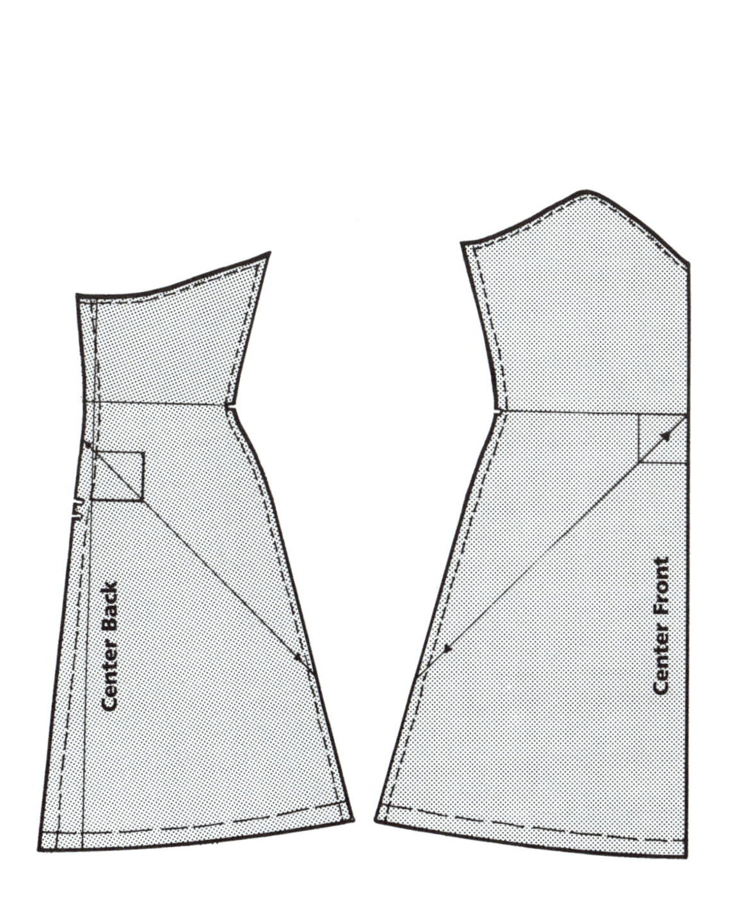

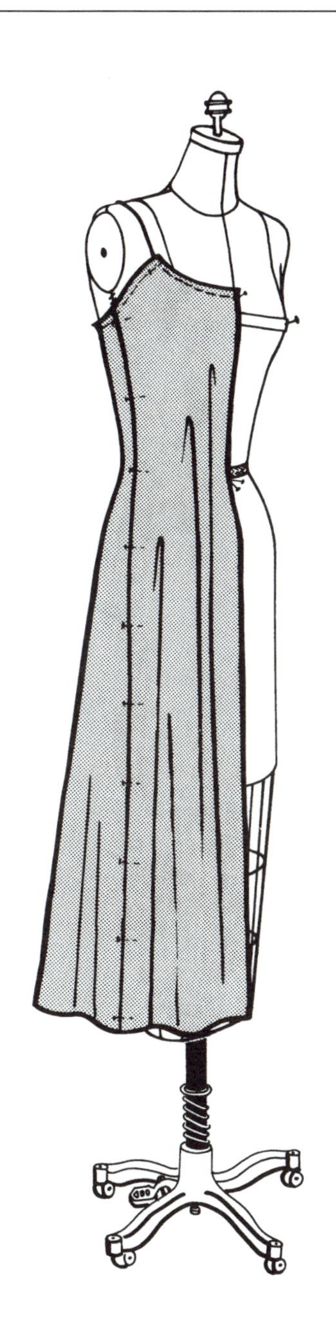

15 **True up the front and back dress.** Remove the fabric drape from the dress form. True up all seams, add seam allowances, and trim excess fabric. Pin the front drape to the back drape.

Return the finished drape to the dress form and check for accuracy, fit, and balance.

"Sculptured" Dress

A "sculptured" dress has excess fabric tucks or pleats around the bust area that radiate from a shaped motif and blend to nothing at the side seam. The tucks or pleats distribute and shape the fabric around the bust and creates a smooth molded effect in the waist area of the dress. These multiple folds will hug, wrap, and drape the body to produce a sultry, sexy, and provocative dress.

"Sculptured" Dress—Preparing the Fabric

1 Measure, along the straight of grain, 60 inches to 88 inches, which is the length for the front and back. Snip and tear the fabric at this length.

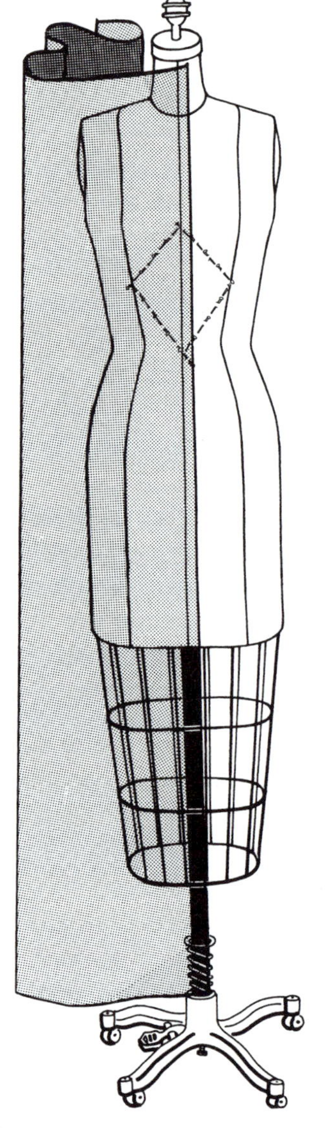

2 Measure, along the cross-grain, the width for the front and back.

a. For the front drape, it will be necessary to use the full width of the fabric goods.

b. For the back drape, measure from the center back to the side seam, and add 8 inches. Snip and tear the fabric at this width. The measurement will be at least 18 inches.

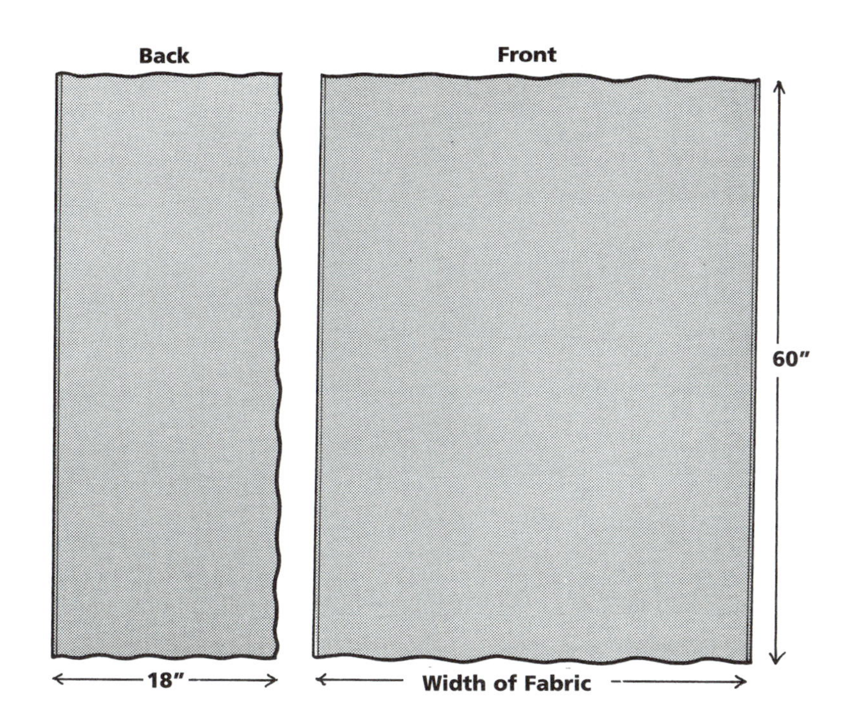

3 Draw the grainline for the front in the middle of the fabric piece.

4 Draw the grainline for the back panel 10 inches from the torn edge.

5 Draw the crossgrain for the back panel 9 inches from the top edge of the fabric.

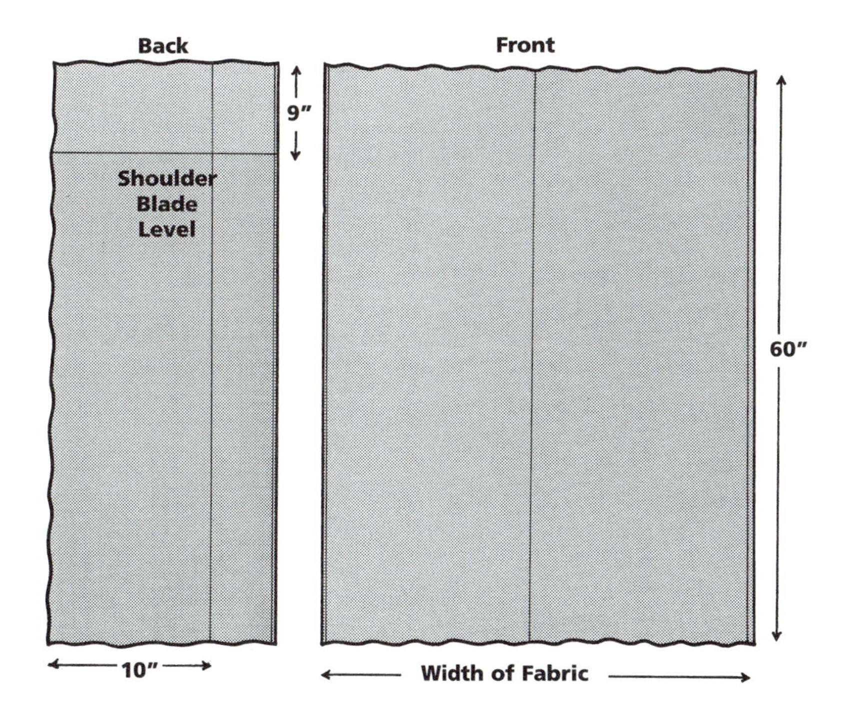

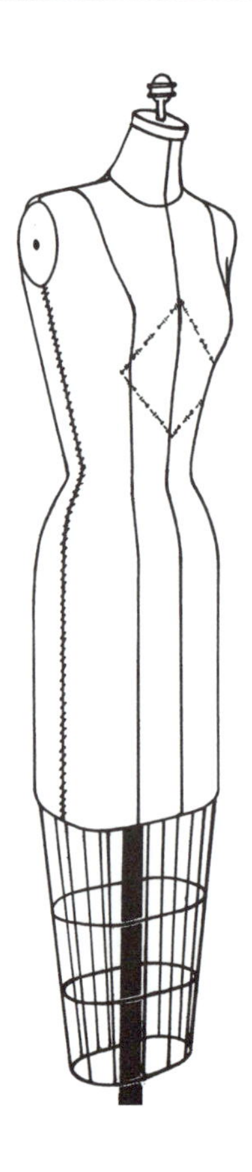

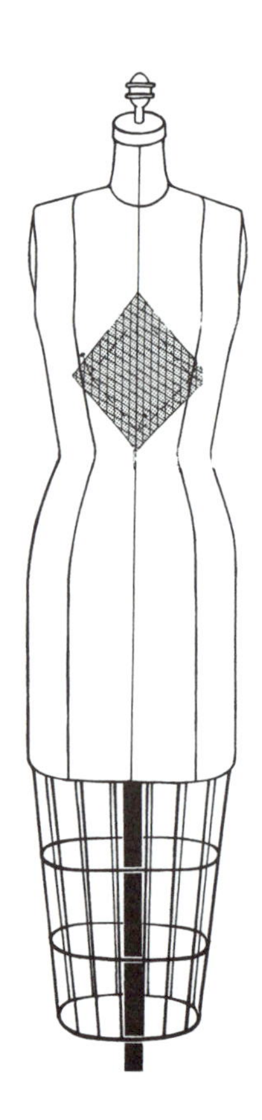

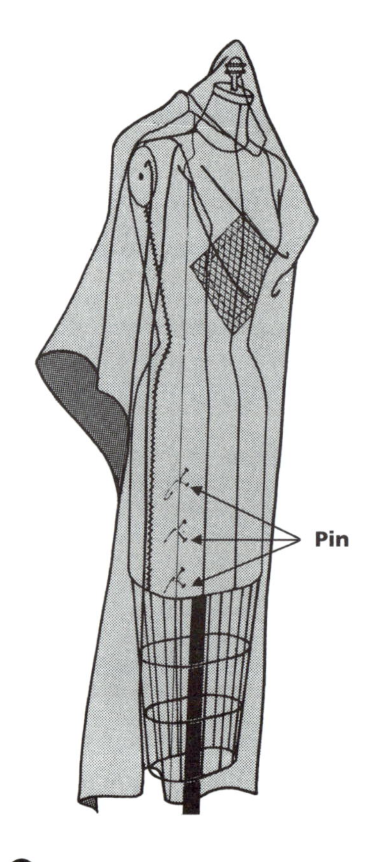

Prepare the dress form.
Refer to the garment design and note on the dress form the area of emphasis from which the drapes will radiate.

1 **Design and drape in the desired motif** (with all necessary seam allowances). Place this motif on the dress form. (This area was previously noted.)

2 **Place the grainline for the front dress.**

a. Position the grainline on the center of the princess panel on the dress form. Pin this grainline from the bottom of the dress form up to the hipline with at least three pins.

b. Allow all excess fabric to fall over the shoulder and the top of the dress form while draping the lower area of the design.

c. Drape and pin the fabric across center front of the dress form. Keep the grain of the fabric parallel to center front. Secure pins on the center front position with a couple more pins.

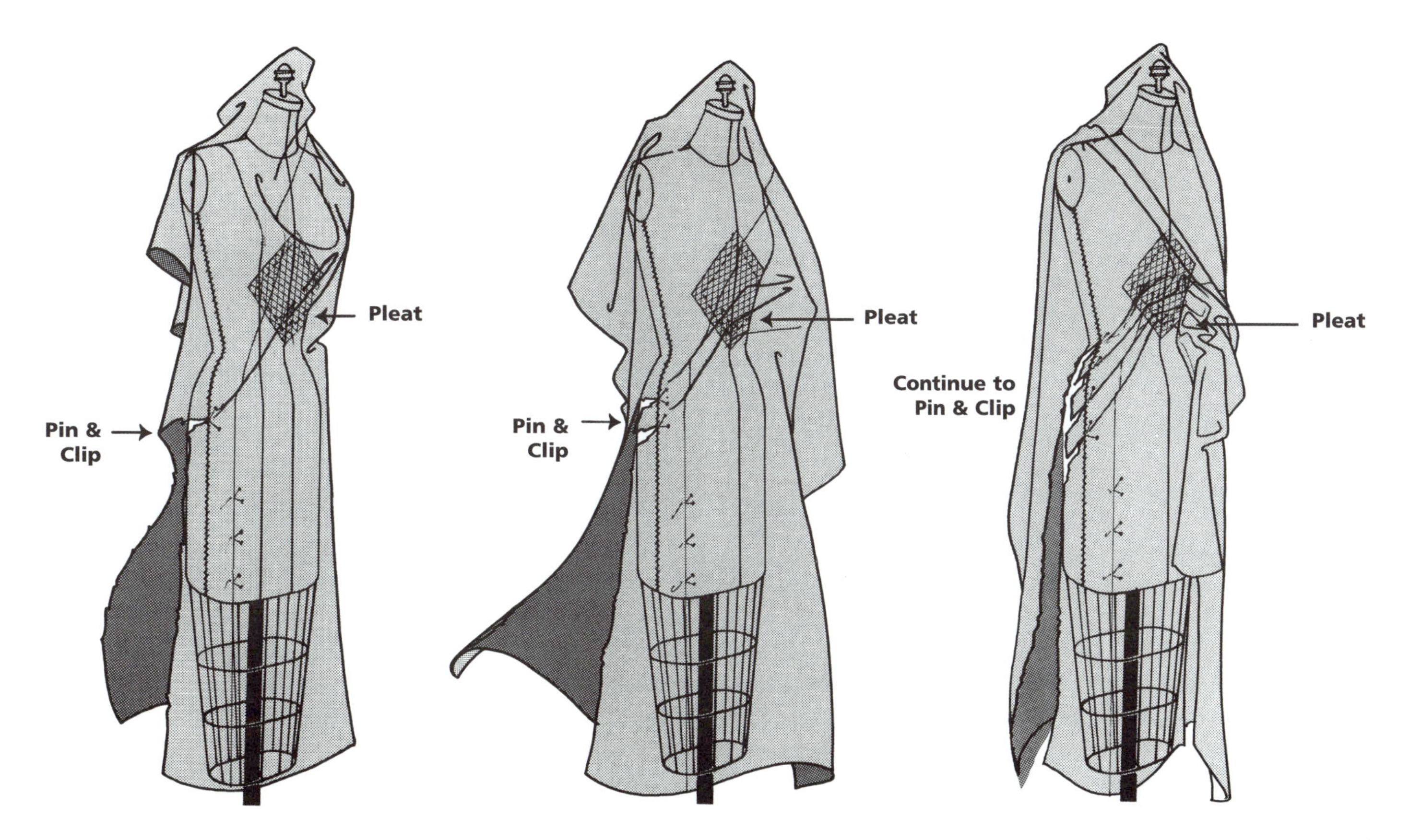

3 Trim, clip, and the create first pleat.

a. Clip the fabric approximately 2 inches from the side seam of the dress form. Clip fabric up from the bottom edge to where the lowest pleat will radiate.

b. Place a pin on the side seam at the point from where the lowest pleat will radiate.

c. Clip into the side seam to this pin.

d. Fold the first drape from the design motif to nothing at the pinned side seam.

NOTE: The grainline will start to angle toward the center front and become more exaggerated in this direction as the pleats are continued. Also, this first pleat is the most difficult of the pleating process. Be patient.

4 Create the second pleat.

a. Smooth the fabric up on the side seam at the point from which the second pleat will radiate.

b. Place a pin on the side seam at this point.

c. Clip into the side seam to this pin.

d. Fold the second drape from the design motif to nothing at the second pin on the side seam.

5 Continue to pin, clip, and place the remainder of the pleats. Pin and clip the side seam about every inch or so. At each pinning and clipping, fold a new drape, each radiating from the design motif. Also, continue to clip and trim the side seam past the waistline.

6 **Smooth the fabric upward in a clockwise direction,** flat over the armplate and shoulder, after the side seam area has been draped. Be careful not to stretch the fabric.

7 **Trim away the excess fabric** that is falling toward the back of the dress form, leaving approximately a 4-inch excess. Recheck the shoulder draped area.

8 **Clip the fabric** to the center of the design motif from the edge of the fabric near the grainline.

9 **Trim the fabric around the design motif** area that has been draped. Leave enough fabric for seam allowances and the upper bodice drape.

10 **Create pleats at the design motif.**

a. Use the excess fabric that falls below the bustline. Working left to right, pin and place pleats at the design motif stitchline. Allow each pleat to fall over the bust area and radiate to nothing over the bust.

b. Trim excess fabric at the design motif (one pleat at a time) as pleats are pinned and draped in place.

11 **Trim neckline area.** Leave at least 2 inches of excess fabric for possible neckline shape changes and seam allowances.

12 **Pin and drape in the desired neckline.** Trim excess fabric at the neckline, shoulder, and side seam.

13 **Mark key areas** of the dress form to the fabric.

Shoulder
Desired Front Armhole Shape
Desired Front Neckline Shape
Side Seam
Motif (Stitchline) and Pleats

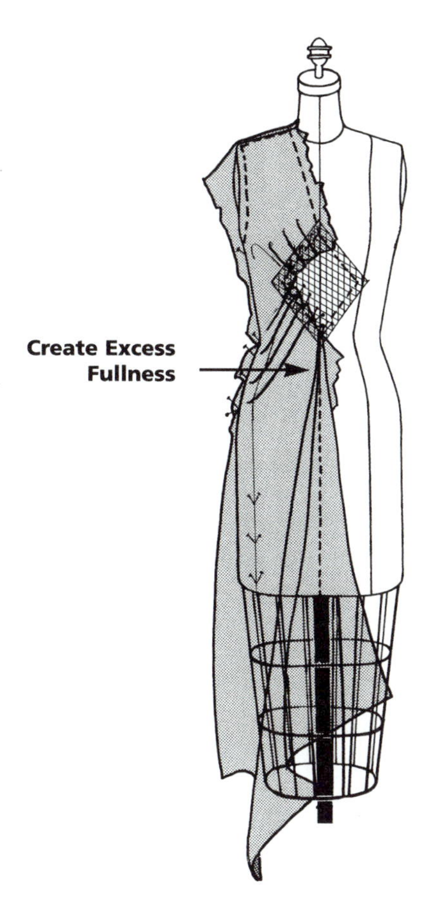

14 Create more fullness in the center front. Clip, pin, and allow excess fabric to fall from nothing at the lowest section of the design motif and to flow as extra fullness to the hem/center front area. Transfer and draw in a new center front position of the dress form to the fabric drape.

NOTE: The skirt area will cascade easier if a slight pulling up of the fabric at the design motif is used.

"Sculptured" Dress—Back Draping Steps

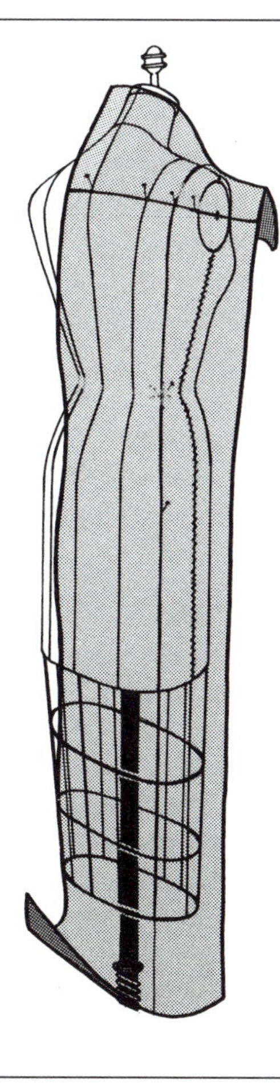

1 Place the back crossgrain at the shoulder blade level. Pin in place.

2 Place the back straight grainline in the center of the back princess panel. Pin in place. Pin center back near the hem on the dress form rung.

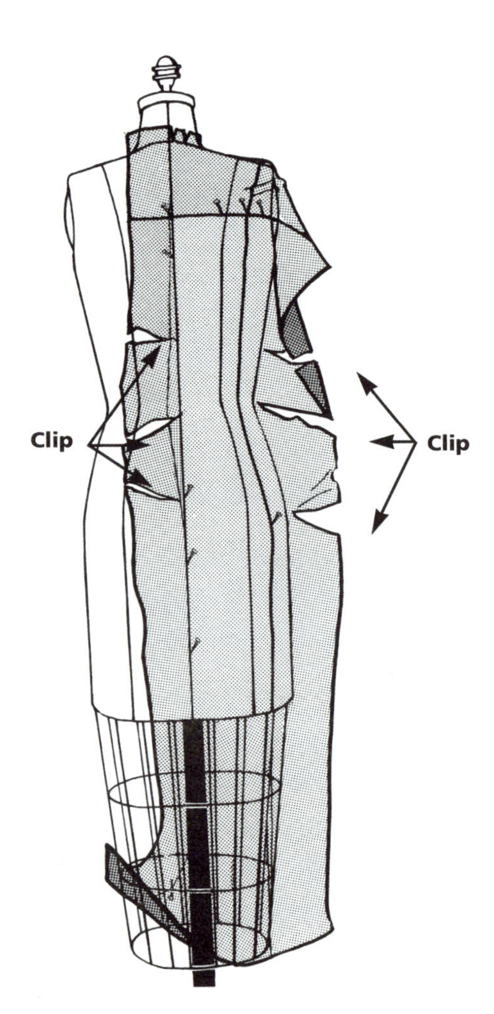

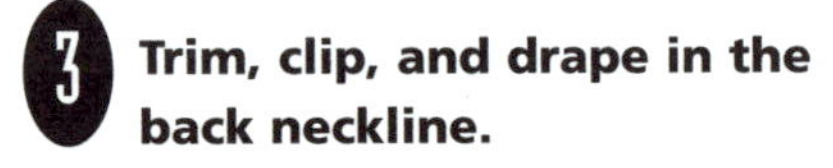
3 Trim, clip, and drape in the back neckline.

4 Drape the back shoulder area. Smooth the fabric over and past the shoulder seam and drape in the shoulder area.

5 Clip the waistline area at center back and the side seam. Also, clip once above and once below the waist area at the side seam and center back.

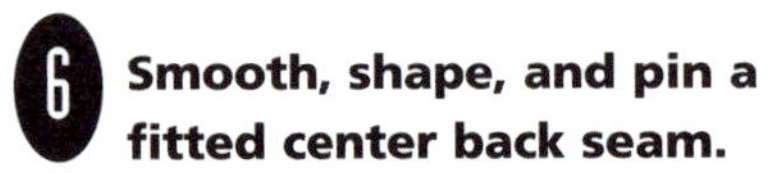
6 Smooth, shape, and pin a fitted center back seam. Approximately 3/4 of an inch will be smoothed out at the center back/waist area. The waist area will extend up and drape to nothing at the crossgrain line and down to nothing at the hipline.

7 Smooth, shape. and pin a fitted side seam. Finish draping the side seam by pinning the front side seam to the back side seam.

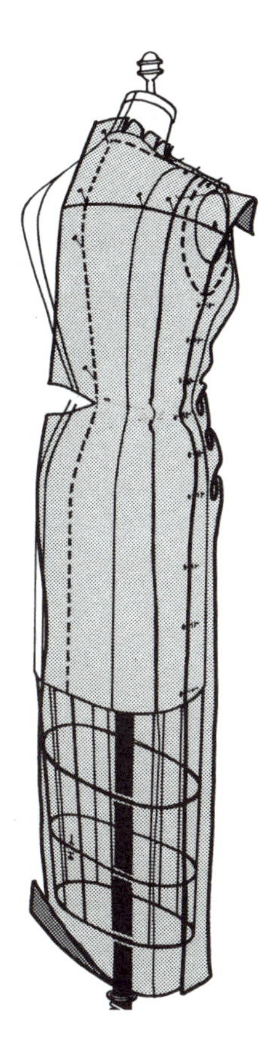

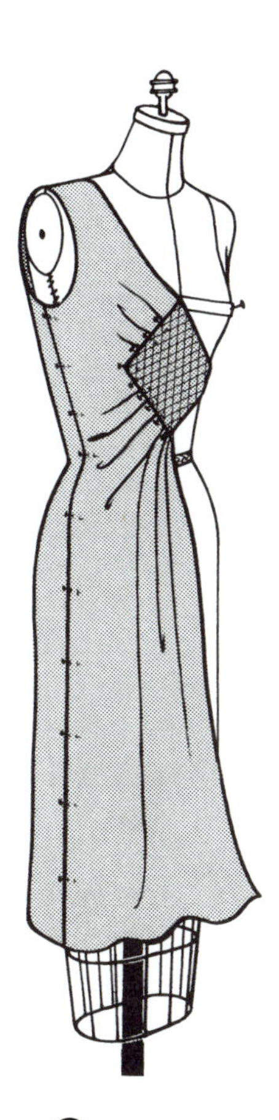

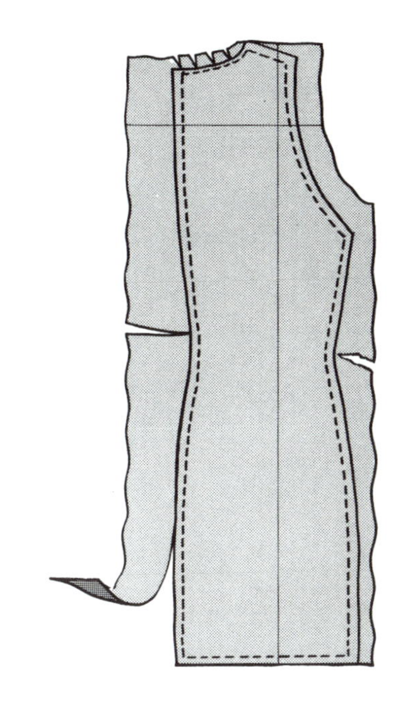

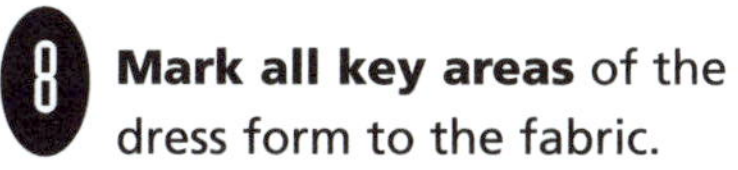

8 **Mark all key areas** of the dress form to the fabric.

Desired Back Neckline Shape

Shoulder Seam match front shoulder seam.

Desired Armhole Shape

Side Seam

9 **True up** motif, front and back dress. Remove the fabric drape from the dress form. True up all seams, add seam allowances, and trim excess fabric. Pin the front drape to the back drape.

Return the finished drape to the dress form and check for accuracy, fit, and balance.

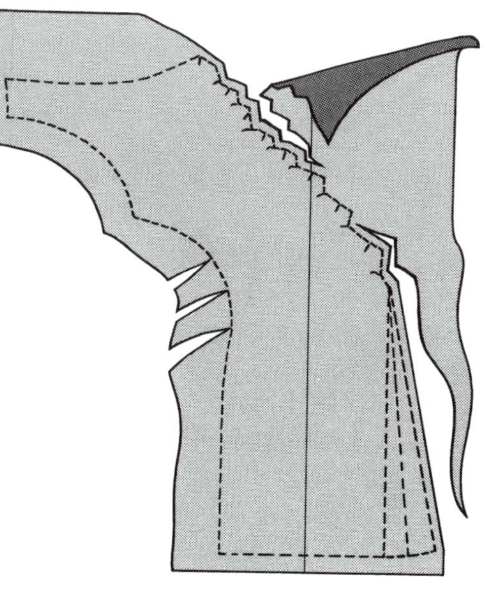

Bustier

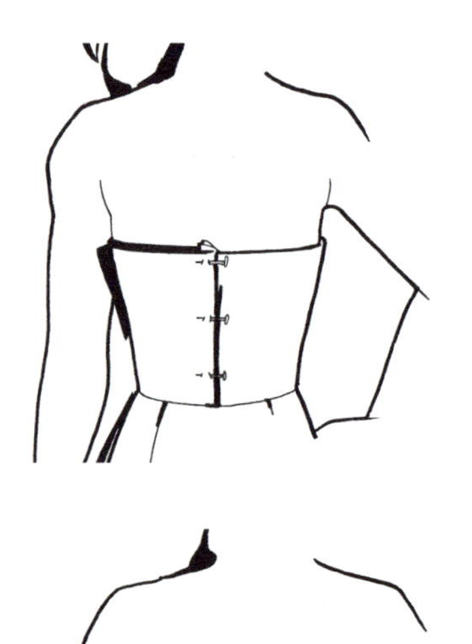

The bustier is a form-fitting strapless princess bodice that fits snugly around the rib cage. A traditional bustier foundation garment has a low-cut front and back neckline. Front princess seams are always used to create and support an extra tight fit at the princess seams and side seam. The back design is usually one piece that allows for either a center back/zipper or an elasticized back area.

Special boning and sewing techniques help support the foundation section of this classical bodice. A bustier foundation is the garment sewn between the actual bustier design (that is, the layer between the outside of the garment and the lining).

Bustier—Preparing the Fabric

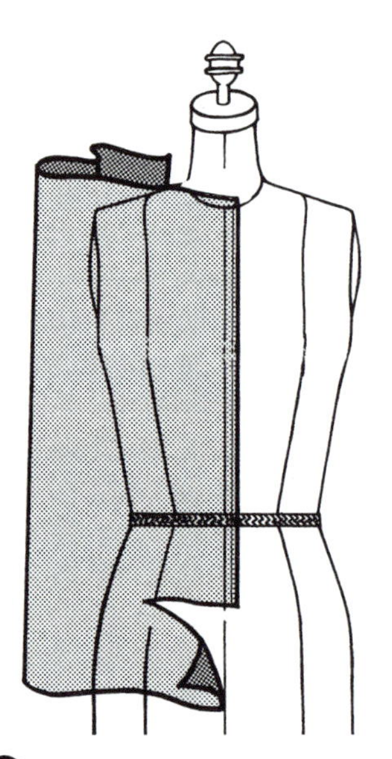

1 **Measure the length** (along the straight of grain) from the neckline to the waist, and add 4 inches.

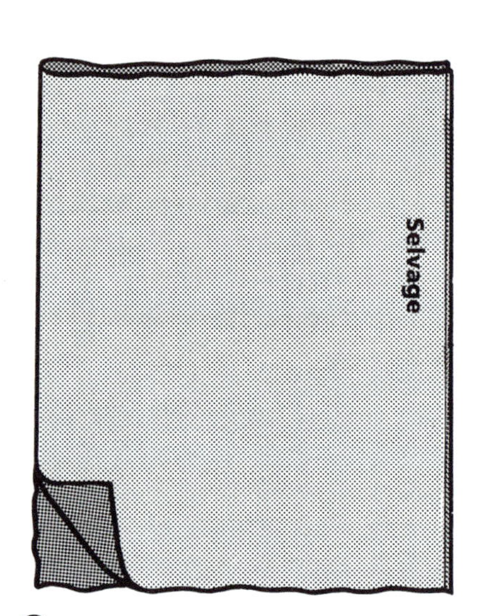

2 **Divide the fabric piece in half.** Fold the fabric from selvage to selvage, and snip and tear the fabric piece in half lengthwise.

One piece will be used for the front panels and the other piece will be used for the back panels.

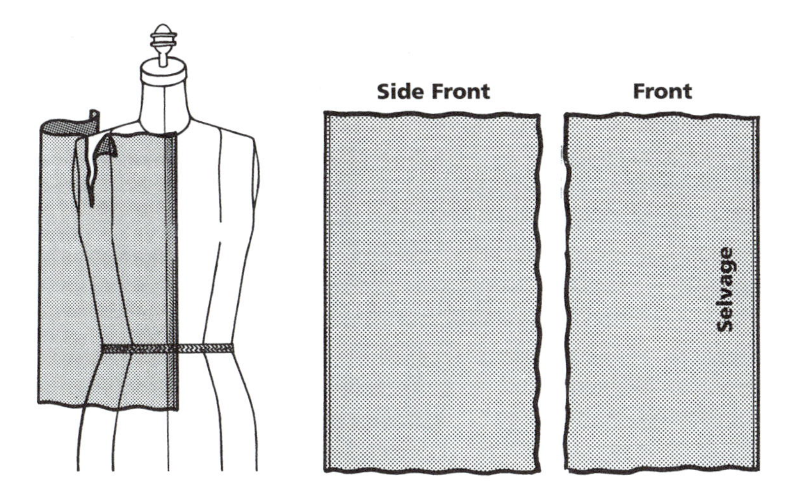

3 **Measure the width** for the center front panel (along the crossgrain) from the center front of the dress form to the princess seam at the apex, and add 4 inches.

Use the remaining front fabric piece for the side front panel.

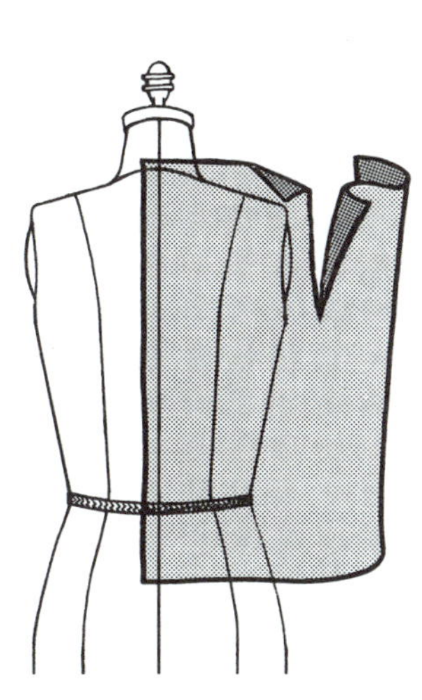

4 **Measure the width for the back panel,** using the fabric piece prepared in Step 2. Measure from the center back of the dress form to the side seam, and add 4 inches. Snip and tear the fabric at this width.

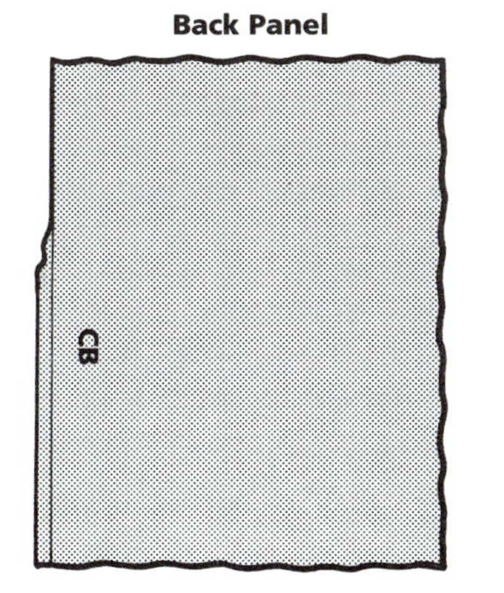

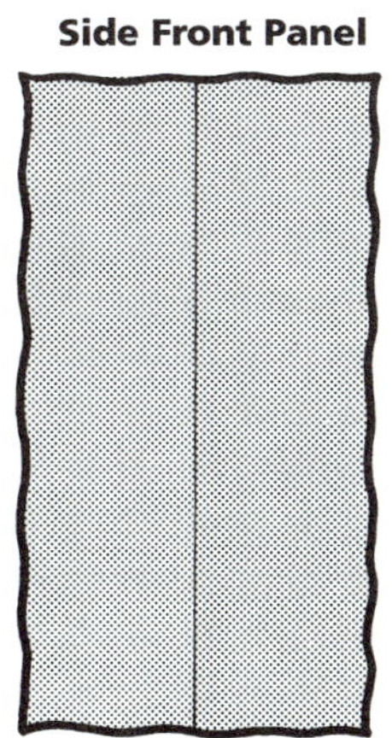

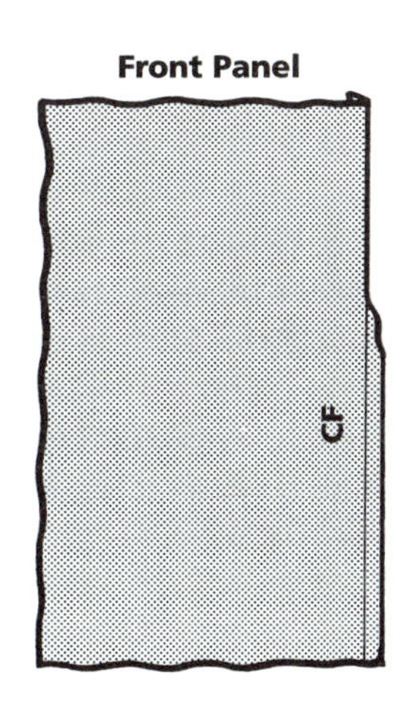

5 **Draw the grainlines for the fabric pieces.**

a. Draw the grainline for the center front panel 1 inch from the torn edge, and press under.

b. Draw the grainline for the side front panel at the center of the fabric piece.

c. Draw the grainline for the back panel 1 inch from the torn edge, and press under.

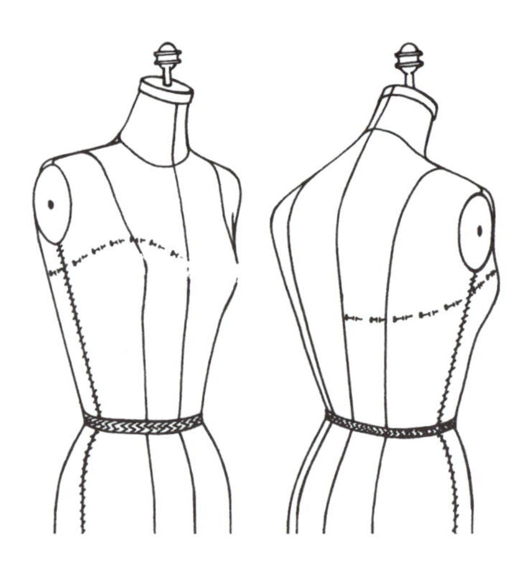

Prepare the dress form.
Place pins on the dress form at the desired bustline. Remove the bust level (bra) tape from the dress form.

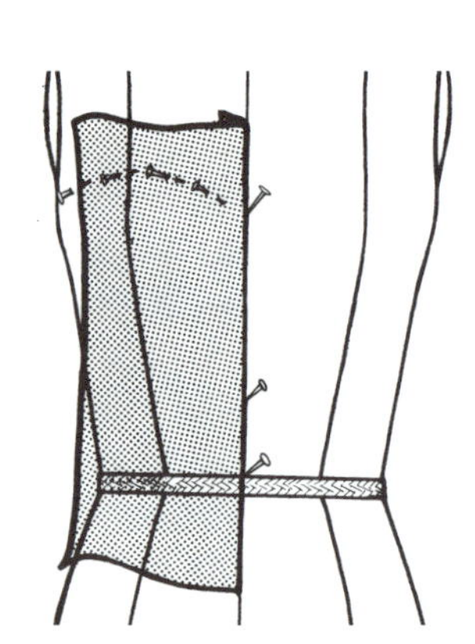

1 **Pin the center front grainline fold** of the fabric to the center front position of the dress form. The fabric piece should extend at least 3 inches above the styled bustline and at least 3 inches below the waistline seam.

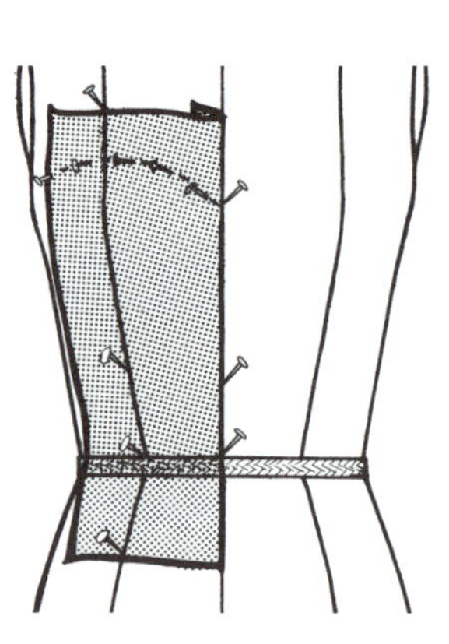

2 **Drape to the princess seam.** Smooth the fabric across the dress form from center front to just past the princess seam, and pin.

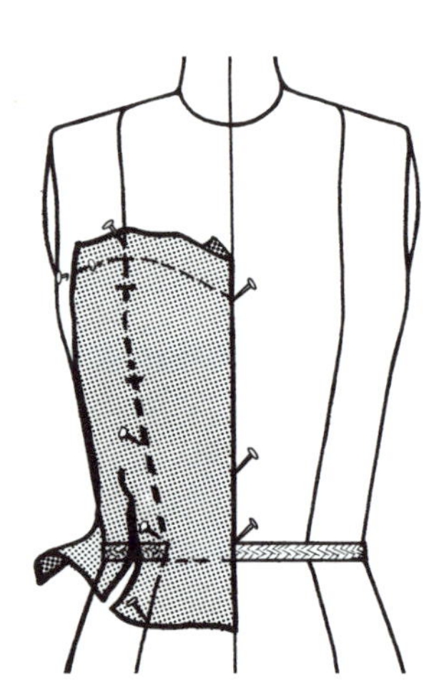

3 **Mark all key areas** of the dress form on the center front panel.

Bustline Styled Area

Princess Seam and Style Line Notches 1 1/2 inches above and below apex.

Waistline

Trim excess fabric, allowing for seam allowances.

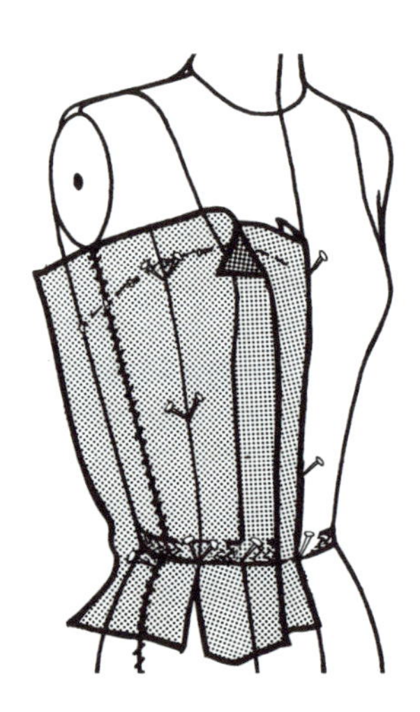

4 **Pin the grainline of the side front panel** to the center of the princess panel on the dress form. The side front panel should extend at least 3 inches above the styled bustline and at least 3 inches below the waistline seam.

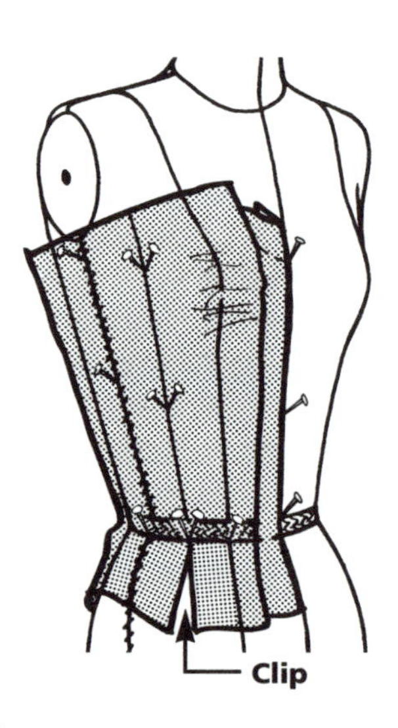

5 **Clip and drape the waistline.**

a. Clip the waistline fabric at the center of the front princess panel up to the bottom of the waist seam tape.

b. Drape and smooth the waistline in place. Smooth the fabric across the waistline from the grainline to the side seam. Also, smooth the waistline from the grainline to the princess seam.

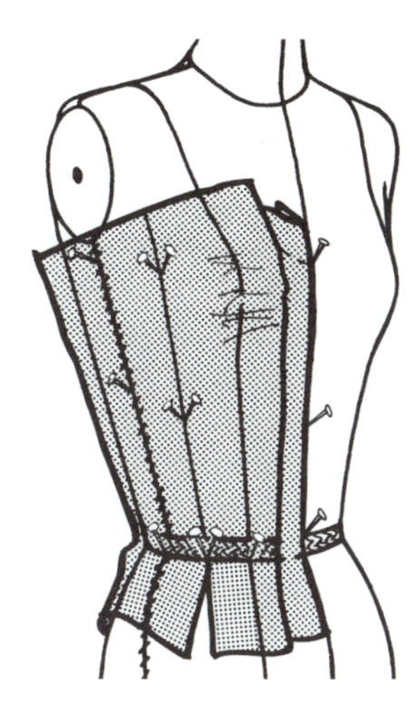

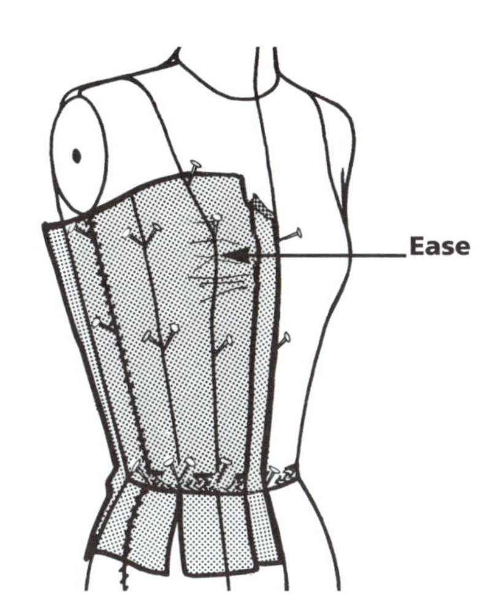

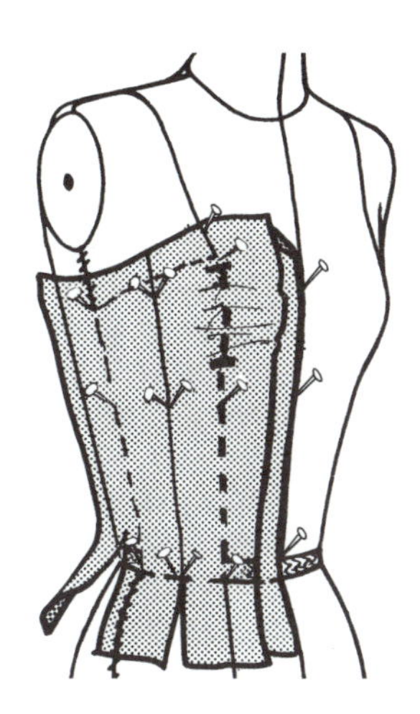

6 **Smooth and pin the side seam in place.** From the grainline of the side front panel, smooth the fabric past the side seam of the dress form. Do not allow the grainline to slip out of position. Pin the side seam in place.

7 **Smooth and pin the princess seam in place.** From the grainline of the side front panel, smooth the fabric past the princess seam of the dress form. Do not allow the grainline to slip out of position. Pin the princess seam in place.

8 **Mark all key areas** of the dress form to the side front panel.

Bustline Styled Area

Princess Seam and Style Line Notches Match to center front panel notches.

Waistline

Side Seam

Trim excess fabric, allowing for seam allowances.

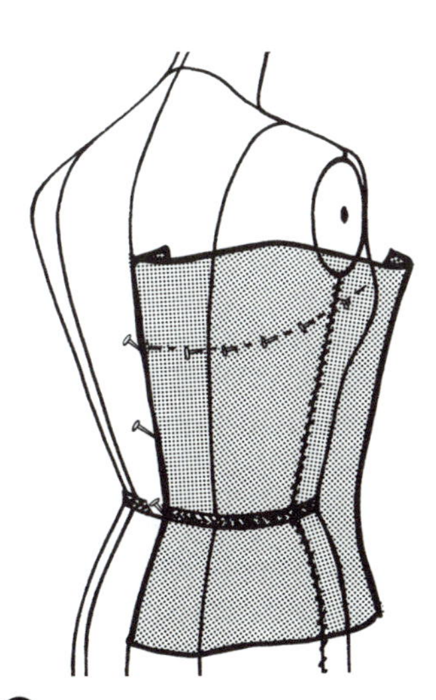

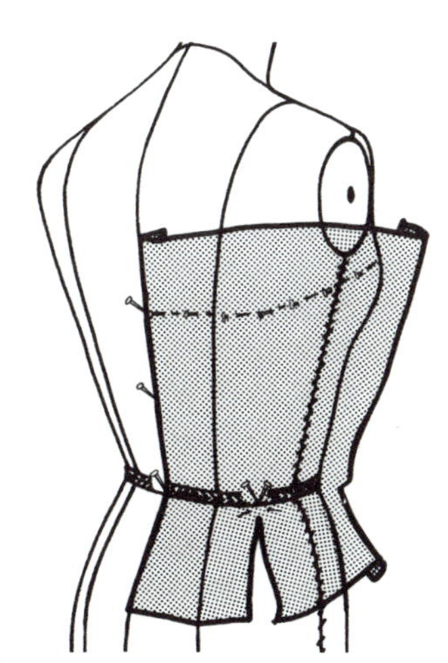

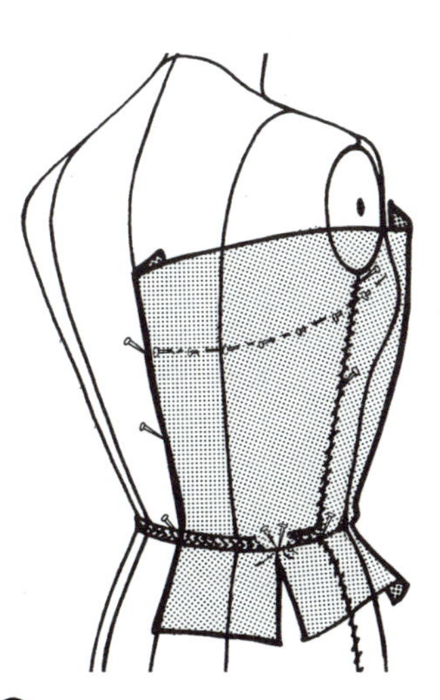

9 **Pin the center back grainline** fold of the fabric to the center back position of the dress form. The center back panel should extend at least 3 inches above the styled bustline and at least 3 inches below the waistline seam.

10 Clip the fabric at the center of the back princess panel up to the bottom of the waist tape. Smooth the fabric across the waistline tape and pin at the side seam/waist.

11 **Pin the side seam in place.** Smooth the fabric past the side seam. Be careful not to distort the grain of the fabric.

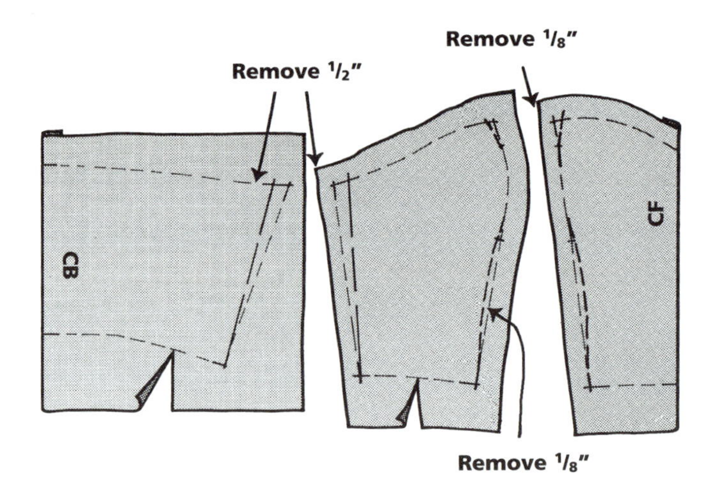

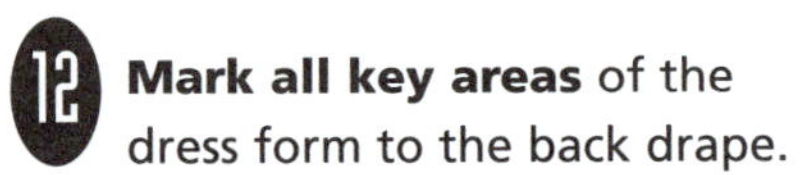

12 Mark all key areas of the dress form to the back drape.

Styled Bustline
Waistline
Side Seam

13 True up all seams. Remove the entire drape from the dress form and true up all seams.

a. To ensure a well-fitted bustline, readjust the princess seam by eliminating 1/8 inch above and below the notches. Blend in a new princess seam.

b. To ensure a secure underarm fit, eliminate 1/2 inch at both the front and back side seam bustline area. Blend this new side down to the waistline.

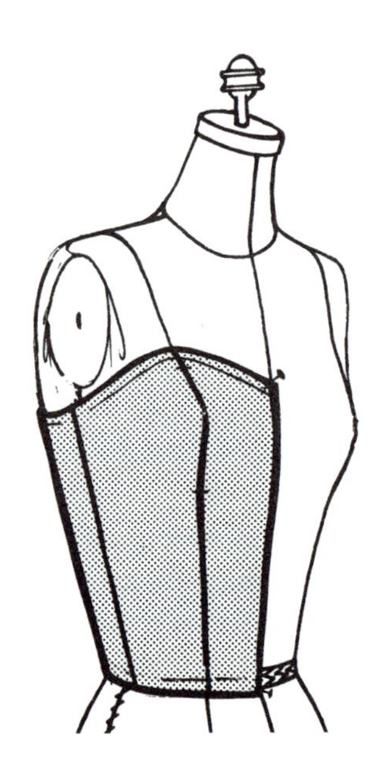

This drape should be transferred to paper. The pattern will be used as a guide for the foundation garment and the lining. As future reference, this princess bodice with be referred to as the bustier pattern.

14 Add seam allowances and trim excess fabric. Match the notches and pin the fabric pieces together. Return the fabric drape to the dress form and check for accuracy, fit, and balance.

NOTE: It is advisable to collapse the shoulders of the dress form to check this final drape.

Bustier—Draping Steps

The outside bustier design needs to be draped separately from the foundation garment **if the outside design does not include a princess seam.** The outside bustier design could be darted, ruffled, pleated, or gathered to create a sculptured bustier design that does not include a princess seam.

1 Drape the outside garment design by referring to the desired bustier design as a guide.

NOTE: The neckline bustline shape must be the same shape as the bustier pattern neckline. However, within this shape, the bustier may be pleated, tucked, ruffled, or gathered. Also, the princess seams are not mandatory, but the side seams are necessary.

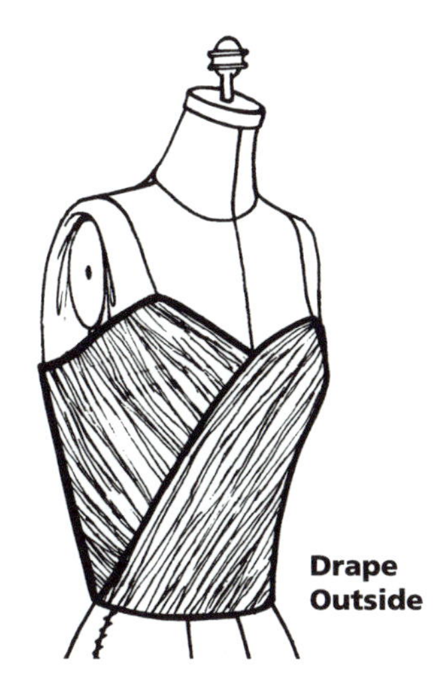

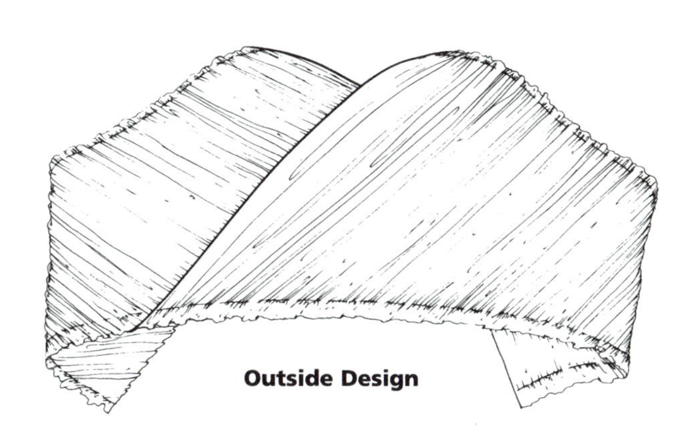

2 **Mark all key areas** and remove the fabric from the dress form.

3 **True up,** add seam allowances, and trim excess fabric.

4 **Sew the garment design together,** leaving an opening at center back (usually for a zipper).

Bustier Foundation

In addition to draping the bustier design, bustier styled dresses need to have special attention given to the sewing techniques.

A **bustier foundation** is necessary to correctly add boning. Boning is added in the princess and side seams to help keep the bodice on the body and ensure the fit and wearability of the garment.

This boned foundation is sewn between the outside design of the garment and a prepared lining.

Cut a copy of the bustier pattern out of a strong, woven fabric, such as kettle cloth.

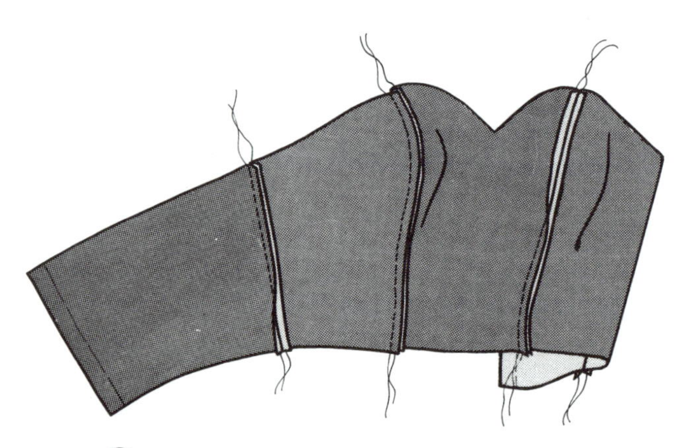

1. **Sew the bustier foundation pieces together.** This includes the princess seams and the side seams, leaving an opening at the center back seam. Press all seam allowances open.

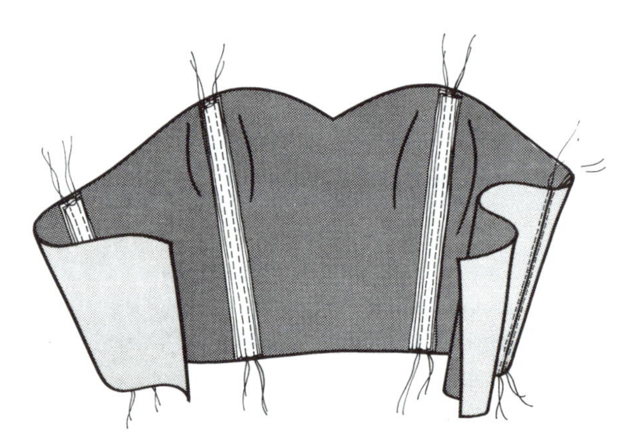

2. **Pin strips of boning to each princess seam and side seam.** The strips of boning should lay on the wrong side of the garment covering the seam.

NOTE: The boned end of each strip should be trimmed at each end (approximately 1/2 inch) and the excess fabric at each end should be turned over the boned edges.

3. **Stitch the boning to the princess seams and side seams,** using a zipper foot.

Variations: As more strength or support is needed, boning may be placed and attached in a variety of areas. For example, across the side bust panel from top to bottom.

Bustier Lining

Lining the bustier is necessary to cleanly finish all outer edges of the bustier bodice. It also adds strength to the overall bodice and hides the foundation garment. The lining is the same as the foundation garment, but does not have boning and is made out of a fabric of your choice—usually a lighter weight fabric than the garment.

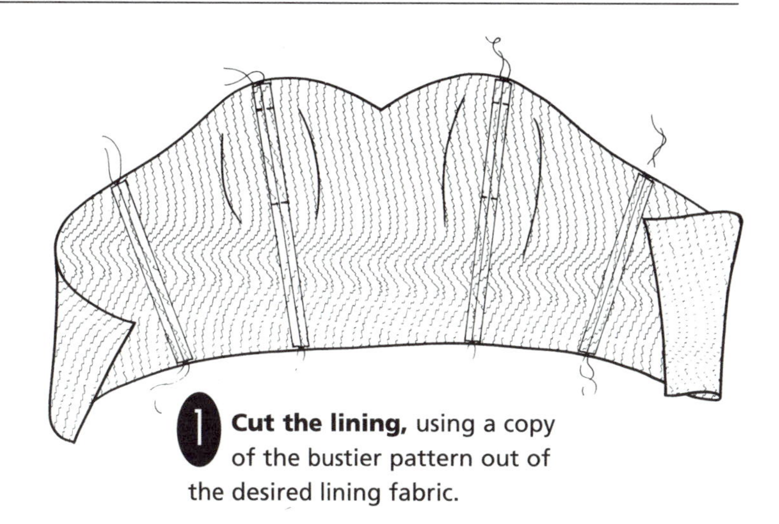

1. **Cut the lining,** using a copy of the bustier pattern out of the desired lining fabric.

2. **Sew all lining pieces together,** leaving an opening at the center back. Press all seam allowances open.

***Bustier**—Sewing Steps*

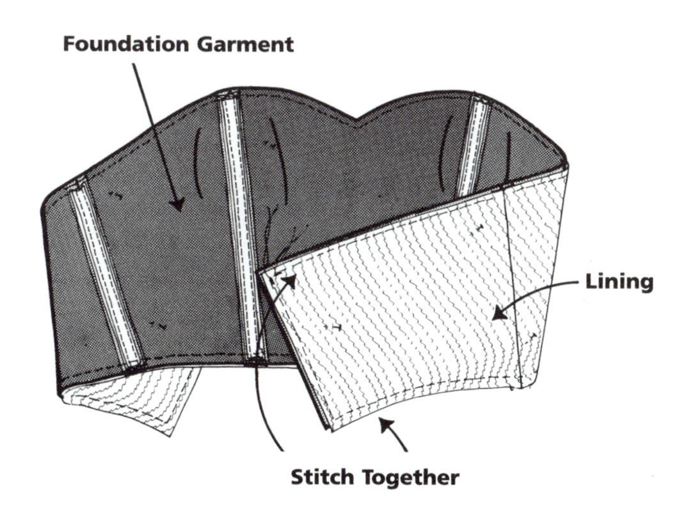

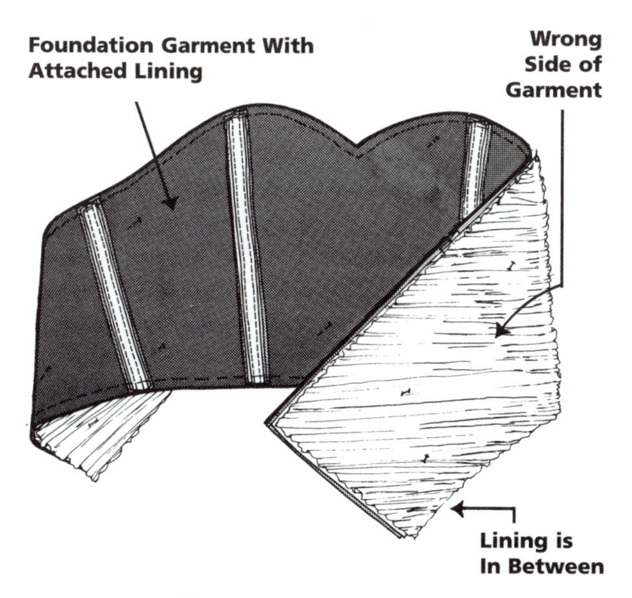

1. **Pin the foundation garment to the wrong side of the lining.** Stitch all outer edges together so that the lining and the foundation garment will act as one.

2. **Place the lining,** with the attached foundation garment, to the outside garment design, matching correct sides.

3. **Sew the neckline seams together,** using a 1/4 inch seam allowance.

4 Understitch all the layers of the seam allowance to the lining. Understitching is accomplished by first placing the lining (with the attached foundation garment) flat. Then, fold the entire neckline seam allowance to the lining side and stitch close to the seam edge.

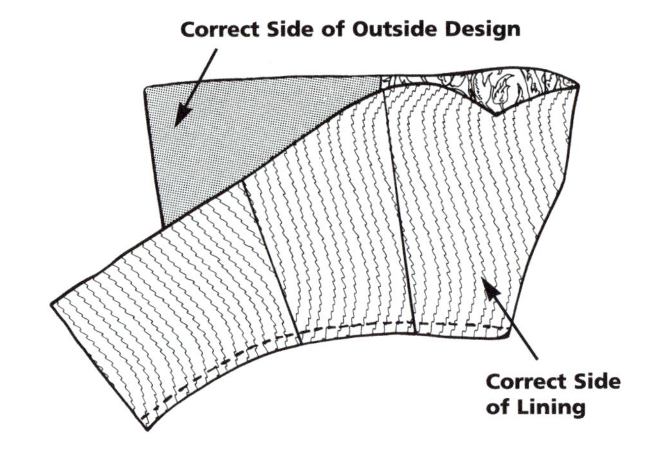

5 Turn the garment pieces so the correct side of the lining and the garment design are facing out.

NOTE: Raw edges will remain at the center back seams and the waistline seams.

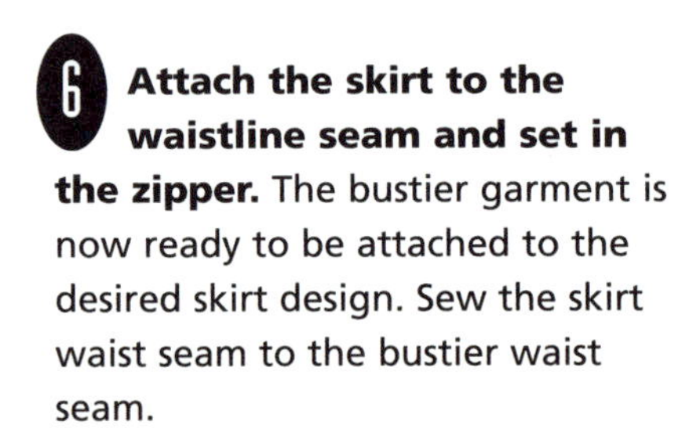

6 Attach the skirt to the waistline seam and set in the zipper. The bustier garment is now ready to be attached to the desired skirt design. Sew the skirt waist seam to the bustier waist seam.

Pin and sew in a zipper that will extend at least 7 inches into the skirt seam and the center back seam.

Chapter Eighteen

Knits

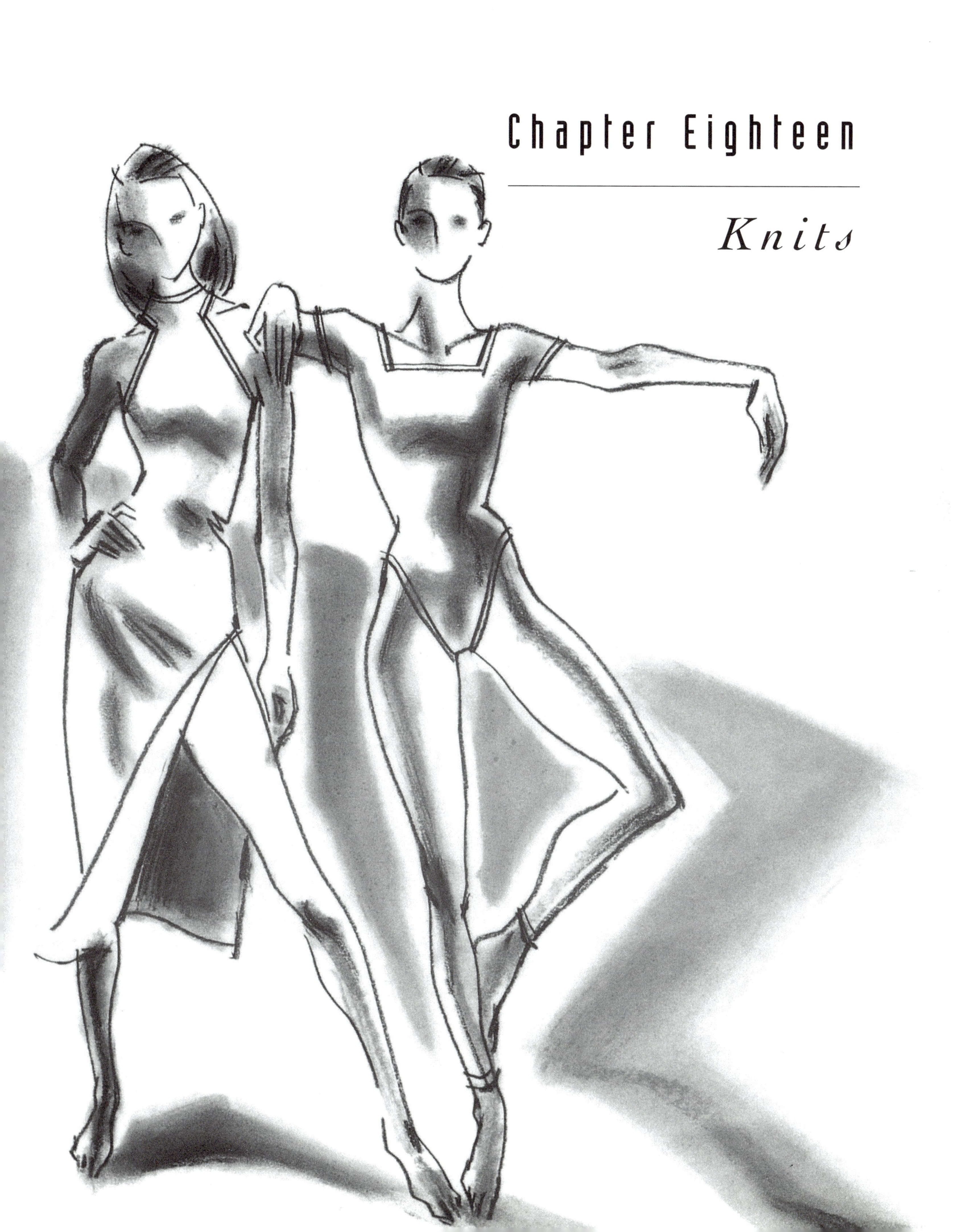

Objectives

By studying the various draping steps in this chapter, the designer should be able to accomplish the following:

- Mold and manipulate knit fabric on the dress form.
- Drape the knit fabric close to the body shape without the need for darts or complex seaming construction.
- Maintain the grain of knit fabric to create a smooth design without overworking the fabric.
- Explore the fit and shape of the finished pattern with regard to the different degrees of stretch in the knit fabric.
- Handle pliable fabrics to define a design and determine the most flattering style for the figure.
- True up and check the results of the draping process and its relationship to fit, hang, balance, and proportion.

Basic Knit Bodice/Dress

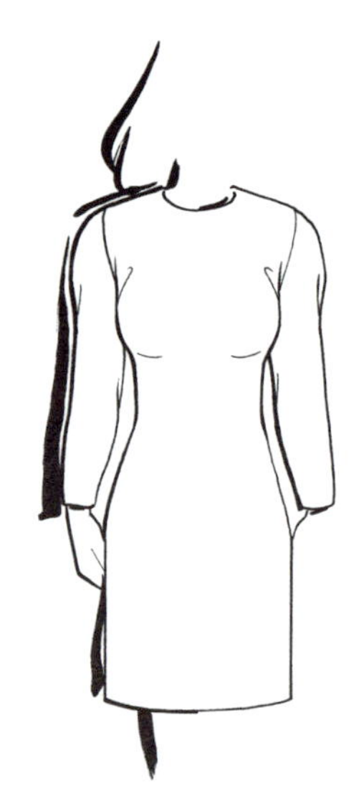

The basic knit bodice/dress is a tight-fitting garment that offers crisp, close-to-the-body comfort, without the need for darts or complex seaming construction. A wide variety of knit fabrics are available with different degrees of stretch. Therefore, the degree of stretch must be considered before designing and draping a knit garment. The newest double knits may be cut to look tailored for suits and dresses, casual for shirts and sportswear, or glamorous with added glitter for evening wear. The shoulders may become extreme, with the use of shoulder pads, or discreet, as the design demands. A knit garment may be fabricated, colored, and shaped to specifically suit a mood, occasion, or environment.

The fitted knit bodice sloper is a hip-length pattern that is developed by draping knit fabric of your choice into a fitted body shape. A variety of necklines, sleeve lengths, style lines, and hem lengths can easily be adapted to this foundation pattern.

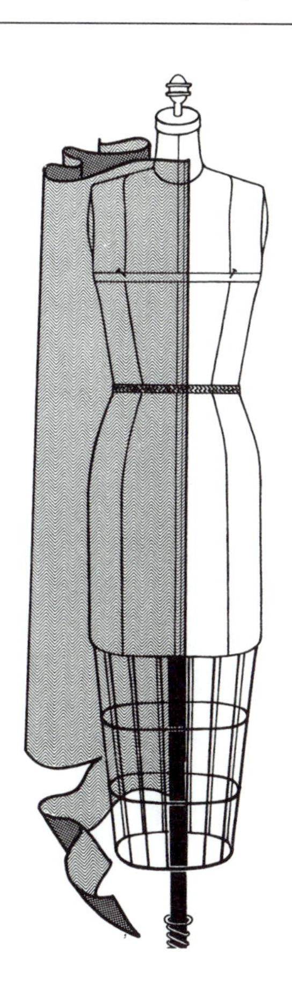

NOTE: The stretch quality of the sample fabric should be the same as the stretch quality for the desired finished garment.

1 **Measure the length** for the front and back from the neckband on the dress form to the desired length of the garment. Add 2 inches. Cut the fabric at this length.

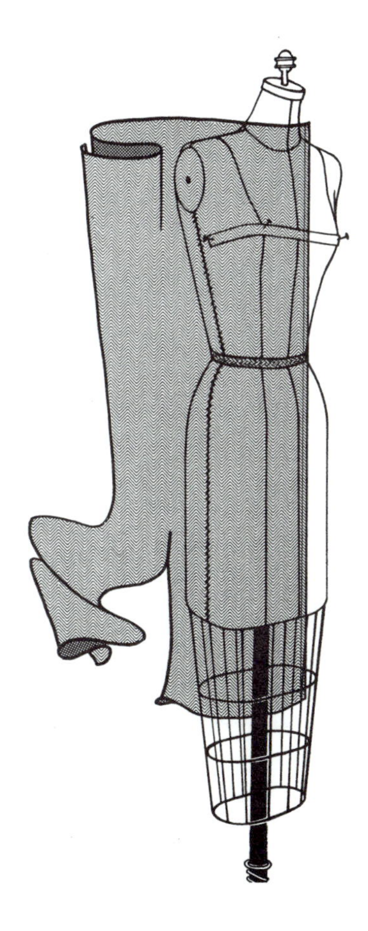

2 **Measure the width** for both the front and back from the center of the dress form to the side seam. Add 3 inches. Cut the fabric at this width.

3 **Draw the center front and center back lines** for the front and back bodice 1 inch from the edge. Keep fabric pieces flat.

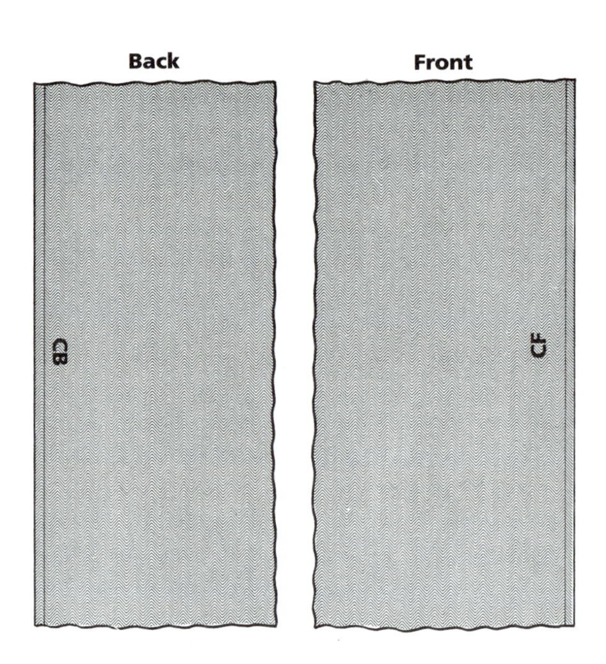

4 **Draw the front crossgrain** 12 inches from the top edge of the fabric.

5 **Draw the back crossgrain** 9 inches from the top edge of the fabric.

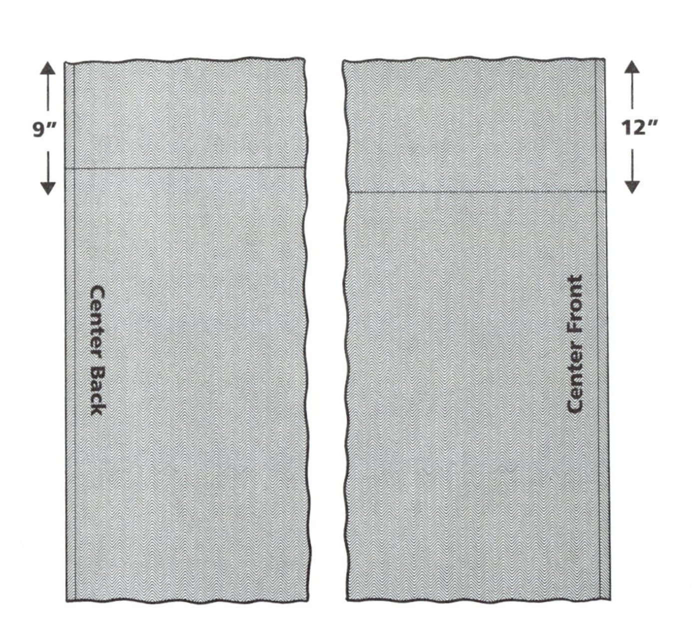

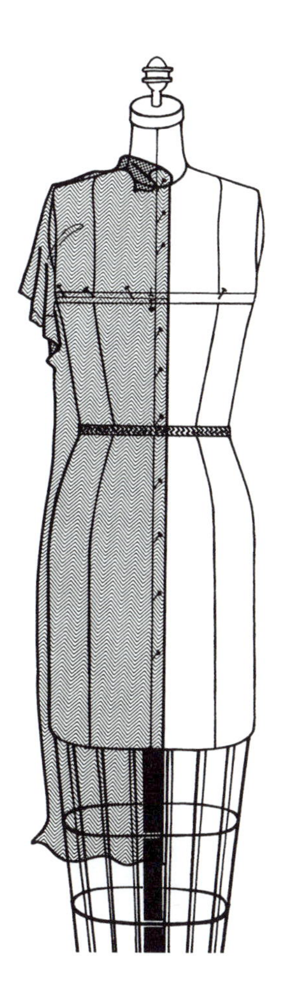

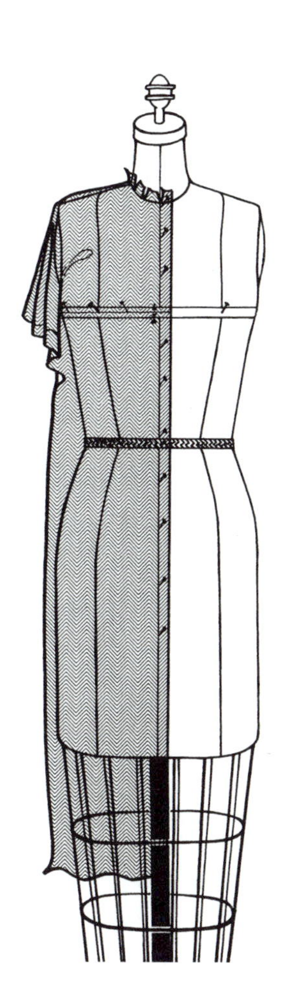

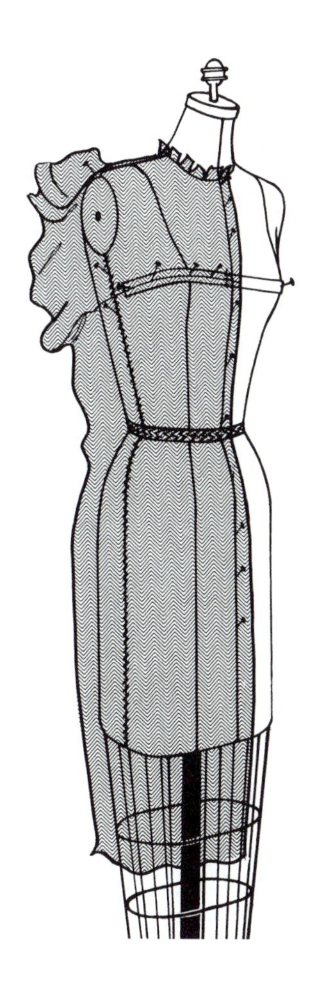

1 **Pin the center front line** of the fabric on the center front position of the dress form.

2 **Align the crossgrain** at the bust level. Pin at frequent intervals—approximately every 2 inches.

3 **Drape the front neckline.** Trim and clip the front neckline. Smooth the fabric around the neckline past the shoulder seam of the dress form.

4 **Drape the front shoulder seam and the front armhole areas.**

a. Smooth the fabric up and over the shoulder seam of the dress form.

b. Smooth all excess fabric over the armhole ridge and flat past the armplate.

NOTE: Be sure to drape out all excess ease.

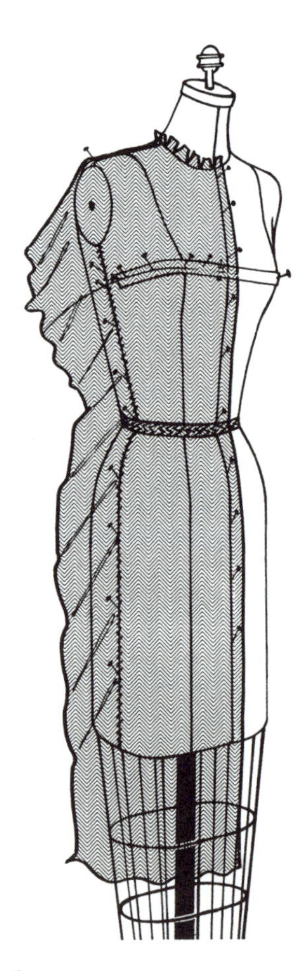

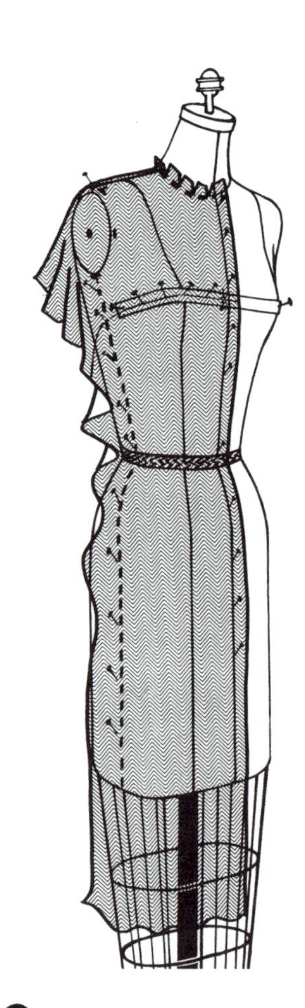

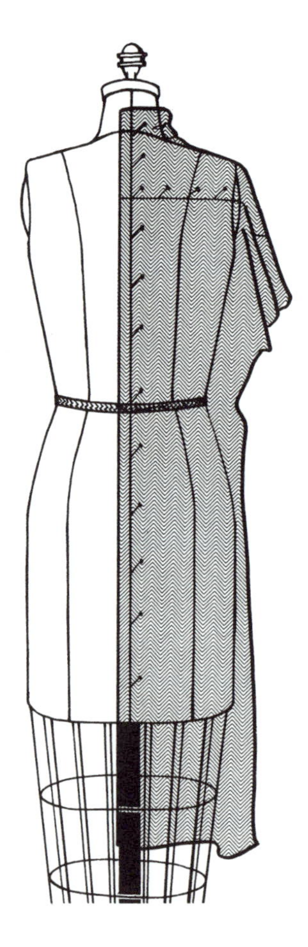

5 **Drape the front bodice side seam.** Smooth all excess fabric past the side seam at the crossgrain and underneath the armplate. Continue to smooth the side seam into the side seam shape desired.

6 **Mark all key areas** of the dress form to the fabric.

Front Neckline

Armplate

a. Top at shoulder seam ridge.
b. Middle at screw level.
c. Crossmark bottom at side seam.

Front Side Seam

Hem

7 **Pin the center back line** of the fabric on the center back position of the dress form.

8 **Align the crossgrain** at the shoulder blade level. Pin at frequent intervals—approximately every 2 inches.

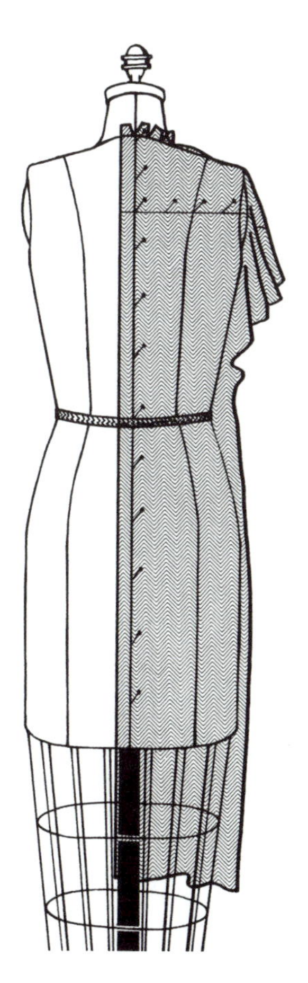

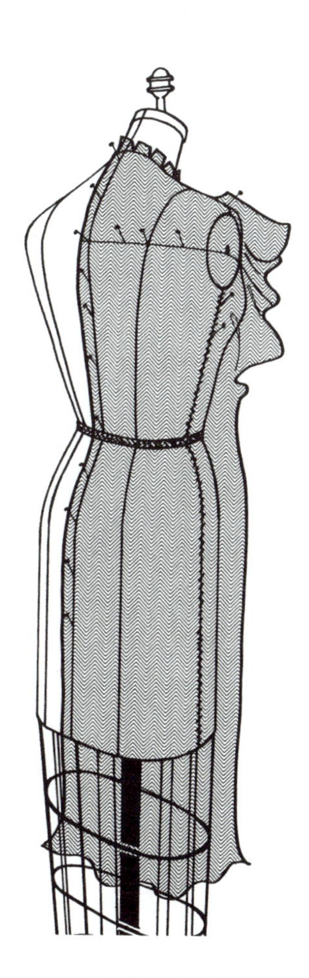

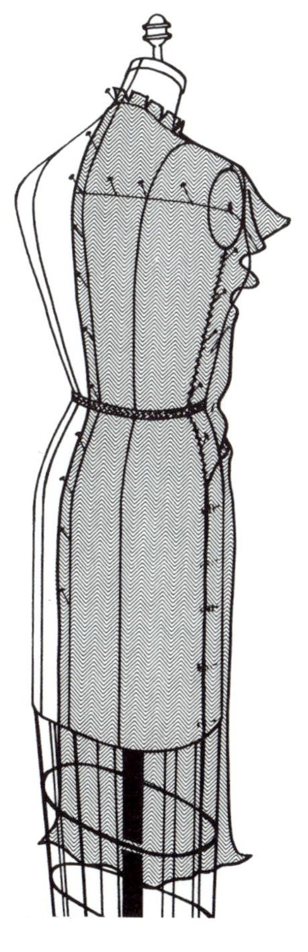

9 **Drape the back neckline.** Trim and clip the neckline. Smooth the fabric around the neckline past the shoulder seam of the dress form.

10 **Drape the back shoulder seam and back armhole areas.** Smooth the fabric up and over the shoulder seam of the dress form. Smooth all excess fabric past the side seam at the crossgrain and underneath the armplate.

11 **Drape the back bodice side seam.** Continue to smooth the side seam into the side seam shape desired. Match and pin the front side seam to the back side seam.

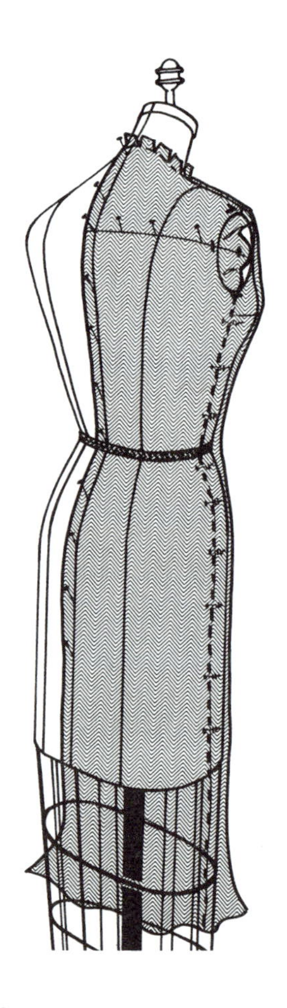

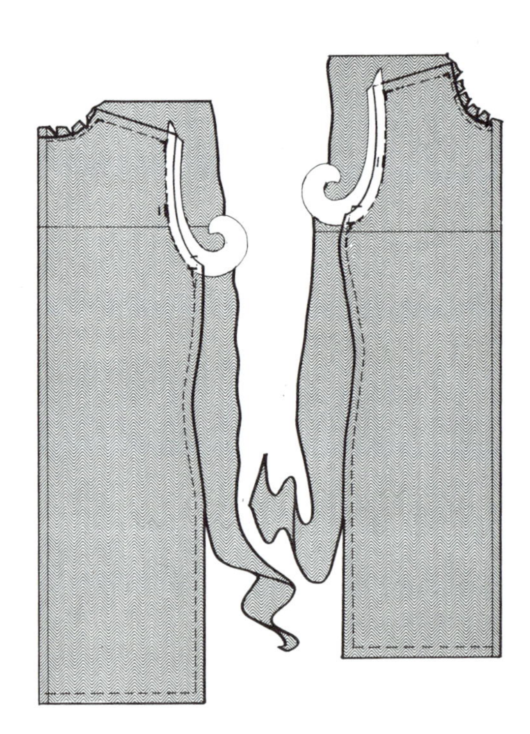

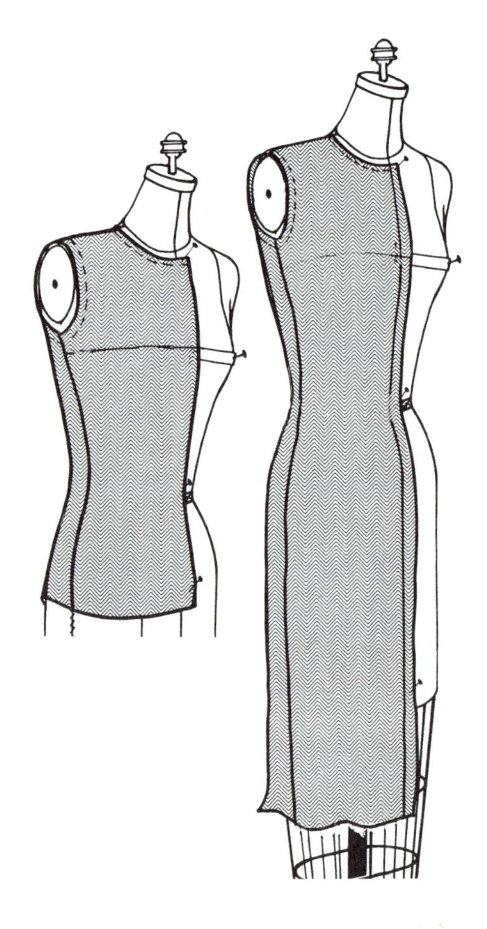

12 **Mark all key areas** of the dress form to the fabric.

Back Neckline

Shoulder Seams

Armplate
a. Top at shoulder seam ridge.
b. Middle at screw level.
c. Bottom at side seam.

Back Side Seam

Hem

13 **True up all lines.** Remove the knit drape from the dress form and true up all lines. True up the armhole by dropping the side seam position 1 inch and removing 1/4 inch from the dropped side seam/armhole corner. Add seam allowances and trim the excess fabric.

NOTE: The technique of removing 1/4 inch at the side seam/armhole corner ensures that a smooth non-gapping armhole is created.

NOTE: For an armhole that is balanced front and back, measure the armhole distances. The armhole distances should either be equal in length or the back should be slightly longer.

14 **Sew together the front and back shoulder seams.** Insert a piece of twill tape at the shoulder seam using a ball needle.

15 **Sew together the front and back side seams.** Using a ball needle, sew the seam with a "stretch and sew" process.

16 **Place the knit drape on the dress form** and check for accuracy, fit, and balance.

NOTE: For a knit top, choose the desired length and cut the drape at that length.

Basic Knit Sleeve

The basic knit sleeve is specially developed to fit into the smaller armhole created in a knit bodice. Traditional sportswear made out of knit fabrics requires a knit sleeve, unless the design is sleeveless.

The measurements used for this sleeve are for maximum stretch for double or single knit fabrics and fit into a basic knitted bodice armhole. Therefore, when using a fabric with less stretch, use slightly larger numbers (1/8 or 1/4-inch increments) in the direction with less stretch.

Knit sleeves, such as the muscle sleeve or the cap sleeve, can be developed from a basic knit sleeve pattern. The basic knit sleeve pattern can be developed from the basic sleeve pattern, steps 1 through 13, pages 80-83. However, use measurements provided in the chart. The front and back cap shapes will remain the same, since the armhole shapes are so similar. An elbow dart is not required in knit sleeves.

Basic Knit Sleeve Measurement Chart

Before you draft the Basic Knit Sleeve, study the following four important measurements.

1. Overarm length (distance from the shoulder to the wrist)

Size	8	10
Overarm length	22 3/4"	23

2. Cap height (remaining distance from the underarm armpit to the shoulder)

Size	8	10
Cap height	5 1/4"	5 3/8"

3. Elbow circumference (measurement around the elbow plus 2 inch ease)

Size	8	10
Elbow circumference	4 1/4"	4 3/8"

4. Bicep circumference (measurement around the upper arm plus 2 inch ease)

Size	8	10
Bicep circumference	5 1/4"	5 3/8"

Note: Drafting a size 8 or 10 sleeve will serve as a guide to create and drape a correct sleeve cap for knit fabrics. Refer to step 2, page 308, for detailed instructions.

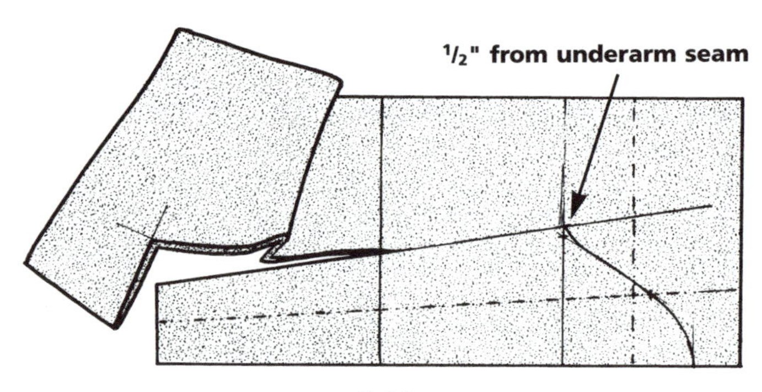

The basic Knit sleeve is developed from the basic sleeve, pages 80–83. However, refer to chart, page 309, for measurments.

1. When preparing the cap shape, crossmark the bicep line 1/2-inch in from the underarm seamline. An elbow dart is not required.

2. **Determine the sleeve cap notches** and sleeve cpa distance**.** Pivot the stitchline of the sleeve cap into the stitchline of the desired armhole. Refer to the Pivoting Steps, **pages 85–86,** for a clear example of pivoting technique and notch placement. If the sleeve cap is too short, add measurements at the underarm seams.

3. **Sew together the underarm seams** and then sew the sleeve into the basic knit bodice.

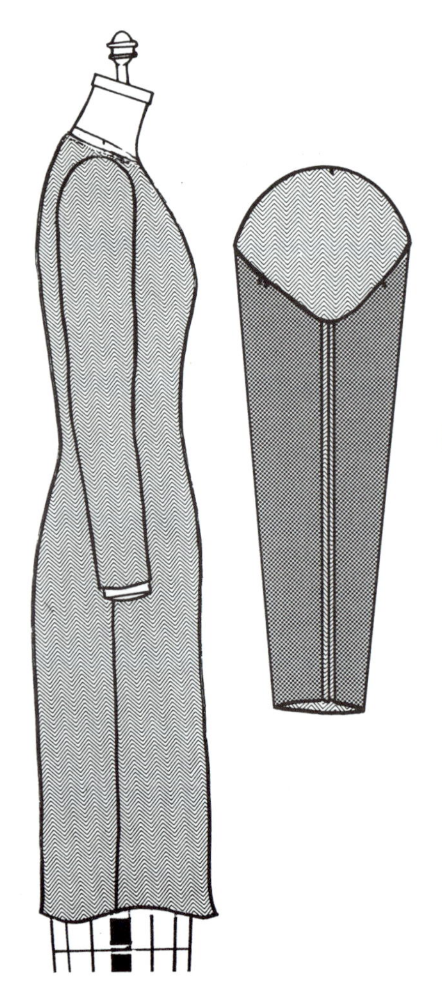

4. **Place the knit garment with the attached knit sleeve onto the dress form** and check for a clean, smooth fit and hang. The armhole area should not show any gapping or overstretching.

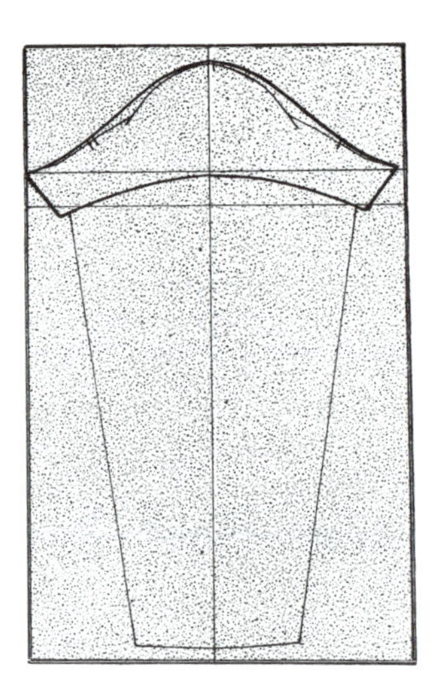

Sleeve Variations

A very common sleeve used in knit garments is the cap or muscle sleeve. **Illustrated here is the completed muscle sleeve.** Using the Basic Knit Sleeve, raise the bicep level 2 inches and pivot the sleeve bicep level. Draw a new cap and underarm seam. For more details in pivoting a bicep line, refer to Sleeves, page 197.

Knit Halter

The description for a halter made with knit fabric is the same as the bias halter discussed on pages 262-264. The differences is the fabric, grainline, and measurements. Almost always the outer edges are finished with bias binding to give all edges extra strength and body with minimum expense.

Knit Halter—Preparing the Fabric

1. **Measure and cut a perfect 44-inch square** of knit fabric, which is wide enough for an entire front and back.

2. **Draw a center front grainline** in the middle of the piece of fabric. This line will be the center front line of the garment.

3. **Draw a crossgrain line** in the middle of the fabric piece opposite direction (crossgrain) from the grainline. This line will represent the bust level line of the garment.

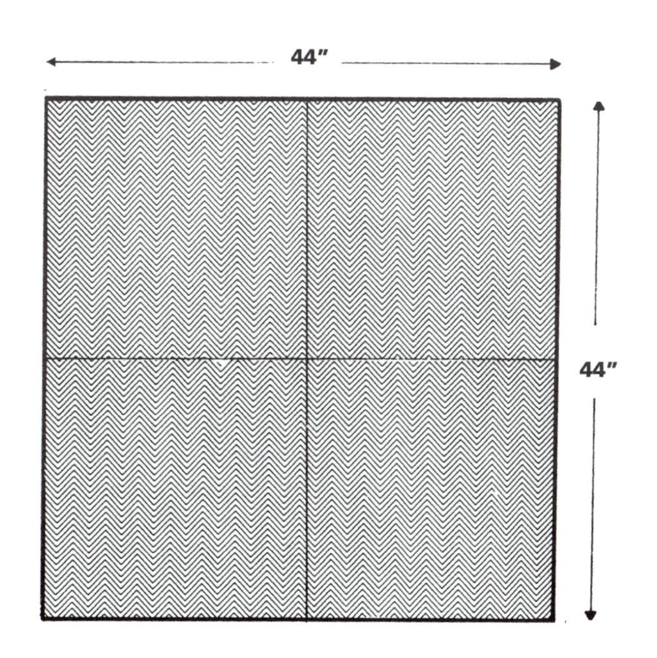

Knit Front and Back Halter—Draping Steps

Prepare the dress form.
Remove the bra tape on the dress form. Pin or use style tape to indicate the desired neckline and/or armhole shapes.

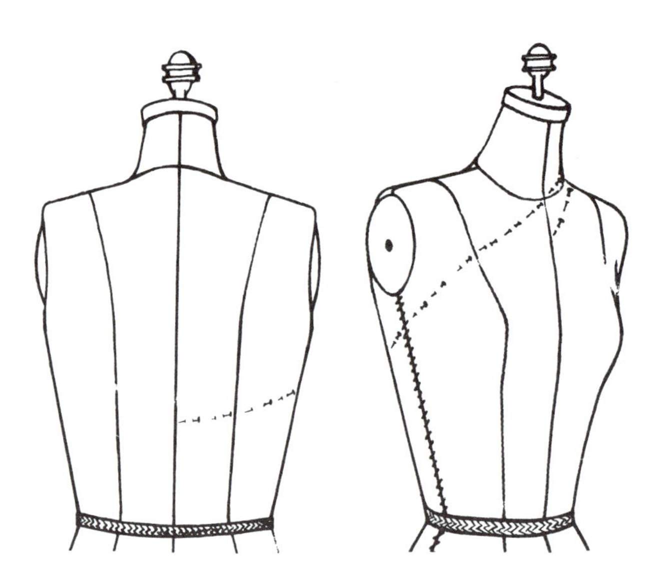

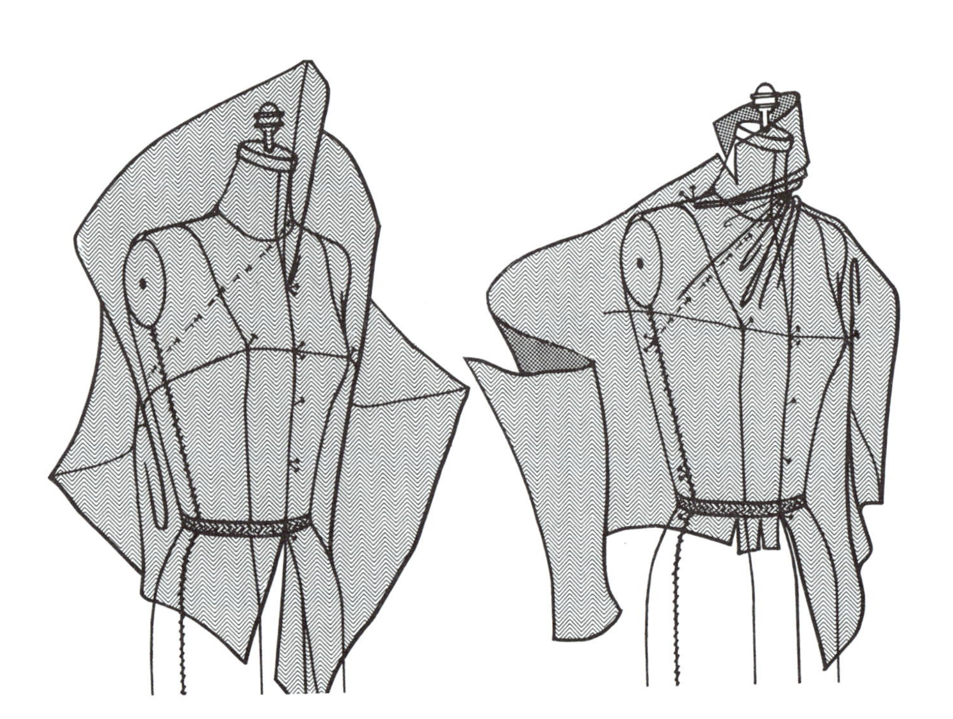

1 **Pin and drape the center front grainline** on the center front position of the dress form.

2 **Align the crossgrain line** on the bust level of the dress form.

3 **Trim, clip, and drape the waistline.** Drape the entire waistline from side seam to side seam. Pin in place.

4 **Smooth and drape the fabric up and across the side seam.** Excess fabric will now be falling toward the neckline above the bust level.

NOTE: The direction of the bust level line is now angled upward.

5 **Trim away the fabric at the premarked bare armhole** from center back to the front shoulder near the neck area, leaving a 2-inch excess.

6 **Smooth and drape the fabric around the trimmed armhole.**

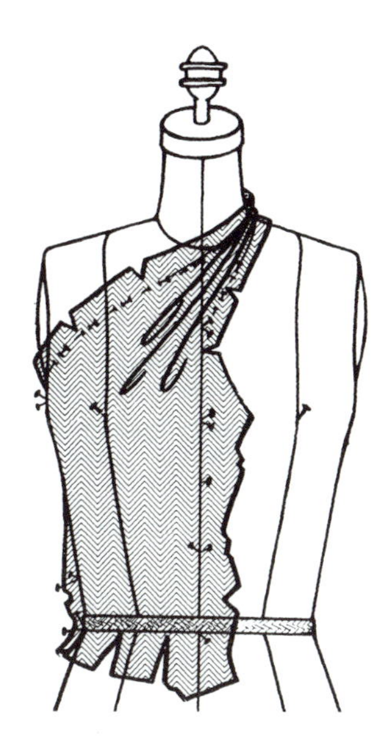

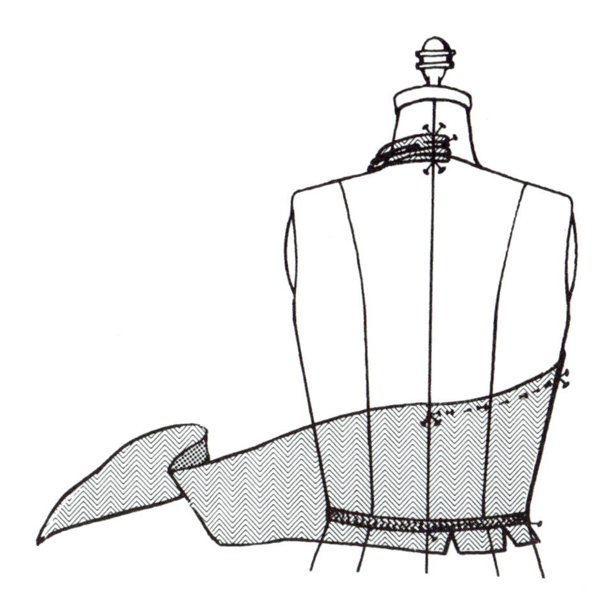

7 **Fold, tuck, pleat, or gather in the fullness** around the neckline finishing at the center back neck area.

8 **Drape and smooth across the side seam.** Extend the excess fabric across the side seam to the desired length of the back halter waist tie.

9 **Clip and shape the fabric around the back waistline** to the desired styled shape of the garment.

10 **Drape and smooth the back side seam flat.** Match the side seam of the back bodice to the front side seam of the halter top.

11 **Mark all key areas** of the dress form to the fabric.

Armhole/Neckline Follow the bare shoulder style-line up and around the front and back neckline.

Side Seam Lightly crossmark.

Waistline Lightly crossmark the entire waist area of the drape.

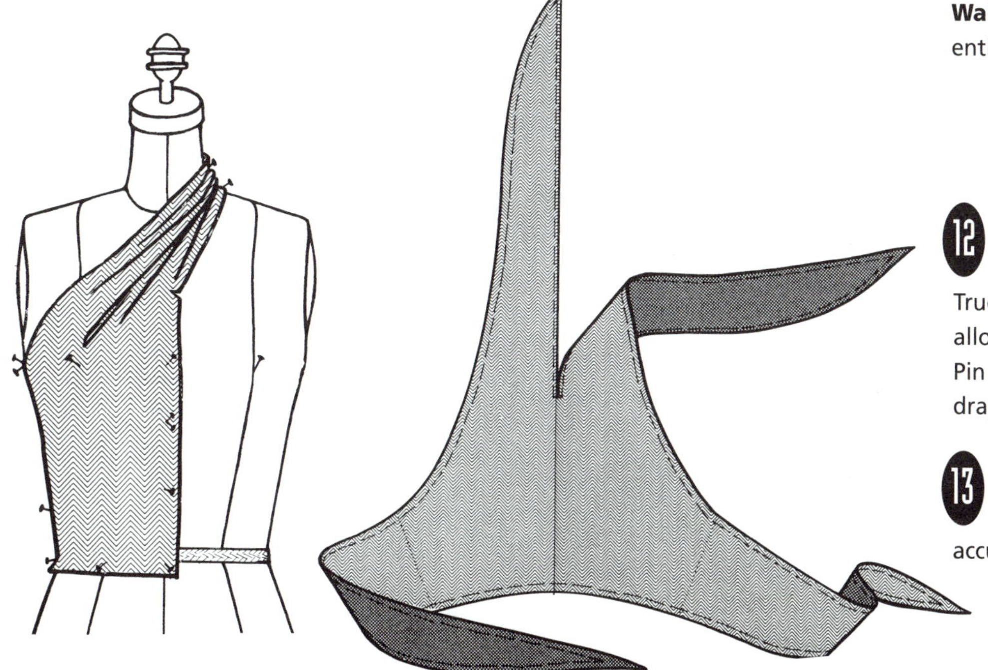

12 True up. Remove the fabric drape from the dress form. True up all seams, add seam allowances, and trim excess fabric. Pin the front drape to the back drape.

13 Return the finished drape to the dress form and check for accuracy, fit, and balance.

Knit Leotard

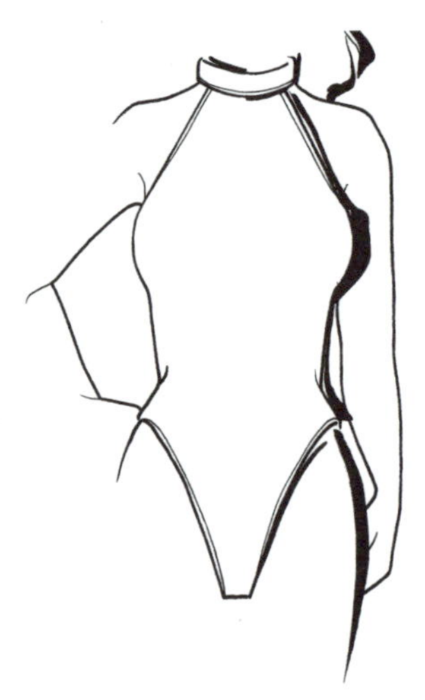

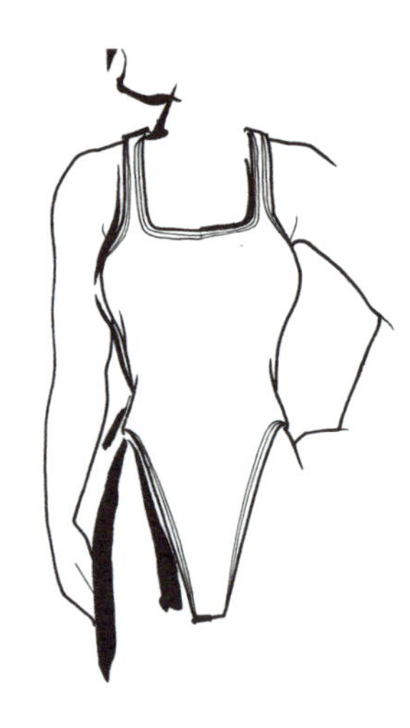

The knit leotard and/or bathing suit is a one-piece garment without legs and sometimes with sleeves. The knit leotard is the newest looking style in exercise wear and bathing suits. This popular knit garment exposes the legs completely and allows the designer to use many different leg cuts. Knit fabrics, such as spandex or latex, are ideal fabrics for this clean-cut simplistic actionwear.

The leotard is developed from the dartless knit top to achieve a close-to-the-body fit. It is then fitted and adjusted on the dress form. This method offers a fast and easy method for achieving an accurate knit leotard block.

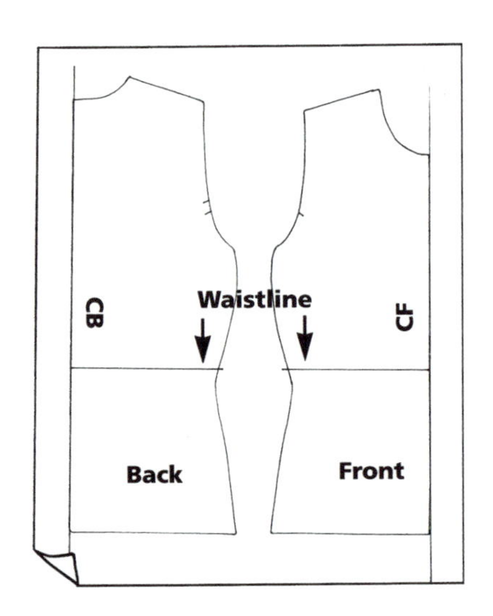

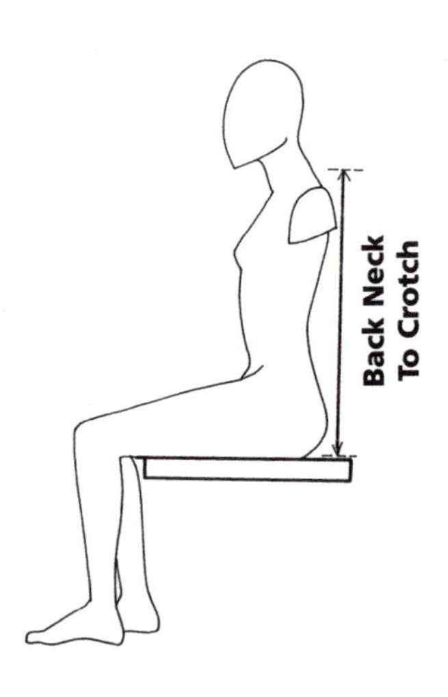

1 **Trace front and back onto pattern paper.** Using the fitted knit pattern, which is made of the same knit quality as your desired leotard, trace onto pattern paper.

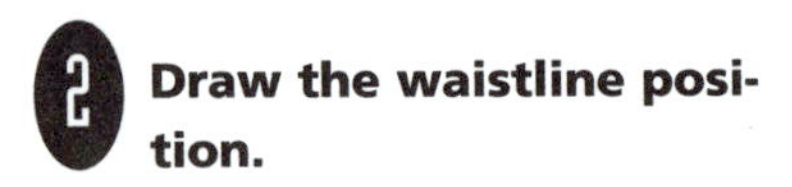

2 **Draw the waistline position.**

3 **Measure from the natural back neck position to the crotch,** while sitting straight on a chair. This measurement should be approximately 27 inches. Subtract 1 1/2 inches from this measurement.

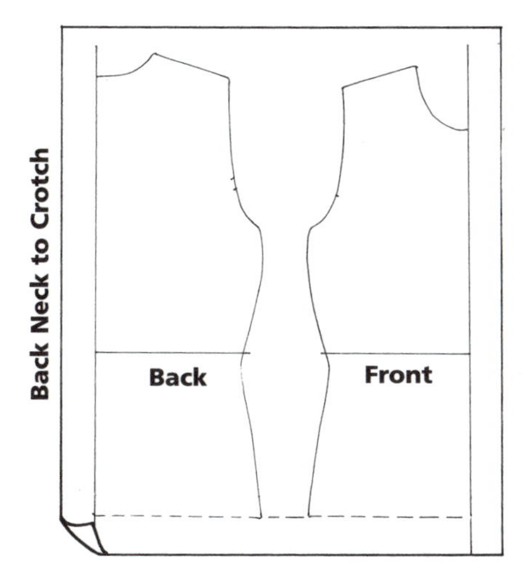

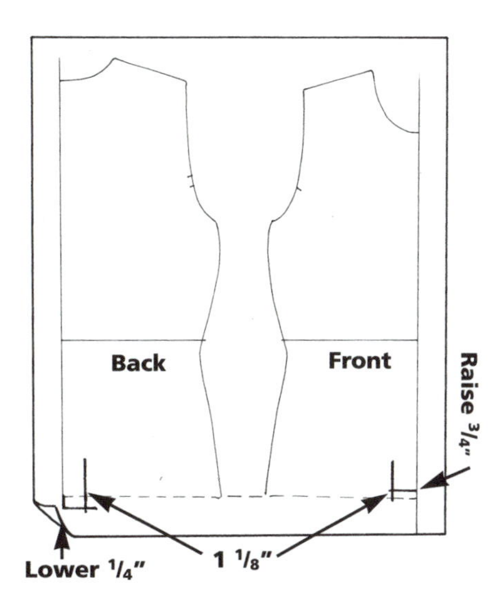

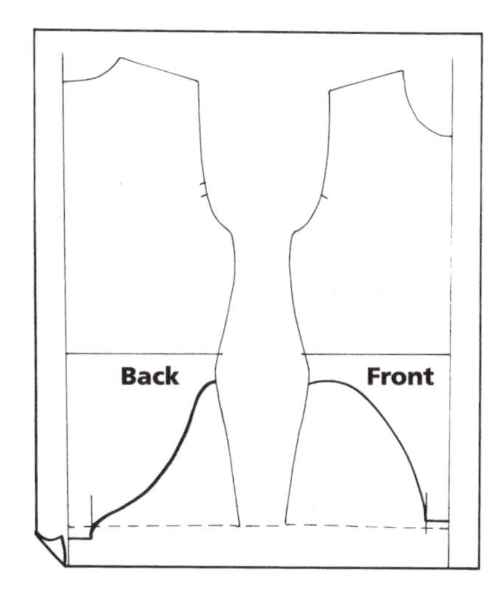

4 **Transfer the back neck to crotch length onto the back pattern.**

a. Measure down from the back neckline of the pattern the measurement determined in the previous step. Crossmark this measurement.

b. Square a line across the pattern for front and back at this crossmark.

5 **Draw the front crotch.** Raise the front crotch up 3/4 inch and measure in 1 1/8 inches toward the side seam at the crotch depth line. Crossmark and draw these positions.

6 **Draw the back crotch depth.** Lower the back crotch 1 1/4 inches from the original crotch level and measure in 1 1/8 inches toward the side seam at the crotch depth line. Crossmark and draw these positions.

7 **Draw the desired legging—french cut.** Using a curved ruler, this line should start at the crotch crossmark, extend into a 90 degree angle, and move up to or just below the waistline (see illustration).

NOTE: To ensure maximum coverage over the back buttocks, the line drawn for the back will drop considerably (see illustration).

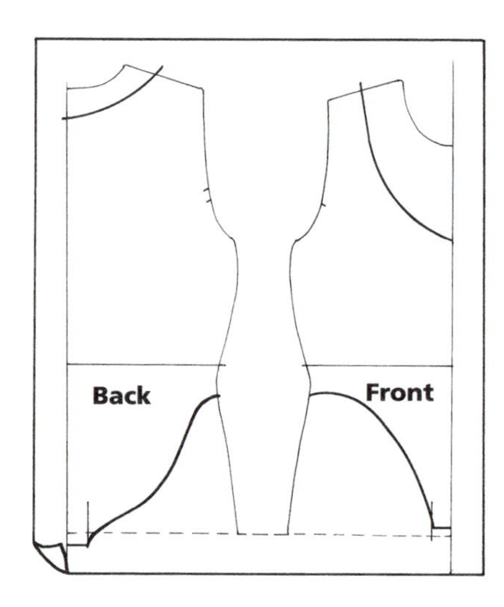

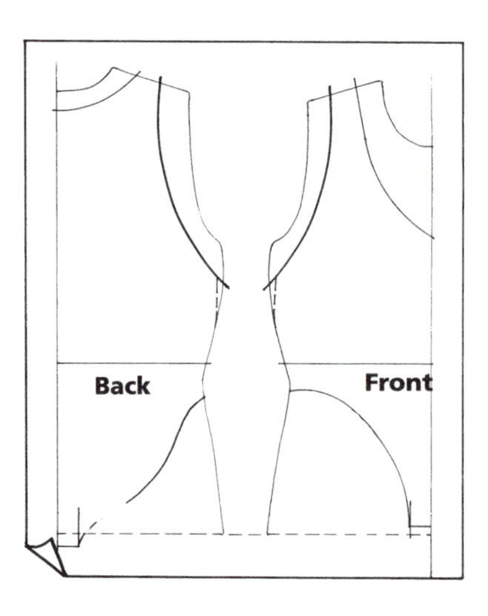

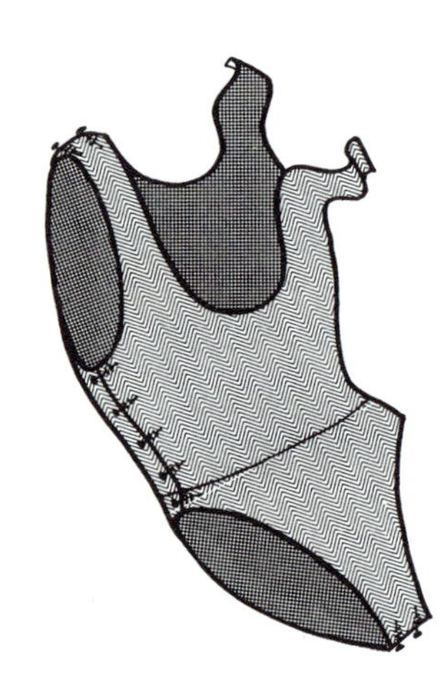

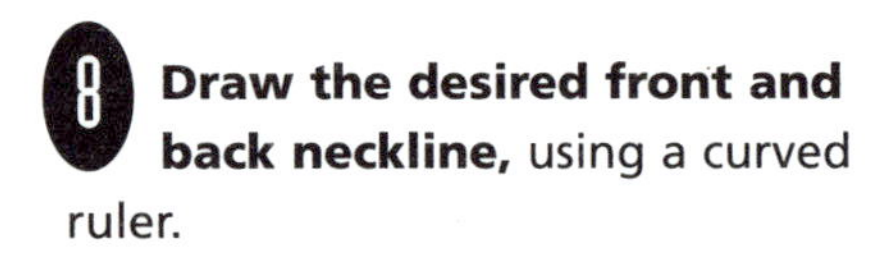

8 **Draw the desired front and back neckline,** using a curved ruler.

NOTE: If a low front neckline is desired, then a higher back neckline is necessary, and vice versa, because structurally the leotard will gap and fall off the shoulders.

9 **Draw the desired front and back armholes,** using a curved ruler. At this time, once again remove 1/4 inch at the new armhole/side seam corner. Blend in a new side seam/armhole corner.

NOTE: This is done to take out any excess ease that was created by dropping the armhole.

10 **Cut out a full pattern** (left to right) of a knit fabric. Pin together the shoulders, side seams, and crotch.

NOTE: The stretch quality of the sample fabric should be the same as the basic knit pattern and the same as the desired garment.

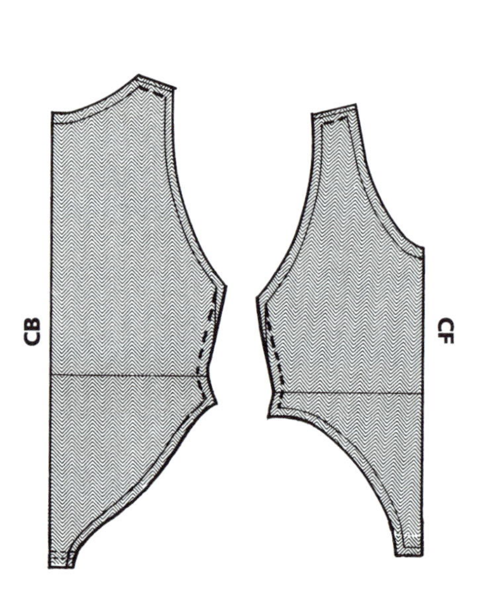

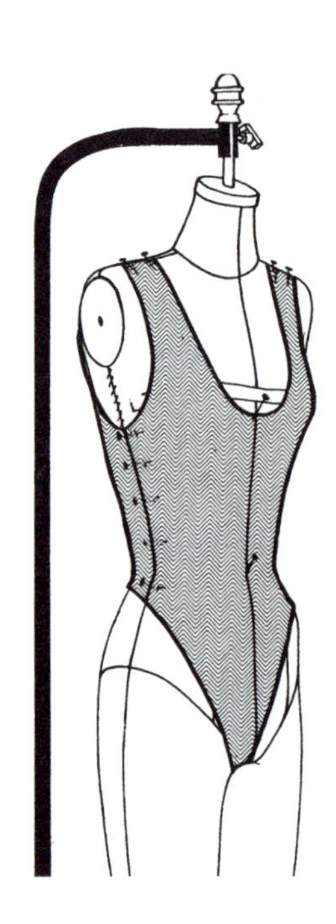

11 **Place the leotard onto a pant form.** Be very careful to pin the center positions.

12 **Fit the shoulders, side seams, and crotch** by repinning the desired changes. With a felt tip pen, draw all corrections and adjustments.

13 **Retrue all altered changes.** Remove the drape from the pant form. Retrue all seams and add a 3/8-inch seam allowance. Because of the changes when fitting, a new pattern may be necessary.

NOTE: Refer to page 323 for detail information on elastic for the legging.

The fitted knit bodysuit is a form-fitting, one-piece garment with legs that may have sleeves. The legging may be short, three quarter length, or long.

Style, practicality, and comfort are part of what makes the bodysuit so inviting. This one-piece knitted garment is worn by the fashion minded, the sports minded, and also by the serious competitive athlete. It can be made in a variety of knit fabrics such as mohair, jersey, or tricot to maintain complete freedom of body movement. However, this type of bodysuit cannot be styled or made in woven fabrics, which use a completely different pattern theory.

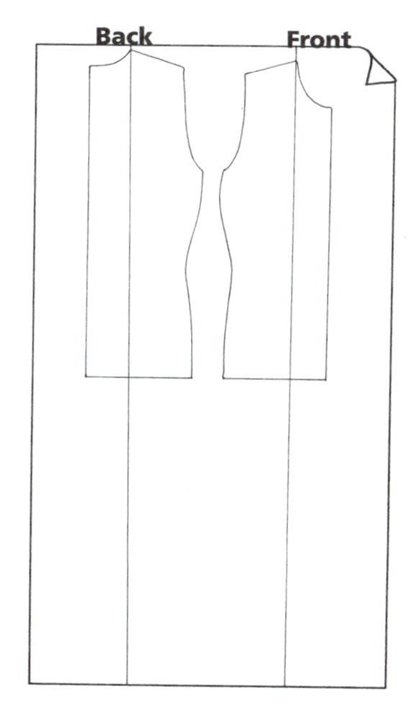

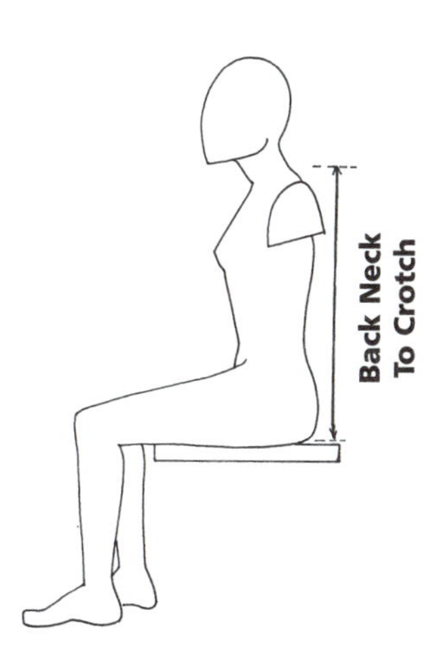

1. **Cut a piece of pattern paper** 60 inches long by 30-inches wide.

2. **Draw two straight of grainlines** the length of the paper and 11 inches in from each end.

3. **Trace front and back bodice pattern onto pattern paper.** Use a fitted knit bodice pattern that is made of the same knit quality as your desired bodysuit.

4. **Align the grainlines at the shoulder/neck corners** and parallel to center.

5. **Measure from the natural back neck position to the crotch** while sitting straight on a chair. This measurement should be approximately 27 inches. Subtract 1 inch from this measurement.

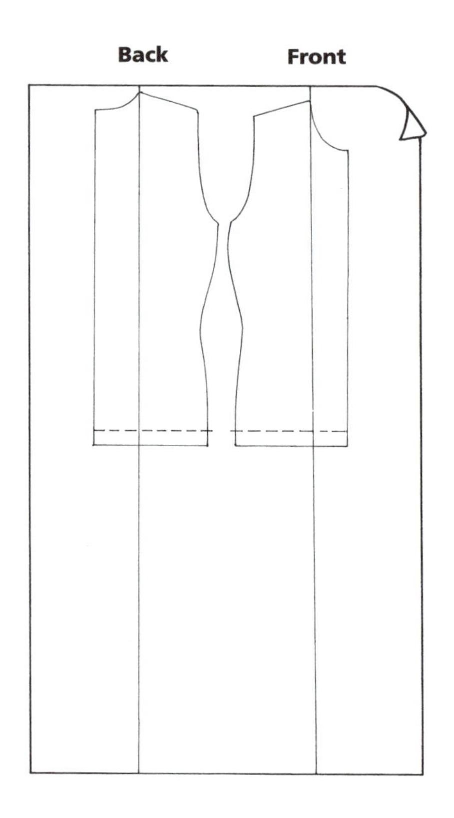

6 **Transfer the back neck-to-crotch length onto the back pattern.** With a ruler, measure down from the back neckline of the pattern. Mark this measurement and square a line across the pattern for the front and back.

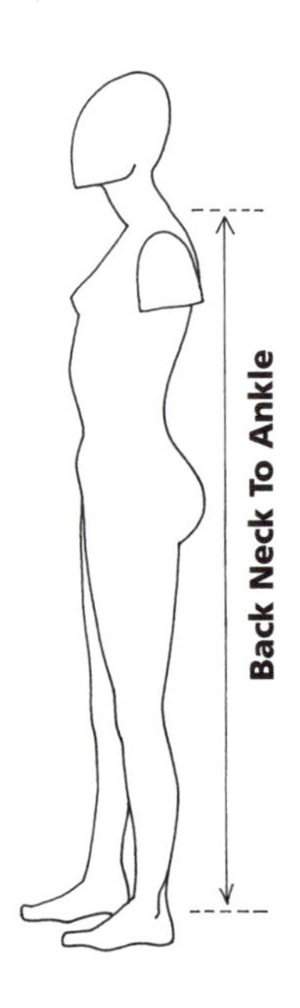

7 **Measure from the natural back neck position to the ankle** while standing straight. Subtract 1 1/2 inches from this measurement.

NOTE: This measurement may change slightly, depending upon the stretch quality of the desired knit fabric.

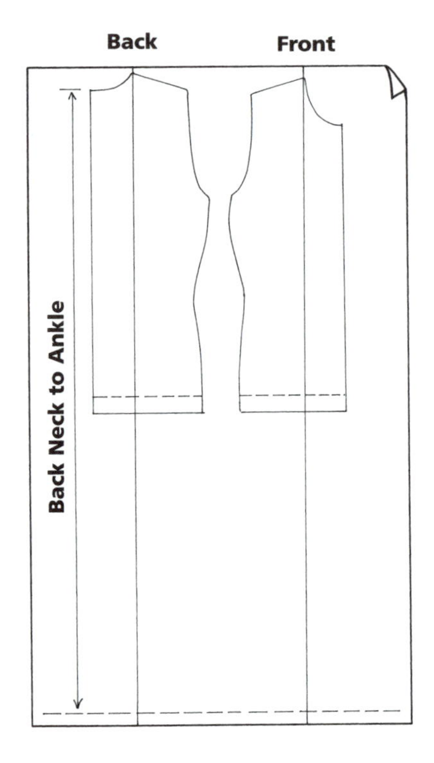

8 **Transfer the back neck-to-ankle length onto the back pattern.** With a ruler, measure down from the back neckline of the pattern the overall length. Mark this measurement and square a line across the pattern for both the front and back.

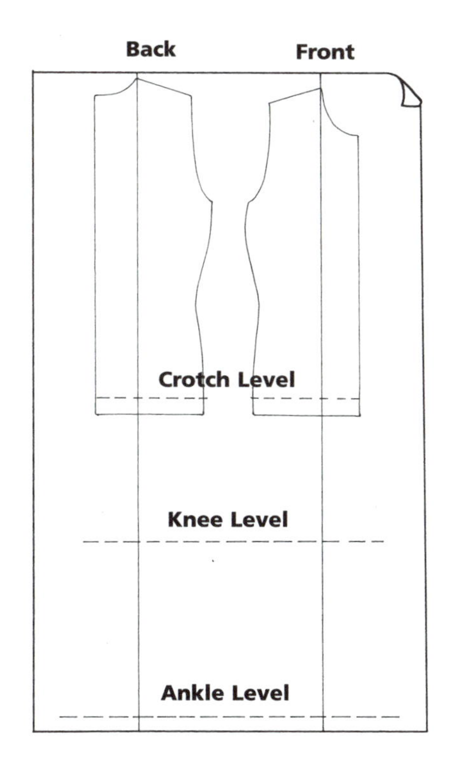

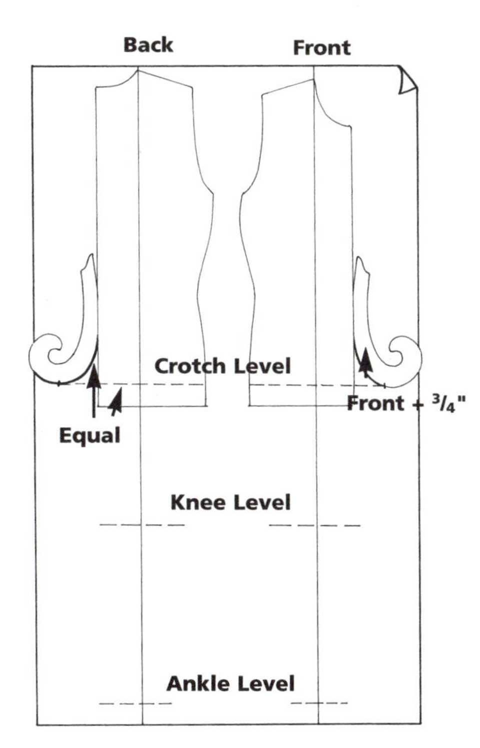

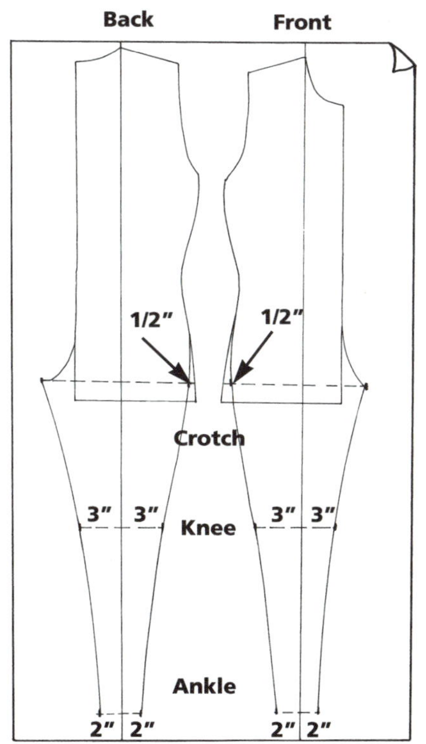

9 Locate the knee level line.

a. Measure from the crotch line to the ankle line, and subtract 2 inches. Divide this measurement in half, and add 3 inches to this measurement.

b. Measure up from the ankle line this measurement. Mark this measurement, and square a line across the pattern for both the front and back.

10 Develop the crotch.

a. To develop the front crotch, measure from center front to the straight of grainline, and subtract 3/4 inch. Extend this new measurement from the center front toward the edge of the paper.

b. To develop the back crotch, measure from the center back to the straight of grainline. Extend the measurement from the center back toward the edge of the paper.

c. Draw these new extended lines up into the center lines, using a french curve ruler.

11 Develop the legging.

a. At the ankle line, measure 2 inches on both sides of the grainline. Crossmark this position.

b. Crossmark a new side seam position. At the crotch line from the side seam, remove 1/2 inch from the side seam.

c. Measure 3 inches on both sides of the grainline. Crossmark this position on the knee line.

d. Blend the crotch line to the knee level, using a long, curved ruler.

e. Blend a new side seam up to the waistline and down to the knee line, crossing the new side seam crossmark. Using a straight ruler, blend from the knee level to the ankle level.

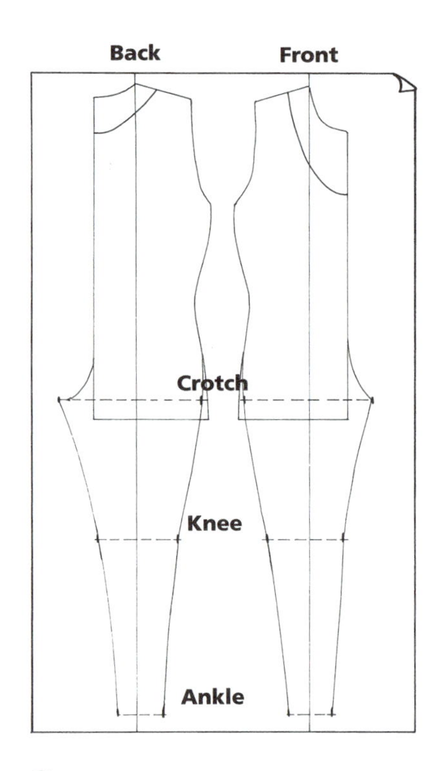

12 **Draw the desired front and back neckline,** using a curved ruler.

NOTE: If a low front neckline is desired, then a higher back neckline is necessary, and vice versa, because structurally the body suit will gap and fall off the shoulders.

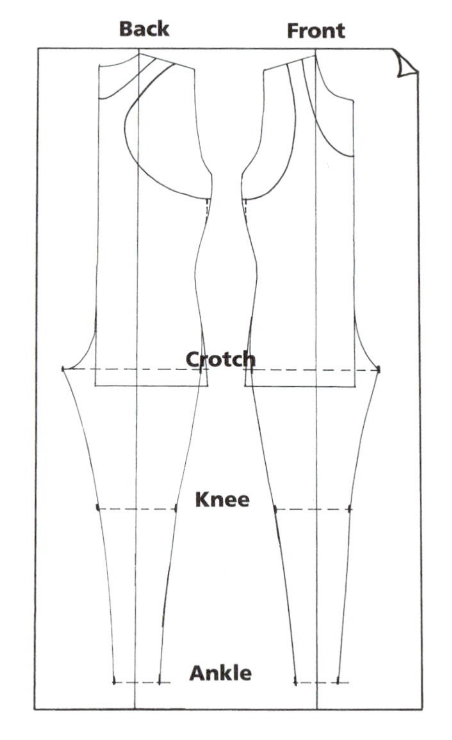

13 **Draw the desired front and back armholes,** using a curved rule. Remove 1/4 inch at the new armhole/side seam corners. Blend in a new side seam/armhole corner.

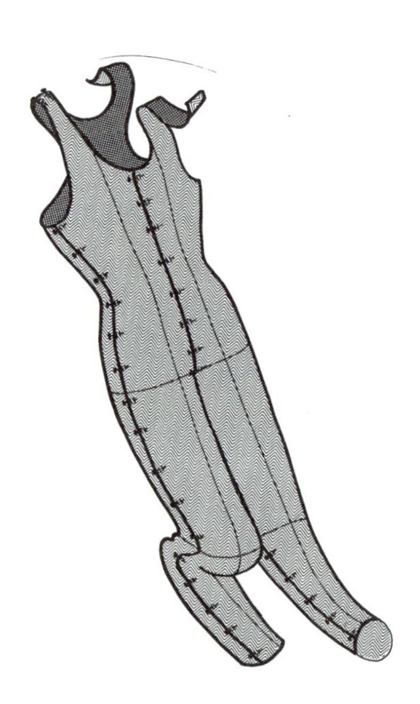

14 **Cut out a full pattern** (left and right) of a knit fabric. Pin together the shoulders, side seams, and inseams.

NOTE: The stretch quality of the sample fabric should be the same as the basic knit pattern and the same as the desired garment.

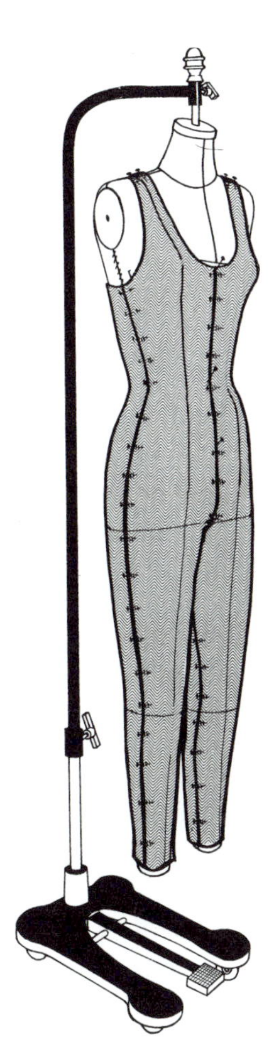

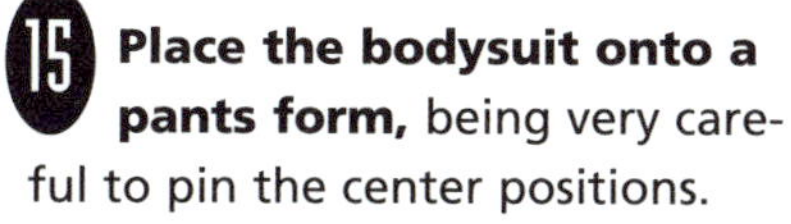

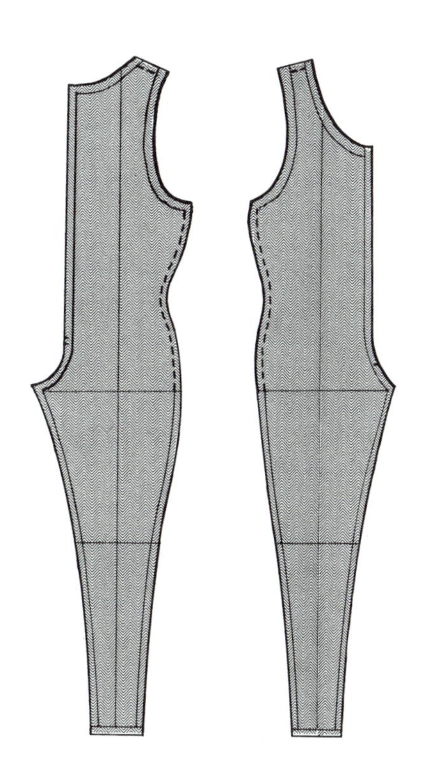

15 **Place the bodysuit onto a pants form,** being very careful to pin the center positions.

16 **Fit the shoulders, side seams, inseams,** and crotch by repinning the desired changes. With a felt tip pen, draw all corrections and adjustments.

17 **Retrue all altered seams.** Remove the drape from the pant form. Retrue all seams, and add 3/8-inch seam allowances. Because of the changes when fitting, a new pattern may be necessary.

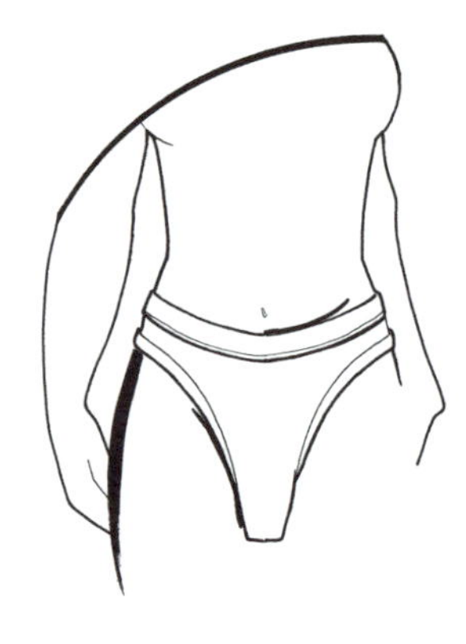

Knit fabrics are becoming increasingly important for their easy wear qualities. Lightweight knit fabrics provide gentle shaping and maximum elasticity for the hiphugger, bikini style briefs, or the soft stretch brief. Designing briefs can be a real joy if the basic drape and fit are well done.

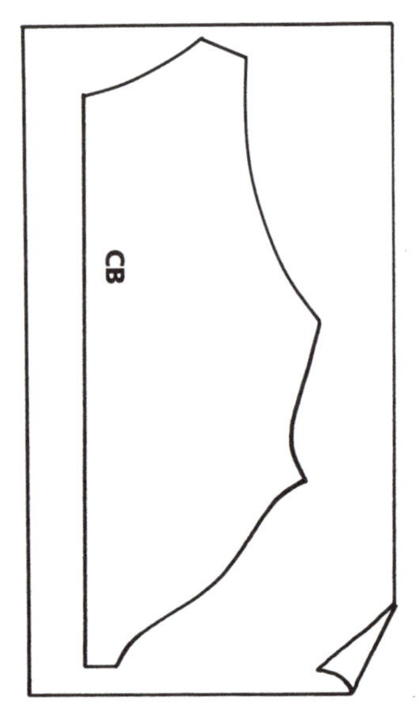

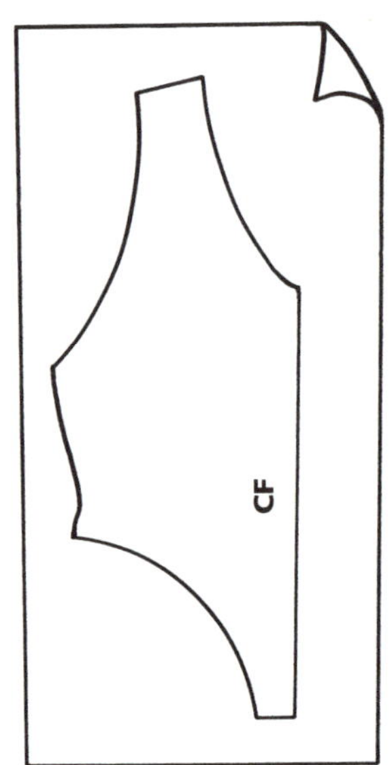

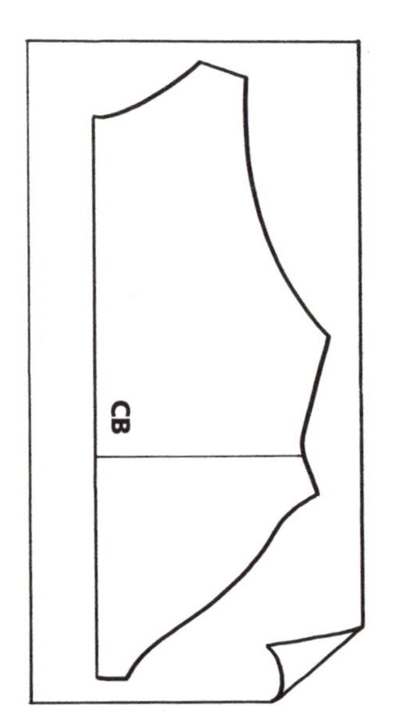

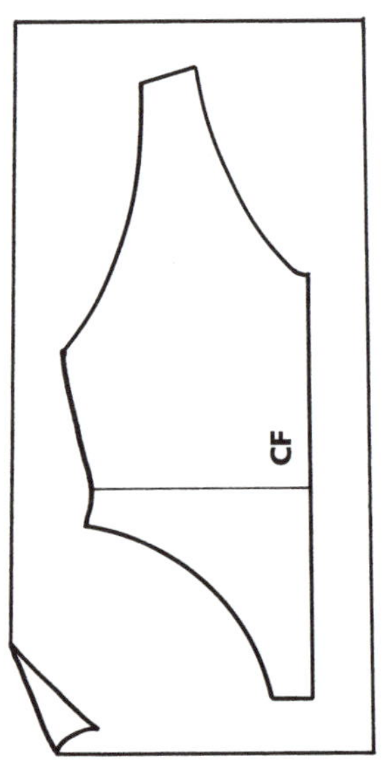

1 **Trace front and back leotard pattern** onto a new piece of pattern paper.

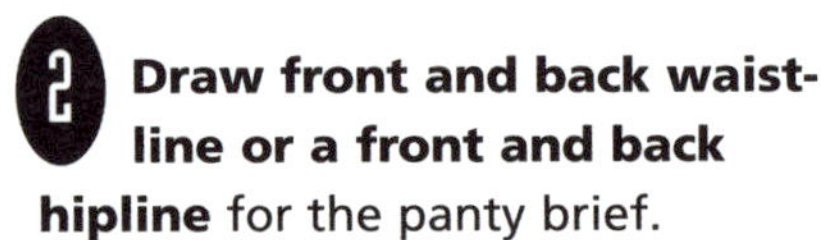

2 **Draw front and back waistline or a front and back hipline** for the panty brief.

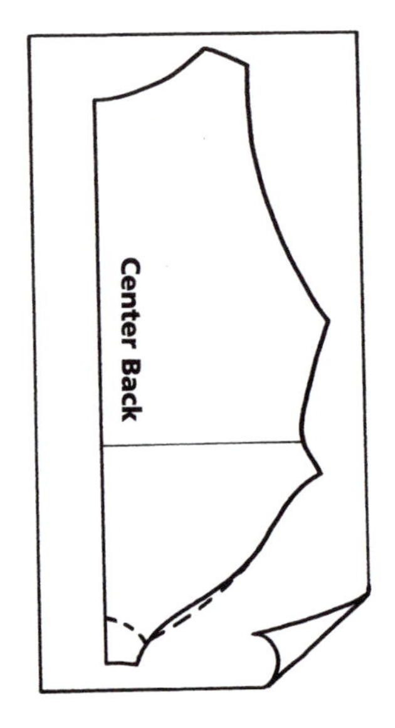

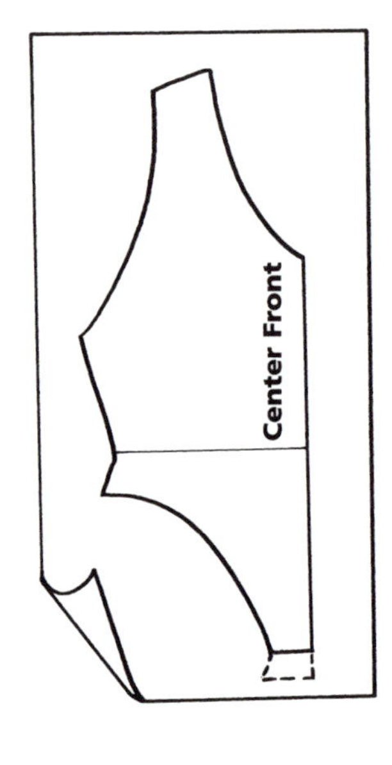

3 **Reshape the front and back crotch seams.**

a. For a body-fitting front crotch, extend and shape the front crotch seam approximately 2 inches (see illustration).

b. For a body-fitting back crotch, subtract approximately 2 inches and draw a concave line at the back crotch seam (see illustration).

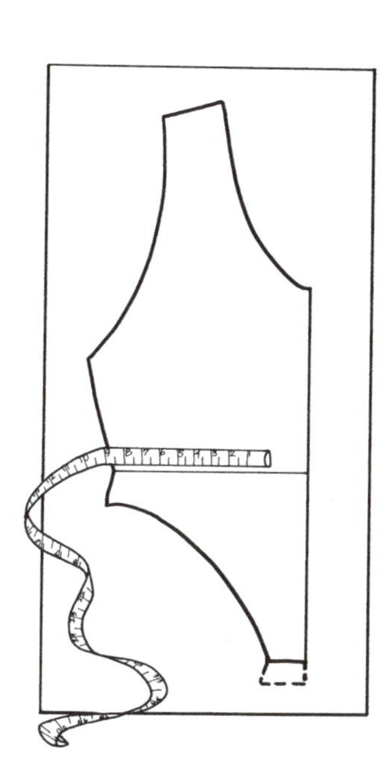

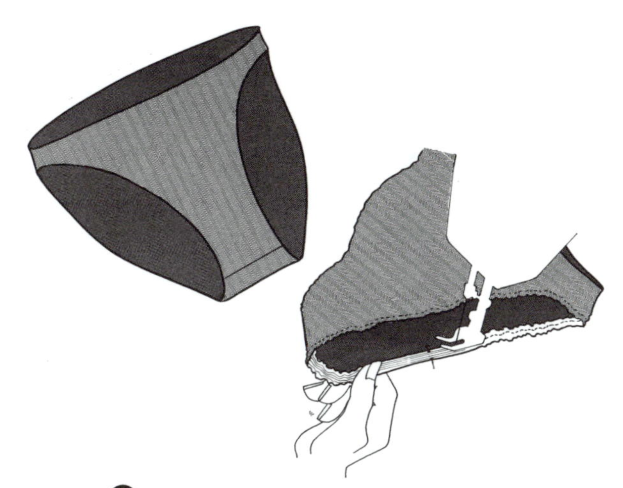

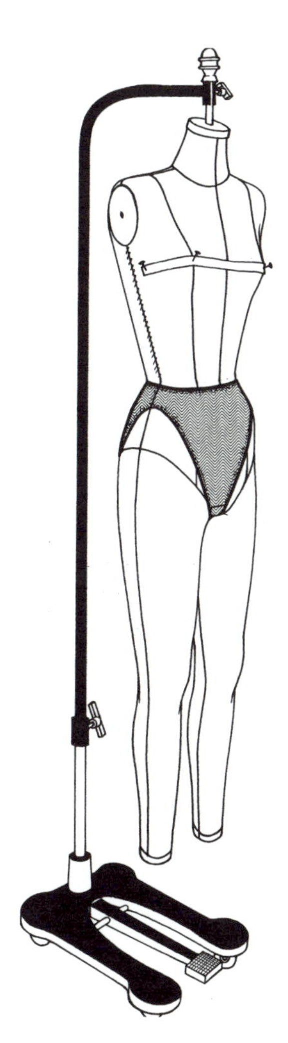

4 **Measure the waistline elastic and legging elastic.**

a. The waistline or hipline elastic should measure approximately 2 inches smaller than the desired finished measurement.

b. When sewing the legging, elastic should measure approximately 22 inches per leg.

5 **Cut the entire panty out** of the same stretch quality fabric in which the finished panty will be produced.

6 **Sew the crotch and side seams together.** Using a stretch and sew method, single-needle serge the elastic into the waistline and the two legging areas. Sew less elastic into the lower back legging area to provide a more secure back fit.

7 **A final fit of a panty should be done on the human body.** Place the sewn panty onto the dress form and make any fitting corrections.

Chapter Nineteen

Yokes and Midriffs

Objectives

By studying the various draping steps in this chapter, the designer should be able to accomplish the following:

- Drape a front bodice yoke; a separate front and back bodice yoke; an all-in-one bodice yoke; a hip yoke; and a waist midriff.
- Recognize grain and crossgrain in the relation between the yoke or midriff and the garment.
- Drape an accurate side seam and have it hang straight from the bust level line at the front; the shoulder level line at the back; and down to the hem.
- Drape the front and back bodice yokes that cross the shoulders in the front and back.
- Drape a circular and pleated skirt design into the front and back yokes with the correct amount of ease and side seam allowance.
- Drape a flared, gathered, and pleated skirt into a hip yoke with the correct amount of ease and side seam allowance.
- True up and check the results of the draping process with regard to fit, hang, balance, and proportion.

Front Bodice Yoke

A bodice yoke is a portion of a garment fitted at the shoulders. Yokes are used to support the lower section of the garment, which may be designed in a variety of lengths and styles.

There are many shapes used to enhance or create a particular design. Choose them with the principles of line and learn the tricks that help create a most flattering silhouette.

Shown here are three different front yoke style lines. All three yokes are draped following the same instructions.

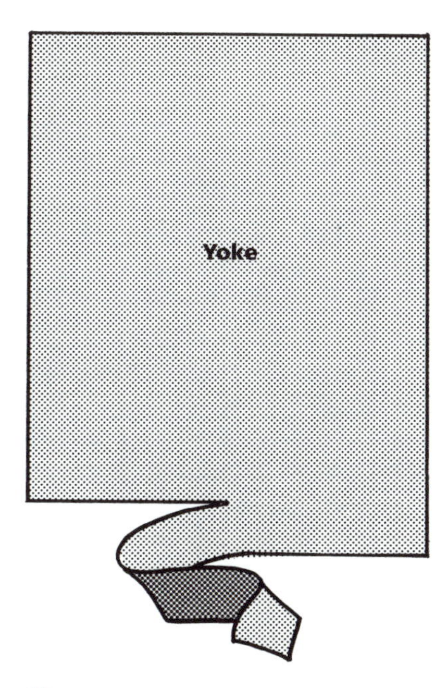

1 Measure the length for the yoke (along the straight of grain) from the neckband to the yoke style line, and add 3 inches. Snip and tear the fabric at this length.

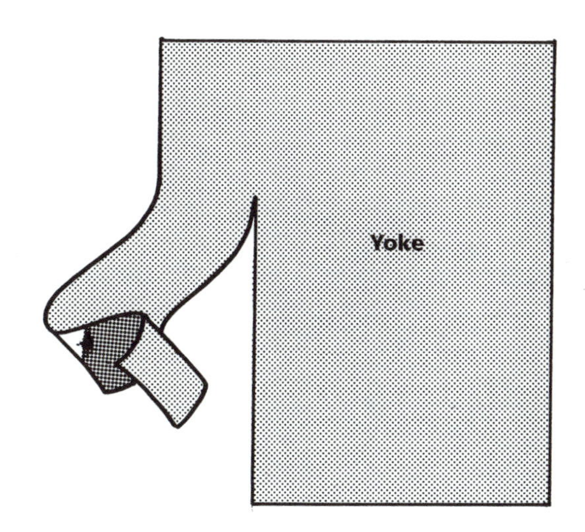

2 Measure the width for the yoke (along the crossgrain) from the center front to the armhole, and add 3 inches. Snip and tear the fabric at this width.

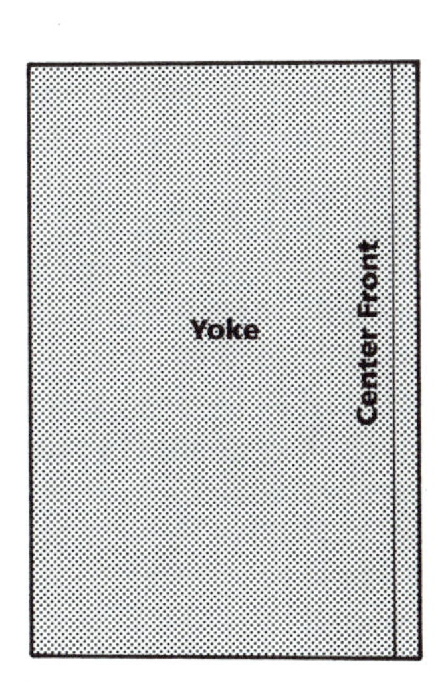

3 Draw a center front grainline 1 inch from the torn edge on the prepared yoke piece. Press under.

4 Measure down on the grainline 4 inches. Crossmark at this measurement on the prepared yoke piece.

Front Bodice Yoke—Draping Steps

Prepare the dress form. Referring to the design sketch, pin the desired yoke style line on the dress form.

Drape a bodice to match the desired yoke design. Follow the bodice instructions for the bodice of either the Pleated Blouse (pages 334-338) or Circular Bodice (pages 339-342) or the All-in-One Bodice Yoke (pages 343-348).

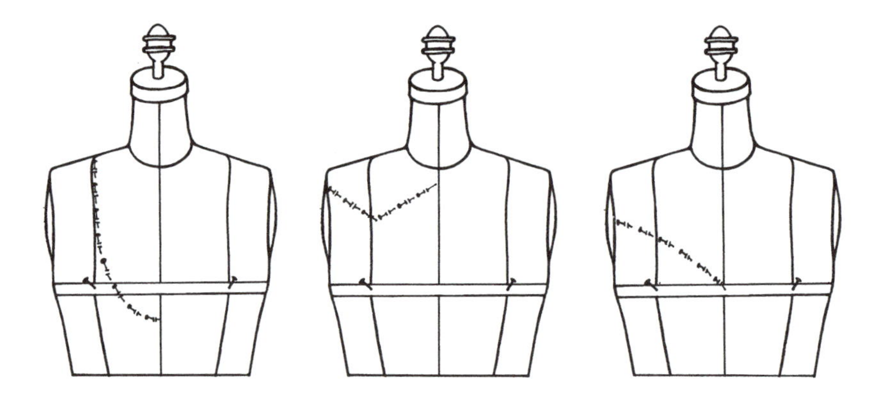

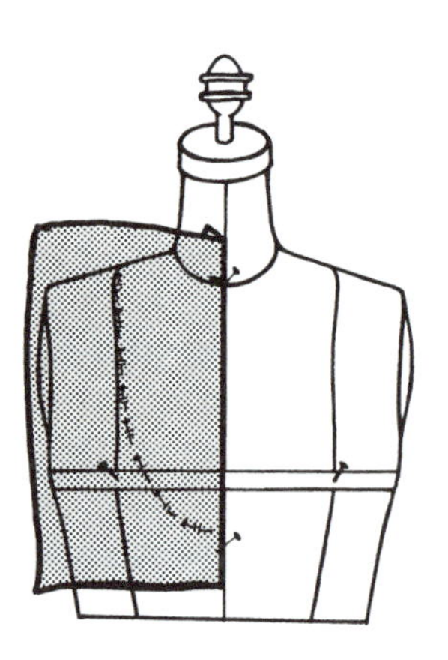

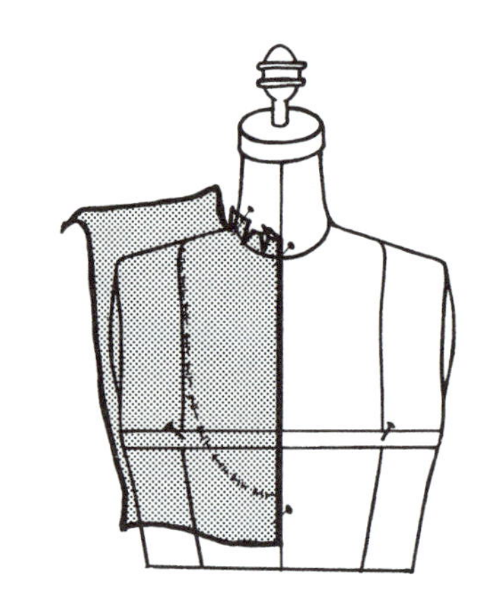

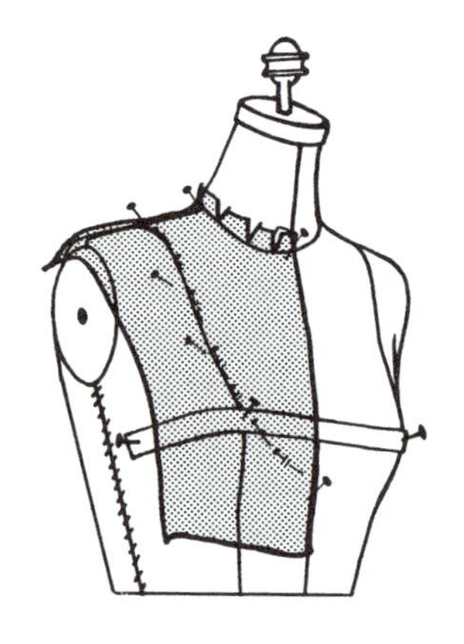

1 Place the center front yoke grainline to the center front position of the dress form. Align the center front neckline position crossmark of the yoke to the center front neckline position of the dress form.

2 Clip, smooth, and pin the neckline of the yoke.

3 Smooth the fabric over and past the shoulder seam of the dress form. Pin in place.

4 Smooth the fabric past the desired yoke style line. Pin in place.

5 **Mark all key areas** of the dress form to the fabric of the yoke.

Neckline

Shoulder Seam and Shoulder Ridge

Yoke Style Line

Yoke Style Line Notch

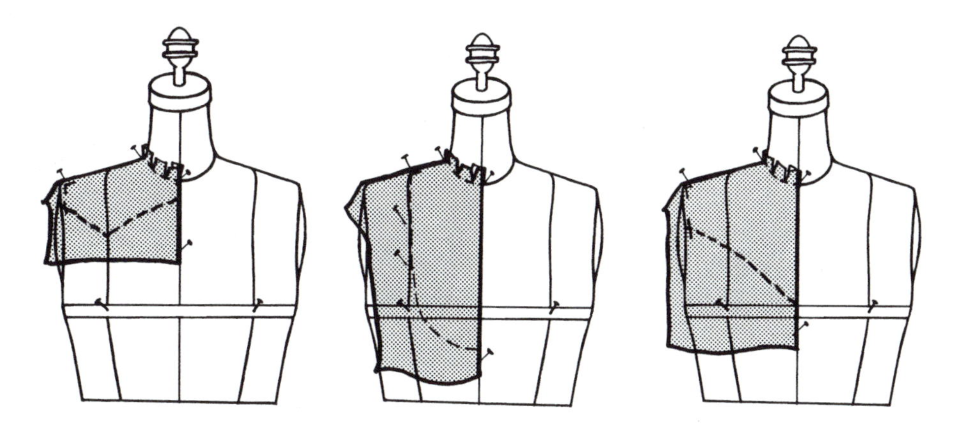

6 **True up all seams.** Remove the yoke drape from the dress form. True up all seams, add seam allowances, and trim excess fabric. Return the yoke to the dress form and check for accuracy, fit, and balance.

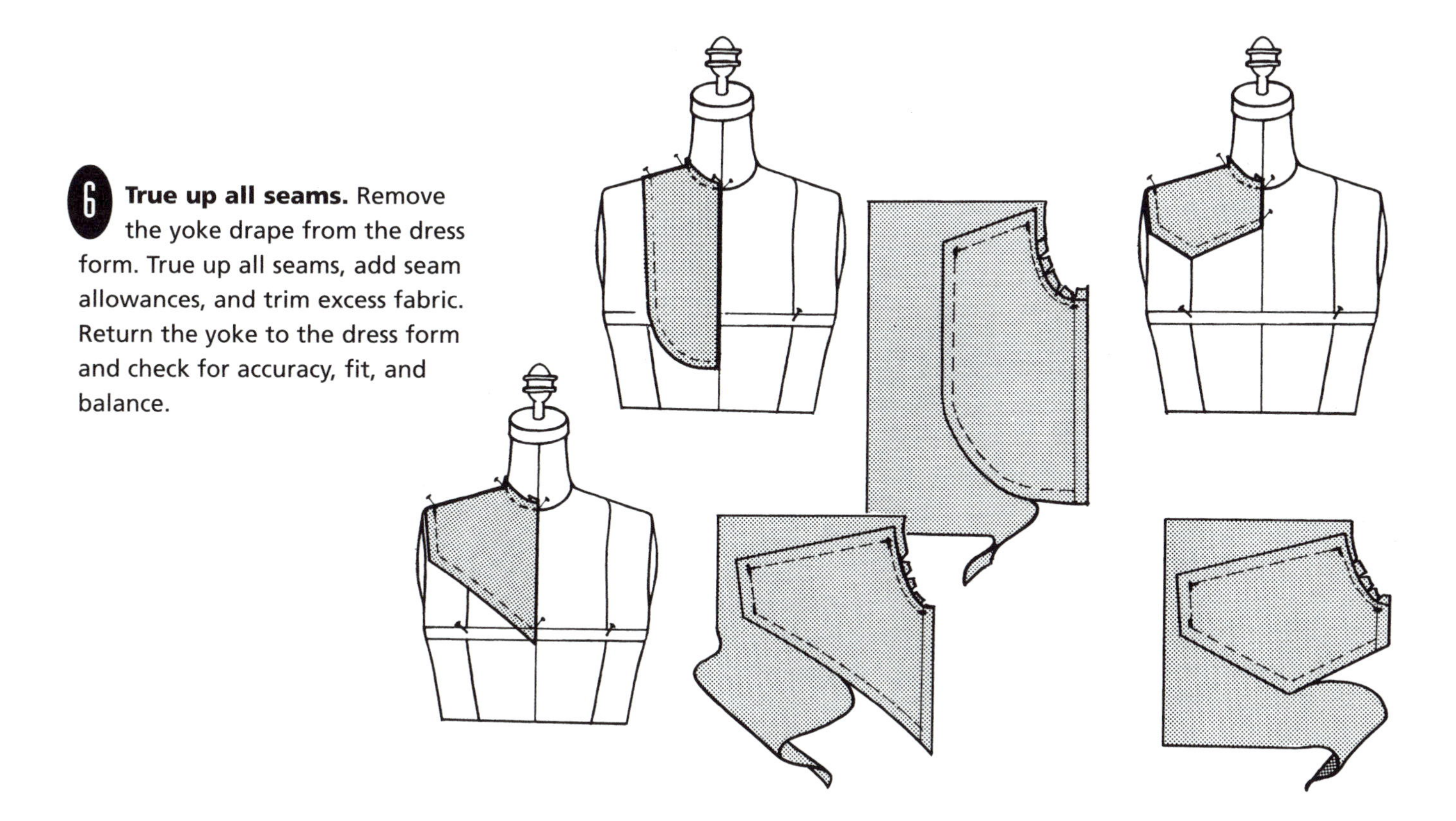

Separate Front and Back Bodice Yoke

Front and back bodice yoke with circular bodice

Front and back bodice yoke with pleated bodice.

A separate front and back bodice yoke crosses the shoulders in the front and the back. The front and back yokes are attached by a shoulder seam, which allows the front and back yoke pieces to maintain a straight of grain at both the front and back seams.

Often the lower section of the garment will be designed with gores, gathers, pleats, or circular shapes, and are sewn to the yoke.

Instructions are provided in these projects for sewing a separate front and back bodice yoke into a circular and pleated bodice. To create gathers rather than pleats, follow the same draping steps for pleats, but drape in fullness rather than pleats.

Separate Front and Back Bodice Yoke—Preparing the Fabric: Front and Back Yoke

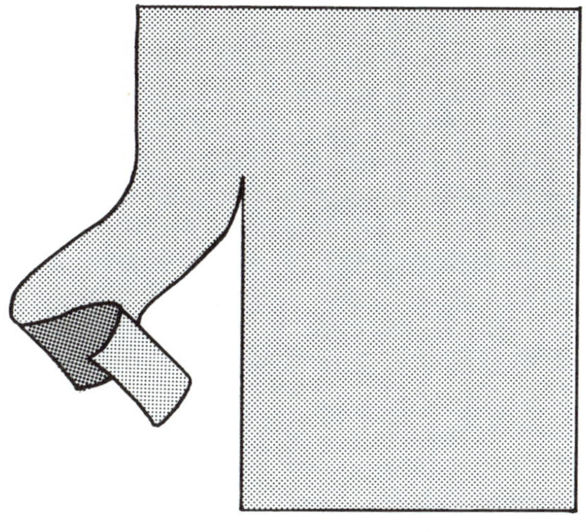

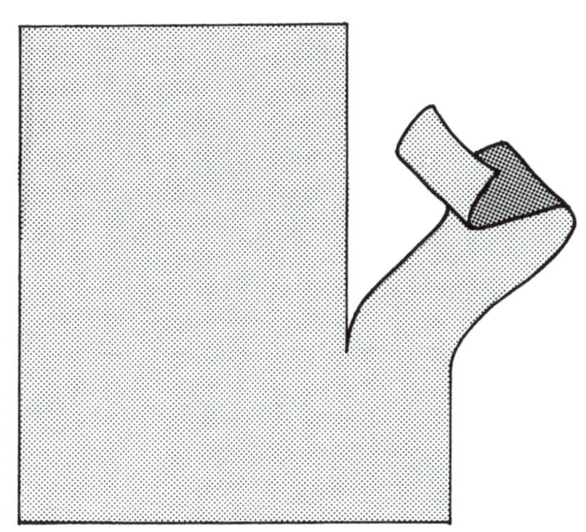

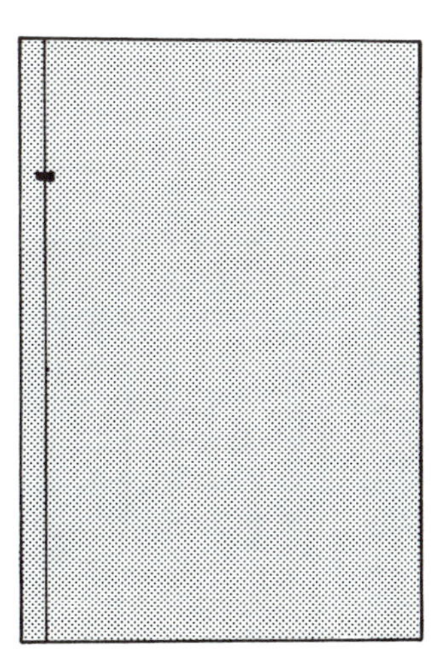

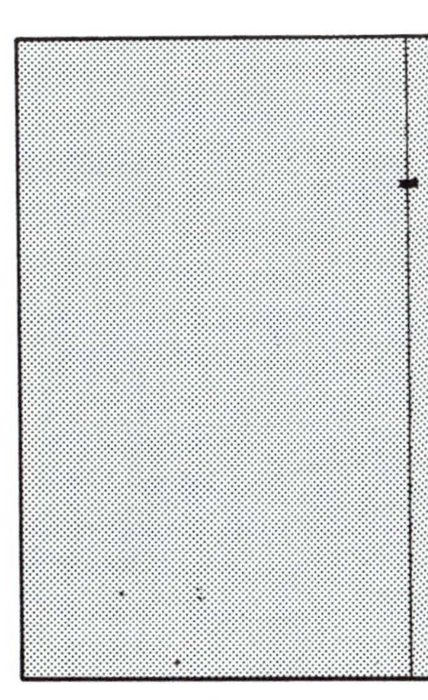

1. **Measure the length for the front and back yokes** (along the straight of grain) from the neckband to the yoke style line. Add 3 inches. Snip and tear the fabric at this length.

2. **Measure the width for the front and back yokes** (along the crossgrain) from the center front to the armhole. Add 3 inches. Snip and tear the fabric at this width.

3. **Draw a center front and center back grainline** 1 inch from the torn edge on the prepared yoke piece, and press under.

4. **Measure down on the grainline** 4 inches. Crossmark this measurement on the prepared front and back yoke pieces.

Separate Front and Back Bodice Yoke—Draping Steps: Front and Back Yoke

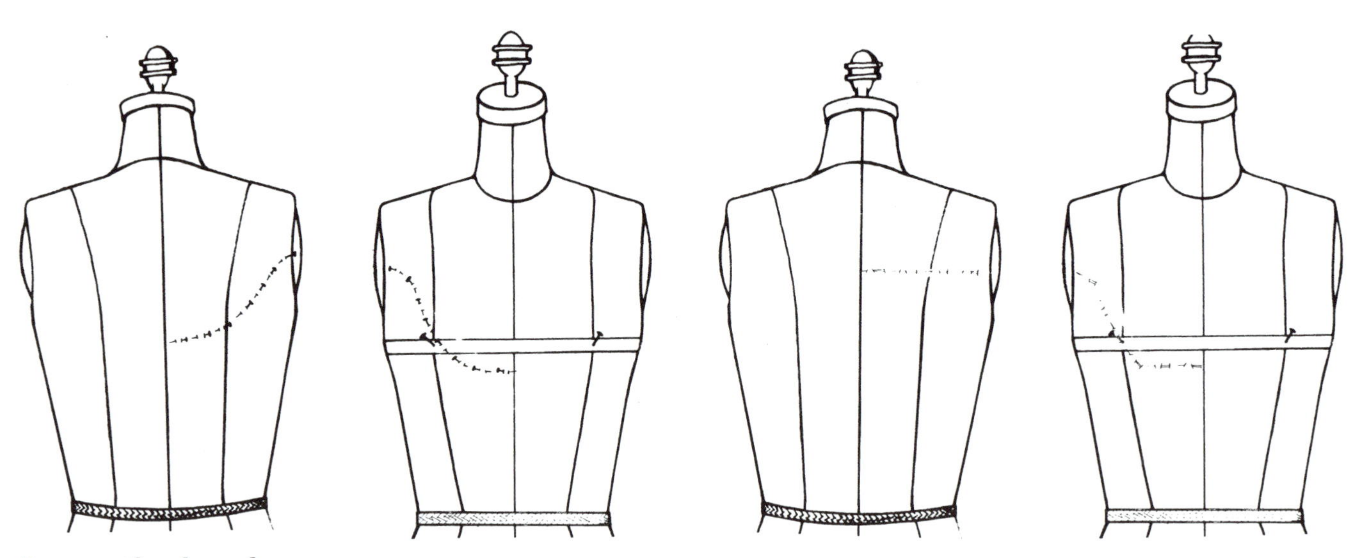

Prepare the dress form.
Referring to the design sketch, pin the desired yoke style line on the dress form front and back.

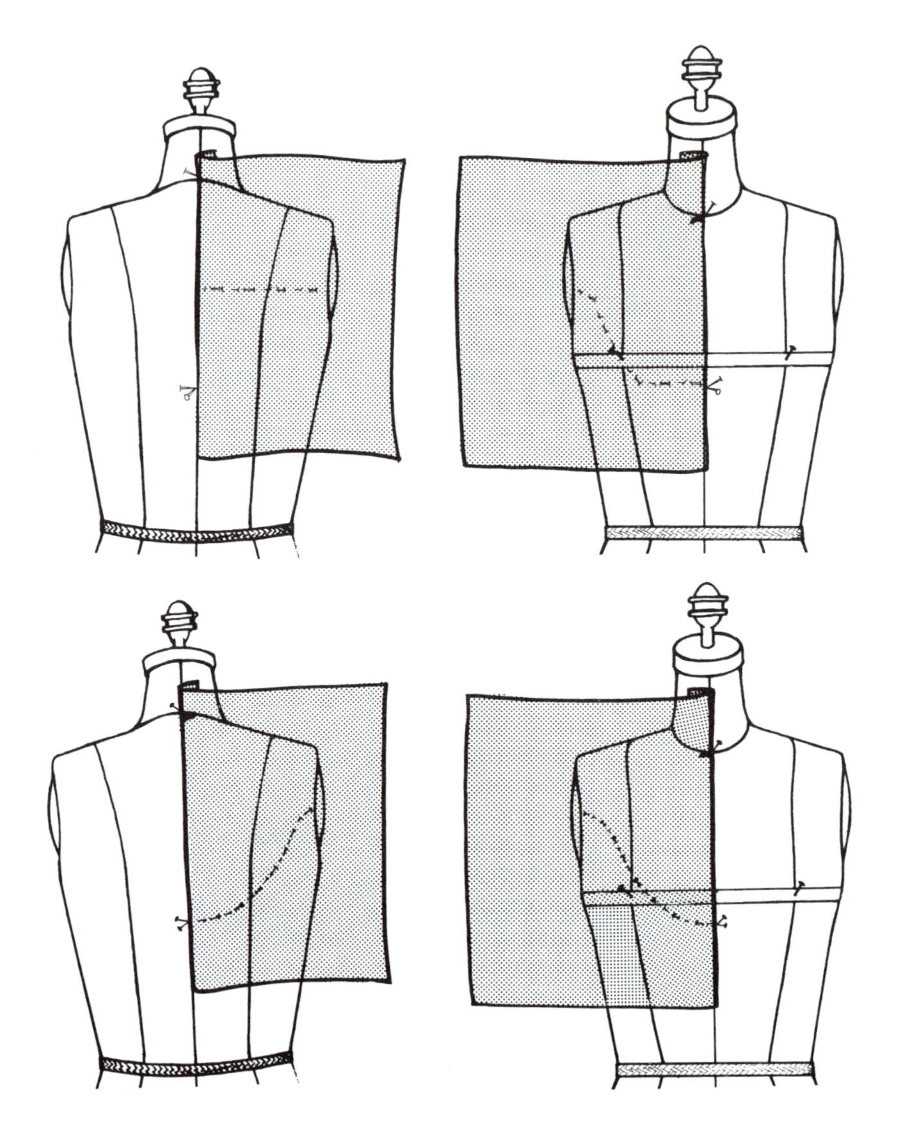

1 Place the center front and center back yoke grainline.

a. Place center front grainline fold of the front yoke piece to the center front position of the dress form. Align the center front neckline crossmark of the yoke to the center front neckline position of the dress form.

b. Place the center back grainline fold of the back yoke piece to the center back position of the dress form. Align the center back neckline crossmark of the yoke to the center back neckline position of the dress form.

2 **Clip, smooth, and pin the front and back neckline** of the yoke pieces.

3 **Smooth the yoke fabric over and past the shoulder seam** of the dress form. Match the front shoulder seam to the back shoulder seam.

4 **Smooth the yoke fabric past the desired yoke style line for both the front and back.** Clip at the style line if necessary. Pin in place.

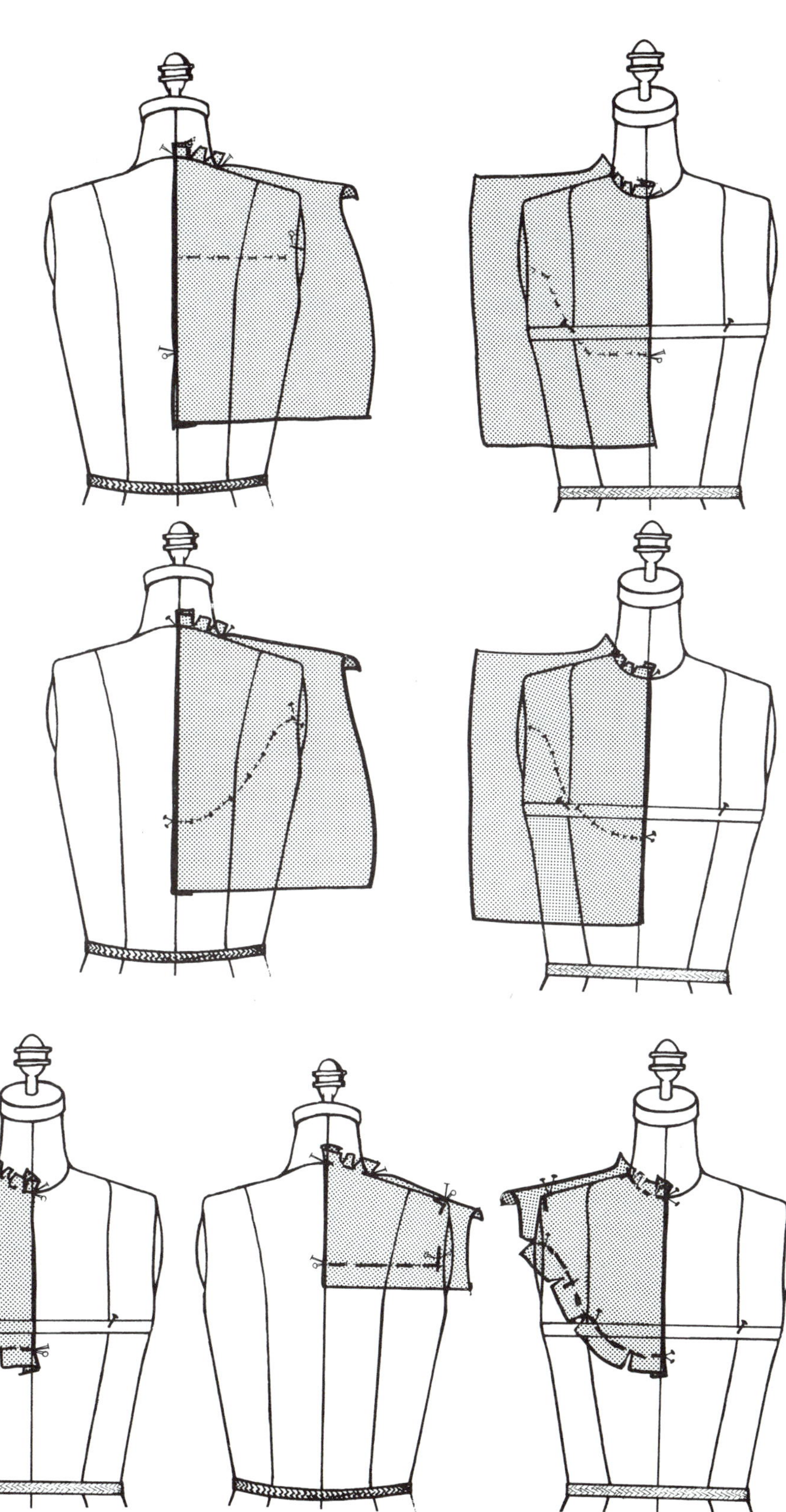

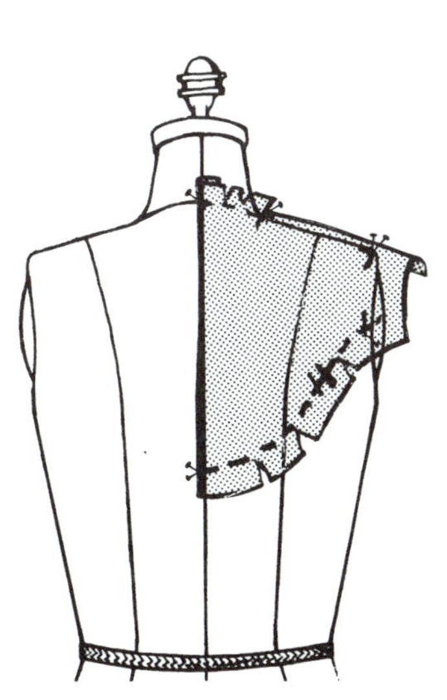

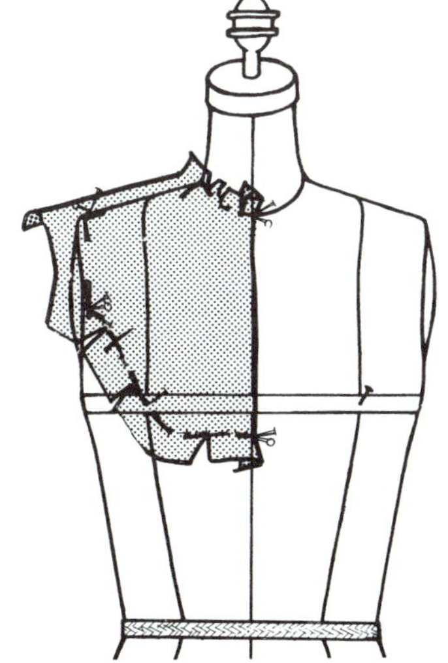

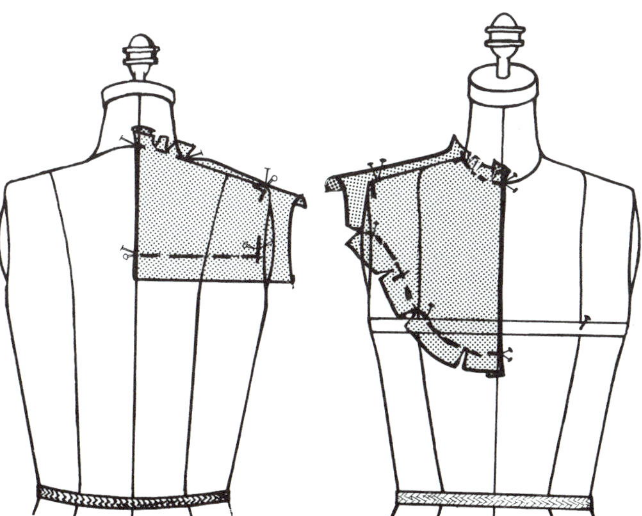

5 **Mark all key areas** of the dress form to the front and back yoke fabric pieces.

Neckline Lightly mark.

Shoulder Seam and Shoulder Ridge

Yoke Style Line Lightly mark.

Yoke Style Line Notches One for the front and two for the back.

6 **True up all seams.** Remove the yoke drape from the dress form, true up all seams, add seam allowances, and trim excess fabric. Return the yoke to the dress form and check for accuracy, fit, and balance. The chosen bodice style should be draped with the trued up yoke on the dress form.

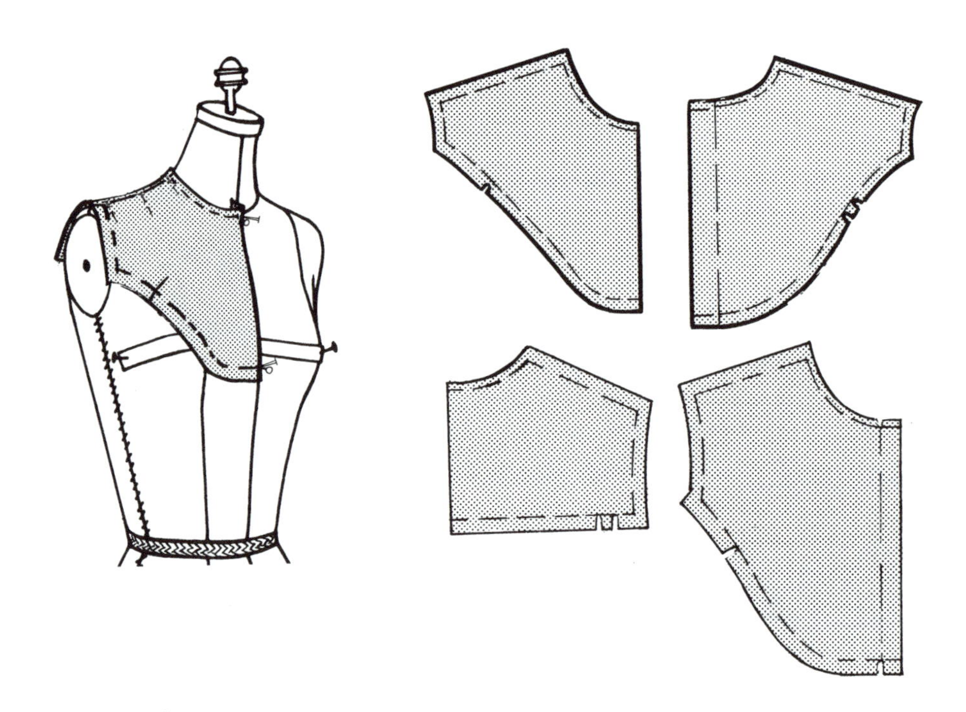

Pleated Bodice—Preparing the Fabric

1 **Measure the length desired for a front and back blouse.** Measure the length (along the straight of grain) from the neckband to the desired length, and add a few inches. Snip and tear the fabric at this desired length.

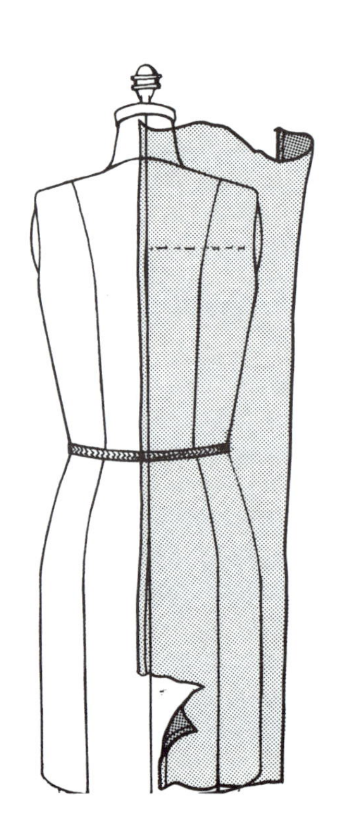

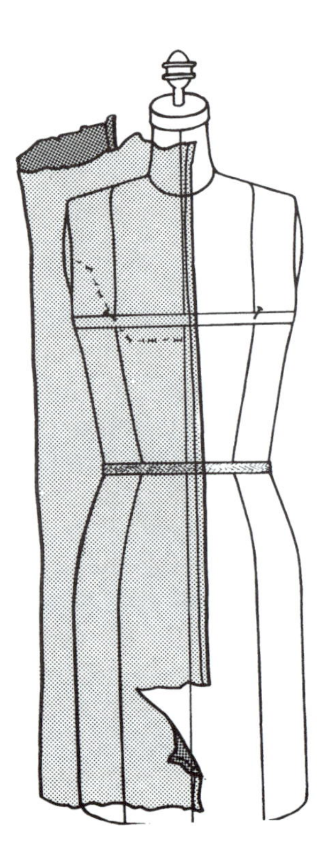

2 **Divide the fabric piece in half.** Fold the fabric from selvage to selvage. Snip and tear the piece in half lengthwise.

One piece will be used for the bodice front and the other piece will be used for the bodice back.

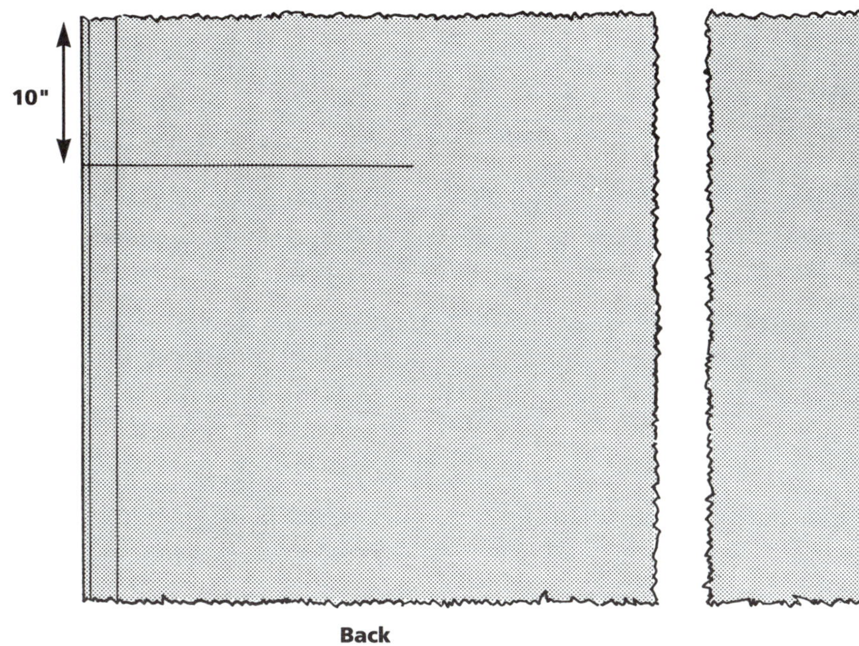

Back

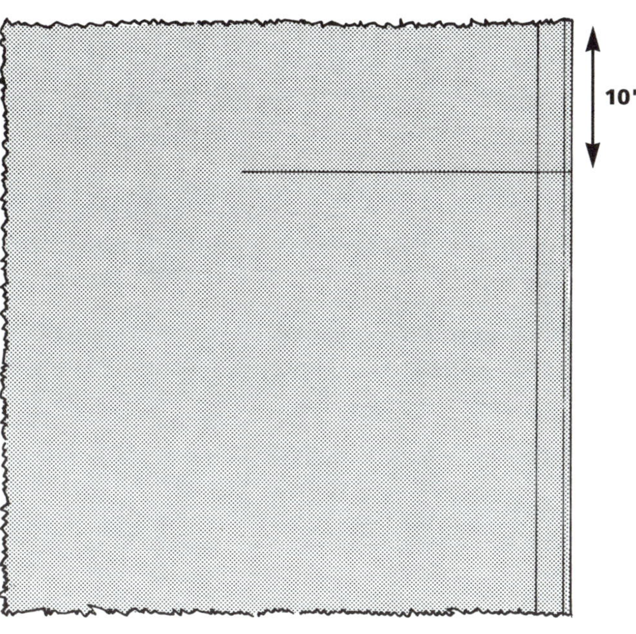

Front

3 **Draw the center front and center back grainlines** on the fabric 1 inch from the torn edge, and press under.

4 **Draw the crossgrain for the front and back bodice fabric pieces** 10 inches from the top of the fabric edge. Draw the crossgrain across the fabric piece for the front bustline level and the back at the shoulder blade level.

Draping Steps—Pleated Bodice

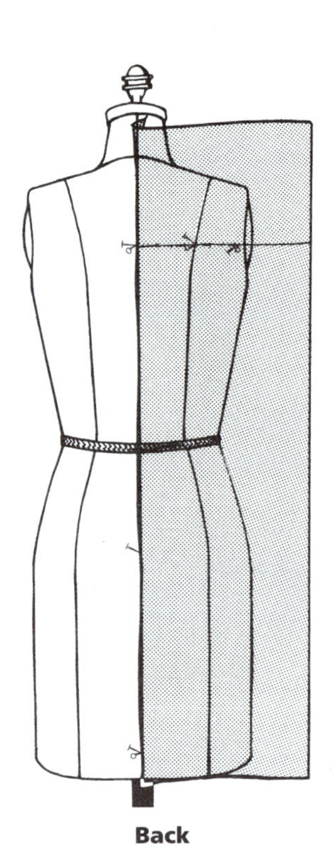

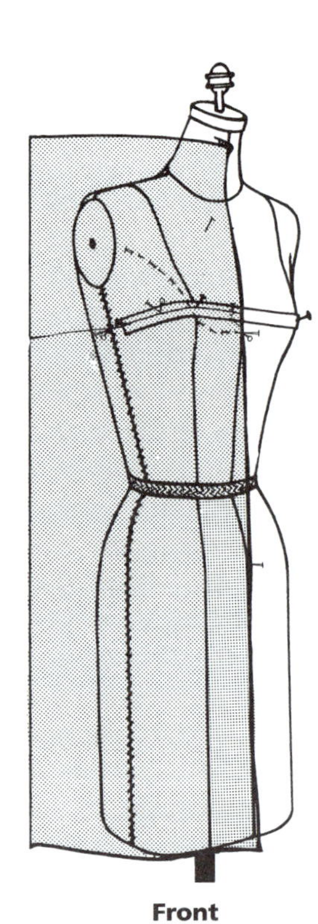

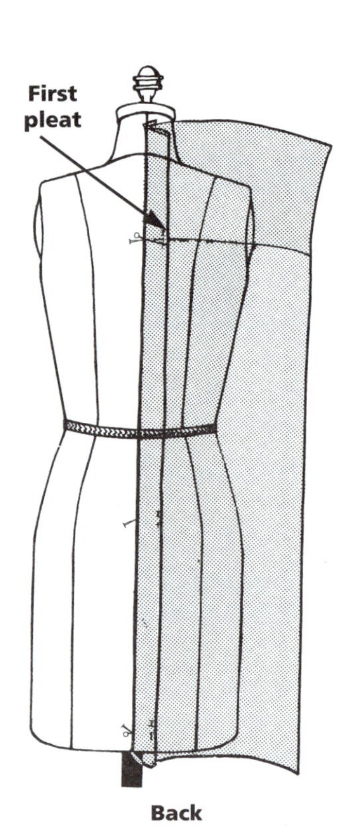

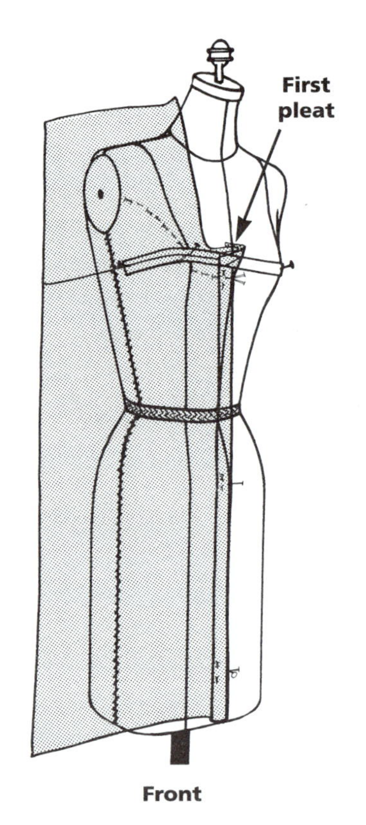

1 Pin the grainlines to the dress form.

a. Pin the center front grainline fold of the bodice to the center front position of the dress form.

b. Pin the center back grainline fold of the bodice to the center back position of the dress form.

2 Align and drape the cross-grain.

a. For the front drape, align the crossgrain at the bustline level. Allow the fabric to hang smoothly and evenly from the bust level. Pin at the side seam.

b. For the back drape, align the crossgrain at the shoulder blade level. Allow the fabric to hang smoothly and evenly from the shoulder blade level. Pin at the side seam.

3 Drape the front bodice pleats.

a. Drape the desired number of pleats at the bust level of the bodice. Be sure to leave approximately a 3/4-inch space from each pleat.

b. Pin each pleat straight up and down and parallel from center front.

NOTE: The width of the pleat should be two times the desired final width of the pleat. Example: 1 1/2 inches will yield a 3/4-inch pleat.

4 Drape the back bodice pleats.

a. Drape the desired number of pleats at the back shoulder blade level of the blouse. Be sure to leave about 3/4-inch space from each pleat.

b. Pin each pleat straight up and down and parallel to center back.

NOTE: The width of the pleat should be two times the desired final width of the pleat. Example: 1 1/2 inches will yield a 3/4-inch pleat.

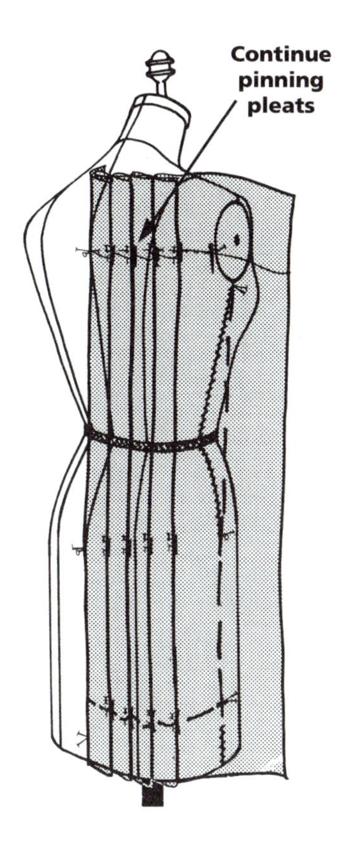

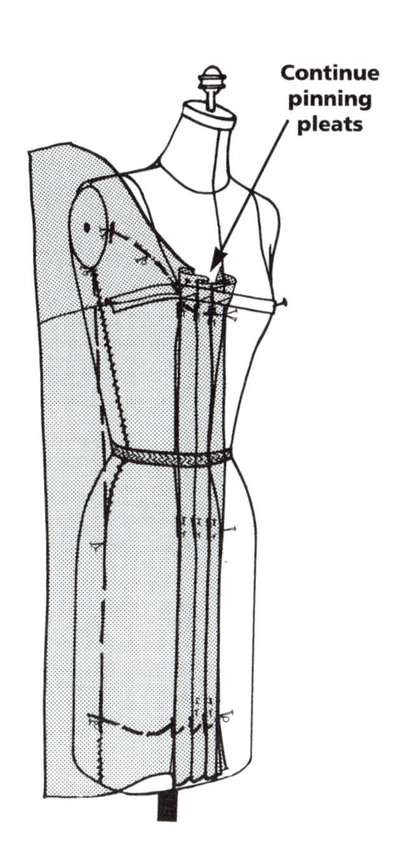

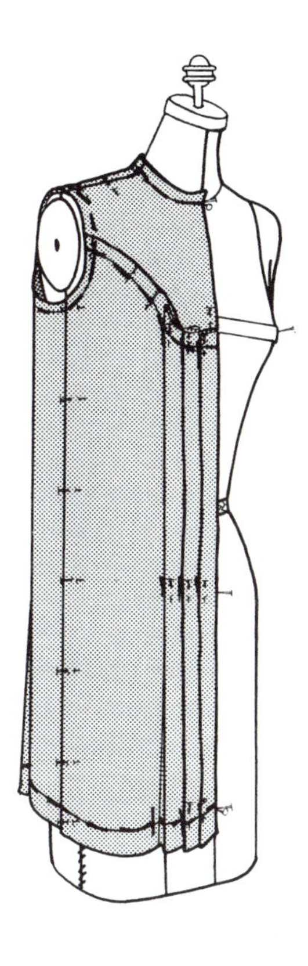

5 **Drape the remainder of the front bodice.**

a. Pin the pleats at the front style line.

b. Pin the remainder of the front and back yoke. Keeping the crossgrain in place at the bust level, continue to drape the remainder of the front yoke style. The blouse should remain parallel to center front. The side seam should remain parallel to center front.

c. Trim away the excess fabric around the front yoke.

6 **Drape the remainder of the back bodice.**

a. Pin the pleats at the back style line.

b. Pin the remainder of the back yoke. Keeping the crossgrain in place at the shoulder blade level, continue to drape the remainder of the back yoke style. The bodice should remain parallel to center back. The side seam should remain parallel to center back.

c. Trim away the excess fabric around the back yoke.

7 **Mark all key areas** from the dress form to the fabric.

Bodice Style Seam Will match the yoke style line seam.

Matching Notches Match to the yoke notches.

Bottom of Armplate at the Side Seam

Side Seam

Hem Follow the bottom of the dress form as a guide.

8 **True up the front and back bodice drape.** Remove the front and back bodice drape from the dress form. True up all seams, add seam allowances, and trim excess fabric.

When trueing the front armhole: Pin the front bodice style line to the front yoke style line. Then, true up the armhole.

When trueing the back armhole: Pin the back bodice style line to the back yoke style line. Then, true up the armhole.

9 Pin the front and back yoke to the front and back bodices. Pin the side seams, return the drape to the dress form, and check the fit and balance. If necessary, make corrections.

Notes

Preparing the Fabric—Circular Bodice

1 Measure the length desired for a front and back bodice. Measure the length (along the straight of grain) from the neckband to the desired length, and add a few inches. Snip and tear the fabric at this desired length.

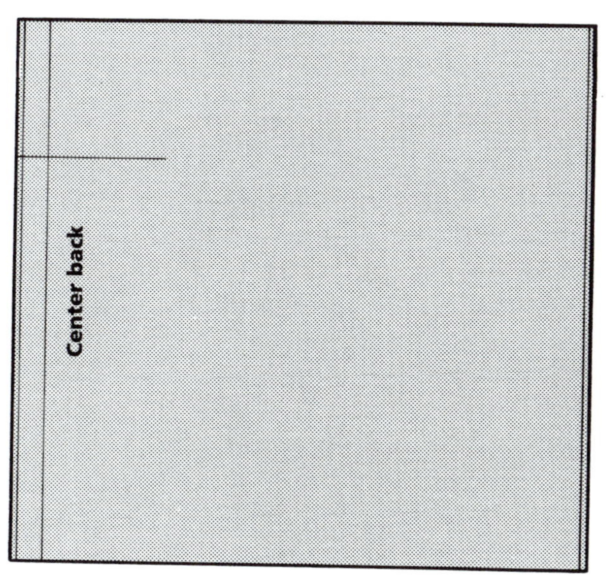

Back

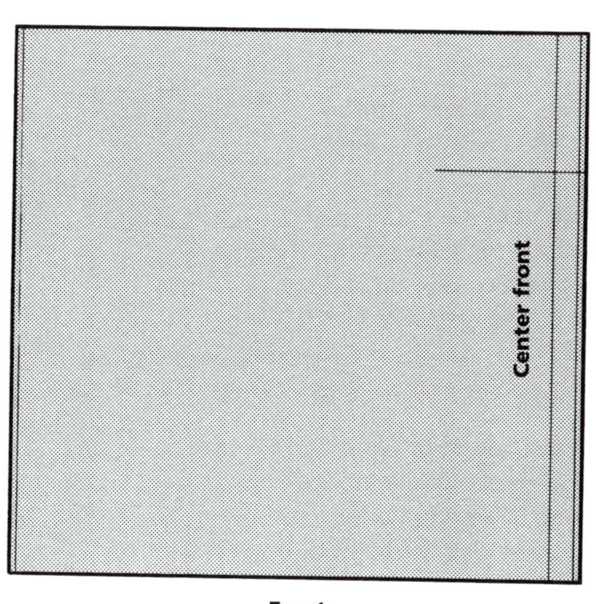

Front

2 Use the entire width of the fabric pieces for the front and back circular bodice drape.

3 Draw the grainline for the front and back bodice fabric pieces 1 inch from the selvage.

4 Draw the crossgrain for the front and back bodice fabric pieces 10 inches from the top of the fabric edge. Draw the crossgrain halfway across the fabric piece for the front bustline level and the back at the shoulder blade level.

1 **Pin the center front/center back grainline fold** of the bodice on the center front/center back of the dress form.

2 **Align and drape the cross-grain.**

a. For the front drape, align the crossgrain at the bustline level. Allow the fabric to hang smoothly and evenly from the bust level. Pin at the side seam.

b. For the back drape, align the crossgrain at the shoulder blade level. Allow the fabric to hang smoothly and evenly from the shoulder blade level. Pin at the side seam.

3 **Smooth, clip, and pin the front and back style line seam.** Approximately 2 inches from center front or center back, clip the fabric from the top edge down to the yoke style seam. Pin the bodice style seam to the yoke style line seam at the clip.

4 **Pivot the fabric down** from the style seam, forming a nice flowing flare. Place another pin on the bodice style seam to the yoke style seam, maintaining this flare.

5 **Smooth, clip, pin and pivot about 1 inch from the first flare.** At the bodice style line seam, smooth the fabric toward the side seam. Clip, pin, and pivot the front and back style line seam at this position, forming a second flare.

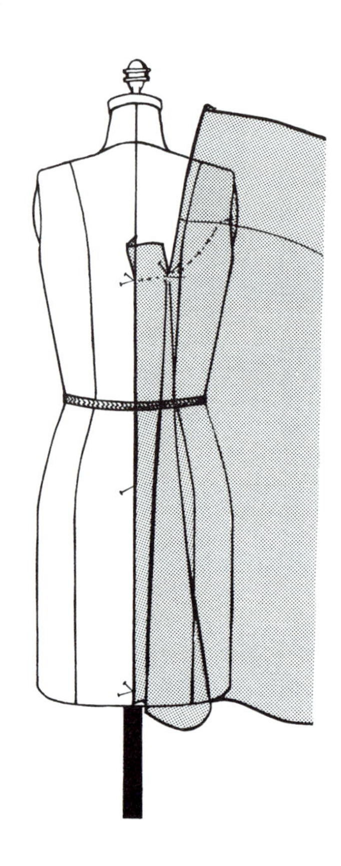

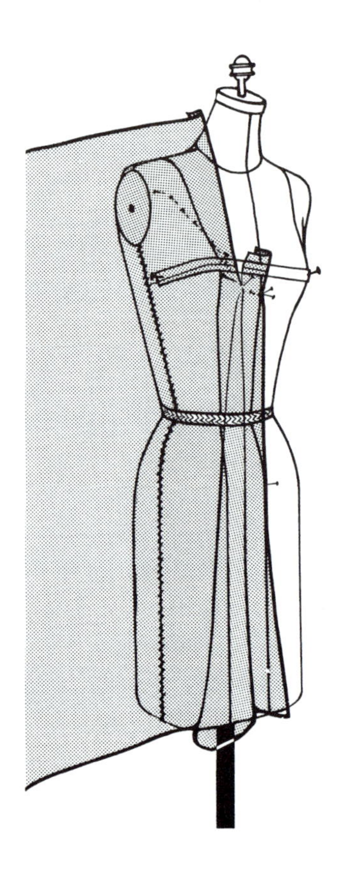

6 **Continue to smooth, clip, pin, and pivot** the front and back style line seam where each flare is desired.

7 **Mark all key areas** from the dress form to the fabric.

Bodice Style Seam Will match the yoke style line seam.

Matching Notches Match to the yoke notches.

Bottom of Armplate at the Side Seam

Side Seam

Hem Follow the bottom of the dress form as a guide.

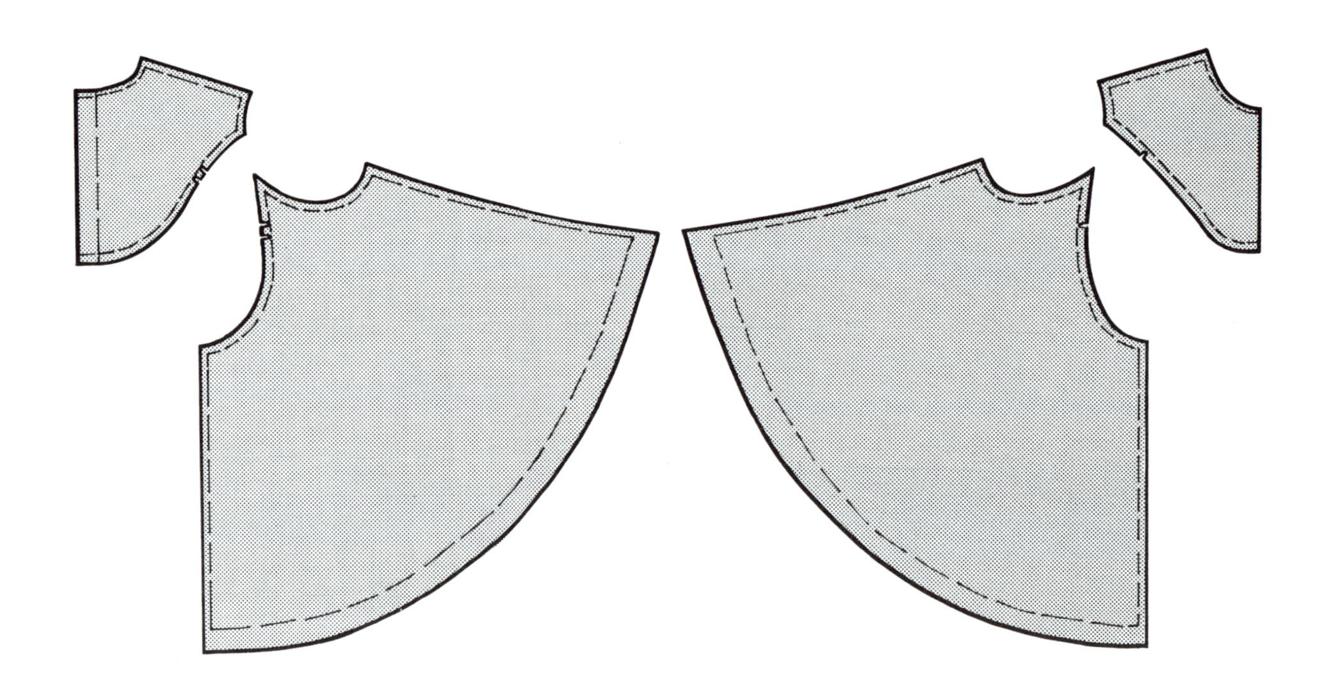

8 True up the front and back bodice drape. Remove the front and back bodice drape from the dress form. True up all seams, add seam allowances, and trim excess fabric.

When trueing the front armhole: Pin the front bodice style line to the front yoke style line. Then, true up the armhole.

When trueing the back armhole: Pin the back bodice style line to the back yoke style line. Then, true up the armhole.

9 Pin the front and back yoke to the front and back bodices. Pin the side seams. Return the drape to the dress form. Check the fit and balance. If necessary, make all corrections.

All-in-One Bodice and Yoke

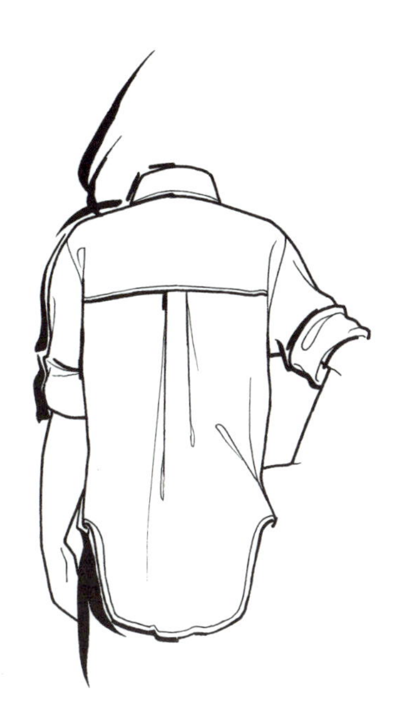

The all-in-one bodice or shirt yoke extends across the shoulder blade level on the back, drapes over the front shoulder, down to the front yoke style line. The all-in-one yoke eliminates the need for the shoulder seam. The technique of draping an all-in-one yoke for either a dartless bodice or a bodice with darts or shirring is the same; the bodice drape is what will differ. Illustrated here are the steps for draping the traditional all-in-one yoke, and then draping a bodice with shirring radiating from the yoke.

The all-in-one yoke is often styled with a dartless shirt (see Shirt Drape, pages 114–115) using neckband collars, shirt armhole, shirt sleeve, front placket openings, and patch pockets. It creates a sporty, carefree, and casual design.

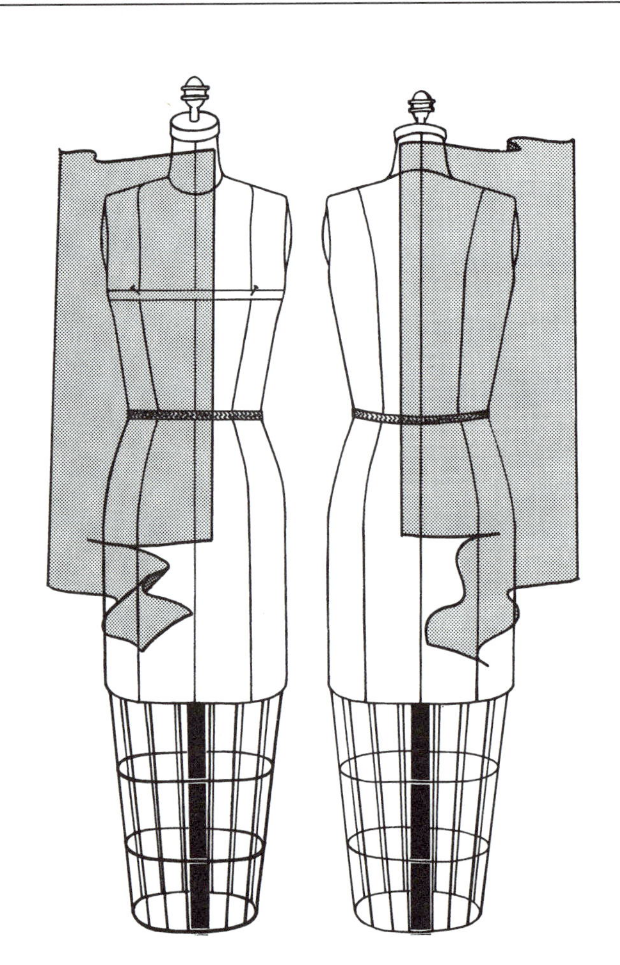

1 **Measure the length and width desired for a front and back bodice piece.** Add a few inches. Snip and tear the fabric at this desired length and width.

2 **Draw the grainline on the front and back bodice** piece 1 inch from the torn edge.

3 **Draw the crossgrain** for the front at the bustline level. Draw the crossgrain for the back at the shoulder blade level.

4 **Mark the apex and side seam. Draw the center of the princess panel line** on the front fabric piece. For more detailed instruction on preparing the bodice fabric pieces, refer to Basic Bodice, page 29.

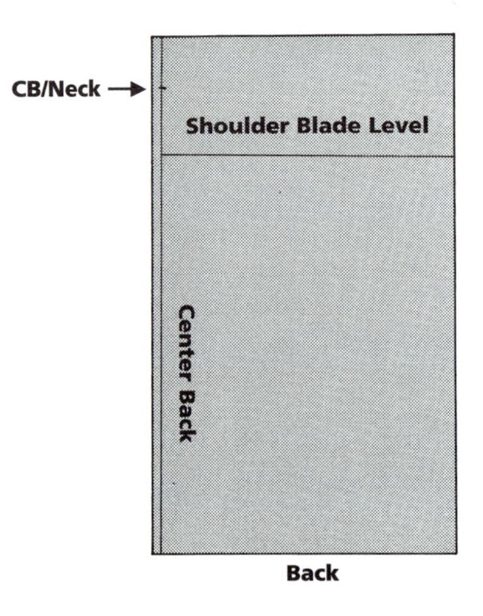

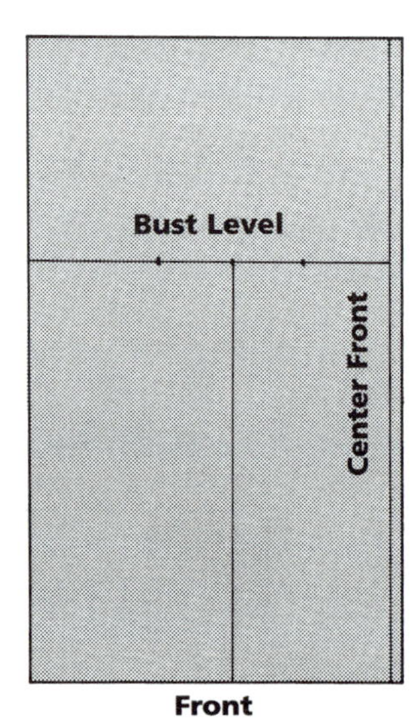

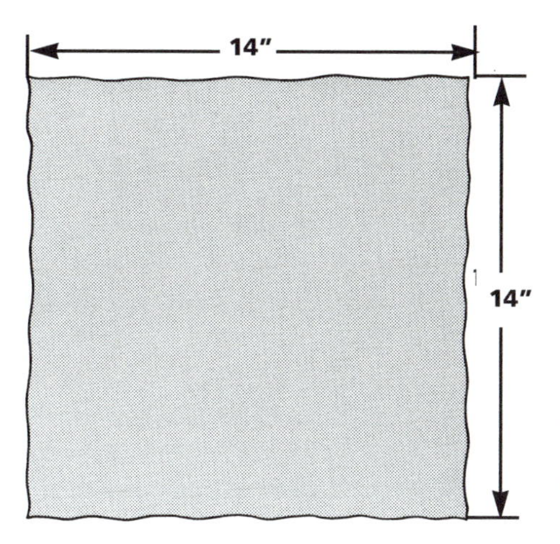

1 **Measure the desired length and width of the yoke.** Cut a perfect square approximately 14 inches.

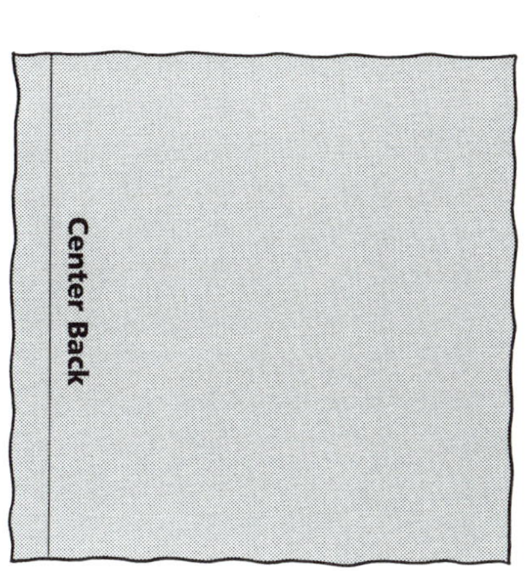

2 **Draw the center back grainline** 1 inch along the torn edge and parallel to the grain of the fabric.

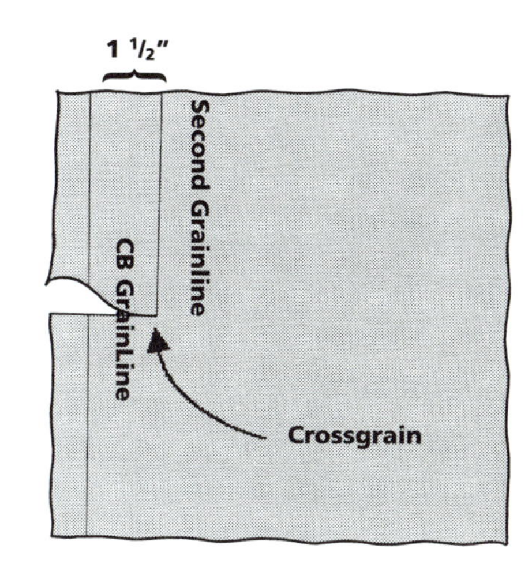

3 **Prepare the back neck opening.**

a. Measure up from the lower edge half the measurement of the fabric piece. Draw a perfect crossgrain 1 1/2 inches long.

b. Draw a second grainline parallel and 1 1/2 inches from the center back grainline.

c. Cut the fabric on the crossgrain line and on the second grainline and remove this rectangular piece of fabric.

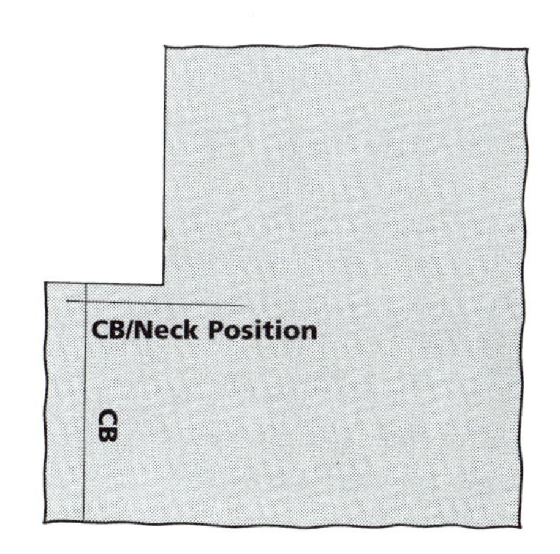

4 **Draw a short crossgrain line** 1/2 inch below the cut crossgrain. This indicates the center back/neck position.

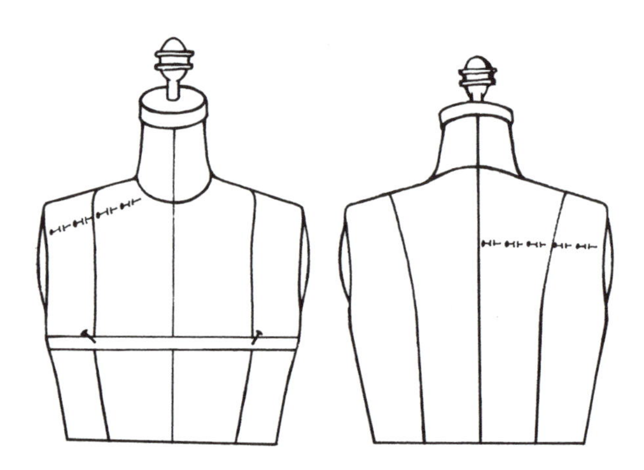

Prepare the dress form.

Pin the desired yoke style line on the dress form.

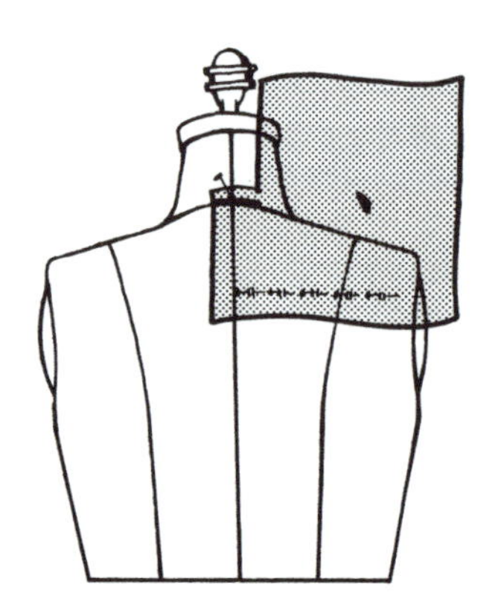

1. **Pin the center back grainline of the yoke** fabric at the center back position of the dress form.

2. **Align the neckline position mark** on the fabric to the neckline seam on the dress form.

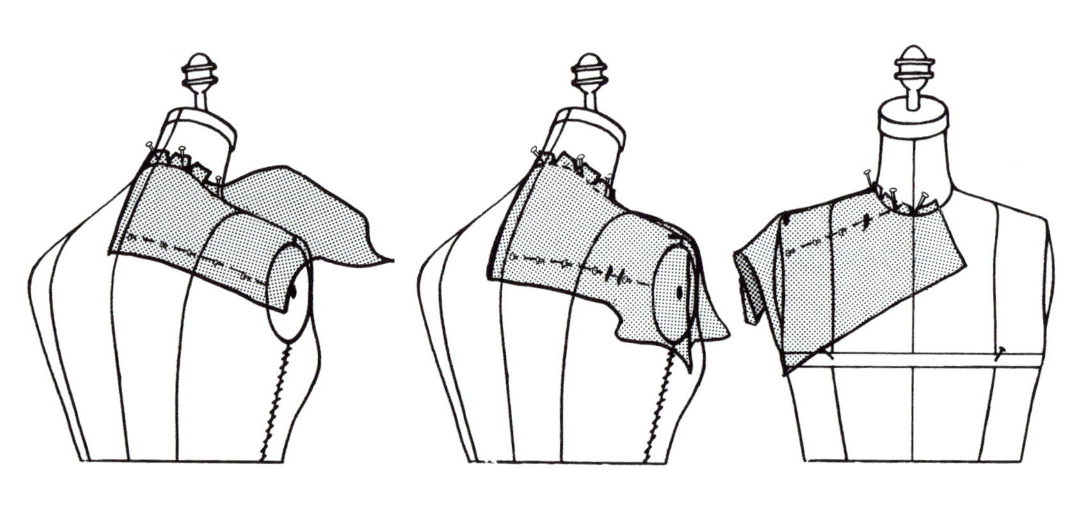

3. **Clip, smooth, and pin the neckline** until the fabric lies smoothly over the shoulder of the dress form. Continue to clip, smooth, and pin the front neckline until the fabric touches the front style line.

4. **Mark all key areas** of the dress form to the fabric.

Draw the style line and the style line to notches
Single on front; double on back.

Mark the armhole ridge
Crossmark the ridge on the front and back yoke.

Neckline

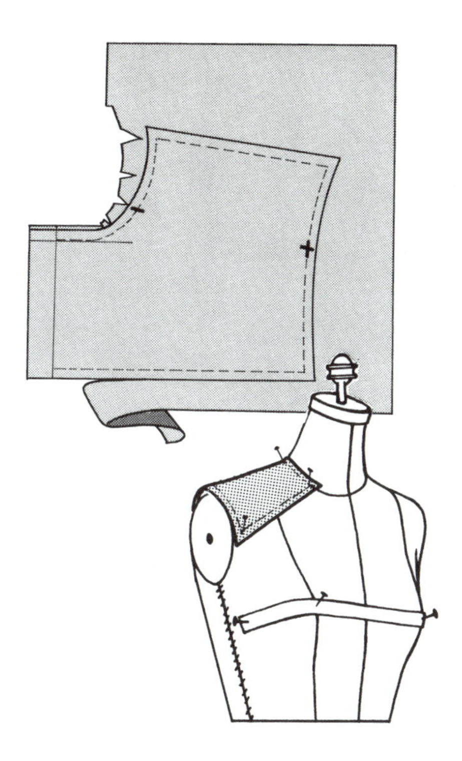

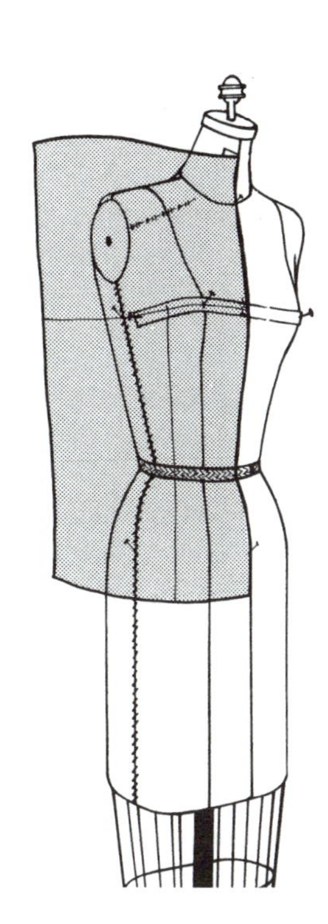

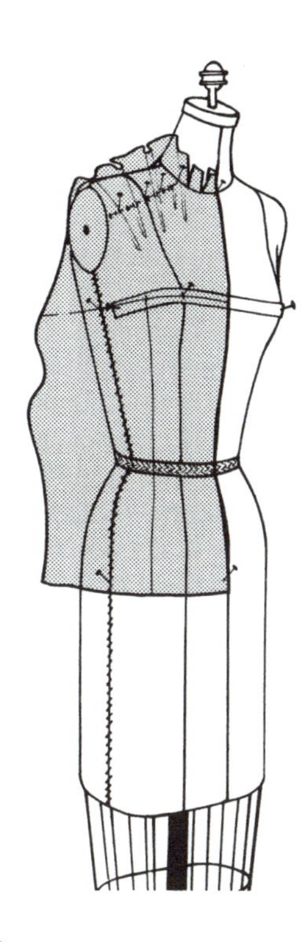

5 **True up all seams.** Remove the yoke drape from the dress form, true up all seams, add seam allowances, and trim excess fabric. Return the finished yoke to the dress form and check for accuracy, fit, and balance.

6 **Drape the front bodice grainline.** Pin the center front grainline fold of the fabric on the center of the dress form.

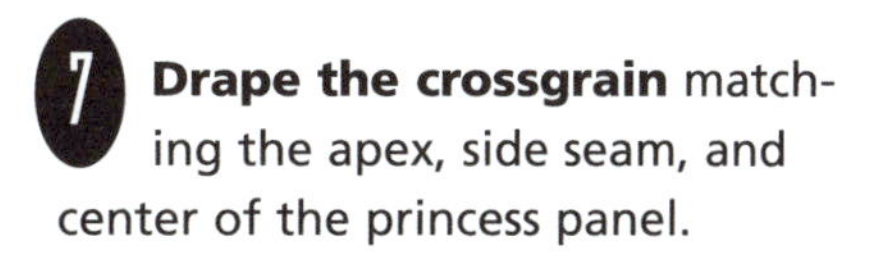

7 **Drape the crossgrain** matching the apex, side seam, and center of the princess panel.

8 **Smooth the fabric up from the crossgrain.** Evenly distribute all excess fabric into the yoke style line. Clip, trim, and smooth in the neckline.

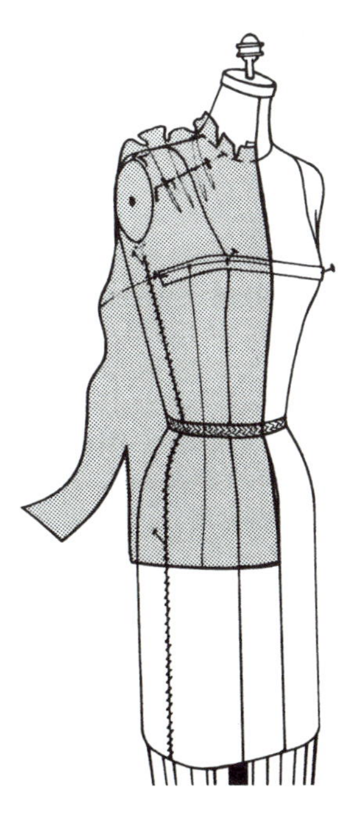

9 **Mark all key areas** of the dress form to the fabric.

Neckline Lightly mark the remaining of the neckline.

Yoke Style Line

Matching Notches Match to the yoke notches.

Armplate
a. Shoulder ridge.
b. Plate at screw level.
c. Plate at side seam.

Side Seam Mark and trim excess fabric, leaving enough for trueing and seam allowances.

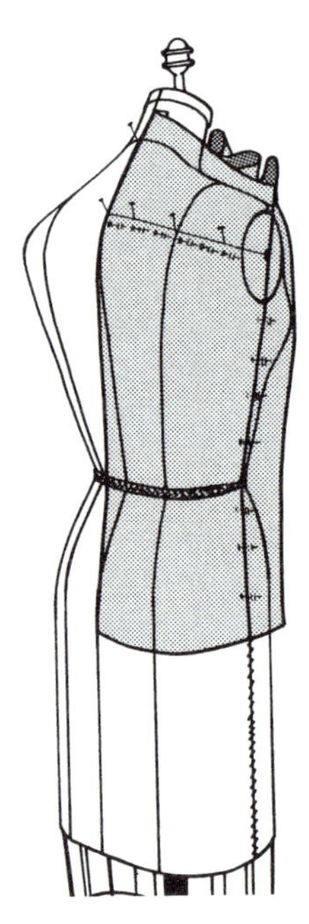

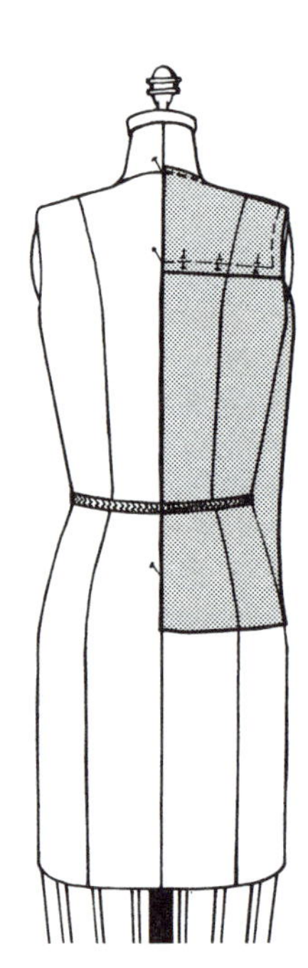

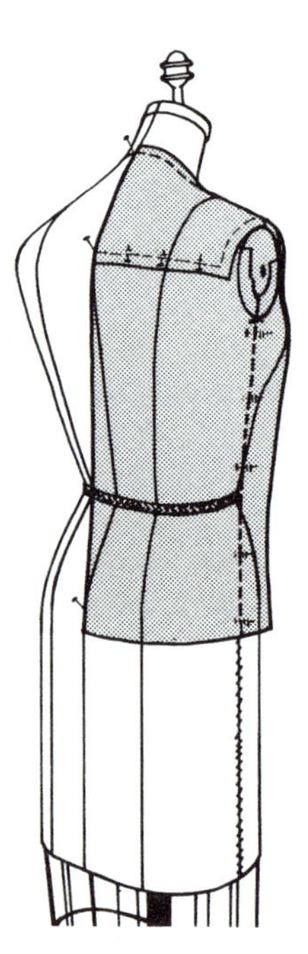

10 **Place the back straight of grainline** to the center back of the dress form.

11 **Align the crossgrain** at the shoulder blade level. Pin in place. Allow the fabric to hang smoothly and freely from the shoulder blade level.

12 **Pin the front side seam to the back side seam.**

13 **Drape and pin the back style line** seam up into the back yoke seam. Pin the yoke to the bodice drape.

14 **Mark all key areas** from the dress form to the fabric.

Back Yoke Style Line

Matching Notches Match to the yoke notches.

Bottom of Armplate at the Side Seam

Side Seam

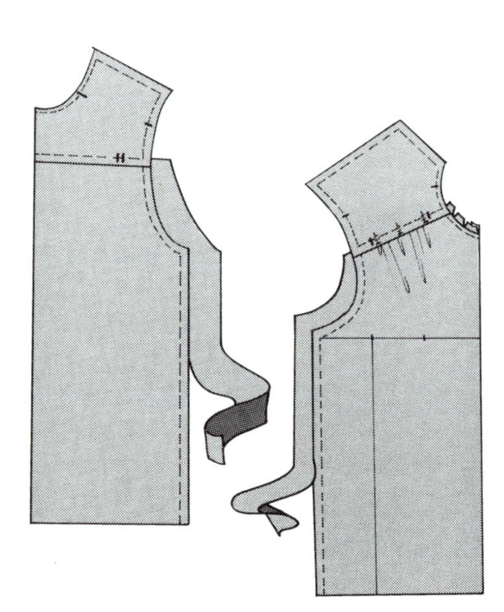

15 **True up all seams.** Remove the fabric drape (front, back, and yoke) from the dress form. True up all seams, add seam allowances, and trim excess fabric.

When trueing the front armhole: Pin the front bodice style line to the front yoke style line. Then, true up the armhole.

When trueing the back armhole: Pin the back bodice style line to the back yoke style line. Then, true up the armhole.

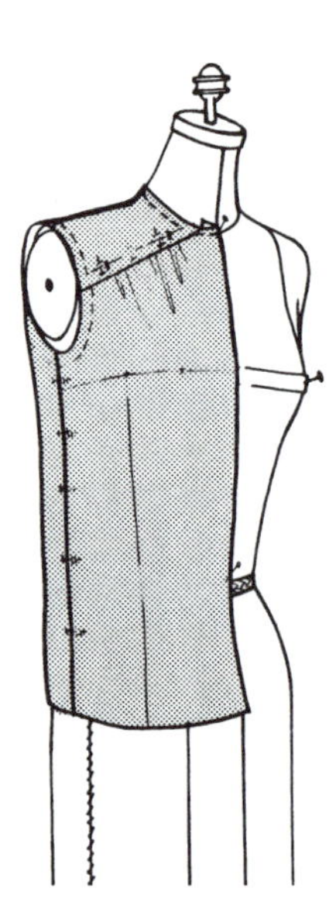

16 Return the finished drape to the dress form and check for accuracy, fit, and balance.

Hip Yoke

A skirt hip yoke is a fitted top portion of a skirt without the use of darts. A horizontal seam in the hip area divides the skirt into two sections. The yoke seam may be designed parallel to the waistline or shaped into any pointed or curved shape desired. The lower portion of the yoke may be connected to a skirt by means of shirring, gores, or pleats, without the use of darts. The hip yoke controls a waistline fit and supports the remainder of the skirt design, whether it is gathered, straight, or circular.

The hip yoke with a gathered skirt section can create many different looks. The yoke may be shaped in a variety of styles and widths. The amount of fullness in the skirt section depends on the particular style. The gathered skirt that falls from a styled yoke enables a designer to complete a style in which the fullness in the skirt hangs straight up and down (hanging plumb). At the same time, the designer can control the amount of fullness desired. The gathered skirt is a classic design, allowing the designer to use border prints.

Hip Yoke—Preparing the Fabric

Prepare the dress form.
Pin or use style tape for the desired yoke design.

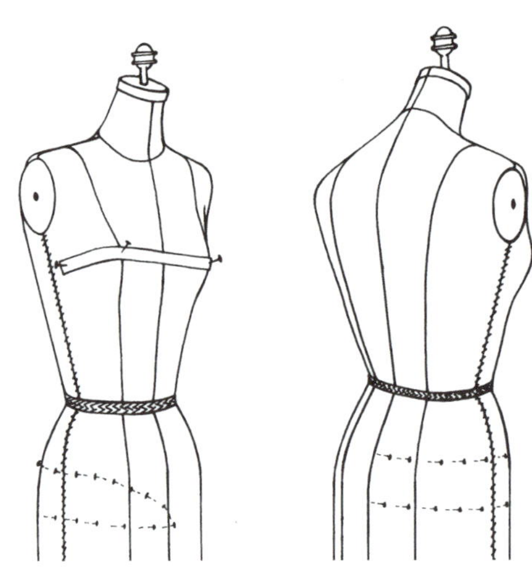

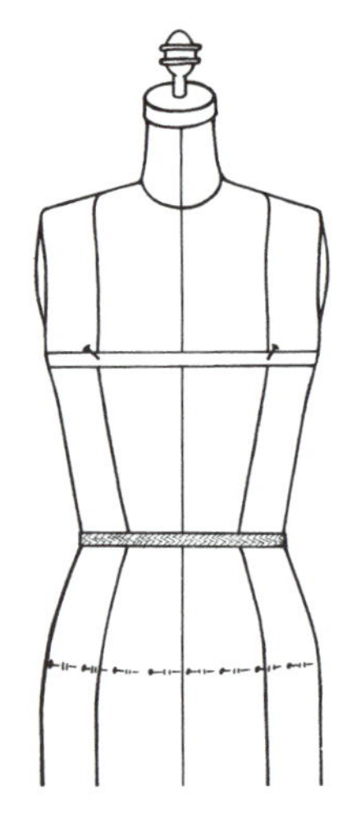

Straight Yoke

1 **Measure the length** (along the straight of grain) for both the front and back yokes, and add 5 inches. Snip and tear the fabric at this length.

2 **Measure the width** of the widest part of the desired front and back yoke area (hip), and add 5 inches. Snip and tear the fabric at this width.

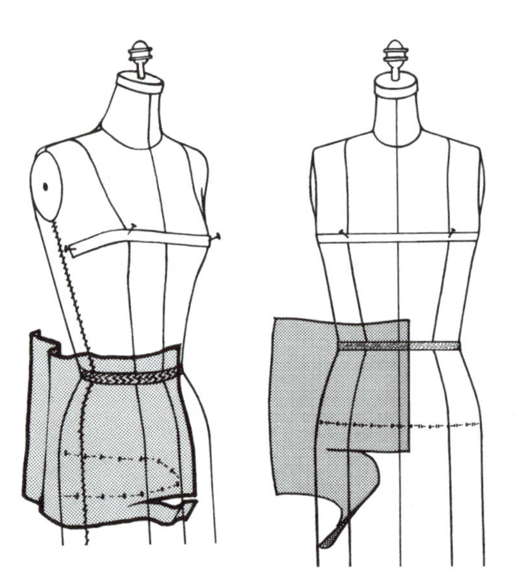

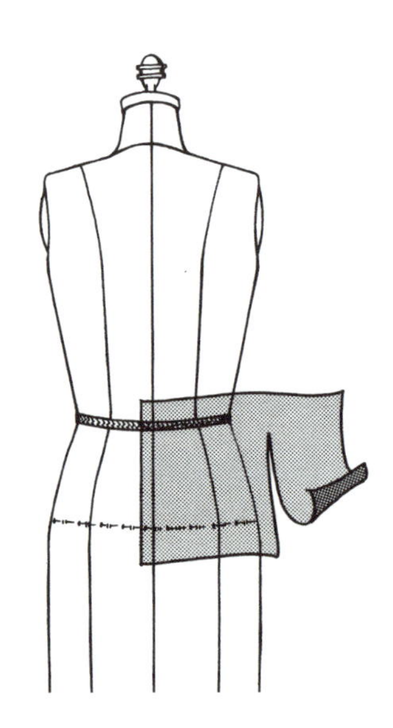

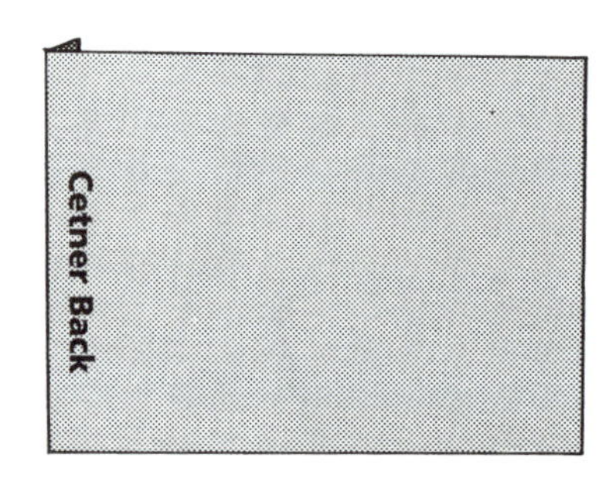

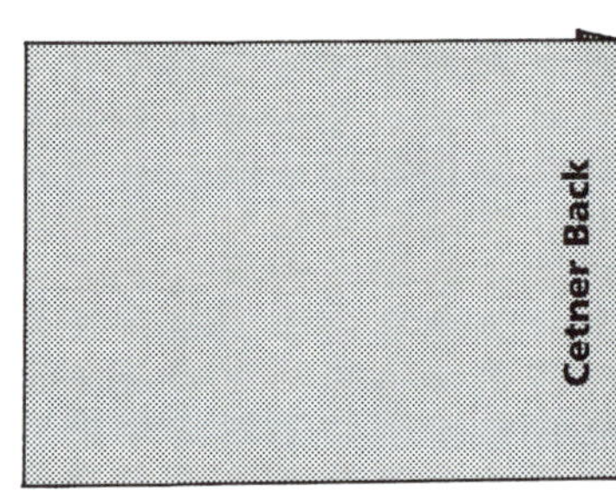

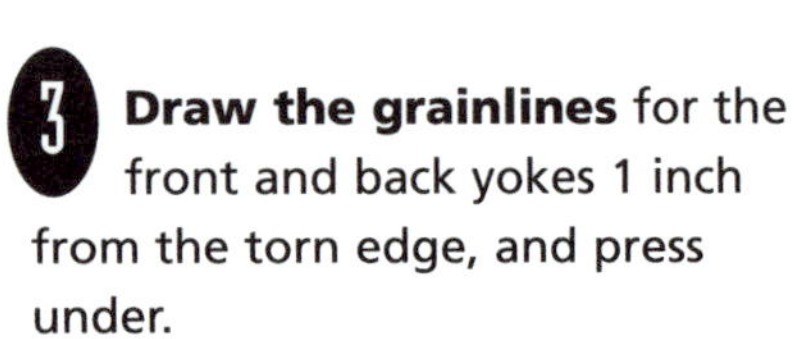

3 **Draw the grainlines** for the front and back yokes 1 inch from the torn edge, and press under.

4 **Crossmark a waistline position.** From the top edge of the fabric (on the front grainline) measure down 5 inches and crossmark.

1 Establish the center front/center back yoke grainline.

a. Place the center front grainline fold of the yoke piece on the center front position of the dress form. Extend the yoke piece 2 inches above the waistline.

b. Place the center back grainline fold of the back yoke piece to the center back position of the dress form. Extend the yoke piece 2 inches above the waistline.

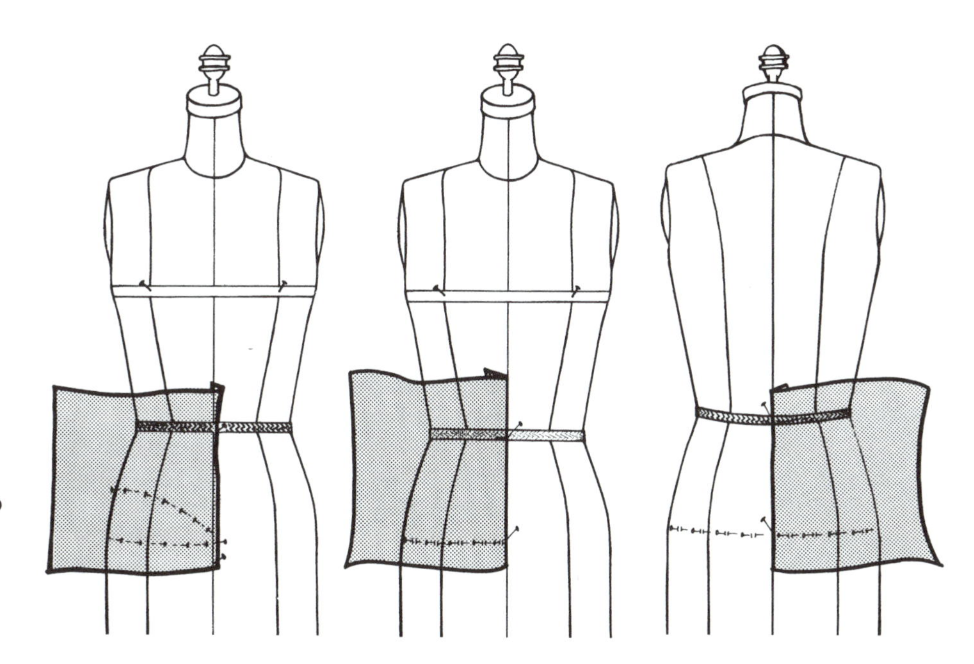

2 Drape the front and back yoke waistline. Trim and clip the fabric from the top of the fabric down to the waistline. (Be careful not to clip past the waistline position.) Drape and smooth the fabric at the waistline from the center of the dress form over to the side seam. Anchor a pin at the side seam/waist corner.

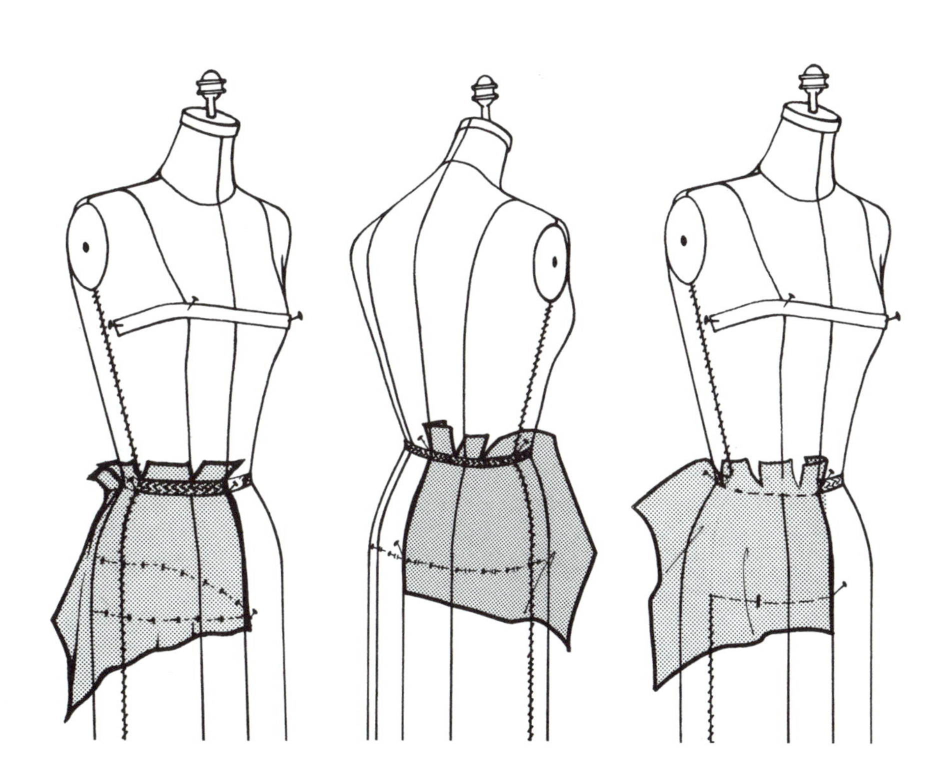

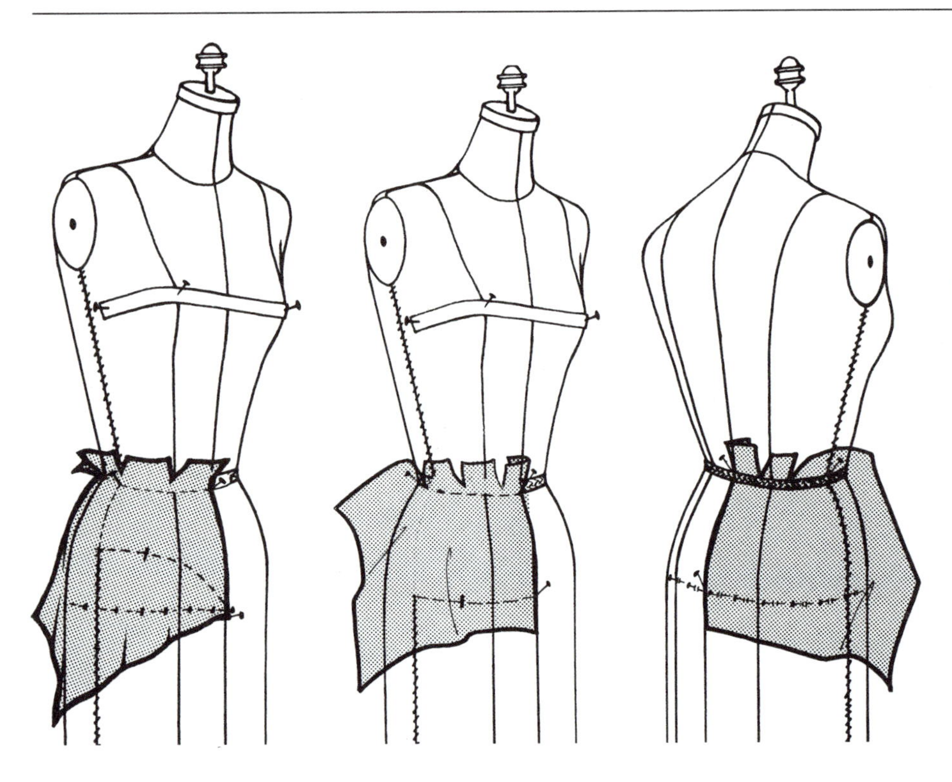

3 **Mark all key areas** of the dress form to the front yoke fabric.

Waistline Front and Back

Side Seam Front and Back

Front and Back Yoke Style Lines

Yoke Style Line Notches One for the front and two for the back.

4 **True up all lines.** Remove the front and back yoke drape from the dress form. True up all lines, add seam allowances, and trim excess fabric. Pin the front and back yoke side seam to each other. Return the yoke drape to the dress form to drape the skirt section.

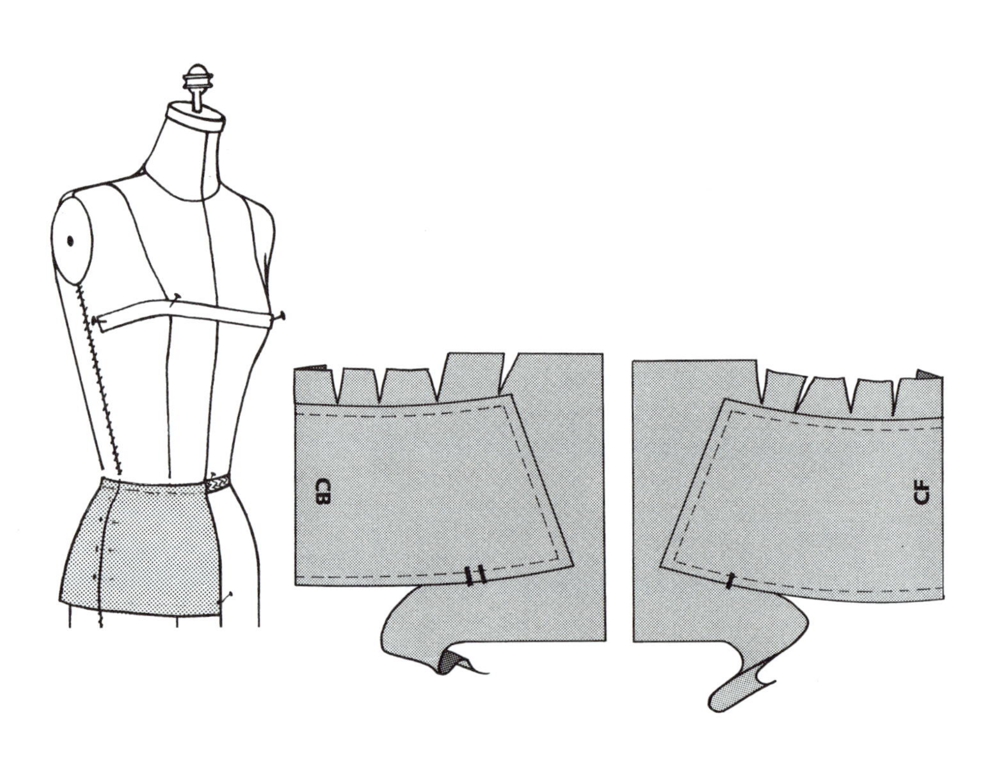

Circular Skirt with Hip Yoke—Preparing the SkirtFabric

For instructions of different skirt designs, refer to Skirts, page 149.

1 **Measure the length** (along the straight of grain) for the front and back skirt.

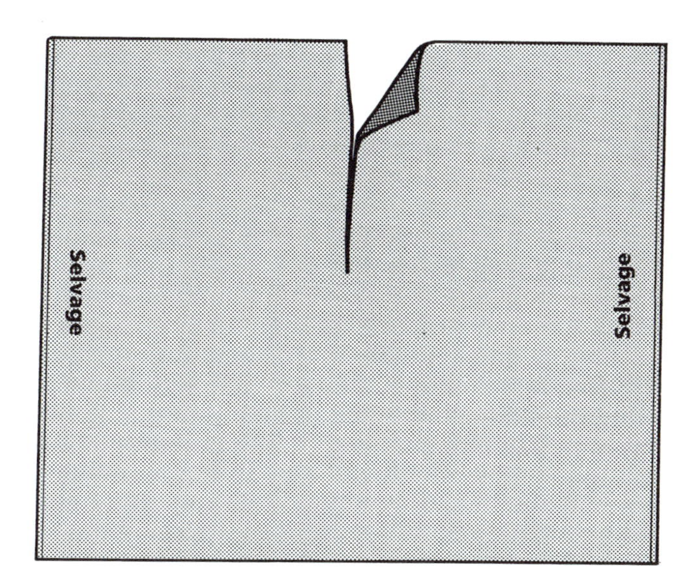

2 **Fold the fabric from selvage to selvage.** Snip and tear the fabric in half. One piece will be used for the front skirt and the other piece will be used for the back skirt.

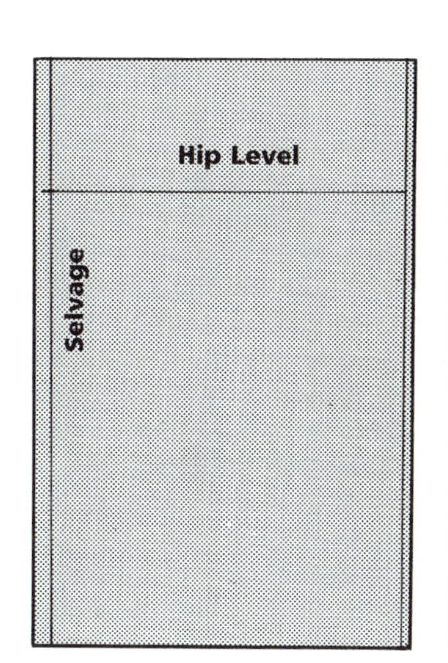

3 **Draw the straight of grainlines and crossgrains** for the front and back skirt.

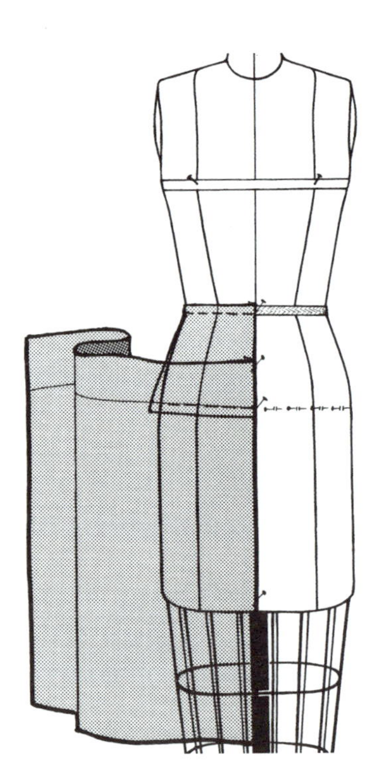

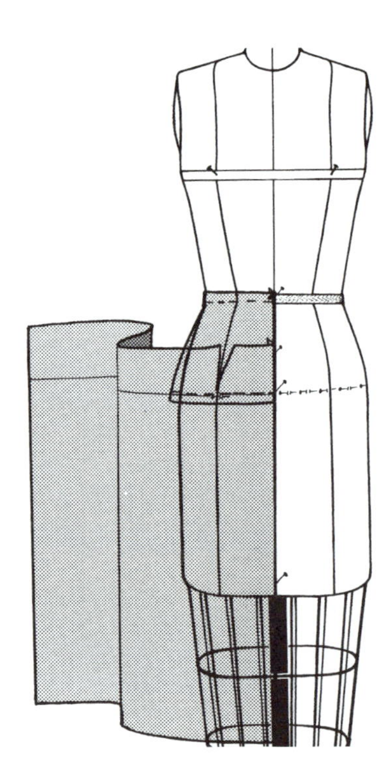

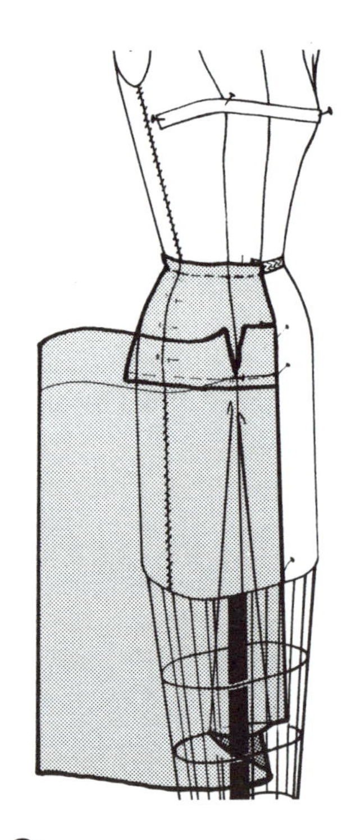

1 Pin the center front grainline fold of the skirt on the center front position of the dress form.

2 Align the crossgrain at the hip level. Pin the crossgrains at the hip level and not the yoke style seam. In this sketch, however, both the yoke style seam and the hip level are the same.

3 Smooth, clip, and pin the skirt style line.
Approximately 3 inches from center front, smooth, trim, and clip the fabric from the top edge down to the yoke style seam.

Pin the skirt style seam to the yoke style seam, and not to the dress form.

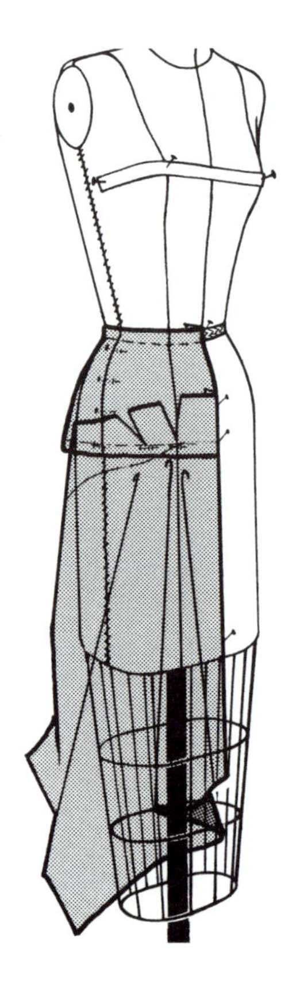

4 Pivot the fabric down from the style seam at the princess area, forming a nice flowing flare. Pin the skirt style seam to the yoke style seam, maintaining this flare.

5 **Smooth, clip, pin, and pivot approximately 1 inch from the first flare.** At the skirt style seam, smooth the fabric toward the side seam. Pin, clip, and pivot the skirt style seam at this position, forming a second flare.

6 **Continue to smooth, pin, clip, and pivot** the front skirt style seam where each flare is desired.

7 **Mark all key areas** of the dress form to the fabric.

Skirt Style Seam and Matching Notches
Side Seam
Hem: Follow a rung on the dress form.

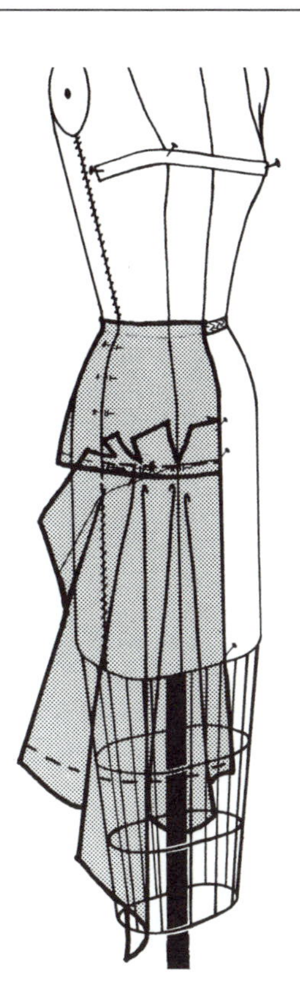

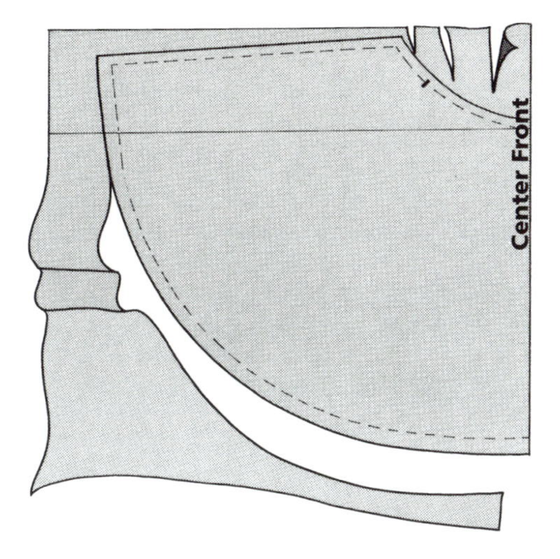

8 **True up the front skirt drape.** Remove the front skirt drape from the dress form. True up the front skirt drape, add seam allowances, and trim excess fabric.

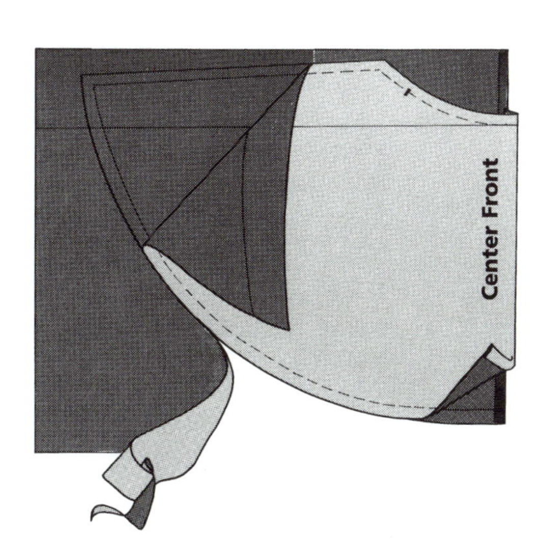

9 **True up the back skirt.**

a. Place the skirt front drape on top of the prepared fabric for the back drape, matching the crossgrains of the front and back skirt.

b. Place the center fold grainlines parallel, allowing the front to extend 1/2 inch over the back grainline, but still parallel. This distance allows for the difference between the back style seam amount and the front style seam amount.

c. Draw in the skirt back stitchlines, following the same markings as the skirt front (style seam, side seam, and hem).

10 **Pin the yoke and skirt fabric piece together** and return to the dress form. Check the fit and balance. If necessary, make all corrections.

Gathered Skirt with Hip Yoke—Preparing the Fabric

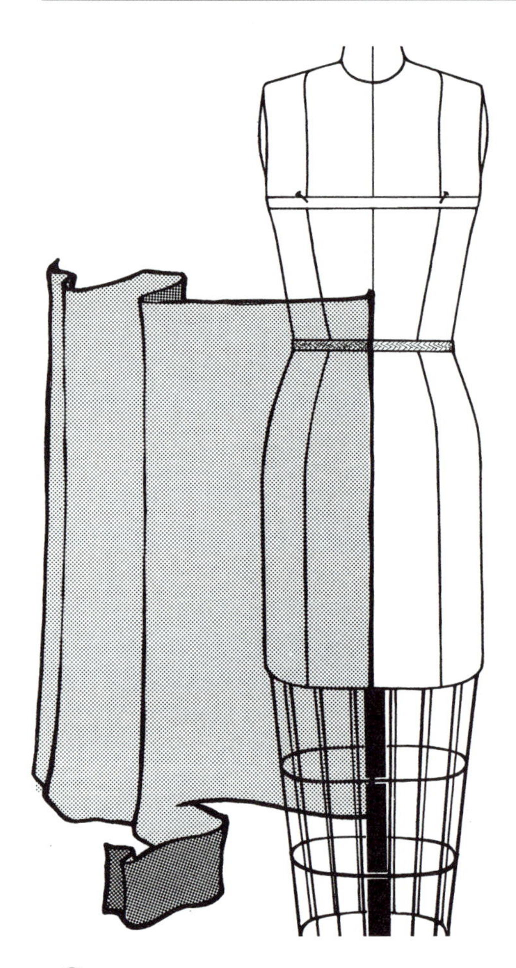

1 Measure the length along the straight of grain for both the front and back skirts.

2 Divide the fabric piece in half. Fold the fabric from selvage to selvage. Snip and tear the piece in half lengthwise.

One piece will be used for the skirt front and the other piece will be used for the skirt back.

3 Draw all the grainlines and crossgrain lines for the front and back skirt. For more detailed instructions in preparing the skirt fabric, refer to The Dirndl Skirt/Preparing the Fabric, pages 167–168.

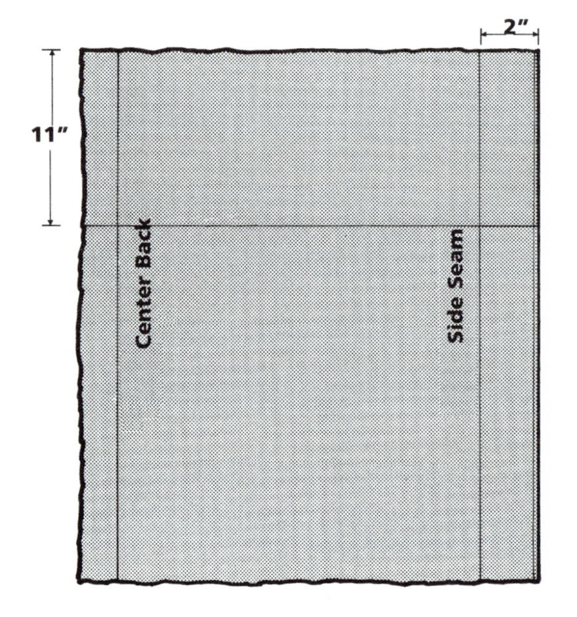

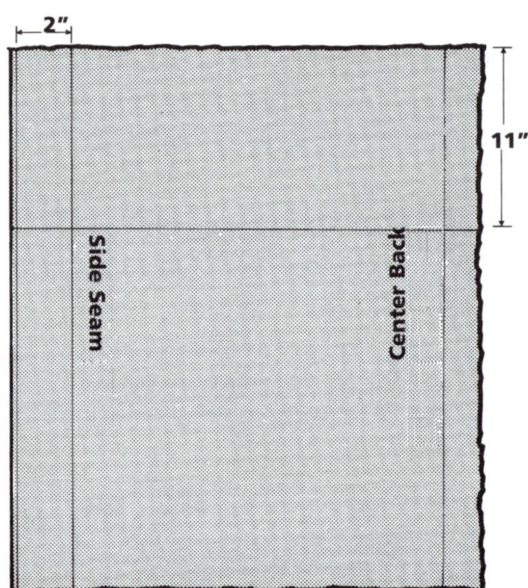

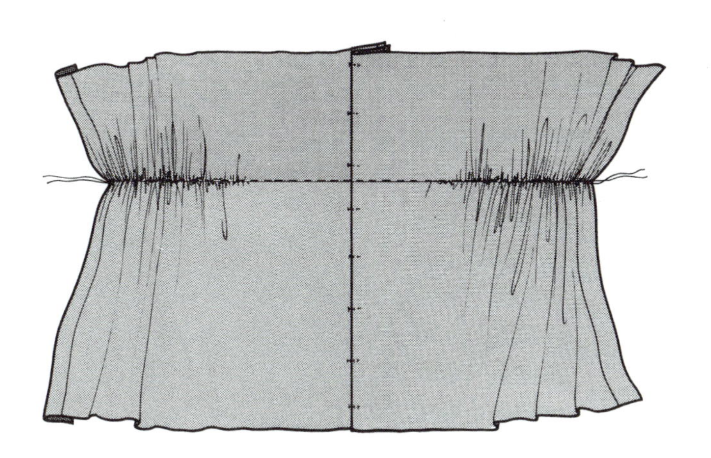

1 **Gather the fabric on the crossgrain line** on both front and back. Pin the side seams together.

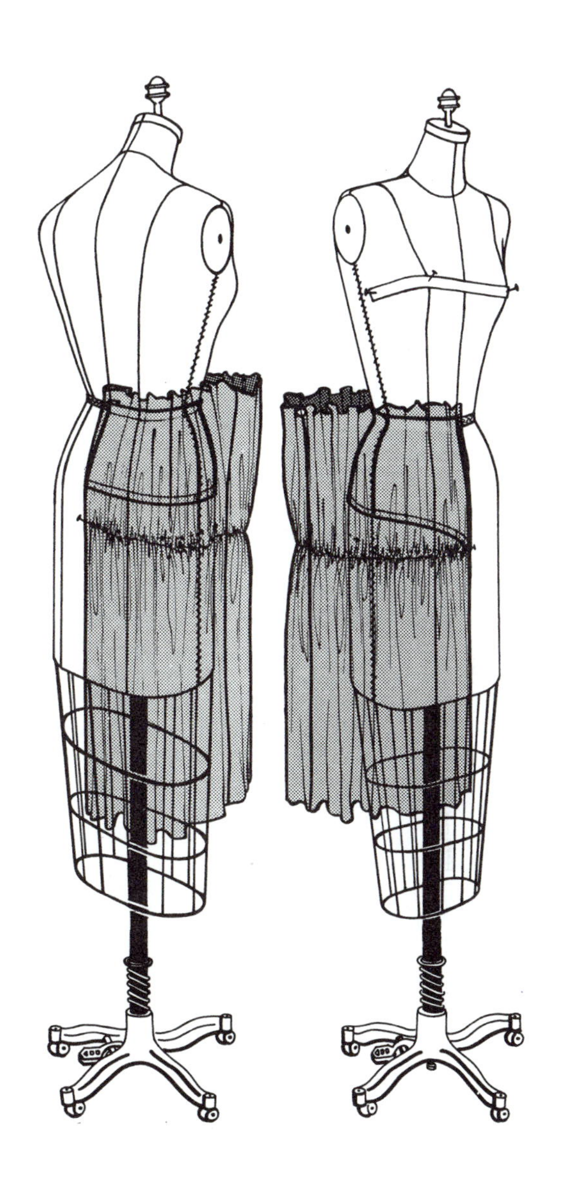

2 **Pin the center front and center back grainline** folds of the fabric on the center positions of the dress form.

3 **Align front and back crossgrains** at the hip level. Pin the crossgrains in place.

NOTE: Be sure to pin the crossgrains at the hip level and not at the yoke line.

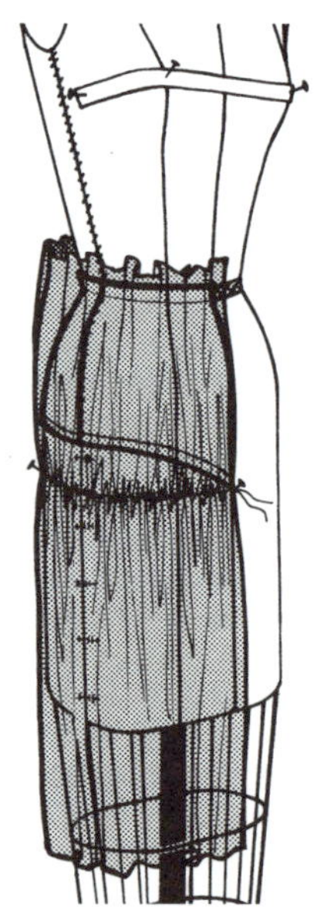

4 **Pin the side seams** of the fabric on the side seams of the dress form. Evenly distribute the gathered fabric across the dress form.

NOTE: Be sure the fabric cross-grains are parallel to the floor and the side seams match the side seams of the dress form.

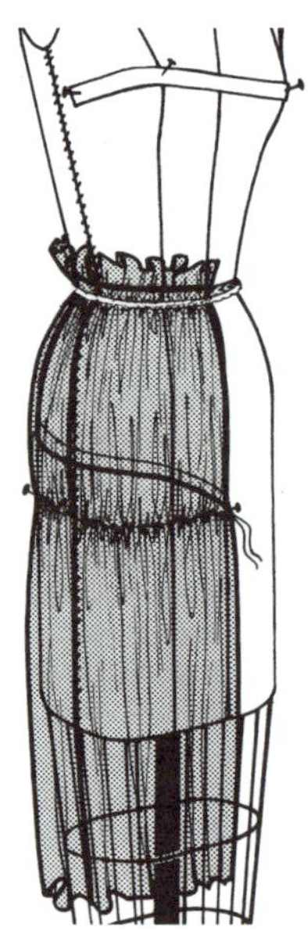

5 **Gather up the fabric at the waistline** with a piece of twill tape. Evenly distribute the gathers.

NOTE: The skirt is draped over the desired yoke.

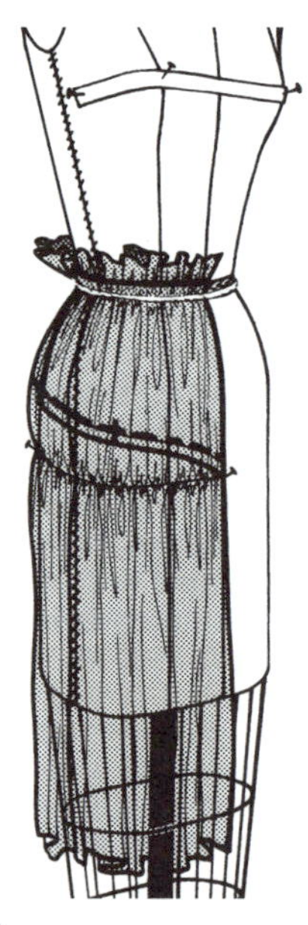

6 **Mark key areas.**

Yoke Style Line Through the gathers.

Style Line Notches

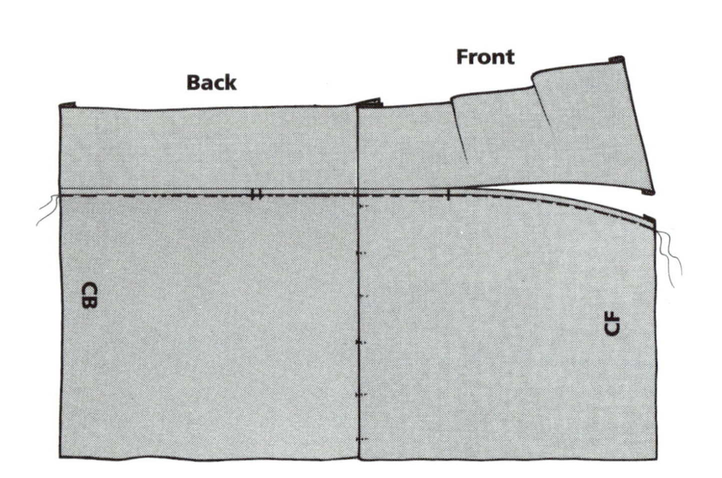

7 **True up the drape.** Remove the fabric from the dress form and true up the drape. Add seam allowances and trim excess fabric.

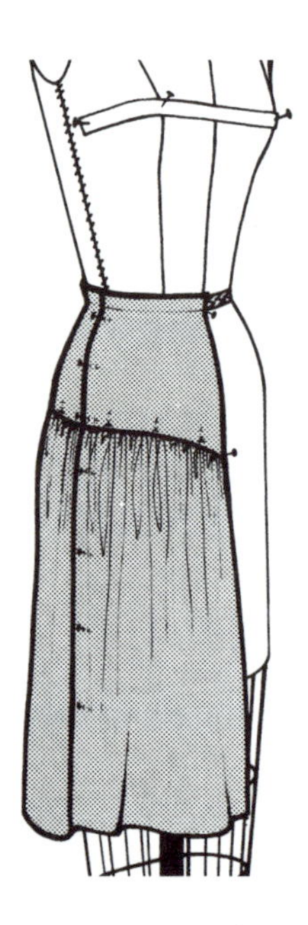

8 **Pin the gathered skirt to the styled yoke** and place on the dress form to check for accuracy, making all necessary corrections.

Pleated Skirt with Yoke—Preparing the Fabric

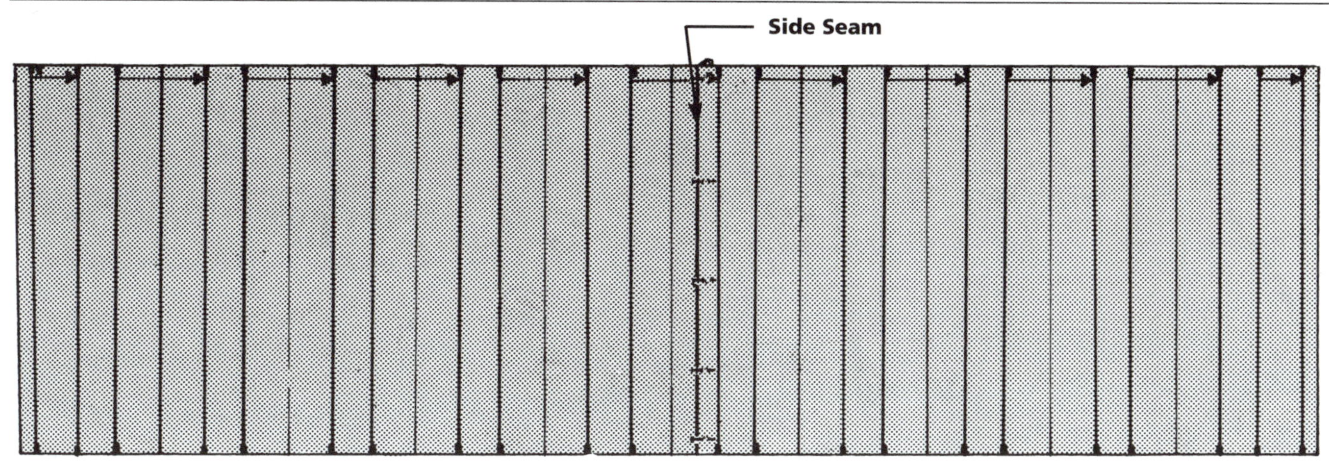

1 Measure the length along the straight of grain for both the front and back skirts. Use the entire width of the fabric for the front and another piece for the back.

2 Pin the side seams together, allowing for the necessary seam allowances.

NOTE: Prepare the hip yoke drape (see pages 349–350). Prepare the dress form.

3 Starting from the side seam, mark two times the width of each pleat on both sides of the side seam.

4 Mark the distance of the space between the pleats. Continue these measurements for the entire width of the fabric.

5 Pleat the fabric for both the front and back until the entire width of the fabric is used.

6 Draw in a crossgrain 9 inches down from the top of the fabric.

Pleated Skirt with Yoke—Draping Steps

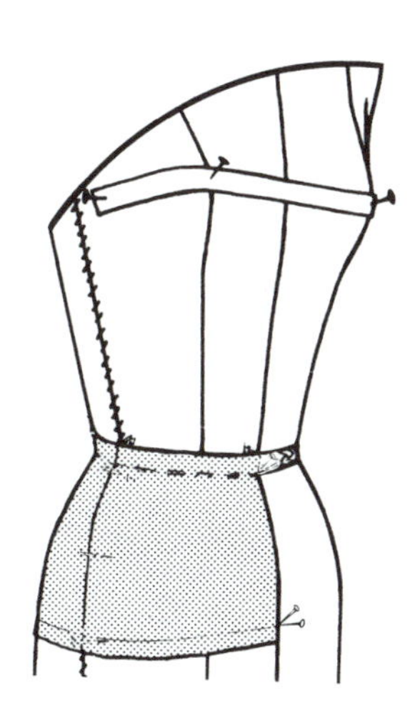

1 Drape the yoke and draw in the desired style line.

2 Pin the center front and center back grainline folds of the fabric on the center positions of the dress form.

3 Align front and back crossgrains at the hip level. Pin the crossgrains in place.

NOTE: Be sure to pin the crossgrains at the hip level and not at the yoke line.

4 Trim the excess fabric at the yoke seam, leaving enough for seam allowances.

Waist Midriff

A waist midriff design has a horizontal seam between the bust and the waistline. A waist midriff traditionally fits snugly under the slope of the bust while maintaining the shape of the waistline and controlling the fit of the remainder of the bodice design. Usually, the midriff is simply styled parallel to the waistline or shaped into any pointed or curved shape desired.

Waist Midriff—Preparing the Midriff Fabric

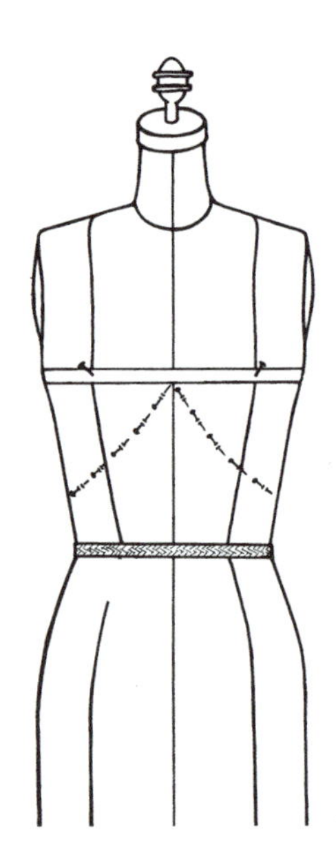

Prepare the dress form.
Pin the desired midriff style line on the dress form front and back.

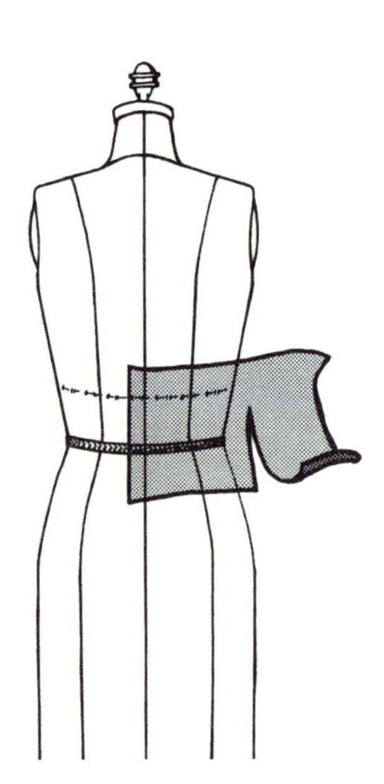

1 Measure the length for the front and back midriff (along the straight of grain) from the top of the midriff to the waistline, and add 6 inches. Snip and tear the fabric at this length.

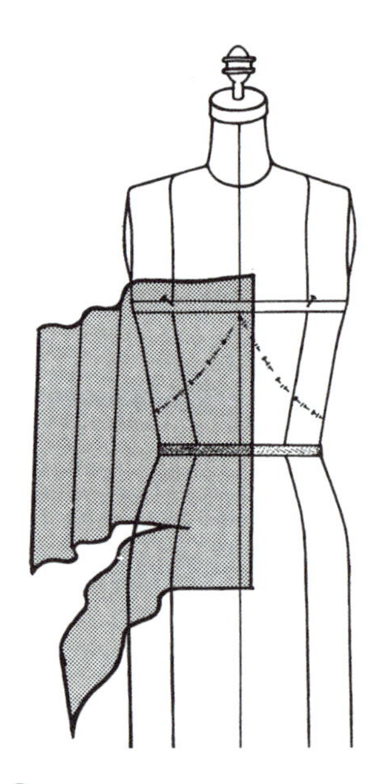

2 Measure the width for the front and back midriff (along the crossgrain) from the center front to the side seam, and add 3 inches. Snip and tear the fabric at this width.

3 **Draw center front and center back grainlines** 1 inch from the torn edge on the prepared midriff pieces, and press under.

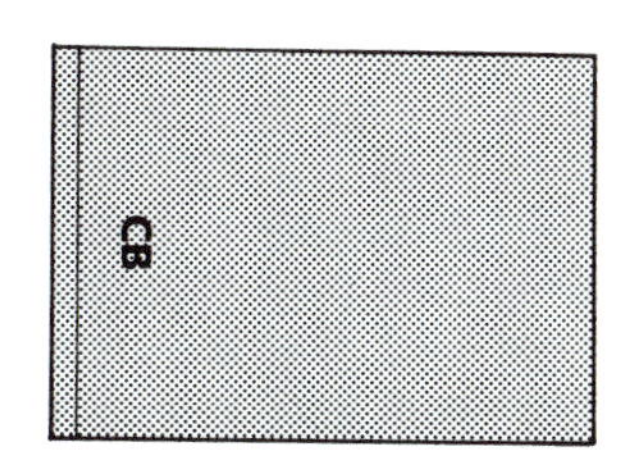

Waist Midriff—Preparing the Bodice Fabric

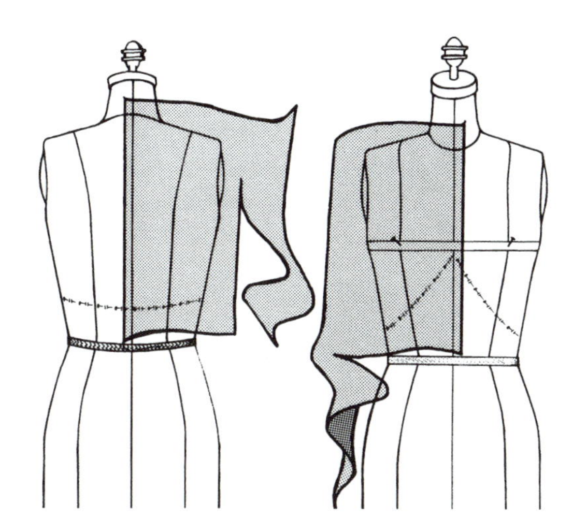

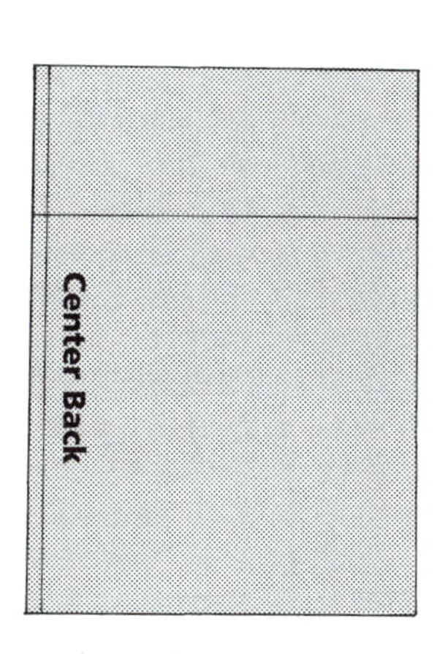

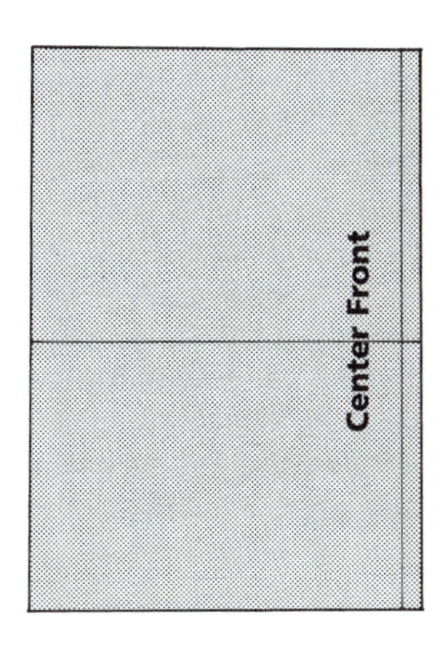

1 **Measure the length and width desired for the front and back bodice,** add a few inches. Snip and tear the fabrics the desired length and width.

2 **Draw the straight of grainlines and crossgrains for the front and back bodice fabric pieces.**

a. Draw the grainline on the front and back bodice 1 inch from the torn edge and press under.

b. Draw the crossgrain for the front at the bustline level and the crossgrain for the back at the shoulder blade level.

For more detailed instructions, refer to Basic Bodice, pages 29.

Waist Midriff—Midriff Draping Steps

1 **Pin the center front grainline of the midriff** to the center front position of the dress form. Align the fabric so it extends above and below the desired midriff section.

2 **Pin the center back grainline of the midriff** to the center back position of the dress form. Align the fabric so it extends above and below the desired midriff section.

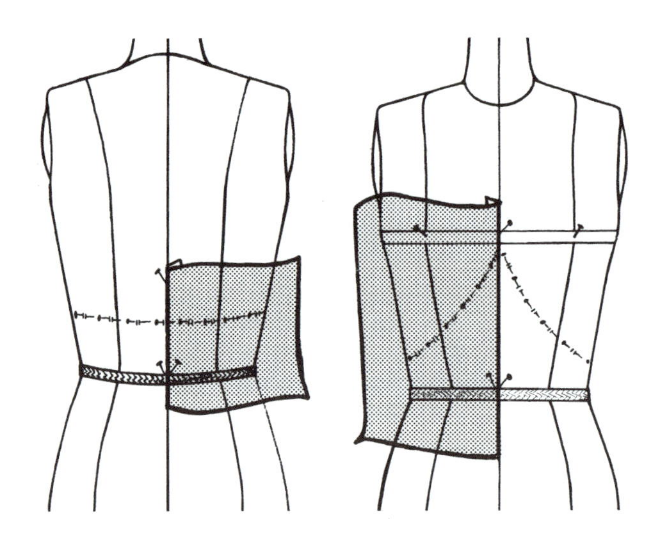

3 **Drape the front and back midriff waistline.** Clip the fabric at the front and back waistline. Smooth the fabric across the waistline tape toward the side seam.

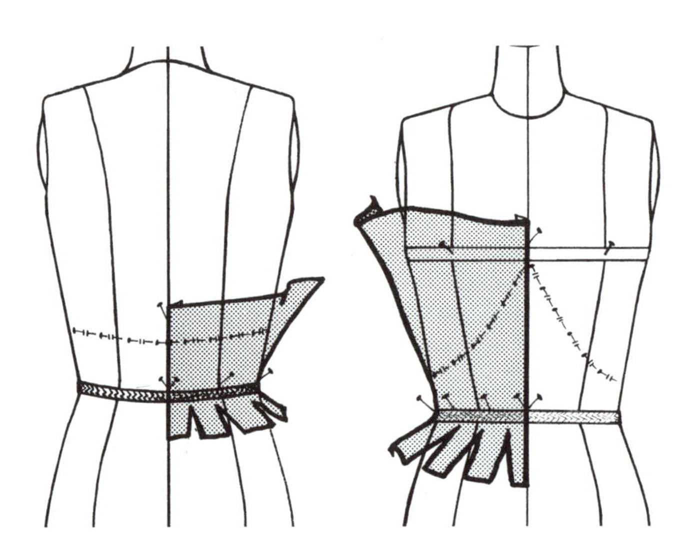

4 **Drape the front and back midriff style line.** Clip the fabric at the front and back style line. Smooth the fabric across the style line seam toward the side seam.

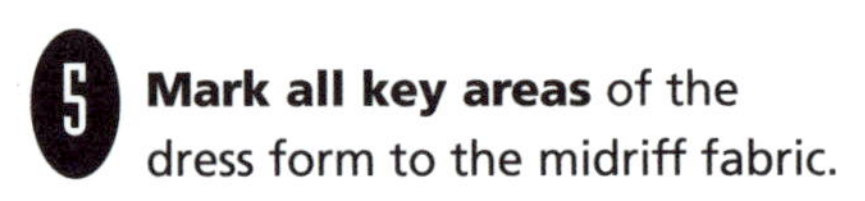

5 **Mark all key areas** of the dress form to the midriff fabric.

Midriff Style Line

Side Seam

Waistline

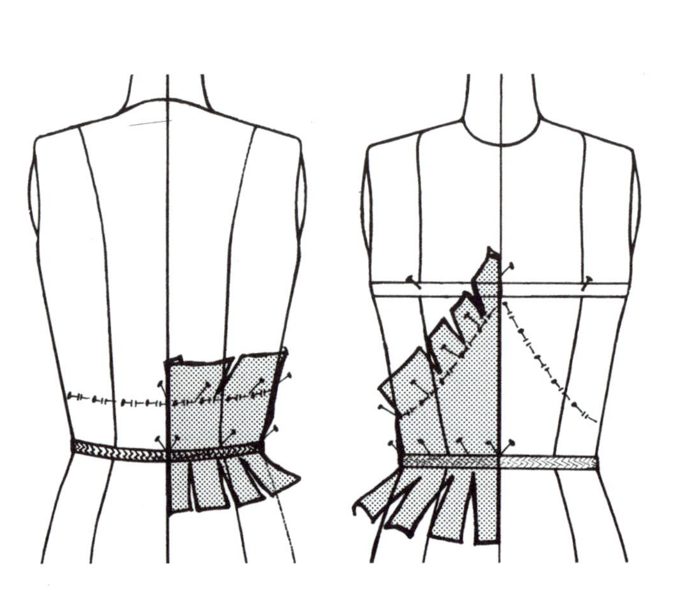

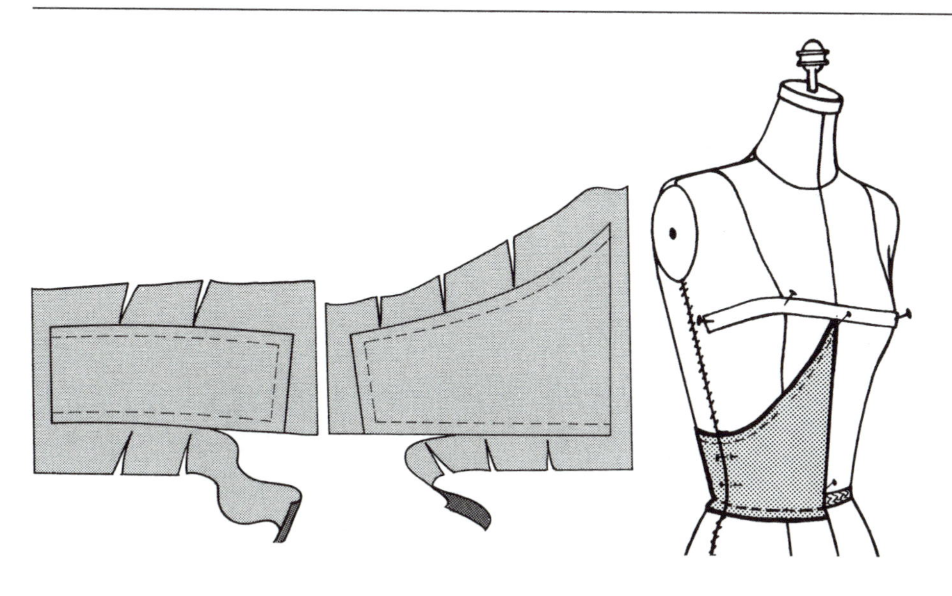

6 **True up all seams.** Remove the front and back midriff drape from the dress form. True up all seams, add seam allowances, and trim excess fabric. Pin the front side seam to the back side seam. Return the midriff to the dress form and check for accuracy.

Notes

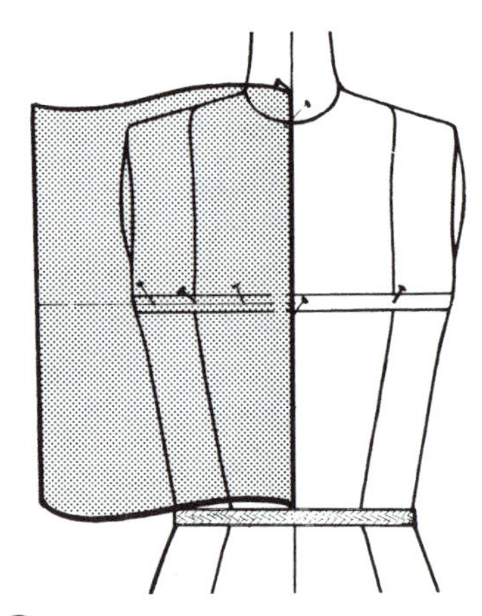

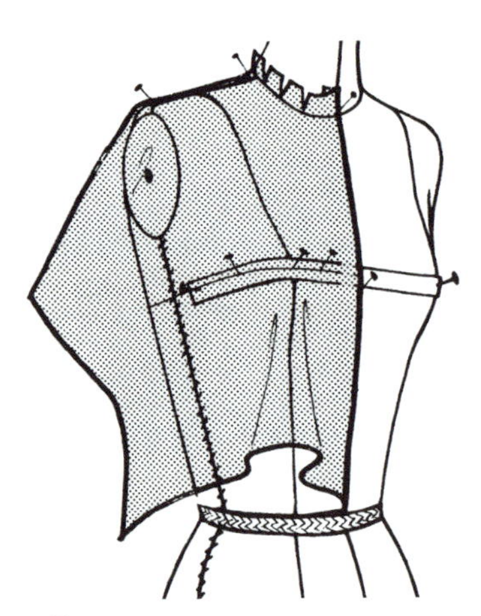

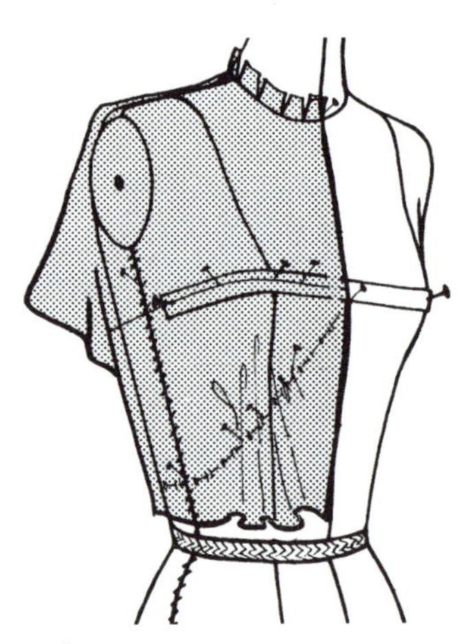

1 **Pin the center front grainline of the bodice** to the center front position of the dress form. Align the crossgrain at the bustline level. Pin in place.

2 **Trim, clip, smooth, and pin the front bodice neckline.**

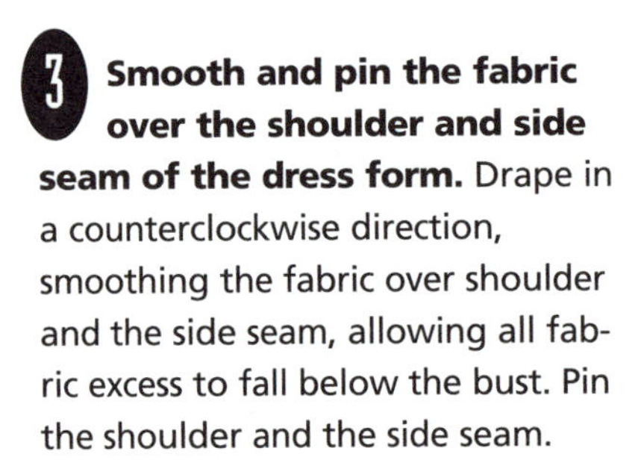

3 **Smooth and pin the fabric over the shoulder and side seam of the dress form.** Drape in a counterclockwise direction, smoothing the fabric over shoulder and the side seam, allowing all fabric excess to fall below the bust. Pin the shoulder and the side seam.

4 **Drape the front bodice into the midriff style line.** With the excess fabric falling underneath the bust area, evenly distribute and pin all fullness at the midriff style line below the bust area. Drape the remainder of the bodice smoothly into the midriff.

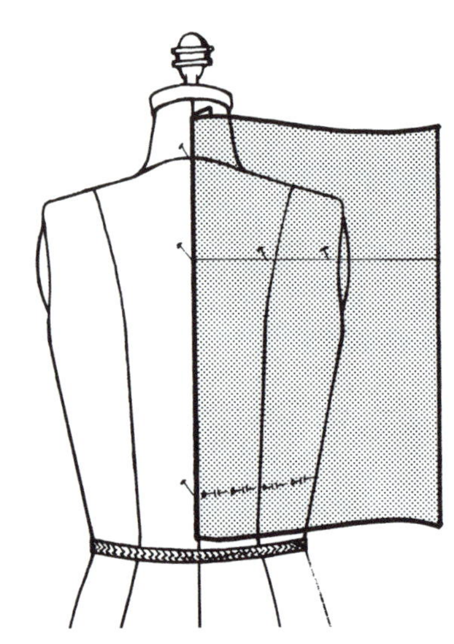

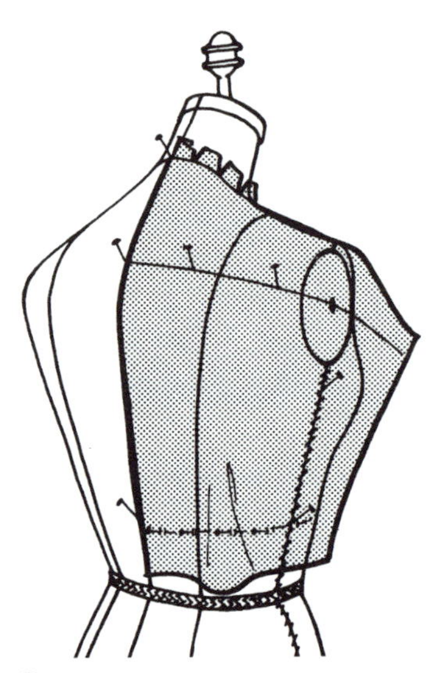

5 **Drape the back bodice.** Pin the center back grainline of the back bodice to the center back of the dress form.

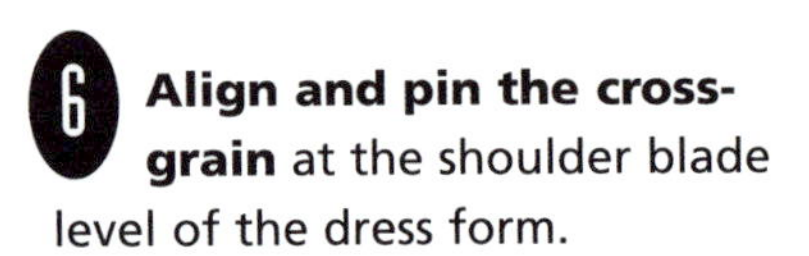

6 **Align and pin the crossgrain** at the shoulder blade level of the dress form.

7 **Trim, clip, smooth, and pin the back bodice neckline.**

8 **Smooth and pin the fabric over the shoulder and side seam of the dress form.** Pin in place. Some excess fullness will fall at the midriff seam in the middle of the back. This excess fullness will be converted into gathers.

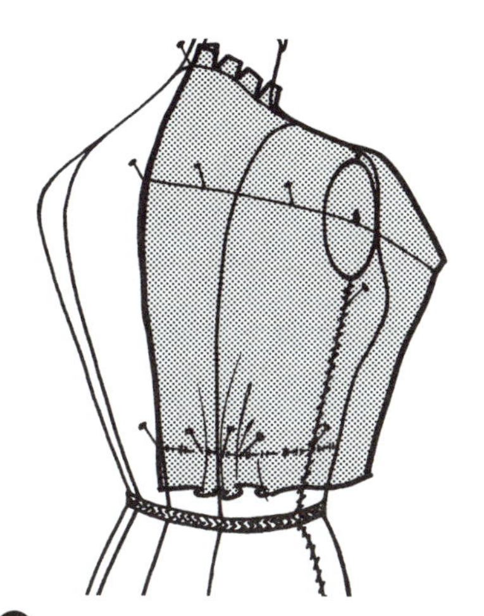

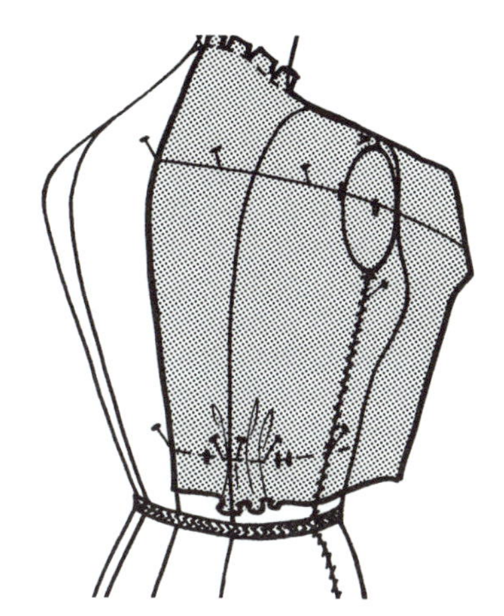

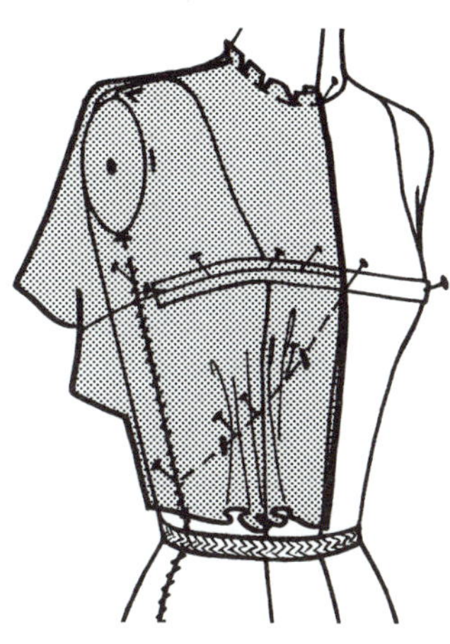

9 **Drape the back bodice into the back midriff style line.** Evenly distribute and pin all fullness at the midriff style line. Pin the entire midriff style line.

10 **Mark all key areas** of the dress form to the front and back drape.

Front and Back Neckline Shoulder Seams

Armplate
a. Shoulder ridge.
b. Center and screw level.
c. Bottom and side seam.

Side Seams

Midriff Style Line and Style Line Notches

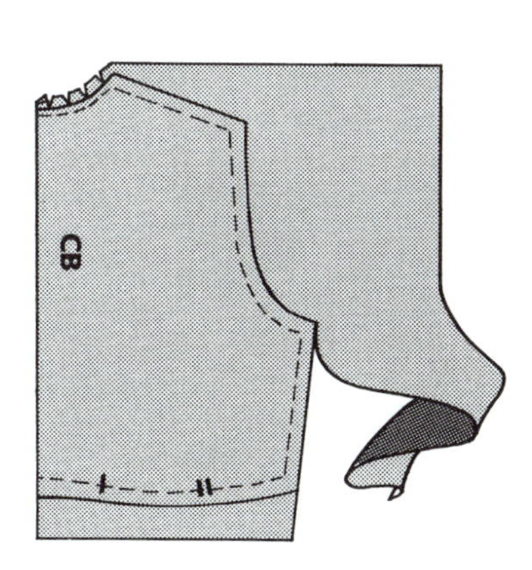

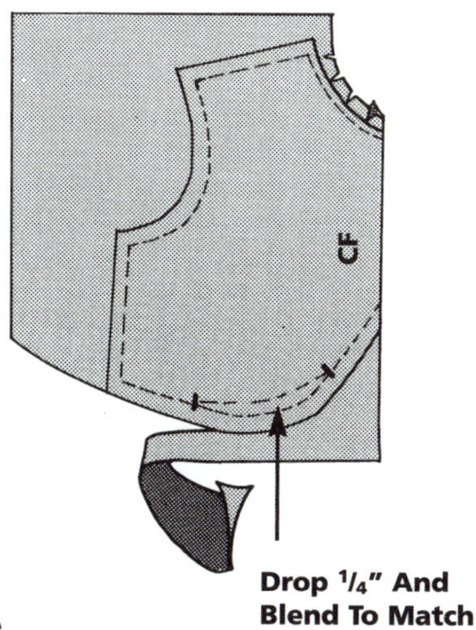

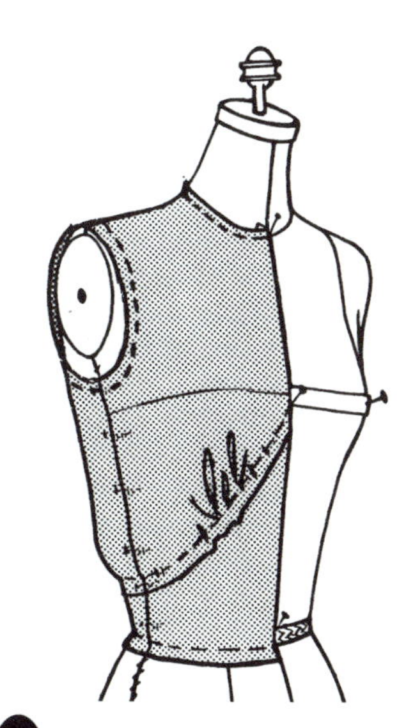

11 **True up all seams.** Remove the drape (front, back, and midriffs) from the dress form. True up all seams, add seam allowances, and trim excess fabric.

NOTE: The front bodice style line, between the midriff notches, may need to be dropped 1/4 inch. This allows the bodice drape to give the illusion of a fuller bust.

12 **Pin the midriff and bodice fabric pieces together** and return to the dress form. Check for accuracy, fit, and balance. If necessary, make all corrections.

Chapter Twenty

Cowls

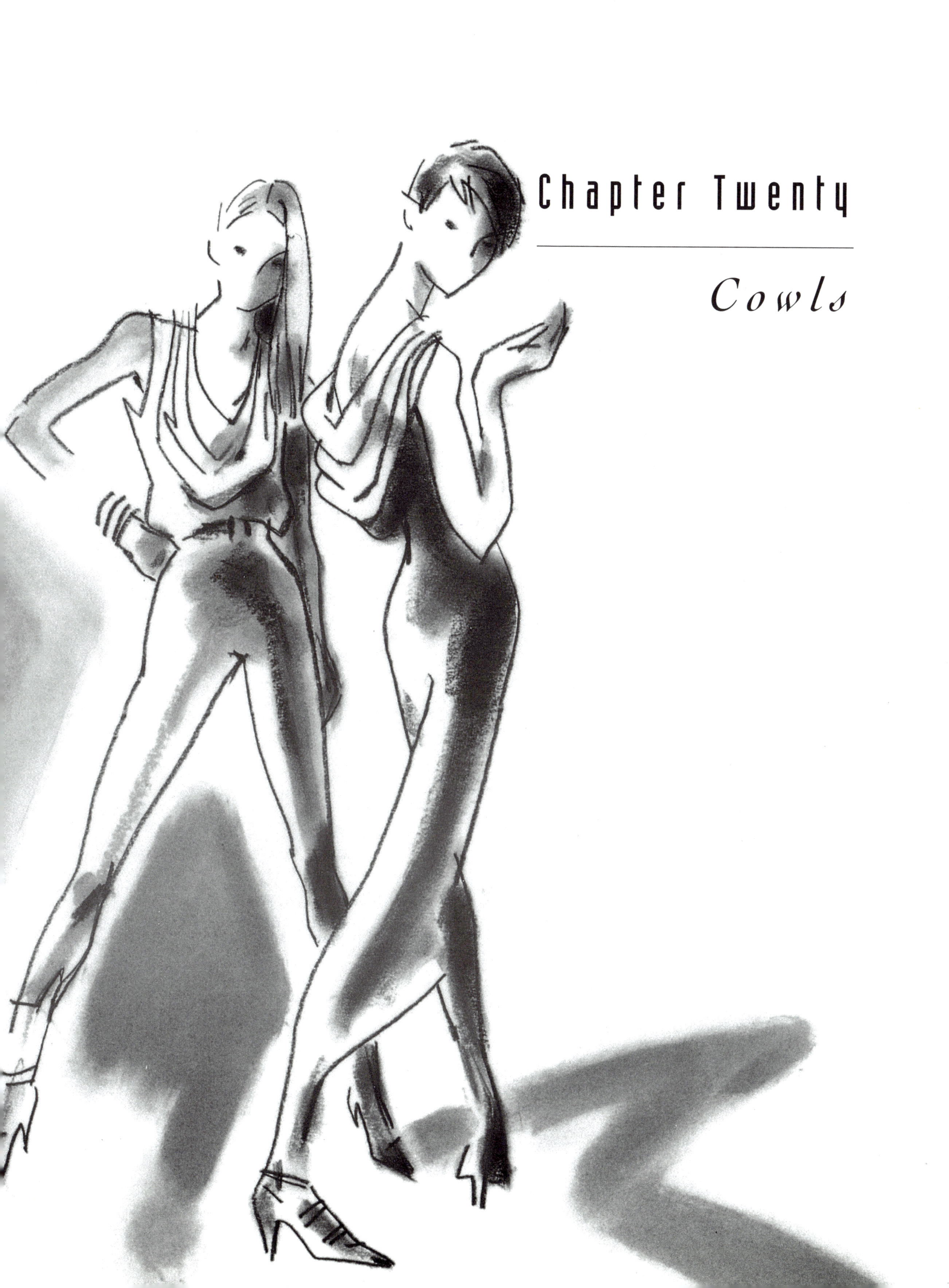

Objectives

By studying the various draping steps in this chapter, the designer should be able to accomplish the following:

- Drape a fitted bodice cowl design utilizing a soft fabric cut on the bias.
- Manipulate the bias fabric to fit the curves of the body over the bust and shape it over the contour of the body with a waistline seam.
- Visualize the front and back neckline cowl in relation to the figure.
- True up and check the results of the draping process with regard to fit, hang, balance, and proportion.

Basic Neckline Cowl

Cowls are draped on the bias, usually in lighter, finer fabrics to enhance a soft, harmonious look. A basic neckline cowl can be used subtly or add imaginative zing to an otherwise low-key garment. The drape should be done in the same quality of fabric as the finished garment.

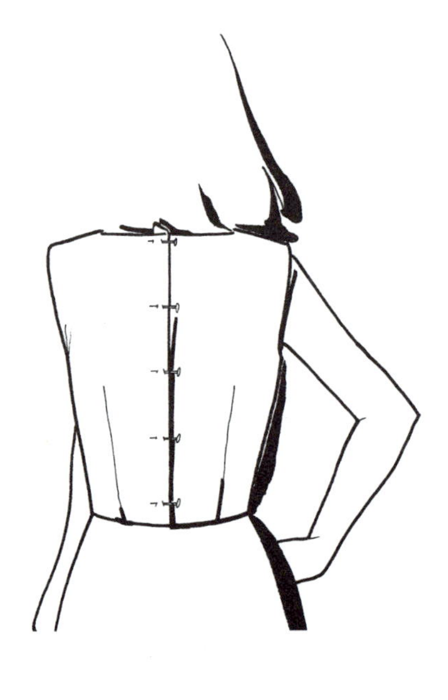

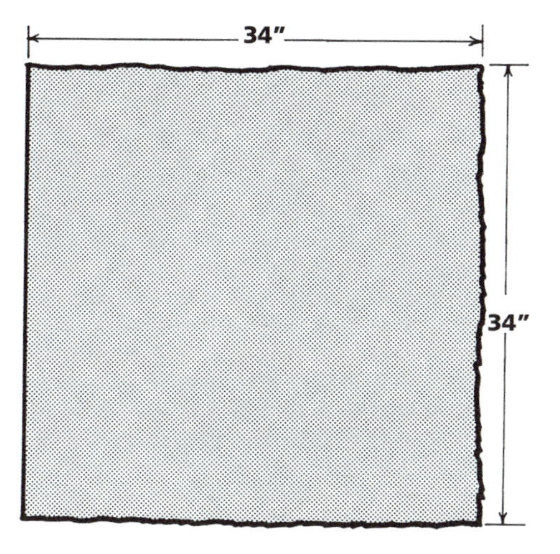

1 **Measure and cut a perfect square** of soft fabric wide enough for an entire front or entire back bodice (approximately 34-inche square).

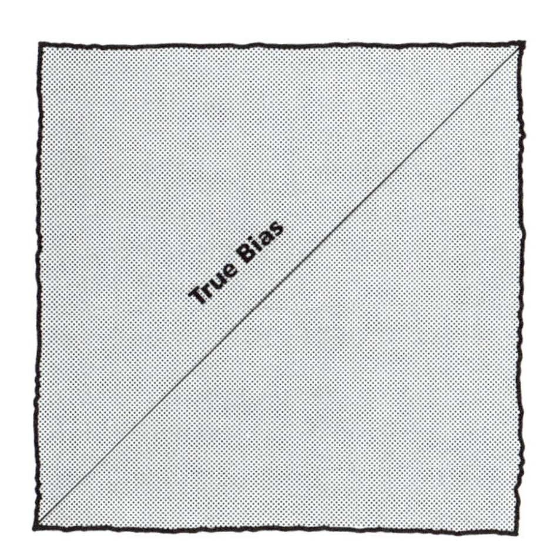

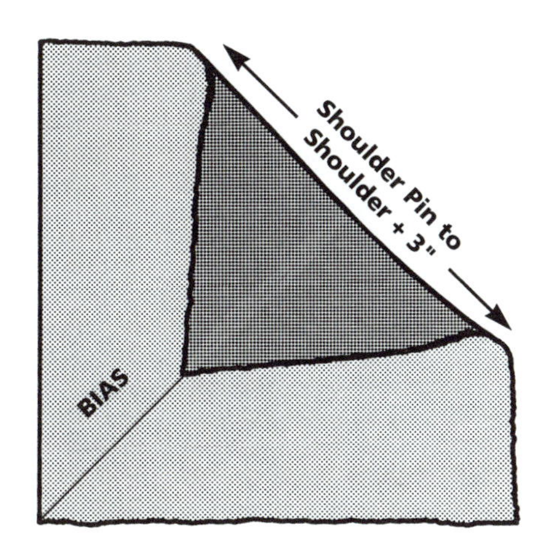

2 **Draw a true bias line** diagonally across the piece of fabric.

3 **Determine the neckline edge and facing area.** Turn a corner of the fabric deep enough to reach from one shoulder pin through the neckline pin, and over to the other shoulder pin. Add 3 inches for ease, and press in place.

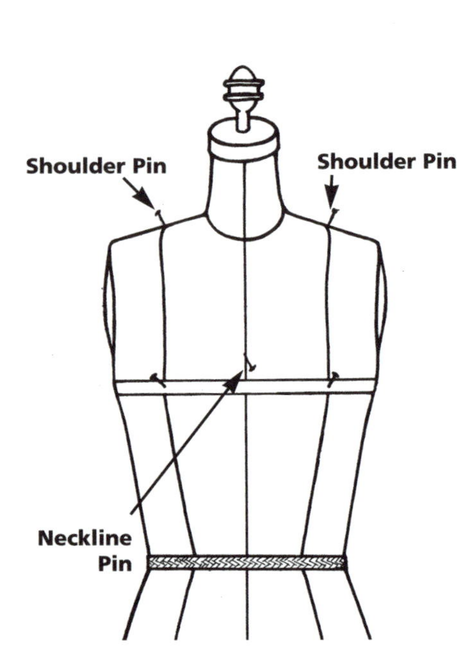

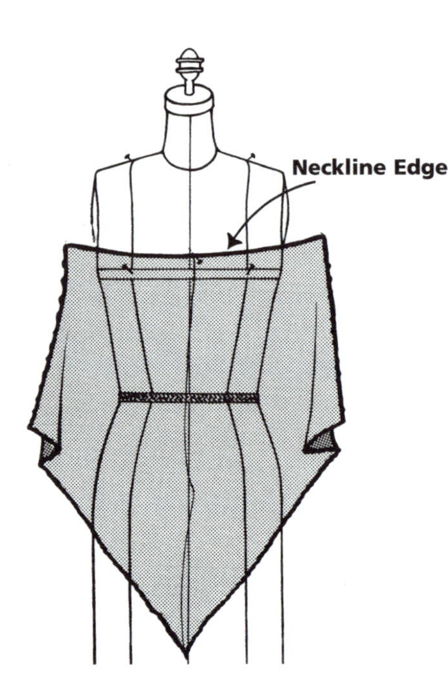

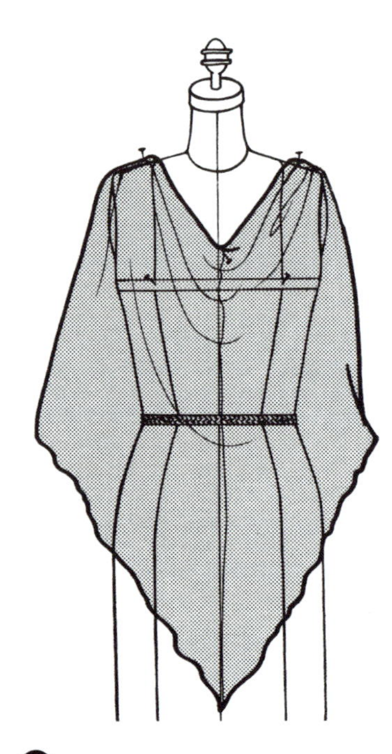

Prepare the dress form.
Determine the desired neckline depth. Place a pin on the dress form at this neckline position. Also, place a pin on each shoulder seam the width of the

1 **Drape the center front neckline.** Place the folded edge of the fabric on the dress form.

2 Match the center front bias line of the fabric to the center front neckline pin on the dress form.

3 **Drape and pin the shoulders** into position by holding the fabric at each end of the foldline of the fabric edge.

Swing the fabric up and onto the shoulders. Allow the neckline cowl to fall in gently. Be sure to keep the center front bias line on the center front of the dress form.

NOTE: The pleating process in Step 4 is optional. If no shoulder pleats are desired, continue draping with Steps 5 and 6.

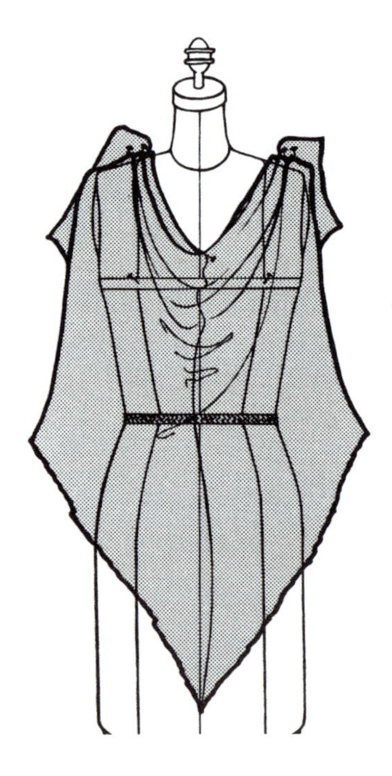

4 **Lift and pleat each shoulder** to form additional desired cowl drapes.

NOTE: Refer to the garment design to determine the number of cowl drapes desired.

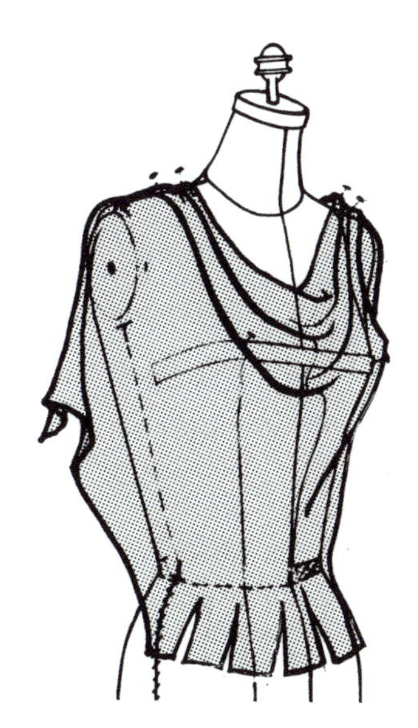

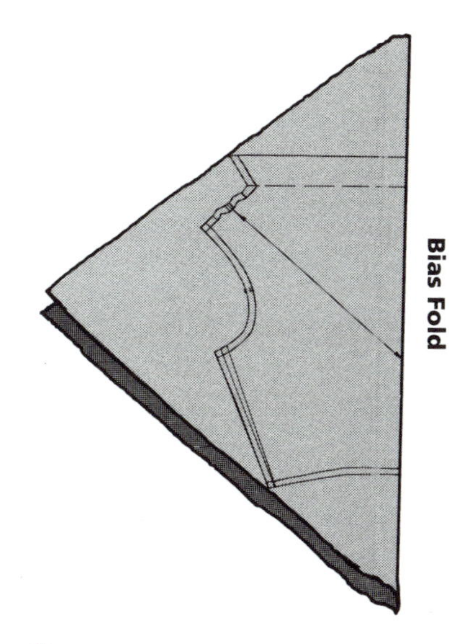

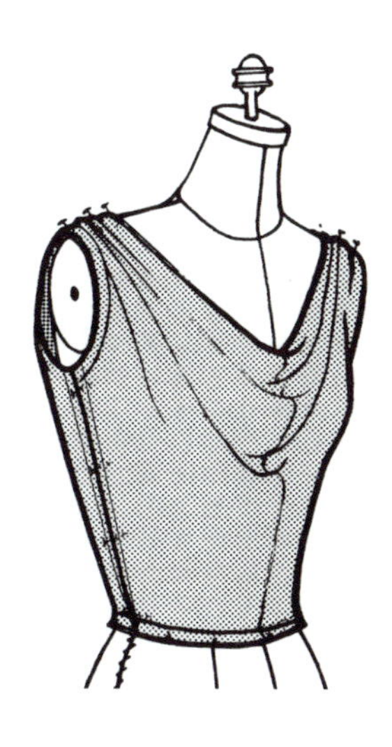

5 **Clip the waistline fabric.** Pin and drape the waistline, side seam, and armhole areas.

6 **Mark all key areas** of the dress form on one side of the drape only.

Shoulder Sea
Side Seam
Waistline
Armhole Area and Desired Armhole Shape

7 **True up the front cowl drape.**

a. Fold the drape on the center front bias fold.

b. True up all seams, and add seam allowances.

c. At the neckline fold, determine the width of the desired neckline facing. Keep the bodice drape folded. Trace all necessary markings from the trued side to the unmarked side. Trim excess fabric.

d. Place the drape back on the dress form. Check for accuracy and make all necessary corrections.

NOTE: Refer to the Basic Bodice, page 40, for trueing the shoulder, side seam, and waistline areas.

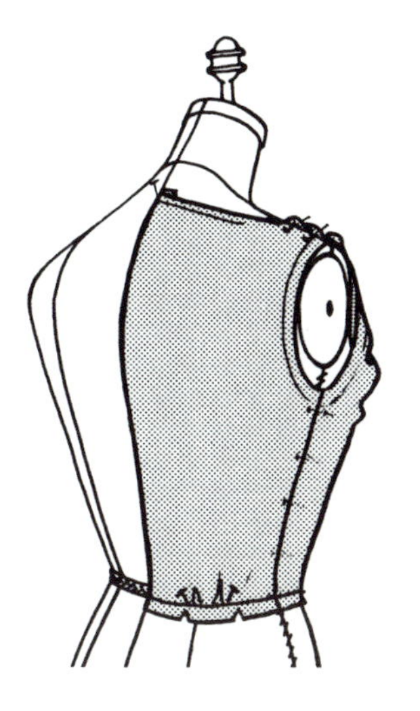

8 **Drape a back bodice design.** Refer to one of the basic back drapes to correctly drape the back bodice design.

NOTE: A low back neckline cannot be used because the drape will fall off the shoulders. Also, the neckline shoulder areas should match.

A yoke cowl becomes quite effective when a cowl design requires the remainder of the garment to be dartless and free flowing. It also allows the grainline of this garment area to remain parallel to the center front position.

1 **Draw in the desired yoke style line,** after completing the cowl drape. Add seam allowances and trim excess fabric.

2 **Drape the desired garment style into the yoke cowl,** keeping the cowl yoke in place. The garment style grainline will remain parallel to the center front position of the dress form.

Underarm/Side Seam Cowl

The underarm/side seam cowl drape produces soft curved bias folds at the underarm seam. The fabric is placed on the true bias and is draped without a side seam. The underarm/side seam cowl is effective on a soft and sumptuous drape without looking overdone. It offers design inspiration for soft and fluid fabrics, and creates a mood of easy elegance.

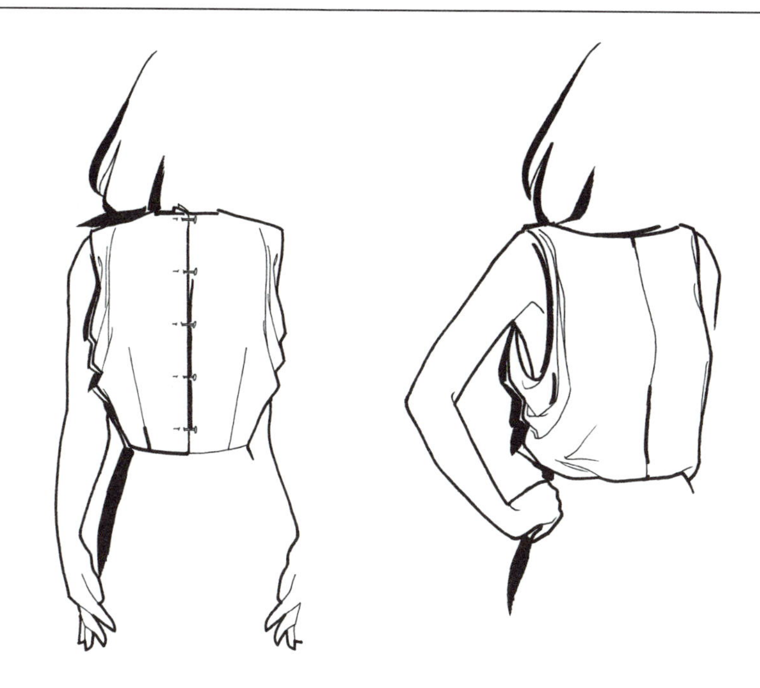

***Underarm/Side Seam Cowl**—Preparing the Fabric*

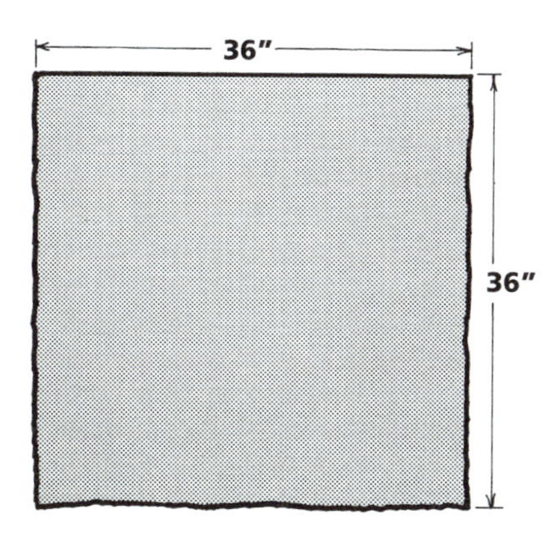

1 **Measure and cut a 36-inch square** of soft fabric. This will be enough fabric to drape a front and back waist seam design forming an underarm cowl.

NOTE: The drape should be done in the same quality of fabric as the finished garment.

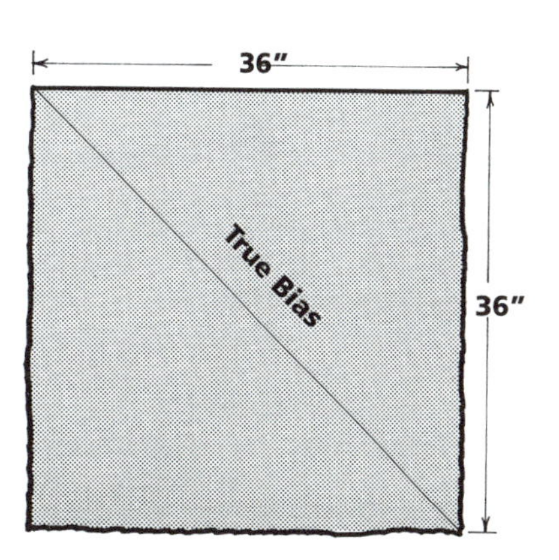

2 **Draw a true bias line** diagonally across the 36-inch piece of fabric.

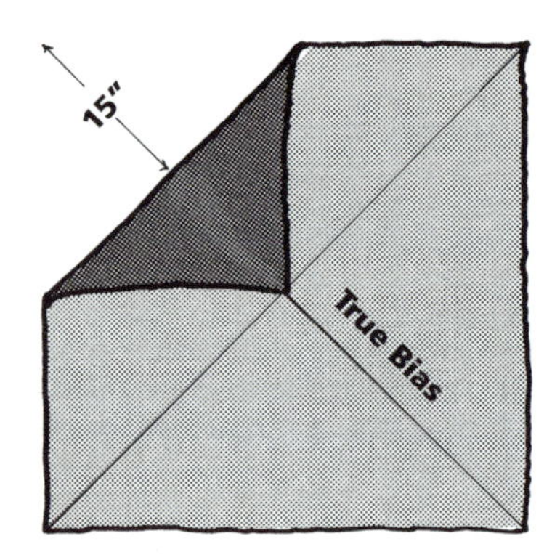

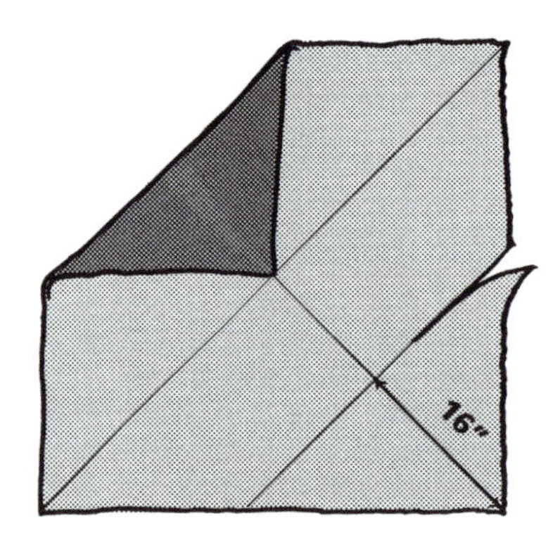

3 **Measure down 15 inches** from the top edge on the bias line.

4 **Draw a perfect cross bias line on the 15-inch position.** Fold back the fabric on this line.

5 **Measure up 16 inches** from the bottom edge on the bias line.

6 **Draw a perfect cross bias line at the 16-inch position.** Trim the fabric on this line.

Underarm/Side Seam Cowl—Draping Steps

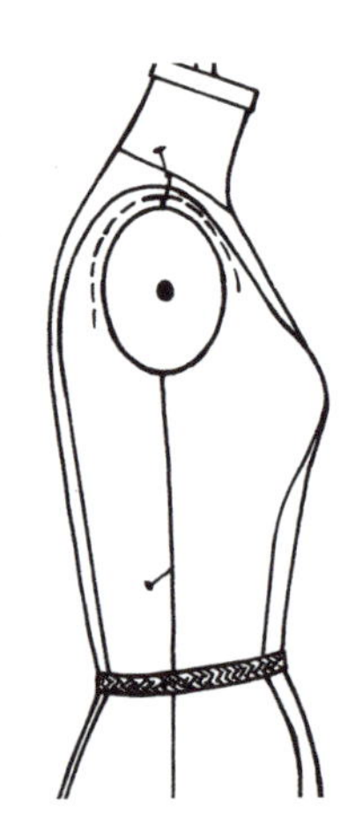

NOTE: **Prepare the dress form.** Determine the depth of the underarm cowl desired. Place a pin on the dress form at this underarm/side seam position. Also, place a pin on the shoulder seam at the desired shoulder/armhole position.

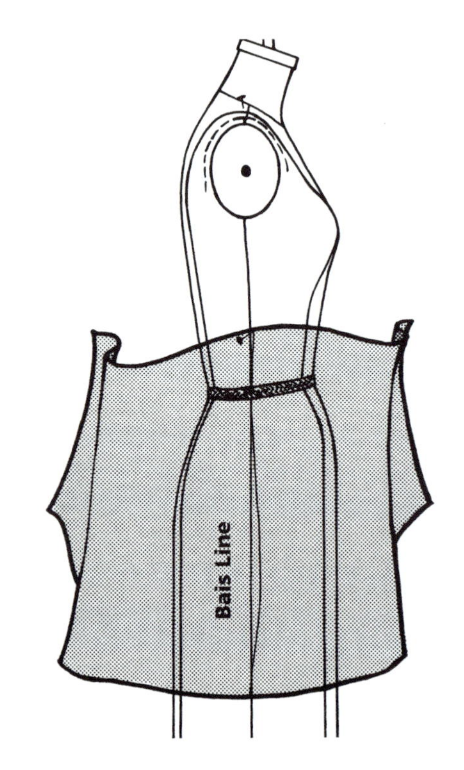

1 **Pin the fabric on the dress form at the underarm side seam pin.**

2 **Position and match the bias line** at the foldline to the side seam pin of the dress form.

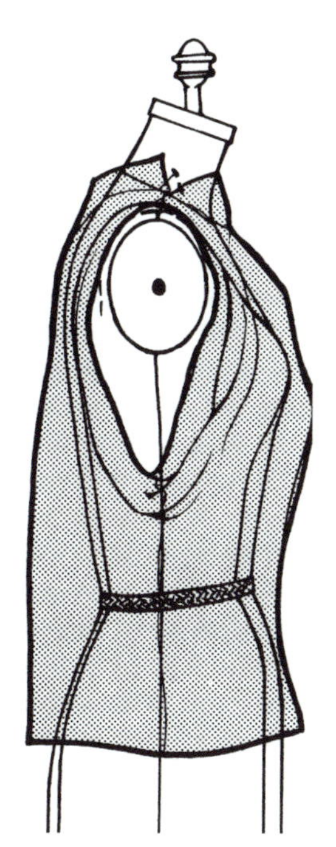

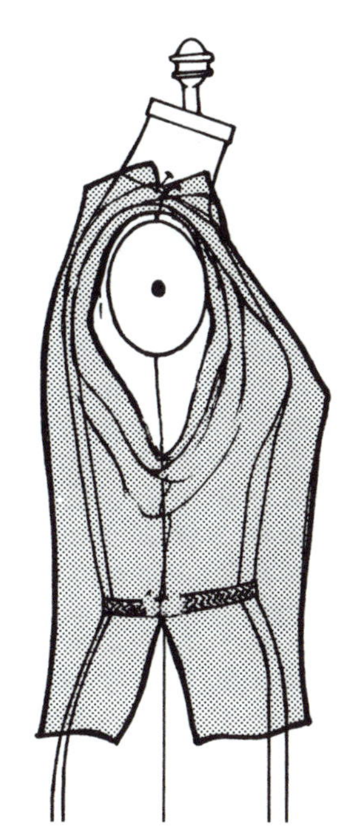

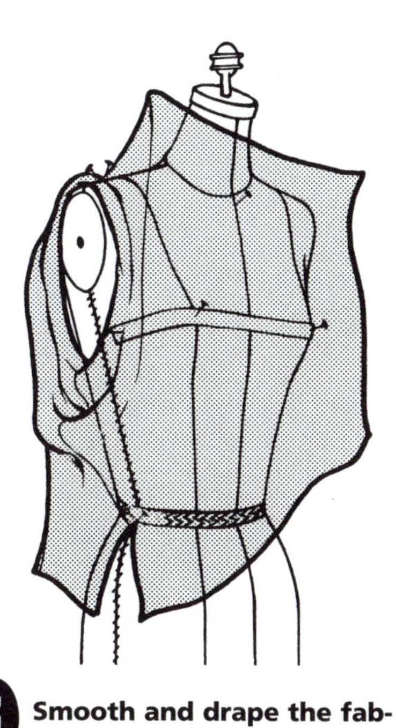

3 Drape the shoulders.

a. Hold the fabric at each end at the foldline of the fabric edge.

b. Swing the fabric up and onto the shoulders. Place anchor pins at this shoulder position.

c. Cowls will automatically form at the underarm.

NOTE: For deeper side seam cowl drapes, it will be necessary to form pleats at the shoulder.

4 Clip the fabric on the side seam, from the bottom of the bias line up to the waistline. Pin the bias line of the fabric to the side seam/waist position of the dress form.

5 Smooth and drape the fabric past the center front line until the grain of the fabric is parallel to the center front of the dress form.

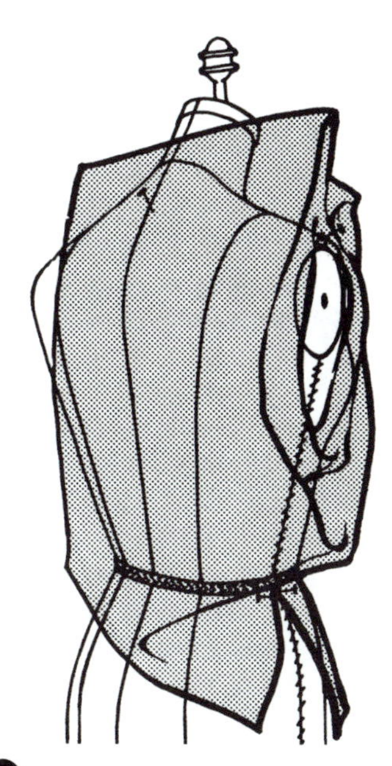

6 Smooth and drape the fabric past the center back line until the crossgrain of the fabric is parallel to the center back of the dress form.

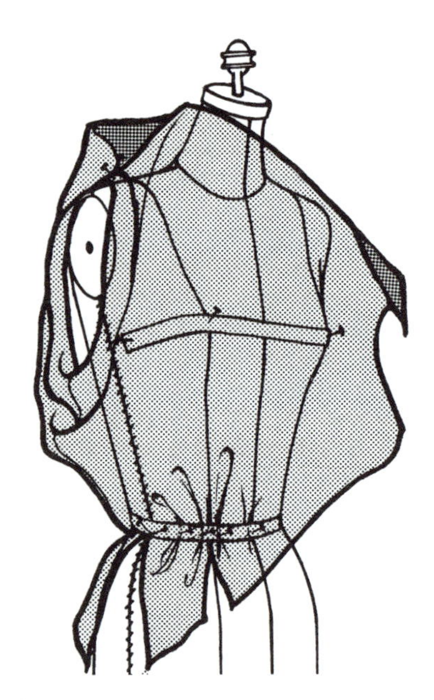

7 **Clip and pin in place the waistline** for the front and back.

NOTE: It will be necessary to form tucks, darts, or shirring as shown here when draping in the waistline.

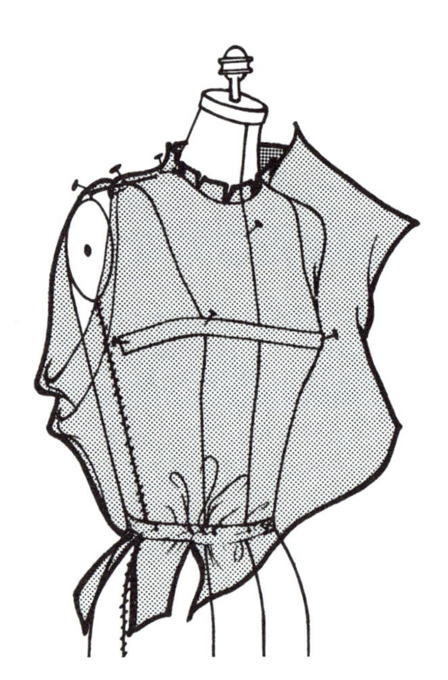

8 **Clip the front and back necklines, and drape in the shoulders.**

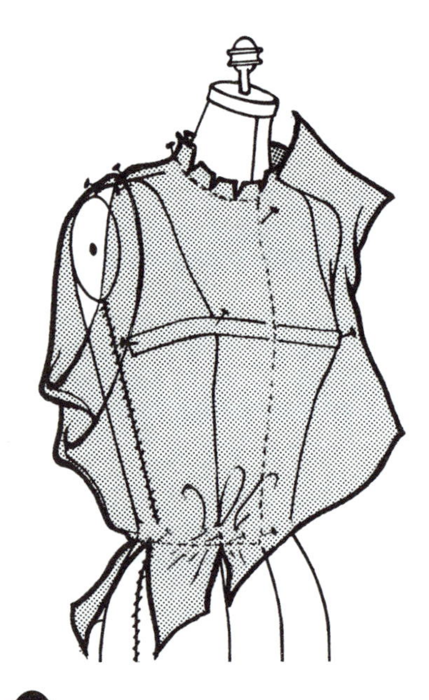

9 **Mark all key areas.**

Front and Back
Center Front
Center Back
Front and Back Waistline
Shoulders and Pleats

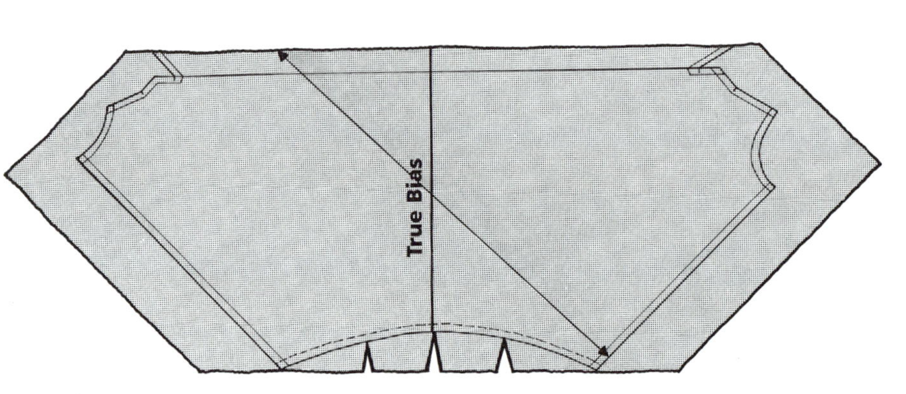

10 **True up all lines.** Refer to the Basic Bodice, page 40, for trueing up the shoulder, neckline, side seam, and waistline areas. Add seam allowances and trim excess fabric. At the underarm cowl foldline, determine the width and shape of the desired facing amount.

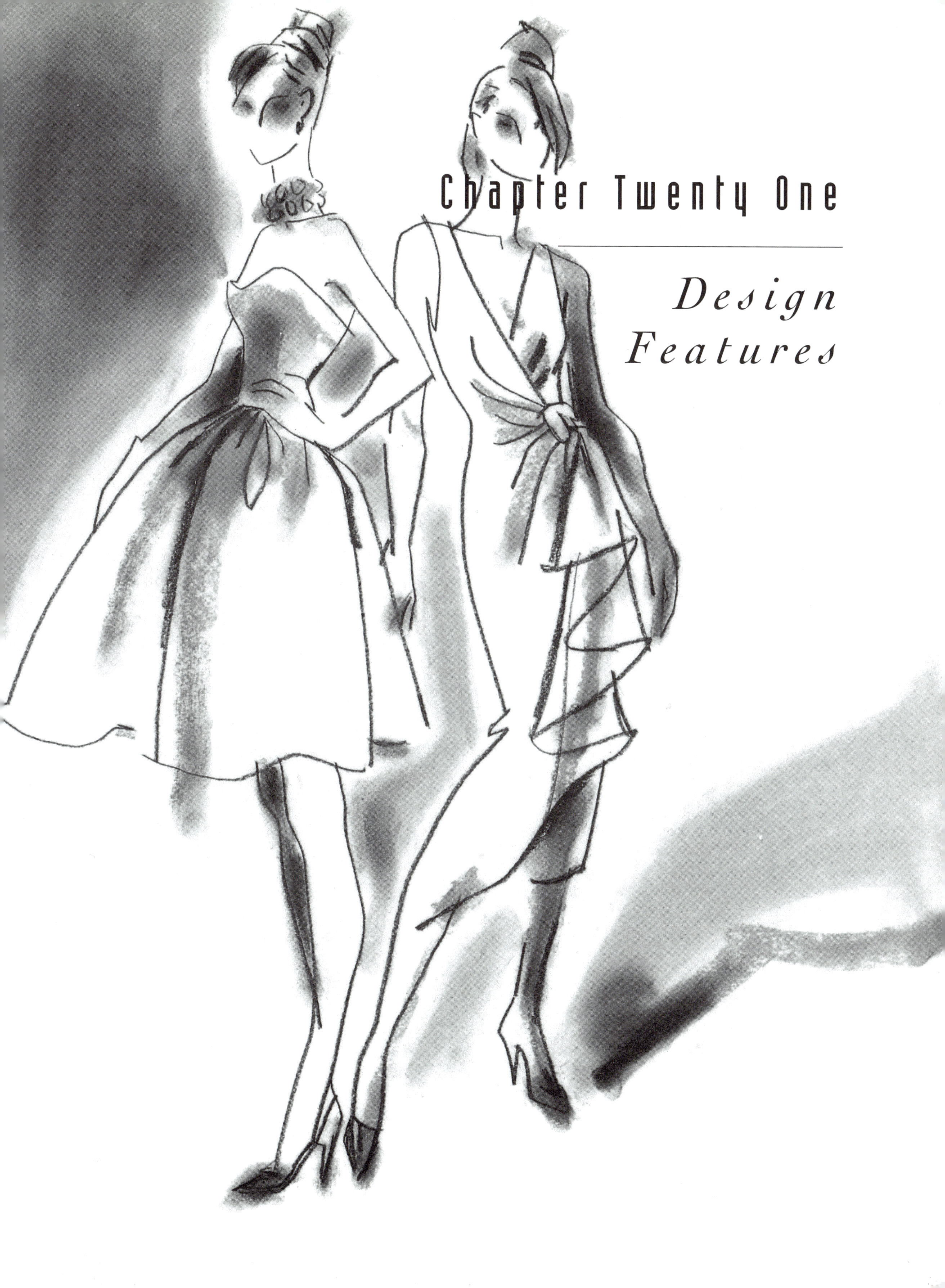

Chapter Twenty One

Design Features

Objectives

By studying the various draping steps in this chapter, the designer should be able to accomplish the following:

- Prepare and drape a circular piece of fabric into a relatively straight edge, and create a cascading flounce.
- Determine the ratio of the length of the ruffle and the length of the seam into which it is being sewn.
- Prepare and drape a straight piece of fabric into almost any edge—necklines, armholes, style lines to create a ruffle.
- Trim and shape the outside style line to the desired design of a circular flounce or ruffle.

Circular Flounce

A circular flounce is a curving, cascading part of the design and can be draped into almost any edge—necklines, armholes, style lines. Flounces are created by draping a circular fabric piece into a relatively straight line. This creates a cascading flow. The outside final shape is then created by trimming and shaping in the desired design. A circular flounce can be draped by using one circle or several circles and can be designed with singular or multiple layers.

The design of a circular flounce is the stuff of romance. Flounces recall a mood of elegance with a rich, dramatic graceful flare.

Circular Flounce—Preparing the Fabric

1 Measure the style edge on the garment for the desired circular flounce.

a. Neckline flounces (example is 18 inches, from center back neck edge to center front neck edge)

b. Large armhole flounce (example is 24 inches, the entire circumference)

c. Princess seam flounce (example is 17 inches, from the shoulder to the waistline)

2 Determine the amount of circle needed. Take the measurement from Step 1, subtract 1 inch, and divide that new number by 6. This figure will be used for the next step.

a. Neckline flounce
18" minus 1" = 17". Divide 17" by 6 = 2.8 or 2 3/4".

b. Large armhole flounce
24" minus 1"= 23". Divide 23" by 6 = 3.8 or 3 3/4".

c. Princess seam flounce
17" minus 1" = 16". Divide 16" by 6 = 2.6 or 2 5/8".

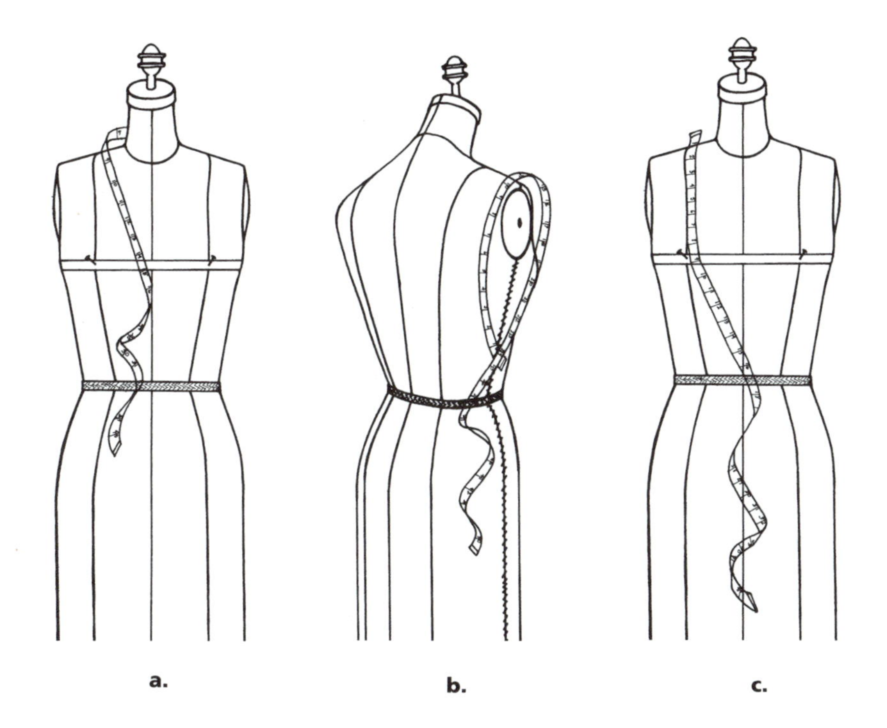

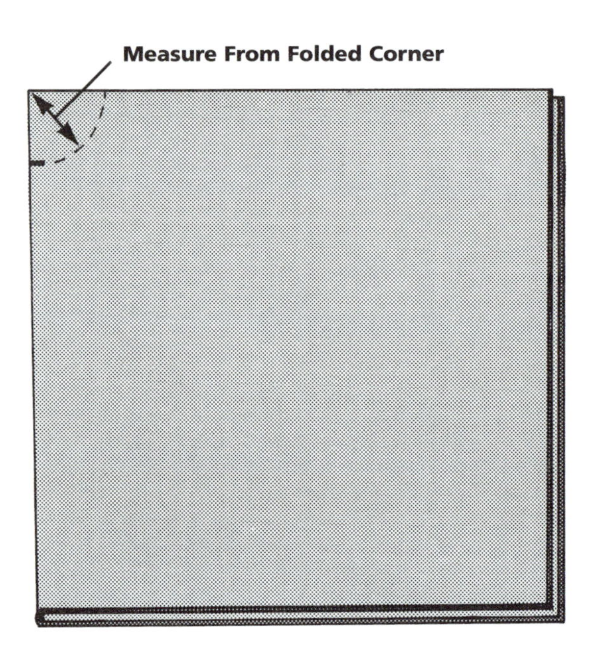

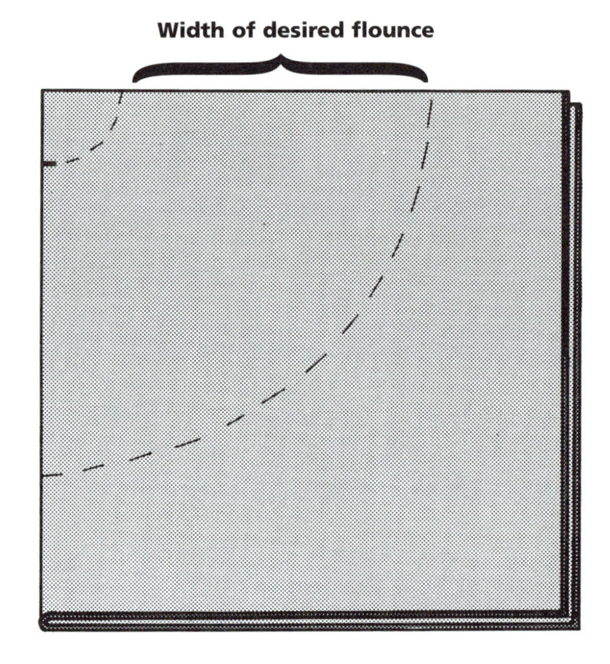

3 **Fold the muslin** in half and then in half again in the other direction.

4 **Measure down from the folded corner edge.** Using a ruler or tape measure, measure the desired measurement. Draw this measurement in a circular manner from folded edge to folded edge.

5 **Determine the desired width** of the flounce, and add 2 inches. Draw this width parallel to the first circle.

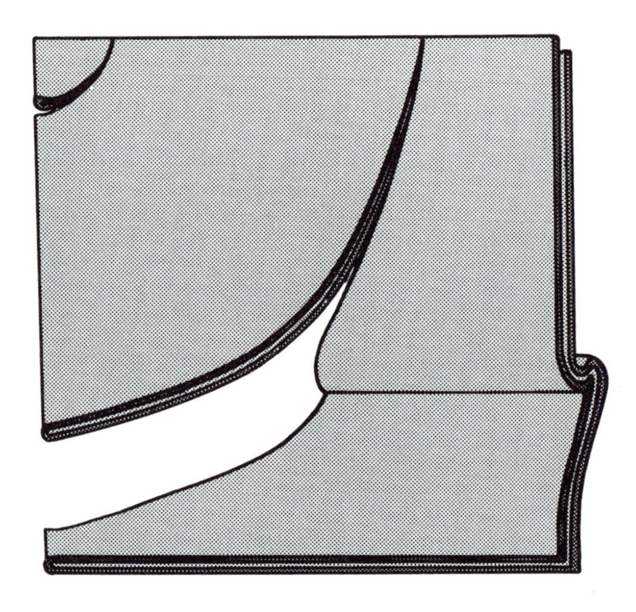

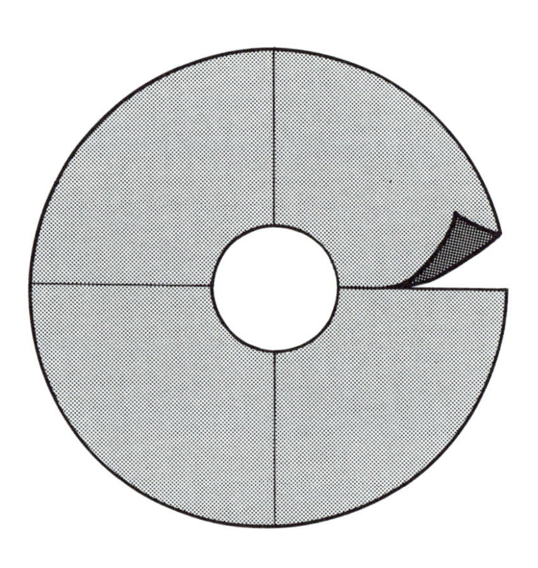

6 **Cut out the fabric** on the two circular lines.

7 **Open the fabric,** exposing a full circular fabric piece. Cut the fabric on one of the folds.

Circular Flounce—Draping Steps

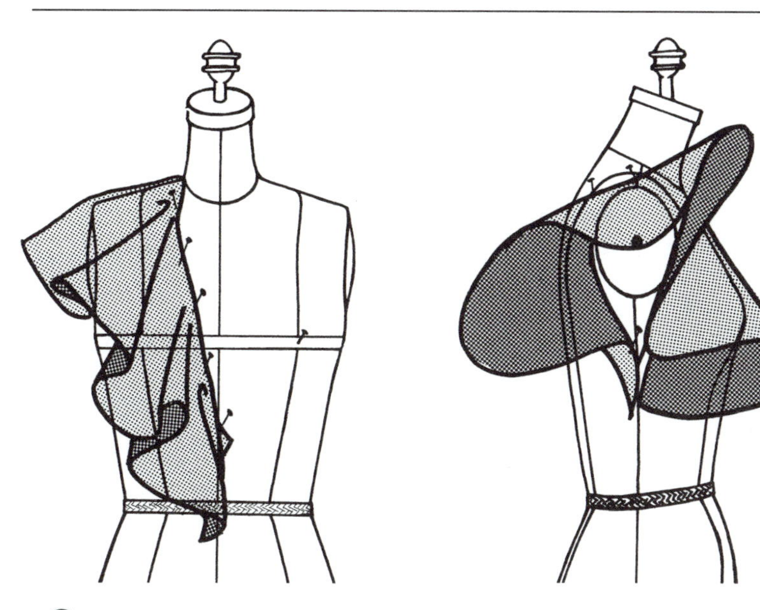

1 **Place the fabric circle on the dress form** along the desired styled edge. Pin approximately every inch.

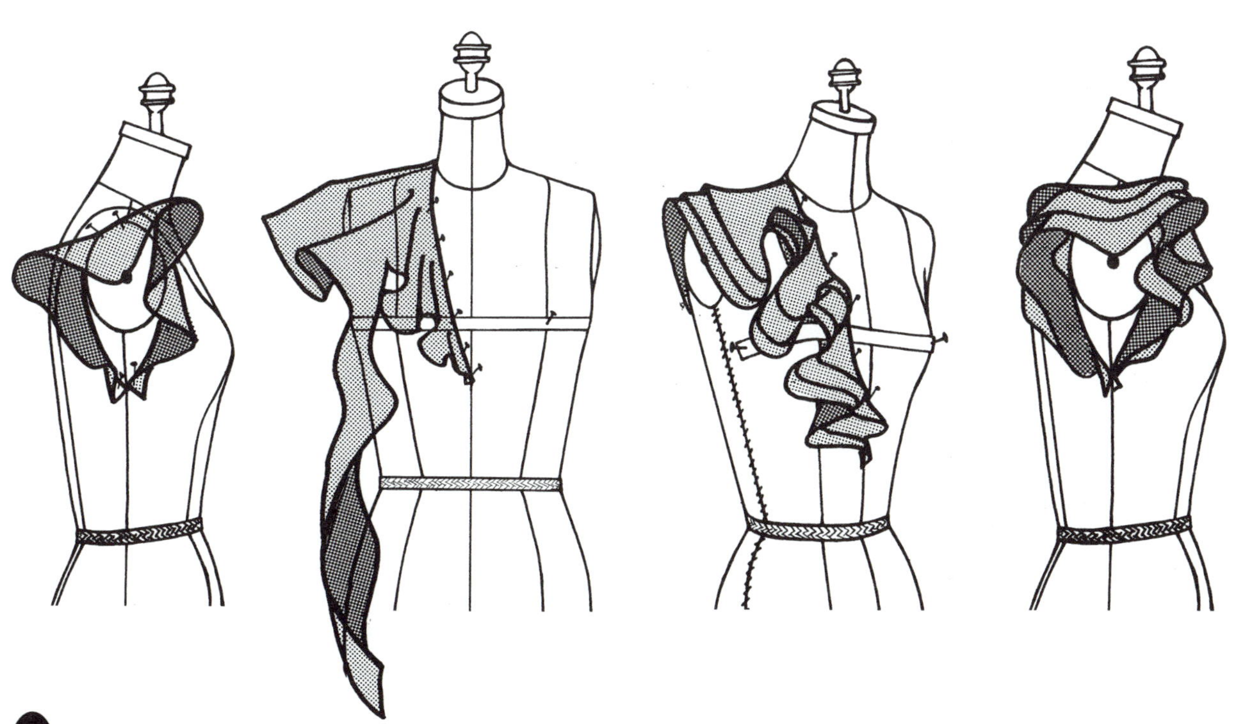

2 **Trim the outside edge** of the flounce into the desired shape of the design.

NOTE: There may be multiple layers required, depending upon the design. Each layer is usually shaped and layered using different widths.

There are times when a designer may want more fullness in the flounce. In this case, apply the following pattern preparations.

Shirred Flounce—Preparing the Fabric

1 Fold fabric, determine circular measurement, and cut out the circle. Refer to Circular Flounce, pages 376–379.

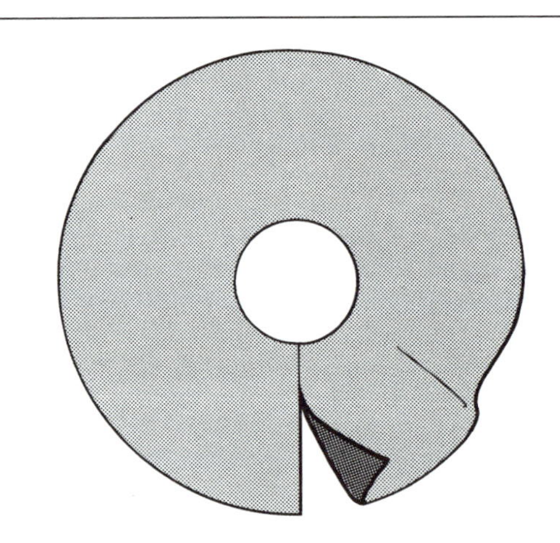

2 Slash and spread the circle until the desired amount of fullness is achieved. Lay the circle flat. From the inner circle edge, slash and spread circle open (this is usually two times the original amount or an additional half of the original amount).

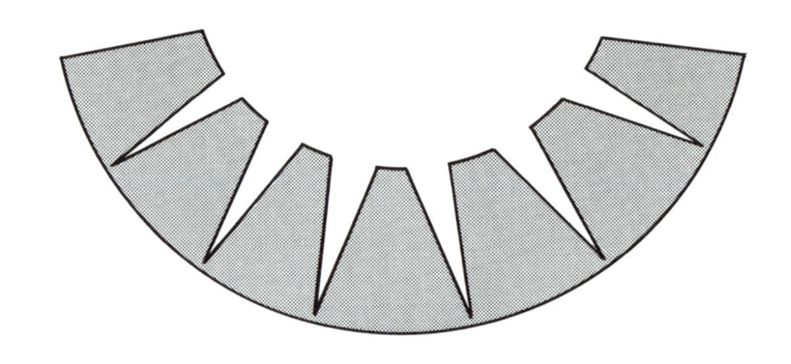

3 Cut the new circular pattern out of fabric.

4 Sew a row of gathers on the inner circle edge. Gather circle untill the inner circle measures the same distance as the seam it will be sewn into.

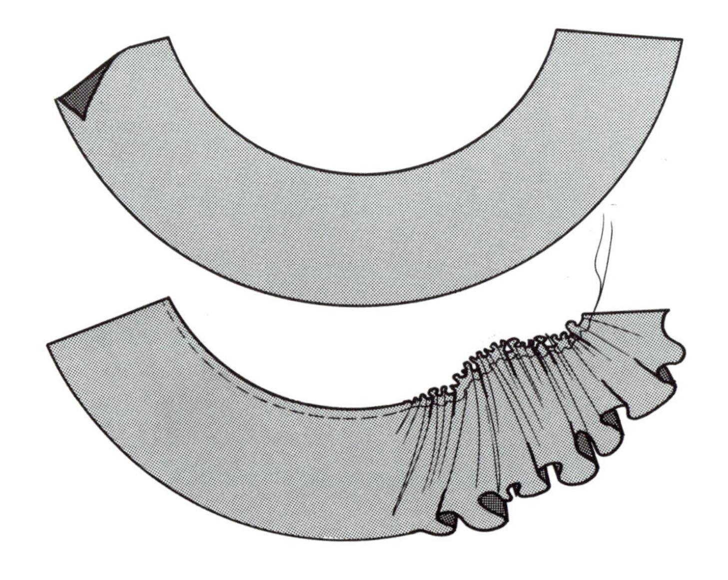

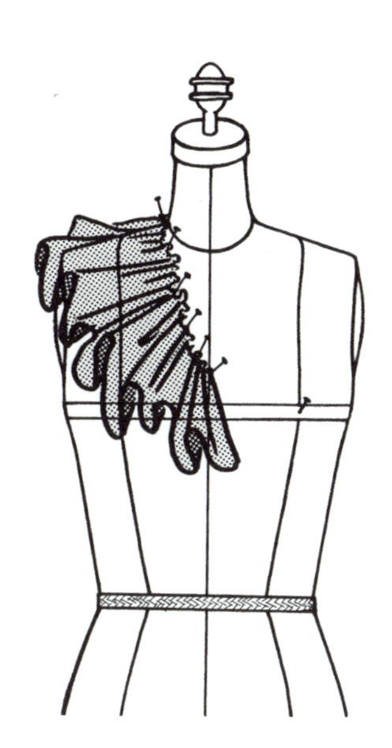

5 **Place the gathered fabric circle along the desired style edge of the dress form.** Pin approximately every inch.

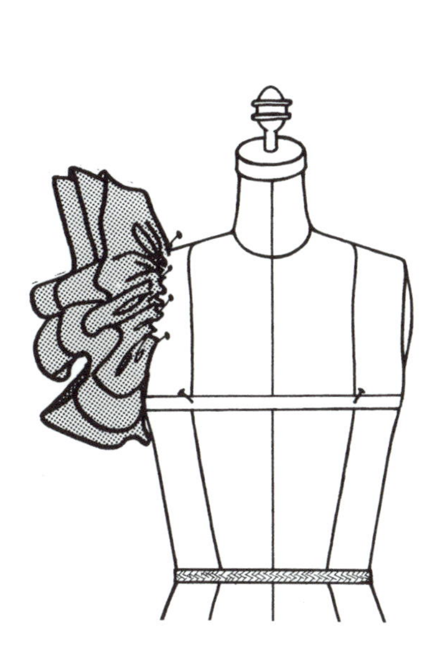

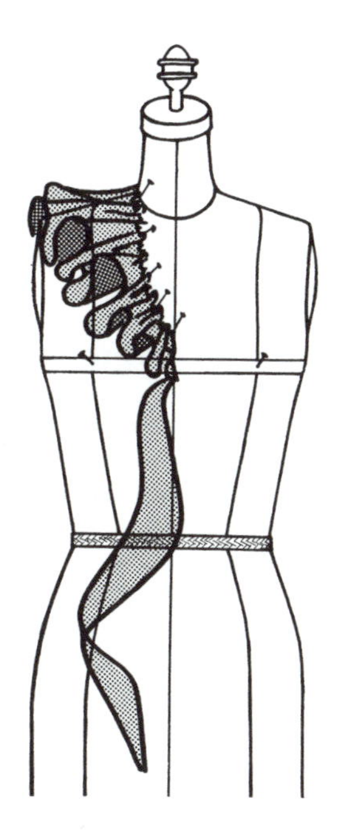

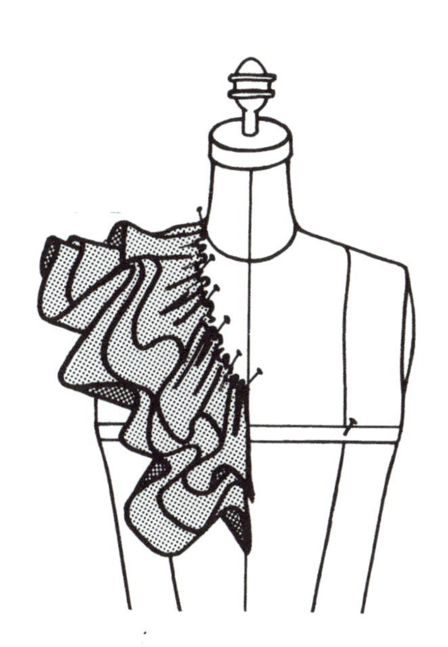

6 **Trim the outside edge** of the flounce till it represents the desired shape of the flounce design.

NOTE: Multiple layers may be required, depending on the design. Each layer is usually shaped and layered using different widths.

Ruffles can be the perfect solution for finishing a neckline, collar, skirt, or cuff. It is a straight piece of fabric gathered into a seam. Depending upon the type of fabric and style, the ruffle can be designed in any width or length. However, the ratio for determining the length is 1 1/2 or 2 times the length of the seam it is to be sewn into.

Ruffles lend a graceful touch to inspire a softer, more romantic look in fashion.

Ruffles—Draping Steps

1. **Measure the area of the garment** where the ruffle will be applied.

2. **Add the fullness.**

   a. Double the amount, using the measurement in step 1, for maximum fullness (2 to 1).

   b. Add half the amount to the measurement from Step 1, for less fullness (1 1/2 to 1).

3. **Determine the desired width.** This should be in proportion to the design of the garment.

4 Transfer the length and width measurements to the fabric. The width is placed on the straight of grain, so that the gathering will be done on the cross-grain. This ensures a clean and even fabric fullness.

NOTE: If the length measurement is longer than the width of the fabric, then the fabric length should be divided into sections.

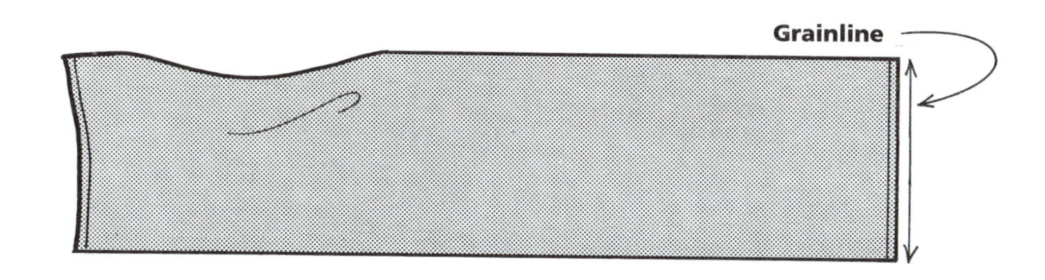

5 Gather the ruffle into the same length as the area where the ruffle is desired. Pin the ruffle into the garment.

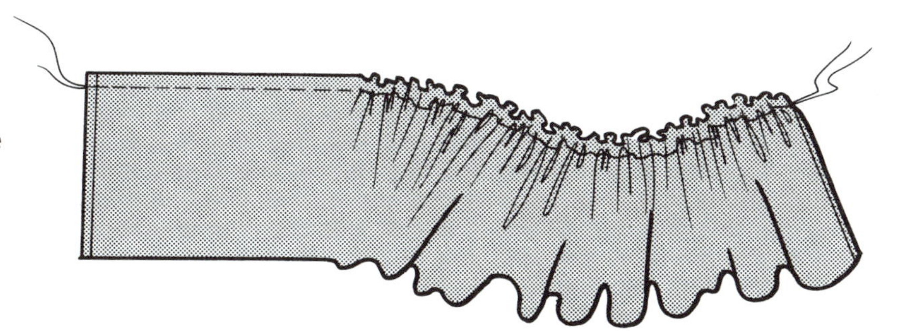

Various Ruffle Finishes

a. A ruffle may be baby hemmed on the outer edge.

b. A ruffle may be doubled in width and folded in half. Therefore, both raw edges are sewn into the desired styled area and no hemming is required.

c. A ruffle may have a double ruffle technique.

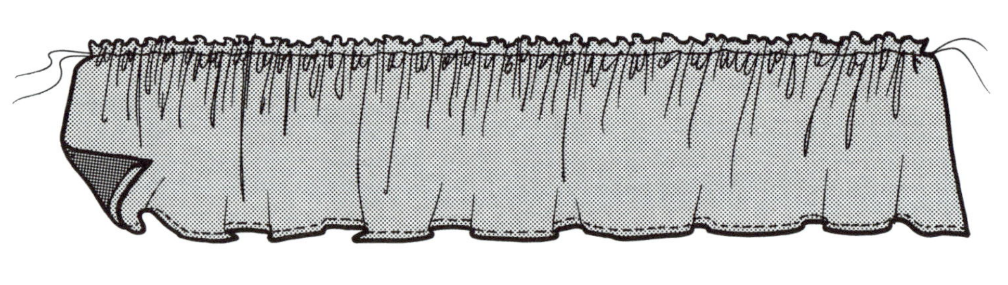

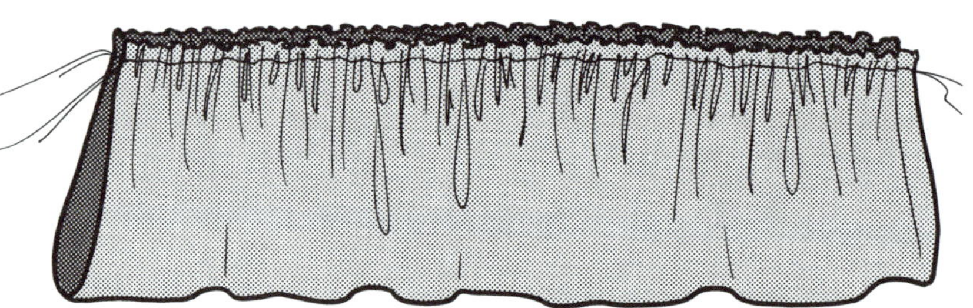

Notes

A peplum is a short-fitted circular skirt attached to the waist seam of a bodice or jacket. Peplums are cut in a circle and then draped for a desired flare. A soft-draped peplum will often add a smashing touch to an otherwise traditional garment. The peplum moves in and out of the fashion limelight, but designers welcome this fashion emphasis periodically.

Peplums—Draping Steps

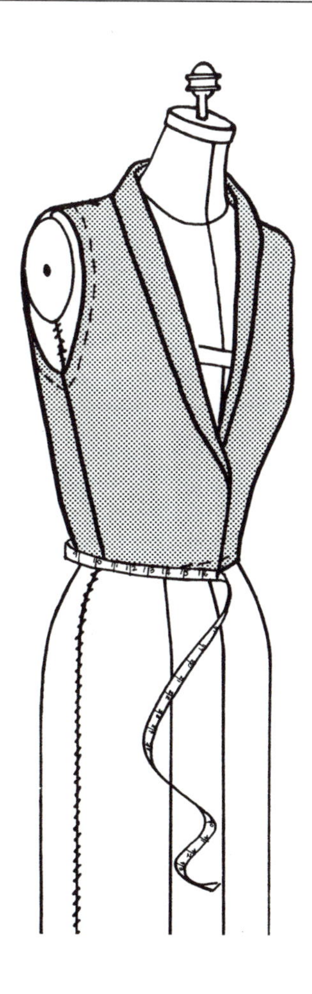

1. **Measure the style edge on the garment** for the desired peplum. In most cases, this is in a waist area of a jacket or dress.

2. **Determine the amount of circle needed.** Take the measurement in Step 1, subtract 1 inch, and then divide that new number by 6. For example: 27″ minus 1″ = 26″. Divide by 6 = 4 3/8″.

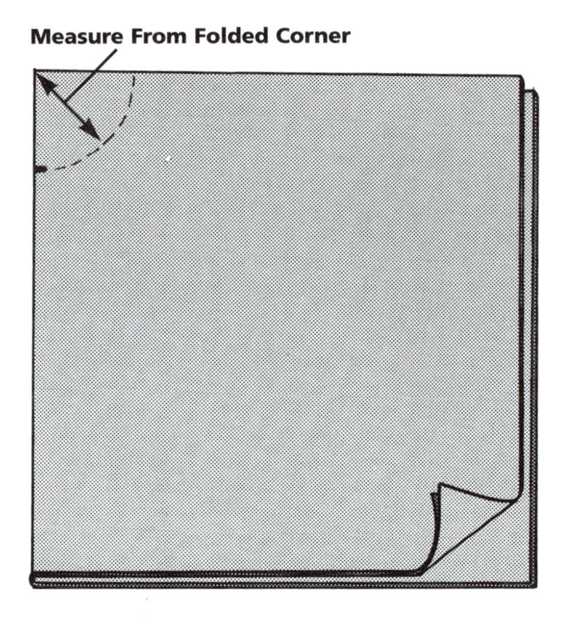

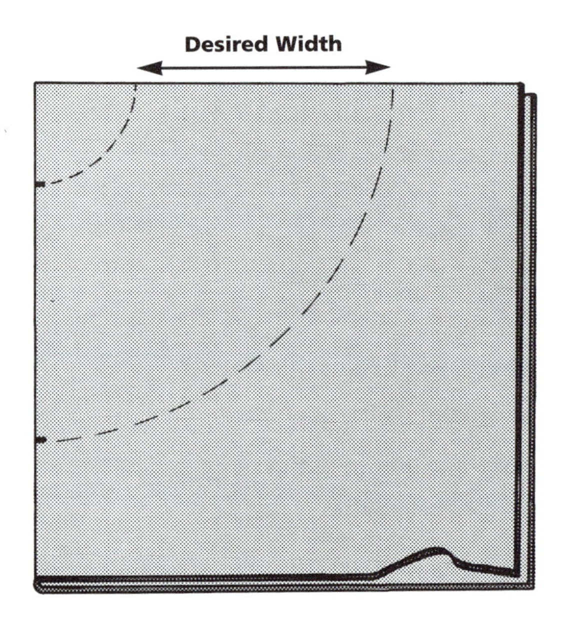

3 **Fold the muslin in half, and then in half again** in the other direction.

4 **Measure down from the folded corner edge.** Using a ruler or tape measure, measure the desired measurement. Draw this measurement in a circular manner from folded edge to folded edge.

5 **Determine the desired width of the peplum.** Draw this width parallel to the first circle.

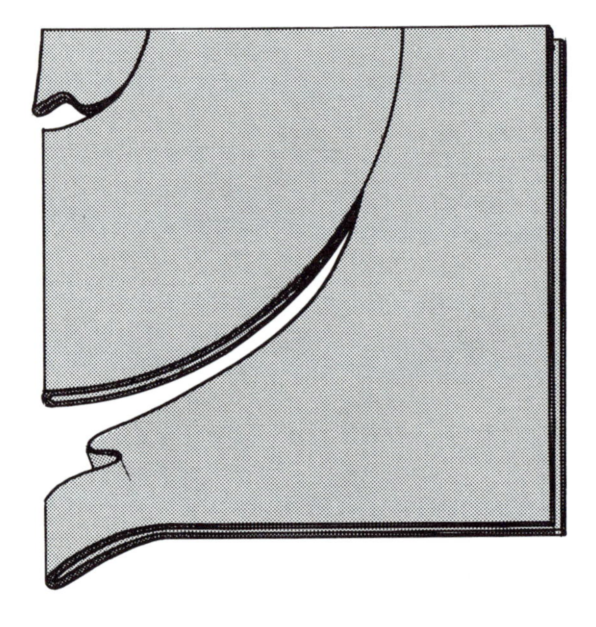

6 **Cut out the peplum** on the two circular lines.

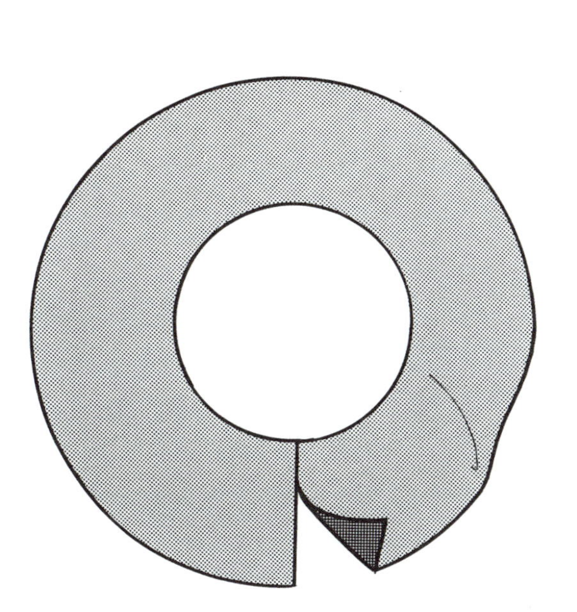

7 **Open the fabric,** exposing a full circular fabric piece. Cut the fabric on one of the folds.

8 **Drape and pin** the prepared peplum circle fabric along the desired styled edge.

9 **Check the peplum drape for the desired amount of circular fullness.**

a. If more fullness is required, slash and spread from the outer edge to the styled edge.

b. If less fullness is required, slash and close from the outer edge to the styled edge.

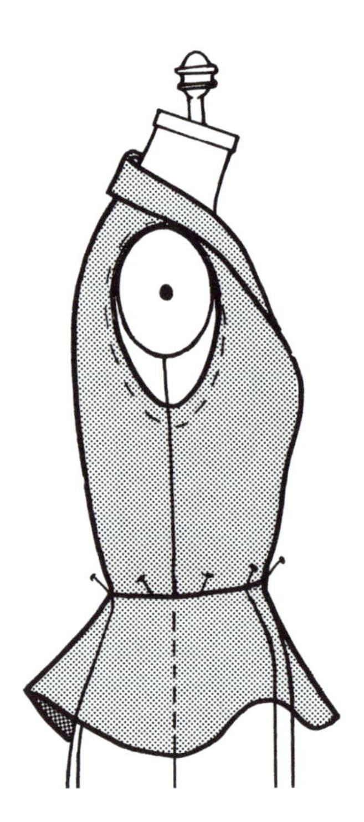

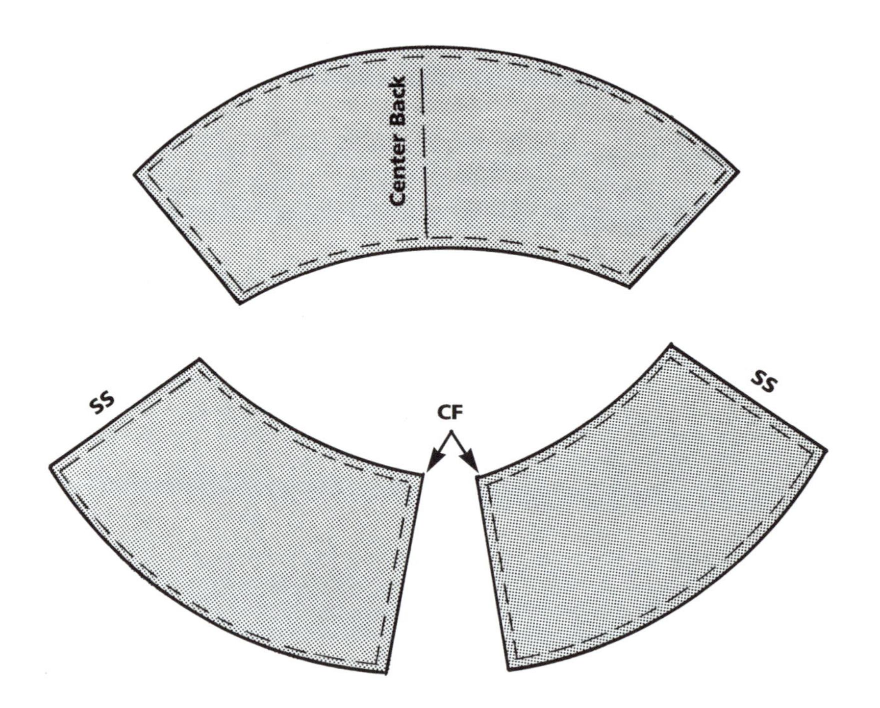

10 **Pencil in the side seams.** Following the side seam of the dress form, pencil the side seam position on the fabric.

11 **Remove the peplum drape** from the dress form. Cut drape at the side seam.

12 **Prepare a pattern piece for the front peplum** (from center front to the side seam).

13 **Prepare another pattern piece for the back peplum** (from center back to the side seam). Usually center back is placed on the fold and an opening is required for the front.

14 **Return the peplum drape to the dress form.** Pin the side seams together. Pin the peplum back to the garment. Check the peplum for correct length and movement.

Appendix

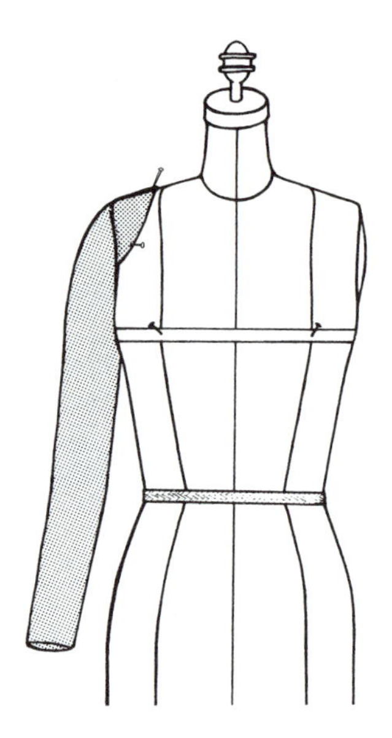

An arm is often not included with the dress form. An arm pattern is included on these pages. This arm, when cut, sewn, stuffed and attached to the dress form, will allow you to check the drape of sleeves. By following the instructions, you will be ready to drape and check-fit many types of sleeves.

1 Cut arm pattern pieces out of heavy muslin and transfer all notches and dart drill hole. Be sure to follow the grainlines when placing the pattern pieces onto fabric.

a. Cut 1 arm pattern.

b. Cut 2 shoulder stay patterns.

c. Cut 1 top arm circle pattern.

d. Cut 1 wrist arm circle pattern.

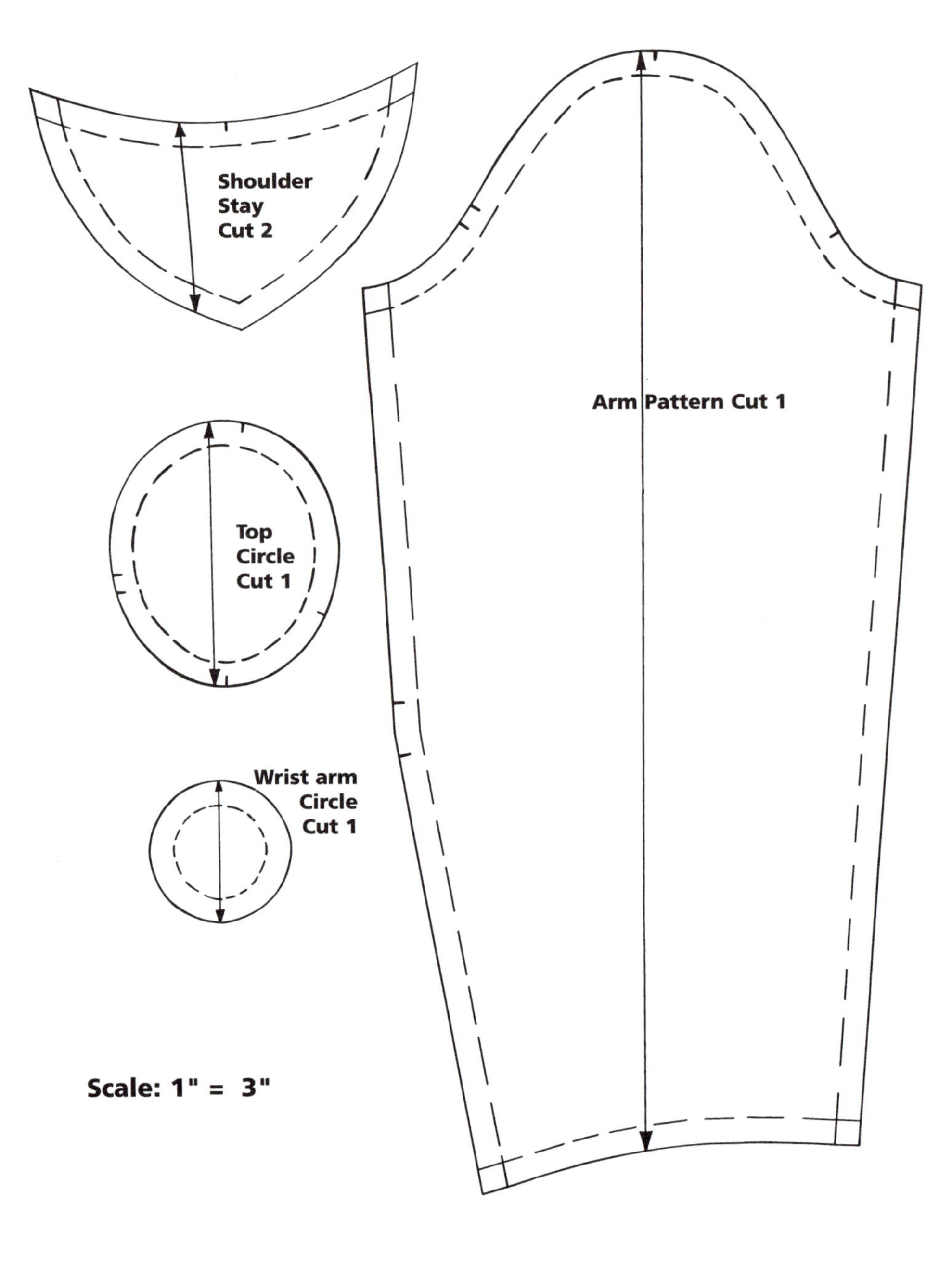

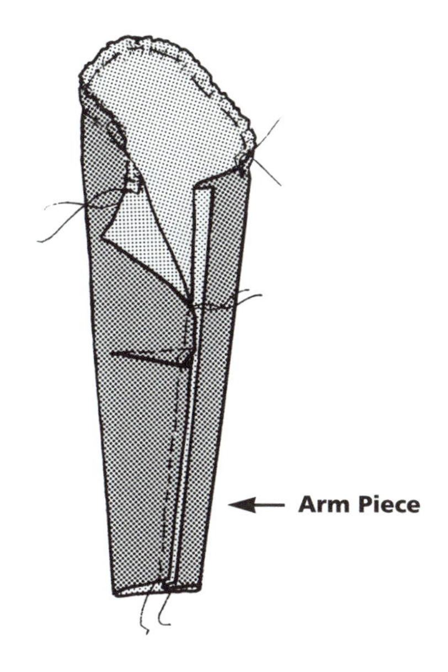

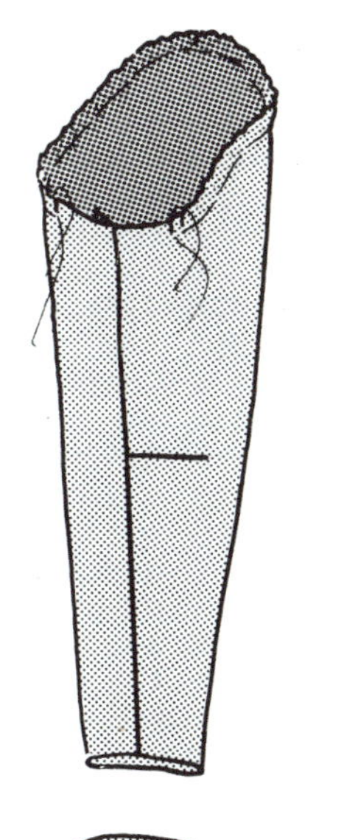

2 Sew the arm piece.

a. Crimp the cap of the arm.

b. Sew the elbow dart and the underarm seam. Be sure to sew the underarm together so that when the arm is completed, it will fit the **right side** of the dress form.

3 Turn the arm correct side out.

4 Sew the wrist area of the arm.

a. Clip and press under (to the inside) the wrist seam allowance of the arm.

b. Clip and press under the seam allowance of the Wrist Arm Circle (smaller circle).

c. Hand sew the Wrist Arm Circle (smaller circle) to the bottom at the wrist level of the arm. Be sure the wrist level at this stitchline remains 7 inches.

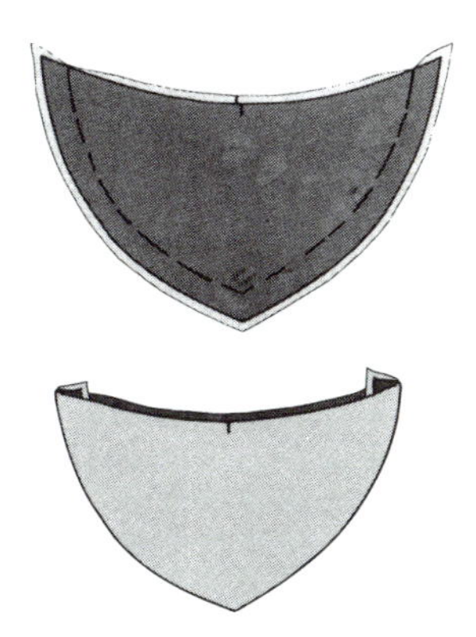

5 Sew the Shoulder Stay.

a. Sew the outer edges of the shoulder stay (pointed edge).

b. Turn the stay correct side out.

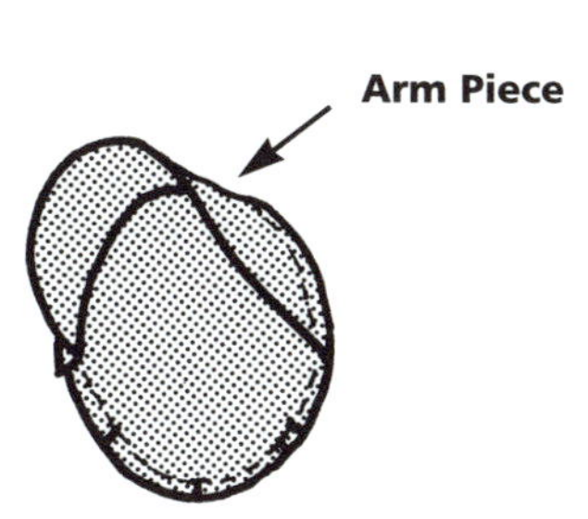

6 Sew the shoulder stay to the larger circle (top arm circle), matching shoulder position notches.

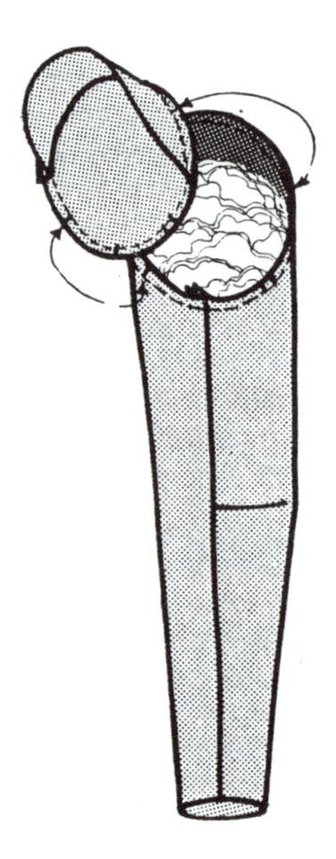

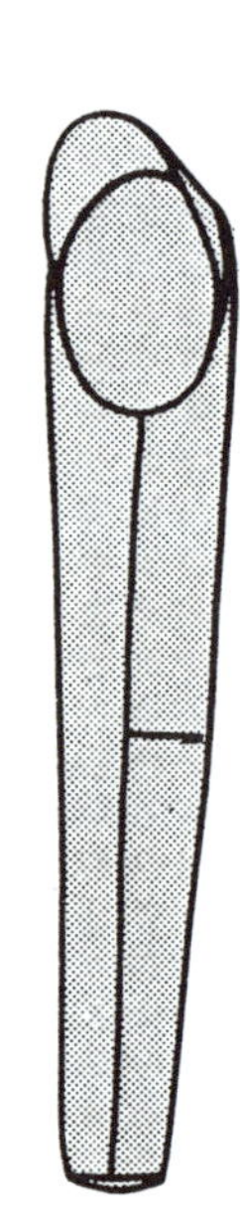

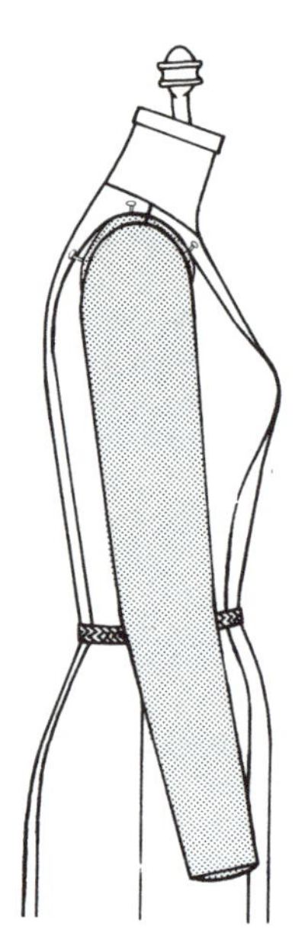

7 Sew the shoulder stay with the attached larger circle (top arm circle), to the cap of the arm.

a. Place the shoulder stay between the arm cap (previously crimped) and the larger circle.

b. Stitch the shoulder stay to the arm cap from the edge of the shoulder stay across to the opposite edge of the shoulder stay.

8 Fill the arm with polyfill. Be careful not to overstuff as the arm may become distorted.

9 Match the bottom area (unsewn section) of the larger circle to the underarm section of the arm (notched area).Hand sew the underarm section of the arm to the lower section of the larger circle, matching stitchline to stitch-line.

10 Pin the arm to the right side of the dress form when the arm is completely sewn.

Index